Windows 3.1:
The Complete Reference

Tom Sheldon

Osborne **McGraw-Hill**

Berkeley New York St. Louis San Francisco
Auckland Bogotá Hamburg London Madrid
Mexico City Milan Montreal New Delhi Panama City
Paris São Paulo Singapore Sydney
Tokyo Toronto

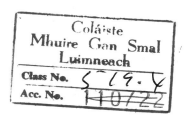
Osborne **McGraw-Hill**
2600 Tenth Street
Berkeley, California 94710
U.S.A.

For information on translations or book distributors outside of the U.S.A., please write to Osborne **McGraw-Hill** at the above address.

Windows 3.1: The Complete Reference

1234567890 DOC 998765432

ISBN 0-07-881747-1

Publisher ────────────
Kenna S. Wood

Acquisitions Editor ────────────
Frances Stack

Associate Editor ────────────
Jill Pisoni

Technical Editor ────────────
John Heilborn

Project Editor ────────────
Kathy Krause

Copy Editor ────────────
Ann Krueger Spivack

Proofreading Coordinator ────────────
Nancy Pechonis

Proofreaders ────────────
K.D. Sullivan
Valerie Haynes Perry

Indexer ────────────
Richard Shrout

Computer Designer ────────────
Peter F. Hancik

Illustrator ────────────
Susie C. Kim

Cover Design ────────────
Bay Graphics Design, Inc.
Mason Fong

Contents
at a Glance

Contents

Part II
Setup and Configuration

8

How Windows Works 143

9

Memory Management
Commands and Techniques 163

10

Optimizing Windows 183

11

Updating and Customizing Windows 203

12

Hard Disks 239

13

Video Graphics Displays 259

14

Multimedia 285

15
Printers 323

16
Fonts 341

17
Networks 361

22

The Bitmap Editor:
Paintbrush   481

23

Connections and
Communications   505

24

Windows Desktop
Accessories   535

Acknowledgments

I would like to acknowledge all the users in the CompuServe forums. Over the course of a year, we discussed features, talked about problems, and came up with solutions.

Special thanks to John Heilborn for his technical review and comments, and for trying the examples.

I would also like to thank all the hardworking people at Osborne/McGraw-Hill who managed to remain cheerful and keep all the material flowing through the publishing process. Special thanks to Frances Stack who kept pushing and pushing for more, and to Jill Pisoni for keeping track of everything. In addition, thanks to Ann Spivack and Kathy Krause for copy editing.

Last, but not least, thanks to Alexandra, who kept everything in working order, including me, and for her copy editing and work on several chapters in this book, including the reference section.

Introduction

Welcome to *Windows 3.1: The Complete Reference.* This book is an in-depth reference to the much-anticipated Windows 3.1 graphical user interface. Windows is easy to learn and makes your computer more fun to use. It provides a consistent user interface, so once you've learned the essentials, you'll be able to use them when working in most Windows applications. *Windows 3.1: The Complete Reference* is designed to get you up and running with Windows, starting with an overview of the basic interface and leading you into advanced topics. Each chapter has examples you can follow to learn about Windows. You'll also find discussions of important topics that can help you use Windows more efficiently and optimize it for your system.

Microsoft sent out 12,000 beta copies of Windows 3.1 for evaluation and testing before releasing the final product. They also tested over 800 products for compatibility during the beta-testing program. It is possible that Windows 3.1 is the most thoroughly tested software package in history. The beta-testing program required testers to use Windows in day-to-day operations and to provide bug and test reports during those tests. Special CompuServe forums for programmers and users provided a place for beta testers to present problems and share solutions. The result is an extremely reliable and efficient product. Microsoft has undoubtedly set a trend in product development that many companies will follow.

You must look beyond just the interface to see most of the enhancements in Windows 3.1. It is a major upgrade to Windows 3.0 that provides better applications support and protection from disasters. The 386 enhanced mode has been vastly improved and provides performance on a par with standard mode, even when running several applications. Add to that its ability to provide more memory to applications than your system actually has (virtual memory) and the ability to run DOS applications in resizable windows, and you've got a terrific environment to use at all times—you may never again use the DOS prompt for anything but starting Windows.

Windows is just the beginning of a new line of operating systems from Microsoft. It sets the trend for applications development. Newer operating systems in the works provide access to the resources of high-end 32-bit systems that use the Intel 80386 and above processors. Windows NT and Windows for Pen Computing are just examples. This strategy provides upward compatibility for Windows applications. Developers and users can start designing or using applications now that will work on advanced systems in the future. These new operating systems will not have the restrictions of DOS—they will use more memory and the full potential of modern microprocessors to provide better performance and processing.

Windows 3.1 Features

Many of the new features in Windows 3.1 are part of Microsoft's "information at your fingertips" strategy. Computer systems now provide access to a wide variety of information in a wide variety of formats. The Windows graphical user interface helps integrate those media to provide easy access to large volumes of information, including sound, graphics, animation, and text. It also provides a platform for the development of even more sophisticated applications. The following sections define some of the new features in Windows 3.1.

Common Features

Microsoft has gone to great lengths to make Windows 3.1 as intuitive as possible. Many Windows commands, like Open, Save, and Print, now use common dialog boxes—they look the same no matter what application you're using. That means you only need to learn how to use the feature once. This book takes advantage of common features by teaching them to you up front so you can start using Windows applications right away. Later sections then concentrate on advanced features as well as tips and tricks.

Enhanced Performance and Reliability

Windows 3.1 is improved in performance and is more capable of recovering from errors. For example, in 386 enhanced mode (the mode that Windows runs in on 80386 or higher processors), you can press CTRL-ALT-DEL to end an application that is misbehaving or that won't respond to keyboard or mouse commands. Windows will close the application but will keep running so you can save open documents in other applications before restarting Windows. (Restarting Windows in this situation is usually a good idea to prevent further problems.)

To prevent problems of this type from happening in the first place, Windows implements a powerful new feature called *parameter validation*. Windows checks all information passed from an application to the operating system to ensure that it is valid. If it is not, Windows requests correct information from the application. If the application doesn't supply it, Windows displays an appropriate error message. The message gives you a chance to ignore the problem and continue so you can save any open work. At this point you could also choose to close the application.

Compatibility is an important new feature. Microsoft has designed the upgrade so that Windows 3.0 applications will be able to run under Windows 3.1. At the same time Windows 3.1 provides better support for non-Windows applications. For example, you can now use a mouse in a DOS application window as well as change the font size while using the application.

TrueType Fonts

Windows 3.1 comes with a set of 14 TrueType fonts that provide what-you-see-is-what-you-get (WYSIWYG) capabilities. This means that the font you see on the screen will print as well as or better than you see it on the screen, depending on your screen and printer resolution. No special font cartridges or software fonts are required, and the fonts will print on any dot-matrix or laser printer. TrueType allows users to scale a font on the screen to any size without distortion, then print that font. The font is sent to the printer as graphic information, so any dot-matrix or laser printer will support TrueType.

TrueType also provides document interchange capabilities. A document formatted on one machine with a specific printer can be sent to another user with a different printer. The printouts will look almost identical. The author of a document has the assurance that a document created on one Windows system will look and print the same on another Windows system.

Embedded TrueType provides a further extension to document interchange capabilities. Embedding a font allows the recipient of the document to view the font even if that font is not available on his or her system. The 14 TrueType fonts supplied with Windows 3.1 are read-write fonts, meaning that they can be embedded in a document and sent to a recipient.

Object Linking and Embedding

While TrueType provides document interchange, a new Microsoft standard called Object Linking and Embedding, or OLE for short, provides compound document capabilities. A *compound document* is one created with elements from many different applications. Now one document can hold all the files (graphics, spreadsheets, and text) for a single project. You can even edit the elements without leaving the application and document you're working with. While Windows 3.1 contains the latest OLE implementation, it is not yet complete. Microsoft is expanding the concepts of linking, embedding, and compound documents, and Windows 3.1 is designed to take advantage of any improvements.

Embedding is the process with which you can paste a drawing from Paintbrush into a Write document, then double-click the picture to open Paintbrush and edit the picture. *Linking* is more dynamic. It lets you change the picture in Paintbrush and automatically update every document where that picture has been pasted. Of course, OLE is available in more sophisticated applications than Paintbrush and Write. It is being implemented by every major Windows application developer.

Multimedia Support

Windows 3.1 provides new multimedia capabilities and comes with several new utilities and accessories for creating and playing back sounds in documents and multimedia presentations. You can record and play sounds using the Sound Recorder (or more sophisticated accessories from other vendors), and you can include those sounds in your documents using OLE. For example, you could send a message that includes voice greetings or instructions to another user on a network.

The multimedia extensions to Windows 3.1 provide MIDI (Musical Instrument Digital Interface) support. MIDI technology has been around for some time as a way to connect electronic keyboard synthesizers and sound modules. MIDI technology allows one person to control many different devices—keyboards, mixers, stage lighting systems, and other electronic devices—from a single system. MIDI is such a unique and easy-to-use interface that it will undoubtedly be used to control other, non-music related devices. You can think of the MIDI port as an additional input and output source, like the serial and parallel ports, on the back of your system.

Many Windows applications are taking advantage of this new capability. For example, a spreadsheet program could include voice-annotated cells that you click to hear a description of the values in the cells. Such voice annotation is useful for training or presentations.

With the introduction of Windows 3.1 and the multimedia extensions, sound board are sure to grow in popularity. Some manufacturers of sound boards, such as Media Vision (Pro Audio Spectrum) and Creative Labs (Sound Blaster), provide sound boards with record and playback capabilities. These boards also provide connections for CD-ROM (an important aspect of multimedia) and MIDI devices.

Drag-and-Drop Functionality

With the advent of drag-and-drop features, you can easily open or print documents using a mouse. To open a document, simply click and drag the document's icon from the File Manager to an open application. To print a document, drag the icon to the Print Manager. (Note that either the application or Print Manager must be running on the desktop.) You no longer need to open a list of files and search through them for the document you want to access; now you simply drag the icon for the document from the Windows file management system, File Manager.

File Manager provides a much better way to organize and locate files in your system. You can create a window that displays the icons for documents related to a project, or another window that displays the icons of your personal documents.

Improved Application Startup

Windows now includes a Startup group in the Program Manager. In this group you can place any programs you want to start when Windows starts. Simply drag the icon for the program from any other Program Manager group into the Startup group.

The icons that start applications have new features as well. You can add a shortcut key to quickly start an application using keyboard keys, even if its icon is not visible. You can also specify a working directory for an icon. In this way, you can specify exactly where the application can access files. You can even create several startup icons for an application, each accessing files in a different directory. This feature lets you organize files more efficiently at the directory level.

Display Enhancements

The video display market is growing rapidly, mostly due to Windows' ability to support many different display resolutions and color capabilities. You can use any display and video card from any manufacturer, as long as the manufacturer provides a Windows 3.1 compatible driver. Competition is strong and prices are dropping; at the same time, video display performance is improving. A common video display system now supports 256 colors, has a screen resolution of 1024x768, and provides accelerated performance with the use of graphics coprocessors. With more colors, you can display natural-looking images for multimedia desktop presentations or full color brochures and pamphlets. With a bigger Windows desktop, you can display more windows at once in a side-by-side arrangement, not one on top of another. Many video cards are being accelerated using processors from S3, Western Digital, Texas Instruments, and other companies. These accelerated boards relieve the system's processor of many graphics routines and vastly increase the performance of Windows.

Enhanced Communications

Those who use communication applications will appreciate Windows 3.1's support of the 16550 UART (Universal Asynchronous Receiver Transmitter). This special chip can vastly improve the performance of communication transfers. In addition, Windows applications can now set transfer speeds higher than 19.2 Kbaud—up to 57.6 Kbaud. Previous problems with I/O addresses and interrupt settings on serial ports have also been resolved.

32-Bit Operation

Windows is moving toward the implementation of 32-bit operation. Future Windows versions such as NT will provide this technology to take full advantage of 32-bit processors like the Intel 80386 and 80486. Some of these new operating system features are already implemented in Windows 3.1. The FastDisk option in Windows 3.1 is a good example. It bypasses the slower BIOS routines for accessing the disk and uses its own disk routines to improve performance. It also provides another important feature: the ability to support multiple-disk accesses by non-Windows applications. Users benefit by being able to run more Windows and non-Windows applications together. Unlike in previous versions, in Windows 3.1 a non-Windows application can be partially swapped out to disk to conserve memory and allow other applications to run. In the past, the non-Windows application had to reside completely in memory before it could make a disk access. While you could still load other applications simultaneously, the non-Windows applications used so much memory that the number of other applications you could run was limited.

Requirements for Running Windows

You'll need the following equipment and peripherals to run Windows. Most systems that run MS-DOS will also run Windows. (A file called SETUP.TXT on Windows Disk 1 provides more information about equipment that Windows may or may not be compatible with.)

- You should have Microsoft MS-DOS version 3.1 or later. However, it is highly recommended that you use MS-DOS version 5.0, especially if your system has less than 4 megabytes of memory and you plan to run non-Windows applications from within Windows.

- Generally, you need two megabytes or more of memory, but it is recommended that you have at least four megabytes of memory for optimum performance. Memory should be configured as extended memory except in special cases, as described in Chapters 8 and 9.

- You'll also need six megabytes or more of disk space, but this is for the minimum Windows installation that doesn't include some of the optional accessories.

- You must have a graphics adapter and display, preferably VGA or better.

- A mouse is a vital component to any Windows system, although not absolutely required. This book assumes you are using a mouse.

Where to Get Additional Information

This book provides tutorials and other essential information to get you up and running with Windows 3.1. Other sources of information are included with the Windows 3.1 software and are in the form of text files copied to the hard drive, as listed below.

SETUP.TXT   This file contains information about installing Windows and about any software or hardware that may cause problems. You'll find this file on Windows Disk 1. Open it with any text editor and read it before installing Windows.

README.WRI   This file contains information about any updates to Windows. You can read this file using Windows Write.

PRINTERS.WRI   This file contains information about specific printers and fonts. You can read this file using Windows Write.

NETWORKS.WRI   This file contains information about using Windows with computer networks.

SYSINI.WRI   This file describes settings in the SYSTEM.INI file and how to change them. This file contains hardware settings and other settings that Windows uses every time it starts. You'll also find a detailed index of this file in Appendix E of this book.

WININI.WRI   This file describes settings in the WIN.INI file and how to change them. This file contains customized Windows environment settings.

How to Use This Book

Windows 3.1: The Complete Reference assumes you have some familiarity with computers and may have used previous versions of Windows, or that you have read *Windows 3.1 Made Easy* (Sheldon, Osborne/McGraw-Hill, 1992). You'll learn some of the basics of using the interface, but each topic quickly moves to intermediate and advanced features. This approach provides you with the most information.

You'll learn how to optimize hardware and software features to get the best performance from Windows using the new display, disk, and printer technologies. You'll also learn about working with new features like OLE and multimedia. Multimedia and MIDI equipment is discussed in detail. You'll also find a thorough discussion of the graphics production process, including scanning, editing, and printing images. A reference section provides quick help on every command and dialog box option. As you work with Windows during day-to-day operations, you can refer back to this section for a quick reminder of how to use a command. A glossary is also included, along with a unique index to the SYSTEM.INI file.

Because Windows uses a common user interface, Chapter 3 covers the common features up front. You'll learn how to use Open, Save, Print, Font, Edit, and Clipboard commands for *all* Windows applications. Later in the book, you'll learn about features specific to each application. Presenting this common material up front gives you a chance to learn how all Windows applications work so you can start experimenting on your own.

How This Book is Organized

Windows 3.1: The Complete Reference is split into three parts and and a set of appendixes. Each part is discussed below.

Part I

The first part is for beginning Windows users or those who need to familiarize themselves with the new features of Windows 3.1. Chapter 1 opens with a discussion of how to start Windows and how to use its interface. Chapter 2 shows you how to start programs and teaches you skills you can use to begin working with any application that runs under Windows. Chapter 3 then covers the global techniques common to all Windows applications, such as opening, saving, editing, and printing files.

Chapter 4 provides a brief discussion of Object Linking and Embedding to familiarize you with methods of integrating applications. Once you learn the basics, you'll be able to use OLE features as you work through the remainder of the book. (A detailed discussion of OLE is covered in Chapter 25.) Chapter 5 shows you a few tricks and techniques for optimizing your use of Windows and provides a thorough discussion of the Windows Recorder program, which you can use to automate your daily activities using keyboard macros.

To further optimize your use of Windows, Chapter 6 covers techniques for organizing applications and creating startup icons in the Program Manager. You'll learn how to rearrange icons and groups to fit your needs, and how to change the properties of icons so you can work with specific document files. Part I ends with a discussion of files and the File Manager in Chapter 7. You'll learn how to quickly access files that you want to open or print. You'll also see how to organize the File Manager into a powerful application- and document-launching utility that rivals the Program Manager. In fact, you may want to make the File Manager instead of the Program Manager your permanent shell.

Part II

The second part discusses intermediate and advanced topics of concern to more-than-casual Windows users. Chapter 8 starts with a discussion of the Windows architecture. You'll learn about the components of Windows and how they work in the background to manage your applications. You'll also become familiar with memory, microprocessors, and other components. This information is useful to know as you read through the remaining chapters. Chapter 9 discusses memory management under Windows. It contains a detailed discussion of configuring and optimizing memory using new features in DOS 5. You'll also find useful information about optimizing memory for the different Windows operating modes and for when you run non-Windows applications.

Chapter 10 discusses optimizing Windows. This is a topic that should not be taken lightly. A complete list of tips and tricks is presented, and you'll be introduced to some interesting Windows commands and options that can help you get the best performance from your system. Chapter 11 follows with a discussion of customizing Windows with special utilities and options. You'll learn how to change basic system settings like the color of windows and the features of the desktop. You'll also learn about some special settings that aren't covered in most documentation.

Chapters 12 through 15 provide detailed discussions of various hardware components, such as hard disks, video displays, multimedia products, and printers. You'll find the discussion enlightening, and you'll also find details about the underlying Windows settings that determine how your system uses these components. Chapter 16 covers fonts and TrueType.

Part II wraps up with a discusion of networks in Chapter 17. You'll learn how to install Windows on a network and how to access network features with Windows utilities and accessories. If you're a network system administrator, you'll be interested in the methods for installing customized versions of Windows for network users described in this chapter.

Part III

The third part covers Windows and non-Windows applications. The first chapter in the section, Chapter 18, provides a few tips for organizing applications. Chapter 19 then discusses how to start, run, and optimize *non-Windows* applications, which are applications not specifically designed to work with Windows. Chapter 20 covers writing and editing programs like Notepad and Write. Chapter 21 provides a thorough discussion of the graphics process in Windows. This chapter provides essential information for those who need to work with graphics. You'll learn about scanning, editing, file conversion, dithering and halftoning, printing, color separation, and other features. Chapter 22 covers the Windows bitmap editor known as Paintbrush.

Those who need to run Windows communication programs will be interested in Chapter 23. It provides a discussion of communications options and features under Windows and talks about enhanced communications features in Windows 3.1. Chapter 24 discusses the Windows accessories such as Calculator, Calendar, and Cardfile and how you can use them in your day-to-day activities. Chapter 25 then brings together all you've learned about applications and shows you how to integrate their features using Object Linking and Embedding (OLE). Chapter 26 is the command and option reference section, and Chapter 27 is a glossary of terms.

Appendixes

The appendixes include useful information about setting up Windows and customizing the setup process. You'll also find a complete listing of the Windows files and a description of the SYSTEM.INI and WIN.INI Windows startup files.

Windows Update Notes

A set of update notes is available for this book to keep you current with the latest information for Windows. The notes contain the following information:

- Update information from Microsoft Technical Support and the Microsoft Knowledge Base Information service
- Information about known bugs, problems, and solutions
- Software and hardware compatibility information
- System and hardware notes
- The latest tips, tricks, and techniques for Windows and Windows applications

We participate in various online forums where Windows users discuss hardware and software problems and solutions. This "user" information is often vital to running Windows in the most efficient and trouble-free fashion. The first set of notes will be available about two months after the Windows 3.1 release. We constantly update the notes to guarantee the set you receive has the latest information. To further guarantee the accuracy of the information, we print and assemble the notes in-house on an as-needed basis.

To order the notes, use the coupon in the back of this book. Send a $10 check or money order to cover shipping and handling. If you are a California resident, add 72 cents. The price covers our shipping and handling. Make the check payable to Tom Sheldon. This is solely an offering of the author. Osborne/McGraw-Hill takes no responsibility for the fulfillment of this offer.

Part I

Using Windows

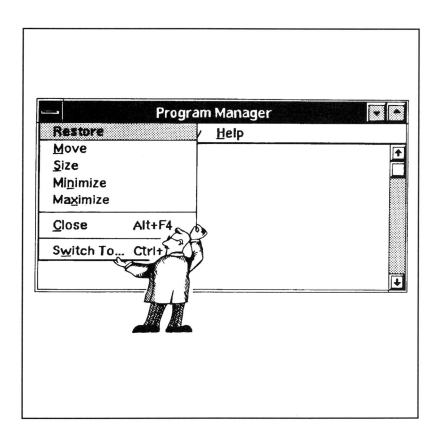

Chapter *1*

Starting and Using Windows

This chapter assumes that Windows is already installed in your computer and you're ready to start using it. First, you'll learn about the Windows startup commands. You'll then learn about window elements, such as menus and scroll bars. You'll also see how to rearrange the windows to fit your own needs.

Starting Windows

To start Windows type **WIN** at the DOS prompt. Windows starts in standard mode or 386 enhanced mode, depending on the processor and memory your system has. You'll learn about these modes next.

The Windows Modes

Windows has two operating modes, standard and 386 enhanced. The mode your system uses depends on its processor and the amount of memory it has available.

- Windows runs in 386 enhanced mode if you have an 80386 computer (or above) with at least 2MB of memory (640K of conventional memory and 1024K of extended memory).

- Windows runs in standard mode if you have an 80286 computer (or above) with at least 1MB of memory (640K of conventional memory and 256K of extended memory). Windows also runs in standard mode on 80386 computers that have less than 2MB of memory.

You can force Windows to start in another mode by specifying a startup parameter. Typing **WIN /S** starts Windows in standard mode. Typing **WIN /3** starts Windows in 386 enhanced mode.

You can't start in 386 enhanced mode if you have an 80286 system, but starting in standard mode on an 80386 system provides a slight increase in speed. However, standard mode doesn't provide the memory and multitasking benefits of 386 enhanced mode, which you may need if you're working with several applications or using graphics or scanning applications that manipulate large images in memory.

If you have an 80386 or 80486 system with between 2MB and 3MB of memory and you don't plan to run non-Windows applications, start Windows in standard mode by typing **WIN /S.**

Startup Command Options

The following sections explain each of the options you can type at the DOS prompt to start Windows.

WIN /S   Type **WIN /S** to cause Windows to start in standard mode.

WIN /3   Type **WIN /3** to cause Windows to start in 386 enhanced mode.

WIN /B   Typing **WIN /B** creates a boot log file called BOOTLOG.TXT that provides you with diagnostic messages while you're booting up. This is called *boot log tracing.* You use this option to diagnose problems. Microsoft technical support may ask you to run this option if you call the support line.

WIN /d:f   This option disables FastDisk for the current session. FastDisk is discussed in Chapter 12.

WIN /d:s   You can use WIN /d:s on 80386 (or above) systems only, and only if instructed to do so when using some memory managers. Windows in 386 enhanced mode normally searches the ROM address space between F000:0000 and 1MB to find a special instruction that is used as a system break point. If this address space contains something other than permanently available ROM, use the /d:s switch. You can also set SystemROMBreakPoint=FALSE in the [386Enhanced] section of the SYSTEM.INI file.

WIN /d:v   You can use WIN /d:v on 80386 (or above) systems only. Some hard drives might require this option in order for interrupts to be processed correctly. If WIN /d:v is used, the ROM routine handles the interrupts, which slows down system performance. If /d:v is not used, Windows terminates interrupts from the hard disk controller, bypassing the ROM routine that handles these interrupts. You can also set VirtualHDIRQ=FALSE in the [386Enhanced} section of SYSTEM.INI. You may need this option when using SCSI drivers, as discussed in Chapter 12.

WIN /d:*x*   If Windows runs erratically, it is usually because of conflicts with devices or programs for the upper memory area, typically the range A000-FFFF. Use the /d:*x* option to exclude a block of upper memory, replacing *x* with the range of memory to exclude. The EMMExclude option in SYSTEM.INI accomplishes the same thing, but gives you more control over the memory area to exclude. Refer to Chapter 9 for a complete discussion of conflicts over upper memory area.

Starting Windows Applications

The Windows command line also supports a run option. You can specify which program you want to start or which document to open when Windows starts by adding the option to the Windows startup command at the DOS command prompt. Starting an application when Windows starts is especially useful in classroom environments when you want students to go directly into the application they're learning. You can place the command in the AUTOEXEC.BAT file if you want it to run when the system starts.

The following command starts Windows and loads Microsoft Word at the same time:

```
WIN D:\WINWORD\WINWORD.EXE
```

To include a startup option on the command line along with a run option, type the startup option first, followed by the run option as shown here:

```
WIN /S D:\WINWORD\WINWORD.EXE
```

Most documents in Windows are *associated* with the programs that create them, which means you can specify the name of the document to open without first loading the application that created it. The application automatically opens with the document you specified in its workspace. For example, to open a document called DAILY.TXT when starting Windows, you would type the following at the DOS prompt:

```
WIN DAILY.TXT
```

Files with the extension .TXT are normally associated with the Windows Notepad text editor. This Windows startup command loads Notepad with DAILY.TXT in its workspace.

6

The Startup Group

Using run commands to start Windows and applications is fine if you're starting only one application. If you use more than one application in your normal work sessions, however, a better method is to place icons for applications you want to start when Windows starts in the Program Manager Startup group, as you'll see in the next chapter.

The Windows Interface

When you first start Windows, you see the Program Manager window, which is shown in Figure 1-1. The basic elements of this window are listed and discussed in the following sections. Note that the appearance of this window may be slightly different on your system.

The entire screen area is known as the *desktop*. The Program Manager window is placed on top of the desktop. Other application windows you open also rest on the desktop. One window is always *active*, which means its title bar is highlighted and it reacts when you use certain keyboard keys. The active window usually overlaps other, non-active windows. Use the mouse to click other windows and make them active. You will learn later how to use several keyboard methods to make other windows active.

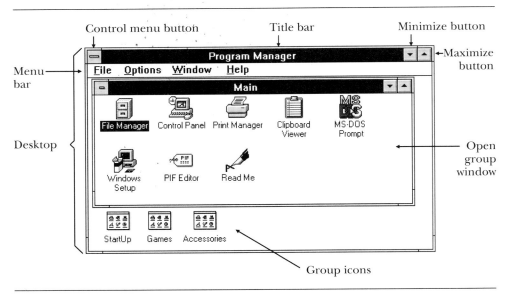

Figure 1-1. *The Program Manager window appears when you first start Windows*

A mouse is almost essential to using the Windows interface. With it, you click window elements such as buttons and scroll bars, or click and drag items on the desktop. Keyboard methods for accessing windows are available, but using a mouse is much easier in most cases. Chapter 5 covers keyboard techniques, but mainly for the purpose of recording macros for playback at a later time. There are three mouse actions in Windows:

- Click a button or option once to select it.

- Double-click an option to execute it.

- Click and drag. This action is the equivalent of grabbing an object such as a window or an icon and moving it to another location. You click, hold, and drag, and then release the mouse to drop the object.

The Program Manager

Think of the Program Manager as the "main menu" for Windows. Its primary purpose is to provide a quick and easy method for starting applications. The Program Manager window holds icons that you double-click to start applications. Find the Read Me icon in the Program Manager Main group and double-click it now. An hourglass appears as the application loads. In a moment, you see a new window overlapping the Program Manager window. Its title bar reads Write - README.WRI.

The active window's title bar is highlighted. The title bars of inactive windows are dimmed or white. You'll see an example of this shortly in Figure 1-2.

Position the mouse pointer over the Write window's title bar, and then click and hold the mouse button. Drag the window on the desktop until you see the title bar of the underlying Program Manager window, then release the mouse button. Click anywhere on the Program Manager window to make it active and bring it to the top of the stack of windows.

The Program Manager contains groups of *program startup icons*, or icons that you double-click to start programs. The group called Main is open in Figure 1-1. Three other groups, Accessories, Games, and StartUp are visible at the bottom of the Program Manager window. These icons are *minimized groups*. You double-click the icons to open them as windows within the Program Manager window. Try double-clicking the Accessories group now to open its window and display the icons within it.

Now the Accessories group window overlaps the Main group window within the Program Manager window. You can double-click any of its icons to start the associated program. Try double-clicking the Clock icon. When the Clock appears, click and drag its title bar to move it off to the side.

Document Windows

The Program Manager is one of many Windows applications that contains its own windows. Notice that the Main and Accessories windows are within the borders of the Program Manager. You cannot drag these subwindows outside the borders of the Program Manager window. Subwindows of this type are called *document windows*. They are most common when working in applications such as word processors or drawing programs that allow you to work on several documents at once. Each document window holds a separate document, letting you quickly switch among those that are open. An application's *workspace* is the area that documents load into. Each document window represents a separate workspace.

Microsoft Word for Windows uses document windows. Figure 1-2 illustrates Microsoft Word for Windows with two open document windows. The title bar of each displays the loaded document name. (Notice that the title bar of the active window, CHAP1.DOC, is highlighted, but the title bar of the inactive window, NETWORKS.DOC, is white.) The important thing to know about document windows is that each has its own window elements, but also shares the commands and menu options of the main application.

The Desktop

The desktop is the underlying background for Windows. It takes up the entire screen. As you open more applications, they'll begin to cover the desktop and overlap one another. If you opened Write and Clock previously, you'll notice that they take up most of the desktop unless you have a high-resolution screen with a large desktop.

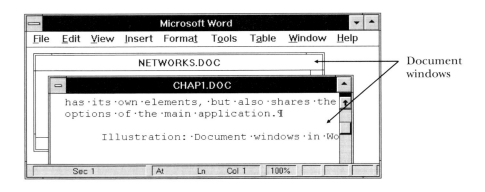

Figure 1-2.   *Two open document windows in Microsoft Word for Windows*

To make a different window active, click any visible portion of that window with the mouse. If you can't see the window, try one of the following to make it active:

- Double-click any visible part of the desktop to display the Task List shown in Figure 1-3. Double-click the name of the application to work with, making it the active window.

- If you can't see the desktop to click it because too many windows are open, press CTRL-ESC. This also opens the Task List.

- Minimize open windows, as discussed next.

Applications on the Desktop

When the screen gets cluttered, you can *temporarily* remove open applications from the desktop by clicking their minimize buttons (the down arrow button in the upper-left corner of the window). When a running application is *minimized*, its icon appears at the bottom of the desktop. This icon looks like the icon in the Program Manager, but don't get the two mixed up. The one on the desktop is a running application. It's still in memory and may contain documents in its workspace.

Click the minimize button of the Clock and Write windows now to see how this works. Note that Write's icon displays the name of the document in its workspace and that Clock still displays the time in its minimized state. To restore a minimized application, double-click its icon.

To *maximize* an application, or display the window of an application full-screen over the entire desktop, use the maximize button. This gives you the maximum amount of room to work with the documents in your applications, and incidentally, provides better performance for the application because Windows no longer needs to update the appearance of other windows on the screen. Try maximizing the Write

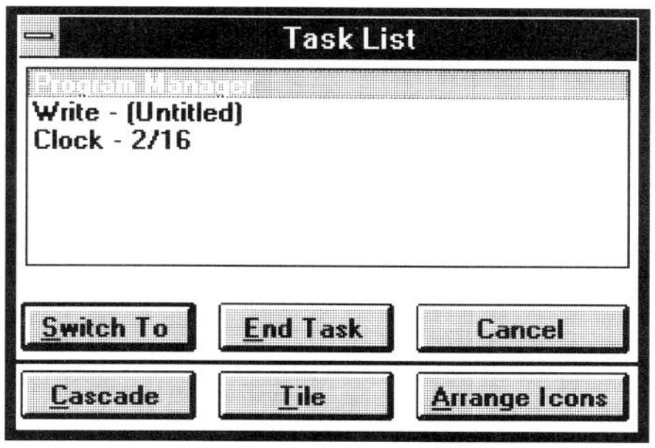

Figure 1-3.   The Task List dialog box

window. First double-click its icon to restore its window, then click the maximize button, which is the upward-pointing arrow in the upper-right corner of the screen.

You can *restore* a maximized window to its previous size by using the restore button. When a window is maximized, its maximize button turns into a restore button. Look at the upper-right corner of the Write window. The double-pointing arrow is the restore button. Click it to restore the window to its previous size, or click the minimize button to place Write as an icon on the desktop.

Sizing and Rearranging Windows

You can resize windows by dragging their borders. If you drag a border inward, you shrink the window. Dragging a border toward the edge of the screen enlarges the window. There are several reasons for resizing windows:

- To work with two applications side by side.
- To make underlying application windows visible for easy switching.
- To show only part of a window while working in other applications.

The Clock is a good example of an application to resize. The Clock displays the time while you work in another window; it doesn't need to be large, so you can resize it to any size you want. Two methods of resizing a window are listed here:

- *Change one side* Point to any side of an open window. When the double-headed arrow appears, click and drag inward or outward.
- *Change two sides* Point to any corner of an open window. When the double-headed diagonal arrow appears, click and drag inward or outward.

As you drag the side or corner of a border, a shadow border follows the pointer to indicate the window's new size. Release the mouse button and the window will be resized.

After resizing a window, you'll probably want to move it or place it beside another window. Click the window's title bar, then drag the window to its new location.

The Task List

The Task List provides a way to quickly rearrange the open windows on the desktop. Before you try using it, restore the windows of the applications you've opened so far (Write, Clock, and Program Manager). Remember, a restored window is neither minimized nor maximized. When you use the restore button, the window reverts to its default size.

Cascade and Tile Arrangements

Double-click a blank portion of the desktop, or press CTRL-ESC to open the Task List as pictured in Figure 1-3. The Task List has six buttons but we're interested in the effects of just two: Cascade and Tile. Click each to see what happens to the open windows.

- *Cascade* Cascading arranges open windows so that they are staggered, one behind another. This arrangement is useful because it keeps windows large enough to work in, but makes them easy to select.

- *Tile* When you tile windows, they align edge to edge, much like ceramic tiles on a floor or countertop. Tiling is useful when you want to see the contents of each open window or place two open windows side by side.

Try this. Minimize the Clock, then open the Task List (CTRL-ESC) and click the Tile button again. Now only two open windows are tiled, assuming you still have the desktop arrangement discussed earlier, making them more reasonable in size and easier to work with.

When windows are tiled or cascaded, click the maximize button of the window you want to use. When done, restore the window, then maximize another.

Other Task List Options

The Task List provides a way to switch to, close, and arrange windows or icons on the desktop. You've already learned how to tile and cascade files, and several ways to move and resize them. Here are alternative techniques:

- An alternative method of switching to an application is to highlight its name, then click the Switch To button. This is really a keyboard method, since mouse users can simply double-click the application's name. In Chapter 5, you'll see how this keyboard method is useful when recording macros.

- To close an application, highlight it and click the End Task button.

- To arrange icons on the desktop, click the Arrange Icons button.

Switching Among Applications

The Task List displays a list of applications to choose from, and has buttons for organizing the desktop. Two other ways to switch among applications are listed here:

- Press ALT-ESC to highlight each open application or application icon, one after the other, until the application you want to use is highlighted.

- Press ALT-TAB to preview each open application or icon. A title box appears in the middle of the screen with the name of each application as you press the keys. The application listed in the title box when you release the keys becomes active. If the application is minimized to an icon, press ALT-TAB to restore it.

Other Windows Elements

There are a few other Windows elements to explore. In this section, you'll take a look at menus and scroll bars.

Menus

The Program Manager has four menus: File, Options, Window, and Help. You can use any of the following methods to open a menu:

- Click the menu name with the mouse.

- Press ALT followed by the underlined letter of the menu name. For example, press ALT-F to open the File menu. (If you refer back to Figure 1-1, you can see that the first letter in each of these four menus is the *mnemonic*, or the letter underlined on screen that you use in a key combination to access that menu.)

Menus like the Program Manager's are often called *drop-down menus* because they drop down from the menu bar. In some applications, you can actually click and drag drop-down menus and places them on the desktop for future use. These are called *tear-off menus*. Menus have *options*, or choices that you select from; the top option is always highlighted when you first open a menu. Do one of the following to choose another menu option:

- Click an option with the mouse.

- Type the underlined letter of the menu option.

- Use the DOWN ARROW key to move the highlight to the option, and then press ENTER.

 If a menu is open, you can press the RIGHT ARROW *or* LEFT ARROW *key to scan across the menu bar and open other menus. Try it. Press the* ESC *key to close a menu if you don't want to use it.*

Keep in mind that keyboard methods are sometimes quicker and easier to use than the mouse. For example, press ALT-F R to select the Run option from the File menu. Keyboard methods are also useful when creating macros, which will be discussed in Chapter 5. A *macro* is a recording of keyboard commands you can play back at any time.

Other items you'll encounter on menus are labeled in Figure 1-4.

Quick Keys   Note that some menu items include *quick keys*, which are keyboard alternatives to using your mouse or the menu to select an option. Click File on the Program Manager menu bar and notice that Move's quick key is F7, Copy's is F8, and so on. So to access the Copy option you can either select Copy with the keyboard keys from the menu, click it with your mouse from the menu, or press F8 on your keyboard.

Unavailable Options   An unavailable option is "grayed out," meaning that it's not currently available for selection. Usually, you must pick an object or file to work with before the menu option becomes available.

Ellipsis Options   The ellipsis (...) in a menu option indicates that a dialog box opens when the option is selected. A *dialog box* is used to enter additional parameters and options for the command, as covered in the next section.

Toggle Options   A toggle option has a check mark when enabled. If there's no check mark, it's disabled. Open the Program Manager Options menu and notice that Auto Arrange and Save Settings on Exit are checked (enabled). Click the Auto Arrange option once to disable it, then again to enable it. Notice that the menu closes when you choose the item, so you need to open it again just to check its status. When you open the menu again, make sure Auto Arrange is enabled. The remainder of

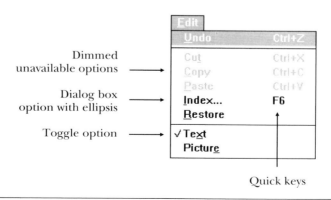

Dimmed
unavailable options →

Dialog box
option with ellipsis →

Toggle option →

Quick keys

Figure 1-4.   *Items you'll encounter on menus*

this book uses the terminology "enabled" and "disabled" to indicate whether these toggled menu options are on or off.

The Control Menu

The Control menu button is in the upper-left corner of every window. When you click it, the Control menu shown in Figure 1-5 appears. You can also press ALT-SPACEBAR on the keyboard to display the menu (ALT-HYPHEN for document windows). The options on this menu are really designed for keyboard users. They provide keyboard methods for resizing, moving, minimizing, and maximizing a window.

To close a window, choose the Close option, or better yet, simply double-click the Control menu button. The Switch To option opens the Task List.

Dialog Boxes

A dialog box opens when you select a menu item that has an ellipsis. Click the About Program Manager option on the Help menu to display the About Program Manager dialog box shown in Figure 1-6. This dialog box indicates the version number of Windows, the serial number of your copy, and the owner's name. The bottom shows important memory and startup information. Open this box when you're concerned about memory problems or what mode you're using, or if Windows seems to be having a problem. System Resources is a measure of all the "objects" on the screen that Windows tracks. Objects are icons, buttons, scroll bars, or any other active elements on a window. The more applications you open, the more resources Windows needs to track.

 If the System Resources percentage falls below 20 percent, close application windows. If System Resources are still low, close all applications and restart Windows.

Program Manager	
Restore	Help
Move	
Size	
Minimize	
Maximize	
Close Alt+F4	
Switch To... Ctrl+Esc	

Figure 1-5.   *The Control menu in the Program Manager*

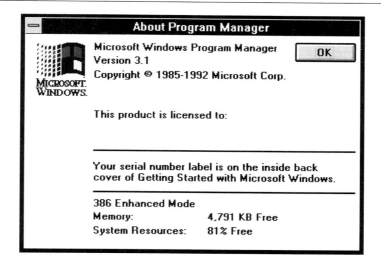

Figure 1-6.   *The About Program Manager dialog box*

Most Windows 3.1 applications have their own About dialog boxes that display the version number and other information.

Figure 1-7 shows a dialog box with a number of different controls. You use these controls to set options or make decisions about how a command should run. The advantage of dialog boxes is that they present you with options so you don't need to look them up in a book.

The options on dialog boxes are discussed in the following sections. Remember that each dialog box is different. Some contain only one or two items, while others contain many items, as does the HP LaserJet dialog box in Figure 1-7.

Command Buttons   You've already used command buttons. You could click the OK button to execute the settings in a dialog box, or click the Cancel button to cancel your changes. Buttons with an ellipsis display an additional dialog box.

Text Boxes   Use text boxes to supply additional information by typing it at the keyboard. You access a text box by clicking it, or by pressing the TAB key until its contents are highlighted. When you type new text, the highlighted text is over-written.

16

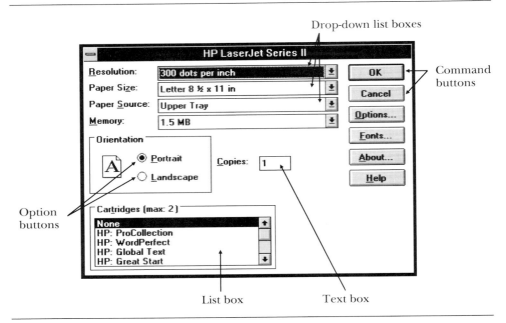

Figure 1-7.   *Controls you'll find in some dialog boxes*

List Boxes   List boxes let you scroll to locate an option in a list of options. To select the option you want, you click it when it appears. A list box has a scroll bar, as discussed in the next section.

Drop-Down List Boxes   A drop-down list box is a one-line text box with a down arrow button next to it. When you click the down arrow button, a drop-down list appears with a more complete list of options. When you click one of the options, it appears in the text box and the drop-down list disappears. Program designers use drop-down list boxes instead of list boxes to save room in dialog boxes.

Option Buttons   Option buttons always come in sets. They are usually within a field that is surrounded by a box. The Orientation field in Figure 1-7 is an example. Only one option button in a group can be enabled. You enable an option button by clicking it; any other button that may have been enabled then disables. The remainder of this book refers to this toggle action as enabling or disabling an option button.

Check Boxes   Some dialog boxes have check boxes. You may see check boxes by themselves or in sets. Each check box can be enabled or disabled. An X in the box indicates it is enabled. Clicking an enabled box disables it. The remainder of this book refers to this as "enabling" or "disabling" a check box.

Warning and Message Dialog Boxes

When you execute illegal commands and options, or if you forget an important step (such as saving a document before closing an application), Windows warns you by displaying a message dialog box, similar to the one shown here:

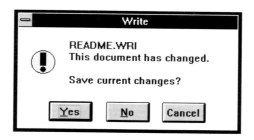

In this dialog box, you can click Yes to save the changes, No to exit without saving changes, or Cancel to return to the application without saving or exiting.

Scroll Bars

Scroll bars come in two varieties: vertical and horizontal. A vertical scroll bar is used to scroll up and down through a document. A horizontal scroll bar is used to scroll left or right in a document that is too wide to fit in a window.

Double-click the Read Me icon in the Main group window of the Program Manager. You can experiment with the scroll bars using this document.

A scroll bar has four active areas, as shown in the following illustration. The horizontal scroll bar is shown here, but the vertical scroll bar's operations are essentially the same.

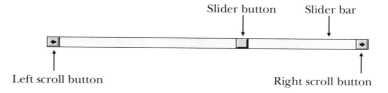

- Click the scroll buttons (either horizontal or vertical) to move through the text. The slider button also moves to indicate the new position in the text.

- Click and hold the scroll buttons for continuous scrolling.

- The slider bar is a measure of the document width or length. You can click it to scroll one page or screen at a time.

- Click and drag the slider button anywhere in the slider bar. The document view changes to display text relative to the position of the slider button in the slider bar. For example, if you move the slider button halfway down the slider bar, when you release it the information onscreen will be about halfway into your document.

Once you're done working with Write's scroll bars, click its minimize button to remove it from the desktop.

Customizing with Control Panel Options

In this section, you'll get a chance to work with some of Windows' features by changing the colors of windows, and by placing a picture on the desktop. The options for doing these things are located in the Control Panel. Open the Control Panel now by double-clicking the Control Panel icon in the Main group window of the Program Manager. A window similar to Figure 1-8 appears.

The Control Panel holds utilities used to change the settings of printers, ports, the keyboard, sound devices, the mouse, and many other features. A full discussion of the Control Panel utilities is covered in Chapter 11.

Changing Colors

To change the colors of Windows, double-click the Color icon. The Color dialog box opens. At the top is the Color Schemes drop-down list box. You can click its down arrow button to show a list of color schemes, or you can press the DOWN ARROW key on your keyboard. As you press the key, various color scheme samples appear in the middle of the dialog box. When you find one you like, click the OK button.

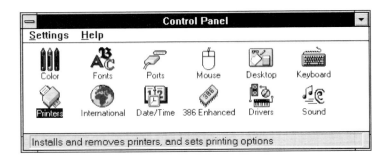

Figure 1-8. *The Control Panel window*

You can create custom color schemes beyond those defined in the Color Schemes list box. Creating your own custom color scheme is covered in Chapter 11.

Pictures on the Desktop

Now try placing a picture on your desktop. The Control Panel should still be open from the last example. Double-click the Desktop icon. The Desktop dialog box appears with a wide range of options. Click the down arrow button on the File drop-down list box in the Wallpaper field. Scroll through the drop-down list until you see the LEAVES.BMP file entry. Click it to make its name appear in the File text box. Now click the OK button at the upper-right section of the Desktop dialog box. A leaf pattern appears on your desktop. Take a few moments to try some of the other options; if you want to experiment further with the options in the Desktop dialog box, refer to Chapter 11.

Rearranging the Program Manager

The Program Manager arrangement you see when Windows first starts is fine for new users, but you can resize its window and rearrange its group windows to fit your own needs. There are also a few options to enable, as discussed in the next sections.

Setting Options

The first thing to do is set the Program Manager options. Click the Options menu and note the enabled/disabled status of the following items.

Auto Arrange   When Auto Arrange is enabled, icons within Program Manager groups automatically rearrange themselves to fit within a resized window. If Auto Arrange is disabled, you must manually click and drag icons to rearrange them, or choose the Arrange Icons option from the Window menu.

Minimize on Use   When Minimize on Use is enabled, the Program Manager shrinks to an icon when you start an application. When Minimize on Use is disabled, the Program Manager stays on the desktop. It's sometimes best to minimize the Program Manager to make it easier to find when the desktop gets crowded.

Save Settings on Exit   When Save Settings on Exit is enabled, any changes you make to the size and arrangement of windows are saved for the next session. For example, if you leave the Accessories window open on top of the Main group window when exiting, that's how it will be the next time you start Windows. Disable this option if you've made an arrangement you don't want to keep.

Saving Arrangements

After making changes to the arrangement of groups or the size of windows, you'll want to make sure they are saved for the next session. One way to do this is to enable the Save Settings on Exit option and exit Windows. Another way to save the changes *without* exiting Windows is to hold down the SHIFT key and click Exit Windows on the File menu. The changes are saved, but you don't actually exit Windows.

Resizing and Rearranging Group Windows

You can resize and rearrange the group windows in the Program Manager in the same way you resize and rearrange application windows on the desktop. Try the following examples to get an idea of the options available.

 Before getting started with the following examples, make sure Auto Arrange on the Options menu is enabled.

Tiling Group Windows

Open the Main group and the Accessories group (double-click their icons if a group is not open). Click Tile on the Window menu to automatically arrange the open group windows. If the Program Manager window is small, the new tiled windows will contain scroll bars for scrolling icons into view. To see all the icons at once, enlarge the Program Manager window, then choose Tile again. You can see how these steps help you find the right arrangement for the window.

Cascading Group Windows

Now try cascading the group windows. Open the Games group, then choose Cascade from the Window menu. Now the windows are staggered. Resize the Program Manager and choose Cascade again. Note that the last window selected is at the top of the cascade. Click the Main group window, then choose Cascade to place it at the top of the stack.

Custom Group Arrangements

You don't need to rely on the Tile and Cascade options for your group window arrangements. You can resize each group window to a size that's appropriate for the number of icons they hold, then place them side by side in a custom tiled arrangement as shown in Figure 1-9.

Taking this a step further, you can even create your own groups, then copy the icons in the Main, Accessories, and Games groups into them. Thus, you might have a Daily group that contains the File Manager, MS-DOS Prompt, Write, Calendar,

Chapter 1:   Starting and Using Windows

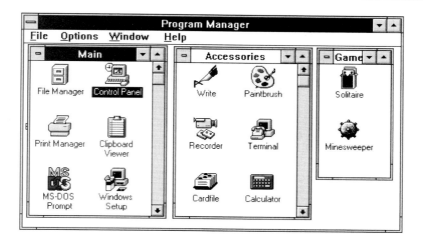

Figure 1-9.   *A custom tiled window arrangement*

Calculator, and other programs you use on a daily basis. You can create your own icons to add to this group, as well. Creating custom groups and icons is covered in Chapter 6.

Closing Applications and Exiting Windows

Always exit from Windows using the procedures described here. Applications open on the desktop may contain documents that haven't been saved. In addition, the SmartDrive disk caching utility may hold information that must be written to disk. If you turn the system off, this information will be lost.

Check the status of the Save Settings on Exit option of the Options menu. If you don't want to save the changes you've made to the windows, disable this option.

Choose the Exit Windows option from the Program Manager's File menu or double-click the Control button (upper-left corner) to exit Windows. If applications are open with documents that haven't been saved, Windows displays a message that prompts you to save the documents before exiting.

Chapter 2

Starting Programs

Chapter 1 covered the basics of starting Windows. Recall that it's possible to start a program when you start Windows by including the program's startup command with the Windows startup command. Other methods of starting programs are covered in this chapter.

Starting Applications from the Program Manager

Once Windows loads and the Program Manager window is on the screen, you start applications by double-clicking their icons. Program Manager groups have an interesting feature. The icon of the last program executed in a group is highlighted the next time you open that group. To start the program, just press ENTER. You can highlight any icon in a group by pressing the arrow keys, and then press ENTER to start it, but this increases the number of keystrokes; the mouse is more convenient for this.

Other ways to start programs in the Program Manager are to assign and use quick keys (covered in Chapter 1) or to place the icon for the program in the Startup group so it loads every time Windows starts.

Using Quick Keys

You can assign a quick-key sequence to icons in the Program Manager, making it possible to start any program from the keyboard. When starting a program with quick keys, it's not necessary to have the group window open. Quick keys reduce the number of steps you must perform to start a program from the Program Manager by eliminating the need to open or arrange windows when looking for a specific icon.

To assign quick keys to an icon, first select it. Click the MS-DOS Prompt icon in the Main group by clicking it now (click it once). The icon's name is highlighted. Now choose Properties from the File menu to display the Program Item Properties dialog box, as shown in Figure 2-1. Use TAB to get to the Shortcut Key field, or click it, then type a letter on the keyboard (such as **D** for DOS). The quick-key sequence CTRL-ALT-D is automatically inserted in the field. Click OK to save your changes, then press CTRL-ALT-D to start the DOS Prompt. When you get to the DOS prompt, type **EXIT** and press ENTER to return to Windows.

The Shortcut Key field adds CTRL-ALT to your quick key so it doesn't conflict with Windows key assignments. For example, ALT by itself highlights the menu bar, so it can never be assigned to a quick key. Try assigning quick keys to your other icons, but be sure to write them down for reference. If you forget a quick-key sequence, just click the icon and choose Properties from the File menu to view its quick-key sequence.

Starting Minimized Applications

The Program Item Properties dialog box, as you've seen, is the place to make changes to the startup properties of icons in the Program Manager. One interesting option is the Run Minimized check box. When enabled, the application starts, but immediately minimizes to an icon on the desktop. You don't need this setting if you use an application as soon as its starts. However, when you're working on a project that requires several applications, it's easier to start all the applications before you start working. Enabling the Run Minimized option places those applications on the desktop as icons so you can quickly get to them when you need them.

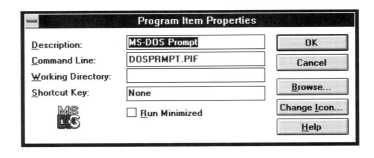

Figure 2-1.   *The Program Item Properties dialog box holds the startup parameters of an icon*

In the previous section, you added a quick-key sequence to the MS-DOS Prompt. When you execute the quick keys, the DOS prompt immediately appears. To return to Windows, type **EXIT**, (or press CTRL-ESC, as described later). Click the MS-DOS Prompt in the Main group again, then choose Properties from the File menu. Enable the Run Minimized check box and click the OK button to save your changes. Now double-click the icon or press CTRL-ALT-D to start MS-DOS. It appears as a minimized icon on the desktop. When you're ready to work with it, double-click the icon.

Enable Run Minimized only if you have a need for it. It's a hassle to double-click an icon twice when you need to use its program immediately.

The Startup Group

The Startup group provides a way to start any application when Windows starts. Unlike adding a command to the Windows startup command in DOS, by using the Startup group method you can start more than one application simultaneously.

The Startup group is like any other Program Manager group, except that icons in it are executed automatically at startup. To copy icons to the group, first open the group window that holds the icon you want to start. In this example, you'll open the Main group and copy the File Manager icon to the Startup group. Follow these steps:

1. Make sure the Startup group icon is visible in the Program Manager window.

2. Hold the CTRL key, then click and drag the File Manager icon to the Startup group.

3. Release the mouse button when the icon is over the Startup group.

4. Double-click the Startup group to see the File Manager icon in it. Click the icon, then choose Properties from the File menu, enable the Run Minimized check box, and click OK.

5. Close the Startup window. You don't need it open during normal operations.

The next time you start Windows, the File Manager will load automatically. Note that holding the CTRL key while dragging makes a copy of the icon in the Startup group. If you don't hold CTRL, the icon is "moved" to the Startup group and removed from the Main group. Never move icons into the Startup group; always copy them. This leaves a copy of the icon in the group where you would most expect to find it if you need to restart the application later. To restart all the applications in the Startup group if you've closed them, choose New Group from the File menu, enter the path to the Startup group file (\WINDOWS), hold down the CTRL key, and press ENTER.

To prevent applications in the Startup group from loading when Windows starts, hold down the SHIFT *key when you start Windows.*

The Load= and Run= Options in WIN.INI

The Startup group did not exist in previous versions of Windows. Instead, you specified the programs you wanted to start when Windows starts in the WIN.INI file. The names of programs to start were placed on the following lines under the [windows] section in the WIN.INI file. WIN.INI is Windows' initialization file. It's located in the \WINDOWS directory and it contains parameters and startup options Windows uses when it starts.

```
[windows]
load=
run=
```

The load= option specifies programs that should load as minimized icons. The run= option specifies programs that should load as open windows. The reason these options are mentioned here is that older applications may still make entries to these settings during setup. If a program automatically starts and you don't see its icon in the Startup group, check the load= or run= entry in the WIN.INI file. For more information on WIN.INI, refer to Appendix D.

The Run Command

If an icon doesn't exist for an application you want to run, choose the Run command from the Program Manager File menu. This will open the Run dialog box shown in Figure 2-2.

Type the name of the command that starts the program in the Command Line field in the same way you would type the command at the DOS command line. You can also include parameters and options (such as document filenames). Click the Run Minimized check box if you want the application to start as a minimized icon

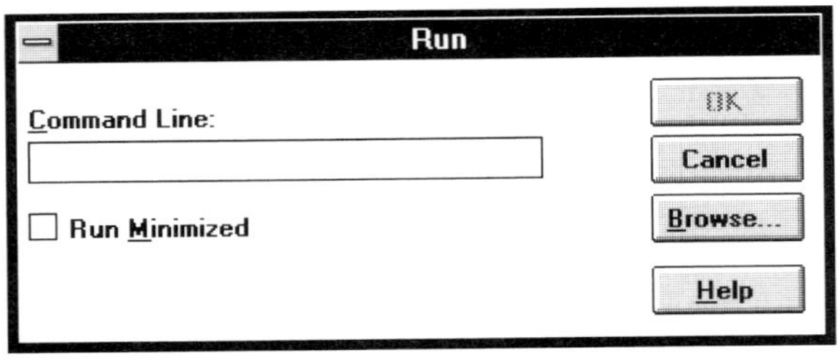

Figure 2-2.   *The Run dialog box is used to start applications that don't have Program Manager icons*

on the desktop. The following command starts Microsoft Word for DOS and loads the file REPORTS.DOC in its workspace:

```
C:\WORD5\WORD.EXE  C:\DOCS\REPORTS.DOC
```

The path to WORD.EXE is specified, along with the path to the document files. Seasoned DOS users know this is not all necessary. If Word is on the DOS path, you can just type **WORD**. The path to the document file is necessary, however.

If you can't remember the name of a program to start, use the Browse button to scan for executable files on your hard drive. The Browse option is used in the same way as the Open option covered in Chapter 3, with the Run command used as an example.

Opening Associated Files

One of the best features of Windows is its ability to open associated document files by typing the filename in the Run command. Remember from Chapter 1 that associated files are linked to the applications that created them by their filename extensions. The most common associated extensions are listed here:

.BMP	Paintbrush
.CAL	Calendar
.CRD	Cardfile
.HLP	Help
.INI	Notepad
.PCX	Paintbrush
.REC	Recorder
.TRM	Terminal
.TXT	Notepad
.WRI	Write

You can try this now by opening the Run dialog box and typing **README.WRI** in the Command Line field. When you click OK, Write opens with README.WRI in its workspace. This produces the same results as double-clicking the Read Me icon in the Main group window. Next, you see how to create startup icons for associated files instead of using the Run command. Before doing so, double-click the Control button on the Write window to close it. You don't need it for now, and since it uses memory when open it's best to close it when you can.

If you're curious about how the Read Me icon loads an application, click the icon once with the mouse, then choose the Properties option from the File menu. Note that the Command Line field lists only the name of the file that opens. This file is associated with Write and automatically opens. Click Cancel to close the window.

Creating Your Own Startup Icons

It's time to learn how to create your own startup icons. In this section, you'll create a startup icon for a Windows editing program that Microsoft left out of the Main group. It's called SysEdit (System Editor) and it's used to edit the system startup files (AUTOEXEC.BAT and CONFIG.SYS) as well as the Windows initialization files (SYSTEM.INI and WIN.INI). You'll use SysEdit extensively in future chapters to make changes to these files as you learn methods for optimizing your system and its resources. Follow these steps to create the icon:

1. First, make sure the title bar of the Main group window is highlighted. New icons are always inserted in the active group window.

2. Choose New from the File menu.

3. The New Program Object dialog box appears with the Program Item option highlighted. You would only click the Program Group option if you wanted to create a new group. Since Program Item is selected, click the OK button.

4. The Program Item Properties dialog box appears as shown in Figure 2-3. This is the Properties box you've already seen, but with blank fields.

5. In both the Description field and the Command Line field, type **SYSEDIT**. Use the TAB key to move to the next field.

6. Don't worry about the remaining options for now. Click the OK button to create the icon.

The icon appears in the Main group. You'll use this same technique later to create icons for your own applications. You can also create icons for documents you work with every day.

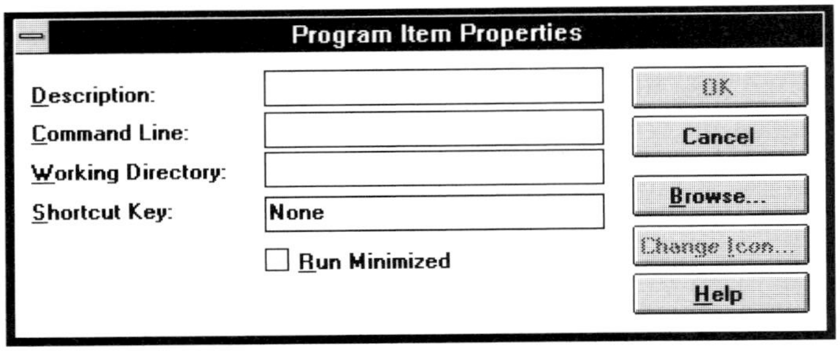

Figure 2-3.   *Use the blank Program Item Properties dialog box to create new startup icons*

Starting Applications from the File Manager

The File Manager is the Windows file handling utility. You use it to list and manipulate the files in your system. The File Manager provides a whole new way to copy, move, rename, delete, and execute documents or program files. The mouse is instrumental in these actions. You click a file icon and drag it to another folder to make a copy, or double-click a program file to execute it.

Start the File Manager now by double-clicking its icon in the Main group. The File Manager window appears as shown in Figure 2-4.

A complete description of the File Manager is presented in Chapter 7. This section concentrates on using it to start programs and open documents.

The File Manager has a menu bar and a document window in its workspace with the C:\WINDOWS*.* title. This document window contains drive icons, a directory tree, and a list of files. Document windows in the File Manager are more commonly referred to as *directory windows.* We're interested in the file list here.

Click and drag the lower-right corner of the directory window down and to the right to make it larger. This improves the file view.

Locate the icon called CALC.EXE in the file list and double-click it with the mouse. The Calculator opens. Minimize the Calculator and take another look at its

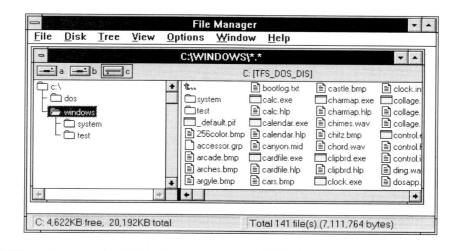

Figure 2-4.   Use the File Manager to manipulate files

File Manager icon. This icon, as shown here, represents *executable* program files, or those you can double-click to start a program.

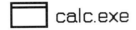

calc.exe

Now locate the icon for the file README.WRI in the file list. You'll need to scroll the list to the right using the scroll bar techniques learned in Chapter 1. The files are listed in alphabetical order, so you should be able to locate it easily. Double-click the icon when you find it. Once again, the README.WRI file opens, demonstrating yet another way to open a document and start applications. Double-click the Control button of the Write window to close it for now.

All associated document files are listed with the following icon in the File Manager. Any file with this "page" icon can be opened using the double-click method.

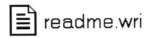

readme.wri

Locating Files to Run

Instead of searching through the list of all files, you can list only executable files or only associated document files. Try the following to see how this works. Choose By File Type from the View menu to display the dialog box shown here:

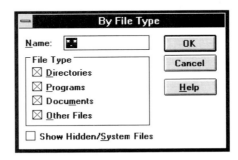

In the File Type field, disable all the options except Programs, then click the OK button. The file list changes to show only program files.

Now open a new window and change the file listing so only associated document files are listed. First, choose New Window from the Window menu (or double-click the icon of the drive that holds your Windows directory). A second directory window appears. Choose By File Type from the View menu, disable the Programs check box, enable the Documents check box, and then click OK. The second directory window now shows only associated document files. Choose Sort by Type from the View menu to sort these files in order of their filename extensions. This helps locate files associated with each application.

You can do two other things to arrange the directory windows you've opened in these exercises:

- Choose Directory Only from the View menu to remove the tree from the current directory window. Click the other directory window to make it active and remove the tree from it as well.

- Choose Cascade from the Window menu to fit both directory windows in the File Manager workspace, as shown in Figure 2-5.

With this arrangement, you can easily start any program or open any document from the File Manager. Why use the File Manager instead of the Program Manager? The File Manager lists files in directories, and shows associated document files as well. While you can create associated document icons in the Program Manager, doing so takes time. It's easier just to keep a directory window in the File Manager open to the documents you want to open in this way.

Drag-and-Drop Method

When the File Manager is open, you can use "drag-and-drop" to open files for viewing or printing. You click and drag an icon over the application it is associated with,

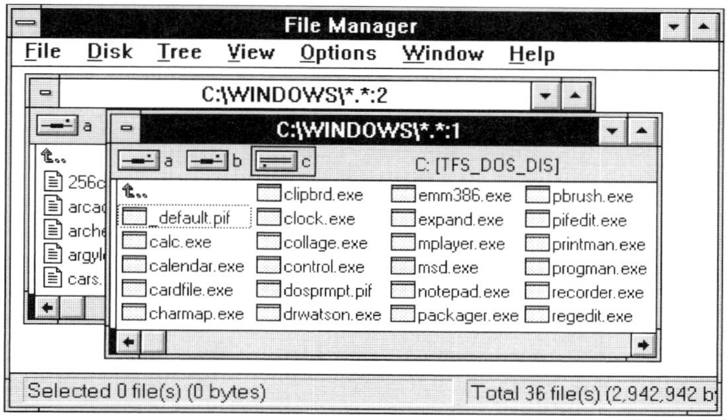

Figure 2-5. *Arrange File Manager directory windows so you can easily open the files you use on a regular basis*

assuming that application is open on the desktop. Try this now using the following steps:

1. Double-click the Notepad icon in the Accessories group of the Program Manager.

2. When the Notepad window opens, drag it so you can see part of it and part of the File Manager.

3. Click the File Manager to make it active, and then locate the file WIN.INI.

4. Click the icon and drag it over the Notepad window. The file loads immediately in Notepad's workspace.

5. Make the File Manager active again, and then find SYSTEM.INI and drag its icon over Notepad. The file loads into the workspace.

The advantage of this method is that only one Notepad window is used. Double-clicking icons in the File Manager opens a separate Notepad window for each document. Use the drag and drop method to quickly view the contents of files.

You can also use this method to print documents by dragging a file's icon over a running copy of the Print Manager, as discussed in Chapter 3.

Non-Windows Applications

Non-Windows applications are DOS applications not specifically designed to work with Windows. If you run these applications from Windows, Windows opens a DOS session and removes most of itself from memory unless you're running in 386 enhanced mode. In 386 enhanced mode, several Windows and DOS applications can run at once, each with its own block of memory and allocation of processor time.

You run DOS applications from Windows for several reasons. The first is because you prefer to work in Windows most of the time and it doesn't make sense to quit Windows and return to DOS to run a DOS application. Another reason is that Windows allows both Windows and non-Windows applications to share information using cut and paste techniques. Third, it's easy to switch from one task to another in Windows. You can work with a DOS-based word processor, and then switch to Windows to use a draw or paint program.

Running MS-DOS

To work at the DOS prompt, double-click the MS-DOS Prompt icon in the Main window. Windows removes itself and DOS appears over the full screen. A message box at the top reminds you to type **EXIT** when you're done with DOS. You can also switch back to Windows and leave the DOS session open by pressing CTRL-ESC to switch back to Windows. The DOS session then minimizes and appears as an icon on the desktop. Double-click that icon to return to the DOS session.

You can run DOS commands or start applications normally from the DOS prompt. Be careful of applications that might crash your system, although this is less of a problem when running 386 enhanced mode since each session is protected from other sessions. DOS sessions inherit the environment that was present before you started Windows. If your applications need more environment space or other options when running in DOS sessions, you can create a batch file that loads another command processor with these specifications.

Running a DOS Window

A Windows DOS session normally runs full-screen. If you need to work in other Windows, and if you have an 80386 or 80486 system, you can press ALT-ENTER to place the DOS session in a resizable window like the one shown in Figure 2-6. Now you can both see your DOS work and click on other applications to make them active.

If the DOS window is too large, or so small that you can't read the text, change its font and size by choosing Fonts on the window's Control menu. The Font Selection dialog box in Figure 2-7 opens.

Click a new font size in the Fonts list box. When you do, the Window Preview and Selected Font fields change to show you a sample of the new font size. Click OK to make the changes. If you don't want to use these settings in your next session, disable the Save Settings on Exit check box before you click the OK button.

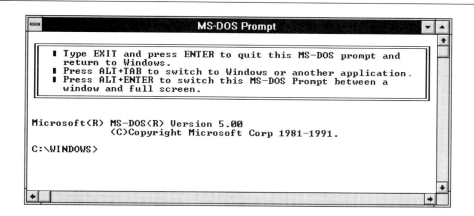

Figure 2-6.   *Use the MS-DOS Prompt to work with commands at the DOS level*

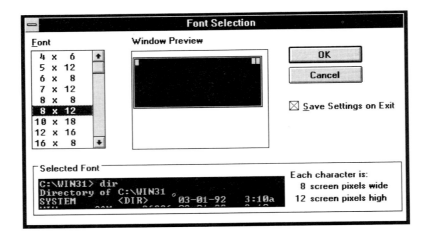

Figure 2-7.   *Use the Font Selection dialog box when working with DOS applications to change the font and size of windows (in 386 enhanced mode only)*

Chapter *3*

Global Techniques

One of the best features of Windows is its common user interface. Features used to access files, change fonts, and print documents are the same from one application to another. For example, Figure 3-1 illustrates the File menus from three different Windows applications. Not only are the options on the menus similar, but the menu bar of each application contains the same menu titles of File, Edit, and View.

This chapter shows you *global techniques*—actions that work the same way in word processing applications, spreadsheets, and many other types of programs—so you'll know how to start, access and work with files, change fonts, and print in just about any Windows application. Let's start with the Help system.

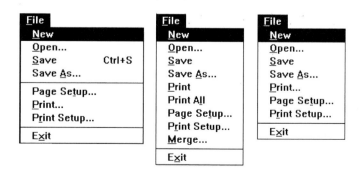

Figure 3-1. *Many Windows applications have similar menus and commands*

Using the Help System

When you need some additional information before proceeding with whatever action you are doing, you can access help by clicking the Help option on an application's menu bar, or by highlighting a specific command on a menu and pressing F1. Many dialog boxes also contain a Help button.

For example, choose Properties on the Program Manager File menu. You see the Program Item Properties dialog box for the selected icon. Click its Help button to display a complete set of help information on how to change properties. Notice that help information displays in its own window, so you can resize the window for viewing as you work with applications, or minimize it to an icon. Minimize the help window now; it appears on the desktop as a question mark with the title of the program it belongs to.

Each application has its own help file in the Windows directory. These help files have names such as CONTROL.HLP (Control Panel help), or NOTEPAD.HLP (Notepad help). When you press F1 to open help files, they reflect the action you were doing when you requested help. For example, when you pressed F1 to get help for the Properties command, Windows opened PROGMAN.HLP, and displayed the help information for the Properties dialog box. Once help is open, the entire PROGMAN.HLP file is available for browsing. Use the help menu options and buttons to quickly search for and jump to the specific area of help you need.

The other method for opening help files is to choose Help from the menu bar. You then see options for accessing any part of the help system. Click Help now to display this menu:

Help
Contents
Search for Help on...
How to Use Help
Windows Tutorial
About Program Manager...

With these options you can see the table of contents for help (Contents), search for specific topics (Search for Help on), get help on how to use the Help system (How to Use Help), or run a tutorial (Windows Tutorial). The About Program Manager option displays information about Windows.

Other applications have similar help menus. Here's the help menu for Microsoft Word for Windows. Notice the tutorials (Getting Started and Learning Word); there's even a section for WordPerfect users who are using Word.

Help Options

The features of help windows are listed in Figure 3-2, using Program Manager Help as an example. The menu bar has options for opening other help menus, copying the help text to other applications, and for setting bookmarks so you can quickly return to sections that you mark. You can even add your own help information. You use the buttons to navigate through the help text. Help text also has "hot spots," which are the green (or colored) underlined text items. You click the text to jump to another topic or display a glossary reference.

Choose Contents from the Program Manager to display the table of contents for the help file. Your window should appear similar to Figure 3-2. To display a topic, click its title in the contents list. For example, click Start an Application under the

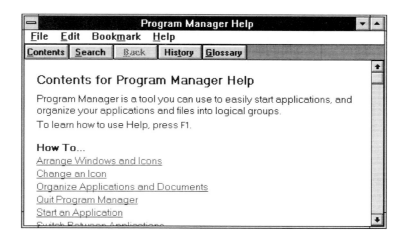

Figure 3-2. *A typical help menu and its features*

How To heading. You see a brief description and a further list of topics. Click the topic Starting an Application from A Group. A description appears with step-by-step procedures.

Notice the colored underlined glossary references in the text. You click these to display a short description of the term. Click again to remove the description.

Now that you've "stepped" into the help text, you can use the buttons on the help menu to step back through it or to call up other topics. The buttons are described here:

Button	Action
Contents	Return to the table of contents
Search	Search for a topic
Back	Move back one step
History	Display a history list of topics viewed
Glossary	Display the complete glossary list

On some help menus, you'll see buttons with left and right pointing arrows (<< or >>). Click these buttons to browse forward or backward through help text that consists of several pages of information.

Topics you view while browsing through the help text are logged into a history file. Click the History button to view this file. To jump back to any topic, double-click it with the mouse.

Using Search

The Search button displays the Search dialog box shown in Figure 3-3. The dialog box is divided in half. The upper half is used to search for topics. The lower half displays topics that match what you type in the upper half; you choose a topic from the list in the lower half the topic you want to view.

Type search text in the field on the upper half of the dialog box. As you begin typing, a matching topic is highlighted in the list box. When the topic you want is highlighted, either press ENTER, double-click the item, or click the Show Topics button. A subset of topics then appears in the lower window. To view a topic, double-click it, or highlight it and click the Go To button. The help topic then appears onscreen.

Using the Help Menu Options

The menu items on help windows are described here:

- The File menu has options for opening other help files or for printing portions of the current help file.

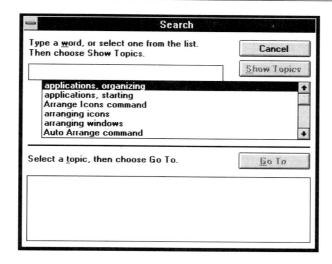

Figure 3-3.   *Use the Search dialog box to search for topics in the help text*

- The Edit menu has options for copying a block of help text to another application and annotating (adding to) help text.

- The Bookmark menu is used to insert a place holder in help text so you can quickly refer back to the help text at any time.

- The help menu provides help information for the Help system.

This section steps you through the menu options. Make sure the Program Manager help window is still open. Choose Contents from the help menu if it isn't already chosen.

Opening Other Help Files

You can look at the help information for any application, even if the application is not running. Choose Open from the File menu. Instructors who are creating help manuals may want to open other help menus to extract information and procedures. When the Open dialog box appears, use the scroll bar to scan through the list of files, and then double-click the help file you want to open. Instructions for using the Open dialog box are covered later in this chapter.

Printing a Help Topic

Printing a help topic is useful if you like to keep help information posted next to your computer or in a binder. For example, you can print the entire set of keystrokes for the Calculator, or the procedure for creating new icons. Follow these steps to see how this works:

1. Using the Open option on the File menu, open the help file CALC.HLP.

2. Make sure the table of contents for Calculator help is visible by clicking the Contents button.

3. Click the topic "Standard Calculator Functions" under the Keyboard heading to display the keyboard methods for accessing the Calculator.

4. Choose Print Topic from the File menu to print the topic.

To print other topics, first select a topic to display, then choose the Print Topic command.

Copying Topics

You can copy and paste the text of any help topic into another application. In this way, you can create your own manuals based on the information in the help files.

First display the topic to copy, then choose Copy from the Edit menu. The Copy dialog box appears with the text of the topic in its workspace. To copy all the text, click the Copy button. To copy only part of the text, click and drag the mouse through the part of the text you want, then click Copy. Switch to the application where you want to paste the text, then choose the Paste command from its Edit menu. Copy and Paste procedures are covered later in this chapter.

The Annotate Option

The Annotate option lets you add notes and comments of your own to any help topic. When an annotation is added, a green (or colored) paper clip appears at the beginning of the help text for the topic. Try adding a comment to the current help window by following these steps:

1. Choose Annotate from the Edit menu. The Annotate dialog box appears.

2. Type the text that makes up your annotation, then click the Save button.

3. Scroll to the top of the help text until you see the green paper clip.

4. Click the paper clip to display the Annotate dialog box, then press ESC when you're done reading the annotation.

You can remove an annotation at any time by opening the annotation text and clicking the Delete button. The Copy and Paste buttons are used to copy existing annotated text from one annotation dialog box to another.

Defining Bookmarks

Use bookmarks to mark a place in the help text you want to return to later. You give titles to bookmarks that are added to the Bookmark drop-down menu. To move to a marked location in the text, simply choose the bookmark title from the Bookmark menu.

Try this now. First locate the help text you want to return to later, then click the Define option on the Bookmark menu. Type a short bookmark title, then click the OK button. To see the new bookmark, open the Bookmark menu. The next time you open the help file, this bookmark will be available.

Create bookmarks for any topic you need to access quickly. Bookmarks are saved from one session to the next. When you don't need to reference a bookmark any longer, open the Bookmark Define dialog box, click the bookmark you want to delete, then click the Delete button.

Working with Files

Because Windows runs on top of the DOS operating system, file specification and methods of access are similar. This section shows how files are accessed and provides a brief explanation of file types.

Files Under DOS and Windows

A *file* is a collection of information, initially created in the memory of the computer, then saved to a disk storage device. All files must have unique names that follow the DOS naming conventions described in your DOS manual. Files are stored in directories that are part of a directory tree. A *directory tree* has branching directories and subdirectories that separate and organize the hundreds of files stored in your system.

Files stored in the same location must have unique names; if you give a file the same name as an existing file, the new file will overwrite the old file. The location of a file is important. You may need to specify its drive letter and directory name when accessing it. This is referred to as specifying the *search path* (or just *path*) to the file.

This book categorizes files into two broad categories: *program files* and *document files*. Applications such as Windows Write and Notepad are stored on disk as program files. The files you create with these applications are document files, and may contain text, graphic information, or other types of data. Within these categories are the file types described here.

Program File Types

Program files contain computer instructions or commands and have the extensions .EXE or .COM.

Support Files   Some programs use auxiliary support files that also contain program code. Support files are program files with different filename extensions such as .OVL (overlay), .SYS (system), or .DRV (driver). You cannot "run" these files by typing their names on the command line. They are accessed only by the application they are associated with.

Document File Types

Document files may contain text, graphics, numbers, or other data. Document files are loaded into the workspace or document windows of Windows applications.

Text Files   Text files contain human-readable alpha-numeric characters that follow the American Standard Code for Information Interchange (ASCII) format. These files are often referred to as ASCII files and can be opened by a wide range of programs on a wide range of computers, not just DOS systems. They are easily transferred over telephone modems to other systems and have the extensions .TXT, .DOC, or one of several other extension possibilities.

Graphics Files   Graphics files contain graphic information in several possible formats. The most common is the bitmap format, which saves the actual dot-by-dot representation of the image on the screen to a file. Another graphic file format called vector stores the series of commands required to rebuild the image on the screen. Graphic files have extensions such as .BMP, .TIF, .GIF, .EPS, and others as discussed in Chapter 21.

Data Files   Data files contain information, usually created by a database program such as dBASE or a spreadsheet program such as Microsoft's Excel. These files are readable only by the applications that create them, or applications that can translate the information in the files to their own format. Information in data files is separated in various ways to form the fields of a database or cells of a spreadsheet. Common formats are comma-delimited files for databases and SYLK (SYmbolic LinK) or DIF (Data Interchange Format) for spreadsheet data. Data files have many extensions such as .WRI, .WKS, and others. These files are discussed further in your applications manual.

File Naming Conventions

It is important to understand the conventions used to name and refer to files. Files within the same directory cannot have the same name, but you can use names that have characters in common as part of a strategy to keep your files organized. Windows warns you if you try to create a file with a name that's already in use by another file.

The basic filename consists of eight characters, followed by an optional three-character *extension*. The filename may be fewer than eight characters, but any characters beyond the maximum eight are truncated. Here is a typical filename:

YOURFILE.TXT

Another important part of a filename is its location or path. When referring to a file not in the current directory, you need to include the drive and directory along with the actual filename. For example, the complete path of YOURFILE.TXT when located in the WINWORD directory on drive D is as follows:

D:\WINWORD\YOURFILE.TXT

Backslashes separate the drive, directory, and filename. If you need more information on file naming conventions, refer to your DOS manual.

File Naming Strategies

To keep your files organized and track their contents, its helpful to develop a naming strategy that uses descriptive filenames and extensions. Many programs automatically add filename extensions when a file is saved, as shown in Table 3-1. You can usually specify your own extension to override those added by the application.

Table 3-2 lists other common extensions you can use when creating files with the Windows accessories or with other programs. Recall from Chapter 2 that a filename

Program	Extension	Meaning
Paintbrush	.BMP	A new Paintbrush bitmap image
Paintbrush	.MSP	An older Paintbrush bitmap image
Paintbrush	.PCX	A PC Paintbrush bitmap image
Calendar	.CAL	A Calendar file
Clipboard	.CLP	A saved Clipboard image
Cardfile	.CRD	An index card file
Program Manager	.GRP	A group information file
PIF Editor	.PIF	A Program Information File
Recorder	.REC	A set of Recorder macros
Notepad	.TXT	A Notepad text file
Terminal	.TRM	A Terminal file
Write	.WRI	A Windows Write text file

Table 3-1.   *Filename Extensions Used by the Windows Accessories*

extension is used to associate a document file with the program that created it. You can double-click an associated document file in the File Manager to open that file without first opening the application. You'll want to retain the extension used by Windows applications for this reason, or create another extension association, as discussed in Chapter 7.

Use the filename itself to describe and categorize the contents of a file. Adopt a file naming strategy for yourself or others in your company that makes a file's contents readily apparent and avoids duplication of names. A common strategy is to code the date and file type into the filename. Consider the following filenames used in Microsoft Excel:

    RA92130.XLS
    RB92130.XLS
    RC92130.XLS
    RA92228.XLS
    RB92228.XLS
    RC92228.XLS

Assume these are files created every month. The R designates the files as reports (budget files might begin with B). The second letter is a code that indicates the type of report; here three separate reports are created at the end of each month (A, B, and C). Next comes the report date, followed by the .XLS extension added by Excel. Usually, for listing purposes, you'll want to put the year first, followed by the month, then the day; thus, the file RC92228 is a C-type of report entered on February 28, 1992.

Extension	Usage
.BAK	A generic extension for the backup of an edited file
.BAT	A reserved extension for DOS batch files
.DAT	A generic extension for data files
.DTA	Another generic data file extension
.DOC	A generic extension for document files
.HLP	A commonly used extension for help files
.MNU	A generic extension for menu files
.MSG	A generic extension for message files
.TMP	A generic extension for temporary files

Table 3-2.   *Common Filename Extensions*

Listing Files with Wildcard Characters

A *wildcard* character is a substitute for any letter or group of letters in a filename. The question mark (?) can represent a single letter and the asterisk (*) can represent two or more letters. Veteran DOS users are familiar with wildcard characters and their usefulness in listing groups of files. Windows also accepts wildcard characters.

Using the previous list of files as an example, you can see how wildcard characters can be used to list or access specific files. The specification RA*.* includes the following files:

    RA92130.XLS
    RA92228.XLS

The specification R???1*.* includes these files:

    RA92130.XLS
    RB92130.XLS
    RC92130.XLS

Finally, the specification RA??1*.* includes only this file:

    RA92130.XLS

Notice how ? serves as a place marker; that is, any character may occupy its position. The *, on the other hand, designates a group of letters in the filename or extension. You'll use wildcard characters when opening files in applications, or listing files in the File Manager.

Directory Concepts

Directories provide a way to separate files on drives in much the same way you would organize paper files in a filing cabinet. The following illustration shows a typical directory structure for the hard drive where Windows is located.

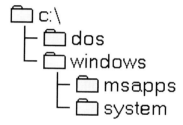

The top folder is the *root directory*. All disks have a root directory, and all other directories on the disk branch from it. In the illustration you can see that the DOS directory and the Windows directory branch from the root directory. They are *subdirectories* of the root. The Windows directory has two subdirectories of its own, MSAPPS and SYSTEM.

Files in a directory include as part of their filenames the complete path to the directory. You may need to use this full path when referring to files outside of your current directory. For example, a file called JANBUDG.XLS in the MSAPPS subdirectory of the previous illustration has the complete filename shown here, assuming it is stored on drive C:

C:\WINDOWS\MSAPPS\JANBUDG.XLS

In most cases, you don't need to specify the whole name. The dialog boxes used to open and save files handle this for you. All you need to do is type the filename, as you'll see.

Organizing with Directories

Directories keep program files and data files separate. Always create a separate directory when installing a new program, although this is often done automatically by the program's setup routine when you install the application. Data files should also have their own directory to prevent files from mixing with program files or other types of data files. The danger of combining data files and program files in one directory is that in deleting data files, you might accidentally delete program files.

Also, separating data files from program files makes backup easier, since you only need to back up the directories that contain the data files, which change often. Program files rarely change, and you can always restore from the original floppy disks, or a master backup set. Backing up data files is easy if they all branch from a single directory as shown here:

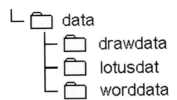

With this directory arrangement, you only need to back up the data directory, making sure that its subdirectories are included in the backup. Don't forget to perform an occasional "full system" backup. This would make it easy to reinstall all your programs the way they are if the hard drive should fail.

Using File Menu Options

This section describes dialog boxes used to open, save, browse, and search through files. What you've learned about files and directories so far will help you access the common features of these dialog boxes.

For the exercises in this section, activate the Notepad accessory now by double-clicking its icon in the Accessories group of the Program Manager. When the Notepad window appears, click on the File menu option, or press ALT-F. The first four options are used to open and save files and are found throughout a wide range of Windows applications. What you learn about using them in Notepad applies to other applications as well.

The New Option

The New option clears the application's workspace or opens a new document window. If the existing work has not yet been saved, Windows asks if you want to save it before clearing the screen.

Some applications, such as Word for Windows, let you open two or more documents at once. Consequently, the workspace is not cleared when you select New. Instead, another document window is opened for the new file. In this way, you can edit two documents at once, compare their contents, or cut and paste text or graphics between them. Keep in mind that each new document window requires additional memory, so the amount of memory you have may limit the number of new windows you can open.

In some applications, you can press CTRL-N *to select the New option.*

The Open Option

The Open option is used to open an existing file. Select Open on the Notepad File menu to display the Open dialog box shown in Figure 3-4.

There are four areas where you enter or select options:

- In the File Name field, type the name of the file to open, or choose a file from the list. You can change the listing by entering wildcard characters.

- In the List Files of Type field, choose from a list of wildcard specifications. This is an optional step.

- In the Directories field, choose a new directory by clicking its icon.

- In the Drives field, choose the drive you want to use.

The typical procedure for using the Open dialog box is given here:

1. Select the drive.

2. Select a directory on that drive.

3. Specify the type of files you want to see listed by choosing an option in the List Files of Type field or by typing your own file specification in the File Name field. When you type your own specification, press ENTER to change the file listing.

4. When a valid filename is listed in the File Name text field, pressing ENTER or clicking the OK button opens that file.

Some of these steps are optional, of course. If a file is in the current drive and directory, you can simply type its filename or select it from the list and click the OK button. If you need to switch drives, the last directory you accessed on that drive in the current session is still selected in the Directories field.

If you're searching for a file because you can't remember the drive or directory where you saved it, first type the wildcard specification for the file in the File Name field, then click on different directories or drives. The file list will change to show matching files each time you change drives or directories.

The following sections describe how to use the features in each field of the dialog box. Keyboard methods are useful when working with dialog boxes. You can easily jump from one field to another. To access a field, press ALT and the mnemonic (the underlined letter) in the title of the field. For example, to jump to the Drives field, press ALT-V.

Always make sure you're connected to the correct drive and directory before opening or saving files.

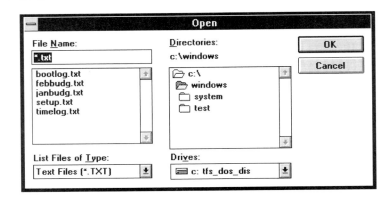

Figure 3-4.   The Open dialog box is used throughout most Windows applications

Choosing a Drive   To choose a drive, click the down arrow button on the Drives list box, or press ALT-V to highlight the field, then press the DOWN ARROW key on the keyboard. A list similar to the following appears:

Drives:

```
| c: silicon            | ↓ |
| c: silicon            | ↑ |
| d:                    |   |
| e:                    |   |
| f:                    |   |
| g:                    | ▮ |
| h:                    |   |
| i:                    | ↓ |
```

The current drive is highlighted. Highlight other drives by clicking them with the mouse, or moving the highlight with the arrow keys on the keyboard.

Choosing a Directory   The current drive and directory are in the Directories field. To select a new directory, double-click its folder with the mouse. Keep in mind that subdirectory folders may not be visible. You must double-click the "parent" folder to open it and display branching subdirectories. You then double-click the subdirectory to list them. Once you've selected a directory, its files appear in the File Name list.

Changing the File Listing   Once you've selected the correct drive and directory, you're ready to type a name in the File Name list, or pick a file in the list box.

When you first open the Open dialog box, the highlight is in the File Name field. This makes it easy to just type the name of the file you want and press ENTER. In addition, you can type the full drive and path name of a file, rather than picking a drive or directory icon as described earlier. In some cases this may be the quickest way to open a file. For example, to open README.WRI in the Windows directory on drive C, you could type the following and press the ENTER key.

C:\WINDOWS\README.WRI

To get a listing of files, type the wildcard specification in the File Name field and press ENTER. For example, to see all executable files with the extension .EXE, type ***.EXE** and press ENTER. To see files with the text extension, type ***.TXT** in the field. To list other types of files, choose an option in the List Files of Type list box.

When the file list appears, use the scroll bar to scan through it if necessary. Click the file and its name appears in the File Name text box. Press ENTER or click OK to open it.

Here are some other examples that demonstrate the use of wildcard characters. Before proceeding, make sure the Windows drive is selected in the Drives box and the Windows directory is selected in the Directories box.

1. Type **PROG*.*** in the File Name field and press ENTER to view files related to the Program Manager, as shown here:

File **Name**:

| prog*.* |

| progman.ann |
| progman.exe |
| progman.hlp |
| progman.ini |

2. Type ***.BMP** to see all .BMP files, as shown here:

File **Name**:

| *.bmp |

| 256color.bmp |
| arcade.bmp |
| arches.bmp |
| argyle.bmp |
| boxes.bmp |
| cars.bmp |
| castle.bmp |
| chess.bmp |

3. Type **A*.BMP** to see files that start with "A" and have the extension .BMP, as shown here:

File **Name**:

| a*.bmp |

| arcade.bmp |
| arches.bmp |
| argyle.bmp |

4. Now restore the list so that all files are visible. Choose All Files (*.*) in the List Files of Type box.

The Save Option

The Save option is used to save a file using the name that appears in the title bar. This assumes you have previously saved the file and assigned a name to it using the Save As option. If you choose Save, and the file has not yet been named, the File Save As dialog box appears. Keep in mind that the Save option saves changes without asking for verification. In most cases, this will be fine, but there may be times when you want to load a file, make changes to it, then save it under a different name so you can retain the original. Use the Save As option in this case.

Some applications have a Read Only check box that you enable for precautionary reasons. When enabled, you can't save the file using its current name, which means you can't overwrite that file—it stays safely in its original form. The application forces you to rename it and opens the Save As dialog box discussed next. You use this option when working with template files, which are files you use over and over again.

The Save As Option

Use the Save As option on the File menu to save a file for the first time by specifying its new filename. It also lets you save an existing file under a new name. The Save As dialog box has the same features as the Open dialog box. You type the new name for the file in the File Name box and specify the drive or directory location.

The Save As dialog box lists the names of files on the current drive and directory. The list lets you see what filenames have already been used when deciding on the new file's name.

Editing Techniques

The techniques you use to edit documents are similar among a wide variety of applications. In this section, you learn editing techniques used in Notepad, Write, SysEdit, and many other applications. Start by opening Write with the README document. Double-click the Read Me icon in the Program Manager Main group.

When the window opens, you see the text of the document in the workspace. The blinking insertion point is at the beginning of the text. You reposition the insertion point by clicking elsewhere in the document with the mouse, or by using one of these keyboard methods:

Arrow keys	Scroll in any direction, one character or line at a time
CTRL-RIGHT ARROW	Jump to next word
CTRL-LEFT ARROW	Jump to previous word
PGUP/PGDN	Scroll up or down one window full of text or options
CTRL-PGUP	Scroll left one window

CTRL-PGDN	Scroll right one window
HOME	Jump to the beginning of a line
END	Jump to the end of a line
CTRL-HOME	Jump to the beginning of a document
CTRL-END	Jump to the end of a document

Once you've positioned the insertion point, you can press the DEL key to remove the character to the right or the backspace key to remove the character to the left. To insert new text, just type the text. It is automatically inserted. Some applications have an Overtype mode that is toggled on or off with the INS key. When on, any text you type overtypes existing text.

Selecting Text

In Windows, operations such as character formatting, deleting, and moving take place on text that is highlighted. For example, to delete a block of characters, first highlight the block using the following techniques, then press the DEL key. The simplest method of highlighting text is to click and drag over it with the mouse. Try this now in the Write document. Click anywhere in the text, hold the mouse button, and drag to another location. All text in between is highlighted.

The Selection Bar

In Write and many other Windows applications, a selection bar exists between the left edge of text and the window border. You click in this bar to select either a line or paragraph. Try this now by clicking once in the selection bar just to the left of text. Note that the mouse pointer converts to a right-pointing arrow in the selection bar. Now click once and drag the mouse pointer down to select multiple lines.

To select an entire paragraph, double-click to the left of the paragraph in the selection bar.

Selecting Text with the Keyboard

The keyboard methods for selecting text are listed next. Text selection starts at an "anchor" point and extends outward from there, depending on the keys you use. Try both to determine whether mouse or keyboard methods are easier for you to use when selecting text. The mouse is sometimes awkward to use when selecting over multiple screens because it's easy to overshoot your target or loose track of how far you've scrolled.

SHIFT-DOWN ARROW	Extend the selection to the next line
SHIFT-UP ARROW	Extend the selection to the previous line

SHIFT-END	Extend the selection to the end of a line
SHIFT-HOME	Extend the selection to the beginning of the line
SHIFT-PGDN	Extend the selection down a window
SHIFT-PGUP	Extend the selection up one window
CTRL-SHIFT-RIGHT ARROW	Extend the selection to the next word
CTRL-SHIFT-LEFT ARROW	Extend the selection to the previous word
CTRL-SHIFT-END	Extend the selection to the end of the document
CTRL-SHIFT-HOME	Extend the selection to the beginning of the document

Using the Edit Menu and the Clipboard

The Edit menu has options for undoing mistakes, as well as copying, cutting, and pasting text within a document or among other documents. Click Edit on Write's menu bar to display the following menu:

Edit	
Undo Editing	**Ctrl+Z**
Cut	Ctrl+X
Copy	Ctrl+C
Paste	**Ctrl+V**

The next section looks at how to use the Undo option. There are other options on this menu, but they are discussed in Chapter 4. Other applications may have additional features.

The Undo Option

The Undo option is used to cancel the last editing change you made. If you deleted text or part of a graphic, or if you changed the format of a block of text, it is restored when you select Undo.

As an example, delete a character in the text of the Notepad window, then press CTRL-Z to undo the deletion. You can even press CTRL-Z again to cancel the undo.

The Clipboard Options

The Cut, Copy, and Paste options are called the Clipboard options. The *Clipboard* is a temporary holding area used to hold text until you paste it elsewhere. Its options are the same on all Windows menus and do the following tasks:

- Cut removes the selected text or graphics from the document and places it on the Clipboard. You can also press CTRL-X to cut (think of "X"ing out a portion of text from your document).

- Copy places a copy of the selected text on the Clipboard. You can also press CTRL-C.

- Paste copies the contents of the Clipboard to the position of the insertion point. You can also press CTRL-V (think of V as a caret or insertion mark to remember this keyboard method).

Some Edit menus have the Select All item described here:

- Select All selects all the text or graphics objects in a document or workspace. You then choose Cut or Copy to place them on the Clipboard.

Typically, you cut or copy an object or text from one window, press ALT-TAB to switch to another window, then paste.

Transferring information to and from non-Windows applications requires special procedures covered in Chapter 4.

The Clipboard is a powerful tool for transferring information between applications. The application that provides the Clipboard information may supply several formats that the receiving application can use to maintain formatting or graphic content.

Try experimenting with Cut and Paste by selecting a part of the text in README.TXT, and then copying it to the Clipboard and pasting it elsewhere. The following takes you through cutting and pasting step by step. Make as many changes as you want to README.TXT, but don't save those changes when you're done.

1. Highlight a portion of text using mouse or keyboard methods.

2. Press CTRL-C to copy it to the Clipboard.

3. Move to a new location in the text and press CTRL-V to paste the text block.

The procedure for copying between applications is similar. After placing text or graphics on the Clipboard, switch to the other applications by clicking the application or by pressing ALT-TAB. If the document contains text, click where you want to paste and press CTRL-V.

The Clipboard Window

You can open the Clipboard by double-clicking its icon in the Main group window. You'll see the current text or graphic in the Clipboard window. If you want to save the image for later use, choose the Save option on the File menu. This is a convenient way to save graphics or text that you use all the time. The other Clipboard menu items are described here:

- Choose Open on the File menu to open a previously saved Clipboard image.

- Choose Save on the File menu to save the image currently in the Clipboard for future use.

- Choose Delete on the Edit menu to clear the Clipboard. The image on the Clipboard can use quite a bit of memory, so it's a good idea to clear it if you don't need it anymore. Note that copying a single character to the Clipboard effectively clears a larger image and is easier than choosing Delete.

- Choose Display on the Edit menu to list the available image formats supplied by the program you're working in. You can click one of the formats to see how the image will look if pasted with that format. Select Auto to get back the original format.

Capturing a Window or Screen to the Clipboard

You can capture a picture of the entire Windows desktop, or a picture of the active window using the keystrokes described shortly. (The screen images in this book were captured using these methods, then pasted into Microsoft Word for Windows.) To edit captured screen images, paste them into Paintbrush. For example, you can convert colors to dot patterns that print on single-color printers. These methods are covered in Chapter 21.

Capturing the Screen   Make sure the information you want is visible on the screen, then press the PRINT SCREEN key. The entire screen is captured to the Clipboard. Keep in mind that high-resolution screens (1024 by 768) require a lot of memory. After pasting the image in an application such as Paintbrush, crop it down as much as possible before saving it to disk. Then copy a single character to the Clipboard to free up the memory used by the Clipboard image. If you can't capture with just the PRINT SCREEN key, try ALT-PRINT SCREEN or SHIFT-PRINT SCREEN.

Capturing the Active Window   To capture just the active window, press ALT-PRINT SCREEN. If this method doesn't work, try pressing SHIFT-PRINT SCREEN.

Fonts and Special Characters

When working in applications such as Write that support character formatting (Notepad does not), you highlight text and change its character formatting with the Font dialog box shown in Figure 3-5. Make sure Write is open with the README.TXT file in its workspace, then highlight some text and click the Character menu option. This menu has several options for quickly changing the style of characters, but to change fonts and accurately control the font size, choose Font.

Use the Font dialog box to choose a TrueType or regular font, to change its style, and to change its size. The text must be highlighted before opening this dialog box. In the Font field, scroll through the list to choose a font. Two types are listed.

- TrueType fonts are designated with the TT symbol. They are scalable fonts that print at high-resolution on dot matrix and laser printers. Use TrueType fonts whenever possible. Documents formatted with TrueType fonts can be sent to other users and printed on their dot matrix or laser printers without making any special changes.

- Printer fonts are designated by an icon that looks like a printer. These are the built-in fonts for the currently selected printer. The type of printer font listed in the Fonts list box changes when you choose another printer in Print Setup, as discussed under the "Printing" section later in this chapter. Chapter 16 includes a more thorough discussion of fonts.

When you choose a different font, a sample appears in the Sample window. To choose a different style or size, select it in the Font Style or Size list box. Note that

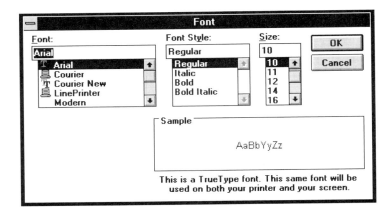

Figure 3-5.   *Use the Font utility to change the font, style, and size of selected fonts*

you can also type an unlisted font size in the Size dialog box. The TrueType fonts list even numbers in this box, but because they are scalable, you can enter any value from 4 points to 127 points. Sizes outside this range may not print properly. Once you've selected a font, click the OK button. The text in the document then changes to the new font.

In Write, superscript and subscript formatting is applied from the Character menu only. These options are not available on the Font dialog box. The Reduce Fonts and Enlarge Fonts options are used to quickly resize a font, but the increments are not always multiples of two. For more accurate font sizing, use the Font dialog box.

The Character Map

The Character Map utility helps you locate and insert special foreign language characters and symbols into your documents. You can keep the utility open on the desktop while you write documents in Write, Word for Windows, or other Windows applications. Character Map does not work with non-Windows DOS applications.

Double-click the Character Map icon in the Accessories window to display the utility, as shown in Figure 3-6.

The first thing to do is choose a font. Click the down arrow button in the Font field to display and choose from a list of fonts. In most cases, you'll probably use the Symbol or WingDing font because it contains many characters not available on the keyboard. As you choose different fonts, note that the table of characters changes in style and content. Compare the Symbol font map to a text font such as Courier.

To insert a character into your document, do one of the following:

- Click on the character in the table, then view its keystroke requirement at the bottom-right of the Character Map. In Figure 3-6, note that the heart is selected

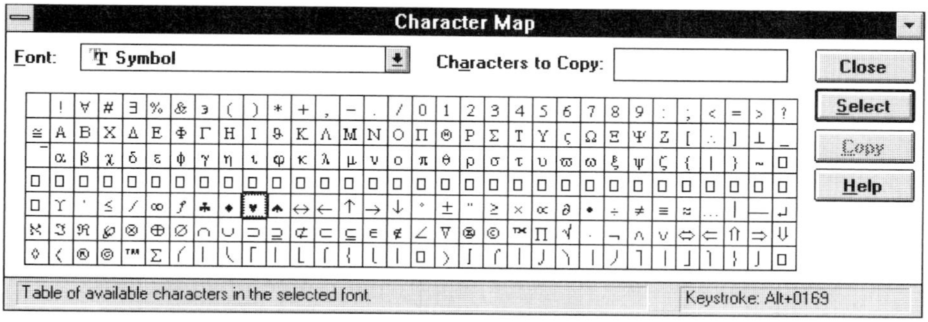

Figure 3-6.   *Use the Character Map to insert special characters in your documents*

in the table, and its keystroke is listed on the bottom right as Alt+0169. Switch back to your application and type this keystroke.

- The second method involves the Clipboard. Double-click the character or characters you want (or click the Select button). This places the characters in the Characters field at the top. Click Copy to place the selected characters on the Clipboard, then switch back to your application and paste (CTRL-V).

The second method is useful when you need more than one character, as when building complex strings or mathematical expressions using the Symbol font. When you switch back to your application, be sure to position the cursor before pasting the characters.

 If the characters are too small to see, hold the mouse button and click on a character. It appears enlarged. You can also drag the mouse over the Table of Characters using this method. Each character is displayed as the mouse pointer touches it.

Printing

Printing a document is as simple as choosing Print on the File menu and clicking the OK button. However, in most cases, you want to make sure the printer is set up properly, or change some of the printing parameters, such as the number of copies or range of pages to print. That's where the Print Setup commands come into use.

 You'll print the README.WRI file in this section. It is a useful document you should have around. However, if you changed it in the previous exercises, reload a fresh copy using the Open option. When asked if you want to save changes you made to the previous copy, select No.

Printer Setup

Choose Print Setup on Write's File menu to display the Print Setup dialog box shown in Figure 3-7. The printer listed in your Print Setup dialog box may be different, depending on the printer selected during your setup. If more than one printer is connected to your system on a different port or on a switchbox, click Specific Printer and choose the printer in the drop-down list box. If you're connected to a network, one or more of these optional printers may be a network printer.

After choosing a printer, click Portrait (upright) printing or Landscape (sideways) printing in the Orientation field. In the Paper field, pick a paper size and paper source in the drop-down list boxes.

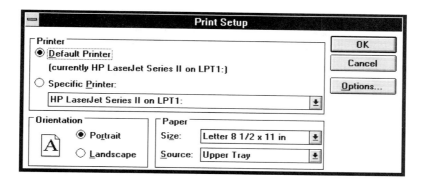

Figure 3-7.   *Use the Print Setup dialog box to set printer options before printing the current*
print job

Options for Printing Graphics

Click the Options button to set the printing resolution of the printer. A dialog box
similar to the one shown here appears unless you have a PostScript printer or a
Hewlett-Packard LaserJet III (some models). Use this dialog box to adjust the printing
resolution of graphics in your document. The options are discussed in this section.

Dithering

Dithering is a process of converting colors (and true gray shades) into dot patterns
that simulate gray shading on black-and-white printers (also called halftoning). A full
discussion of dithering appears in Chapter 21.

- If None is selected in the Dithering field, graphics print in black and white
  with no dithering.

- When Coarse is selected, the dithering is done with larger dots, and printing is quicker than when using the Fine setting.

- Choose Fine to print with finer dots, giving the effect of a true gray, but slowing down printing.

- Choose Line Art using various dithering patterns. You'll need to experiment with this option.

The dot size of the dithering pattern also depends on the printer resolution selected in the Print dialog box discussed in the next section.

Intensity Control

Use the Intensity Control to adjust how light or dark the dithered pattern is. You need to experiment with this control to find the right setting for your printer. Dithered patterns range from loose dots to tight dots, with tight dots giving the smoothest grays. Each adjustment of the Intensity Control adds or subtracts dots from the pattern. Often, a color will be "on the verge" of being a smooth gray. To create a smooth gray, adjust the Intensity Control one or two clicks with the mouse.

Printing TrueType as Graphics

If you enable the Print TrueType As Graphics check box, TrueType text is sent to the printer as a bitmapped image, thus improving the printer's speed. The cost of faster printing may be that the resolution of the type drops. Try this option both enabled and disabled to see what kind of quality you get each way on your printer.

When the Options dialog box settings are correct, click OK. Then click OK on the Print Setup dialog box. Now you're ready to print.

Printing

Choose Print on the File menu. The dialog box shown in Figure 3-8 appears. Note that this box may not look the same from application to application, but its features are similar.

In the Print Range box, choose All to print the entire document, choose Selection to print only a highlighted part of the document, or choose Pages to specify a range of pages. If you choose Pages, type the starting page number in the From text box and the ending page number in the To text box. Set the other fields as follows.

- You can choose a Print Quality on some printers. Printing at higher resolutions takes more time, but gives better results than low resolutions when printing pictures.

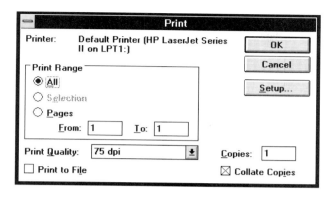

Figure 3-8. *Use the Print dialog box to specify printing parameters such as number of copies and page range*

- In the Copies field, type the number of copies you want. If Collate Copies is enabled, each copy prints separately. If disabled, Windows prints all the page 1s together, then the page 2s, and so on.

- Enable the Print to File option to send the print information to a file on disk. You can then print this document at any time or on another system without starting Windows or Write. (You can even print it on a system that doesn't have Windows or Write.) When you print to a file, Windows opens a dialog box in which you specify the filename.

Chapter *4*

Linking Applications
with OLE

This chapter covers special techniques for linking pictures and information between applications, but first it gives you a brief introduction to some of the Windows accessories. You've already had a chance to work with Windows Write and Notepad. This chapter introduces Paintbrush and Cardfile, then shows you techniques for integrating text, graphics, and other data using Object Linking and Embedding (OLE) techniques.

The Picture Editor

This section is about Paintbrush, but giving it a title such as "Painting with Paintbrush" is a little misleading. That might indicate that you'll use Paintbrush only to create pretty pictures or exercise your artistic skills. While you can paint and create with it, Paintbrush actually lets you do much more. You can use Paintbrush to change your wallpaper images or create technical drawings for your Write documents. You can even capture pictures of windows on the desktop, paste them into Paintbrush for editing, and then paste them into documents. Think of Paintbrush as an editor of graphics in the same way that Notepad and Write are text editors.

To get started, double-click the Paintbrush icon in the Accessories window. In a moment, you'll see the Paintbrush window as shown in Figure 4-1.

The Paintbrush window consists of a work space or *canvas* where pictures are painted. On the left of the canvas is the *Toolbox*, which contains a set of painting tools. At the bottom is the *Color Palette*, where you select which colors you'll paint with, and

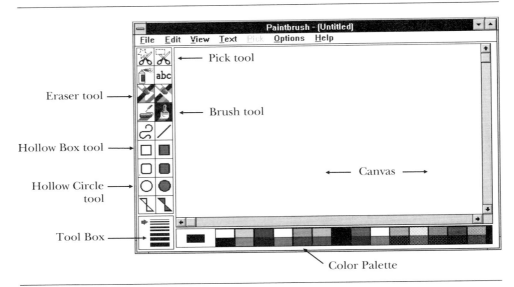

Figure 4-1. *Paintbrush is an editor for graphics files in the same way that Write and Notepad are text file editors*

to its left is the *Linesize box*, where you select the width of line to paint. Once you select a tool, color, and line width, point to the canvas, click and then drag the tool around in the canvas. Follow these steps to see how each works:

1. Click the Hollow Box tool in the Toolbox. (Refer to Figure 4-1 to locate this tool.)

2. Click red in the Color Palette and note that red appears in the foreground color box.

3. Point to the canvas, then click and drag to create a box. When you release the button, a red box appears.

4. Now click a wider line size and create another box on the canvas.

5. Hold down the SHIFT key, then click and drag to create another box. Notice that holding SHIFT causes the tool to paint squares instead of rectangles.

6. Click the Hollow Circle tool, another line size, and another color. Then click and drag in the workspace. Before releasing the mouse, press the RIGHT ARROW key several times. Pressing the arrow keys moves the painting tools in small increments, which is often too difficult to do with the mouse.

7. Now try selecting part of the drawing and moving it elsewhere. Click the Pick tool, then click and drag in the workspace so that an object you've drawn is surrounded by a dotted-line box. If the object is not completely surrounded, click and drag again. When the object is surrounded, click inside the dotted-line box and drag. The surrounded object moves.

8. Now create a copy of an object on the canvas. Repeat step 7 to select an object, then hold the SHIFT key, click the selected object, and drag.

9. Now click the Eraser tool and select a large line size in the Linesize box. Point in the workspace, then click and drag to erase. Hold the SHIFT key to erase along a straight line, or press the arrow keys to erase in small increments.

10. Erase the entire painting by double-clicking on the right Eraser tool.

Continue experimenting on your own. You'll use these techniques in a later section to transfer pictures to other applications using cut-and-paste techniques. To learn more about Paintbrush, refer to Chapter 22.

The Cardfile Accessory

Cardfile is similar to an index card filing system. Each card has an index header that determines its alphabetical order in the stack. Under the header is a blank area where you can type text, place pictures, or both. You can scan through the cards one by one; when you get to the end of the stack, the first card reappears like a rotary card filing system. You can also search for keywords in the index header or in the body text of the card. Double-click the Cardfile icon in the Program Manager Accessories group. The window shown in Figure 4-2 appears.

The following sections give the basic procedures for using Cardfile:

Adding a New Card   To add a new card, choose Add from the Card menu, or press F7. The Add dialog box appears. Type a descriptive name for the information you'll place on the card, since this information is used to sort the card alphabetically in the card stack. Type one of the names in your personal phone list, for example.

Typing Card Body Text   When the new card appears, type text in the body of the card. If you like, you can also paste graphics at this point (as discussed in the "Linking Objects Between Applications" section of this chapter), but you must first choose Picture from the Edit menu.

Saving Cards   Now that you've created cards and added some text, you're ready to use Object Linking and Embedding techniques with both Cardfile and Paintbrush.

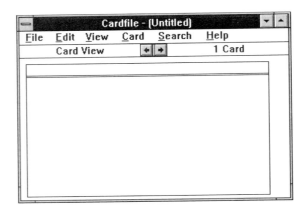

Figure 4-2. *Cardfile is like an index card filing system*

Save this file before proceeding. For more information on the Windows accessories, refer to Chapter 24. Use the Save option on the File menu to save the cards.

The remainder of this chapter concentrates on integrating Paintbrush, Cardfile, and Write information.

Linking Objects Between Applications

Windows 3.1 provides a method of copying and pasting graphics and text between applications that maintains links between the pasted "object" and the application that created it. *Linking* an object in a block of text, numbers, or a picture you've copied from another application simply means that your computer system knows that you want to keep these objects connected—even though they are in different applications. What these links later allow you to do is to change one of the links and therefore automatically change all the others.

For example, say you pasted an Excel chart showing your company's annual income into three different documents created in Microsoft Word. Each document is intended for a different audience, but contains the same chart. You later change the numbers in your spreadsheet, which causes the chart to change. Because the Word documents are linked to Excel, the chart is automatically updated there as well.

These graphic and text *objects* that you paste must originate from an application that supports Microsoft's Object Linking and Embedding (OLE) specification.

Microsoft's Object Linking and Embedding

OLE sets up a communications link between an object created in an OLE-compatible application, and the pasted version of that object in a document created in another application. OLE is part of Microsoft's "Information at Your Fingertips" strategy, which defines ways of integrating many different types of applications, data, and media in desktop computer systems. While Chapter 25 contains a more complete discussion of OLE, we'll cover it briefly here as an introduction.

Nearly any Windows application can supply OLE objects. For example, graphic images created in Paintbrush, tables and graphs created in Excel, or even sounds created in Sound Recorder can all be OLE objects. To supply OLE objects, an application must conform to Microsoft's Object Linking and Embedding specifications. When pasting an OLE object in an OLE-compatible document, you can simply *embed* the object, or paste it with an *active link*. An embedded object does not update when you update the original, but if you double-click it, the originating application opens so you can change it.

Embedded Objects

When you paste an object (such as a picture from Paintbrush) into an application that supports embedding (such as Write or Cardfile), you create an embedded object. To make changes to or edit the object, double-click it. The application used to create it immediately opens for editing.

Active Links

An active link is more dynamic than an embedded link. If you make changes to or edit an object that has been linked into one or more applications, the objects pasted into those applications also change.

In previous versions of Windows, pasted objects were difficult to change in this way. To update a pasted object, you had to open the original file, edit it, and then repaste the object over the old object in each application in which you'd used it. With OLE, you simply double-click the pasted object to make editing changes. Windows 3.1 lets you create *compound documents* that hold all the text, graphics, and data in one document, or at least provide a quick link to all those components. This makes it easier to keep track of your documents and projects.

The Two Types of Applications

An application that allows pasting of linked objects is called a *client* application; the applications from which these objects come are called *server* applications. Windows Write and Cardfile are client applications, while Paintbrush and Sound Recorder are server applications.

Client Applications

Client applications appear to have features they don't actually have. For example, you can copy sound files from the Sound Recorder into a Write document. This creates an icon for that sound file in the Write document. When you double-click it, the sound plays! It appears that Write has sound capability, when in fact, Write simply calls up Sound Recorder and lets it do all the work. This process happens in the background; all you have to do is double-click the object. Think about how you might use sound in your documents. For example, you could send voice-annotated electronic mail messages to other Windows users, or include verbal instructions in a tutorial file.

Server Applications

Server applications are applications that are OLE-compatible. They are capable of creating objects that you can paste as embedded or linked objects into OLE client applications.

Embedding Objects

To embed an object from a client application to a server application, you use the normal copy and paste procedures. If both applications support OLE, the pasted object becomes embedded. If the applications don't support OLE, the pasted object becomes static (in other words, you can't change it without deleting it and repasting an updated version). Follow these steps to embed an object from Paintbrush in a Write file:

1. Open Write and Paintbrush.

2. In the Paintbrush window, open the file ARCHES.BMP.

3. Use the Pick tool (the right pair of scissors in the Toolbox) to select part of the image. The mouse pointer converts to a cross hair. Point in the picture, then click and drag to surround part of the image with a dotted line.

4. Choose Copy from the Edit menu to place the selected object on the Clipboard.

5. Switch to Write and choose the Paste command from the Edit menu.

OLE embeds the image in the document because both Paintbrush and Write support OLE. Now try editing the image in the Write document. Follow these steps:

1. Double-click the pasted image in the Write document. The Paintbrush window becomes active and the image sits in its workspace, ready for your edits.

2. Change the image using any tools that you want from Paintbrush's Toolbox.

3. Now open the File menu and choose Exit and Return. When you see the message "Update open embedded object before proceeding," click the Yes button. The image is updated in Write and the Paintbrush window closes.

Remember, one of the advantages of using this method is that compound documents hold all the information for a document. You don't need to keep track of a set of separate picture files or data files (from Excel, for instance).

Linking Objects

The procedure for creating a linked object is the same as the procedure for creating an embedded object, except that you choose Paste Link instead of Paste when pasting the object. Try the following with Paintbrush and Cardfile. Keep in mind that you can use this procedure to create a catalog of graphic images in Cardfile, then update those images whenever necessary. Follow these steps to paste and link a Paintbrush file into Cardfile:

1. Open Cardfile and Paintbrush.

2. In Paintbrush, open the WINLOGO.BMP file.

If you modify the image, you must save the changes to disk by choosing the File Save option. This is an important step. Paste-linked objects maintain a connection to the original file, unlike embedded objects.

3. Use the Pick tool (the right pair of scissors in the Toolbox) to outline the image, then choose Copy on the Edit menu to place the image on the Clipboard.

4. Switch to Cardfile, then choose Picture from its Edit menu. This lets you paste a picture, rather than text.

5. Next, choose Paste Link from the Edit menu to paste the object—and link it—in the card.

Now experiment with the linked object. Because the picture object in Cardfile is linked to the file WINLOGO.BMP, any changes you make to the file in Paintbrush are reflected in Cardfile (or any other place where the object is paste-linked). If both applications are open at the same time, you can watch the linked object change as you edit the original. If you change an object that is pasted into an unopened document, the pasted image is updated the next time you open the document. To see how this works, try the following steps:

1. Double-click on the linked image you just pasted in Cardfile. The Paintbrush window becomes active with the image in its workspace.

2. Arrange the Cardfile and Paintbrush windows side by side so you can see both images at once.

3. Now make some changes to the image in the Paintbrush file. Click the Brush tool, then a color, and paint some lines. The changes are immediately updated in Cardfile.

You can continue this example further by opening Write and paste-linking the image from Paintbrush. Then make changes to the image in Paintbrush and watch how the linked object in both Cardfile and Write changes simultaneously.

Now consider ways in which you might use these features. If you're working on a project that contains several documents, and each of the documents contains the same graphic image (a logo or product picture) or table of data (a schedule or budget), you can easily update all the documents at the same time by editing just the original files. OLE automatically updates the pasted object in the other documents.

Embedding Icons

Windows 3.1 also lets you embed icons into documents like those you see in the Program Manager. Embedded icons contain instructions for executing commands or opening documents. When you double-click an embedded icon, the application or document associated with it opens or plays. If you have a sound board or have the Speaker driver installed as discussed in Chapter 14, you can copy a sound from Sound Recorder and embed it in a document. The sound will appear in the document as an icon.

You can easily create a document, written for kids, that shows pictures of cows and dogs next to icons the children click to hear the sounds of those animals. In the business environment, you could attach voice instructions or greetings to documents.

Methods for Embedding Icons

There are several methods for placing embedded icons in documents. First, you can click and drag icons from the File Manager to your documents. Second, you can use the Packager accessory in the Program Manager Accessories group to create embedded icons. The first method is covered here. The second method, the Packager accessory, is discussed in Chapter 25, which covers this topic in more detail.

The following example demonstrates how you might create a catalog or directory of documents using Cardfile. You'll place an icon for a document on a card, then add an index header to the card to explain what the document is. Follow these steps:

1. Open Cardfile and the File Manager and arrange their windows side by side.

2. Locate the file README.WRI in the \WINDOWS directory. If the Windows directory is not visible, choose New Windows from the Window menu, then click the drive icon where the Windows directory is located, and finally, click the folder for the Windows directory in the directory tree on the left.

3. When you find the file, click and drag it from the File Manager over the top card in the Cardfile stack. The Write icon with the title README.WRI appears as shown in Figure 4-3.

Now double-click the icon in Cardfile to open the file you just pasted. Try the same procedure with another text file, a sound file with the extension .WAV, or even an application such as Notepad. Any of these files or programs automatically start when you double-click their icons. Keep in mind that you can paste icons in this way to other OLE applications such as Windows Write.

If you're still wondering how you can apply all this, think about ways to organize your applications and documents. For example, you could create a Cardfile for a project, then add icons to cards in the stack for each document associated with it. Cardfile also makes a good application organizer on the order of the Program Manager. You could create a stack of cards for a novice user that includes icons for starting applications, along with descriptions of what the applications do or how the user should put them to use in their daily tasks.

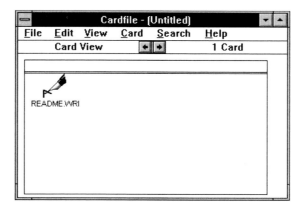

Figure 4-3.   *An embedded icon in Cardfile*

Chapter 5

Optimizing and Automating Windows

This chapter helps you use Windows more effectively. It starts off with a few tips and tricks for working with applications, editing documents, and organizing your activities. You then learn keyboard techniques, and how to automate your use of Windows by recording frequently used keystrokes or macros.

Useful Tips

The tips presented here are optional and follow no particular order of importance. They're just useful techniques you can use in your day-to-day Windows activities. While Windows accessories are used in the examples, you can apply these techniques to any of the applications you use.

Printing Help Topics

You've already seen how to work with the Help system, but don't forget that it contains useful information in an easy to use format. What's more, you can print any topic, or copy the information to a word processor for further editing. The next section uses the copy technique to place help information on the desktop.

The help information for Windows accessories is the most appropriate help information to print out and keep on hand. For example, you can easily print out a complete list of Write keystrokes. Simply open Windows Write and choose Contents from its help menu. Scroll to the bottom of the Contents list until you see Keyboard, then click on Write Keys. The complete list of Write keystrokes is displayed. Turn your printer on and choose Print Topic from the File menu. You'll find that this printed keystroke list will be handy later when you create macros.

While most Windows tasks are easier with the mouse, some keyboard methods may be quicker and easier to execute. For example, creating macros is generally best done using the keyboard rather than the mouse.

Click the Program Manager window and choose Contents on its help menu. When the help window opens, scroll to the bottom of the Contents list until you see the Keyboard topic as shown in Figure 5-1. Each topic in this list is worth printing. Most of the keyboard lists in the Program Manager are generic; the keys are applicable to many Windows applications.

Editing Help Text

An alternative to printing each topic is to copy them to a word processor, edit out the text you don't need, and combine several topics together. First open each help topic, and then choose Copy from the Edit menu. The Copy dialog box opens with the complete text in its viewing window. Click and drag through the text you want, and then click the Copy button.

Now switch to Write or another text editor and choose the Paste command. You may need to edit the text somewhat; this usually involves adding extra tabs to align columns. Highlight and delete any text you don't want. Add additional help text to the document by using Copy as described in the previous paragraph. Print the document when done.

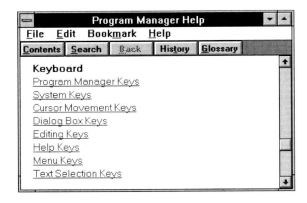

Figure 5-1.   *A typical Program Manager help menu*

Adding Reference "Pictures" to Your Desktop

You can place patterns, repeating pictures, scanned photographs, or artwork on the desktop, but a more practical idea is to place the most important help information or keystroke sequences there. Here's how.

Follow the procedure under Editing Help Text in the previous section to copy a list of keystroke definitions or other information you want onto the desktop. Remove unnecessary text and change formatting so you can fit as much text on one screen as possible. Maximize the window for best results. When you've got it just right, press the ALT-PRINT SCREEN key combination. This places a "picture" of the entire current window on the Clipboard.

Now open Paintbrush. You'll use it to remove the window borders and other parts of the picture you don't want. It would be confusing to have a picture of a window on the screen that's not really a window!

To paste the picture into the Paintbrush workspace, first maximize its window, and then choose Zoom Out from the View menu and Paste from the Edit menu. You must zoom out to paste the complete picture of the screen, otherwise its edges will be cropped. The image appears as a crosshatched pattern in the Paintbrush workspace. Click any tool in the toolbox. The image appears, but you must choose Zoom In from the View menu before you can edit it.

Now use the Eraser to remove the window borders. To change the size of the Eraser, pick a larger line size in the Linesize box. Use the scroll bars to move other parts of the image into view for editing. When you're done, save the image with an appropriate name such as KEYHELP.BMP.

To attach the image to the desktop, open the Control Panel and double-click the Desktop utility. In the Wallpaper field, choose KEYHELP.BMP in the File text box, then click the OK button. The help text appears on the desktop.

Note that this same technique can be used to place any text on the desktop, such as a list of phone numbers or important dates. It's easier to edit the text in an application such as Write than to type it on the Paintbrush canvas, plus you can use the full editing capabilities of Write.

Side-by-Side Editing

You can place documents side by side in separate application windows to make text comparisons or editing easier. For example, if you have two versions of a file and you're not sure what the differences are, place them side by side and scan through each. Try this now by opening two copies of README.WRI. Follow these steps:

1. Start by double-clicking the Read Me icon in the Program Manager Main group.

2. When the Write window opens, make the Program Manager active and double-click the Read Me icon again.

3. Now minimize all windows on the desktop except the two Write windows, then press CTRL-ESC to open Task List and click its Tile button. The two Write windows are sized the same and placed side by side.

To determine where a new section of text has been added, you scroll through each document until you find the new text. There's an easy way to do this that keeps the text in each window synchronized so you can quickly scroll and view the differences. In the active window, press the PAGE DOWN key to scroll the text. Click the title bar of the other window to make it the active window, and then press the PAGE DOWN key to scroll its text by the same amount you scrolled the other window's text. Continue this process of making one window active, then the other as you scroll to keep the windows in synchronization. Be sure to click the title bar when switching windows; clicking in the text could cause the text to go out of sync.

 If the windows aren't wide enough to display all the text, rearrange them so they are the width of the screen and so one is above another. You'll have to do this manually, since neither Tile nor Cascade produces this arrangement. However, Cascade may be good enough for your needs.

Saving Reusable Text and Graphics

You can save blocks of text or graphics using one of two methods with the Clipboard. The first method is to save the image on the Clipboard in a separate file, or to paste the text or images into a "master" document where you can easily get them in the future.

To save a Clipboard image, first open the Clipboard viewer. Its icon is located in the Program Manager Main group. You'll see the image you copied to the Clipboard. Choose Save As from its File menu, and then save the image with an appropriate filename.

The second method makes it easier to keep track of the text or images. You paste the Clipboard image to a Write document or a Cardfile card. Cardfile is used in this example. Follow these steps:

1. Open Paintbrush and draw an image you'll need often, such as your company logo, or create some text in Write that you use often, such as your name and address.

2. Capture the text or image to the Clipboard, then start Cardfile.

3. Choose Add from the Card menu, and then type an appropriate name for the text or image in the Add field. This name will appear at the top of the card. For example, type **Company Address** or **Company Logo** in the field.

4. Click OK to create the new card. If you're pasting text, choose the Paste command from the Edit menu. If you're pasting graphics, first choose Picture from the Edit menu, then choose Paste.

Save the Cardfile file with a name such as CATALOG.CRD, and then add all your reusable text and graphics to it.

Keeping the MS-DOS Prompt Handy

The MS-DOS Prompt is useful for several reasons. First, you can use it to quickly return to DOS and run DOS applications or utilities. It also provides an alternative method of listing and printing files and directories if you're not using the File Manager. Also, if you haven't yet learned all the features of the File Manager, you might want to revert back to DOS commands to format disks (FORMAT), check the memory of your system (MEM), or copy files (COPY, XCOPY, and DISKCOPY).

Be careful when executing commands in DOS. Don't remove .TMP files because these may be in use by your Windows applications, and don't run the CHKDSK command with the /F option as this may corrupt your disk. The README.TXT file covers these topics in more detail.

If you execute the MS-DOS Prompt in standard mode, DOS opens in a full screen. You can't run it in a window. Press ALT-TAB or ALT-ESC to return to Windows. You'll then see the MS-DOS Prompt as an icon on the desktop. Double-click the icon to return to DOS.

If you're running 386 enhanced mode, you can run DOS in a resizable Window. Double-click the MS-DOS Prompt, then press ALT-ENTER to convert DOS in a full screen to DOS in a window. To change the size and fonts of the window, click the Control button and choose Fonts from the Control menu, then choose a different font size in the Font list.

Keeping Notepad Handy

Notepad is another utility you can leave on the desktop during your Windows sessions. It doesn't take a lot of memory, and you can use it to jot down quick notes, reminders, and other information.

To quickly view a Notepad document, double-click the Notepad icon to open it, then open File Manager as well. Drag the icon of a file with the .TXT extension over the Notepad window. The document immediately opens in its workspace, as discussed in Chapter 2.

Creating a Time Log File

Notepad has a time logging feature that lets you create a file to track the time and date of entries. Whenever you open the time log file, the current date and time are automatically added to the file. You can then make entries under the date and time and save the file. The next time you open it, the current date and time are again added to the end of the file. You can use this feature to track billable events, phone calls, or other activities.

To create the time log file, open Notepad and type **.LOG** on the first line, in uppercase and with the period as shown. Then save the file, giving it a name such as TIMELOG.TXT. Now open the file and you'll see the current time and date.

You can create an icon for TIMELOG.TXT and place it in the Program Manager Startup group to open the time log every time Windows starts. This is covered in Chapter 6.

Keyboard Techniques

You can use Windows without a mouse. Some keyboard techniques provide quicker access to menu options, fields in dialog boxes, and window items, if you can remember the keystrokes. For example, press ALT to access the menu bar, then press F R to execute the Run command on the Program Manager's File menu. (For many people, it's easier to remember File Run than to use the mouse.)

Other options have quick-keys, such as the Move option (F7) and the Copy option (F8). You should check menus for these options. This section presents a short discussion of keyboard techniques, mainly to prepare you for the section on recording keystrokes that follows since you'll use keyboard techniques almost exclusively to create macros that speed up your everyday activities.

When working in dialog boxes, press TAB to move among fields, or SHIFT-TAB to move backward through fields. Try this now by clicking an icon in the Program Manager, and then choosing Properties from the File menu. Press TAB or SHIFT-TAB to move between fields. Also note that each field or button name has an underlined letter, or mnemonic. You access the field or button by pressing ALT followed by this letter.

Start Write and choose the Print Setup option on the File menu. Press ALT-Z to access the Size list box, then press the DOWN ARROW key on the keyboard and continue pressing it to scroll through the list. Press ALT-O to access the Options button, then press ENTER to open the Options dialog box. Press ALT-I to access the Intensity slider control, then press the RIGHT ARROW or LEFT ARROW key on the keyboard to move it. TAB to the Cancel button and press ENTER, then cancel from the Print Setup dialog box as well.

You should review the keyboard techniques for applications before you start recording keystrokes. Some keyboard techniques are extremely useful. In Write and many other word processors, you can jump from word to word, to the end of the current sentence, the next paragraph, or the next page, and you can jump forward or backward.

If you need to move, resize, minimize, maximize, or close a window, press ALT-SPACEBAR to open the Control menu. If the window is a document window, press ALT-HYPHEN to display the Control menu. You'll find a discussion of the Control menu keyboard techniques in the Program Manager help window.

The Recorder

The Recorder lets you record a series of frequently used keystrokes and mouse movements, which you can play back at any time using just one or two keystrokes. These key sequences, called *macros*, are assigned to CTRL or SHIFT key combinations. For example, you could record the sequence of keystrokes used to format a paragraph or change a font in Windows Write, assign the macro to the keyboard, then press the shortcut keys at any time to have Windows repeat the entire sequence of keys. Once you record your macros, all you do is press the CTRL or SHIFT key combination that triggers the macro you want.

This section explains the Recorder's features and how to use them. In most cases, you'll use the keyboard techniques discussed previously when recording macros; mouse movements don't record well because you can never be sure the window on the desktop will be in the same place when you play them back. Keystrokes are not dependent on the position or size of a window. You can record mouse movements too, but limit them to a single window, or a macro that's used only during the current session when the window size and position stays the same.

You can create macros for a specific application such as Write; a good macro to create is one that types in your name and entire return address. You can also create common macros that work with many different applications. A common macro could be used to set features in the Print Setup dialog box or to choose a font in the Fonts dialog box because these boxes are the same throughout most Windows applications.

Macro Sets

Macros are saved to files in sets and only one set of macros can be open at once. That means you can create a set of macros for Write and another set for Cardfile. Open each set of macros when working in the application they are designed for. But if you don't want to do this switching, you can create a general set of macros for use in all applications.

You can automatically load this macro set when Windows starts by including the macro file in the Startup group. In addition, one macro in the set can run automatically when the startup macro file is loaded. In this way, a set of keystrokes can execute when Windows starts. For example, you could create macros that do the following upon startup:

- Open the Calendar accessory and print your daily appointments

- Log onto a network to access your daily messages

- Access an online service such as CompuServe to access e-mail (electronic mail) or get information on stock activities

Startup and Overview

Start the Recorder by double-clicking its icon in the Program Manager Accessories window. The Recorder window appears as shown in Figure 5-2. The Recorder window includes a large workspace where macro names appear after they are recorded.

Recording a Macro

In the following example, you'll create a macro that formats selected text with the 24-point Arial TrueType font in Windows Write.

Preparing to Record

When you start recording, all keystrokes and mouse movements are recorded. Therefore, you need to prepare your desktop before you start recording. Follow the steps below to prepare for the Write macro:

1. Minimize the windows of any open applications.

2. Start Recorder if it is not already running.

3. Start Write and move its window so you can see the Macro Record window.

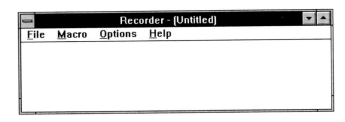

Figure 5-2.   *The Recorder window*

The Recorder switches to the most recently active window when it starts recording. Do not click an unnecessary window before executing the Record command.

Opening the Recorder Dialog Box

The process of recording a macro starts by choosing Record on the Macro menu. The Record Macro dialog box opens as shown in Figure 5-3.

In the Record Macro Name box, type **Arial 24 Point Font**. In the Shortcut Key box, type **F1** (or click the down arrow button and choose F1 from the list). Make sure the Ctrl box is checked in the Shortcut Key box to assign the macro to the CTRL-F1 keystroke. Click the Start button or press ENTER. All keystrokes and mouse movements are now recorded until you press CTRL-BREAK to stop recording.

Assuming the Write window was the last active window, it reappears as the active window. Recorder minimizes itself to a flashing icon, indicating that it is in record mode. Now follow these steps to create the Write macro:

1. Press ALT-C to select the Character menu.

2. Press F to select the Fonts options.

3. Type **Arial** in the Font Name field, even if it is already there. Keep in mind that this dialog box may not look the same when you run the macro later.

4. Press TAB twice to access the Size field, then type **24**.

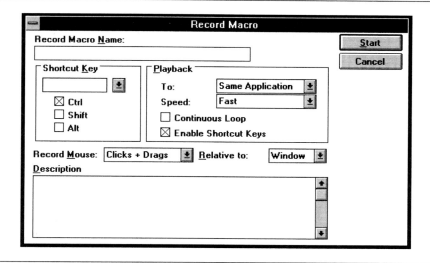

Figure 5-3.   *The Record Macro dialog box*

5. Press ENTER to accept the changes. Do not click the OK button with the mouse since the button may not be in the same place relative to the screen when you play the macro later.

Now stop the recording by pressing CTRL-BREAK. The Recorder dialog box appears, as shown here:

Click the Save Macro button, then the OK button to save the macro. Now restore the Recorder window, which lists the new macro in its workspace. To save the macro, choose Save As from Recorder's File menu. Type **WRITE** in the File Name field since this file contains macros for use with Write, then click OK to save the file. Recorder adds the extension .REC to all macro files. Keep in mind that you can add more macros to this file at any time.

Playing the Macro

To play the macro, switch to the Write window, then choose another font such as Courier from the Character menu. Type some text and highlight it using the mouse. Press CTRL-F1 to format the text with the macro.

The highlighted text converts to 24-point Arial font. Another way to play the macro is to open the Recorder window and double-click on the macro name in the workspace. The Recorder immediately switches to the most recently active window and plays the macro. Use this method if you can't remember the keystroke that runs the macro.

Press CTRL-BREAK *to stop a running macro.*

Using the Macro in Other Applications

By default, macros play back only within the application where they were recorded. However, some macros are useful in other applications. The macro you just created opens the Font dialog box on Character menus, which is a common task in other applications. To use this macro in other applications, change its properties using these steps:

1. Highlight the macro in the workspace.

2. Choose Properties from the Macro menu to open the Properties dialog box.

The Macro Properties dialog box has most of the same features as the Record Macro dialog box shown in Figure 5-3.

3. Choose Any Application in the To field of the Playback box.

4. Click the OK button.

This is one of many changes you can make to a macro after it has been created. You can also change its description, shortcut keys, and other playback options.

The Record Macro Dialog Box

The remaining features of the Record Macro dialog box pictured in Figure 5-3 are discussed in the following sections. Macro settings are made before recording, or after using the Macro Properties dialog box, which is discussed next.

Shortcut Keys

The Shortcut Key field in the Record Macro or Macro Properties dialog box holds the key assignment for the macro. The number of possible assignments is practically unlimited if you create multiple macro files. You should assign similar tasks to keystrokes in each macro file to make them easier to remember. For example, a print setup macro can be assigned to CTRL-F2 in both the Write and Paintbrush macro files.

Always assign a macro key in combination with the CTRL, SHIFT, or ALT key. Assigning a key like "A" by itself would prevent the letter "A" from being typed. In addition, use the ALT key sparingly or not at all since many Windows options use ALT. Don't assign keys that your application uses since the Recorder's assignments will override them. For best results, use a standard sequence such as CTRL-SHIFT, followed by the letters of your various macros.

The Description Field

Type an explanation of the macro or instructions for its use in the Description field.

The Record Mouse Field

As mentioned, only record mouse movements in special cases. To set the level at which mouse movements are recorded, use the Record Mouse box as follows.

- Choose *Ignore Mouse* to prevent the recording of mouse movements. If you choose this option, you can use the mouse while recording but it won't be recorded. This is useful for making "unrecorded" changes to windows or other options while recording.

- Choose *Everything* to record all mouse movements. Use this option to record demonstration macros or one-time only macros, as described later. In a demonstration, it's useful to show the mouse pointer moving across the screen and pointing to different options. A demonstration also runs at the recorded speed so viewers can see what's happening.

- The default option is *Clicks + Drags*, which records the position of the mouse when it is clicked. Not all mouse movements record and play back correctly, but setting the Relative To options described next enhances the ability to use the mouse in macros. On the other hand, some mouse movements and actions always play back correctly, such as dialog box selections or options that require a click of the mouse without first positioning the mouse.

The Relative To Field

You record the mouse relative to the borders of your screen, or the borders of a window. Choose Screen if the macro will work between windows and with objects on the desktop. Choose Window to restrict mouse movements to a single window. When Screen is selected, the x and y position of the mouse is measured from the screen border. When Window is selected, the x and y position is measured from the window border. Note the following:

- The *Screen* option provides accurate playback of mouse movements among objects on the desktop. However, make sure that objects you select during recording are in the same place during playback. This shouldn't be a problem if you play the macro back during the current session. Playing it in future sessions is difficult if the screen arrangement changes.

- The *Window* option replays mouse movements within a window. You can move the window anywhere on the desktop, but its size must remain the same. If, for example, you recorded a Paintbrush macro, and then resized the Paintbrush window before playing it back, mouse movements in the macro won't work because the location of the tools change when the window is resized. If the window size changes, a mouse action that selected the Brush during recording might select the Eraser during playback, so be careful.

The secret to recording and successfully playing back macros with mouse movements is to maximize the application window and choose the Relative To option. Include the keystroke ALT-SPACEBAR-X *(the Control menu Maximize option) as the first step in the macro so the window is always maximized.*

When to Use the Mouse

Macros are classified into three types. Whether or not you use the mouse depends on the type of macro you're creating.

- One-time only macros
- Keyboard and mouse macros
- Keyboard-only macros

One-Time Only Macros

Not all macros are played back over and over again in different sessions. For example, you might need a macro to help you copy and paste blocks of text between side-by-side windows. With a macro, all you would need to do is highlight the text to copy, then press the keys for the macro. A *one-time only* macro performs a temporary task, and is then discarded. Since the macro is based on your current screen arrangement, and not a future arrangement, use the mouse as much as you want and place windows in any arrangement. However, once you've recorded the macro, the arrangement of the desktop and the size of windows cannot be changed until you're through playing the macro. Since mouse movements are used extensively in one-time only macros, choose Everything in the Record Mouse field of the Record Macro dialog box.

Keyboard and Mouse Macros

In some cases, it makes sense to use both the mouse and keyboard. The keyboard is used to select options that would be hard to select with a mouse during playback, and the mouse is used to perform actions that are awkward with the keyboard. When using the mouse, choose Window in the Relative To box if the macro is limited to an application, and choose Screen if the mouse is used to select objects on the desktop or in another window. Choose Clicks+Drags in the Record Mouse field of the Record Macro dialog box.

Keyboard-Only Macros

Keyboard-only macros are played back often on a variety of desktop and window arrangements. Since you can never be sure of the exact position of Windows, the mouse is never used. Instead, all options and commands are selected with keyboard commands. Choose Ignore Mouse in the Record Mouse field to ensure that mouse movements are not recorded.

More About Playing Back a Macro

Playback options for macros are specified in the Playback box on the Record Macro dialog box. To change the options after a macro has been recorded, highlight the macro, then choose the Properties option from the Macro menu. The options for the Playback box on the Record Macro dialog box are described next.

The Playback To Field

Some macros are designed for use in one application and may cause problems if run when the application is not active. To avoid problems, designate a macro for use only in the applications where it was recorded by choosing Same Applications from the To field in the Playback box on the Record Macro dialog box. If that application is not open when the macro is played, an error message displays. Choose Any Application to allow playback in applications other than the one a macro was recorded in. Macros always play back in the current window. If Recorder is the current window, the macro plays in the next window. You can preview the order of windows on the desktop by pressing ALT-TAB.

The Playback Speed Field

You can play the macro back at fast speed, or at the speed it was recorded. The default playback mode is Fast; use the Recorded Speed option to play macros at the speed they were recorded, which is useful for demonstrations or training sessions in which you want to follow the mouse movements. An example showing how this is helpful appears later in this chapter.

The Playback Continuous Loop Option

Check this box to repeat the macro continuously until CTRL-BREAK is pressed. Set this option to continuously play a macro or to repetitively execute a command until you stop it. For example, a software vendor could continuously replay a running demo of a software feature, or you could use it to perform a repetitive formatting or replacement task in a document until you tell it to stop (or until it reaches the end of the document).

The Playback Enable Shortcut Keys Option

To include the shortcut keys of other macros in the macro you are recording, check this box. In this way, macros can include other macros so you don't have to record the keystrokes over again. Up to five other macros can be included in a macro.

Other Recorder Options

The following toggled items are located on the Options menu.

CTRL-BREAK Checking

Click this option to keep Recorder from detecting CTRL-BREAK. When set, a macro cannot be stopped until it finishes.

Shortcut Keys

Choose this option to turn Recorder shortcut keys off until you're done with an application. Keyboard conflicts can occur when macro key assignments are the same as those in an application you intend to run.

Minimize on Use

Set this option on to minimize Recorder to an icon when a macro starts.

Setting Preferences

The Preferences option is used to set *default* options for the Record Macro dialog box. Make these changes based on the previous discussion and on your own needs. They will be the default settings on the Record Macro dialog box, which will appear with these settings whenever you record a new macro.

Playback To   The To option in the Playback box lets you set the default for macro playback to either Same Application or Any Application.

Playback Speed   The Speed option in the Playback box lets you set the default to be either Recorded Speed or Fast.

Record Mouse   The Record Mouse option lets you set the default for mouse movements. You can ignore all mouse activities, record everything, or record just clicks and drags.

Relative To   The Relative To option lets you set the default for the recording of mouse movements. You can record over the entire desktop or restrict recording to the current window.

Loading a Macro File at Startup

Once a set of macros is created, you can load them every time Windows starts by creating a document icon for the Recorder file and placing it in the Program Manager's Startup group. Assume you've created a series of macros for general use in Windows, not for a specific application. The macro file is called MAIN.REC. Follow the steps here to create a startup icon in the Startup group:

1. Open the Startup Group in the Program Manager.

2. Choose New from the File menu.

3. Choose Program Item on the New Program Object dialog box.

4. When the Program Item Properties dialog box appears, type **MAIN** in the description field, and then click the Browse button to locate the MAIN.REC file in the Windows directory or the directory where it is located.

5. Click OK.

The next time you start Windows, the MAIN macro file is loaded and its macros are available for use. Creating startup icons is covered in more detail in Chapter 6.

Running a Macro at Startup

You can run an individual macro in a macro file when Windows starts. To do so, click the icon for the macro in the Startup group, then choose Properties from the Program Manager File menu and type the keyboard sequence for the macro in the Command Line field. Use the following keys to designate the ALT, CTRL, and SHIFT keys in the Command Line field:

For	Use
ALT	%
SHIFT	+
CTRL	^

For example, to start a macro with the key sequence CTRL-F1, type the following line in the Command Line field, assuming the macro filename is MAIN.REC:

```
RECORDER -h ^F1 MAIN.REC
```

You must include RECORDER in the field, not just the associated macro filename. The -h option executes the key sequence. Following the -h is the key sequence to be executed, and then the macro filename. Specify the path for the macro file if necessary.

Macro Examples

The following examples are presented to familiarize you with the macro recording process and give you ideas for your own macros. Create the macros in a single macro file called MAIN.REC.

A Macro that Opens Dialog Boxes

In this example, you'll create a macro that opens the Open dialog box and changes its file listing method. The macro can be used in any application that has an Open option on its File menu. For this recording, use the Open option on Notepad. Follow these steps:

1. Start Notepad.

2. Start Recorder or make its window active.

3. Choose Record from the Macro menu.

4. In the Record Macro Name field, type **List all files on Open boxes**.

5. In the Shortcut key box, press O, then click the Ctrl and Shift options to make the macro keystroke CTRL-SHIFT-O.

6. Choose the Any Application option in the To field of the Playback box. This makes the macro available for use in any application.

7. Click the Start button. The Recorder window reduces to an icon and Notepad becomes active.

8. Type ALT-F O to open the Open dialog box.

9. Type *.* in the File Name field and press the ENTER key. The list changes to display all files.

10. Click the Recorder icon or press CTRL-BREAK to stop recording, then click Save Macro and the OK button.

11. Finally, test the macro by running it in an application other than Notepad.

You can use the macro to list all files in a directory for any application. You can create additional macros that change the drive or directory as well. For example, if you keep all your document files in a directory called DOCS on drive D, you could create a macro similar to the one just given that opens the Open dialog box, changes the drive field to drive D, changes the directory field to the DOCS directory, then types *.* in the File Name field to show all files.

A Continuous Demo Macro

The following macro is of interest to those who create demonstrations or tutorials. You'll open Paintbrush and record the mouse movements necessary to create a box. You'll then replay the macro repetitively at the recorded speed.

1. Start by opening Paintbrush.
2. Start Recorder or make its window active.
3. Choose Record from the Macro menu.
4. Type **Repeating Demo** in the Record Macro Name field.
5. In the Shortcut Key field, click the down arrow button and choose a key from the list. For this example, choose Scroll Lock. Click Ctrl and Shift to make the demo startup keys CTRL-SHIFT-SCROLL LOCK.
6. Choose Recorded Speed in the Speed field of the Playback box.
7. Click the Continuous Loop check box.
8. In the Record Mouse field, choose Everything.
9. In the Relative To field, make sure Window is selected.
10. Click the Start button to start recording. The Paintbrush window appears.
11. Press ALT-SPACEBAR X to maximize the window. Since the mouse will be used, this ensures the coordinates will be the same during playback.
12. Drag the mouse to the Filled Box tool and click. Remember that the mouse movements are visible during playback, so use slow steady mouse movements.
13. Choose a foreground and a background color.
14. Click in the workspace and draw a box.
15. Leave the box on the screen for about five seconds, and then click white with the right mouse button, click a wide line in the Linewidth field, select the Eraser tool, and erase the box.
16. Press CTRL-BREAK to stop recording, click the Save Macro box, and click OK.

Now you can play the macro back by pressing CTRL-SHIFT-SCROLL LOCK. The macro repeats until you press CTRL-BREAK. You can create similar macros to display messages such as the words "I'm out to lunch" typed continuously across the screen.

Boilerplate Macros

Boilerplates are blocks of prewritten text you insert into your documents. In this example, you create a boilerplate macro to type your company name and address, then center it and change the font.

1. Start Write.

2. Start Recorder or make it the active window.

3. Choose Record from the Macro menu.

4. Type **Company Logo** in the Record Macro Name field.

5. Choose Caps Lock in the Shortcut Key field and click the Ctrl and Shift options.

6. Click the Start button. The Write Window appears.

7. Press ALT-C F to open the Font dialog box.

8. Type **Arial** in the Fonts field, then TAB to the Size field and type **14** and press ENTER to make the changes.

9. Now press ALT-P C to center the logo.

10. Type your company name and address.

11. When you're done, press CTRL-BREAK, click the Save Macro box, and click the OK button to end recording.

You can play this macro back in any Write file. You can also create similar macros that assign different type styles or type different text. Because boilerplates are so useful, creating a separate macro file to hold them may be necessary.

Chapter 6

The Program Manager

The Program Manager is Windows' graphical program launching utility. You use it to start applications and open documents. This chapter shows you how to arrange and organize Program Manager groups and icons to fit your needs.

Arranging Groups and Icons

Chapter 1 covered methods of resizing and arranging group windows in the Program Manager. To reiterate:

- Enable the Auto Arrange option on the Options menu to automatically rearrange icons to fit within a resized window.

- If Auto Arrange is disabled, choose the Arrange Icons option on the Window menu to rearrange the icons.

- Enable the Minimize on Use option to reduce the Program Manager to an icon when starting applications.

- Enable Save Settings on Exit to save any changes you've made to the Program Manager for the next session.

Copying, Moving, and Deleting Icons

You can copy or move icons from one group to another by using the mouse or by using the Copy and Move options on the File menu.

Copying an Icon Using the Mouse

To copy an icon using the mouse, press the CTRL key, click the icon, and drag it to another group. This makes a copy of the icon in the target group and leaves the original where it is. To move an icon, just click and drag it to a new group. The icon is then removed from its original group.

Copying an Icon Using the File Menu

You use the Copy option on the File menu to achieve the same results. There is little reason, however, to use the menu method, unless you can't see the group icon. Try this now by copying the MS-DOS Prompt icon from the Main group to the Startup group. Click the icon, then choose Copy on the File menu. The Copy Program Item dialog box appears, as shown here:

    You see the icon and group name of the selected icon (MS-DOS Prompt and Main, respectively). At the bottom is a drop-down list box where you select the destination group. Press the DOWN ARROW key on the keyboard until Startup appears in the field, and then press ENTER or click the OK button. Verify that the icon is now in the Startup group by double-clicking the Startup icon.

Moving an Icon

The steps for moving an icon are exactly the same as copying an icon, except that you choose Move from the Program Manager File menu instead of Copy.

Deleting an Icon

To delete an icon, click it with the mouse, then press the DEL key on the keyboard or choose Delete from the File menu. To delete an entire group, reduce it to an icon, click it with the mouse, and follow the same procedure. Before deleting a group, move any icons you might need to other groups. If you don't want the MS-DOS Prompt icon in the Startup group, click it now and choose Delete from the File menu.

Creating New Groups

To create a new group, choose New from the File menu. The New Program Object
dialog box appears, as shown here:

Click the Program Group button, and then click the OK button. Next, you see
the Program Group Properties dialog box, as shown here:

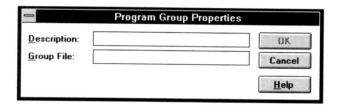

In the Description field, type a name for the new group. For this example, type
Tools in the Description field. You'll use this group to organize the icons of programs
and documents you'll use as you read this book. The Group File field is used to specify
the name of the file that holds group information. If you leave it blank, Windows
names the group with the name found in the Description field, up to the first eight
letters. For this example, click OK to create the new group, named Tools.

The Tools group window appears in the Program Manager. Now you can add icons
to it by following the exercises in the next few sections. Drag the SysEdit icon you
created in Chapter 2 to the Tools group.

Creating New Icons

In Chapter 2, you saw how to create the SysEdit icon in the Main group. This section
covers the details of creating a new program icon in the Tools group. In the examples
that follow, you'll create an icon for the Windows tutorial. The tutorial's filename
is WINTUTOR.EXE and it is located in the Windows directory.

Creating Program Icons

To create the WinTutor icon, first open the group that will contain the icon. For this example, open the Tools group you created in the previous section, or click on its window if it's already open. Next, choose New from the File menu to display the New Program Object dialog box. Make sure the Program Item option is selected; it should be if you first opened the Tools group, and then click OK to display the Program Item Properties dialog box, shown in Figure 6-1.

The fields of the Program Item Properties dialog box are described in the next sections.

The Description Field   In the Description field, you type the name that will appear under the icon in the group window.

The Command Line Field   In the Command Line field, type the name of the executable file used to start the program, along with drive letters and path names if necessary. You don't need to specify a path if the file is in a directory on the DOS path. If you don't know the executable filename, you can click the Browse button to activate a search. You can also include the name of a file to load with the application when it starts, thus creating a document icon. For example, to create an icon that opens an Excel document called BUDGET.XLS, type **EXCEL BUDGET.XLS**.

The Working Directory Field   In the Working Directory field, type the name of the directory where the application should access document files. The directory becomes the current directory while the application runs.

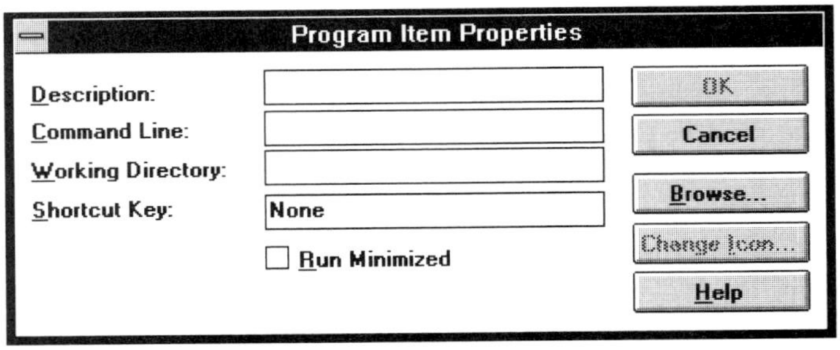

Figure 6-1.   *Use the Program Item Properties dialog box to define the name and other properties of a program startup icon*

The Shortcut Key Field   In the Shortcut Key field, you specify a keystroke used to start the application. Only CTRL-ALT key combinations are allowed.

The Run Minimized Box   Check the Run Minimized box to reduce the application to an icon on the desktop when it starts. This option is useful for icons placed in the Startup group if you don't need to use them as soon as they open.

The Browse Button   Click the Browse button to browse for executable filenames. A Browse dialog box that looks similar to the Open dialog box opens.

The Change Icon Button   Click the Change Icon button to choose an icon.

To create the WinTutor icon, Type **WinTutor** in the Description field. This name will appear under the icon. In the Command Line field, you can also type **WinTutor**. A path is not necessary since the executable file is in the Windows directory on the DOS path. However, for this example, click the Browse button to search for the filename.

The Browse dialog box opens with a list of files in the Windows directory. If you're creating icons for other programs, use the Browse dialog box to look for executable files on other drives and directories.

The Browse dialog box lists files with the extensions .EXE, .PIF, .COM, and .BAT. You can create icons for each of these file types. Files with the extensions .EXE and .COM are DOS executable files. The PIF files (Program Information Files) start non-Windows applications and contain special settings for doing so. DOS users are familiar with .BAT files, or batch files. A batch file *contains a series of commands that execute one after the other at the DOS level. Chapter 19 gives more information about PIF and .BAT files.*

Scroll to the bottom of the File Name list and double-click the WINTUTOR.EXE file. The filename then appears in the Command Line box with its complete drive and path.

In this example, it doesn't make sense to specify a directory in the Working Directory field since the WinTutor command simply starts the Windows tutorial. You specify working directories for applications that create and store files. Tab to the Shortcut Key field and enter **T** (for tutorial). The key sequence Ctrl+Alt+T appears in the field. It's not necessary to enable the Run Minimized option.

The WinTutor utility comes with its own set of icons. To see them, click the Change Icon button. The Change Icon dialog box appears as shown in Figure 6-2.

In the case of WinTutor, the first icon is appropriate because the others are already in use by the Windows accessories. However, you can scroll the list and pick any icon you want. Double-click the icon you want to use. In the next section, you'll see how to open files that contain other icons. When you return to the Program Item Properties box, click OK to create the new icon. It appears in the group and you can double-click the icon to start the tutorial.

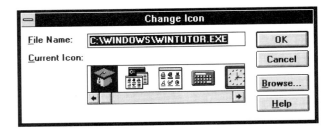

Figure 6-2. *Use the Change Icon dialog box to select an icon for the program item*

The WinVer Utility

As long as you're creating icons, assign one to the Windows Version utility. Its file is called WINVER.EXE and it's in the Windows directory. This will give you practice in creating icons and give you an icon that shows the current version number for Windows.

Choose New on the File menu, and then make sure Program Item is selected on the New Program Object box. Click OK. Type **WinVer** in both the Description field and the Command Line field of the Program Item Properties dialog box. This particular utility has only one icon so you don't need to click the Change Icon button. At the Shortcut Key field, type **V** to create the CTRL-ALT V shortcut key sequence.

The fields for the WinVer utility are now complete. Click the OK button. The WinVer icon appears in the Tools group. Double-click the icon to see the WinVer dialog box as shown in the following illustration. Click the OK button to close the dialog box.

Changing Icon Properties

You can change the properties of an icon at any time. Its *properties* include all the items listed on the Program Item Properties dialog box shown in Figure 6-1. You can change the icon, icon name, shortcut key sequence, or other listed options of any existing icon.

You can make a copy of an existing icon, and then change its properties. This is especially useful when you need icons that start the same program but open different documents; in the command field, simply change the name of the file to load.

Try changing the properties of the Read Me icon in the Main group. First click the icon, then choose Properties from the Program Manager File menu. To change the title that appears under the icon, type **Win Info** in the Description field. Tab to the Shortcut Key field and type **W**. The key sequence Ctrl+Alt+W appears in the field. Changing the icon itself is discussed next.

Changing the Icon

To choose a new icon, click the Change Icon button in the Program Item Properties dialog box. The Change Icon dialog box appears with the Write icon. Note that Write's icon is automatically used because Write is the program used to create the document. Changing the icon does not affect how the document loads. Write still starts with the README.WRI file loaded in its workspace.

To choose a different icon, click the Browse button. When the Browse dialog box appears, notice that three file types are listed: .ICO, .EXE, and .DLL. Hidden within the listed files are icons. For example, double-click CALC.EXE and you'll see the Calculator icon. But once again, only one icon is available and it's already in use by Calculator.

Click Browse again and scroll through the file list until you see PROGMAN.EXE. This is the Program Manager executable file. Double-click the filename to see the extensive list of icons shown in Figure 6-3. Use the scroll bar to scan through the list.

There's one other file that has an extensive list of icons. Click the Browse button again, and then double-click the file MORICONS.DLL. The numerous icons shown in Figure 6-4 are available in this file. Note that MORICONS.DLL is used by the Setup utility to create startup icons for non-Windows applications; therefore, most of the icons in this file represent specific products.

Note that the icons in PROGMAN.EXE are for general use while the icons in MORICONS.DLL are for third-party applications. You can try opening other .ICO, .EXE, or .DLL files. The .ICO files are created with an icon editor and are commonly found on bulletin boards. Icon editors are also available on bulletin boards.

For now, find an icon you like that provides a representation of the Windows information file. Double-click the icon to return to the Program Item Properties dialog box. You see the selected icon in the lower left. Click the OK button to complete the change of properties and the new icon appears in the Main group.

Figure 6-3. *Icons in the PROGMAN.EXE file*

The Working Directory

Recall that the Working Directory field is used to specify where a program will access files. If a working directory is not specified, the directory of the program is used. Type the data directories where the program should access files. It helps keep your data files separate from program files. You may have noticed that the Windows accessories automatically access the Windows directory.

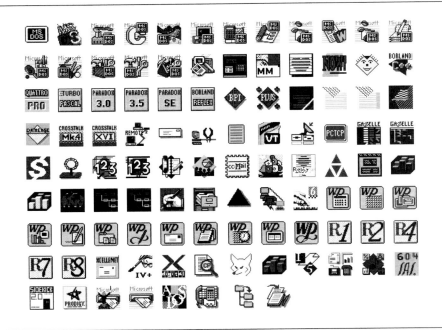

Figure 6-4. *Icons in MORICONS.DLL*

You should change the working directory of the accessories, such as Write and Paintbrush, to ensure that files you create using these accessories are stored in a directory other than the Windows directory. Chapter 18 discusses this further.

Creating Document Icons

In this section, you create icons for documents rather than programs. In a way, document icons are more useful than program icons because they load the exact document you want to work on, thus saving you steps. The following steps lead you through the creation of a startup icon for the time log file you created in Chapter 5:

1. Open the Tools group, or click it to make it the active group.

2. Choose New from the File menu. When the New Program Object dialog box appears, make sure Program Item is selected and click OK.

3. On the Program Item Properties box, type **Time Log** in the Description field. This will be the title of the icon.

4. Tab to the Command Line field, and then click the Browse button. Use Browse to locate TIMELOG.TXT, which should be in the Windows directory. In the List Files of Type field, choose All Files (*.*) to display all files, and then scan the list and double-click the file.

Because TIMELOG.TXT is associated with Notepad, only its name needs to appear in the Command Line field. You'll need to type a program name and document name when creating unassociated documents, as you'll see in the next section.

5. Assign a shortcut key if you like.

6. Click the Change Icon button to pick an icon for the document. If you don't do this, the Notepad icon will be used. You could pick the phone icon in PROGMAN.EXE.

7. Click OK when done.

The new icon appears in the Tools group. Double-click it to open the time log.

Creating an Unassociated Document Icon

If a document is not associated with any application, you must specify a program to load on the Command Line field, followed by the document name. In the following example, you'll do that by creating an icon for SETUP.INF, an unassociated file.

SETUP.INF is the Setup information file Windows uses when you change its configuration. You'll refer to this file in Appendix B, so create an icon for it in the Tools group by following these steps:

1. Click the Tools group to make it active.

2. Choose New on the File menu and use the normal procedure to get to the Program Item Properties box.

3. In the Description field, type **SETUP.INF**. In this case, we want the icon to indicate the exact file it opens.

4. In the Command Line field, type the following to specify the program and filename with full path:

    WRITE C:\WINDOWS\SYSTEM\SETUP.INF

5. Click OK to save the changes. You don't need to change the icon.

The icon appears in the Tools group window. If you double-click the icon, you'll see the following dialog box. It appears because Write does not recognize SETUP.INF as one of its files. Click No Conversion to maintain the text-only format of SETUP.INF.

Never convert the SETUP.INF file to Write format. It must remain in text-only format to be readable by SETUP.

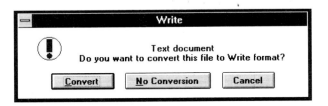

Using the File Manager to Create Icons

The File Manager provides one of the best methods for creating document icons. You simply locate the documents you want to create icons for, and then drag them from the File Manager onto your Program Manager group. In the following example, you'll create startup icons for the WIN.INI and SYSTEM.INI files. You'll work with these files in future chapters, so it's a good idea to make them available as icons in the Tools group.

Start by opening the File Manager and making sure you have a directory window open for the Windows directory. If you do not, double-click the drive icon where your Windows directory is located, then click the folder for the Windows directory. Reduce the file list in this directory window by following these steps:

1. Click By File Type on the View menu.

2. In the Name field, type ***.INI** and click the OK button.

Now you see only the .INI files in the Windows directory. Resize and move the File Manager window so you can see part of the Tools group in the underlying Program Manager window. Now follow these steps to create icons for the .INI files in the Tools group:

3. Click the first file in the list.

4. Hold the SHIFT key and click the last file in the list. This selects all the files.

5. Click any one of the file icons and hold the mouse while dragging the icon onto the Tools group in the Program Manager.

In a moment, an icon appears for each file in the Program Manager's Tools group. Try double-clicking any of the icons to open its associated file.

Using Setup to Create Icons

The Setup utility offers yet another way to create startup icons for applications. You may already be familiar with it from the installation routine. Setup can search your hard drive filing system for executable files, and then create startup icons for the executable files you select. If Setup finds non-Windows applications, it creates PIF files for those it recognizes.

Start Setup by double-clicking its icon in the Main group window of the Program Manager. This opens a window similar to the one shown next. Setup displays configuration information about your system, so your Windows Setup dialog box may appear different than the one shown here:

Windows Setup	
Options **Help**	
Display:	VGA
Keyboard:	Enhanced 101 or 102 key US and Non US
Mouse:	Microsoft, or IBM PS/2
Network:	No Network Installed

Follow the steps given next to set up a new application startup icon using Setup. Choose Set Up Applications from the Options menu. When the Setup Applications dialog box appears, make sure Search for Applications is selected, then click the OK button. The next dialog box, Setup Applications, displays a list of drives, or the Path entry as shown in Figure 6-5.

You can limit the search to a single drive or multiple drives, or to just the directories specified in the system path. Click one or more options in the box and click the Search Now button. In a moment, a dialog box similar to the one shown in Figure 6-6 appears.

On the left side of the dialog box shown in Figure 6-6 is a list of applications that are not currently set up. Because every system is different, you'll need to pick the name of a file that you want to install. If you have DOS 5, QuickBASIC (QBASIC) should appear in the list. Click it, and then click the Add button to place it in the right list box. Continue selecting applications. If you decide you don't want to add one of the applications, click its name on the right, then click the Remove button. When done selecting, click the OK button or press ENTER.

Icons are created for the applications in the Applications group or in the Non-Windows Applications group. You can open these groups now to see any new icons that were added.

Setting Up a Single Application

You can use the Setup Utility to create a startup icon for a single application, and, if it's a non-Windows application, create a PIF file for it in the Windows directory. Follow these steps:

1. Start the Setup utility from inside Windows.

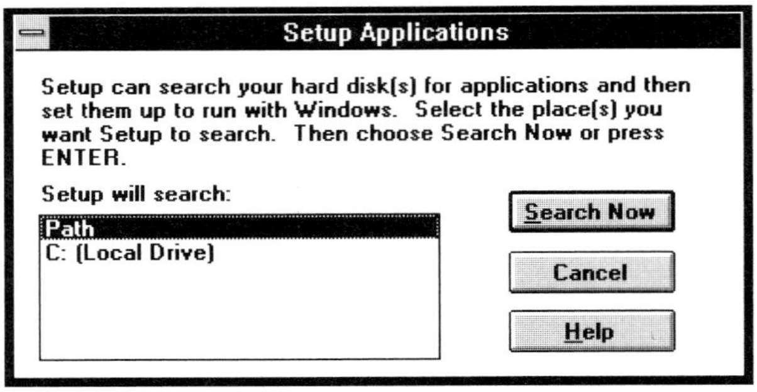

Figure 6-5. *The Setup utility will search for programs on the path or in specific drives*

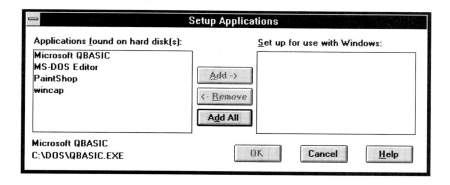

Figure 6-6.   *Use the Setup Applications dialog box to add applications*

2. Choose Setup Applications from the Options menu.

3. The next dialog box has the option "Ask you to specify an application." Click this option and click the OK button.

4. Next, you see the Setup Applications dialog box shown in Figure 6-7.

5. Type the path and filename for the application, or click the Browse button to locate the startup file.

6. In the Add to Program Group field, select the group window where the icon should be placed.

7. Click OK to create the icon.

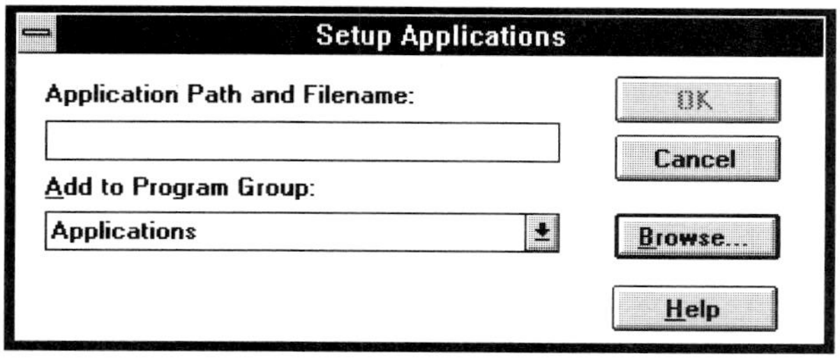

Figure 6-7.   *Use the Setup Applications dialog box to install a single application*

If the application is known to the Windows Setup program, an appropriate icon is selected and a PIF file is created. Setup gets its instructions from the APPS.INF file in the Windows SYSTEM directory. This file is covered in Appendix B. If you need to change the settings of the new startup icon, click it, then choose Properties from the File menu.

Deleting Groups and Icons

When you don't need an icon or group window, make sure you delete it. Windows must keep track of each icon during a Windows session and this requires memory and resources. The more icons cluttering your system, the slower Windows runs.

- To remove an icon, click it with the mouse, then press the DEL key, or choose Delete from the File menu.

- To remove a group, first reduce it to an icon, then click the group and press the DEL key or choose Delete from the File.

Chapter *7*

Files and the File Manager

The File Manager is a program that displays and manages files on your local drives or the drives of remote network file servers. Here's a partial list of what you can do with the File Manager:

- Copy or move single files or groups of files by clicking and dragging their icons to other drives or directories.

- Delete or rename files or groups of files.

- Start executable program files by double-clicking their icons.

- Open documents by double-clicking their icons.

Of course, the File Manager has many other features, which you'll learn about as you read this chapter and do the examples.

To start the File Manager, double-click its icon in the Program Manager Main menu. The first time the File Manager starts, it looks similar to the window shown in Figure 7-1. If yours doesn't look like this, refer to the section called "Resetting File Manager Defaults" later in this chapter. The File Manager has document windows like the Program Manager and many Windows applications, but these windows are called *directory windows* in the File Manager because each displays the contents of a single directory. Directory windows have the following features:

The Drive Icon Bar   The drive icon bar depicts each of the floppy drives, hard drives, RAM memory drives, and network drives available to the File Manager. You

107

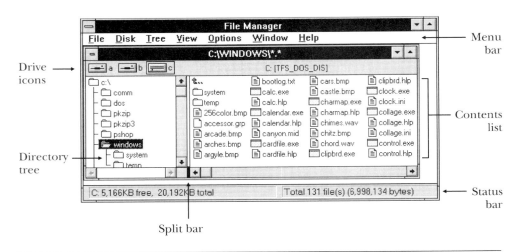

Drive icons

Directory tree

Split bar

Menu bar

Contents list

Status bar

Figure 7-1.   *The File Manager startup window*

click the icon once to see its contents in the current directory window or twice to open a new directory window.

The Directory Tree   The directory tree depicts the directories on the drive that is currently selected in the drive icon bar.

The Contents List   The contents list shows the files for the directory selected in the directory tree.

The Split Bar   The split bar separates the directory tree and the contents list. You may click and drag the split bar left or right to enlarge one side of the directory window, or remove it completely to display only directories or only files.

The Status Bar   The status bar displays important information about the selected drive such as the number of files and their total disk space.

Resetting File Manager Defaults

The following steps prepare the File Manager for the exercises in this chapter. The file WINFILE.INI holds the startup information for the File Manager, such as what its window size and shape should be, and which directory windows it should open. By renaming this file, the File Manager reverts to its default settings the next time it starts, displaying the window you see in Figure 7-1. Follow these steps:

1. Start the File Manager by double-clicking its icon in the Main group.

2. Disable the Save Settings on Exit option on the Options menu.

3. Choose Rename from the File menu.

4. When the Rename dialog box appears, type the following in the From field. If your Windows directory is on a drive other than C, replace C with the correct drive letter.

   C:\WINDOWS\WINFILE.INI

5. Type the following in the To field, once again substituting the drive letter if necessary.

   C:\WINDOWS\WINFILE.TMP

6. Exit, then restart the File Manager.

The File Manager re-creates its startup file with the default settings. You are now ready to continue with the exercises. If you want to restore the previous settings at any time after finishing this chapter, first delete the WINFILE.INI file, then rename WINFILE.TMP to WINFILE.INI using the Rename command.

Customizing the File Manager

You can customize the File Manager by changing its fonts, setting its status bar on or off, or changing the way the File Manager confirms your commands. The options discussed in this section are on the File Manager's Options menu.

Suppressing Confirmation Messages

Warning messages appear when you delete or copy files in the File Manager. Often, these messages are a nuisance if you are sure about the actions you're taking, or if you are copying or deleting large groups of files. You can turn off messages by choosing the Confirmation option on the Options menu. The Confirmation dialog box in Figure 7-2 appears.

Each option in the Confirmation dialog box is described next. When these options are enabled (or checked), warning messages appear when you execute the commands or actions.

The File Delete Option　Remove the X from the File Delete option, and you'll no longer get a warning message when you remove files with the DEL key or the Delete option on the File menu.

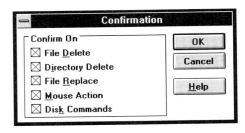

Figure 7-2.   *Use the Confirmation dialog box to enable or disable warning messages*

The Directory Delete Option   Disable the Directory Delete option to prevent warning messages when you remove subdirectories with the DEL key or the Delete option on the File menu.

The File Replace Option   If you disable the File Replace option, you won't get a warning message when you save a file with a filename already in use for an existing file. Disabling this option lets you copy over existing files without warning.

The Mouse Action Option   Disable the Mouse Action option to prevent warning messages when copying or moving files using mouse click-and-drag techniques.

The Disk Commands Option   Disable Disk Commands, and you won't be warned when performing any disk-related actions, such as formatting.

New users should leave these options set until completely comfortable with File Manager techniques. It can be handy to disable confirmation messages when deleting large groups of files, but be sure it is safe to make the deletions. For example, if you're deleting an entire directory and you leave Delete Confirmations on, a warning message appears for every file in the directory. Once you've deleted the files, you can set the confirmation back on.

Controlling Individual File Deletions

The confirmation messages provide an excellent way to selectively control file operations. You can pick and choose the files to delete or copy. A dialog box similar to the Confirm File Delete dialog box shown here appears when deleting more than one file (assuming File Delete confirmation messages are enabled):

Selectively delete files by clicking the Yes or No button as the message box appears for each file. Click the Yes to All button if you're sure the remaining files should be deleted. Click Cancel to keep the remaining files and stop the Delete command.

Changing Fonts

To change the font used to display filenames in directory windows, choose the Font option on the Options menu. The Font dialog box appears. Note that it's similar to the Font dialog box discussed in Chapter 3.

Choose a font, style, and size in the appropriate boxes. Fonts are displayed in lowercase by default. Disable the Lowercase check box to display fonts in uppercase. When the options are set the way you want them, click the OK button.

To align characters in a file listing, use monospaced fonts. This is useful when comparing the names of different files for length or similarity. Courier is a monospaced font, but choose a small font size such as 8 or 10 to make sure characters fit and don't overlap in the directory window.

Displaying the Status Bar

The status bar at the bottom of the File Manager window displays useful information about disk space and file sizes for the currently selected disk.

- When a directory is selected, the status bar displays information about the drive on the left and the directory on the right.

- When a file is selected, the status bar displays the size of the file.

- When multiple files are selected, the status bar indicates the number of files and their total number of bytes.

If your desktop becomes crowded, you can gain a little more room by disabling the Status Bar option from the Options menu.

Minimizing File Manager on Use

The Minimize on Use option, if enabled, reduces the File Manager to an icon when you start an application or open an associated file. Enable this option to reduce screen clutter if you use the File Manager as a program launcher.

Saving Settings on Exit

The Save Settings on Exit option saves changes you make to the File Manager for your next File Manager session. The following options and settings are saved:

- Enabling or disabling Option menu items

- Adding new directory windows

- Changes you make to file listing methods in directory windows

- Window resizing and arrangement

You should determine your need to enable this option during each File Manager session. If you've created an arrangement you like, enable the setting and exit. If you've opened several directory windows as part of a non-standard procedure and don't want those windows open the next time you start the File Manager, then disable the option, or close the windows before exiting.

You can save changes to the File Manager arrangement without exiting by holding the SHIFT *key and choosing Exit from the File Manager. Use this method if you create an arrangement you like.*

Getting just the right arrangement of directory windows and option settings takes time. To ensure that you don't accidentally change the settings (by exiting with the Save Settings on Exit option enabled), make a backup of the WINFILE.INI file. Give it a name such as FMSETUP.INI. Then if you loose your settings, just make a copy of this file and call it WINFILE.INI. Then disable the Save Changes on Exit option and restart the File Manager. The settings in the new file will then be used.

Working with Directory Windows

The first time you start the File Manager using its default settings, only one directory window is open and it displays the files in the Windows directory. This section shows you how to open new directory windows or change the contents of existing windows.

Opening and Arranging Directory Windows

To open a new directory window, choose New Window from the Window menu. A duplicate of your current window opens. Note that its title bar includes a number 2, indicating it is the second window for the directory listed. Do the following to change the window arrangements:

- Choose Tile from the Window menu to arrange the two windows side by side. Using Cascade in the File Manager places windows one on top of another.

- In the upper window, click the DOS directory icon in the directory tree (or another directory if you don't have a DOS directory).

- Choose All File Details from the View menu to list the filenames, file sizes, and file dates.

Another way to open a directory window is to double-click a drive icon on an existing directory window. Double-click the icon of the drive you want to list files on. A new directory window opens with a list of files for that drive. The new directory window takes on the characteristics of the original, such as its file type listing or directory contents.

The Split Bar

The split bar divides the directory tree and the contents list in the directory window. You control its position with the mouse or with options on the View menu.

Moving the Split Bar

Click and drag the split bar left to enlarge the file area or right to enlarge the directory tree. When the mouse pointer is over the split bar, a double-headed arrow icon appears. Adjust the split bar in both windows to remove the excess white space next to the directory tree.

Another way to adjust the window split is to choose the Split option on the View menu. A large split bar appears in the current directory window that you can adjust with the RIGHT ARROW or LEFT ARROW key on the keyboard, or by moving the mouse. Press ENTER or click the mouse to set the new split.

Removing the Window Split

You can remove the window split entirely to display the tree only or files only using one of these methods:

- Choose Tree Only from the View menu to display only the directory tree.

- Choose Directory Only from the View menu to display only files for a selected directory.

Try the following to create a unique arrangement:

1. Double-click the icon for the drive that has your Windows directory. A new directory window opens.

2. Choose Tree and Directory from the View menu, and then adjust the window split to remove any excess white space on the tree side.

3. Click the other directory windows and choose Directory Only from the View menu for each.

4. Now choose Cascade from the Window menu to arrange the directory windows as shown in Figure 7-3.

This arrangement is unique because it lets you browse through the directory structure using just one window. The other windows display files only. Since the tree is removed, you see more files in each.

 You can resize and rearrange directory windows in any configuration you want. Use the techniques discussed in Chapter 1 for arranging windows.

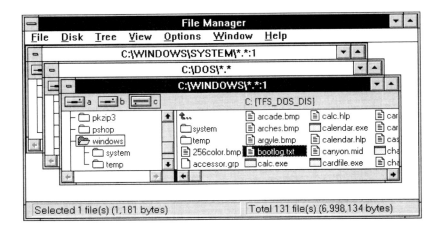

Figure 7-3.   *Arrange directory windows to display the files you work with on a regular basis*

Refreshing Windows

The Refresh option on the Window menu is used to update the contents of a directory window. You'll probably use the Refresh option in the following situations:

- When you perform a file operation outside the File Manager that would cause a directory window's contents to change.

- When you restore a minimized directory window.

- When a directory window lists files for a disk drive and you change the disk.

- Because the File Manager does not automatically update the directory list for network drives to help reduce network traffic, you must update these drives manually using the Refresh option.

By default, non-Windows applications do not update the file listing when they create, rename, or delete a file. You'll need to press F5 *to update the list. You can set the FileSysChange option on in the SYSTEM.INI file to get automatic updates, but this will slow performance.*

Climbing the Directory Tree

The directory tree displays the directories and subdirectories of the currently selected drive. To display the tree of a different drive, click the drive icon of the drive you want displayed at the top of the directory window. To open a directory window on a different drive, double-click the appropriate drive icon.

To display the files for another directory, click the directory icon in the tree. Alternatively, move the highlight in the directory tree by pressing the arrow keys on the keyboard. To view branching subdirectories, use the methods discussed next.

Expanding and Collapsing Branches

You can expand or collapse the directory tree using mouse, keyboard, or menu methods. An *expanded* directory tree shows some or all of the directories and branching subdirectories. A *collapsed* tree shows only the top level directories of your choice. The Tree menu has options for changing the directory tree. To see the entire directory tree for a drive, choose Expand All from the Tree menu, or press CTRL-*. All directories and branching subdirectories are listed.

Use the following methods to further change your view of the directory tree:

- Collapse the entire directory tree by double-clicking the root directory folder.

- Double-click the root directory folder again to expand its branches. Now only first-level directories are shown.

- Double-click any directory folder that has a branching subdirectory to display its subdirectories. Double-click the folder again to close the branch. Try this on the Windows directory.

- You can use keyboard methods to expand and collapse the directory tree.

- Move to a folder with the arrow keys, then press the PLUS (+) or MINUS (−) key to expand or collapse the branching directories. You can also press ENTER to expand or collapse a directory branch.

Indicating Expandable Branches

The Indicate Expandable Branches option on the Tree menu provides another way to view the directory structure. Selecting this option causes a plus sign to appear in directories that have branching subdirectories, or a minus sign if the directory is already fully expanded. In this way, you don't need to display the directory icon for every branching subdirectory to know that subdirectories exist.

Indicating expandable branches causes the File Manager to run slower, so disable this feature if you don't need it.

Working with the File List

You use directory windows to list files on your drives, and then execute commands on those files. To make file manipulation easier, you can change the way files are listed in the directory window as described in this section.

Showing All File Details

Use the Name, All File Details, and Partial File Details options on the View menu to alter the way information is displayed in a directory window. The default is Name, which displays just the names and icons of files and allows you to see more files at once. Choose All File Details to change the listing method so it displays all the details shown in Figure 7-4:

- The first column lists the filename and icon.

- The second column lists the size of the file in bytes.

- The third column lists the date the file was created or the date it was last modified.

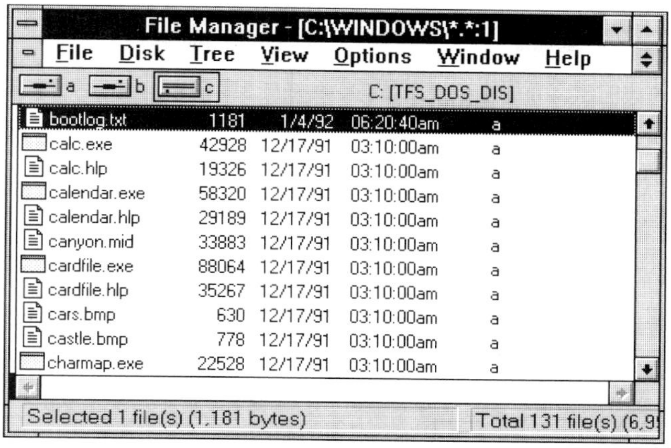

Figure 7-4. *You can change the way information is displayed in a directory window by switching options in the View menu*

- The fourth column lists the time the file was created or the time it was last modified.

- The final column lists the attributes, or *status flags* of a file, which indicates whether it can be changed and erased, or whether it has been backed up. In Figure 7-4, each file has the a (archive) attribute. These attributes are covered later in this chapter in the section called "Viewing and Changing File Properties."

Showing Partial File Details

To display only specific information about a file, choose the Partial Details option from the View menu. It lets you choose which columns of information to display in the file listings. By removing columns, you can reduce the size of directory windows if you're short on space. The Partial Details dialog box is shown here:

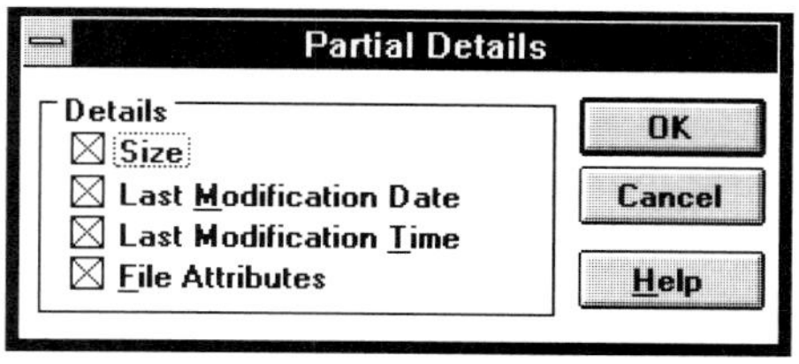

If you previously selected All File Details from the View menu, each check box is enabled. Click the items you want to remove from the file listing and click the OK button.

Sorting the File List

To change the order in which files are listed, enable one of the following options on the View menu. Sorting file lists makes it easier to see groups of files and select them from the list.

Sort by Name   Sort by Name is the default option. Files are sorted alphabetically by the first eight characters of the filename.

Sort by Type   The Sort by Type option sorts the file list by the filename extension. For example, all executable files with the extension .EXE would be listed together and all Write files with the extension .WRI would be listed together.

Sort by Size   Sort by Size means all files are sorted in size order with the largest file first. This option is useful if you need to find and delete large files to make room on a disk.

Sort by Date   Use the Sort by Date option to sort files by date, which may be the date they were first created or the date they were last changed. This option lists the most recent files first and the oldest files last. You can scroll to the bottom of the list to see if there are any old files that can be deleted.

Listing Specific Files

The By File Type dialog box lets you specify exactly which files to list, using wildcard characters or special check box options. Choose the By File Type option on the View menu now to display the dialog box shown in Figure 7-5.

The Name field is highlighted when this dialog box first opens. Try the following to see how wildcard characters affect the file list. Make sure the Windows directory is still current.

1. Type ***.TXT** in the Name field and press ENTER to view all files with the extension .TXT.

2. Choose the By File Type option again, and then type ***.BMP** in the Name field and press ENTER to list Paintbrush bitmap files.

3. Choose the By File Type option again and type ***.EXE** in the Name field and press ENTER to list program files with the extension .EXE.

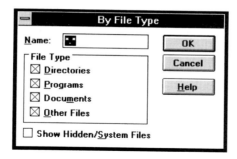

Figure 7-5.   *The By File Type dialog box*

4. Click the DOS directory icon in the directory tree, and notice how the same file specification is used to list .EXE files there. You can use this feature to scan for files on your hard drive.

5. Choose the By File Type option once more and type the wildcard characters ***.*** to list all files.

An alternative method of listing files is to enable or disable the options in the File Type box in the By File Type dialog box, as discussed next.

The Directories Option   Enable the Directories option to display a list of all your directories.

The Programs Option   Enable the Programs option to list executable files with the extensions .EXE, .COM, .BAT, or .PIF. Use this option to create a directory window that you can use to start applications. If you want to list other file types for this category, change the Programs= option in WIN.INI, as discussed in the following section.

The Documents Option   Enable the Documents option to list associated documents. Recall from Chapter 1 that associated documents are those created by Windows accessories. You can double-click them to open the documents for editing. You can create directory windows that only list documents by enabling this option and disabling others. If you want to list other document types for this category, change the Documents= option in WIN.INI, as discussed in the following section.

The Other Files Option   Enable the Other Files option to list all other files not included in any other category.

The Show Hidden/System Files Option Enable the Show Hidden/System Files option to display files with the Hidden or System attribute. DOS creates these files and typically hides them in directory listings at the DOS level. Important files are marked in this way to prevent accidental deletion.

Enable the File Type options by themselves or in combination with the other options on the dialog box. For example, type **WIN*.*** in the Name field and enable all the File Type options to show all files that start with WIN. To reduce the list so that only document files are visible, disable all but the Documents option in the File Type box.

Be sure to keep track of which file options you've disabled for a window. For example, you might disable document file listings for a window, then forget. Later, when you look at the file list, you might panic when you can't find your document files. They are in the directory, but just not listed.

You can control which files are listed when the Programs or Documents option is enabled. By default, files with the extensions .COM, .EXE, .BAT, and .PIF are listed when Programs is enabled. When Documents is enabled, all associated files are listed. To change these specifications, open the WIN.INI file for editing and locate the following lines under the [windows] heading.

```
Programs=com exe bat pif
Documents=
```

In the Programs= line, you can remove an extension so its type of file doesn't show up in the list. You can add an extension, but the four executable program file extensions are already included.

In the Documents= field, include any document extension you want to include in the listings. For example, to list files with the extension .XYZ, you would change the line to read as follows.

```
Documents=xyz
```

In most cases, you won't need to add extensions to the Documents line. Most documents created by Windows applications are associated with those applications, so their names automatically appear in file listings when the Documents option is enabled. If not, you use the Associate option on the File menu to create an association, as discussed later in this chapter in the section on "Program and Document Associations."

Selecting Files

Before any command can be executed on a file or on multiple files, you must first highlight (select) the files. Single files are selected by clicking them with the mouse. Methods for selecting multiple files are explained here. Before proceeding, reset the Windows directory window by following these steps:

1. Choose By File Type from the View menu.
2. Type *.* in the Name field.
3. Check all the options in the File Type box.
4. Click the OK button or press ENTER.

Selecting Contiguous Files

Contiguous files are easy to select. Simply click the first file you wish to select, hold down the SHIFT key and click on the last file. You can scroll the list if the last file you want to select is not visible in the window. The following exercise demonstrates this selection technique using the files in the Windows directory:

1. Rearrange the file list by choosing Sort by Type from the View menu. This is an important step because it rearranges the files in groups, making them easier to select. Notice that files with the extension .BMP are listed at the top.
2. Click on the first .BMP file in the list.
3. Now press and hold the SHIFT key, then click on the last .BMP file in the list. If you can't see the last file, scroll the list until you can.

This method selects all files in between the two selected files. You could then perform a copy, move, rename, or delete operation on the selected files.

To quickly jump to a file in a list, type the first letter of the filename.

Selecting Noncontiguous Groups of Files

To select *noncontiguous* files, hold the CTRL key and click each file you want to select. Again, it's important to sort the file list correctly. However, some files don't follow an order, so it's probably best to sort the list by filename to easily locate the files.

Files remain selected until you click another file without holding the CTRL key. They also remain selected as you scroll through the file list looking for other files to select. Try the next few uses of the SHIFT and CTRL keys to select executable files.

You can combine the contiguous and noncontiguous file selection methods. If you've previously selected a contiguous group using the SHIFT key, press CTRL and continue selecting. If you've previously selected noncontiguous files using the CTRL key and want to add a contiguous group to your selection, hold both CTRL and SHIFT, and then click the first file in the contiguous group. Continue holding the CTRL and SHIFT keys, and then click the last file in the contiguous group.

Removing Files from a Selection

If you select a file by mistake, remove it from the list by pressing the CTRL key and clicking the file's icon. Similarly, you can remove a group of selected files by holding the SHIFT key. These methods are useful because it is often easiest to select a large group of files, then remove one or two you don't want from the selection.

Using the Select Files Option

The Select Files option on the File menu provides an alternative way to select files in the contents list, instead of clicking files with the mouse. Choose the Select Files option now to display the Select Files dialog box, shown here:

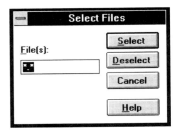

To make selections in the Select Files dialog box, type a file specification using wildcard characters. Initially, the specification *.* is given in the File(s) field, but you can type over it. These steps demonstrate how to use the Select Files dialog box:

1. If there are files selected in the contents list, click the Deselect button on the Select Files dialog box.

2. Double-click in the File(s) field and type ***.EXE**. Press the Select button to select all the executable files.

3. You can continue to add more selections. Double-click in the File(s) field and type ***.BMP**, then click the Select button.

4. Now deselect the .EXE files that begin with WIN. Type **WIN*.EXE** in the File(s) field and click the Deselect button.

5. Close the Select Files box and the files remain selected.

The Select Files dialog box can be closed and reopened without losing your current selection.

Use the Select Files dialog box when you know the names or extensions of the files you want to select. Use the mouse selection methods when filenames are unknown or you prefer to scroll through the file list in search of files. You can also combine both methods to select files.

Copying and Moving Files with the Mouse

Use the mouse to copy and move files by clicking and dragging their icons to other directories or drives. Use the Move and Copy options on the File menu when it's easiest to specify the source or destination by just typing it, such as when you don't have a directory window open.

A Moved File   When moved, a file is copied to the destination and removed from the source. Move is the default—just click and drag the file to its destination and it will be deleted from its old original location.

A Copied File   When copied, a duplicate of the file is placed in the destination, and the original stays where it is. To copy, hold down CTRL while dragging file icons.

When dragging file icons to other drives, the default is to copy the files. Press ALT while dragging if you want to move—and not copy—files to another drive.

In the following exercise, you'll create a new directory and copy files to it; then later, you'll see how to remove files and delete the directory. Make sure the Windows directory window is active and that it lists the Windows directory. Also make sure all the options are selected on the By File Type dialog box and *.* is listed in its Name field.

1. Choose Create Directory from the File menu to display the Create Directory dialog box, as shown below. The current directory (Windows) is listed in the

Current Directory field at the top of the dialog box and the new directory will branch from it.

Create Directory

Current Directory: C:\WINDOWS

Name: [   ]

OK

Cancel

Help

2. Type **TEST** in the Name field and click the OK button or press ENTER.

The new TEST directory icon appears, branching from the Windows directory. Now you can copy files to it using mouse click-and-drag methods.

1. The Windows directory should still be selected. Choose Sort by Type from the View menu.

2. Select the files that have the extension .TXT.

3. Hold the CTRL key, click anywhere in the selection, and drag left. An icon appears when you start dragging.

4. Drag the icon to the TEST directory icon in the directory tree.

5. When a rectangle surrounds the TEST directory icon, release the mouse. You'll then see the Confirm Mouse Operation dialog box on which you must confirm the mouse operation:

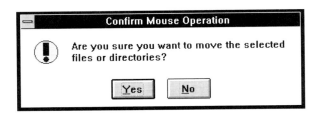

Confirm Mouse Operation

Are you sure you want to move the selected files or directories?

Yes   No

6. Click the Yes button to confirm the copy.

Remember, to move files, follow the steps just given, but don't hold the CTRL key in step 3. Move operations are useful when you want to reorganize the files on your drive (because files are removed from their original locations). Later, you'll see how to reorganize your hard disk filing system by moving and copying files.

File Commands

The File menu holds a set of options that execute file commands like those used in DOS. You use these commands to manipulate the files and directories you've selected in directory windows. Each command is discussed in the following sections, along with other topics of interest.

One thing to keep in mind is that some commands on the File menu act on the currently selected directory in the directory tree. For example, if you click the Windows directory in the directory tree, and then choose the Delete option, the dialog box will suggest deleting the Windows directory! So be careful.

Open Selected Items

The Open command is a substitute for double-clicking or using the ENTER key. Choose it to open a selected directory in the tree, start a selected program, or open an associated document file.

Moving and Copying Items

Use the Move and Copy commands instead of a mouse to move or copy files from one location to another. The Move and Copy commands have the following advantages over using a mouse:

- You can move or copy without opening directory windows.

- You can use wildcard characters to specify files to copy or move.

Before choosing the Move or Copy command, you can click a file in the directory list, or click a directory icon in the tree. The name of the file or directory will then appear in the Move or Copy dialog box. Don't worry about this step if you're going to move or copy files or directories that aren't currently listed in a directory window. You can just type them when the dialog box opens.

Choose Copy from the File menu to display the Copy dialog box shown here:

The Move box is the same except it lacks the Copy to Clipboard option.

The currently selected directory or file appears in the From field. To type a different specification, double-click the field to highlight its contents, and then type over it. If one or more files are selected in the directory window, their names appear in the From field. Type the drive and directory where the files should be moved in the To field.

Try these steps to copy the Paintbrush .BMP files in the Windows directory to the TEST directory you created earlier:

1. Choose Copy from the File menu.

2. Type **C:\WINDOWS*.BMP** in the From field.

Replace C with the letter of your Windows drive if it is different.

3. Type **C:\WINDOWS\TEST** in the To field.

4. Click OK to copy the files.

Use the Copy to Clipboard option on the Copy dialog box to copy the icon of a file to the Clipboard so you can paste it as an embedded object in another application. Refer to Chapter 25 for more information.

Deleting Files

To delete a file, simply click its icon and press the DEL key on the keyboard. A warning message appears, asking you to confirm the deletion, unless you have set confirmations off as described earlier in this chapter under the section "Suppressing Confirmation Messages."

Use the Delete command on the File menu to name specific files to delete. The Delete command opens a dialog box so you can type specific path and filenames. Try deleting the Paintbrush .BMP files that you copied to the TEST directory. Follow these steps:

1. Choose Delete from the File menu to display the following dialog box:

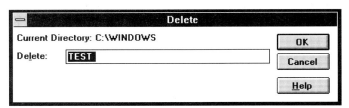

The names of currently selected files appear in the Delete field, so be careful when using this option.

2. Type **C:\WINDOWS\TEST*.BMP** in the Delete field, making sure to specify the correct path and file specification for the file(s) you wish to delete.

3. Click the OK button to delete the files.

Assuming that File Delete confirmations are still set on, the Confirm File Delete dialog box appears for each file to be deleted, as shown here:

Click the Yes button to delete a file or No to keep a file. This dialog box helps you selectively delete files.

4. To delete all remaining files that match the specification, click the Yes to All button.

Renaming Files

Use the Rename command to change the names of files and directories. If a directory or file is highlighted when you choose the Rename command, its name appears in the From field of the Rename dialog box. In the following illustration, two files were selected before choosing Rename, JANBUDG.TXT and FEBBUDG.TXT. A wildcard specification then renames the files using the existing filenames and the new extension .DOC.

Be careful when renaming program files. Other programs may call these files expecting a specific name. For example, don't rename files in the Windows directory since specific filenames are called when you double-click icons in the Program Manager.

You can rename groups of files by using wildcard characters in the Rename box. For example, you could specify NEWDATA?.DBF in the From field and OLD*.* in the To field to rename NEWDATA1.DBF, NEWDATA2.DBF, and NEWDATA3.DBF files to OLDDATA1.DBF, OLDDATA2.DBF, and OLDDATA3.TXT.

Viewing and Changing File Properties

Files and directories have attributes that protect them from accidental deletion or indicate whether they have been backed up. You can view and change these properties by first selecting a file, then choosing the Properties option on the File menu.

Files Marked Read Only   Files marked Read Only cannot be changed or deleted unless the attribute is removed.

Files Marked Archive   When a file is first created, or anytime it is altered, its Archive flag is set on. DOS commands such as BACKUP or XCOPY look at the Archive flag to determine if a file should be included in an *incremental backup*, which is a periodic backup that backs up the files that have changed since the last backup. During the backup, the flag is set off so the file is not included in the next backup. If the file does change, its Archive flag is once again set on and it will be included in the next backup.

In most cases, you won't need to worry about the Archive bit. However, there may be occasions when you want to set the bit on or off to include or exclude files from a backup. For example, to create a second set of backup disks, it may be necessary to set the archive bit on for files in directories you want to backup.

Files Marked Hidden   Files marked Hidden will not appear in DOS file listings, and will only appear in directory windows if the Show Hidden/System check box is marked on the By File Type dialog box. This dialog box is discussed under "Listing Specific Files" earlier in this chapter.

Files Marked System   Files marked System are usually DOS files that are hidden in DOS listings and in directory windows if the Show Hidden/System check box is marked on the By File Type dialog box.

To view or change a file's properties, follow these steps as an example:

1. Click the Windows directory in the directory tree.

2. Click the file README.WRI as an example.

3. Choose Properties from the File menu. A dialog box similar to Figure 7-6 opens.

Properties for README.WRI

File Name:	README.WRI
Size:	80,768 bytes
Last Change:	12/17/91 03:10:00AM
Path:	C:\WINDOWS

OK
Cancel
Help

Attributes
☐ Read Only   ☐ Hidden
☒ Archive   ☐ System

Figure 7-6.   *The Properties dialog box displays information about files and lets you change file attributes*

The Properties dialog box displays information about the file such as its size, creation date or last modification date, and path. Any attributes set for the file are check marked in the Attributes field. Apply the Read Only attribute with this step:

4. Click the Read Only check box in the Attributes field, then click the OK button or press ENTER.

Next see what happens if you try to edit the file, now protected with the Read Only attribute:

5. Double-click the README.WRI file to start Write and load the file.

6. Type your name (or any text) at the blinking cursor, and then choose the Save option from the File menu. The Write dialog box appears, as shown here:

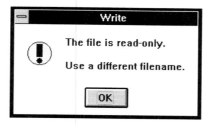

Write

The file is read-only.

Use a different filename.

OK

As long as the file has the Read Only attribute, it cannot be changed. Click OK to close the dialog box. You can save this file using a different name, but for now, just close the window without saving.

This demonstrates how to protect template files from accidental erasure or change. A *template* is a document used to create other documents. For example, a template might contain just your company logo and address. You open the template file to create letters, but always save the completed letter under a different filename to preserve the template for the next letter. Protecting the template file with the Read Only attribute keeps you from accidentally overwriting your template.

Printing from the File Manager

You can print associated files in the File Manager by dragging the icon of the file over the top of the Print Manager, but the Print Manager must be running as a window or icon on the desktop for this to work. Here are the steps for using this method:

1. Start the Print Manager by double-clicking its icon in either the File Manager or the Program Manager. The file is called PRINTMAN.EXE in the Windows directory. You can reduce the Print Manager to an icon.

2. Make the File Manager window active, then click the file to print and drag it over the Print Manager icon.

3. Release the mouse; the file prints.

Another way to print in the File Manager is with the Print option on the File menu. Click the file to print, then choose Print. When the Print dialog box appears, the file you selected is listed in the display field. Click the OK button to print the file. Note that this option only supports printing text files.

Program and Document Associations

Recall that associated document files automatically open into the workspace of the application used to create them when you double-click the file's icon in the File Manager. Associations are formed by the filename extension. Here's a list of common associations:

Extension	Application
.BMP	Paintbrush
.CAL	Calendar
.CRD	Cardfile
.HLP	Help
.INI	Notepad
.PCX	Paintbrush

Extension	Application
.REC	Recorder
.TRM	Terminal
.TXT	Notepad
.WRI	Write

Documents created by Windows applications are already associated. Use the Associate command to associate other file extensions to applications, or to change associations. For example, assume you want to use Write to create documents for a project, but you want to give those files the extension .PRJ instead of .WRI, the normal Write extension. To automatically load those files, or to have them appear in document file listings, you must first associate the extension with Write.

The Associate command is also used to create associations for non-Windows applications. Assume you use a DOS word processor that creates document files with the extension .XYZ. These documents appear in the File Manager, but you can't open them by double-clicking until you associate the .XYZ extension with the DOS application. After associating the extension, the icons for the files appear as associated icons in the File Manager.

You can also use the Associate command to resolve conflicts between extensions. For example, both Word for DOS and Word for Windows use the .DOC extension. If you double-click a .DOC file, it most likely loads in Word for Windows, even if the file was created in Word for DOS. To resolve this conflict, rename your Word for DOS files with another extension, such as .DOK, and then associate the .DOK extension with Word for DOS using the Associate command.

Here's an example showing how to associate a file. In this example, the extension .LOG is associated with Notepad so you can automatically start the time log files discussed in Chapter 5.

1. Choose Associate from the File menu to display the Associate dialog box shown in Figure 7-7.

If a file is highlighted in the contents list, its extension is displayed in the Files with Extension field. In the future, you can save a step when associating files by first clicking a file that has the extension you want to associate.

2. The cursor should be in the Files with Extension field. Type **LOG**.

3. Locate Text File (notepad.exe) in the Associate With field and click the option.

4. Click **OK** or press ENTER to create the association.

Note the following:

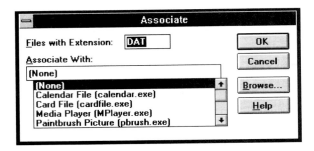

Figure 7-7.   *Use the Associate dialog box to create associations between document files and the programs used to create them*

- You can type the name of the program in the Associate With field or click the Browse button to locate the program filename.

- To remove an association, choose None in the Associate With field.

Searching for Files and Directories

Use the Search option on the File menu to locate files and directories within your filing system. You can search for a file by specifying its full name, or by specifying a partial name using wildcard characters. Once the File Manager locates the files, it displays them in a separate window. You can then open, copy, rename, delete, or perform other operations on the listed files.

Try the following steps to search for .SYS files:

1.   Choose Search from the File menu to display the Search dialog box:

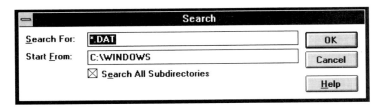

2.   Type ***.SYS** in the Search For field.

3.   Type **C:** in the Start From field.

If your Windows directory is in another drive, replace C with its drive letter.

4. Make sure the Search All Subdirectories box is enabled, and then click the OK button.

The Search Results dialog box soon appears with a listing similar to that shown in Figure 7-8.

Scan through the list and note that .SYS files are listed in several different directories, including the DOS and Windows directories (assuming the DOS directory is on the same drive as Windows).

You might use the Search command when organizing your hard drive. For example, if you've created .DOC files in several different directories, you could easily combine them into a single directory. First search for .DOC files. When the Search Results window appears, select all the files and move them to the new consolidated directory. Note that Move is used to remove them from their original location. Be sure to avoid duplicate filenames before moving the files.

Working with Directories

As you've seen, you can create directories using the File Manager. In addition, you can copy or move entire directory branches from one directory or drive to another, and selectively delete the contents of directories.

Creating Directories

Use the Create Directory option on the File menu to create new directories. You must click the directory that the new directory will branch from, or type the full path for the new directory in the Create Directory dialog box.

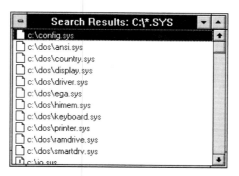

Figure 7-8.   *The listing that appears after activating a search*

In previous exercises, you created the directory TEST that branches from the Windows directory. In this exercise, you'll create a new directory that branches from TEST. Follow these steps:

1. Make sure a directory window is open to the drive that holds the Windows directory.

2. Double-click the Windows directory icon in the directory tree to display its subdirectories.

3. Click the TEST subdirectory.

4. Now you're ready to create the new directory. Choose Create Directory from the File menu.

5. In the Name field, type **LEVEL3**. Note that this name is used as an example only and has no significance except that this is a level 3 subdirectory.

6. Click OK or press ENTER.

Note that you can also type the full path name of the directory you want to create in the Name field of the Create Directory dialog box. For example, in the exercise you just completed, you could have skipped steps 1 through 3 and typed **C:\WINDOWS\TEST\LEVEL3** in the Name field to create the directory.

Copying and Moving Directories

When a directory is copied, a duplicate is made at a new location. When a directory is moved, once the directory is set in its new location, the original directory is deleted. Copying and moving directories is a useful way to create a new directory structure on another drive or to reorganize the current drive. Remember that any branching subdirectories are copied or moved unless you specify otherwise.

In this exercise, you'll move the TEST directory and its branching subdirectory LEVEL3 to the root directory. In this way, the directory will branch from the root, not from the Windows directory.

1. Click the drive icon for the Windows directory if it is not active.

2. Double-click the Windows directory if you can't see its branching subdirectories, including TEST.

3. Click and drag the TEST directory icon over the root directory icon. When the rectangle appears over the root directory icon, release the mouse.

4. A warning message asks whether you are sure you want to move the directory. Choose Yes.

In a moment, you'll see the new structure of the directory tree. If you can't see the LEVEL3 directory, scan down through the list or double-click the TEST directory to open its subdirectory tree.

Typically, you'll move, rather than copy, directories from one location to another. Copying creates duplicates of every file, which wastes disk space. But when you really want to copy an entire directory, hold down the CTRL key and drag the directory icon.

Directories are copied to other disks by default since Windows assumes you want to keep the original directory in place. To move a directory to another disk, hold the ALT key while dragging the directory icon.

You can use the Copy or Move command on the File menu to copy directories. The advantage to this is that you can type the exact path where the directory should be placed.

Deleting Directories

In this section, you'll delete the TEST directory. Previously, you copied and moved files to it, and you moved the directory to another location. Now you'll delete the directory so it doesn't take up space on your hard drive (that your real directories will need).

To delete a directory, highlight its icon in the directory tree and press the DEL key. Alternatively, choose the Delete command from the File menu and type the path and directory name. When deleting directories, be aware of the current confirmation settings. Choose Confirmation from the Options menu now to display the Confirmation dialog box, then note the following settings.

The File Delete Option   If the File Delete confirmation option is set on, the File Manager will ask you to confirm the deletion of the files in the directory and its subdirectories. Make sure this option is checked since it's best to make choices about deleting all files when the confirmation message appears during the delete operation.

The Directory Delete Option   If the Directory Delete confirmation option is set on, the File Manager will ask you to confirm the deletion of the directory and each of its subdirectories. It's probably best to always leave this option on. This way, you'll be warned before an important subdirectory that you may have forgotten about is deleted.

Make sure all the confirmation options are set, then follow the steps here to delete the TEST directory:

1. Click on the TEST directory and press the DEL key. The Delete dialog box appears to verify the name of the directory to delete:

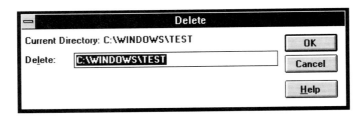

2. Click the OK button or press ENTER. You then see the following warning message:

If you click the Yes button, the File Manager will start deleting files in the TEST directory. If you click the Yes to All button, the File Manager will automatically delete all the remaining files.

3. Click the Yes to All button on the Confirm Subdirectory Delete dialog box. The File Manager will display a Confirm Directory Delete dialog box similar to the one shown here:

All of the remaining files are deleted and the TEST directory is removed. Windows doesn't ask for confirmation to delete the files in the LEVEL3 directory since you clicked the Yes to All button. To delete files in a directory but not its branching subdirectory, click the No button when the Confirm Subtree Delete dialog box appears for the directory you want to keep. This leaves the directory structure intact.

Disk and Network Commands

Commands on the Disk menu are used to format, label, and copy disks. In addition, commands are available for connecting to network drives and accessing network resources. Each command is described in this section.

If you are connected to a network, additional options appear on the Disk menu. Refer to Chapter 17 for more information.

The Copy Diskette Option

The Copy Diskette option on the Disk menu is similar to the DOS DISKCOPY command. It copies the contents of one disk onto another, deleting any files that might be on the destination disk. If your system has one floppy disk drive or two different types of floppy drives, type **A** in the Source In and Destination In fields. You'll be asked to switch disks during the copying process.

The Label Disk Option

The Label Disk option on the Disk menu is used to add or change the electronic name assigned to a disk. Disk labels appear at the top of directory listings and are used by some programs to ensure that the correct disk has been inserted in the drive. To label a disk, place the disk in a drive and click the drive icon. Choose the Label Disk command on the Disk menu, then type the new label for the disk.

The Format Disk Option

Use the Format Disk option on the Disk menu to format any disk. The Format Disk dialog box is shown in Figure 7-9.

Choose formatting options on the Format Disk dialog box based on the type of disk you want to format, as noted here:

- Choose the drive in the Disk In field.

- Choose the disk type in the Capacity field.

- Specify a label in the Label field.

- Click the Make System Disk option to create a bootable disk that includes the system files.

- If a disk is already formatted and you want to remove any existing files and directories, enable Quick Format to completely erase the disk.

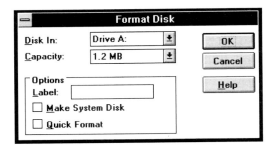

Figure 7-9. *Use the Format Disk dialog box to format new disks or quick-format (erase) previously formatted disks*

The Make System Disk Option

The Make System Disk option copies the system files to a previously formatted disk. A disk with the system files is a bootable disk you can use to start a system from the floppy drive. Keep in mind that the system files take up disk space, so if you don't need to boot a system with the disk, leave them off.

Organizing with the File Manager

Now that you're familiar with File Manager features, you can start thinking about ways to organize your filing system. First decide whether you want the File Manager to start every time you start Windows. If so, copy the File Manager startup icon into the Startup group. If you do start the File Manager in this way, it becomes a useful tool for launching applications or opening documents that can replace the Program Manager. Chapter 11 even discusses a method for replacing the Program Manager shell with the File Manager.

The File Manager directory windows can become your program and document "launch windows" if you follow these suggestions:

- Set up a directory window that lists all the program files in the Windows directory. Open the By File Type option on the View menu, then enable the Programs option and disable the rest. List the files alphabetically and remove the tree from the window.

- Store all your documents in separate directories, and then create a directory that lists each directory. Use these directory windows to open applications. Remove the tree from the document windows.

- If your system has multiple drives, or is connected to network drives, create a directory window for each drive. These directory windows should show both the directory tree and files so click Tree and Directory on the View menu. Use these directory windows to list and work with files on each of the drives.

- Minimize the directory windows to avoid clutter.

- Save your arrangement by holding the SHIFT key and choosing Exit on the File menu, or enable the Save Settings on Exit option when you exit.

- To avoid accidentally changing the arrangements, disable Save Settings on Exit unless you've made changes you want to keep. Any changes you make during one session will not be saved for the next.

Part *II*

Setup and Configuration

Chapter *8*

How Windows Works

Windows is a graphical user interface that runs on systems that use the Intel 80286, 80386, and 80486 microprocessors. Unlike DOS, Windows uses these processors to their full potential by making more Random Access Memory (RAM) available to applications and by using built-in features that allow multiple applications to run simultaneously. While Windows runs under DOS, in most cases Windows uses its own functions to read keyboard and mouse input, to produce printer and display output, and to manage disk files. Windows' built-in functions for handling these tasks are much more efficient than those provided by DOS.

This chapter covers the terminology and concepts behind microprocessors and memory. This information is important in understanding bits and bytes and the features of memory and microprocessors, but you don't need to get too involved in the technical details unless you plan to write Windows applications of your own. There are many books that cover programming in more detail. The topics covered here are designed to help you understand the Windows operating modes (standard or 386 enhanced), how Windows uses memory, and the technical jargon you're likely to face when upgrading or purchasing new systems and peripherals.

Microprocessors and Memory

The Intel line of microprocessors has provided the core of DOS personal computing since IBM announced its Personal Computer in 1981. Earlier versions of Windows (up to version 3.0) ran on slower Intel 8088, 8086, 80286, 80386, and 80486 systems, but Windows 3.1 breaks from this tradition. It works solely on 80286, 80386, and 80486 processors. To understand the workings of Windows, it's worth looking at these processors and the way they use memory.

Because the Intel 8088 and 8086 microprocessors were used in the IBM Personal Computer, they are usually referred to as PC processors. The 80286 was first used in the IBM AT (Advanced Technology) computer and is called the AT processor. Systems that use 80286, 80386, and 80486 processors are referred to as AT compatibles.

Processor Features

When an 80286 (or above) processor starts, it does so in *real mode*. In this mode, the processor can emulate the functions of earlier 8088 and 8086 processors and run applications written for DOS. Real mode operation has limitations, however. The most notorious is its inability to address more than one million bytes (1MB) of memory. (Think of a *byte* as a unit of memory that is roughly equivalent to one character—you'll learn more about memory later in this chapter.) Also, only one application can run at a time because there is no built-in protection that prevents one application from using memory in use by another application.

1K or 1KByte refers to a kilobyte, which is one thousand bytes. 1MB or 1MByte indicates a megabyte, which is one million bytes. A typical DOS personal computer has anywhere from 1MB to 16MB of memory.

The AT processors (80286, 80386, and 80486) provide *protected mode* operation, which addresses larger amounts of memory and allows multiple tasks to run at once (referred to as *multitasking*). The important point is that each task is protected (at least in theory) from interruption by other tasks. Each task gets its own segment or block of memory, and access to that memory is verified by the processor.

An operating system must be specifically designed to access the protected modes of a processor, and DOS is not designed in such a way. Attempts have been made to run older DOS applications in a protected mode. Windows is the first popular DOS enhancement to take advantage of advanced processor features, provide backward compatibility to DOS applications, and provide an environment that fosters the development of new types of applications. Applications now operate with 16 times the memory available to DOS applications; they can also run simultaneously with other tasks.

Memory

When the 80286 processor operates in protected mode, it can access up to 16MB of memory. When the 80386 and 80486 operate in protected mode, they can access up to 4 gigabytes (4GB, or four billion bytes) of memory. The amount of memory a processor can access is determined by the maximum address value it can store in its internal "memory" registers or send out to external devices such as memory boards. Let's take a look at how this works.

Memory Addressing Methods

Microprocessors hold information in either on or off electrical states, which are represented as either 0 (off) or 1 (on). Thus, the *binary numbering system* (simply meaning that there are only two numbers in the entire system—0 and 1) is used to represent numeric values in processors. (You'll see more about how the binary numbering system applies to bits and bytes in the following paragraphs.)

Registers are used to manipulate these numbers. Some registers store memory addresses while others perform mathematical operations like the memory buttons on your calculator. Think of registers as sets of switches that can be either off (0) or on (1). The *bit-width* of a register is the number of switches it has. The wider the register, the larger the value it can hold. A register that has only one bit or switch can hold one of two values—either 0 or 1. A two-bit wide register can hold one of four possible 2-bit combinations, as shown here:

```
00   01   10   11
```

These values represent decimal 0 through 3 (00=0, 01=1, 10=2, and 11=3). A 3-bit register has eight possible combinations of on and off states representing decimals 0 through 7, as shown here:

```
000    001    010    011    100    101    110    111
```

So the number of bits in a register determines how large a value it can hold. You'll see shortly how the size of registers relates to memory in the various Intel processors. But first you need to know what a bus is.

An *address bus* is the transfer line that sends memory addresses and data from one place to another within the processor, or externally to memory or adapter cards. As you can see in Table 8-1, the size of this address bus differs with each processor. Internally, a memory address is formed as a binary value (a string of 0's and 1's), then sent out over this bus, so the bit-width of this bus determines the maximum amount of memory the processor can address, as shown in Table 8-1.

Processor	Register Size	Address Bus Size	Addressable Memory
8086	16 bits	20 bits	1MB
80286	16 bits	24 bits	16MB
80386/80486	32 bits	32 bits	4GB

Table 8-1.   *Intel Processor Specifications*

Internally, the 16-bit registers of the 8086 and 80286 can store values as high as 65,636. Larger values can be calculated in multiple operations by loading the registers several times, but this requires extra CPU "cycles." Notice that the address bus to external memory is 20 bits wide on the 8086. A 20-bit wide bus can address memory up to 1MB. The 24-bit address bus on the 80286 addresses memory up to 16MB. The 80386 and 80486 are full 32-bit processors. They can address, operate on, and move up to 32 bits of data at one time. The largest value you can send over a 32-bit bus will address 4GB of memory.

You can perform these calculations yourself with the help of the Windows Calculator. Start Calculator and choose Scientific from its View menu, then click the Bin (Binary) button. Type **1** 24 times to represent the highest possible number you can send on the 24-bit address bus of the 80286. Now click the Dec (Decimal) button to convert the number to decimal. You'll see the value 16777215, which is 16MB.

Bottlenecks occur when data on the processor transfers to external adapters on a bus that doesn't match the bit-width of the processor. The Industry Standard Architecture (ISA) bus in AT-compatible systems is only 16 bits wide, which doesn't match the address width of the processor. IBM's Micro Channel Architecture (MCA) and the Extended Industry Standard Architecture (EISA) bus designs each provide full 32-bit external bus support. Generally, memory and auxiliary chips attached directly to the motherboard are connected to a bus that is the width of the processor's address bus, so there is no bottleneck when transferring to these devices.

Processors normally work with 8-bit chunks of memory (or multiples thereof). So a byte (8-bits) is the normal unit of reference when discussing memory. The *hexadecimal* system is a base 16 numbering system that works well when referring to bytes. The hexadecimal numbering system uses the digits 0 through 9 and the letters A through F. Thus, the first byte in memory is at address 0, the eleventh byte is at address A, and the sixteenth byte is at address F. Note that 0 is counted as an address.

Memory Layout on DOS Systems

Because DOS was originally written for the Intel 8088, it is restricted to working with less memory than 1MB (the 8088 has a 20-bit wide address bus). Even though more advanced processors have been designed, software manufacturers and users have been reluctant to leave their DOS applications behind. So the burden of slow software and compatibility issues that existed with the original IBM PC still exist. The "640K barrier" is part of that burden. When the IBM designers mapped out the 1MB address space accessible by the 8088, they gave the first 640K to applications and reserved the rest for system use. Unless you use special memory extension techniques, the 640K workspace will limit the amount of memory available to your DOS applications.

Since Windows is built on the memory structure of the DOS operating system, it's important to understand how it functions. The Intel 8088 microprocessor on the first IBM PC addressed up to 1MB of memory. As the operating system for the PC, DOS also worked within the 1MB limits of the 8088 processor. The designers of the system made the first 640K of memory available to applications and reserved the remaining 384K for add-in cards and program code. Each type of memory is listed here:

Conventional memory	The first 640K of memory addresses.
Reserved memory	The 384K block of memory addresses from 640K to 1MB, sometimes called the *adapter area*.
Extended memory	Memory above 1MB on 80286 and above processors.
Virtual memory	An extension of memory, stored on a hard drive. Virtual memory is hard disk space that appears to applications as RAM memory.
Expanded memory	A technique used to make additional memory available to DOS applications. Windows does not use expanded memory, but you may need it to run your non-Windows applications.
High memory	A 64K block in the extended memory area that DOS can access when HIMEM.SYS is loaded.

Figure 8-1 shows the memory structure of a DOS-based system. The types of memory—conventional memory, reserved memory, extended memory, and virtual memory—are depicted. Recall that virtual memory is not RAM memory, but disk space masquerading as RAM. A fifth type of memory, expanded memory, is really a technique to make extended memory or memory on an optional memory card available to DOS applications specially designed to use it.

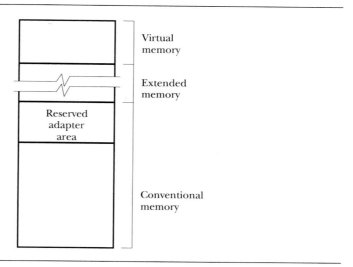

Figure 8-1.   *Memory map for a DOS system*

The Traditional Hexadecimal Memory Map

This chapter makes many references to specific locations in memory. While you can refer to these locations in decimal bytes, the more traditional method is to use hexadecimal numbers. As discussed earlier, hexadecimal numbering is a base 16 system, so it works well with 8-bit bytes. Common references to memory are in multiples of 8 (16K, 32K, 64K, 640K, and 1024K, for example). We can divide the 1MB of memory into 16 *pages* of 65,536 bytes each, numbered 0, 1, 2, 3, 4, 5, 6, 7, 8, 9, A, B, C, D, E, F, as shown in Figure 8-2. (Recall that hexadecimal A is decimal 10, hexadecimal B is decimal 11, and so on). The first 640K of conventional memory is address range 0 through 9, and the reserved memory area from 640K to 1024K is address range A through F. For this discussion, you don't need to know the details of hexadecimal numbering, just that the 16 segments of the memory map shown in Figure 8-2 are labeled 0 through F.

While you might refer to a page as the "F" page, the actual value for a memory location is in thousands or millions depending on how much memory you have. So the byte at the beginning of the second 64K memory block is 65,536, or 10,000 hexadecimal, and the last byte of conventional memory is 1,048,575, or hexadecimal FFFFF. Here's a conversion list to give you an idea of the byte value at each segment.

Hexadecimal	Decimal
100000	1,048,576
FFFFF	1,048,575
F0000	983,040
E0000	917,504
D0000	851,968
C0000	786,432
B0000	720,896
A0000	655,360
90000	589,824
80000	524,288
70000	458,752
60000	392,216
50000	327,680
40000	262,144
30000	196,608
20000	131,072
10000	65,536

In Chapter 9, when you work with the EMM386.EXE command, you'll specify hexidecimal addresses by using only the first four digits of the number. For example, to refer to physical address D0000, you'll specify D000. You do this because a 16-bit processor can't directly address a number higher than FFFF. Instead, the micropro-cessor uses a segmenting scheme to calculate the first four digits, then the remainder. The same scheme is used to reference memory locations when using EMM386.EXE.

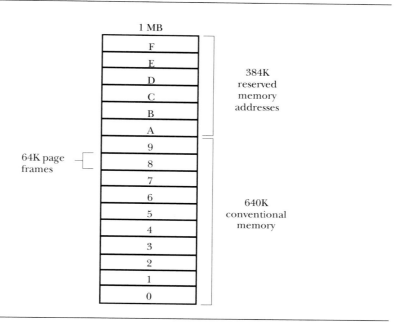

Figure 8-2.   *A memory map showing addressing scheme*

Conventional Memory

As mentioned, the first 640K of memory addresses is conventional memory. DOS, device drivers, and TSRs load into this memory when you turn your system on, based on lines in the CONFIG.SYS and AUTOEXEC.BAT files.

DOS applications use any remaining conventional memory. If a shortage of conventional memory exists, DOS applications may not run and you'll need to install more memory. If your system physically does not have 640K of conventional memory, purchase more to fill this range. If 640K is still not enough, you can take the following steps to make more memory available to DOS applications.

- If your DOS applications support expanded memory, add an expanded memory board to 80286 systems and add an expanded memory manager command to your boot files. On 80386 and above systems, use the EMM386.EXE driver to emulate expanded memory (special boards are not necessary), assuming you have enough extended memory for this purpose.

- Upgrade to DOS 5 and use its LOADHIGH and DEVICEHIGH commands to move drivers and TSRs into reserved memory and free up conventional memory.

When Windows starts, it adds all conventional memory and extended memory together to form a continuous block of memory used by Windows applications. When you run a DOS application, Windows either steps aside and lets DOS run (standard mode) or creates a virtual DOS machine (386 enhanced mode). In either case, DOS sessions inherit the environment that was available before starting Windows so it's a good idea to optimize that environment, but only when necessary. (This will all be discussed in Chapter 9.)

Reserved Memory

Reserved memory addresses stretch from 640K to 1024K (the "A" page to the "F" page in Figure 8-2). Video adapters, disk controllers, network interface cards, and other add-in cards use addresses in this range for their BIOS (Basic Input/Output System). When IBM mapped out the original reserved memory area, they set aside areas for video and other devices. Over time, additional areas of reserved memory became commonly accepted as "in use," and board manufacturers avoided mapping their own cards into these areas. This means that reserved memory contains many addresses that are used and some that are unused.

Keep in mind that most systems do not have physical memory mapped into the reserved memory address range. That would be a waste of memory because video, network, and other adapter cards map their own program code into these areas. A ROM chip soldered onto the adapter itself contains hard-wired programs for running the adapter. You can make these programs available to your system by assigning them addresses in the reserved area. The important point is that the code remains on the card and the processor accesses it over the bus.

The code on the card can also be copied to system memory. This improves performance because accessing system memory is faster than accessing the adapter via the bus. But if an adapter's code is transferred to system memory, a process called *shadowing*, then you must map physical memory into the reserved area where that code will reside. Some systems that have 1MB of memory installed already make physical memory available in this area. The Expanded Memory Management (EMM) scheme provides a way to do this for DOS applications. By setting aside a block of memory addresses, usually 64K, that memory on an expansion board can be mapped into. A good way to visualize this is to think of an office desk surface. Space is limited, so you might move some of your work onto another table until you need that work again. That extra table is like expanded memory—it's not part of your desktop (conventional memory), but you can use it to keep your papers on as if you had a bigger desktop.

Upper Memory Blocks

Now we can take a closer look at the reserved memory area where the upper memory blocks reside. Figure 8-3 shows how 64K segments are further divided into four 16K

F000	FFFF FC00	1024K 1008K	ROM BIOS area used by DOS
	FBFF F800	1007K 992K	
	F7FF F400	991K 976K	
	F3FF F000	975K 960K	
E000	EFFF EC00	959K 944K	Not available on PS/2 and some other machines
	EBFF E800	943K 928K	
	E7FF E400	927K 912K	
	E3FF E000	911K 896K	
D000	DFFF DC00	895K 880K	Available on most systems
	DBFF D800	879K 864K	
	D7FF D400	863K 848K	
	D3FF D000	847K 832K	
C000	CFFF CC00	831K 816K	
	CBFF C800	815K 800K	8514/A up to CBFF Non-PS/2 VGA up to C7FF EGA up to C3FF
	C7FF C400	799K 784K	
	C3FF C000	783K 768K	
B000	BFFF BC00	767K 752K	EGA/VGA text and low resolution Hercules page 2 CGA
	BBFF B800	751K 736K	
	B7FF B400	735K 720K	Monochrome adapter Hercules page 1
	B3FF B000	719K 704K	
A000	AFFF AC00	703K 688K	Reserved for EGA/VGA video adapters
	ABFF A800	687K 672K	
	A7FF A400	671K 656K	
	A3FF A000	655K 640K	

Figure 8-3.   *A reserved memory map*

segments. This is because many programs placed in upper memory blocks require 16K or less, and we need to refer to some of the in-between addresses.

Notice that the entire A and B range and most of the C range are already reserved for video adapters. In some cases, you can use small blocks of memory in these areas, but only if you're sure they are not being used on your particular system. Every system uses reserved memory addresses in a different way. For example, if you don't have a monochrome video card, the block from B000 to B7FF is not in use. You'll be referring to this map often as you configure and optimize your memory in Chapter 9.

Shadow RAM is available on many 80386 and 80486 systems. As mentioned, it allows the code embedded in the ROMs of video and other adapters to be moved to the fast 32-bit RAM of your system. Without shadowing, access to the ROM on the adapters would be in 8- or 16-bit chunks of memory that could take up to 20 percent longer to fetch.

Extended Memory

Extended memory starts at 1024K and extends up to 16MB in both Windows standard and Windows 386 enhanced mode. Windows combines extended memory with any available conventional memory and makes it available to Windows applications as a single block of continuous memory. This memory, however, is still beyond the reach of DOS applications, so Windows switches back to real mode when running DOS applications.

The Extended Memory Specification (XMS) defines access to extended memory. It includes a definition for Upper Memory Blocks (UMBs), High Memory Area (HMA), and Extended Memory Blocks (EMBs), as defined in the following sections.

Upper Memory Blocks   Upper memory blocks reside in the reserved memory area from 640K to 1MB. DOS drivers, TSRs, and programs can use these blocks if DOS 5 or a third-party memory manager such as Quarterdeck's QEMM-386 or Qualitas' 386Max is used. The location and availability of memory blocks depend on your hardware and software configuration and are rarely the same from one machine to the next.

In some cases, over 600K of conventional memory is available to DOS applications after DOS is loaded into the High Memory Area and drivers are loaded into upper memory blocks.

High Memory Area   The HIMEM.SYS driver provides access to extended memory and the High Memory Area, or HMA. The HMA is a 64K block of memory from 1024K to 1088K available to DOS. A special processor feature tricks DOS into seeing this memory within its addressable range. You don't need to know the technical details of this trick to take advantage of it. DOS 5 users can load part of DOS itself in the HMA to free conventional memory for applications. If the HMA is not in use when Windows starts, Windows adds it to the global memory heap and makes it available to its applications.

Extended Memory Blocks   Extended memory blocks start at 1088K and are only addressable by the processor when it is running in protected mode. DOS does not have direct access to this area unless memory management schemes are used.

Windows Architecture

Windows consists of a layered architecture, as shown in Figure 8-4. Each layer provides a service, either to the user or to the hardware, or both. The Device Independent layer, configured during setup to match the hardware and components of your system, is at the bottom of this scheme. At the top is the Applications layer, which presents a consistent interface (windows, menus, icons, dialog boxes, and so on) to users. In between is the Core layer, which interfaces the top and bottom layers and provides most of the functions for running Windows itself.

The Applications Layer

All Windows programs operate in the Applications layer, which appears as the Windows Common User Interface. This interface provides drop-down menus, icons, windows, dialog boxes, and other features used by all programs.

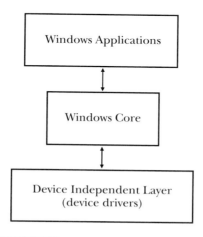

Figure 8-4.   *Windows' layered architecture*

The Core Layer

The Core layer is the interface between the drivers in the Device Independent layer and Windows applications. It consists of the following:

- *Kernel* The Kernel schedules tasks, manages memory, controls file access, and communicates with DOS. The disk file for this module is KRNL286.EXE for standard mode and KRNL386.EXE for 386 enhanced mode.

- *User* This portion of the Core layer manages the presentation of windows, menus, icons, and dialog boxes to the user. The disk file is USER.EXE.

- *Graphic Device Interface (GDI)* The GDI draws graphics, such as lines and curves, on the screen and interfaces with hardware. The disk file is GDI.EXE.

The Device Independent Layer

The Device Independent layer allows Windows to be compatible with many brands and types of computer systems. This layer provides support for keyboards, mouse devices, video equipment, printers, communications devices, and networks. When adding new hardware devices to your system, support for those devices is linked into Windows at this layer through the use of *device drivers*. Device drivers are small programs written for a specific type of hardware. For example, a Hewlett-Packard LaserJet III printer driver passes descriptive information about the printer to the Core layer, which then displays a list of matching features in a dialog box at the Applications level.

Device independence is extremely important to the development of Windows as a standard. It frees programmers from the need to provide support for every conceivable hardware configuration and gives users the freedom to choose the hardware configuration they want. Software becomes more readily available and hardware does not stay locked into specific configurations just to remain compatible with software.

Windows Modes

Windows 3.1 runs in two operating modes: *standard mode* and *386 enhanced mode*. In standard mode, Windows takes advantage of the protected mode operation of Intel 80286 (and above) processors. 386 enhanced mode is available only on 80386 (and above) systems. It uses protected mode and the virtual-86 mode of the processors to multitask non-Windows applications (run several applications at once) and to provide virtual memory, which is a process of using disk space as an extension of RAM memory. The two modes are discussed in the following sections.

Virtual is an adjective used to describe a device or service that is perceived to be something it is not. For example, a RAM memory drive is a virtual disk. Alternatively, virtual memory is disk space perceived as memory.

Standard Mode

To run in standard mode you must have a system with an 80286 processor or above, 256K of free conventional memory, and 192K of free extended memory. To provide support for extended memory, always load the HIMEM.SYS (or compatible) driver before any other driver. Include the HIMEM command on the first line of your CONFIG.SYS file, if possible.

Windows automatically runs in standard mode on 80286 systems. Windows supports both standard mode and 386 enhanced mode on 80386 and 80486 systems. There is good reason to choose standard mode, even though it may not appear to be the mode of choice for the 80386/80486: standard mode is about 20 percent faster than 386 enhanced mode.

To start in standard mode, type **WIN /S** at the DOS prompt.

When Windows runs in standard mode, it breaks the 640K barrier imposed by DOS and lets Windows applications access up to 16MB of memory. Windows and Windows applications see memory as a continuous memory pool and use any amount they need within the amount available on your system.

Standard Mode Components

The following is a list of standard mode files. These files exist in the \WINDOWS or \WINDOWS\SYSTEM directory.

HIMEM.SYS	Driver for accessing extended memory
DOSX.EXE	Interfaces Windows to HIMEM.SYS
KRNL286.EXE	Provides memory management, file input/output, and program loading functions
USER.EXE	Handles user input
GDI.EXE	Draws screen images

Recall that drivers are also necessary to provide the interface between your system hardware and Windows. These drivers, located in the \WINDOWS\SYSTEM directory, have the extension .DRV. Typical drivers are MOUSE.DRV (mouse support), VGA.DRV (VGA video support), COMM.DRV (communications support), and NETWARE.DRV (Novell Netware support). Setup normally takes care of installing drivers, but you can also use the SETUP program or the Drivers utility (Control Panel) to install additional drivers.

Running DOS Applications in Standard Mode

Executing a DOS application from Windows switches the processor to real mode. In the processor's real mode (not to be confused with the real mode of Windows 3.0), Windows removes all but a small part of itself from memory to make room for the DOS application. A "stub" of about 50K remains in memory to hold the information used to switch back to Windows. A disk swap file holds information about DOS applications when you switch from them back to Windows. Placing the swap files in a RAM drive (a virtual disk drive) improves performance. This will be fully discussed in Chapter 10.

DOS applications inherit the environment that existed before you started Windows (environment means both the size of memory and the way memory is used by DOS). In other words, drivers and utilities (TSRs, or terminate-and-stay-resident programs) loaded when you first started your computer system reduce the amount of memory available to DOS applications. These same reductions in memory occur when running DOS applications from Windows. Chapter 9 covers methods of optimizing memory to make more available to DOS applications.

Some DOS applications require expanded memory. Windows does not use expanded memory itself, but allows applications that need it to use any expanded memory you may have configured on an optional expanded memory board. If you have applications that need expanded memory and you want to run them in Windows standard mode, install an optional memory board that supports expanded memory and configure that memory before you start Windows. Windows allows the applications to access the memory on the board even though Windows doesn't access it.

Program Information Files (PIFs) provide important run-time information about DOS applications to Windows. Windows will create PIF files for a large number of third-party applications it knows about, or you can create your own PIF files for those DOS applications that need special settings. For example, you can specify the amount of expanded memory required by an application so it doesn't take more than its share. You can also specify such things as whether it is possible to switch back to Windows while the application is running. This is important if you are running a process such as a communications session that should not be interrupted. Since standard mode does not support multitasking, switching back to Windows from a DOS application suspends the application until you return to the DOS application.

386 Enhanced Mode

To run in 386 enhanced mode you must have a system with an 80386 processor or above, 256K of free conventional memory, and 1024K of free extended memory.

The 80386 and 80486 processors have a virtual-86 capability that allows them to mimic the performance of one or more Intel 8086 processors. A separate "virtual machine" is set up for Windows and for each DOS application you start. The virtual-86 capability allows multitasking of non-Windows applications and allows those applications to run either in full-screen mode or in a resizable window. Each application runs in its own virtual 8086 session and has access to 640K of memory. If a DOS application needs expanded memory, Windows 386 enhanced mode will emulate expanded memory as needed, taking it from the extended memory area. There is no need to add an expanded memory board to your system, but you must have enough extended memory available.

Windows 386 enhanced mode takes advantage of the virtual memory capabilities on 80386 and 80486 processors to provide additional memory to applications. This memory is simulated on disk in a high-speed transfer file. Virtual memory is useful when running applications that require more memory than your system has, such as a graphics package. Windows sets up a swap area on disk and treats it as extra memory. While not as fast as the real thing, virtual memory is essential when running applications that require more memory than your system has physically available.

The kernel modules used to manage virtual memory and multitasking in 386 enhanced mode use 32-bit accessing schemes, which means they are written to access the processor at its full 32-bit capability, improving performance and reducing the number of instructions required to perform a task. However, most current Windows applications are written as 16-bit applications to ensure compatibility on both 80286 and 80386 systems. Future versions of Windows are being designed to support only 32-bit applications on 32-bit systems to provide the best performance possible.

One thing to keep in mind is that standard mode on an 80386 system can outperform 386 enhanced mode on the same system. This is because virtual memory and multitasking add overhead to the system, which slows it down when compared to standard mode. However, speed is relative and you may be perfectly happy with the performance you get from your system in 386 enhanced mode. If performance degradation is a concern, use 386 enhanced mode only in the following situations:

- When you need to run more than one DOS application at the same time.

- When you need to run a DOS application in a resizable window beside other applications windows (for comparing or transferring text or graphics). Standard mode supports only one full-screen DOS application.

- When you're running low on memory and need the virtual memory capabilities of 386 enhanced mode.

- When you need to run a DOS application that requires expanded memory, but expanded memory is not hardware-configured on your system.

To start Windows in 386 enhanced mode, type **WIN /3** at the DOS command prompt.

386 Enhanced Mode and Virtual Machine Mode

Windows 386 enhanced mode uses the virtual machine (VM) mode of the 80386 and 80486 processors. This mode provides one virtual machine called the *System VM* for Windows and Windows applications, as shown in Figure 8-5. Windows creates a separate virtual machine for each DOS application as needed until there is no system memory or resources to support further applications.

The System VM and each DOS virtual machine receives a portion of the processor's time called a *time slice*. It is possible to change the amount of time (scheduling) the processor spends in each virtual machine, but Windows treats all the Windows applications in the System VM as a single application. There are two ways to change the scheduling parameters for DOS applications: from the Control Panel while the application is running or in the Program Information File (PIF) used to start the DOS application. You'll learn how to set these features in Chapter 19.

Windows applications are managed by a *task manager* that runs in the System VM. It tracks the current tasks and provides efficient messaging and CPU time sharing. Windows transfers control to each task and prevents other tasks from running until the time slice for the current task elapses.

386 Enhanced Mode Components

The 386 enhanced mode uses the following software modules, which are stored in the \WINDOWS directory or the \WINDOWS\SYSTEM directory.

HIMEM.SYS	Driver for accessing extended memory
WIN386.EXE	Provides access to extended memory by bridging Windows to HIMEM.SYS
KRNL386.EXE	Provides memory management, file input/output, and program loading functions
USER.EXE	Handles user input and output
GDI.EXE	Draws screen images

As with standard mode, various drivers are also necessary to provide the interface between the equipment of your system and Windows. The drivers have the extension .DRV and are stored in the \WINDOWS\SYSTEM directory.

System VM running Windows applications	DOS virtual machine	DOS virtual machine	DOS virtual machine	Others as requested

Figure 8-5.   *Virtual machines in 386 enhanced mode. Each DOS virtual machine runs a separate DOS application in a protected memory partition.*

Running DOS Applications in 386 Enhanced Mode

Windows allocates a virtual 8086 machine with 640K of memory when you start a DOS application in 386 enhanced mode. However, the memory available to the application in the 640K block depends on the device drivers and TSRs loaded before starting Windows. For example, if your system has 550K of available conventional memory before starting Windows, each DOS virtual machine started from within Windows will have 550K of memory. Chapter 9 discusses several ways to optimize memory. One method is to load the DOS EMM386.EXE device driver (on 80386 and 80486 systems only) when your system starts. You can then load DOS device drivers into the upper memory area, thus freeing memory needed by DOS applications.

DOS applications running in 386 enhanced mode connect with system resources such as video displays, disk drives, and printers through a *virtualization layer,* as shown in Figure 8-6. This layer helps multiple DOS applications share resources, and provides support to a *virtual* number of machines. Normally, a DOS application expects full access to and control of a resource, but under Windows, applications that are being multitasked need to share resources. The virtualization layer provides mechanisms that manage how applications access the same device at the same time.

As mentioned previously, foreground and background control of processing time allotted to each DOS application is possible by changing the settings of a Program Information File (PIF), or by changing the scheduling options when it is running. The foreground and background priorities determine the amount of processor time each application gets when running in the foreground (when it is the active application) or running in the background. For example, an application might use 100 percent of the processor while in the foreground, but only 50 percent when in the background. These options are discussed in Chapter 19.

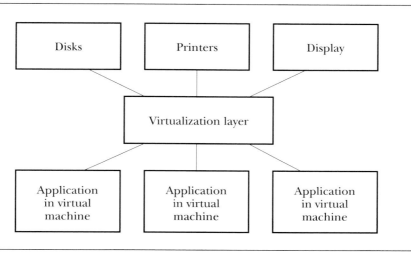

Figure 8-6. The virtualization layer allows multiple virtual machines to access the same devices

Setup and Customization

The SETUP program determines the type of hardware your system has, then asks you to confirm its findings. You can change most of the settings if necessary. You must also specify the drive and directory where you want the Windows files installed. If your system has special hardware that requires drivers not available with Windows, you'll need to have the drivers available on a special diskette during the setup process.

If your system does not contain special equipment that requires special drivers or settings, you can run a quick installation procedure. To gain more control over the setup process, you can run a custom installation procedure. The custom installation procedure lets you choose not to install certain files, such as games or help files if you're running short on disk space or will never use them. Setup is discussed in Appendix A.

The file SETUP.INF has parameters that direct the complete installation procedure. Technically inclined readers or those with special requirements, such as the need to install custom versions of Windows for network users, can change the installation procedure in SETUP.INF. Appendix B discusses SETUP.INF in more detail.

After installing Windows, you can change many of its features by running the SETUP utility from within Windows. However, changes to video drivers and other hardware-dependent drivers require that you run SETUP in the Windows directory from the DOS level, then restart Windows. Making changes with SETUP in this way is relatively simple. Windows does not need to reinstall itself completely; it asks only for the disk it needs to make the change.

The SYSTEM.INI and WIN.INI files in the \WINDOWS directory hold setup and customization information. Some users find it beneficial to maintain two or more setup configurations by keeping several copies of these .INI files on hand, each with a different setup.

The .INI Files

Windows keeps track of its current configuration by logging settings in various files that have the extension .INI. The files are stored in the \WINDOWS directory and are listed here:

SYSTEM.INI   Holds current hardware specifications such as the type of video equipment and printers in use.

WIN.INI   Holds current graphical interface settings such as the color scheme, desktop patterns, font specifications, and port settings. These settings are usually changed with the Control Panel.

Program Manager, File Manager, and many other Windows applications create their own .INI files to store configuration information. These are the most common .INI files:

CLOCK.INI	Clock
CONTROL.INI	Control Panel
DOSAPP.INI	Non-Windows applications running in Windows
MOUSE.INI	Mouse settings
MPLAYER.INI	Media Player
NETWARE.INI	Network file (name depends on network)
PROGMAN.INI	Program Manager
SYSTEM.INI	System hardware settings
WIN.INI	Windows interface settings
WINFILE.INI	File Manager

While applications normally change these files (according to settings you select from within the application), you might sometimes need to edit the files manually using Notepad or Sysedit. As you read through the remaining chapters, you will see many references to changes you can make in the SYSTEM.INI file. The Control Panel is used to change the setting in WIN.INI, but there are a few you can make yourself, as you'll see. One thing to keep in mind is that changes you make to the .INI files do not take effect until you restart the application. You must restart Windows to see changes to SYSTEM.INI or WIN.INI. The WIN.INI file is covered in Appendix D, and the SYSTEM.INI file is covered in Appendix E.

Chapter *9*

Memory Management Commands and Techniques

A clear understanding of memory and memory-related topics is helpful when working with Windows. Memory is often at a premium because Windows runs multiple programs simultaneously. In addition, DOS programs have special memory requirements since they don't take advantage of the way Windows allocates memory. This chapter fills you in on a few tricks and techniques to get your programs running when you're short on memory.

Memory Management Commands

This section provides details of the HIMEM.SYS and EMM386.EXE commands. Refer to this section as you work with the commands in the remainder of this chapter.

HIMEM.SYS

HIMEM.SYS is an extended memory manager (XMM) that gives programs access to extended memory. Windows uses HIMEM.SYS for its access to extended memory. The Windows setup procedure automatically installs the HIMEM.SYS driver in your

CONFIG.SYS file, but you can make changes to its settings if necessary, as described in this section.

The HIMEM.SYS command takes the following form:

DEVICE=C:\DOS\HIMEM.SYS *options*

Options can be replaced by any of the parameters discussed shortly. The first two options, /hmamin and /numhandles, are the most important.

> *The example above shows the DOS directory as the location of HIMEM.SYS. The Windows directory also contains a copy of HIMEM.SYS that may be more recent. Be sure that the path points to the version with the latest date. Some models of computers may have trouble with Windows' version of HIMEM.SYS. You may need to use the version of HIMEM.SYS supplied with your computer.*

/hmamin=n (High Memory Area Minimum program size)   In this option, you set the value n to the minimum number of kilobytes an application must take up in order to be placed in the HMA. If, for example, you have a 5K program and another larger program, you can prevent the small program from loading into the HMA by setting n higher than 5 since only one program can reside in the HMA at a time. The most efficient way to use the HMA is to set n to the size of the largest program you can place in the HMA. If n is omitted, the first available application that can load in the HMA is placed there.

/numhandles=n   In this option, n specifies the maximum number of Extended Memory Block (EMB) handles that can be used simultaneously, with a range of 1 to 128 and a default of 32. Each handle requires 6 bytes of memory. You should set aside 16 handles per megabyte of memory. The default value is 32, which is sufficient for 2MB of memory. Upgrade this value if you have more memory, or if Windows runs out of extended memory in standard mode. The /numhandles option has no effect when Windows is running in 386 enhanced mode.

/int15=n   This option reserves memory for older non-Windows applications that use Interrupt 15h to access extended memory. Use the option to ensure that enough memory is available to them by setting n to 64K larger than the amount required by the application. Set this option only if your application has trouble accessing extended memory when HIMEM.SYS is used. The range is 64 to 65,535 and the default value is 0. Zero is used if you specify a value less than 64.

/shadowram:on|off   This option enables or disables shadow RAM. Some computers copy their system BIOS from ROM into faster system memory to increase performance, a technique called *shadowing*. Since shadow RAM uses extended memory, less is available to Windows applications. However, disabling shadow RAM will slow performance.

/**machine:***name* Use this option to specify a particular computer, if necessary. Currently, systems that require this option include Acer 1100, Wyse, and IBM 7552. Replace *name* with one of the codes or numbers listed in Table 9-1.

/**a20control:on|off** This option enables or disables control of the A20 line, even if A20 was on when HIMEM.SYS was loaded. The A20 handler gives your computer access to the HMA. Specifying /**a20control:off** gives HIMEM.SYS control of the A20 line only if A20 is off. The default setting is /a20control:on.

/**cpuclock:on|off** HIMEM.SYS may affect the clock speed of your system. Setting this option to on may correct the problem, but will slow the performance of HIMEM.SYS.

EMM386.EXE

This section lists the options for the EMM386.EXE command. If you use EMM386, you should disable or remove any other command lines for expanded memory management software. Note that EMM386.EXE can be included as a command in

Code	Number	Computer Type
at	1	IBM AT or 100% compatible
ps2	2	IBM PS/2
pt1cascade	3	Phoenix Cascade BIOS
hpvectra	4	HP Vectra (A & A+)
att6300plus	5	AT&T 6300 Plus
acer1100	6	Acer 1100
toshiba	7	Toshiba 1600 and 1200XE
wyse	8	Wyse 12.5 MHz 286
tulip	9	Tulip SX
zenith	10	Zenith ZBIOS
at1	11	IBM PC/AT
at2	12	IBM PC/AT (alternate delay)
css	12	CSS Labs
at3	13	IBM PC/AT (alternate delay)
philips	13	Philips
fasthp	14	HP Vectra
ibm7552	15	IBM 7552 Industrial
bullmicral1	16	Bull Micral 60

Table 9-1. *Name Codes for Specific Computers*

the CONFIG.SYS file or executed at the DOS prompt. EMM386 uses an extra 48K of extended memory in addition to the amount needed for emulating expanded memory (if used). It also allocates memory so that at least 64K of extended memory always remains free.

The SYSTEM.INI file contains the following lines that control many of the same features as EMM386.EXE. Refer to Appendix E and the information file SYSINI.WRI for more information.

EMMInclude makes upper memory available for use.
EMMExclude excludes upper memory.
ReservedHighArea excludes 4K ranges of upper memory.
UseableHighArea specifies range that Windows will scan for EMS page frame placement.
NoEmmDriver disables EMS memory.

The EMM386.EXE command line has the following form:

DEVICE=EMM386.EXE on|off|auto *memory / options*

Include a driver and path with the EMM386 command if it is not located in the root directory.

on|off|auto

Use these options when executing EMM386 at the DOS prompt. Use on to activate EMM386, and off to suspend it. Auto enables expanded memory support only when a program calls for it. Typing the command at the DOS prompt without an option sets EMM386 on.

memory

This option specifies memory in kilobytes used by EMM386. The range is 16 to 32,768 with a default value of 256K. Note that EMM386 rounds the value down to the nearest multiple of 16.

options

These options control various aspects of EMM386 and its use of memory. While you usually won't need to bother with them, you can use them to fine-tune memory management. The following sections explain each option.

/w=on or /w=off   This option enables or disables support for the Weitek Coprocessor. The default is off.

/frame=*address*   This option specifies the location of the expanded memory page frame in upper memory. Using this option precludes the use of the /m option or the /p option. The /m option can be used in place of /frame. Recall from Chapter 8 that a page frame is one of the 64K reserved memory areas labeled A through F.

/m*n*   This option provides an alternative to the frame option. Enter one of the following one- or two-digit values to specify the location of the expanded memory page frame to use. The address each value represents, in hexadecimal, is listed next to it.

1 -	C000h	8 -	DC00h
2 -	C400h	9 -	E000h
3 -	C800h	10 -	8000h
4 -	CC00h	11 -	8400h
5 -	D000h	12 -	8800h
6 -	D400h	13 -	8C00h
7 -	D800h	14 -	9000h

Values ranging from 10 through 14 should be used only on computers with 512K of memory. This option precludes the use of the /frame or /p option.

/p*n*   Replace *n* with a value that specifies the starting address of the expanded memory page frame. This option precludes the use of the /frame or /m option.

/p*n*=*address*   This option defines the segment address of a specific page. Replace *n* with the number of the page, and *address* with the segment address. For example, to place page 4 at the address CC00, type **/p4=CC00** on the EMM386 command line. Valid values for *n* range from 0 through 255. Valid values for *address* are in the ranges 8000h through 9C00h and C000h through EC00h, in increments of 400h. The addresses for pages 0 through 3 must be contiguous in order to maintain compatibility with version 3.2 of the Lotus/Intel/Microsoft Expanded Memory Specification (LIM EMS). If you use the /frame, /m, or /p option, you cannot use the /p option to specify addresses for pages 0 through 3.

/x=*mmmm-nnnn*   This option excludes addresses that might be used by EMM386 and conflict with other memory settings. Replace *mmmm* with the starting address and *nnnn* with the ending address of the range you want to exclude. Valid values for *mmmm* and *nnnn* are in the range A000h through FFFFh and are rounded down to the nearest 4K boundary. The /x option takes precedence over the /i option if the two ranges overlap.

/i=*mmmm-nnnn*   This option includes addresses that might normally be ignored by EMM386. Replace *mmmm* with the starting address and *nnnn* with the ending address of the range to exclude. Valid values for *mmmm* and *nnnn* are in the range A000h through FFFFh and are rounded down to the nearest 4K boundary. The /x option takes precedence over the /i option if the two ranges overlap.

/b=*address*   Replace *address* with the lowest address available for EMS *bank-switching* (swapping of 16K pages). Valid values are in the range 1000h through 4000h, with 4000 being the lowest possible address.

/L=*minXMS*   Replace *minXMS* with the amount of extended memory that must still be available after EMM386 is loaded. For example, to ensure that 640K of extended memory will be available after loading EMM386, type the value **/L=640** on the command line.

/a=*altreg*   Replace *altreg* with the number of fast alternate register sets to allocate to EMM386. The range is 0 to 254 and the default is 7. Each set adds about 200 bytes to the size in memory of EMM386.EXE.

/h=*handles*   Replace *handles* with the number of handles EMM386 can use. The range is 1 to 255 handles and the default setting is 64.

/d=*n*   Replace *n* with the number of kilobytes to reserve for buffered direct memory access (DMA). This value should reflect the largest DMA transfer that will occur while you use EMM386.EXE, not counting floppy disk DMA. The range is 16K to 256K and the default setting is 16.

/ram   This option provides access to both expanded memory and the upper memory area, and is valid only if you are running MS-DOS version 5.0 or later. It is covered extensively later in this chapter.

/noems   This option provides access to the upper memory area but does not install expanded memory. Expanded memory that conforms to the LIM specification version 4.00 is still available. This option is valid only if you are running MS-DOS version 5.0 or later.

DOS 5 Memory Management

This section describes methods used in DOS 5 to increase conventional memory for DOS applications. If you run DOS applications from Windows, you still need to free conventional memory because Windows provides these DOS applications with the same memory environment that was available before you started Windows. If you have a previous version of DOS, upgrade to DOS 5 if possible. Microsoft went all out to make DOS 5 the operating system for Windows by adding features that improve performance and capabilities. The majority of improvements benefit 80386 system users, but 80286 users will find a few tricks as well.

DOS 5 does a good job of freeing conventional memory, but third-party applications that work well with DOS and Windows, such as QEMM386 and 386Max, are also available and give you more options. For example, you can specify the exact order and placement of drivers in upper memory with one of these third-party applications. This is important if you want to efficiently fit those drivers in the upper memory blocks to fully use memory.

In addition, QEMM386 and 386Max automatically determine the best way to load upper memory using a trial-and-error method. During installation, you're asked to restart your system several times while the programs determine the best load order. For more information, refer to "Using Third-Party Memory Managers" at the end of this chapter.

Why You Might Not Want to "Load High"

The ability to "load high" is a great new feature of DOS. Freeing conventional memory provides more memory for DOS applications. However, if you don't plan to run DOS applications, or if your DOS applications run fine now with your current conventional memory configuration, you may not want to install EMM386 and load drivers and TSRs high. Here's why.

Since Windows pools conventional memory with extended memory, you might think that loading high would also provide additional memory for Windows. This is not necessarily true. DOS, through the HIMEM.SYS driver, allocates part of extended memory for use as upper memory blocks. This cuts down on the total amount of extended memory available to Windows unless you have enough drivers to fill all the upper memory blocks, which is unlikely, simply because it's hard to make them fit just right. First, just installing the EMM386 driver even without loading drivers high allocates extended memory. On one system, extended memory was reduced by 254K. You can try this yourself by starting your system with and without the EMM386 driver loaded. Run the DOS MEM command to see how much extended memory is available in both cases.

Next, loading drivers high on the system just referred to made 94K of conventional memory available, at a cost of 254K extended memory! Starting Windows and displaying the About Program Manager dialog box revealed that Windows had 3978K available in its memory pool. Turning EMM386 off increased the pool to 4196K. So on this system, loading high robbed memory from Windows. Keep in mind, however, that if your DOS applications run out of memory, EMM386 and the load high commands are the way to go, so you should continue reading the next section.

Loading DOS High

HIMEM.SYS makes the High Memory Area available on 80286 systems or above. You then use the command DOS=HIGH to load portions of DOS into the HMA. The DOS 5 install procedure probably inserted the command in your CONFIG.SYS file. If not, both commands appear as they should appear in the CONFIG.SYS file.

```
DEVICE=C:\DOS\HIMEM.SYS
DOS=HIGH
```

Loading DOS high frees up about 50K of conventional memory for your DOS applications. To see a list of available memory, switch to DOS (by exiting Windows or double-clicking on the MS-DOS Prompt icon) and type **MEM**. If DOS is loaded high, you'll see a listing of memory ending with the statement "MS-DOS resident in High Memory Area." If DOS isn't loaded high, perhaps another driver got access to the HMA before DOS. (Remember that only one program can reside there, so rearrange your CONFIG.SYS file.) You should also make sure you're using the version of HIMEM.SYS supplied with Windows, or a newer version obtained from Microsoft.

Upper Memory Block Loading

If you have an 80386 or 80486 system and DOS 5, you can use the EMM386.EXE driver to load drivers and TSRs into upper memory blocks. First, you must initialize the upper memory block area so drivers and TSRs (herein called simply "drivers") will load into it. The DOS=HIGH,UMB and EMM386.EXE commands perform this. You then use the DEVICEHIGH (in the CONFIG.SYS file) or LOADHIGH (in the AUTOEXEC.BAT file) commands to load drivers into upper memory.

The process of loading high is easy when you have just a few drivers, since they will probably all fit in upper memory. You change the DEVICE= command in the CONFIG.SYS file to DEVICEHIGH= for drivers to load high. In the AUTOEXEC.BAT file, insert the command LOADHIGH= in front of program names to load high. You can then reboot your system and run the MEM command to see how much conventional memory is available.

When drivers don't load high, it is probably because you've filled upper memory blocks and DOS has loaded the drivers into conventional memory instead. You can take another shot at loading the driver high by rearranging the order of the CONFIG.SYS or AUTOEXEC.BAT file. Reboot your system to see if they all fit in the UMB. If they still don't fit, read through the section "Optimizing Upper Memory Blocks" for tips on optimizing the use of the UMBs and overcoming space problems.

There are two other things you need to be aware of before you start this process. First, when Windows runs in 386 enhanced mode, it needs some space (from 12K to 24K) to place buffers used to run DOS applications. Technically, these are called *translation buffers.* If the UMB is full, Windows puts the translation buffers in conventional memory, depriving DOS applications of needed memory. Just be aware of this as you work through the next examples. You'll see how to use the /x (exclude) option to reserve areas of the UMB for Windows.

Quick Steps for Loading High

You should try running through the following quick procedure to load your drivers high before proceeding to the more advanced topics in the next section.

Before starting, create a bootable DOS disk in case your system locks. Also make backup copies of your current CONFIG.SYS and AUTOEXEC.BAT files.

Use a text editor to make the following changes. Make sure your editor does not save any formatting codes or special characters of its own with the file. Usually, you select a "save as text file" option when saving the file. Add the following lines to the beginning of your CONFIG.SYS file if they don't already exist. Make sure that the HIMEM.SYS driver comes before the other commands.

```
DEVICE=C:\WINDOWS\HIMEM.SYS
DOS=HIGH,UMB
DEVICE=C:\WINDOWS\EMM386.EXE /NOEMS /Y=C:\WINDOWS\EMM386.EXE
```

The UMB parameter in the second line signals DOS to use UMBs; it sets the stage for loading the EMM386 driver in the third line. In the third line, the /noems parameter specifies upper memory blocks loading but prevents expanded memory emulation. If you need expanded memory support, refer to the section "Using Expanded Memory" later in this chapter. The /y option specifies where the EMM386.EXE file is located on disk. This option is necessary when running Windows 386 enhanced mode.

While still editing the CONFIG.SYS file, change the DEVICE= command to DEVICEHIGH= for each driver you want to load high. For example, to load the MOUSE.SYS driver high, you would change the command

```
DEVICE=C:\MOUSE.SYS
```

to

```
DEVICEHIGH=C:\MOUSE.SYS
```

Open your AUTOEXEC.BAT file for editing and add the command LOADHIGH in front of each TSR or program you want to load high. For example, the following command loads the DOSKEY utility high. (Note that the equal sign is not required for commands in the AUTOEXEC.BAT file.)

```
LOADHIGH C:\DOS\DOSKEY
```

After making changes, reboot your system. If everything loads correctly, type **MEM /C | MORE** to see if your drivers loaded into upper memory (the more option allows you to view the screen one page at a time). Drives that are loaded high appear near the end of the listing and have an address greater than 09FFF0. If any driver didn't make it to upper memory, edit the CONFIG.SYS or AUTOEXEC.BAT file to change the load order.

Load the biggest driver into the UMB first and the smallest last. This ensures that only small drivers get pushed to conventional memory if all the drivers don't fit.

The following DOS 5 device drivers are safe to load into upper memory:

ANSI.SYS
DISPLAY.SYS
DRIVER.SYS
EGA.SYS
PRINTER.SYS
RAMDRIVE.SYS

The following DOS 5 programs are safe to load into upper memory:

APPEND.EXE
DOSKEY.COM
DOSSHELL.COM
GRAPHICS.COM
KEYB.COM
MODE.COM
NLSFUNC.EXE
PRINT.EXE
SHARE.EXE

The HIMEM.SYS and EMM386.EXE commands can't be loaded high, but hundreds of other drivers and programs can. You'll need to experiment with drivers until you find a setup that works.

Optimizing Upper Memory Blocks

To best use the UMB and gain the most conventional memory, you must find the most efficient way to fit drivers and TSRs into the UMB. That's where the MEM or

MSD (see Appendix F) command comes in. It shows the current size of your drivers and TSRs and helps you determine which will fit best in the UMB. The DIR command also shows memory, but its listing is not as useful as MEM's.

Determine the areas of upper memory already in use by your video cards and other adapters, then write down their locations. First, pull out the documentation for your existing adapter cards and mark the locations used by these cards on a copy of the memory map in Figure 8-3 in Chapter 8.

If there are large gaps between the locations used by the cards, move their address locations closer together in memory by changing switches on the cards. This is an optional step, but it creates large areas of the contiguous memory that will accommodate large drivers.

For example, if one adapter uses addresses up to CC000, then set the switches on the next adapter (a network card, for example) to address CC000. If the network adapter requires 16K, it fits in the range CC000 to D0000. (Remember, the last 0 in the address is commonly dropped when referring to these addresses.)

Now use the EMM386 command to see where UMBs start, then use the MEM /p command to see how the UMBs are being used. Type **EMM386** at the DOS command line to display a listing similar to the following:

```
MICROSOFT Expanded Memory Manager 386   Version 4.40
Copyright Microsoft Corporation 1986, 1991

Expanded memory services unavailable.

  Total upper memory available . . . . . .   79 KB
  Largest Upper Memory Block available . .   71 KB
  Upper memory starting address . . . . . .  C800 H

EMM386 Active.
```

The second to the last line indicates that upper memory starts at C800. Now you can run the MEM /C (classify) command to see the size of your existing drivers and TSRs. To print the listing, type **MEM /C > PRN** (> PRN sends the listing to the printer).

You'll see a printout similar to the following:

```
Conventional Memory :
  Name          Size in Decimal        Size in Hex
  ----------    --------------------   -----------
  MSDOS         14592    ( 14.3K)      3900
  HIMEM          1072    (  1.0K)       430
  EMM386         8512    (  8.3K)      2140
  NECCDR         6672    (  6.5K)      1A10
```

Name	Size in Decimal		Size in Hex
SETVER	400	(0.4K)	190
HHSCAND	8784	(8.6K)	2250
COMMAND	2624	(2.6K)	A40
HDILOAD	18320	(17.9K)	4790
MSCDEX	36208	(35.4K)	8D70
DOSKEY	4128	(4.0K)	1020
EP	8352	(8.2K)	20A0
FREE	64	(0.1K)	40
FREE	192	(0.2K)	C0
FREE	545104	(532.3K)	85150

| Total FREE : | 545360 | (532.6K) | |

Upper Memory :

Name	Size in Decimal		Size in Hex
SYSTEM	172064	(168.0K)	2A020
RAMBIOS	33360	(32.6K)	8250
SMARTDRV	24384	(23.8K)	5F40
MOUSE	11120	(10.9K)	2B70
LOGITECH	5568	(5.4K)	15C0
RAMDRIVE	1184	(1.2K)	4A0
VANSI	2624	(2.6K)	A40
FREE	6128	(6.0K)	17F0
FREE	5504	(5.4K)	1580

The important information in this listing is the size of the drivers. Using these sizes, you can determine how and where to fit them at the upper memory block starting address. To look at the actual placement of drivers in memory, use the MEM /p (Program) command, or MEM /P > PRN, which directs output to the printer.

You should get a listing similar to the following. While this listing may seem confusing at first glance, simply match up the hexadecimal addresses on the left to the copy you made of the upper memory map in Figure 8-3.

Address	Name	Size	Type
000000		000400	Interrupt Vector
000400		000100	ROM Communication Area
000500		000200	DOS Communication Area
000700	IO	000CC0	System Data
0013C0	MSDOS	001490	System Data

```
002850          IO            007450      System Data
                HIMEM         000430        DEVICE=
                EMM386        002140        DEVICE=
                NECCDR        001A10        DEVICE=
                SETVER        000190        DEVICE=
                HHSCAND       002250        DEVICE=
                              000940        FILES=
                              000100        FCBS=
                              000200        BUFFERS=
                              000420        LASTDRIVE=
009CB0          MSDOS         000040      System Program

009D00          COMMAND       000940      Program
00A650          MSDOS         000040      -- Free --
00A6A0          COMMAND       000100      Environment
00A7B0          HDILOAD       000040      Environment
00A800          MSCDEX        008D70      Program
013580          HDILOAD       004750      Program
017CE0          MEM           0000C0      Environment
017DB0          DOSKEY        001020      Program
018DE0          EP            0020A0      Program
01AE90          MEM           0176F0      Program
032590          MSDOS         06DA50      -- Free --
09FFF0          SYSTEM        028010      System Program

0C8010          IO            00E1B0      System Data
                RAMBIOS       008250        DEVICE=
                SMARTDRV      005F40        DEVICE=
0D61D0          IO            004600      System Data
                MOUSE         002B70        DEVICE=
                LOGITECH      0015C0        DEVICE=
                RAMDRIVE      0004A0        DEVICE=
0DA7E0          MSDOS         0017F0      -- Free --
0DBFE0          SYSTEM        002020      System Program

0DE010          IO            000A50      System Data
                VANSI         000A40        DEVICE=
0DEA70          MSDOS         001580      -- Free --
```

Examine your memory map and take note of drivers currently in upper memory. Note that reserved memory starts roughly at 9FFF0 and that upper memory blocks begin at the address you just found using the EMM386 command. In the listing just given, upper memory blocks start at C8000. Almost all the drivers fit into the upper memory area. The exceptions are NECCDR, SERVER, and HHSCAND, which require more room than was available at the end of upper memory blocks. (Note the last line, which indicates that only 1580 hex bytes are free.)

In this example, it may be worth changing the load order. Look at the driver sizes and rearrange them so the largest load is first. Smaller drivers then have a better chance of being configured into the remaining memory. If they don't fit, only small drivers are loaded into conventional memory.

Upper memory blocks are often not contiguous. Blocks may be split into two or more separate sections if addresses are already in use by adapters. It may not always be possible to reconfigure the addresses used by the adapters. In this case, filling upper memory is like trying to fit blocks into slots. You simply rearrange the load order of the drivers to get the blocks to fit within the boundaries set by existing adapters, as shown in Figure 9-1.

Some drivers take up a lot of memory while loading, but need little afterward. If you're having unexplainable problems getting your drivers to load, one or more drivers may not have enough upper memory to install themselves, even though the MEM listing shows they take little room. You'll need to experiment to find which drivers are the culprits, then try loading them first while a lot of upper memory still exists.

Including and Excluding Memory Blocks

You can include or exclude addresses by using the /i and /x parameters with the EMM386 command. The /i parameter is used to include memory addresses that it normally detects as reserved. Use the /x parameter to *exclude* memory areas and avoid conflicts. Excluding areas is important to avoid memory conflicts because some adapters place code in upper memory after the system has already booted.

*The Microsoft Diagnostics Utility (MSD.EXE) can show available space in the UMB. Type **MSD** to start the utility, then exclude any address space identified as "RAM" or "ROM."*

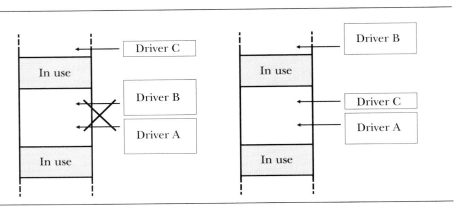

Figure 9-1. *Fitting upper memory blocks*

*If Windows will not start in 386 enhanced mode, try starting the program with the command **WIN /D:X**. This excludes the entire adapter area. If Windows then boots, you can begin the exclude routine described here.*

For example, on some machines (like the IBM PS/2), the 64K block of memory in the range E000 to EFFF is not available for use. But on other systems, you can make this range available if it is not being used by an adapter or other driver, by adding the following command to your EMM386 line in CONFIG.SYS:

```
I=E000-EFFF
```

Note that some VGA cards use E000. Check your video card manual before using this area. Another possible candidate for inclusion is the area from B000 to B7FF if a monochrome adapter is not installed on your system. This 4K area is normally used to hold the buffer for text on the monochrome screen. Add the following option to EMM386.EXE before the /y parameter:

```
I=B000-B7FF
```

Note that although the address range B000-B7FF comes before the normal starting address of upper memory blocks, DOS may not fill it first because it is only 32K in size. DOS always starts placing drivers in the largest contiguous upper memory block, and continues placing drivers up to the end of upper memory. It then fills the B000 area with any drivers that will fit.

While your system's ROM code usually takes up the entire F range, in some cases you can use parts of it after your system boots. The AMI BIOS, for example, frees F000-F800 after booting. On the IBM AT, ROM BASIC resides in the F600 to FC00 range. If you don't use BASIC, include the area with an /i option in the EMM386 command. Treat the use of this area experimentally until you're sure there are no conflicts (i.e., your system doesn't lock up).

To exclude an area of memory that might be used later by an adapter or program, use the /x parameter, followed by the range of addresses to exclude. Some hardware and software assume areas in the video address range are available for use and load code into them. For best results, exclude the entire video area with the following command:

```
X=A000-CBFF
```

Later, if you need more upper memory blocks to load high, you can try using areas in the video range that might be available.

Running Windows with the New Configuration

Once you've loaded upper memory, try running Windows and your DOS applications in 386 enhanced mode. If the system crashes, you may need to make room for translation buffers by excluding a range of memory with the /x parameter on the EMM386 command line. If you previously included the range E000 to EFFF, try including only half of this range. Windows will then use the other half when it runs. Remember, if you used the /noems parameter with EMM386, expanded memory won't be available to DOS applications. You may need to set an expanded memory page frame aside before starting Windows, as discussed next in the "Using Expanded Memory" section.

It's possible that drivers in upper memory are sharing the same space, which can cause your system to crash or display error messages as soon as you start a program. If your system exhibits strange intermittent behavior, remove one by one any drivers you've loaded high until the problem goes away. Closely evaluate the memory address range used by your adapters and programs and make changes to avoid conflicts. A process of elimination may flush out the source of the problems, as described next.

The following procedure uses Windows commands to exclude areas of memory. You can also follow a similar procedure using the EMM386 /x option at the DOS level.

To search out and eliminate memory conflicts, include the EMMExclude option in the [386Enh] section of the SYSTEM.INI file with the range of addresses to exclude. You then restart Windows to see if the problem is eliminated; if so, you know you've found the area of conflict. Start by excluding all upper memory with the following command:

```
EMMExclude A000-EFFF
```

Restart Windows. If the problem goes away, follow the next few steps to narrow down the exact area where the conflict exists. If the problem doesn't go away, contact Microsoft or the manufacturers of any special equipment installed in your system.

Replace the previous EMMExclude command with the one listed here, which excludes the first half of reserved memory. This method gives you a 50 percent chance of finding the conflict area when you restart Windows.

```
EMMExclude A000-C7FF
```

If the problem still exists after restarting Windows, try excluding the other half of memory with the following command:

```
EMMExclude C800-EFFF
```

You now know that the conflict exists in either the upper or lower range. Now exclude half of the known range and start Windows again. For example, if the conflict was resolved when you excluded D000-EFFF, check the first half of that section by changing the EMMExclude command as follows.

```
EMMExclude C800-DBFF
```

If that doesn't work, try excluding the second half with the following command:

```
EMMExclude DC00-EFFF
```

Continue this process of elimination until you find the memory block where the conflict occurs. Keep in mind that the conflict may involve more than one 16K block of memory, meaning that more than one of the last areas you check may contain conflicts.

Using Expanded Memory

Expanded memory is a scheme that lets DOS access large amounts of memory using a method called *bank switching*, as defined by the Lotus/Intel/Microsoft Expanded Memory Specification (LIM EMS). Bank switching provides expanded memory through a 64K "window." This window, or *page frame*, is an address range in reserved memory that points to memory on an optional memory card or in extended memory. The 64K page frame consists of four 16K pages. The processor accesses expanded memory through these 16K pages. Expanded memory is not a continuation of extended memory. It is a scheme for providing extra memory to DOS applications that support the EMS specification. Recall the analogy, from Chapter 8, of temporarily moving paper stacks from your desk to another table.

In standard mode, DOS applications can only use expanded memory on an expanded memory board. Install the board and drivers before starting Windows. Windows will then let DOS applications use the expanded memory as normal. However, Windows never uses the expanded memory for its own use and never makes it available to Windows applications. Typical expanded memory boards are the Intel Above Board and the AST RAMpage.

The EMM386.EXE driver provides another way to provide expanded memory to applications, but only on 80386 and 80486 systems. You specify expanded memory by including the /ram option on the EMM386 command line. Your DOS applications can then use this expanded memory when you run those applications at the DOS level, before starting Windows.

EMM386 is a LIM 4.00 expanded memory manager and is capable of implementing large-frame EMS. EMM386 can use up to 384K of the conventional memory addressing area for mapping expanded memory page frames. When EMM386 installs with the /ram option, you'll see a report of this memory allocation listed as "System Memory Allocated."

The remainder of this section covers the EMM386.EXE command and is of interest only to those who use 80386 and 80486 systems and have a need for expanded memory. The following command installs EMM386 and provides expanded memory. Remember to include the name of the directory that has the most recent version of EMM386.EXE and any other options you need to load drivers high, as discussed previously.

```
DEVICE=C:\WINDOWS\EMM386.EXE /RAM
```

The /ram parameter does two things. First, it sets up a 64K expanded memory page frame. Second, it makes upper memory blocks available in the same way the noems switch does, so don't use /noems with /ram. You can specify exactly how much expanded memory you need for applications by including the memory amount before /RAM on the command line. For example, to specify 512K of expanded memory, use the following command:

```
DEVICE=C:\WINDOWS\EMM386.EXE 512 /RAM
```

The /ram option requires a 64K block of upper memory to provide the page frame for expanded memory. EMM386 locates the page frame in the C000 to F000 upper memory range, which may be in use by adapters or other programs. If so, you'll see an error message that EMM386 can't locate the page frame. Use the /frame option to specify a 64K contiguous and available area of upper memory for the page frame. You can try making areas of upper memory available to make sure you still have room to load drivers high. The following option, as mentioned previously, makes the E range available for use. Note that you can't use this option on PS/2 machines.

```
I=E000-EFFF
```

The following options are in the [386Enh] section of the SYSTEM.INI file.

ReservePageFrame=on|off   This option tells Windows whether to give preference to EMS page frame space or conventional memory when it has to use one of the two to allocate DOS transfer buffers. This choice is necessary when Windows cannot find space between 640K and 1MB other than EMS page frame space. If enabled, this setting will preserve EMS page frame space at the expense of conventional memory. If you are not going to run non-Windows applications that use expanded memory, you can disable this setting to give non-Windows applications more conventional memory.

NoEMMDriver=on|off   When this option is on, Windows in 386 enhanced mode is prevented from installing its expanded memory driver. This differs from setting

EMMSize (another SYSTEM.INI option) to zero, which does not prevent the EMM driver from being loaded.

You can specify expanded memory usage for DOS applications in PIF files. Chapter 19 covers this in greater detail.

Using Third-Party Memory Managers

There are a number of alternatives to HIMEM.SYS and EMM386.EXE when it comes to memory management. You should evaluate your system's needs before using third-party memory managers over DOS 5 memory commands.

QEMM-386 from Quarterdeck and 386Max (or BlueMax for IBM PS/2s) from Qualitas are the most-used third-party packages. These managers give you more control when loading drivers high. MS-DOS 5 uses an algorithm that first loads drivers into the largest available contiguous block of memory. The third-party memory managers let you specify which upper memory block to load a program into. In addition, these managers include an automatic configuration program that determines the best loading procedure for your system. The programs try many different configurations, rebooting your system each time to find the optimal fit. This is a useful feature, especially when dealing with drivers that require more memory when loading than during normal operation.

One thing to keep in mind is that Microsoft made MS-DOS 5 and Windows compatible and ensured that their memory manager components work together. Third-party memory managers can cause unforeseen problems and conflicts. You should make sure these packages are compatible with your configuration before you purchase any of them.

If you decide to use a third-party memory manager, remember to disable HIMEM.SYS and EMM386.EXE. You'll also need to remove the DOS=UMB, DEVICEHIGH, and LOADHIGH commands from your startup files.

System Resources ("Out of Memory" Messages)

A shortage of system resources may occur when too many applications are open. Windows displays an "Out of memory" message when you try to open another application. You can check system resources by opening the About Program Manager dialog box. What you'll probably find is that Windows still has available memory listed in the Memory field, but very few system resources. In fact, the Free System Resources field should never drop below 15 percent.

System resources consist of two 64K memory blocks used to track menus, graphics, icons, and other graphical user interface components for each application you start.

The programs GDI.EXE and USER.EXE generate system resources each time you start a new application, so the more applications you open, the more system resources diminish. To resolve this problem, close applications when they are not in use.

If you have a continuing resource problem, there are two steps you can take:

- Program Manager is a system resource hog. Each icon uses about one percent of the system resources, but only when it is visible. To minimize this impact, keep unused groups minimized and remove unnecessary icons.

- Place programs you use often in the Startup group. This means you never have to display their icons for startup, which greatly saves your system resources.

Chapter *10*

Optimizing Windows

This chapter covers a range of topics that help you optimize your system for Windows. You'll learn about the RAMDrive and SmartDrive utilities and see how to streamline your system startup files.

Tips for Improving Performance

The following tips and hints will help you gain better performance and speed from Windows in your everyday activities. Keep in mind that you don't need to implement all the suggestions presented here. This chapter provides a range of things you can do if your system seems to be running slower than normal, or if you just want to make sure it's running efficiently.

System Startup   Follow the procedures covered under the "Optimizing Startup" section later in this chapter to learn how to best use the CONFIG.SYS and AUTOEXEC.BAT.

Windows Startup Mode   On 80386 and above systems, run in standard mode whenever possible to gain performance. Use 386 enhanced mode to run more than one DOS application or to run DOS applications in a resizable window. Also use 386 enhanced mode if your applications run out of memory in standard mode. The virtual memory capabilities of 386 enhanced mode provide applications with additional memory by simulating it on disk. Always start in 386 enhanced mode if you're manipulating large graphics images like those imported with a scanner.

Accessories   Close accessories that rob your system of performance. The clock, for example, must be constantly updated to keep its time correct, so if you don't need it, close it.

Applications   Minimize applications not in use, or close them.

Maximize the applications you're currently using. Applications that don't run full-screen run slower.

The Clipboard   The Clipboard retains its contents even after you've pasted, taking up valuable memory. Clear the Clipboard after copying and pasting a large graphic or block of text. This is easy to do: just copy a single character to the Clipboard, or choose Delete from the Clipboard Edit menu.

The Desktop   Remove wallpaper and desktop patterns if you're short on memory and don't really need them. A wallpaper image can use as much as 150K of system memory.

The Disk Drive Cache   While Microsoft recommends 2MB as the largest Smart-Drive cache (anything more increases the cache overhead), other cache utilities such as Hyperdrive may let you increase the cache further. For example, a 6MB cache can hold so many Windows files that you can exit Windows and restart with virtually no disk activity.

Disk Drives   If your disk drive controller has its own large cache, it's probably fastest to use that instead of SmartDrive, but only if it's a "smart cache." Refer to either your manual, Chapter 12 of this book, or the manufacturer for recommendations on which you should use.

If you have a Western Digital 1003 controller or compatible, make sure the FastDisk options are enabled in SYSTEM.INI, as discussed in Chapter 12. Setup does not automatically install FastDisk. To install it, start the 386 Enhanced utility in the Control Panel, then click the Virtual Memory button, the Change button, and finally, enable the Use 32-Bit Access option. Check with the drive's manufacturer if you're not sure you can use this option.

DOS Applications   In 386 enhanced mode, run DOS applications full-screen and exclusively.

Review the Program Information File settings used by DOS applications as described in Chapter 19. The default settings used by Windows may not be appropriate and will slow performance.

Multitasking   Running applications in the background (multitasking) will drastically reduce performance. Multitask only when necessary, such as when you need to complete one task (a print job or data base sort), but still need your computer available for periodic use.

File Updates   DOS applications do not normally update file lists in File Manager directory windows. You must use the Refresh command on the Window menu after adding or deleting files. The FileSysChange= option in the [386Enh] section of SYSTEM.INI specifies automatic or manual file updates. Normally, Windows sets the option off during setup, but you can turn it on to update file lists automatically. Be aware, however, that performance will suffer. Check the status of the setting; another user may have set it on, causing File Manager to run slower. The FileSysChange option should read as follows for best performance (but don't forget to refresh your file lists by pressing F5):

```
FileSysChange=Off
```

Fonts   Remove fonts you don't use. Windows scans for the fonts during bootup to make sure they're available; this can take time. Use the Fonts utility to remove fonts, as discussed in Chapter 16. You don't need to remove the fonts completely from disk, just from the list that Windows holds in memory. This way you can easily reinstall them later.

Hard Disk Cleanup   Remove any unnecessary files from the hard disk to free up space. Unnecessary files may include .BAK (backup) or .TMP (temporary) files. Choose the Add/Remove Windows Components option on the Setup utility Options menu to remove unnecessary help, graphic, and program files in the Windows directory. Note that you must run the Setup utility from Windows to see the Options menu. Run it from DOS only when changing or upgrading drivers.

   Run the DOS CHKDSK command to recover lost files, but exit Windows before doing so. Refer to your DOS manual for details.

Hard Disk Optimizing   Periodically run a hard disk defragmenting utility to optimize the read/write performance of your hard drive. Also run the utility after removing old files. If you don't have a disk optimizer, refer to Chapter 12 for instructions on optimizing with the DOS BACKUP and RESTORE commands.

Hardware   Check your system ROM BIOS and upgrade to the latest version if necessary. Check your manual or call the system manufacturer for details. Older BIOS chips can cause Unrecoverable Applications Errors (UAEs). Before upgrading the BIOS be sure the motherboard manufacturer authorizes the upgrade.

Printing   Determine whether you really need to use Print Manager. It can slow performance.

Swap Files   Use a permanent swap file instead of a temporary swap file when setting up virtual memory in 386 enhanced mode.

Temporary Files   Specify a RAM drive as the location for temporary application files (not to be confused with virtual memory swap files), but only if you have enough extra memory to make the RAM drive large enough to hold all the temporary files that are placed there. A method for determining swap file size is covered later in this chapter.

The WIN.INI File   The most recent entries, those you're most likely to use, are often placed at the end of the file. Move these to the beginning of the file so Windows and applications can find them faster.

Windows holds the WIN.INI file in memory. To conserve memory, edit the WIN.INI file to reduce it in size, removing unnecessary lines that might remain from applications you've removed from your system.

Hardware Improvements

Windows 3.1 will run on 80286 and above systems, but it performs best on 80386 and 80486 systems. Windows' performance can be noticeably slow on 80286 systems, even to a first-time user. Upgrading to a faster CPU with more memory is the best way to improve Windows' performance, but if that doesn't fit your budget, there are ways to gain more speed from your existing system.

Adding memory to any system is the best solution. Running out of memory in DOS produces error messages. Windows, on the other hand, allocates available memory to its applications as needed, swapping information to and from disk to make room. So while you don't get error messages, Windows performance drops due to the disk swapping.

If you notice the disk drive light running when you're not loading or saving files, your system probably needs more memory. If you're on a budget, try to install at least 4MB. This gives Windows enough room to handle several applications without swapping. If you buy more memory than this you may not use it, unless you run a lot of applications at once, or run graphics applications and load large images. While 3MB is also acceptable, you'll probably find the additional cost of upgrading from 3MB to 4MB to be minimal, especially if you need to add an optional memory board.

Since the minimum amount of extended memory required by Windows is 256K, 2MB rarely provides acceptable performance unless you have a disk cache large enough to relieve disk swapping. 386 enhanced mode requires 1280K of extended memory. If you don't have that amount, Windows runs in standard mode.

Upgrading the hard disk will improve Windows' performance by 15 to 25 percent, if you add a fast-access drive (15 to 20 millisecond access range). The speed of Windows startup, file accesses, and disk swapping improves considerably. However, adding drives is expensive, and futile if the drive you buy outperforms your system. In other words, don't buy an expensive fast disk if the rest of your system can't take advantage of it (that is, if you have an 80286 system).

Upgrading your video hardware is another way to improve Windows' performance. If you have an EGA video card, break your budget and buy at least a VGA card and a new monitor to go with it. The performance of EGA cards is unacceptable for most Windows applications. VGA also offers better screen resolution. Used and inexpensive VGA monitors and video cards should be abundant as users with big wallets upgrade to newer, faster video equipment. Windows has prompted the development of video cards with graphic coprocessors to dramatically improve performance and higher screen resolutions that let you work with documents side by side without the need to reduce windows to an unworkable size.

Optimizing Startup

If your system does not have enough memory, it will operate inefficiently, or prevent you from running some applications. In addition, you may be limited in the number of applications you can run at once. To improve performance, you can alter your system startup files with the changes described here. There are a number of ways to gain extra memory from your system. Drivers and TSRs loaded at the DOS level are duplicated in every DOS virtual machine created by Windows in 386 enhanced mode. You can often remove these drivers from the CONFIG.SYS or the AUTOEXEC.BAT file, then run them from within Windows instead, thus providing more memory for DOS applications.

To change the way your system starts up, modify the AUTOEXEC.BAT and CONFIG.SYS files. These are the DOS startup files located in the root directory of your startup drive (usually C). Before you make any changes, be sure to make a backup by copying the files to a floppy disk.

The CONFIG.SYS file is used to load device drivers for peripherals attached to your system, such as a mouse or special video equipment. The file may also hold commands that configure the operating parameters of DOS. The Windows setup process makes the following changes to your startup files:

- Adds the line DEVICE=HIMEM.SYS to CONFIG.SYS. This command may contain special parameters as discussed in Chapter 9.

- Adds the SMARTDRV.EXE command to CONFIG.SYS or AUTOEXEC.BAT or both, depending on your hardware. This command may contain special parameters, which are discussed later in this chapter.

- Updates the RAMDRIVE.SYS file. Setup does not add the RAMDrive command to your startup files. If you want a RAM drive, you need to install it yourself, which is discussed later in this chapter.

- Updates EMM386.EXE, if appropriate.

- Updates your Microsoft or Hewlett-Packard mouse driver.

- Removes any commands that load incompatible drivers, programs, or third-party memory managers.

- Adds or updates your EGA.SYS driver if you are using an EGA display or a Mouse Systems mouse.

- Adds the appropriate parameter to the 386Max line, if it is present.

- Adds the Windows directory to the path in the AUTOEXEC.BAT file.

- Creates a TEMP directory in the Windows directory and sets the TEMP variable to it (if you have not already set a TEMP= variable). You can change the TEMP= variable to point to the drive and directory of your choice, such as a RAM drive to improve performance.

Using Windows SysEdit

The SysEdit utility is a convenient tool for changing the contents of your startup files, the SYSTEM.INI files, or the WIN.INI files. When you start SysEdit, the startup files are automatically loaded into four separate Notepad windows. If you know Notepad, you know how to use SysEdit.

To start SysEdit, double-click the icon you created in Chapter 6 or choose Run from the Program Manager or File Manager File menu and type **SYSEDIT** in the Command Line box.

You can disable some commands in the startup files once Windows is installed. For example, the command to load a mouse can be removed since Windows provides its own mouse support. (However, remove this command only if you don't run mouse applications at the DOS level, or non-Windows applications from Windows.) To disable a command, either delete the line, or type **REM** at the beginning of its line. Typing **REM** effectively disables a command and is preferable to just deleting the line, since you can enable the line at any time by removing REM.

 A REM statement in the CONFIG.SYS file displays a message that the line is unrecognizable. Your system will ignore the command and you can ignore the error messages.

Once you've made changes to the files, close the SysEdit window. SysEdit will ask if you want to save changes. Answer yes, and restart your computer to enable the changes. Whenever you make changes to SYSTEM.INI or WIN.INI, you must restart Windows to see your changes.

Recommended Changes to CONFIG.SYS

The following changes to the startup files are very general recommendations. You should evaluate your own needs based on your system and its hardware. If you have an 80386 or 80486 system, and want to emulate expanded memory, don't forget to include the EMM386.EXE command as described in Chapter 9. Also, don't remove the HIMEM.SYS command from the CONFIG.SYS FILE.

Some drivers have the .EXE extension. You can run these from the DOS command line or from within a Windows DOS session. Drivers with the extension .SYS only load with a command in the CONFIG.SYS file.

Mouse Support

Remove MOUSE.SYS from your CONFIG.SYS file or MOUSE.COM from your AUTOEXEC.BAT file if you run Windows-only applications, and never run DOS applications. This will free some memory. Windows has its own built-in mouse support. If you have a DOS application that requires a mouse and you want to run it at the DOS level or from within Windows, you'll need to load the mouse driver. However, you can save memory part of the time by loading the driver only when you intend to run the DOS application, either from DOS or from Windows. Type **MOUSE** at the DOS prompt before starting the application or starting Windows, assuming MOUSE.COM is in the Windows directory.

   With some applications, you can load the mouse driver and the application from Windows at the same time by including their commands in a batch file. The mouse support is then only loaded for that application and removed when you exit the application. Batch file techniques are discussed in Chapter 19.

File Handle Settings in CONFIG.SYS

The FILES option is used to specify the maximum number of file handles that can be open at once. Set its value to 30 by including the following command line in your CONFIG.SYS file.

```
FILES = 30
```

   Set this value higher only if you receive insufficient file handle messages when running the application at the DOS level. Each additional file handle uses 48 bytes of memory.

   If you run the DOS application from Windows and it needs more file handles, increase the value of the PerVMFiles= setting in the [386Enh] section of SYSTEM.INI. This setting controls how many additional file handles are allocated to each DOS session running in a virtual machine. PerVMFiles= is described further in your SY SINI.WRI file.

   Insufficient file handle errors are not as recognizable in Windows. Instead, an Unrecoverable Application Error (UAE) will occur if file handles are depleted. Try increasing file handles when this occurs.

Buffer Settings in CONFIG.SYS

The BUFFERS command is used to specify the number of buffers used to improve disk access. If you are using SmartDrive, you don't really need a lot of buffers, which take up memory (512 bytes each). Set BUFFERS to 10 by including the following command in CONFIG.SYS:

```
BUFFERS = 10
```

Environment Space in CONFIG.SYS

Windows displays an Unrecoverable Applications Error when an application runs out of environment space. This is another instance where you may not know the exact cause of the problem when running Windows. To avoid this problem, set environment space high when your system starts by including the following command in your CONFIG.SYS file:

```
SHELL=C:\DOS\COMMAND.COM /P /E:1024
```

The SHELL command specifies the location of the command processor. Some programs temporarily unload COMMAND.COM to gain memory. SHELL specifies the location of COMMAND.COM for reloading. The /p switch keeps it resident in memory and the /e parameter sets the environment space. In the example given earlier, the environment space is set to 1024 bytes. This is a substantial increase from the default environment space of 160 bytes. Increase the setting further if you experience problems running DOS applications. Keep in mind that memory set aside for the environment is taken from the conventional memory used by DOS applications, so there is a trade-off in memory usage when setting the environment variable high. If you run low on memory, set the environment to 512 bytes.

The LastDrive Setting in CONFIG.SYS

The LastDrive command is used to specify how many drives your local system has. When you log onto a network, this setting is read by the network operating system to determine what drive letter it should assign to the first network drive. The default is drive E. Set its value as high as the last drive on your system. The network then makes its drives available using letters that follow your last drive setting. For example, if drive F is your last drive, you should insert the following command in CONFIG.SYS. Drive G will then be the first network drive.

```
LASTDRIVE = F
```

The Stacks Setting in CONFIG.SYS

If you are using DOS 3.3 or higher, include the following command. It prevents DOS from allocating additional memory to handle hardware stacks, which Windows usually does not need.

```
STACKS=9,256
```

If you see the message "Internal Stack Failure, System Halted," when running DOS applications, remove the command and let DOS use its default settings for stacks, or increase the settings. While STACKS=9,256 is a normal setting, you may see parity errors, or your mouse may stop working if the value needs to be higher. Try the following settings in the order listed until the problem goes away:

STACKS=12,128
STACKS=12,256
STACKS=0,0

The AUTOEXEC.BAT File

The AUTOEXEC.BAT file starts programs automatically that you would normally execute at the DOS prompt. Typical commands in AUTOEXEC.BAT are terminate-and-stay-resident utilities (TSRs). Remove these commands from AUTOEXEC.BAT and start the utilities from Windows, if possible. This will save conventional memory for DOS applications and prevent program conflicts.

Commands for loading SmartDrive from the AUTOEXEC.BAT file are covered later in this chapter. If you install a RAM drive, you can include a command similar to the following in AUTOEXEC.BAT to direct standard mode temporary application files to the RAM drive. In this case, temporary files are swapped to RAM drive E. More on this topic is covered under the "Swap Files" section later in this chapter.

```
SET TEMP=E:
```

Setting TEMP= to a RAM drive can speed up printing if you use Print Manager since it will write its temporary files to fast RAM during a print job rather than to a slower drive. Some older applications swap to TMP, not TEMP. You can include the additional command SET TMP=E: to support these applications.

The WINSTART.BAT File

To start memory-resident utilities in 386 enhanced mode, use the WINSTART.BAT file. It makes utilities available to Windows applications (but not non-Windows applications), and prevents the utilities from using conventional memory needed by non-Windows applications. The file is ignored if you start in standard mode.

Programs and utilities used by Windows 386 enhanced mode should be placed in WINSTART.BAT, which you can create with any text editor (DOS EDIT, Notepad, and so on). SysEdit cannot be used.

Swap Files

In standard mode, Windows uses a temporary *application swap file* to hold information about DOS applications when you switch back to Windows. Application swap files are created and removed automatically, so you don't need to be too concerned about them. However, you can improve performance by directing Windows to place application swap files in a RAM drive.

The following sections explain application and virtual memory swap files.

 Don't confuse application swap files with virtual memory swap files *used in 386 enhanced mode. Virtual memory swap files are either temporary or permanent, and you can control their size and location using the 386 enhanced icon in the Control Panel.*

Application Swap Files

Application swap files exist on disk as hidden files to prevent accidental deletion (they don't appear in the directory listing). Their filenames start with the characters ~WOA, which stands for "Windows Old Application." Application swap files are temporary—when you quit the application or quit Windows, the swap file is removed. Windows stores application swap files in the directory specified by the swapdisk= line in the [NonWindowsApp] SYSTEM.INI file. If this option is not set, Windows places the files in the directory specified by the SET TEMP command line in your AUTOEXEC.BAT file.

A RAM disk improves switching between DOS applications and Windows. As mentioned earlier, if temporary files are directed to a RAM disk, make sure the RAM disk is large enough to hold all the swap files placed there during any given session.

 As a rule, set aside at least 1MB for a RAM drive. If you have less than 4MB of memory, swap to a physical hard disk.

In addition, Windows applications may create their own temporary swap files and place them in the drive or directory specified by the TEMP= line.

To determine an appropriate size for your RAM drive, first set up swapping to a physical disk and directory with the following command in SYSTEM.INI. Be sure to specify a drive and directory appropriate for your system.

```
SWAPDISK=C:\WINDOWS\TEMP
```

Next, start Windows, then start the non-Windows applications you expect to run at any one time and load documents into their workspace. Switch back to Windows (ALT-ESC) and start other DOS applications you expect to use at the same time. When you've got a typical work environment set up, start File Manager and open a directory window on the temporary directory. Choose By File Type from the File Manager View menu and enable Show Hidden/System Files so you can see the hidden temporary application files. If you can't see the file size, enable All File Details on the View menu.

Now you can determine approximately how much room the temporary files require. Add up the file size lists, then add an additional 500K if you feel you might need more room. Make your RAM drive this size, if possible (this procedure is discussed under "Setting Up a RAM Drive" later in this chapter). Figure 10-1 shows the contents of a RAM drive when two DOS applications and the MS-DOS Prompt are loaded. The ~doc*.tmp files are temporary files created by the applications, not by Windows. Make sure you provide room for them as well. A typical document swap file ranges in size from 1K to 10K.

Don't forget to refresh the file listing if you open additional applications by pressing the F5 key.

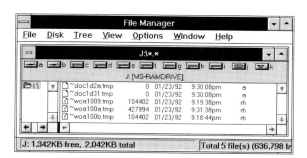

Figure 10-1. *The contents of a RAM drive when two DOS applications and the MS-DOS Prompt are loaded*

If your system crashes, your temporary files on a hard disk may still be intact. Occasionally check the temporary file location and delete files that have the .TMP extension. However, never do this while Windows or another application is running, since the temporary files may still be in use!

Setting Up a RAM Drive

A RAM drive is a phantom drive. Your system and Windows see it as physical disk drive, but in fact, it is located in memory. The advantage of placing files in a RAM disk is speed. Files placed there are accessed almost immediately. The disadvantage is that a RAM drive is volatile. Like anything in memory, its contents are lost when the power goes down.

Never place important data files in a RAM drive unless you absolutely save those files to a physical disk immediately after making changes.

Typically, you place read-only files in a RAM drive. These are files you access but don't change, such as a reference database or Windows program files.

As discussed previously, there is some advantage to placing application swap files in a RAM drive. The RAM drive must be large enough to accommodate all the files that might be placed there, however. This means creating a RAM drive that is 1MB or more in size. If you have less than 4MB of memory, there is no advantage to setting up such a large RAM drive since memory would be robbed from Windows and its applications. If you have more than 4MB, and you plan to direct temporary files into the RAM drive, determine its size using the techniques discussed in the previous section. If you plan to put program files in the RAM drive, add up the size of each file and create a RAM drive that will hold them all.

Before installing a RAM drive, let's clarify the difference between it and disk caching. A disk caching program, like SmartDrive, sets aside part of memory to hold disk information you access often. If you need the information again, it's read from the cache, not from the disk. A disk caching program is "intelligent" if it does a good job of determining which disk information you'll need next. It then loads that information into the cache in addition to the information you requested. The important point here is that a disk cache automatically writes changes to permanent disk storage. Refer to the section "SmartDrive" later in this chapter for more information on disk caching.

A RAM drive is best for program files, read-only data files, and temporary files (which are removed) because you must manually save files that have changed in a RAM drive.

The Command to Load a RAM Drive

The RAM Drive utility for Windows is RAMDRIVE.SYS. The following command loads a 1024K RAM drive. Place this command in the CONFIG.SYS file after the command that loads HIMEM.SYS. The /e parameter loads the RAM drive in extended memory.

```
DEVICE = C:\WINDOWS\RAMDRIVE.SYS 1024 /E
```

After making changes to the CONFIG.SYS file, always restart your system to enable the changes.

RAMDrive Options

Each parameter of the RAMDrive command shown here is discussed in the sections that follow.

DEVICE=C:\WINDOWS\RAMDRIVE.SYS
[*DiskSize* [*SectorSize* [*NumEntries*]]] [/e|/a]

Typically, RAMDRIVE.SYS is stored in the Windows directory. If a more recent version is located elsewhere, change the drive and path as necessary.

DiskSize Replace *DiskSize* with the amount of memory in kilobytes you want to allocate to the RAM disk. In the previous example, 1024 was specified, but you could specify, for example, 512 or 2048. Don't specify a number larger than the amount of memory your system has, or Windows won't have enough memory for its own use.

SectorSize It is usually not necessary to specify this option. The default is 512 bytes. If you have reason to change the sector size, replace *SectorSize* with a value in bytes, such as 128 or 256, then specify a *DiskSize* parameter as well.

NumEntries Replace *NumEntries* with the number of files and directories allowable in the RAM disk's root directory. The limit can be from 2 to 1024 entries, which is rounded up to the nearest sector size boundary. Up to 64 entries are created if this value is not specified. If you specify a NumEntries value, also specify values for *DiskSize* and *SectorSize*.

/e Use the /e parameter to create the RAM disk in extended memory. Use this option whenever possible, because it leaves conventional memory free for DOS applications.

/a   If expanded memory is configured, use the /a option to create the RAM disk in expanded memory.

SmartDrive

SmartDrive, which comes with Windows, is a disk caching program that sets aside part of memory as a cache thereby improving disk access even when you're not using Windows. SmartDrive keeps the most recently accessed hard disk information in memory where it can be accessed again if necessary, thus reducing access to the physical disk drive. SmartDrive also holds disk writes if the hard drive is being accessed for data. It then writes the data to a physical disk as soon as the drive is free.

A disk cache utility must have some "intelligence" to anticipate the information you'll need from disk and information that must be written back to disk. For example, imagine working from a database file. If you're listing fields in records sequentially, the disk cache should anticipate the information you'll need in subsequent records and load those records, along with the records you requested when accessing the disk. A disk cache must also know what to remove from the cache to make room for new information. This is done on a "least-used" basis.

In addition, a cache must write to disk information that you've changed. To improve performance, a cache may withhold writes until it has enough to make a disk access worthwhile, but means that information is not written to disk immediately.

When using a cache, never turn your system off without first closing applications and making sure the cache has written its contents to disk. Usually, this takes a second and happens automatically. But never just turn your system off in the middle of a program!

SmartDrive is automatically installed in the AUTOEXEC.BAT file during Windows setup unless another disk caching program is installed. You should evaluate your need for third-party cache programs over SmartDrive, which is designed to work with Windows. The setup program does not optimize SmartDrive for use on your system, but SmartDrive uses various default values that should be sufficient for most systems. Review the parameters and options listed in the following section to determine if SmartDrive needs to see if any are appropriate for your system.

Installing SmartDrive

You can install SmartDrive from the DOS prompt or by placing its command in the AUTOEXEC.BAT file. In one special case, a SmartDrive command is placed in the CONFIG.SYS file (this particular case will be discussed later in this chapter). The following command loads SmartDrive using default parameters:

SMARTDRV

The default cache size set up by SmartDrive is based on the amount of extended memory in your system, as listed here:

Extended Memory	ICS	WCS
1MB	All	(no caching)
2MB	1MB	256K
4MB	1MB	512K
6MB	2MB	1MB
> 6MB	2MB	2MB

The ICS (Initial Cache Size) parameter is the amount of memory SmartDrive uses for its cache. The WCS (Windows Cache Size) is the minimum size for a cache. This option is necessary because Windows reduces the cache when it loads to gain more memory for its own use. The cache is then resized as necessary during the Windows session and restored to the Initial Cache Size when you exit Windows.

The larger the cache, the less often information is read directly from disk. Initially, all information must be read into the cache, but subsequent reads come from the cache. If the cache is too large, the system may spend as much time searching for information in the cache as it would accessing the information directly from disk. Microsoft recommends 2MB as the largest SmartDrive cache.

*Information in a cache must be written to disk before you shut your system off. Never turn off your system without first closing Windows and waiting for the cache to write itself to disk. To force the cache to write to disk, type **SMARTDRV /C** at the DOS prompt. Failing to follow this procedure could result in lost data. After all disk activity has stopped, you can safely turn off your computer.*

SmartDrive Options

The SmartDrive command line takes the following form. Note that the SmartDrive command filename is SMARTDRV.EXE.

C:\WINDOWS\SMARTDRV [[*drive*[+|−]]...] [/e:*ElementSize*] [*InitCacheSize* [*WinCacheSize*]] [/b:*BufferSize*] [/L] [/q] [/c] [/r] [/s] [/?]

Typically, SMARTDRV.EXE is stored in the Windows directory. If a more recent version is located elsewhere, change the drive and path as necessary. Each parameter is described in the following sections.

drive   Replace *drive* with the letter of the disk drive to cache. If you don't specify a drive letter, floppy disk drives are read-cached but not write-cached, hard disk drives are read- and write-cached, and CD-ROM and network drives are ignored. You can specify multiple disk drives.

+ | −   Specify either the plus (+) or minus (−) sign to override the default settings. Specifying a drive letter without a plus or minus sign enables read-caching and disables write-caching. Specifying a drive letter followed by a plus sign (+) enables read- and write-caching. Specifying a drive letter followed by a minus sign (−) disables read- and write-caching.

/e:*ElementSize*   Replace *ElementSize* with the amount of cache in bytes SmartDrive moves at a time. The default value is 8192 bytes, but you can use 1024, 2048, or 4096 bytes. The read-ahead buffer discussed next must be a multiple of the element size.

InitCacheSize   Replace *InitCacheSize* with the size of the buffer. If you don't specify an amount, Windows defaults to the values listed in the table given earlier.

WinCacheSize   Replace *WinCacheSize* with the minimum size Windows can reduce the cache to. Windows reduces the size to gain memory for itself. The default values are listed in the table given earlier.

/b:*BufferSize*   Replace *BufferSize* with the size of the read-ahead buffer. SmartDrive will read additional information from disk during a read, anticipating that the information will be needed in a later read. The default size of the read-ahead buffer is 16K. Its value must be a multiple of *ElementSize* and cannot be less than 1024 bytes or more than 32,768 bytes. Setting this value too high may unnecessarily clear other information in the cache.

Making the element size and read-ahead buffer size larger increases performance at a reduction in available memory. If you have 4MB or more of memory, try increasing the values. A fragmented file system will cause performance loss when these sizes are high, so make sure to optimize your drive often. Optimizing drives is covered in Chapter 12.

/L   Add the /L option to prevent SmartDrive from loading into upper memory blocks (UMBs), even if there are UMBs available.

/q   Add the /q option to hide the display of SmartDrive information when the command executes.

Stand-Alone Options

Type the following commands at the DOS prompt to display information about your system and SmartDrive.

/**c**   Type **SMARTDRV /C** at the DOS prompt to force SmartDrive to write its cache to disk. Use this option before shutting down your system if you think information is still in the cache. Note that if you wait a few seconds, SmartDrive usually writes its cache contents. SmartDrive watches the keyboard and intercepts the CTRL-ALT-DEL reboot key sequence, writing its data before allowing the system to reboot.

/**r**   Type **SMARTDRV /R** to clear the contents of the existing cache and restart SmartDrive.

/**s**   Type **SMARTDRV /S** to display additional information about the status of SmartDrive. A table appears showing which drives are cached.

/**?**   Type **SMARTDRV /?** to display online help about the SmartDrive command and options.

Double Buffering

The SmartDrive command has an option called *double buffering* that is used to provide compatibility for older bus mastering ESDI and SCSI disk controllers. This specific option is placed in the CONFIG.SYS file, not the AUTOEXEC.BAT file. When placed there, it does not install the cache; you still need a SmartDrive command in AUTOEXEC.BAT to do that. SmartDrive in CONFIG.SYS provides only double-buffer support. The option is covered in more detail in Chapter 12.

386 Enhanced Mode Virtual Memory

Virtual memory is a feature of 386 enhanced mode made possible by the special design of 80386 and 80486 processors. When an application uses virtual memory, part of its program code or data may exist either in physical memory or in a special swap file on a hard disk. Windows and its applications see the swap file as a continuous extension of RAM memory. The Virtual Memory Manager (VMM) swaps 4K pages of memory between RAM memory and the swap file as needed.

The VMM can free space in RAM if necessary during a swap by moving parts of existing RAM information to disk. A least recently used algorithm is used to determine which information in RAM is swapped to disk. In other words, unused page frames swap to disk, ensuring that most frequently used pages stay in RAM.

Virtual memory provides more memory to your applications than is physically available in memory. You can check how much memory is available in 386 enhanced mode by choosing the About Program Manager option on the Help menu in the Program Manager. If virtual memory is in use, you'll see a large figure for available memory, larger than your system's physical memory.

Virtual memory is ideal when working with applications that require a lot of memory. Many users switch from standard mode to 386 enhanced mode when they need to run applications, such as scanning software or graphics packages, that require more memory than their system has available. They then switch back to standard mode, which runs other applications faster.

The VMM handles virtual memory management in the background; all applications written for Windows are compatible with it.

You can place the swap file on any physical hard disk with available space. Typically, Windows Setup installs the swap file, but you can change the configuration of virtual memory and the location and size of the swap file at any time by choosing the 386 Enhanced icon in the Control Panel. The virtual memory swap file can be either temporary or permanent, as described next.

Temporary Swap Files

Windows creates a temporary swap file when you start in 386 enhanced mode. Windows then removes the file when you exit. Unlike a permanent swap file, it can shrink and grow in size, which is useful if you're running low on disk space. However, access to a temporary swap file is less efficient than a permanent swap file because the temporary swap file may not occupy a contiguous block of space on disk. However, Windows frees disk space for other uses by automatically removing temporary swap files every time you leave Windows.

The temporary swap file is named WIN386.SWP. It's located in the drive and directory you specify during setup. You should never delete this file while Windows is running, but if the file still remains on disk when Windows is not running (perhaps Windows crashed without removing the file), you may delete it.

Be sure the swap file drive has enough space to hold the swap file. Ideally, you could even dedicate an entire drive to the swap file. For example, you could create a 5MB or 10MB disk partition and use it exclusively for swapping. To change the location of the swap file, refer to the section on "Creating or Changing the Swap File" at the end of this chapter.

Permanent Swap Files

A permanent swap file maintains the same size and location on disk until you move it or remove it. Windows does not remove the file upon exit but does discard its contents. Because permanent swap files occupy a contiguous block of disk space, they are faster and more efficient than temporary swap files, but you must sacrifice the disk space they occupy. A permanent swap file can be no larger than the largest available block of contiguous space on a hard drive.

The permanent swap file has the name 386PART.PAR and uses the Hidden attribute, so you won't be able to see it in normal file lists. Windows always places the swap file in the root directory of the selected drive.

A swap file marked read-only can become corrupted. You must exit Windows and create a new swap file using the method described in the next section.

Creating or Changing the Swap File

To set up a temporary or permanent swap file, make sure Windows is running in 386 enhanced mode, then double-click the 386 Enhanced Mode icon in the Control Panel. When the dialog box appears, click the Virtual Memory button to display a dialog box similar to the Virtual Memory dialog box shown in Figure 10-2.

The Current Settings box displays the location, size, and type of the currently installed swap file. To change the location or type, make selections in the Drive or Type drop-down menus.

At the bottom of the dialog box, you'll see the available space, maximum size, and recommended size for a swap file. You can use the value that's already in the Approximate Size field, or type in a new value. When finished, click OK. At this point, Windows will recommend that you restart to make the new settings active.

Enable the Use the 32-Bit Disk Access option if your disk is Western Digital 1003-compatible and supports FastDisk as described in Chapter 12.

```
┌─────────────────────────────────────────────────────────────┐
│ ▭                    Virtual Memory                          │
│  ┌─Current Settings──────────────────────┐   ┌──────────┐   │
│    Drive:     I:                               │    OK    │   │
│    Size:      6,156 KB                         └──────────┘   │
│    Type:      Permanent (using 32-bit access)  ┌──────────┐   │
│  └────────────────────────────────────────┘   │  Cancel  │   │
│                                                └──────────┘   │
│                                                ┌──────────┐   │
│                                                │ Change>> │   │
│                                                └──────────┘   │
│  ┌─New Settings──────────────────────────┐    ┌──────────┐   │
│                                                │   Help   │   │
│    Drive:    [▱ i:              ▼]             └──────────┘   │
│    Type:     [Permanent         ▼]                            │
│    Space Available:          12,412  KB                       │
│    Maximum Size:             12,408  KB                       │
│    Recommended Size:          6,156  KB                       │
│    New Size:              [     6156] KB                      │
│  └────────────────────────────────────────┘                  │
│  ⊠ Use 32-Bit Disk Access                                     │
└─────────────────────────────────────────────────────────────┘
```

Figure 10-2.   The Virtual Memory dialog box

Tips for Using Swap Files

Remember that both temporary and permanent swap files work best when contiguous disk space is available. You should optimize your hard drive before installing a permanent swap file. Windows recommends a swap file size to fit in the largest contiguous space on the disk. If you are using a temporary swap file, periodically optimize the disk that holds the swap file for the best performance.

Windows adds the entry PagingFile=d in the [386Enh] section of the SYSTEM.INI file when creating a temporary swap file. The d parameter indicates the drive letter of the swap file. You can add a directory path to this entry if you want to locate the swap file in a location other than the root of the drive.

The file SPART.PAR in the Windows directory contains information about the swap file. If you happen to delete this file, Windows will create a default temporary swap file in the Windows directory. To reestablish the swap file on the drive of your choice, follow the procedures just described.

Don't swap to a network drive. It is inefficient and increases network traffic. Swap to a local drive only. However, if you're using a diskless workstation, be sure to install the swap file in a server directory that has both read and write attributes, and always locate each user's swap files in a separate directory (such as their personal directory) so they don't overwrite other users' files.

Chapter *11*

Updating and Customizing Windows

This chapter covers a number of methods for upgrading and customizing Windows. Most of the sections discuss Control Panel utilities. While the Control Panel automatically updates the WIN.INI file when you make changes, this chapter gives a number of additional settings that you can make in WIN.INI using an editor such as Notepad or SysEdit. After making these settings, you must restart Windows in order for your changes to go into effect.

Changing Hardware Setup

You'll use one of two utilities to change the setup of Windows hardware. Use the Setup utility to add or change the video, keyboard, mouse, or network drivers. To install other drivers, use the Drivers utility in the Control Panel. A third method of manually copying drivers and making updates to SYSTEM.INI is covered under "The OEMSETUP Procedure" later in this chapter.

The manual OEMSETUP procedure is preferable when the driver update disk contains files that are older than those on your system. For example, when installing a video driver, screen fonts are often copied with it. These font files may be older than the font files on your system. Before installing a driver, compare the dates of its files against those in your \WINDOWS\SYSTEM directory.

This chapter does not cover printer drivers. Use the Printers icon in the Control Panel as covered in Chapter 15.

The Setup Utility

You can run the Setup utility from Windows, or from DOS by first exiting Windows. To run Setup from Windows, double-click its icon in the Main group. To run it from DOS, first exit Windows completely, switch to the Windows directory, then type SETUP. You'll see exactly how to run Setup from Windows in the next section. Use Setup in the following situations: you can run Setup from Windows, but you'll still need to restart Windows to activate the changes, or you can run Setup from DOS (exit Windows first) in most cases. Windows won't let you install drivers that it's using, and to install new drivers, you would need to restart Windows to activate those drivers anyway.

Setup is also used to install Program Manager icons for applications, and to remove components (files) of the Windows system to gain hard disk space, but this can only be done by running Setup in Windows. This section will cover the upgrade procedures. Installing applications is covered fully in Chapter 18. If you need to remove any Windows files to make room on your hard drive, refer to Chapter 12.

Running Setup from Windows

Run Setup from Windows if you prefer to use the graphical user interface. (Remember that after making changes, you'll need to restart Windows in order to activate the changes.) Double-click the Setup icon to open the Windows Setup dialog box shown in Figure 11-1.

Choose Change System Settings from the Options menu. In a moment, you'll see the Change System Settings dialog box shown in Figure 11-2.

```
┌──────────────────────────────────────────────────────────┐
│ ▬            Windows Setup                              ▼ │
├──────────────────────────────────────────────────────────┤
│ Options   Help                                           │
├──────────────────────────────────────────────────────────┤
│ Display:      VGA                                        │
│ Keyboard:     Enhanced 101 or 102 key US and Non US      │
│ Mouse:        Microsoft, or IBM PS/2                     │
│ Network:      No Network Installed                       │
└──────────────────────────────────────────────────────────┘
```

Figure 11-1. *The Windows Setup dialog box*

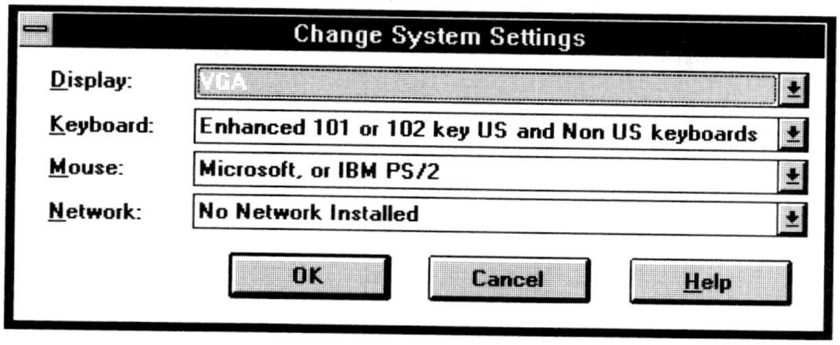

Change System Settings

Display:	VGA
Keyboard:	Enhanced 101 or 102 key US and Non US keyboards
Mouse:	Microsoft, or IBM PS/2
Network:	No Network Installed

OK   Cancel   Help

Figure 11-2.   *The Change System Settings dialog box*

To change any setting, click the down arrow button on one of the drop-down menus, then choose one of the drivers listed. The drivers listed in the drop-down list boxes are available on the Windows disks. At the bottom of each list is an "Other" item, which requires that you supply a disk from the manufacturer of the device. When you select a driver, Setup asks for the appropriate disk. If the driver is already on your hard drive, Setup asks whether you want to use it or install an updated version from a floppy disk.

The item "Other display (requires disk from OEM)" describes a disk from an Original Equipment Manufacturer. The disk should be included with the hardware you're upgrading. If it isn't, contact the manufacturer or obtain the driver from CompuServe or a similar bulletin board system.

Once the new drivers have been installed, you'll be asked to click a button that restarts Windows to initialize the new drivers.

Microsoft provides the Windows Driver Library (WDL), which contains a large number of device drivers released after Windows 3.1. Call Microsoft Customer Support Services at 800-426-9400, or call their electronic downloading service number at 206-637-9009.

The Drivers Utility

Drivers related to the multimedia and sound capabilities of Windows are installed using the Drivers utility in the Control Panel. Open the Control Panel and double-click Drivers to display the Drivers dialog box shown in Figure 11-3.

The Drivers dialog box contains a list of currently installed drivers. To upgrade (replace) existing drivers, first highlight the driver and click Remove. To add new drivers, click the Add button to display the Add dialog box shown in Figure 11-4.

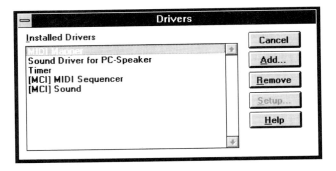

Figure 11-3.   *The Drivers dialog box*

Drivers are normally supplied with the devices you've installed in your system, but the Windows Driver Library may also contain the drivers (the telephone numbers for WDL are given in a note earlier in this chapter). Included on the WDL disk is SPEAKER.DRV, which lets you play .WAV digital sound files from your computer's internal speaker. Windows comes with four .WAV files that you can play by starting the Sound Recorder utility, assuming you have the speaker driver or a sound board installed.

To install new drivers, highlight a driver in the Add dialog box list, or choose "Unlisted or Updated Driver." Place the disk containing the driver in the floppy drive and click OK. Another dialog box appears that lists the drivers on the disk. There

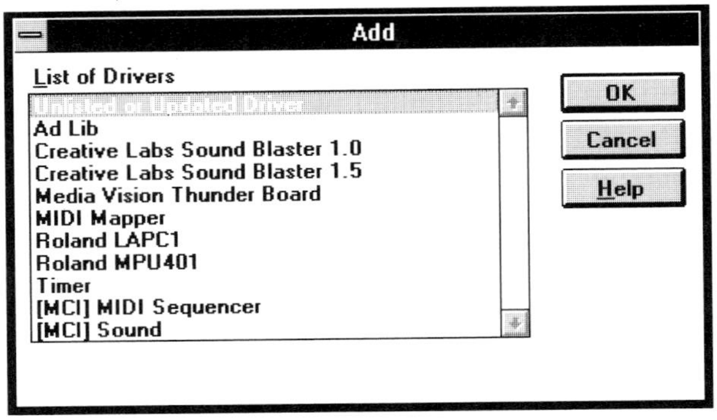

Figure 11-4.   *The Add dialog box*

may only be one. Highlight the driver to install and click the OK button. The driver is installed on your system, but you must reboot to activate it.

Some drivers require setup information, such as the interrupt and I/O port used. Check your device manual for information on these settings. To avoid conflicts with other devices in your system, use the MSD (Microsoft Diagnostic) utility discussed in Appendix F. For example, the speaker driver displays a dialog box in which you can adjust the loudness and pitch of speaker sounds.

The OEMSETUP Procedure

Using the Windows Setup or Drivers utility is not always the best way to install new drivers. It's sometimes best to install drivers manually to prevent the manufacturer's setup routine from copying old files over files on your system that are newer. This section describes the OEMSETUP procedure.

When you install a new driver using Setup or the Drivers utility in Control Panel, it asks you to place the disk containing the new drivers in the floppy drive. It then reads a file called OEMSETUP.INF. This file contains setup information, similar to the SETUP.INF that is used when Windows is installed, as described in Appendixes A and B.

OEMSETUP.INF contains a description of the drivers on the disk along with the names of files to copy and the changes to make to SYSTEM.INI. You can view the file to determine which changes to make, then manually make those changes to avoid problems that might be caused by letting your computer handle the setup.

Here's the OEMSETUP.INF file for the Speaker driver. Normally, you would install this using the Drivers utility; however, it's used here as an example because its contents are simple.

```
[disks]
1=. ,"",speaker.drv

[Installable.Drivers]
; key=filename,        type(s), description
pcwave=1:speaker.drv,  "Wave",  "Wave driver for PC speaker"
```

The first section called [disks] names the disk. In this case, it is assigned the number 1. This number is only important if more than one disk is required for setup; it names (numbers) each disk the setup routine will request. Following this number is the directory (in this case, the period means the root directory), and then the name of the file to copy (speaker.drv). A description is sometimes placed between the quotation marks.

The [Installable.Drivers] section contains two lines. The first is just a description or comment, as indicated by the semicolon. The second line provides a description of the line to add to SYSTEM.INI. The important keyword is under the type(s) column, which is "Wave" for this setup file. It specifies the name for the parameter you insert under the [drivers] section in SYSTEM.INI, as follows:

```
Wave=speaker.drv
```

Driver parameters are always included under the [drivers] section. Video display driver parameters would be included under the [display] heading. Here is a partial listing from an OEMSETUP.INF file for a video driver. (Note: these lines look confusing because they are word-wrapped in the file).

```
[disks]

    u =. ,"Graphics Accelerator Utilities Disk #1",oemdisk1

[display]

ULTRA=u:ultra.drv, "ULTRA: Normal 1024x768", "100,120,120",
u:vgacolor.gr2, u:vgalogo.lgo, u:vddultra.386, u:8514.gr3,,
u:vgalogo.rle
```

The first line names the disk "u". Under [display] is a profile of the video driver. Other profiles are often listed if the video driver supports different resolutions or color schemes. The descriptions in quotation marks are what appear in the drop-down list boxes when you install the drivers using the Setup utility. The file with the .DRV extension is the normal display driver and the file with the .386 extension is the video display driver for 386 enhanced mode. You copy these to your \WINDOWS \SYSTEM directory, then update the SYSTEM.INI file. The others are grabbers and logo files, which usually don't need to be copied if the files already installed on your hard drive are newer. For a further discussion of this process, see Chapter 13.

The OEMSETUP.INF file for video drivers will contain other lines that specify font files for Windows, or DOS running under Windows. Once again, these files may be outdated, so you won't want to copy them. Chapter 13 contains a more thorough discussion of this procedure.

Reinstalling, Upgrading, or Moving Windows

There are a few things you need to know if you plan to move your Windows files to a new directory, or if you plan to reinstall or upgrade Windows. This section describes the files that contain information about your specific setup and how you can preserve that setup if you move, reinstall, or copy over Windows.

Reinstalling and Upgrading Windows

You may need to reinstall Windows over the current copy for various reasons—for example, if files are corrupted and you're not sure which ones to replace, or if you want to install Windows with a new hardware configuration while retaining some of the old settings.

The Program Manager group files and Windows .INI files contain important information about your current setup and applications. The most important files are listed here:

- *Group Files*   Group files with the extension .GRP define the contents of each Program Manager group, including the startup parameters for each icon.

- *PROGMAN.INI*   The PROGMAN.INI file holds information about Program Manager groups such as which are open or minimized, and their location in the Program Manager window.

- *CONTROL.INI*   The CONTROL.INI file holds information about any custom changes made with the Control Panel.

- *WINFILE.INI*   The WINFILE.INI file holds information about File Manager options and directory windows.

- *SYSTEM.INI*   The SYSTEM.INI file contains hardware settings. If you reinstall Windows, the current settings are preserved. If you reinstall Windows to a new directory, transfer settings in this file to the new SYSTEM.INI file to preserve old settings.

- *WIN.INI and SYSTEM.INI*   These files hold hardware settings and information about the Windows interface, desktop, and application settings. The settings in the files are preserved during a reinstall. If you install Windows in another directory, transfer lines from the old files to the new files, depending on which settings you want to preserve.

- *Other*   .INI files are created by applications. Do a file listing to determine which are on your system and back them up before reinstalling. Microsoft is encouraging developers to create their own .INI files, rather than make entries into WIN.INI, so an .INI file may exist for each of your applications.

To manually transfer the settings in an old .INI file to a new .INI file in another directory, open both in separate side-by-side Notepad windows, then scan them. Copy lines from the old file to the new file using Clipboard commands. Save the files and restart Windows to activate the new settings.

Moving the Windows Files

Typically, Windows gets installed on the boot drive in a directory called WINDOWS. At some point, you may decide you would rather have the Windows files on a different drive, or perhaps you want a second copy of Windows that uses different startup settings. You need to copy the files, then make changes to the .INI files before Windows will start on the new drive.

The best way to copy the files is to use the File Manager. Open a window on both the source files and the new destination drive or directory, then drag the Windows Directory icon to the new drive or directory. Windows copies all the files and subdirectories.

Once the files are copied, make the following changes to ensure that Windows boots properly:

1. In CONFIG.SYS and AUTOEXEC.BAT, remove the old Windows directory path and add the new path. If you have two separate copies of Windows installed, each with different settings, be sure to change the path to the Windows directory before starting either copy. The path should point to the copy you want to run. It's not recommended that you keep both directories on the path, but if you must, make sure the copy of Windows you want to run is placed first in the path.

2. In CONFIG.SYS and AUTOEXEC.BAT, check for commands that loaded from the old Windows directory and change the path to point to the new directory.

3. Change the TEMP= variable in the AUTOEXEC.BAT file if the TEMP directory has changed.

4. Check the WIN.INI file for references to the old drive and path. The best way to make these changes is to search for the old drive letter, for example C, then replace it with the new drive letter. Be sure not to change the drive letters of programs that still exist in the old drive.

5. Change the settings in your other .INI files. Some examples are listed here:

    - DOSAPP.INI contains references to PIF files that are often stored in the Windows directory. Change the drive letter to match the new Windows directory.

    - PROGMAN.INI contains a list of .GRP files that hold group information for the Program Manager. Change the drive and directory reference of these entries.

    - WINFILE.INI is the File Manager's information file. It contains information about directory windows, which may not exist after you've rearranged your system. You can change WINFILE.INI, but it is often easier just to create new directory windows in the File Manager.

Customizing Windows

There are two ways to customize the Windows interface. You can open the Control Panel as shown in Figure 11-5, and use its utilities, or you can edit WIN.INI. Control Panel utilities automatically make changes to WIN.INI, but there are a few settings you can make only by editing WIN.INI directly using Notepad or another text editor. Each entry must be inserted under the appropriate heading. For example, the wallpaper settings (discussed later in this chapter) go under the heading [desktop] in WIN.INI.

Each Control Panel utility is described in the following sections. Note that those related to printers, ports, networks, and multimedia are covered in other chapters.

386 Enhanced   The 386 Enhanced mode icon appears in the Control Panel only if 386 enhanced mode is operational on 80386 and 80486 systems. Use it to control multitasking of non-Windows applications. This is more fully covered in Chapter 19.

Color   Use the Color utility to alter the foreground, background, border, and other color schemes of Windows.

Date/Time   Use the Date/Time utility to view or change the date and time.

Desktop   Use Desktop to change the colors and patterns of the background, install a screen saver, and to change blink rates, icon settings, and grid size.

Drivers   Use Drivers to install a CD-ROM drive, sound board, MIDI device, and other multimedia-related devices. It supplements the driver install routines of the Setup utility. Use Setup to install display, mouse, keyboard, and network drivers. Multimedia is covered in Chapter 14.

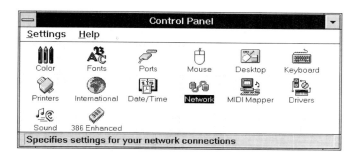

Figure 11-5.   *The Control Panel dialog box*

Fonts   Use Fonts to add, alter, and remove screen and printer fonts. Fonts are discussed more fully in Chapter 16.

International   Use International to change the keyboard, date, time, currency, number features, and formats to U.S. or international standards.

Keyboard   Use the Keyboard utility to change keyboard settings, like the repeat rate of keys.

MIDI Mapper   Use MIDI Mapper to configure settings and mappings for Musical Instrument Digital Interface (MIDI) devices. A MIDI device is typically an electronic keyboard synthesizer. Other MIDI devices include recording studio mixers and stage-lighting systems. MIDI devices are covered in Chapter 14.

Mouse   Use the Mouse utility to control the operating characteristics of the mouse.

Network   The Network utility icon appears if network support is loaded. It is used to control the connection between Windows and the network file system. Networking is covered in Chapter 17.

Ports   Use the Ports utility to change settings for parallel and serial connection ports as covered in Chapter 23.

Printers   Use the Printers utility to add and remove printers or change their settings, as covered in Chapter 15.

Sound   Use Sound to assign sounds to system events such as error messages or the sound you hear when starting or exiting Windows. You need a sound board to hear the sounds, or an optional driver to power your system's internal speaker. This topic is covered later in this chapter and in Chapter 14.

Changes made with Control Panel utilities are recorded in the WIN.INI file. However, Control Panel has its own .INI file called CONTROL.INI. This file holds information about custom configurations, colors, and patterns you create with Control Panel utilities. Since all lines in CONTROL.INI are created with Control Panel utilities, there is little need to manually edit CONTROL.INI yourself. You should include this file in your periodic backup, however, since it holds information about the custom changes you've made.

Screen Fonts

During Windows installation, Setup installs a set of fonts for your system based on the resolution of your display. These fonts are used in title bars, menus, and in some applications such as Notepad. You can change the fonts to make the display text smaller or larger.

Windows 3.1 also includes a new feature for displaying multiple sizes of fonts in DOS applications when you run those applications in a window in 386 enhanced mode. A Fonts option appears on the Control menu. You choose this option to change the size of both the fonts and the window for the application.

Windows Screen Fonts

Windows installs a set of screen fonts during installation based on the type of display resolution your system has. The text in title bars and menus uses these fonts. Don't confuse these system fonts with fonts used by applications to display your documents very close to how they will appear when printed. Windows has screen font sets for the following resolutions:

> EGA resolution (650x350)
> VGA resolution (640x480)
> 8514 resolution (1024x768)

While other resolutions, such as 800x600, are possible, Windows only supplies the fonts just listed. If you have an 800x600 resolution display, Windows installs the 8514 resolution fonts.

There are three types of fonts, as described here:

- *System font* A proportionally spaced font used to display title bar names and menu options. Depending on your display, the fonts are called EGASYS.FON, VGASYS.FON, or 8514SYS.FON.

- *Fixed font* Fixed-pitch characters used in applications such as Notepad and SysEdit that do not support proportional fonts. Depending on your display, the fonts are called EGAFIX.FON, VGAFIX.FON, or 8514FIX.FON.

- *OEM font* A fixed-pitch font related to the U.S. or foreign character set. OEM fonts contain special accented characters and symbols. Depending on your screen display, the fonts are called EGAOEM.FON, VGAOEM.FON, or 8514OEM.FON.

OEM fonts ending in 86x (such as VGA861.FON) contain foreign characters based on the language selected during setup.

You can change the fonts specified in SYSTEM.INI to make fonts larger on low-resolution screens, or reduce fonts on high-resolution screens. Reducing the fonts makes menus take up less space while enlarging fonts makes them easier to see. Locate the following entries in the [boot] section of SYSTEM.INI:

```
fonts.fon=
fixedfon.fon=
oemfonts.fon=
```

You'll see the name of the currently installed font file. For example, if you have a VGA display, you'll see VGASYS.FON, VGAFIX.FON, and VGAOEM.FON listed. To make the fonts smaller so they take up less room on a VGA display, change the lines to read as follows.

```
fonts.fon=EGASYS.FON
fixedfon.fon=EGAFIX.FON
oemfonts.fon=EGAOEM.FON
```

To make the fonts larger and easier to read, change the lines to read as follows.

```
fonts.fon=8514SYS.FON
fixedfon.fon=8514FIX.FON
oemfonts.fon=8514OEM.FON
```

Save the changes to SYSTEM.INI, then restart Windows to make the changes effective. You can experiment with these fonts by trying each of the different font files until you find one you like.

DOS Application Fonts

When you run a DOS application in 386 enhanced mode, you can place it in a resizable window by pressing ALT-ENTER. The application then appears in a window with a Control menu. Click the Control Menu button to display a list of options, then click the Fonts option to display the Font Selection dialog box shown in Figure 11-6.

Use the Font box to choose new screen sizes. The best procedure is to experiment with the sizes listed on the left. When you click a font, the Window Preview box shows how the window will be resized and the Selected Font box shows the size of the font. Click OK to make the changes. If you want to save the font size for all new sessions, make sure the Save Settings on Exit option is checked.

The fonts you select in the Fonts dialog box are contained in the file DOSAPP.FON (or APP850.FON if you selected a French-Canadian, Icelandic, Nordic, Multilingual, or Portuguese language during setup). In the future, other fonts may be available from Microsoft or third parties.

To install a new font, copy it to your Windows directory, using the Expand utility if necessary (Expand is discussed in Appendix C). Then change the following line in SYSTEM.INI to reflect the new font name, like this:

```
woafont=DOSAPP.FON
```

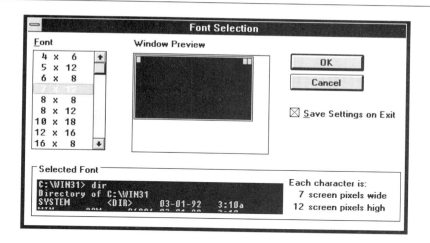

Figure 11-6.   *The Font Selection dialog box*

Changes made to the DOS application window size are stored in the file DOSAPP.INI. If you remove this file or it becomes damaged, the DOS application window reverts to its default size. Choose the size again using the same procedure. Windows will then reset the DOSAPP.INI file when you exit the application, assuming the Save Settings on Exit option is checked on the Font Selection dialog box.

Window Colors

Use the Color utility in the Control Panel to change the colors of window borders, title bars, backgrounds, text, menus, and other features. You can select a predefined color scheme or create your own. The background is the underlying desktop; you can do any of these things to it:

- You can change its color using the Color utility.

- You can install a repeating pattern on the desktop as discussed under the "Patterns" section later in this chapter. The colors of the pattern are set using the Color utility.

- You can overlay the desktop with a graphic image, as covered in the "Wallpaper" section later in this chapter.

Images and patterns on the desktop take up memory. If your system is low on memory, don't install them.

Changing the Color Scheme

You can change the borders, title bars, and other areas of windows using the Color utility in the Control Panel. A set of predefined color schemes is available, or you can create your own custom color schemes.

Double-click the Color icon in the Control Panel to display the basic Color dialog box shown in Figure 11-7. (There are two Color dialog boxes—a basic one and a full one.) Use the basic dialog box to select a predefined color scheme. Press the UP ARROW or DOWN ARROW key on the keyboard to scroll the list. Each color scheme is displayed as you scroll. You can also click the down arrow button on the Color Schemes list box to see a list of color schemes.

When you find a color scheme you like, click OK or press ENTER. The dialog box closes and the new color scheme is installed.

Creating Custom Color Schemes

Windows comes with the color schemes listed in the Color Schemes box as discussed previously. Each color scheme has its own name. If you can't find a combination you like in this list, you can create your own by clicking the Color Palette button in the Color dialog box. Doing so displays the full Color dialog box shown in Figure 11-8.

 It's easiest to choose a color scheme in the Color Schemes list box that is close to the scheme you want to create, then alter it and save it under a different name.

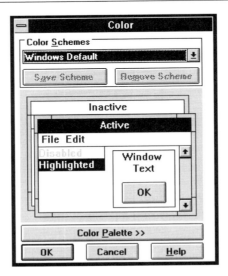

Figure 11-7.   *The Color dialog box*

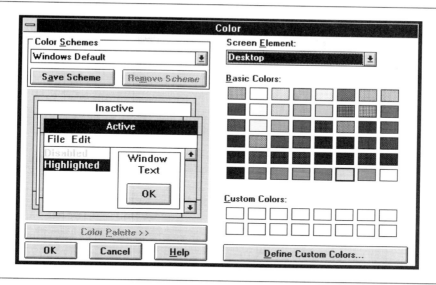

Figure 11-8.   *The Color dialog box with the Color Palette button clicked*

The procedure to create a custom color scheme is to click the window element you want to change (border, title bar, and so on), then click a new color for it from the Basic Colors palette. Once a color is created, save it by clicking the Save Schemes box and name it. Let's take it step by step.

Start by selecting a screen element. Click on that element in the sample window scheme on the left, or press the DOWN ARROW key on the keyboard to scan the list of elements in the Screen Element drop-down list box. If the box is not highlighted, click its down arrow button with the mouse. The Basic Colors palette indicates with a bold box the color currently assigned to the element you've selected.

With the element name in the Screen Element box, click a color in the Basic Colors palette. The sample window scheme changes to reflect your new color selection. After creating a new color scheme, click the Save Scheme button. Type the new color scheme name in the dialog box that appears and press ENTER.

Mixing Custom Colors

You can mix your own colors if those in the Basic Colors field don't suit your needs. Click the Define Custom Colors button to display the Custom Color Selector window as shown in Figure 11-9.

You use the slider bars and text boxes to adjust your color's mix of red, green, and blue (RGB color model), or hue, saturation, and luminosity (HLS color model). When you click the Add Color button, the custom color is added to one of the 16

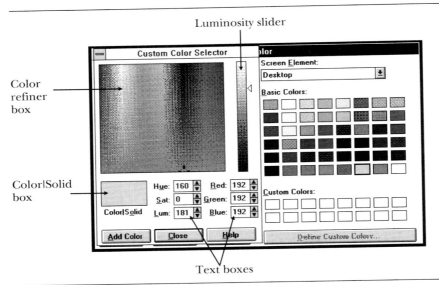

Figure 11-9.   *The Color dialog box with the Custom Color Selector button clicked*

Custom Color boxes in the lower-right corner of the Color dialog box. The Custom Color Selector screen consists of the following:

- The color refiner box in the upper-left portion of the screen.

- The luminosity slider bar in the upper-right section of the screen.

- The Color|Solid box in the lower-left portion of the screen.

- The text boxes (Hue, Sat, Lum, Red, Green, Blue) in the lower-right portion of the screen.

Click the color refiner box and drag the pointer to select different colors. You can also slide the luminosity arrow up or down to adjust the color's brightness. As colors are adjusted, their color values are listed in either the Red/Green/Blue (RGB) text boxes or the Hue/Sat/Lum (HSL) text boxes.

The RGB Color model defines colors with values from 0 to 255 with 0 indicating the minimum intensity and 255 the maximum intensity. The HSL Color model defines colors with values in the range of 0 through 240. The terminology of the HSL Color model is explained here:

- *Hue* relates to the intensity of red, blue, or green in the color and corresponds to a horizontal movement across the color refiner box.

- *Saturation* relates to the purity of a color (or its lack of gray) and to a vertical movement of the cursor in the color refiner box.

- *Luminosity* is the brightness of a color on a scale from black to white, with 0 being black and 240 being white.

The value of a color is known as its *RGB triplet* or *HSL triplet*. When all colors are set to 0, the color is black. When all colors are set to 255 (RGB) or 240 (HSL), they are at their maximum brightest and the color is white. Anything in between is a custom color. Table 11-1 lists the RGB and HSL triplets for the standard colors and their common mixes.

Because some monitors are incapable of displaying the full range of colors supported by Windows, a dot pattern is used to approximate the color as closely as possible. This is called dithering. As you select colors, the Color|Solid box displays the dithered color on the left and the closest non-dithered solid color on the right. Once you've found a color you like, click either the dithered or solid color. The color then replaces the selected color in one of the 16 Custom Color boxes.

Some applications, like Paintbrush, are incapable of displaying the full range of colors and revert to the solid 20 colors provided by Windows' default palette.

Use the text boxes to enter specific color values, make fine adjustments, or to simply note the value of a color for future reference. The values are important if you want to create a similar color later, or in another application. Some of the options in WIN.INI that can't be set from the Control Panel require RGB color values. You can use the Color utility to determine RGB triplets for any color, then open WIN.INI and make those changes manually.

Color	RGB Triplet	HSL Triplet
White	255,255,255	240,240,240
Red	255,0,0	0,120,240
Green	0,255,0	80,120,240
Blue	0,0,255	160,120,240
Yellow	255,255,0	40,120,240
Magenta	255,0,255	200,120,240
Cyan	0,255,255	120,120,240
Black	0,0,0	0,0,0

Table 11-1.   *RGB and HSL Triplets for the Standard Colors and Their Common Mixes*

If screens are printed on a black-and-white printer, dithered patterns appear as black-and-white-dot patterns. You can use this to simulate gray-scaling on your printer by adjusting the Printers Setup utilities Intensity control as discussed in Chapter 15.

To create a color with the mouse, start by placing the luminosity pointer about halfway up the scale, then in the color refiner box point to the color that's closest to the color you want. Click and drag the mouse in the refiner box or slide the luminosity pointer to make adjustments to the color. The Color|Solid box displays the dithered or solid version of the color.

As an experiment to see how hue, saturation, and luminosity relate to the position of the mouse pointer in the refiner box or luminosity bar, click and hold the up or down arrow buttons in Red, Green, or Blue text boxes to change their values.

To add the new color to the Color window, select either the dithered or solid color in the Color|Solid box, then click the Add Color button. To add the color to a Custom Color box of your choice, or to overwrite an existing custom color, click the Custom Color box before clicking the Add Color button.

Be sure to click the Close button to leave the Custom Color dialog box, then click the OK button to leave the Color dialog box. Your changes are then saved.

Patterns

The desktop pattern is an 8x8 pattern of dots that is repeated over the desktop surface. You can change patterns by making a selection in the Pattern box of the Desktop utility, as shown here:

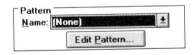

To install a pattern, make a choice from the Name drop-down list box, then click the OK button in the Desktop dialog box. The pattern is repeated over your desktop. Before you decide to keep this pattern, look at the titles of icons on the desktop. If they are illegible due to the pattern, change or remove the pattern, or install wallpaper instead, (you'll see how to use wallpaper shortly).

You can have a pattern and wallpaper installed at the same time; however, wallpaper will always overlay the pattern and both together will use a lot of memory.

Editing a Pattern

You can view patterns before placing them on the desktop or create a new pattern by opening the Edit Pattern dialog box shown in Figure 11-10. Click the Edit Pattern button in the Pattern field to edit patterns.

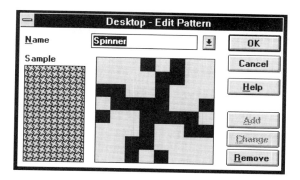

Figure 11-10. *The Desktop dialog box with the Edit Pattern option active*

Press the DOWN ARROW key on the keyboard to scroll through the list of existing patterns. As you scroll, a sample pattern appears in the Sample box on the left. The middle box displays an enlarged view of the pattern. To change the pattern, click in this box with the right mouse button. You'll see that white areas convert to black and black areas convert to white. As you edit a pattern, the Sample box changes to show the new view.

After editing a pattern, use one of the options detailed in the following sections to save or remove it.

Change   Click the Change button to save an existing pattern that you've edited under its current name.

Add   Click the Add button to save an edited pattern under a new name. To do so, begin typing a new name in the Name box; the Add button then becomes available.

Remove   Highlight a pattern name in the Name box and press the Remove button to remove that pattern.

Changing the Color of a Pattern

If you have a white background, the pattern is black over white. To change the pattern colors, open the Color utility and change either or both of the following settings to a color you find more pleasing:

- The Windows Text setting determines the color of the pattern.

- The Desktop setting determines the color that shows through the pattern.

Wallpaper

The Wallpaper box in the Desktop dialog box is shown here:

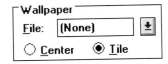

Use this option to place a bitmapped image on the desktop. Bitmapped images are those created in programs such as Paintbrush. There are several images included in the Windows directory that you can try placing on the desktop. Click the File box's down arrow button to display a list of files.

Some of the wallpaper patterns are shown in Figure 11-11. These images are designed to be tiled, which means they are spread out over the surface of the desktop much like tiles on a floor. Choose one of the patterns by selecting it in the File box, then click Tile. Click the Desktop OK button to install the pattern on the desktop.

If you are short on memory, don't use wallpaper. It can take as much as 164K to display a bitmapped picture on the desktop.

Creating Your Own Wallpaper

The bitmapped images used for wallpaper were created in Paintbrush. That means you can load the wallpaper files in Paintbrush for editing. For example, you could change the colors of an existing wallpaper, or combine it with another wallpaper. Try the following example to see how CHITZ.BMP can be combined with MARBLE.BMP. If you're not familiar with Paintbrush, refer to Chapter 22.

1. Open CHITZ.BMP in Paintbrush.

2. Use the Cutout tool to completely surround the image, then choose Copy from the Edit menu.

3. Open MARBLE.BMP in Paintbrush.

4. Choose Paste from the Edit menu in order to paste the Chitz image over the Marble image.

5. Move the upper image until you're happy with the way the underlying Marble pattern shows through.

6. Use the Color eraser to convert the underlying blue in the marble to red, yellow, or any color you like.

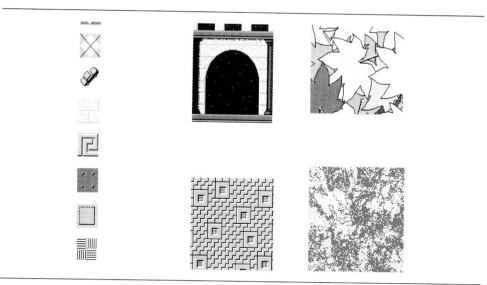

Figure 11-11.   *Wallpaper patterns*

7. When done editing the image, use the Pick tool to surround the overlying Chitz image. Try to be exact since the edges are matched when the image is repeated on the desktop.

8. Save it to a new file by choosing Copy To from the Edit menu.

It's important to use the Copy To command when saving tiled images. Doing so saves only the selected portion so tiles "connect" correctly when placed on the desktop. Using the Save option would include the entire image, including the extraneous marble around the Chitz pattern.

You can use Paintbrush to create a large image that fits on the entire desktop. You can also obtain images from friends or bulletin boards, or scan them using hand or desktop scanning devices. Techniques for working with graphic images are covered in Chapter 21. Here are a few examples of how you might use wallpaper:

- Place your company logo on the desktop.

- Create a list of common keystrokes used in Windows or its applications.

- Scan pictures of your kids and create a collage that includes their birth dates.

- Create a list of important telephone numbers in Paintbrush and place them on the desktop.

- If you're working on a project, place the time table of events on the desktop.

- Create a wallpaper with reference information, such as weights and measures, metric conversions, formulas, and tables.

- Create an "Out to Lunch" or "I'm out for the day" banner.

While these desktop references may not be as visually exciting as the graphic images supplied with Windows, they are definitely more functional.

Saving Wallpaper Files

Public domain utilities such as WinGif (SuperSet Software) and PaintShop (JASC Software) provide a way to convert .BMP files to .RLE (Run Length Encoded) compressed files, substantially reducing the amount of disk space required to store graphic images. To use .RLE files as wallpaper, type the complete name of the file in the Wallpaper File box. Only files with .BMP extensions appear in the File drop-down list box.

Wallpaper Orientation

You can adjust how wallpaper is placed on the desktop by adding or editing in your WIN.INI file the two options listed next. Enter these options in the [desktop] section.

WallpaperOriginX=   Set the WallpaperOriginX= option to the value in pixels that you want the wallpaper image offset from the left edge of your screen. The default value is 0.

WallpaperOriginY=   Set the WallpaperOriginY= option to the value in pixels that you want the wallpaper image offset from the upper edge of your screen. The default value is 0.

Note the following:

- If both of these options are used and Center is selected in the Wallpaper field of the Desktop dialog box, a single non-repeating image appears in the upper-left corner of the screen. The underlying desktop color appears around the top and left side of the image as a border, based on the X and Y placement.

- If only one option is used and Center is selected in the Wallpaper field of the Desktop dialog box, the image remains centered along the opposite axis that has not been redefined with an offset.

- When Tile is selected in the Wallpaper box of the Desktop dialog box, the image repeats over the entire screen. There is no blank border at the offset. The offset merely determines where the image starts repeating.

- When Tile is selected, use the options to adjust where the repeating image starts on the screen. Try experimenting with ARCHES.BMP. You can adjust the X and Y coordinates so the base of the arch aligns with the bottom of your screen or the center of the arch aligns with the left edge of your screen.

To make changes to the X and Y coordinates in WIN.INI effective without restarting Windows, open the Desktop dialog box and temporarily specify a different wallpaper file. Click the Desktop OK button to update the desktop. Changing the file is necessary to make Windows use the new settings. You then change back to your previous wallpaper file after the new X and Y settings have been read.

Icons

The Windows Program Manager uses icons to display applications and utilities. When an application is active, its icon appears on the desktop. This section discusses icons, how to change them, how to create new ones, and how to alter how they appear on the desktop.

Changing an Application's Icon

Application icons are changed in the Program Manager when you first create a new Startup icon, or after an icon already exists. When creating a new icon, the Program Item Properties dialog box appears, as discussed in Chapter 6. This same box appears if you click an existing icon and choose the Properties option on the Program Manager File menu. You then choose the Change Icon button to display the Change Icon dialog box shown. Figure 11-12 shows the icons available in the PROGMAN.EXE file. For this example, the MS-DOS icon prompt was clicked, Properties was selected from the Program Manager File menu, and the Change icon button was clicked. You can see that the MS-DOS Prompt icon uses PROGMAN.EXE, but this can be changed to pick from a list of other icons.

To scan other lists, type the name of a file containing a list of icons, or click the Browse button. When you click the Browse button, files with the extensions .ICO, .EXE, and .DLL are listed. To pick a new icon, scroll the slider bar until the icon comes into view. Click the icon, then click the OK button.

Choose the file MORICONS.DLL to select from a list of third-party application icons.

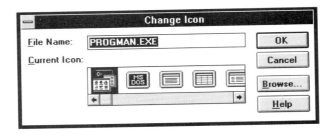

Figure 11-12.   *The Change Icon dialog box*

Creating or Obtaining New Icons

Icons exist in the .EXE files of many Windows applications. You can search for new icons by opening the Change Icon dialog box and specifying the .EXE file that contains the icon list. You can also click the Browse button to scan for .EXE files. For example, if you have Microsoft Excel, click the Browse button, then select the Excel directory. Open each of the files listed to view available icons.

The .ICO file format contains icons created with an icon editor such as IconDraw, which is available in the Microsoft Resource Kit. If you don't have IconDraw or a similar utility, you can obtain them from dealers, bulletin board services, or local users groups. Furthermore, most bulletin boards usually have a large selection of pre-made icon files, so you may never need to use an editor.

Icon Spacing

Icon spacing is used to control the horizontal spacing between icons, whether they are on the desktop or in Program Manager groups. The current setting for your display can be found in the Icons box of the Desktop utility. To change the spacing, enter a new value in the Spacing text box as shown here:

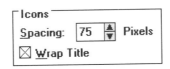

The icon spacing value sets the *horizontal icon spacing*, or the distance between icons in a row, between icons on the desktop, or icons in Program Manager groups. After setting a new value, choose Arrange Icons on the Program Manager's Window menu. To rearrange icons on the desktop, double-click a blank portion of the desktop to open Task List, then click the Arrange Icons button. The IconSpacing= option in

WIN.INI holds the current icon spacing value, but you should always change it with the Desktop utility.

You'll need to increase icon spacing if you enlarge the font for the icon titles as explained in the following sections.

Vertical icon spacing is the amount of space between an upper and lower icon. Vertical spacing can be controlled by adding or editing the IconVerticalSpacing= option to the [desktop] section in WIN.INI. This value cannot be set from the Desktop utility. For example, to increase the vertical spacing to 30 pixels, add the following line to WIN.INI:

```
IconVerticalSpacing=30
```

Changing the Font, Size, and Style of Icon Titles

You can change the font, size, and style of the text used to display icon titles. Doing so may require that icon horizontal and vertical spacing be increased as described in the previous section. To make font changes, add or alter the following options in the [desktop] section of the WIN.INI file:

Icon Font   To change the font of the icon, use the IconTitleFaceName= option. The default font is MS Sans Serif. If you're not sure what the font names are, you can get a listing by opening any Fonts dialog box, for example the one in Write. Write down the name of the new font, then type it exactly as listed in the IconTitleFaceName= entry. For example, to change icon fonts to Arial, insert the following line in the [desktop] section of WIN.INI:

```
IconTitleFaceName=Arial
```

Icon Font Size   To change the size of the font, specify a size using the IconTitleSize= option. The default value is 8, but you can specify any value for the font listed in the common Fonts dialog box as described in the previous paragraph. For example, to change the font to 10 points, insert the following line in the [desktop] section of WIN.INI:

```
IconTitleSize=10
```

Icon Font Style   You can set the style of the icon font to bold with the IconTitleStyle= option. The default is regular, which is a value of 0. To change the font to bold, insert the following line in the [desktop] section of WIN.INI:

```
IconTitleStyle=1
```

Icon Wrap

By default, Windows wraps icon titles that are too wide to fit in the spacing width defined by the current icon spacing. Only titles with multiple words are wrapped. You can turn icon wrap off, although there is little reason to do so. Open the Desktop utility and click the Wrap Title check box in the Icons box to disable icon title wrap.

If a title doesn't want to wrap between the word gap, click the icon, choose Properties from the Program Manager File menu, then add an extra space to the gap between words in the Description field.

Screen Savers

A *screen saver* blanks your screen after a specified period of time and displays moving objects or messages. This prevents screen burn, which can occur if an image is left on the screen too long. Moving the mouse or pressing a key on the keyboard restores your screen.

Use the Screen Saver options on the Desktop dialog box to specify the type of screen saver and the time interval of nonactivity that must pass before a screen saver takes over the screen. To install a screen saver, open the Desktop dialog box to see the Screen Saver field shown here:

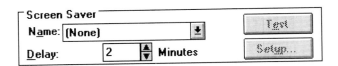

Click the down arrow button in the Name box, then highlight a screen saver, such as Starfield Simulation. Once you've selected a saver, you can test it by clicking the Test button. To stop the test, move the mouse or press any key on the keyboard.

Select the other screen savers and click the Test button to see how they look. The Marquee screen saver has unique features that are covered separately later in this chapter. To install a screen saver, set the desired delay time in the Delay box, then click the OK button on the Desktop dialog box.

Customizing a Screen Saver

You can change the parameters of a screen saver by selecting it, and then clicking the Setup button. For example, select the Starfield screen saver in the Name field of the Screen Saver box, then click Setup. The Starfield Simulation Setup dialog box shown in Figure 11-13 appears.

You can adjust any of the following settings in the Starfield Simulation Setup dialog box. (For a more complete description, click the Help button.)

- Adjust the Warp Speed slider to change the speed of the moving starfield.

- Change the value in the Starfield Density box to increase or decrease the number of stars.

- Set a reentry password in the Password Options field. With this option set, Windows asks for the password before restoring the normal screen. Use this option only if leaving your system for more than several minutes; it is a hassle to retype your password every time your screen blanks.

- Click OK, then click the Test button to see the changes.

You can also make changes to the settings of the Mystify and Marquee options. A complete description of their setup options can be found on the help menu after you click the Setup button. The options for Marquee are discussed later in this chapter.

Setting a Password

Screen saver passwords prevent others from accessing your system, an important issue if an application is left running and should not be disturbed or you have a screen arrangement others shouldn't change. If you're working at your system and expect long periods of nonactivity, extend the delay time of the screen saver.

To add or change a password, follow these steps:

1. Choose a screen saver from the Screen Saver Name box, then click the Setup button.

2. Click the Password Protected check box to make the Set Password button available, and then click the Set Password button.

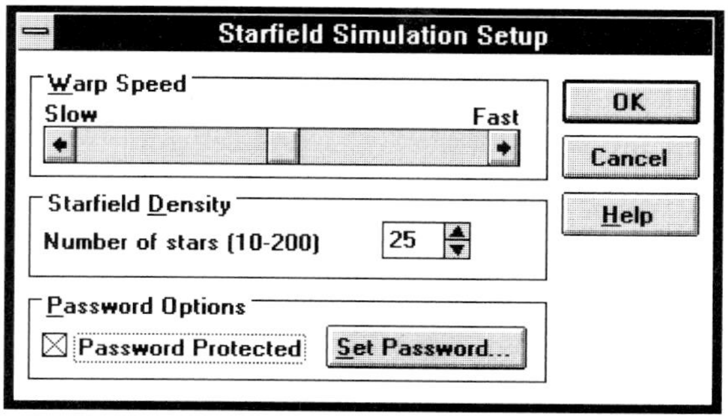

Figure 11-13.   *The Starfield Simulation Setup dialog box*

3. When the Change Password dialog box appears, type a password in the New Password field, then retype it in the Retype New Password field and click OK or press ENTER.

If a previous password was set, you need to type that password in the Old Password field before you can change it.

If You Forget the Password

If you forget the password for a screen saver, you'll need to restart your system to get back into Windows. A small problem occurs when you try to create a new password. You can disable the password completely, but if you want to create a new password, you must first type the old password, which you've presumably forgotten. To get around this, remove the Password= line from the [ScreenSaver] section of CONTROL.INI, and restart Windows. You'll then be able to create a new password.

Creating a Marquee

Use the Marquee screen saver to create a message that scrolls across the screen. The most useful way to use Marquee is as a screen prompt for a demonstration package. For example, the message might say "Press a key to see a demo." Another example might display the opposite message, such as "Hands Off!" or "Don't turn me off" if your system is working on an important task that shouldn't be interrupted.

To create a marquee, select Marquee from the Name drop-down list box in the Screen Saver field. The Marquee Setup dialog box appears. From the Marquee Setup dialog box, you can set these features:

- Select a font and size in the Text Type and Size box.

- Select a text and background color in the Color box.

- In the Position box, choose where you want the text to scroll—either across the center or randomly on the screen.

- Select a speed for the scrolling marquee in the Speed box.

- Type the text you want to display in the Text box.

- If you want a password, fill out the Password Options box as described previously.

Click OK or press ENTER to save the changes and return to the Desktop dialog box. Set a delay if necessary in the Delay box. To test the marquee, click the Test button, then press any key to return to the Desktop dialog box. Once the marquee looks the way you want it to, click the OK button or press ENTER to close the Desktop dialog box and execute the changes.

Sounds

You use the Sound utility to assign sounds to system events, such as when Windows starts or an error occurs. To hear the sounds listed in the Sound utility, install a sound board or the optional Microsoft speaker driver as discussed in the section "The Drivers Utility" earlier in this chapter.

The Sound dialog box is shown in Figure 11-14. Click one of the events in the Events box on the left, then click the sound that you want to assign to that event from the Files box on the right. Click the Test button to hear the sound. When all events have the sounds you want, click the OK button. Sound is discussed further in Chapter 14.

The Keyboard Settings

Use the Keyboard utility to adjust the settings of the keyboard. You can adjust the *delay*, which is how long a key is held down before it starts repeating, and the *repeat rate*, which is how fast the key repeats as you hold it down. To change the delay and repeat rate, double-click the Keyboard icon in the Control Panel to display the Keyboard dialog box shown in Figure 11-15, and follow the instructions in the next sections.

Delay   Drag the Delay Before First Repeat slider button left to increase the time before a key starts repeating when held down. Drag it right to decrease the delay.

Repeat Rate   Drag the Repeat Rate slider button left to decrease the speed that the key repeats when held down. Slide it right to increase the speed. Test the new settings by clicking the Test box and holding down a key.

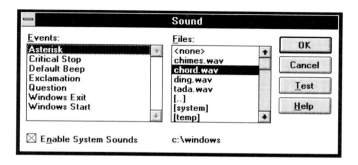

Figure 11-14.   *The Sound dialog box*

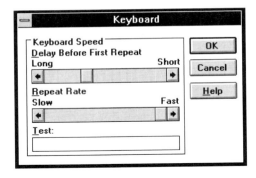

Figure 11-15. The Keyboard dialog box

Setting the Date and Time

To set a new date and time, double-click or select the Date/Time icon on the Control Panel. Double-click on the portion of the date or time to change, then type a new value. Alternatively, click the up or down arrow button to change the values.

Mouse

To change the functions of the mouse, double-click the Mouse utility on the Control Panel. The Mouse dialog box shown in Figure 11-16 appears.

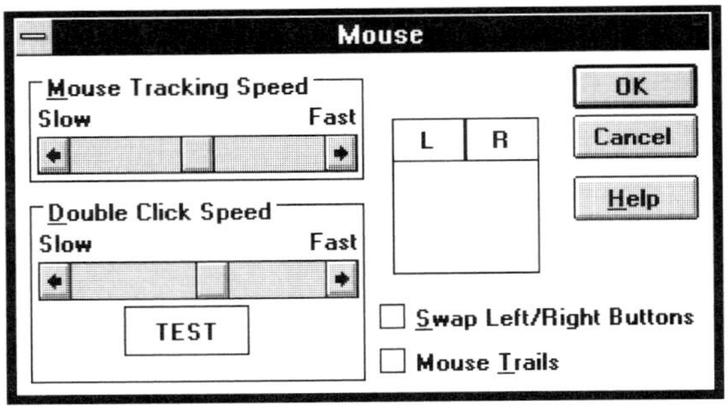

Figure 11-16. The Mouse dialog box

Tracking Speed   Drag the Mouse Tracking Speed slider button left or right to adjust the speed that the mouse pointer moves across the screen in relation to the movement of the mouse. After adjusting the speed, drag the mouse to see how the new setting affects the tracking speed. Adjust the slider button further, if necessary. Try a slow tracking speed if you are a new mouse user, or if you're working on precise graphic images.

Double-Click Speed   Drag the Double Click Speed slider button left or right to adjust when Windows registers a double-click of the mouse button. After adjusting the slider button, double-click in the Test box to check the new setting. The box turns black when it registers a double-click.

Button Swap   If you are left-handed, you can swap the functions of the left and right mouse buttons by clicking the Swap Left/Right Buttons check box. The right button then becomes the button used for the majority of tasks, such as selecting items and executing commands.

Mouse Trails   Enable the Mouse Trails option if you have a liquid crystal display and are having trouble following the mouse. This option leaves a trail of mouse pointers that slowly fade so you can more easily locate the pointer.

After making changes to the Mouse dialog box, click the OK button to save the changes.

Mouse Options in WIN.INI

Most of the mouse options are set with the Mouse utility in the Control Panel. WIN.INI holds two additional options that determine how far the mouse can move between double-clicks. These options are useful if a user has trouble holding the mouse steady while double-clicking, or if you're working on a high-resolution screen. Include the options under the [windows] heading in WIN.INI.

- *DoubleClickWidth=* Set this option to the maximum width in pixels that the mouse pointer can move between double-clicks.

- *DoubleClickHeight=* Set this option to the maximum height in pixels that the mouse pointer can move between double-clicks.

The default setting for both options is four pixels. If the mouse pointer moves out of the specified range, the clicks are treated as two separate single clicks.

Mouse Troubleshooting

If you're having trouble with your mouse, check for these potential troublemakers:

- If the mouse pointer is not active in a non-Windows application resizable window when running 386 enhanced mode, set the MouseInDOSBox= option to 1.

- For a serial mouse, make sure it is connected to COM1 or COM2. COM3 and COM4 do not support a mouse. Open the Ports utility and make sure the settings for the port match those used by the mouse.

- Run the Setup utility to make sure the correct mouse driver is installed. You may need to obtain the latest driver from the mouse manufacturer.

- Make sure the mouse interrupt does not conflict with an interrupt used by another device. Write down the interrupt setting of your other devices for comparison or use the MSD utility described in Appendix F.

Miscellaneous Features

The following features provide ways to further customize Windows.

Windows Border Width

You can adjust the width of window borders to make it easier to differentiate between windows on the desktop. To adjust the width, open the Desktop utility and change the value in the Border width box. The default setting is three pixels. If you have a high-resolution display, or are having trouble clicking on borders to resize a window, increase the border width by a few pixels.

Granularity (Sizing Grid)

The *granularity* of the desktop determines the density of an invisible grid on the desktop that windows snap to when moved or resized. The granularity is initially 0, but you can set it from 1 to 49, with each increment representing eight pixels. To get an idea of pixel size, note that the default border width is 3 or 24 pixels. Generally, setting a granularity of 1 is useful because it makes windows align more evenly and keeps your desktop looking tidy.

To set granularity, open the Desktop dialog box in the Control Panel, then click the up arrow or down arrow button to change the value. Click the OK button to save the changes. At the desktop, try moving windows around with the new granularity settings. If you have a high-resolution display, it may be useful to set a granularity value of 5 or greater.

Drag Full Window WIN.INI

The WIN.INI option DragFullWindow= is used to change what a window looks like when you're dragging it with the mouse. The default setting is 0, which makes the window appear as a gray outline when dragged. When set to 1, the complete image of a window drags with the mouse. Add this line to the [windows] section of WIN.INI if it does not already exist.

Switching Methods

There are three ways to switch among windows:

- Press CTRL-ESC to open the Task List.

- Press ALT-ESC to switch to each window, one after another.

- Press ALT-TAB repeatedly to view the titles of open applications. Release the keys when the title you want to use appears.

You can change the switch method of the ALT-TAB key by opening the Desktop utility and removing the check mark from the Fast "Alt+Tab" Switching option. This saves time because when you then switch with ALT-TAB, the title bar appears for each window, but the entire window is not painted on the screen. Set this option if you need to see part of the window during switching. The CoolSwitch option in WIN.INI holds the value of this setting.

Cursor Blink Rate

You can increase or decrease the blink rate of the cursor so the cursor is easier to locate when you're editing documents in Windows Write or other Windows applications. To change the blink rate, open the Desktop dialog box in the Control Panel, then drag the slider button in the Cursor Blink Rate box. As you adjust the blink rate, watch the blinking cursor on the right until it is set the way you want. Click the OK button or press ENTER to set the new blink rate.

Modifying the Help System

Use the following WIN.INI options to customize the Help system. The first four settings, listed next, are automatically changed when a help window is moved or resized. The settings are then used the next time a help window is opened. You probably won't need to adjust these manually, but if you want more information, refer to WININI.WRI. If you find a help window position and size you like, you can write the values down for future reference in case they change.

M_WindowPosition=	The position and size of the main help window
H_WindowPosition=	The position and size of the History window
A_WindowPosition=	The position and size of the Annotate window
C_WindowPosition=	The position and size of the Copy window

The remaining settings control the colors used by various aspects of the help window. Colors are defined by their red, green, and blue components, or RGB triplet, as discussed earlier in the "Window Colors" section. To determine the RGB triplet of a color, open the Color utility, find a color you like, then note the values in the Red, Green, and Blue text boxes. Use these values when adding or changing one of the following options in WIN.INI:

Option	Meaning
JumpColor=	The color of text you can click to jump to a new panel of help information
IFJumpColor=	The color of text you can click to jump to a new help panel in a different help file
PopupColor=	The color of text you can click to show a pop-up panel (like those used for a glossary reference)
IFPopupColor=	The color of text you can click to show a pop-up panel (like those that are used for glossary references) in a different file
MacroColor=	The color of text you can click to run a help macro

Common RGB values are listed in Table 11-1 in the "Window Colors" section. For example, to make the JumpColor text red in a help file, insert the following line in the [help] section of WIN.INI:

```
JumpColor = 255 0 0
```

Changing the Shell

Now that you've worked with Windows for a while, you're probably used to seeing the Program Manager and its icons appear every time you start Windows. The Program Manager is the default *shell* for Windows. It is the opening program and the one you use to exit Windows. It provides an excellent interface and a quick way to start your applications. However, you don't have to run the Program Manager as your shell; there are good reasons for changing it. While the Program Manager works well, you should evaluate the possible benefits of using other shells.

For example, you could make the File Manager the shell. Then when Windows started, you would have immediate access to all the files on your system. Recall that any program or associated file icon in the File Manager can be double-clicked to start the program or load the file, just as in the Program Manager. In fact the File Manager lets you see more of these files than you can conveniently display in Program Manager. In the File Manager, you can even create directory windows that hold various groups of files for easy selection, as shown in Figure 11-17.

Notice that the left window lists the accessory files in the Windows directory, the middle window lists system files, and the right window holds a directory tree for quick access to other directories and files. You could also use a program such as Microsoft Word for Windows or Excel as the shell. This is useful if you're setting up machines for users who don't need to access other Windows applications, such as temporary employees or students in a word processing class.

The Exit option on the new shell exits you from Windows since the Program Manager is no longer the shell.

To change the shell, specify the new program name using the shell= option in the [boot] section of SYSTEM.INI. For example, to make the File Manager the new shell, edit the shell= line to read as follows:

```
shell=fileman.exe
```

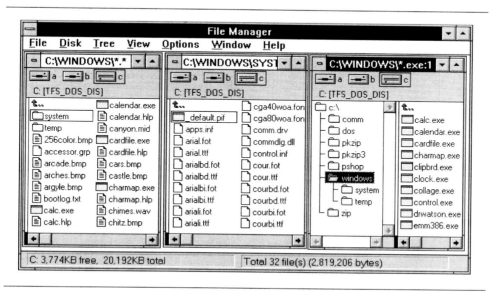

Figure 11-17. *Files displayed in the File Manager*

Chapter *12*

Hard Disks

Your hard disk is probably the slowest component in your system. Of course, floppy drives are even slower, but you don't use them on a continuous basis as you do a hard drive. Therefore any discussion of hard drives eventually turns to methods of improving performance. Using a disk caching program such as SmartDrive will improve disk access tremendously, and has the added benefit of reducing disk wear since the disk is accessed less often.

This chapter discusses hard drive technology and what you need to know if upgrading. It also covers methods for improving the performance of your current hard disk. Since you can't actually make your drive faster unless you upgrade, the goal of disk management is to reduce the amount of time Windows spends accessing the disk. SMARTDRV.EXE and RAMDRIVE.SYS can help you achieve that goal, but there are other methods as well.

A Hard Disk Primer

A *hard disk* consists of internal, magnetically coated platters that store digital information. As the platters spin, a read/write head moves incrementally back and forth over each surface to read and write data. Each incremental move of the read/write head defines a circular track. Tracks are similar to the tracks on an LP record, except that they're not one continuous spiraling loop. Each track forms a distinct circle as defined by the "stepping" of the read/write head.

Tracks are divided into *sectors*, which hold a specific amount of information, usually 512 bytes. A typical hard drive may have from 300 to 2400 tracks per inch and 17 to 26 or more sectors per track. Most of today's drives more than double the sector count of earlier personal computer drives, providing increased storage and access time. Access time has improved with today's drives because more information passes under the read/write head with every spin. The ability to push more data through the transfer lines from a hard drive to a computer system has improved as processor performance has increased data handling abilities.

Hard disks rotate at a constant rate of 3600 revolutions per minute. If sectors hold 512 bytes of information each, you can determine exactly how much information a read/write head can access or transfer as follows.

(rpm x sector size x number of sectors)

Early modified frequency modulation (MFM) drives used in personal computers have transfer rates of 5 megabits per second. Newer drives use advanced methods of encoding data, essentially packing it closer together. While sector size has remained the same, the number of sectors per track has increased from 17 to 26 or higher. Such drives have transfer rates in the 7.5 megabits-per-second range. The biggest benefit, however, is an increase in storage capacity by 50 percent. The encoding scheme used to pack data is defined by the controller card, but a drive must be capable of reading and writing the compressed data, as discussed next.

Encoding converts patterns in bits into codes, rather than storing the information literally bit-by-bit.

Hard Disk Controllers and Encoding Schemes

The hard disk controllers interface and drive combinations determine the method and potential amount of information you can store on a disk. When information is stored on a magnetic disk, tiny magnetic particles on the surface orient themselves toward one of two magnetic poles. The two alignments are used to represent binary data. A flux is the measure of the magnetic field produced by the particles. Encoding schemes are used to reduce the number of flux changes required to store a byte of information on a disk. These encoding methods are commonly used:

- *Modified Frequency Modulation (MFM)* MFM can store 512 bytes per sector and 17 sectors per track with transfer rates of 5 megabits-per-second.

- *Run Length Limited (RLL)* RLL can store 512 bytes per sector and 26 sectors per track, a 50 percent increase over the MFM method with transfer rates of 7.5 megabits per second.

- *Advanced RLL (ARLL) and Enhanced RLL (ERLL)* ARLL and ERLL are less common, but provide yet another increase in data compression and storage.

The hard drive interface defines the methods used to pass information from the hard disk to its controller, and eventually to system memory and the processor. Applications then access information in memory. They never go directly to the hard drive, but instead make requests to DOS for disk services such as reads and writes. The hard drive itself is often rated by its *access time*, which is the time it takes to move the head to a track and read the data. The very fastest drives operate in the 9 millisecond (ms) range, but a more typical rate is about 15 ms. Older hard drives like those used in the IBM XT were rated at 85 ms.

Windows 3.1 provides enhanced disk performance in 386 enhanced mode with FastDisk, a 32-bit hard disk driver that talks directly to the hard disk controller, bypassing slower DOS and BIOS routines. FastDisk can be enabled if your hard disk is compatible with the Western Digital WD1003 interface standard. (See the section on FastDisk later in this chapter.) Almost 90 percent of drives made for personal computers are compatible with this standard, including most ST506, ESDI, and IDE drives. Before purchasing any drive, make sure it is Windows 3.1 FastDisk compatible.

The ST506 Interface

The ST506 drive interface was one of the first to appear in personal computers. It was designed by a company that later became Seagate Technologies. The ST506 interface typically uses MFM encoding when writing data, and delivers data transfer rates of about 5 megabits per second. If RLL encoding is used, data storage and transfer rates increase. ST506 controllers were commonly used on 80286 and early 80386 systems, but are decreasing in popularity because of their slow transfer rates.

The ESDI Interface

The Enhanced Small Device Interface (ESDI) is similar to the ST506 interface, but provides 512 bytes per sector and 34 sectors per track with transfer rates in the 10 to 15 megabits-per-second range. ESDI is an improved, high-speed ST506 interface. ESDI systems are usually high-capacity drives with storage capabilities greater than 100MB. Up to two ESDI drives may be attached to an ESDI controller. ESDI drive technology is decreasing in popularity with the use of IDE drives, as discussed in the section following the SCSI interface.

The SCSI Interface

The Small Computer System Interface (SCSI) differs radically from the ST506 and ESDI interface. It allows up to seven devices such as hard disks, tape drives, and CD-ROM drives, to share the same SCSI interface card, which takes up only one slot in your computer. The card provides a shared bus that all peripherals use to pass data to and from the system. The bus is 8, 16, or even 32 bits wide and supports transfer rates that exceed other standards, giving it the ability to handle faster drives as they are developed and produced. A new SCSI standard called SCSI-II provides even faster throughput of data.

The SCSI interface adapter is not really a controller, but a *host adapter*. That means it provides *bus services* (a connection point) for intelligent devices. Intelligent devices such as SCSI disk drives contain their own control circuitry. In the ST506 and ESDI world, this control circuitry is built on the controller card. The SCSI adapter monitors data throughput and commands between the system and the SCSI devices. Each device handles only the requests assigned to it, not those of other devices. Since the control circuitry is built into each SCSI device, configuration and compatibility issues are minimized. You simply plug the device into an SCSI controller and run.

The IDE Interface

The Intelligent Drive Electronics (IDE) interface is a hybrid that combines features of the other interfaces and offers some new features of its own. IDE interfaces were originally designed as low-cost alternatives to the ESDI drives. However, like SCSI, IDE devices have their own control circuitry. They attach to an IDE adapter, which is usually inexpensive and often built right on to the motherboard, thus saving a slot. An IDE adapter supports only two devices, however. Because IDE is relatively inexpensive to implement, most of the low-priced systems on the market today use it. Don't think that because IDE costs less it is inferior to the other interface methods; when both price and performance are considered, the IDE is probably superior. The IDE interface operates at around 4MB per second, close to the SCSI rate.

A typical IDE drive has an access rate of 16 ms. Some have built-in intelligent caches to improve performance. Systems that use AT ROM BIOS-compatible chip sets will accept IDE drives because the drives provide some backward compatibility with the ST506 standard that was implemented in early IBM PCs. In addition, Windows 3.1 FastDisk supports IDE drives because they are compatible with the Western Digital WD1003 controller. The IDE interface supports two drives and has a 16-bit parallel interface.

There are several implementations of IDE. The AT bus implementation is known as the AT attachment, or ATA interface. Another implementation is for Micro Channel Architecture (MCA).

Obtaining More Information

To obtain more information about hard drive technologies or upgrading your hard disk, consult the following sources:

James McGrath, "The Incredible Shrinking Disk." *Byte Magazine,* October 1991, pp. 255-264.

Winn L. Rosch, "Choosing and Using Hard Disks." *PC Magazine,* December 31, 1991, pp. 313-331.

Robert W. Kane, "SCSI, An Interface Whose Time Has Come." *PC Magazine,* October 16, 1990, pp. 341-347.

Roger C. Alford, "The IDE Hard Disk Drive Interface." *Byte Magazine,* March 1991, pp. 317-324.

For another good source, call the Corporate Data Center in Sunnyvale, California at (408) 737-7312 to purchase *The Hard Drive Bible.* This is a three-ring binder with specifications and configuration information on hard drives.

Evaluating Hardware

If you're buying a new hard drive for your system, the interface design is important, but so is the drive's capacity and speed. Since Windows is a graphical interface, chances are you'll be working with graphic images that require large amounts of disk space. If you work with multimedia sounds and images, you'll need even more disk space. Several years ago, 100MB drives were the high end for personal computer systems. Today, drives in the range of 300MB are more practical for users who create large graphic, sound, and multimedia files.

When evaluating drive performance, the actual speed of a drive may be hard to determine. There are many variables and ways for manufacturers to rate their drives. SCSI drives currently deliver the best performance, but are expensive. IDE drives may be your best choice since they maintain compatibility with older interface designs, have high capacity and speed, and are relatively inexpensive. Refer to one of the articles mentioned earlier to help you with your purchasing decision.

Newer hard drives automatically *park* themselves, which means the heads move away from the data area when the drive shuts down. Non-parking drives require you to run a utility that parks the heads before shutting the system down. This is usually most important if you anticipate moving the system.

A Stepper Motor Versus a Voice Coil System

Hard drives use either a stepper motor or a voice coil actuator to position the read/write heads. A *stepper motor* system relies on a mechanical positioning system to move the head in discrete increments. The mass of the mechanical head places limitations on the speed at which it can access tracks. In addition, the stepper motor mechanism has positioning limitations that minimize track density and limit the capacity of the drive.

Voice coil technology is more expensive than stepper motor technology and provides more accurate positioning on high-performance drives. A *voice coil* positioning system uses magnetic force to move the read/write heads, in the same way an audio speaker reacts to the changes in the magnetic state of its voice coil. Voice coil drives are accurate and react quickly, which makes them ideal for high-capacity drives. To maintain accurate track alignment, a prerecorded pattern on the disk is monitored by the drive's electronics. The drive's read/write heads are constantly and accurately repositioned to maintain alignment to the tracks based on this prerecorded pattern.

The Servo Feedback System

This pattern, often called the *servo feedback system*, is often written on one dedicated side of the drive's platter system. You'll see drives with four disks and eight heads, but only seven heads read and write data. The other head monitors the servo information. If you find a drive with specifications that list an odd number of heads, you can be sure it's a voice coil drive.

The following sections provide other tips for improving the performance of your system.

Caching Controllers

Hard disk controllers with built-in caches are becoming more prevalent. A caching controller stores hard disk data in RAM caches on the controller itself, dramatically boosting access rates. Caching controllers provide features similar to SmartDrive, but usually with better performance since the cache is optimized for the controller and drive. If a caching controller is used, you should disable SmartDrive in most cases. Check with the hard drive manufacturer to determine the optimal way to set up a disk caching system.

Many caching controllers can protect your data if the system should crash, unlike software caching routines. The data that's in a hardware cache is written to disk immediately because the card is able to stay active for the few seconds it needs to write the data after the system has gone down. Any data in a software cache in system memory is lost when a system crashes.

Hard drives are often overrated concerning data transfer rates through the bus. The ratings are written as if the information were immediately available from the drive, that is, in a disk cache. Unless a hard drive controller has a large built-in cache to hold all the information a program needs, it is not running at top bus speeds. Some drives have 32K and 64K buffers, but these are often unintelligent holding areas, not managed caches that anticipate future requests. Many IDE drives come with 256K of RAM on the drive circuit board and provide routines to intelligently cache the disk. That means the cache management software may bring additional disk data into the cache when it physically reads the drive. This anticipation of future data needs reduces physical disk access if the cache manager has preloaded data that is needed later.

Interleaving

Older personal computers such as the IBM XT were relatively slow at writing and reading information to and from a hard drive. If two consecutive sectors of information were needed, the systems would read the first sector, but be incapable of reading the next contiguous sector because the system was still processing the first.

The *interleaving* of data sectors allows slower systems to accurately handle the data stream from fast drives. An interleaved drive skips over sectors, which gives the system a brief interval of time to process the data stream. For example, a drive with 3-1 interleaving skips two sectors. It reads or writes to sector 1, then sector 4, then 7, and so on. As the performance of systems increases, the need for interleaving decreases. 80386 or 80486 systems can handle the normal non-interleaved data transfer rate of a fast hard drive.

The important consideration is to ensure you're not using an interleaved drive on a system that can handle non-interleaved data transfers. Using interleaving when you don't need it reduces performance by introducing pauses in data transfer.

If you're using ST506 drives and controllers, check the interleave to make sure it is set properly for your system. While you may not be able to use a 1-to-1 interleave (basically no interleave), you can often use a reduced interleave that provides a boost in performance. Check with your system's manufacturer to determine the best interleave, how to check it, and how to change it. They may have interleave recommendations to properly match your drive with your system. Alternatively, you can use the utilities listed here to analyze your drive and determine the proper interleave:

- Calibrate in the Norton Utilities

- Spinrite II from Gibson Research

- Mace Utilities from Fifth Generation Systems

If you decide to change the interleave, you'll need to back up the data on your drive and completely reformat it. This formatting must include a low-level format that establishes the new interleave pattern. Low-level formatting completely erases all data on the drive and, in the case of IDE drives, should only be performed at the factory. Use caution when you low-level format drives. There are various parameters and settings you must set to format the drive properly. *The Hard Drive Bible* mentioned earlier provides a good description of both low-level and high-level formatting routines for different types of drives.

FastDisk

FastDisk is a 32-bit driver that operates in the 16-bit world of Windows 3.1. It is a sample of what we can expect from future releases of Windows that will support 32-bit operations more fully. FastDisk bypasses DOS and BIOS for all disk access, including the swap file used when Windows is running in 386 enhanced mode. FastDisk can be installed if your controller is Western Digital WD1003 compatible (the majority of the drives on the market are). Note that boards that follow the WD1003 standard usually have additional features that improve performance beyond the original standard.

 Microsoft decided against automatically installing FastDisk, because it is incompatible with some battery-powered portable computers. Your system may support FastDisk, but if you're not sure and you want to try it, first back up all the data on your drive.

To determine if FastDisk is installed, or to install it, check the virtual memory section in the 386 Enhanced utility. Open the Control Panel, double-click the 386 Enhanced icon, then click the Virtual Memory button. You'll see a dialog box similar to the one shown in Figure 12-1.

Indicates that FastDisk is providing 32-bit disk access

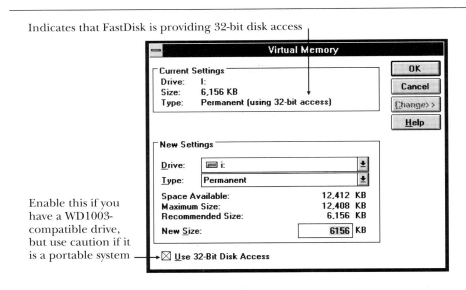

Enable this if you have a WD1003-compatible drive, but use caution if it is a portable system

Figure 12-1. *The Virtual Memory dialog box displays the status of the FastDisk option and lets you install it if necessary*

The Current Settings field indicates one of the following in the type field:

- Using DOS

- Using BIOS

- Using 32-bit access (FastDisk is running)

The last setting indicates that FastDisk is installed. The Use 32-Bit Disk Access check box will also be checked. If it is not, you can check it to install FastDisk, but only if your disk supports it.

Two lines in SYSTEM.INI also indicate that FastDisk is running. Look for the following line in the [386Enh] section of SYSTEM.INI. The first line is set on when you enable 32-bit access on the Virtual Memory dialog box. The second indicates the use of interrupt 13, and the third shows that the Western Digital compatible interface is present.

```
32BitAccess=ON
device=*int13
device=*wdctrl
```

The fact that you use the Virtual Memory dialog box to view FastDisk settings does not imply that virtual memory and FastDisk are one and the same. You can disable virtual memory and still use FastDisk, or vice versa. If you disable FastDisk, the 32 Bit Access option is set off, but the other options remain in the SYSTEM.INI file.

There may be problems using FastDisk with drives over 500MB in capacity. Check with your drive manufacturer for details.

The list of compatible FastDisk drives was incomplete at this writing. A few are listed next. The technical updates that you can order using the coupon at the back of this book provide a more complete listing of compatible drives and FastDisk specifications.

- Compaqs with IDE drives (386s or above) or ESDI drives.

- Conner IDE and Conner CP3204F drives.

- Seagate ST1293, Maxtor LXT-535A, and Maxtor 200MB IDE drives.

- Ultrastor drives, unless the track-mapping feature is used to support drives over 504MB. This inhibits the use of FastDisk since its track mapping depends on Int13, which FastDisk uses.

More About FastDisk and 32-Bit Access

FastDisk is actually part of a system that lets Windows components work directly with hard drives. It is more properly referred to as the 32-bit disk access system. In fact, the component installed in the SYSTEM.INI file to support FastDisk is called WDCtrl and Int13, not FastDisk.

The main purpose of 32-bit disk access is to allow Windows to transfer information directly to and from a hard drive, rather than go through the disk BIOS (Basic Input/Output System), which can slow performance. Without such access, when an application needs information from the disk, it follows the procedure below and pictured in the following illustration.

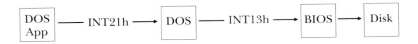

1. The application requests disk service from DOS (using an INT 21H call). (Note that an interrupt (INT) is a request for attention.)

2. MS-DOS determines where to access the information on disk and makes a call (using INT 13H) to the disk BIOS, which can talk directly with the disk controller.

3. The disk BIOS then provides disk services to the application.

FastDisk replaces the disk BIOS and talks directly to the disk controller. It watches for INT 13H calls and intercepts them if it can handle the calls itself, otherwise it passes them on to the BIOS for normal handling. By handling these calls, FastDisk speeds disk access when Windows runs in 386 enhanced mode. It also provides some additional benefits. For example, it lets you run more MS-DOS applications and improves system performance if those non-Windows applications are running in the background.

It is advantageous to bypass the disk BIOS because it provides slow service from the disk. Bypassing the BIOS with a well-written routine provides the first level of disk performance improvement. The second improvement is that disk access can be handled in the protected mode of Windows, which adds all sorts of benefits related to how non-Windows applications can access the disk and run in a multitasking environment. Recall from Chapter 8 that Windows and Windows applications running in enhanced mode use the protected mode of the 80386 and higher processors. This allows them to access more memory and take advantage of features like virtual memory and multitasking. However, DOS applications alone don't have this benefit. When you start a DOS application in 386 enhanced mode, a virtual 8086 machine is created that has 640K of memory and that runs in real mode.

When a DOS application running in Windows needs to access the disk, a series of events occurs similar to that described earlier, except that Windows gets involved in every step to ensure that the operations are correct. Several switches between virtual mode and protected mode take place as Windows checks the calls made by the applications and DOS to the BIOS. All this switching takes time and DOS itself spends a lot of time trying to figure out what to do with the calls. FastDisk helps minimize all the switching by intercepting the INT 13H call that DOS makes to the BIOS. It then handles the disk input and output in protected mode using enhanced routines. The following illustration shows how FastDisk is inserted into the disk access scheme.

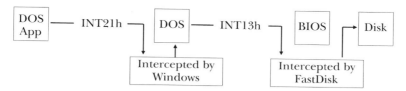

There are some added benefits provided by 32-bit access. One of those is the ability to page non-Windows applications in and out of memory in the same way that Windows applications are paged. *Paging* is a method of moving part of an application that is not in use out to disk in order to free memory for other uses. Before 32-bit access was available, a non-Windows application had to be kept entirely in memory to prevent conflicts when accessing the BIOS. Picture an application that has been partially paged to disk making a request for some disk service to the BIOS. This service requires that the part of the application paged to disk be replaced in memory. Since only one call can be made to the BIOS at a time, making the first call prevents the second call from being made. But the first call can't complete until the second call is complete. It's a no-win situation and the system will most likely lock up.

Windows' 32-bit access solves this problem by handling the BIOS request itself and handling multiple requests at once. This means that a DOS application can now page itself in and out from disk and still make other types of disk requests, just like normal Windows applications. In other words, both Windows and non-Windows applications can use all the virtual memory available to Windows, paging themselves out to disk to make physical RAM accessible to other applications that need it. This prevents out-of-memory messages that would occur when non-Windows applications used all physical RAM (because they could not be paged out to disk). When non-Windows applications use most of physical RAM, Windows applications suffer because they must constantly swap themselves in and out from disk, due to the low amount of memory. This makes the system run more slowly. By allowing non-Windows applications to be paged, 32-bit access improves system performance. Switching between non-Windows applications (using ALT-TAB) also improves because the whole application does not need to be reloaded in memory.

32-Bit Access Components

The following components make up the 32-bit access system. You will find entries for them in the SYSTEM.INI file.

WDCtrl   This is the FastDisk device that works with the standard Western Digital 1003 or ST507 hard drive controllers. This device is only installed if Setup detects a compatible hard drive controller.

BlockDev   This device works between devices that call block I/O services and the FastDisk device, which provides services for specific hard drive controllers. This device is always installed.

PageFile   This device handles the virtual memory paging files and calls through BlockDev if any FastDisk devices are available. It is always installed.

Int13   This device traps and emulates INT 13h BIOS calls by calling BlockDev. It is only installed when a FastDisk device is present (in other words, WDCtrl).

WDCtrl is the FastDisk device supplied by Microsoft. However, other manufacturers may supply FastDisk-like devices of their own to support their equipment.

Potential 32-Bit Access Problems

You should be aware that there are some exceptions to systems that can use WDCtrl. Some hard disk controllers appear to be Western Digital 1003 compatible, but are not. In addition, some portable computers that power down a hard drive to conserve battery power may cause problems. If the drive is tracked by WDCtrl and it is powered down, then powered back up, serious disk write problems can result. Because of these exceptions, Setup does not automatically set FastDisk on, but if you determine that your drive is compatible, you can enable it using the Virtual Memory dialog box as discussed earlier.

Published lists of WDCtrl drives will no doubt be available from many sources. You can order the update notes with the coupon at the back of this book, for example. Always check with the manufacturer of your hard drive if you are not sure about its compatibility.

ESDI and SCSI Drives

When a disk controller supports bus mastering, it takes over the bus on the system so it can directly transfer data to or from system RAM. Many SCSI disk controllers provide this feature. When running Windows in 386 enhanced mode, the read or write address that is passed to MS-DOS is sometimes not the same as the actual physical address, causing data to be written incorrectly. A Microsoft-created standard called *Virtual DMA Services* provides an interface for bus mastering cards that prevents this problem.

However, some older bus mastering cards are not compatible with Virtual DMA Services. As a remedy, Microsoft added a memory buffering feature to SmartDrive that ensures the physical and virtual addresses will be the same when using incompatible bus mastering cards. The SmartDrive double-buffering option shown here is inserted in the CONFIG.SYS file during Windows installation if such drives are found.

```
DEVICE=SMARTDRV.EXE /DOUBLE-BUFFER
```

Note that the option is placed in CONFIG.SYS and does not install a cache. The AUTOEXEC.BAT file contains its own SmartDrive command to install the cache.

Windows installation attempts to determine the need for double-buffering. If it is unable to do so, Windows installs the command in CONFIG.SYS to be safe. Double-buffering is usually required on any drive with a BIOS dated before 1989. However, most drives, including all MFM, RLL, and IDE controllers, do not need double-buffering. Only some ESDI and SCSI devices need this feature.

SmartDrive can display the status of drives to help you determine whether double-buffering is needed. Type **SMARTDRV** at the DOS prompt to display a table similar to the following:

```
Microsoft SMARTDrive Disk Cache version 4.0.091
Copyright 1991,1992 Microsoft Corp.

Cache size: 1,048,576 bytes
Cache size while running Windows: 1,048,576 bytes

             Disk Caching Status
drive    read cache   write cache    buffering
_____

  A:        yes          no            no
  B:        yes          no            no
  C:        yes          yes           no
  D:        yes          yes           yes
  E:        yes          yes           -

For help, type "Smartdrv /?".
```

The last column lists the buffered status of each drive. A Yes indicates that double-buffering is needed, and No indicates it is not. A dash (—) indicates that SmartDrive was unable to determine the need for double-buffering. You should then call the manufacturer of the drive to determine whether you need the option or not. All MFM, RLL, and IDE controllers do not need double-buffering. Only some

ESDI or SCSI drives do, so you should contact the manufacturer of your drive for verification.

If you're not sure whether your ESDI or SCSI drive requires double-buffering, install the command in the CONFIG.SYS file until you can be sure. There will be a slight degradation in performance and a loss of 2.5K of conventional memory.

If a SCSI drive is installed, make sure the following option is in the [386Enh] section of SYSTEM.INI. It prevents Windows from terminating hard disk controller interrupts. When off, interrupts are processed by the ROM.

```
virtualHDIRQ=false
```

CD-ROM Drives

CD-ROM drives have been a part of personal computers for several years, but their use is only just now taking off. This is largely due to an increase in the number of available "CD-ROM titles" and a decrease in the price of CD-ROM drives. Now that Windows supports multimedia, and the industry has defined specifications for a Multimedia Personal Computer (MPC) that include sound and video, the use of CD-ROM is bound to soar. Software vendors are already taking advantage of this by supplying applications on CD-ROM that contain many additional utilities, sample files, and graphic images, due to the large amount of space on the disk.

To provide support for CD-ROMs, DOS requires that the MSCDEX.EXE driver (Microsoft MS-DOS CD ROM extension) be loaded in the CONFIG.SYS file. This driver provides the extensions necessary to access the CD-ROM drive. You should always use version 2.21 of MSCDEX with all configurations of CD ROM drives.

The following setting is required in the [386Enh] section of SYSTEM.INI only if you have a version earlier than 2.20 of MSCDEX. If you have a version later than 2.20, remove this line.

```
device=lanman10.386
```

Manufacturers of CD-ROM drives and sound boards that support the Windows multimedia extensions supply drivers you install using the Control Panel Drivers utility. Refer to your documentation for details.

Windows supports the use of CD-ROM drives for basic file access, but improved specifications are required to meet the Microsoft Multimedia standard. These are outlined here:

- CD-ROM extensions (MSCDEX.EXE) version 2.20 or later

- Average seek time of 1 second or less

- Sustained data transfer rate of 150K bytes per second with limited use of the CPU

The data transfer rate ensures that data streams of the CD-ROM move at a rate sufficient for coordinated motion and audio, yet leave ample processing power to manipulate the data. At most, the CD-ROM drive can use 40 percent of the processor's time.

Optimizing Your Hard Drive

Optimizing your hard drive can improve its performance and free up disk space. It involves removing unnecessary files, checking for and removing corrupted files, and then unfragmenting the disk using backup-and-restore methods or a third-party disk optimizing program. These techniques are all covered in this section.

Cleaning Up Your Disk

Scan your system for files that are no longer of use, or that were left by a terminated application. Use the DIR command at the DOS level, or open the File Manager in Windows and use different file-listing methods on the View menu to scan files. Some of the files you can remove (or back up to floppy disk) are listed here:

- Files that remain in the TEMP directory if that directory is on your hard drive. Only remove these files after exiting Windows.

- Files that start with ~WOA. These are application swap files. Only remove these files after exiting from Windows.

- Files that end in .BAK. These are the most recent backup copies of files you have edited or changed.

- Windows components listed in the Add/Remove Windows Components dialog box. Start the Setup utility to access this dialog box, as discussed next.

Removing Windows Components

The Setup utility includes the option Add/Remove Windows Components. You use this option to remove Windows files you don't need, such as sample Paintbrush graphics files or help files. You should only perform these steps if you're extremely low on disk space or if you are sure you'll never use the components.

Start by opening the Setup utility. Double-click its icon in the Main group. Choose Add/Remove Windows Components from the Options menu. In a moment, the Windows Setup dialog box in Figure 12-2 appears.

You can remove an entire set of components, such as Games, by clicking its check box on the left. To remove individual files, click the Files button on the right for the component group that contains the files. When you're done specifying files to remove, click the OK button.

Running CHKDSK

Before continuing with the next section, run the DOS CHKDSK command to fix and remove lost files. These are incomplete files that were left when an application terminated or your system lost power. CHKDSK renames the files using a numbering scheme. The first file is FILE0001.CHK, the second is FILE0002.CHK, and so on. You use an editor or the TYPE command to view the contents of each file and determine if they are worth saving.

Run the CHKDSK command only from DOS, after exiting Windows. Do not run CHKDSK from a windowed DOS prompt, as some incompatibility may exist between CHKDSK and Windows. Type the following command to find lost clusters:

CHKDSK /F

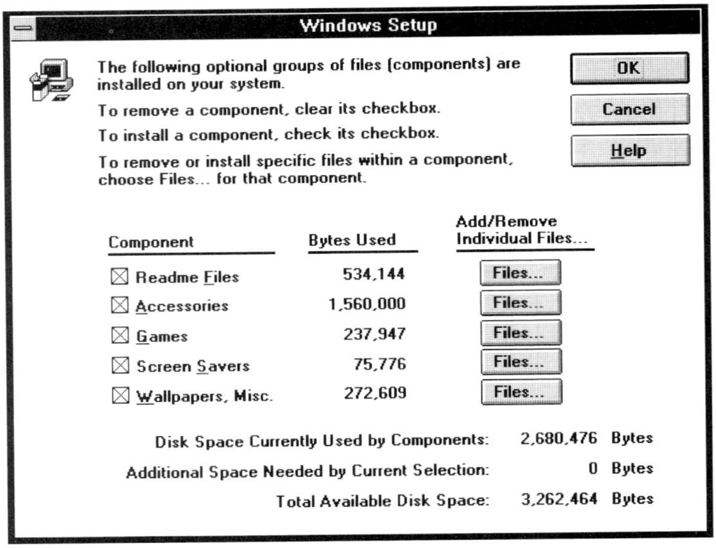

Figure 12-2. *The Windows Setup dialog box used to remove Windows components from the hard drive*

If lost clusters are found, you must answer Yes to convert them to files. Use the TYPE command or an editor to determine if the clusters are usable and rename them if they are.

Unfragmenting Files

After you've found and removed unnecessary files, it's a good idea to unfragment the disk using various third-party utilities or the methods described in this section. In fact, your disk should go on a regular optimizing schedule, say once every month, or whenever you begin to see a slowdown in disk performance. File fragmentation occurs when files are written to disk in noncontiguous sectors. On a newly formatted drive, all available sectors are contiguous and files are stored in a continuous stream in adjoining sectors. As files are removed, sectors are made available between existing files. When new files are saved, they are placed in these available sectors, but if the new file doesn't completely fit, it is fragmented and saved in two or more noncontiguous areas of the disk. Reading and writing fragmented files takes more time, and the slowdown gets progressively worse as more files are deleted and saved.

Disk optimization can be conveniently scheduled to coincide with regularly scheduled disk backup sessions.

Disk optimizing utilities automatically unfragment files by moving them around on the disk until they are all in a contiguous form. This shuffling method ensures that files are not lost should the system crash during the unfragmenting session. Popular disk optimizing programs are made by Peter Norton Computing, Fifth Generation Systems (Mace Utilities), and Softlogic Solutions. If you don't have access to one of these utilities, you can try the methods listed in the next sections.

Note the following before you run a disk defragmenting utility:

- Disable any disk cache utilities such as SMARTDRV before running a disk defragmenting program. A disk defragmenting program needs to manipulate files at the disk level, which the disk cache may inhibit.

- Disable the DOS FASTOPEN command in the AUTOEXEC.BAT file, if it is installed.

- Defragmenting utilities may not be compatible with IDE, SCSI, and ESDI drives. Check with the software manufacturer before preceding. The backup-and-restore method described next is safe to use, however.

The Backup-and-Restore Method

The backup-and-restore method of optimizing a disk can be done with the DOS BACKUP and RESTORE commands, or a tape backup utility. The process involves first backing up your entire hard drive to floppy disk or tape using the Verify option. (Verify ensures that the backup files are correctly copied. You then format the hard disk, and finally restore the data.) When the files are restored, they are restored contiguously.

If you have an ST506 controller or other drive that supports low-level formatting, you can take this opportunity to low-level format the drive as well. This has the benefit of realigning tracks and locating defects that may have cropped up since the last low-level format.

When using a tape drive to back up and restore files, it is important to do a file-by-file backup, not an image backup. An image backup-and-restore would copy the files exactly as they are on the hard drive — that is, in a fragmented format. The file-by-file method gathers together the fragmented portions of each file on the backup medium and then restores them contiguously, assuming the disk has been formatted.

Formatting the hard drive is an important step because it clears the table DOS uses to keep track of files and their location on the disk. This information includes the location of fragmented portions of files. If you restore without removing this table, DOS would simply replace the files in their old locations, based on the table.

Another important step in the process is to remove old files before you perform the backup. In this way, only those files you really want are restored to the drive, thus reducing clutter and increasing available disk space.

The Advanced Backup-and-Restore Method

The advanced backup-and-restore method is the same as the method discussed in the previous section, with the addition of a few extra steps that can help reduce file fragmentation in the future. Consider that your hard drive filing system has two types of files, *permanent* files and *transient* files. Permanent files are files with fixed sizes that will remain on your hard drive in a specific location for a long time. Program files and system files are good examples of permanent files. Transient files are those files that shrink and grow in size and are eventually moved elsewhere or deleted.

Now consider how the effects of file fragmentation can be decreased if all permanent files are kept in one area of your hard drive, and all transient files are kept in another. Since transient files are no longer mixed with permanent files, fragmentation will be confined to the physical area where they exist, which we'll call the *data area.*

Partition your drive using FDISK to include a program-only partition and a data-only partition.

Initially, you can control exactly which files occupy the permanent areas of your hard drive and which occupy the data areas. Start by backing up just program files onto one backup tape, or disk set. Next, back up only data files on a separate tape or set of disks. Format the drive, and then begin restoring files.

Start by restoring all permanent program and system files. If you want, you can restore these from the original program diskettes. In this way, the position of program files on the hard drive is contiguous and centralized. After permanent files have been restored, you can begin restoring data files. Data files can use the remainder of the drive. Thus fragmentation occurs only in the remaining data area of the drive. The next time you need to optimize the disk, all you have to do is back up the data files, delete the data file directory structure, then restore the files, which rebuilds a nonfragmented directory structure.

To make this scheme work, you need to organize your files into distinct program and data groups at the drive and directory levels. If you have two hard drives or a single hard drive partitioned into two, you can store all program files on one drive and all data files on the other drive. Optimizing then becomes a simple task since you only need to optimize the data drive, not the program drive.

If you only have one drive, create distinct program and data directory trees. For example, create two directories at the ROOT level, one called PROGRAMS and one called DATA. Place your program files in subdirectories of the PROGRAM directory, and place your data files in subdirectories of the DATA directory. When you optimize, back up the data directory, erase its files, then restore the files. Note that formatting is not performed unless you also back up and restore the program files.

Chapter *13*

Video Graphics Displays

Before Windows, video graphics resolution on personal computers was determined by a few standards. For example, the first personal computers developed by IBM used the Color Graphics Adapter (CGA). A monochrome monitor was also available, but it was text-only. Software developers wrote applications that were compatible with the adapter. When the Enhanced Graphics Adapter (EGA) was announced, developers scrambled to make their software compatible with it. The same thing occurred when the Video Graphics Adapter (VGA) was announced. Software developers rushed to develop drivers that made their applications compatible.

Windows changed all that by shifting the focus of developers to a standardized graphical user interface (GUI). Software developers simply design their applications to work with Windows and video adapter manufacturers concentrate on making their hardware compatible with Windows. Software developers can be assured that their application will work with Windows as long as video boards provide Windows drivers and support.

There is good reason to consider other video cards and displays. Windows is a graphical user interface, which means it demands more in the way of performance, resolution, and color. New video cards offer acceleration of specific graphics functions that draw, move, and resize images on the screen. In addition, support for more colors lets you display and work with color images using hundreds or thousands of colors for a more natural effect. Windows users have demanded better hardware, and vendors have responded. But the choices can be confusing. This chapter was designed to help you start the search for a display system that fits your needs. At the time of this writing, many new technologies (coprocessor chips, accelerator cards, and color enhancers, for example) were being put to use on a new batch of video cards. Your best sources for the latest information on these are trade journals and computer magazines, which also often provide test results. A listing of several recent articles can be found later in this chapter.

Video Technology

Windows supplies drivers for many different video standards, the most common of which are listed in Table 13-1. But Windows is not limited to just these drivers. Any video manufacturer can create Windows drivers for their cards. You simply run the Setup program to install and configure the driver that comes with the card. The benefit of this scheme is that your applications run as normal, immediately taking advantage of the new video hardware.

The Video Electronics Standards Association (VESA) has developed the Super VGA standard. This standard attempts to maintain a common set of features and functions for video cards throughout the industry. It is an extension of the video BIOS. Manufacturers using this BIOS extension add compatibility to their products.

While VESA ensures compatibility, it's not really important to Windows. The VESA BIOS is a DOS extension that's not used by Windows. Every board must use a specific Windows driver that provides direct support to its hardware features. However, you'll need the VESA compatibility when you exit Windows and run DOS applications. In fact, any board that offers high-resolution Windows modes must also include some sort of VGA (or similar) support so you can run DOS applications. Otherwise, you'll need to purchase a separate card to run alongside the board.

Windows video drivers are supplied by the manufacturer, or you can get a collection of drivers in the Windows Driver Library (WDL), available from Microsoft at 800-426-9400. This library is made available for a minimum shipping charge.

Video Type	Resolution	Colors	Recommended Memory
EGA	640x350	16 color	256KB
VGA	640x480	16 color	256KB
VGA	640x480	256 color	512KB
SVGA	800x600	16 color	256KB
SVGA	800x600	256 color	512KB
8514	1024x768	16 color	512KB
8514	1024x768	256 color	1024KB

Table 13-1.   *Standard Video Card Types and Resolutions*

Other standards are available. The IBM XGA standard, pioneered by IBM is one. TARGA, a 24-bit color technology developed by AT&T is another. A 24-bit color card will display over 16 million colors. Note that 16 million colors includes every color that human eyes are capable of seeing (the transition between each color is not perceptible). However, 24-bit color on a 1024x758 display requires 2MB of video memory.

Color

Color on computer monitors is displayed using the three primary colors: red, green, and blue. A typical color monitor has three electron guns that beam a red-green-blue color mixture to a pixel or dot on the display surface. A color pixel consists of three side-by-side dots (red, green, and blue). These dots are assigned different intensities of each of the electron gun's colors, thus forming a specific combination of red, green, and blue—in other words making that pixel a specific color. If all three color guns are beamed at a pixel with the same intensity, the pixel appears white. We can represent the on or off state of each gun with a three-bit number stored in memory, as shown in Table 13-2.

Table 13-2 illustrates how the number of bits determines the number of colors a monitor can display, as you'll see. The number of bits used to define a color is known as its bit-plane (or bit-depth). A one-bit plane allows only two colors, black and white, which correspond to the on or off state of a pixel.

When IBM designed the Color Graphics Adapter, it used four bits to define the intensity of the color. This bit scheme is known as the Red/Green/Blue/Intensity

Color	R	G	B
Black	0	0	0
Blue	0	0	1
Green	0	1	0
Cyan	0	1	1
Red	1	0	0
Magenta	1	0	1
Yellow	1	1	0
White	1	1	1

Table 13-2.   *Three-Bit Combinations Used to Represent Colors*

(RGBI) color scheme. The extra bit specifies a primary color as either bright (fourth bit = 1) or dark (fourth bit = 0). Thus Table 13-2 doubles in size to 16 possible colors.

The IBM Enhanced Graphics Adapter (EGA) provides higher resolution and up to 64 colors. While the RGBI color scheme is used to define colors, the EGA hardware provides a way of illuminating each screen pixel in one of four states: fully illuminated, partially illuminated, dimly illuminated, and not illuminated. This scheme allows 64 colors (four times the number of colors in the RGBI color scheme).

Both CGA and EGA monitors are digital. They receive color information from the video card over separate wires (there's one wire each for the red, green, and blue bit). The IBM Video Graphics Array (VGA) uses analog signals instead of digital signals to display colors. An analog signal can specify varying color levels, rather than a simple on or off state like digital signals. That means that analog video systems are capable of defining many different colors—in fact, they can display any visible color. However, the color range of a standard VGA card is limited by other factors, including memory size, to 16 colors at a time. A typical VGA system displays 16 simultaneous colors from a palette of 262,144 colors at a resolution of 640 horizontal pixels by 480 vertical pixels. The digital representation of colors on the card is converted to analog signals by a DAC (Digital to Analog converter).

The use of analog display systems opened personal computers to higher resolutions and greater color capabilities. Video cards supporting 800x600 and 1024x768 resolution are now common, as are monitors that work with a wide range of video cards. Interestingly, high video resolutions and color capabilities are now available, but software, including Windows, is often incapable of taking full advantage of it, as discussed next.

How Software Uses Colors

The number of colors is as important as resolution in determining the quality of an image on the screen. By default, Windows only displays 20 colors (and a VGA card displays only 16 of those), so even on high-resolution displays, scanned images show defined boundaries between colors, which detracts from the natural continuous tone of an image like a photograph. When 256 colors are used, image quality improves, but for photographic quality, thousands of colors are necessary. This requires a video card with 2MB or more of memory.

In some cases, a picture on a computer screen may appear less "life-like" than an image on a television monitor even though the computer may have a higher resolution. Ironically, this has to do with the preciseness of digital displays. A lack of colors makes the boundaries between colors stand out. A television monitor, on the other hand, displays images with smooth transitions between colors. To alleviate this problem, some video cards use special chips that smooth the area between color transitions. But these cards slow system performance unless additional measures (such as coprocessors and fast memory) are taken to boost it.

Windows classifies display hardware as being either a *non-palette* or *palette* device. On a non-palette device (the standard 16-color VGA, for example), Windows displays only 20 pure colors, of which only 16 can be displayed simultaneously on a VGA monitor. Windows is able to define a total of 256 colors, but the remaining 236 colors are created using a dithering technique which mixes the available colors using dot patterns. On a palette device, the full range of 256 colors is displayable as pure, undithered colors. This Windows color management system represents a trade-off. It allows individual applications to control their own colors, rather than letting Windows provide 256 colors that no application could change. Out of the 256 colors, 20 are reserved and guaranteed to always be available to any application. The 256-color palette can be manipulated by an application to provide more colors, but currently, few applications go to the extra trouble to do so. Instead, they display the 20 default colors and dither the rest. You can see this when working in Paintbrush, or mixing colors with the Colors utility.

The upshot is that if you purchase a high-resolution card that supports 256 colors, make sure the applications you plan to use are designed to manipulate the full color palette, rather than use its 20 default colors. Alternatively, you can purchase a board that uses the Sierra HiColor RAM DAC (discussed later). Such boards trick Windows into using the full color palette.

Evaluating Your Need for 256 Colors

Any time you work in a color mode that supports 256 or more colors, Windows performance drops. You may not see a slowdown when typing in your word processor, but dragging images across the screen in a graphics applications can take much longer.

Be careful when loading 256-color images into Paintbrush. If you save the image, Paintbrush converts it to 16 colors. In some cases, you can use this to reduce the size of a graphics file if you don't need extra colors, but make sure you don't convert your colors inadvertently.

Install all the drivers available for your video board, and then try each to see which gives the best performance, assuming you can use all those drivers.

Resolution and Screen Size

Windows supports many different screen resolutions, as Table 13-1 has shown. If you upgrade from a 640x480 VGA adapter to an 8514/a-compatible adapter, the size of your desktop increases, which means you can place more windows side by side. But the size of the screen object shrinks so you'll also need to use a larger monitor that basically "magnifies" the view of the desktop. For example, a VGA display only shows a width of about six inches of text while a Super VGA display will display almost eight inches. The relationship of a window on a 14-inch monitor under different resolutions is shown in Figure 13-1. (Monitors are measured diagonally from corner to corner.)

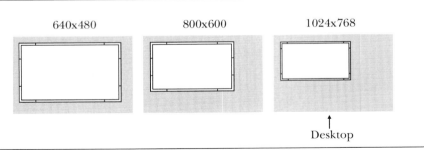

640x480   800x600   1024x768

Desktop

Figure 13-1.   *The relationship of window size to resolution (all three are 14-inch monitors)*

If you intend to use a higher resolution such as 1024x768, it's a good idea to get a larger screen to magnify the image and make it more readable. This relationship is shown in Figure 13-2.

Considering Scan Rate

As screen resolution increases above 800x600, performance can drop. Video cards that offer 1024x768 resolution are often slow performers unless they use special graphics coprocessors, which will be discussed later in this chapter. The higher the resolution, the more information the system needs to paint on the screen and hold in memory. Scan rates (the speed at which the monitor paints the image) become an issue.

Images on a video monitor are drawn by scanning the multiple horizontal lines that run across the screen from top to bottom. The number of times the entire screen is repainted in this way, per second, is known as the *refresh rate*. If the scan rate is low, flickering can occur that results in eye strain. If it is high, flickering goes away, but so does the money in your bank account. However, screen resolutions above 1024x768 are sure to become more popular. Higher screen resolution means a larger desktop

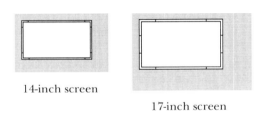

14-inch screen

17-inch screen

Figure 13-2.   *The relationship of resolution to screen size (1024x768 resolution in both cases). A larger screen makes the image more readable.*

(eight inches or ten inches wide, rather than six inches), making it practical to place windows side by side on the desktop, rather than shuffling them around or minimizing them to icons. As coprocessors and fast memory are added to high-resolution cards, performance is increasing.

Video Card Features

The following sections provide important information about video cards and Windows support for those cards.

Video Card Memory

The amount and type of memory on a card plays a large part in determining its color range, resolution, and performance. The relationship of video memory to resolution and color capability is listed in Table 13-3. The video memory holds the image on the display, which may require refreshing up to 72 times per second to avoid noticeable flicker. Video cards use two types of memory: *dynamic RAM* (DRAM) and *video RAM* (VRAM). DRAM is the same type of memory used on the system board.

To improve performance, manufacturers use VRAM. Whereas DRAM is addressed in rows and columns and requires a refresh cycle that reduces performance, VRAM is addressed linearly and can be accessed during its refresh cycle. That's possible because the chips are dual-ported—meaning that the CPU and video refresh circuitry can access it at the same time. VRAM is expensive but cards that use it rate the highest in speed in most tests. Some DRAM boards use various methods to boost performance, such as interleaving and caching, that give them speed ratings comparable to VRAM boards.

Memory	Resolution	Colors
256KB	640x480	16 colors
256KB	800x600	16 colors
256KB	1024x768	4 colors
512KB	640x480	256 colors
512KB	800x600	256 colors
512KB	1024x768	16 colors
1,024KB	1024x768	256 colors
1,024KB	1280x1024	16 colors

Table 13-3.   *The Relationship of Memory to Resolution and Color*

You should evaluate your need for fast graphics. While performance is the ultimate goal, it may not be achievable if you're on a budget. Other boards offer excellent performance at affordable prices compared with what was available on the market only a couple of years ago.

Bus Size Considerations

The Industry Standard Architecture (ISA) systems (IBM AT-compatible) provide an 8-bit or 16-bit bus for the attachment of video cards and other adapters. To get the best performance from a video card, make sure the bus is 16 bits wide. Graphics information is transferred through this bus. Transferring information in 16-bit chunks is faster than transferring in 8-bit chunks. Some systems now include 32-bit video card slots for even faster performance.

One thing to be aware of is that some AT bus systems will run all cards in 8-bit mode if it detects just one 8-bit card. To run 16-bit cards in 16-bit mode in such machines, you'll need to remove or upgrade your 8-bit cards to 16-bit cards. Some video cards are *autosensing* cards, which means they detect the type of slot they are in and switch to the appropriate 8- or 16-bit mode. If your cards can run 16-bit mode, check to make sure they are actually doing that by running the diagnostics utilities supplied with the card. If you're not sure whether your system is taking a performance hit by the presence of 8-bit cards, temporarily remove them to see if performance improves.

A method of improving performance for 8-bit boards, and even 16-bit boards, is to place the card's video BIOS routines into system memory, a process called shadowing. Many boards come with utilities that do this, but shadowing takes up memory in the adapter area that DOS 5 and memory managers such as QEMM may be able to use more efficiently to load drivers high. You'll need to weigh whether you want to speed up video or free conventional memory, a topic covered in Chapter 9.

Maintaining VGA Support

Video cards use various chip sets to provide VGA or Super VGA support. Common sets are provided by Tseng Laboratories, Chips and Technologies, or the manufacturer of the card. The advantage of boards with these common chip sets is that drivers are interchangeable among the different boards and constantly updated to keep up with changes in Windows and hardware. For example, Tseng provides updated drivers to work with Windows 3.1. These drivers can be obtained from most bulletin boards.

High-resolution cards will often contain a VGA chip set to maintain VGA resolution when you exit a high-resolution application such as Windows. When purchasing a card, make sure you can use it with your DOS applications, as well as Windows. Otherwise, you'll need to install a separate VGA card. Not only does this cost more, but you may end up with unresolvable memory and interrupt conflicts with all those boards in your system.

Adding a Graphics Coprocessor or Accelerator

Displaying graphic images on a screen is not an easy task. Drawing lines and moving graphic objects requires many computations and the transfer of information to and from memory, especially as graphic resolution increases. VGA cards rely on your system's processor to handle the display of graphics, so they are notorious for slowing a system down. Using a video card with a graphic coprocessor relieves the system from handling these video tasks.

Some cards provide additional graphics services by handling *graphics primitives*. These are functions that draw lines and circles on the screen, or add shading. Once again, the coprocessor can handle these tasks for the host CPU. You'll often see ratings for how fast a coprocessed card can perform bit-block transfers, or *BITBLT*, which move blocks of bits, like a cutout in a drawing program, around on the screen. Without this feature, clicking an object and moving it can be a frustratingly slow process, especially as screen and color resolution increase. A three- to five-second delay in moving an object is not uncommon for boards without coprocessors. In fact, you can use this as a test when evaluating video cards. Open Paintbrush, and then draw a 1-inch square (approximately). Use the Cutout tool to select it, then move it around on the canvas. The faster video cards move the block in real-time. You'll see a noticeable delay if the video card is not assisting Windows and the CPU with the block move functions.

Graphics adapters based on the IBM 8514/a standard include graphic coprocessors. The coprocessor provides line drawing, area filling, object moving, and alphanumeric data services. The ATI Ultra and Graphics Vantage are both popular and gained the highest rating in many recent tests (see the references at the end of this section). ATI improved on the 8514/a standard by designing and adding its own proprietary coprocessor with improved functions.

Note that proprietary coprocessors are usually locked in functionality, while normal coprocessors are programmable devices that board manufacturers can customize to their own needs by writing C programs. Programmable chips offer some benefit since new drivers can be quickly written to take advantage of changes in software and hardware technology or standards.

Graphic Coprocessors and Accelerators

The following coprocessors and enhancement chips are currently available for video cards. Others are in the works. Board vendors add these chips to their cards for compatibility or enhancement reasons.

The 8514/a Adapter Interface   The 8514/a is an IBM standard that uses a proprietary graphics coprocessor to handle the common line drawing, area fill, and block-move graphics services. This standard is limited because the CPU still handles most of the graphics besides those listed. The ATI Ultra video card is an 8514/a-compatible board that improves the standard by using an enhanced graphics coprocessor.

Texas Instruments' 34010 and 34020   These chips are usually referred to as TIGA (Texas Instruments Graphics Adapter) chips. They are fully programmable. Windows Setup lists two TIGA drivers you install if you have a TIGA-compatible board. The coprocessor executes many of the graphics functions that are normally handled by the CPU, thus increasing performance. Graphics commands optimized for the chips are located in firmware on the board itself and thus provide a performance improvement. A collection of graphics algorithms called the TIGA-340 is developed and maintained by Texas Instruments. Also see the section about DGIS, next.

Direct Graphics Interface Standard (DGIS)   DGIS is not a processor, but an interface to programmable graphics processors such as Texas Instruments' 34010 and 34020, the Hitachi HD63484, and the Intel 82786. DGIS lets programmers write graphics software independent of the type of graphics coprocessor in use. DGIS is a standard of Graphic Software Systems (GSS). It is implemented in Windows as a driver for video cards such as the NEC MultiSync Graphics Engine.

The S3 Incorporated 86C911 Chip   The S3 chip is a graphical user interface controller, which means it was designed specifically for products such as Windows. It is designed after the 8514/a standard and carries a low price, so boards using this chip are relativley inexpensive and provide exceptional acceleration of Windows. The S3 boards are fixed function (non-programmable) and are currently limited to a resolution of 1280x960 or less.

Chips and Technologies' PUMA   The Programmable Universal Micro Accelerator (PUMA) chip set provides enhanced graphics output to printers and acceleration of graphical environments such as Windows. This chip set also sends complex drawings to laser printers eight times faster than normal and provides graphics functions for AutoCAD. The chip set excells in its ability to decrease the number of CPU bus cycles required for some graphics operations.

The Weitek W5086 Graphical User Interface Controller   Weitek's W5086 GUI controller is designed to double the speed of applications running under the Windows GUI. The W5086 chip set supports 16- and 32-bit systems as well as interlaced and non-interlaced monitors with resolutions as high as 2048x1024. This coprocessor is relatively inexpensive, as are the video cards on which it is used. It supports 16 colors. A newer version, the W5186, provides acceleration in 256-color mode.

Enhancement Chips

All video cards have RAM DACs (Random Access Memory Digital-to-Analog Converters). These chips convert digital information into analog signals for display on a monitor. Two chips provide enhancement to this process and are pin-compatible with existing RAM DACs, so you can often swap them out. However, keep in mind that the video driver software must support the enhancement chip, and using the chip can slow performance. Many coprocessed and accelerated cards include one of these enhacement chips.

Edson's RAM DAC   The RAM DAC by Edson provides color enhancement through *antialiasing* functions. These functions blend the borders of colors to reduce the jagged-line effect. The viewer perceives high-resolution images with good blending between colors.

Sierra's High Color RAM DAC   Sierra's RAM DAC provides support for up to 32,768 colors in Windows by bypassing the normal color palette. Applications, including Windows, addressing the RAM DAC see these colors as pure, undithered colors.

Local Bus Video

A recent development is the *local bus video controller*. A video VGA chip set or coprocessed chip set is placed directly on the CPU's local bus (motherboard) where it can run at a faster clock rate than video cards attached to the slower system bus—sometimes as much as ten times faster. The CPU and memory are located on the local bus. You'll see a real boost in memory-to-screen transfers. The Video Electronics Standards Association (VESA), which is largely responsible for Super VGA standardization is working to standardize the local bus design. The advantage of local bus designs is that relatively inexpensive video components can provide excellent performance when mounted directly to the motherboard.

Refresh Rates and Interlacing

As mentioned earlier, the image on a video monitor is drawn by scanning multiple horizontal lines across the screen from the top to the bottom. This scan rate is expressed in thousands of lines per second. Thus, a VGA display rated at 31KHz (kilohertz) produces 31,000 horizontal scan lines per second. The speed of this scanning is a function of both the video card and the monitor, so both must match. In other words, the monitor must be capable of scanning at the rate produced by the card, or the card must be stepped down to match the monitor. Your best bet is to buy a multisynching monitor that exceeds the specification of the video card to accommodate future upgrades. Horizontal scan rates required by the various video standards are listed in Table 13-4.

The scanning rates in Table 13-4 are the minimum for the listed resolutions. To prevent screen flicker, higher scanning rates are necessary.

While the horizontal scanning frequency determines how often the lines are formed, the *vertical scanning frequency* describes how often an entire screen of

Adapter Type	Horizontal Scan Rate
Color Display Adapter (CGA)	15KHz
Enhanced Graphics Adapter (EGA)	22KHz
Video Graphics Array (VGA)	31KHz
8514/a, VESA, and XGA	35KHz
Higher resolutions	48KHz

Table 13-4.   Minimum Required Scan Rates

horizontal scan lines is produced. It is the measure of a monitor's refresh rate. Slow refresh rates produce noticeable flicker that can cause eyestrain. Windows makes flickering displays even more noticeable because it uses white or colored backgrounds that light up the whole screen. For VGA and SVGA modes, you'll need a video card and display that support a 60Hz vertical refresh rate. Higher resolutions require vertical refresh rates of 70Hz or 72Hz to reduce noticeable flicker.

The horizontal and vertical scanning rates of video cards differs widely. You must match the monitor to the video card. A multisynch monitor (also called a multiscanning monitor) is capable of synchronizing itself to a wide range of scanning rates, and is preferred since you don't need to worry about an exact match. In addition, a multisynch monitor can adjust itself to any future video cards you purchase, assuming it is capable of handling the higher scan rates of the new card. You'll see more about multisynch monitors later in this chapter.

Interlacing

Using higher refresh rates is an expensive proposition, so some boards use a method called *interlacing* that draws the screen in two passes. On the first pass, every other line is painted, then on the second pass, the gaps are filled. Interlacing usually produces a noticeable flicker, depending on the scan rate, external lighting, and other factors. Interlaced boards are less expensive and some boards use interlacing to achieve higher resolutions of 1024x768 and above. A typical interlaced scan rate is 87Hz, but even this high rate causes noticeable flicker to some because of the interlacing. Be careful when looking at refresh specifications. A board may be rated at 70Hz or 72Hz in one resolution, but drop down to a lower refresh rate when you use the 1024x768 mode. Also make sure the monitor is capable of handling high refresh rates.

Video Monitors

The front end of the video system is the monitor. While the graphics card dictates many of the features and limitations of the video system, the monitor determines how those features are presented to the user. The next few sections give you important information you'll need to be concerned with when buying a video system and working with Windows.

All VGA-compatible video boards use analog monitors only. Many multiscanning monitors provide both an analog and a digital mode for compatibility with CGA and EGA modes, in addition to VGA.

Dot Pitch

Video monitors form images with dots, or *pixels*. The distance between these pixels is the *dot pitch*. The smaller the distance, the better the display appears to the eye. Dot pitch is really the distance between two like-color pixels in side-by-side RGB triplets.

Typical dot-pitch values are 0.32mm to 0.60mm. Ultra high-resolution monitors have dot-pitch values of 0.28mm, with some as low as 0.26mm. The finer the dot pitch, the less grainy the image looks. Monitors that measure 14 inches diagonally look best when the dot pitch is 0.28mm. Larger monitors are usually rated at 0.31mm dot pitch with some monitors available at 0.28mm, but at a high price. Monitors with dot pitch greater than 0.40 do not provide acceptable screen resolution for day-to-day graphics work.

Multiscanning (Multisynch) Monitors

Multiscanning (or multisynch) monitors are capable of displaying different graphics resolution. Unlike many early VGA monitors, which are locked in at 640x480 resolution, a multiscanning monitor will switch itself to synchronize with the scan rate produced by your video card. This is extremely important if you have a video card that's capable of displaying different modes (for instance, both 800x600 and 1024x768) and you want to switch between those modes. A multiscanning monitor is also important if you plan to upgrade your video card in the future. For example, if you have a VGA card now, you can upgrade to a multisynch monitor now, then later, when your budget permits, upgrade to a higher resolution video card.

As always, the resolution of the card and monitor must be matched. To be on the safe side, look for monitors that have a vertical timing in the range of 50Hz to 90Hz. The higher, the better, but the cost also rises. If you're upgrading the monitor and expect to use the higher resolution of 1024x768, you'll also need to increase the screen size to make images legible, as discussed next.

Screen Size and Style

Monitors are measured diagonally, from one corner to another. Typical monitors used for Windows-based graphics systems are 14 inches to 21 inches. Recently, 16-inch and 17-inch monitors have become the most popular because they display high resolutions at a size that is legible and they are relatively well priced.

Using a large monitor with a standard VGA card really has no benefit unless you have poor eyesight. The 640x400 resolution just looks much larger, as do characters and graphics. The real benefit of large displays is seen when you add graphics cards that display 800x600 or 1024x768 resolution. This resolution looks very small on a 14-inch display, but looks normal when blown up on a 16-, 17-, or 20-inch display.

If you're planning on using a resolution higher than 1024x768 in the future, purchase a monitor larger than 16 inches. A resolution of 1280x1024 squeezes the image down too much on a 16-inch monitor. You'll need a 19-inch to 21-inch monitor to make the most of higher resolutions.

A video display is often defined by its *aspect ratio*, which is a measure of its width to height. A square screen would have an aspect ratio of 1:1. Most screens are rectangular and have aspect ratios of 4:3. Monitors designed for desktop publishing often have the capability to display a full page of text. These monitors have an aspect ratio of 3:4.

Another factor to consider regarding screen displays is their flatness. The larger a screen is, the less appealing the curvature of the display. Flat screens make your images appear more real, and reduce distortion. However, there are penalties; the price goes up and the physical size of the monitor from front to back increases as curvature decreases.

Resources

Because of the changing nature of the video market, trade magazines, and vendors are your best source of information. Refer to the following sources for more information and test results:

Alfred Poor, "Graphics Accelerator: Pump Up the Power." *PC Magazine,* March 17, 1992, pp. 341-392.

M. David Stone, "Boosting Video Performance." *PC Magazine*, February 26, 1991, pp. 207-232.

Winn L. Rosch, "Making the Most of Monitors." *Computer Shopper,* June 1991, pp. 431-458. (Note: This article has one of the most complete listings of monitors and their specifications.)

Winn L. Rosch, "Mainstream Monitors, What Really Matters." *PC Magazine,* July 1991, pp. 103-186.

Mary Kathleen Flynn and Robert W. Kane, "SVGA Boards: Fast Enough for Windows, Cheap Enough for You." *PC Magazine,* September 24, 1991, pp. 247-318.

Doug van Kirk, "Beyond VGA." *PC Computing,* October 1991, pp. 113-119.

Alan Joch, "Tweaking Windows: New Adapters Boost Speed and Clarity." *Byte Magazine,* January 1992, pp. 250-256.

Tips for Using Video with Windows

Windows does a good job of assessing your video equipment during installation and reacting appropriately to your hardware. If a driver is not available, you get a chance to install one from the vendor during installation, or you can run the Setup utility at any time to install a new video driver. Be sure to refer to the README.WRI file if you have any questions about your video hardware or setup. This file contains important video topics that may relate to your hardware.

The drivers listed in Table 13-5 are available when you run the Setup utility. The additional files listed are used to display the startup logo, or to provide 386 enhanced mode virtual display support. Grabber files are used to display text and handle data capture for non-Windows applications. There is a separate grabber for standard mode and 386 enhanced mode.

Expanding Files

If you need to copy, replace, or update any file on your system with a file from the original Windows disks, you must use the Expand utility. The files on the disks are in a compressed form that must be uncompressed before use. The command has a syntax similar to the DOS COPY command. You specify the source and destination for the files. For example, to expand one of the .WRI text files (assuming it was deleted or corrupted), type the following command:

```
EXPAND A:README.WR_ C:\WINDOWS\README.WRI
```

Note that the last character of the extension has an underline character for almost all files on the original disks. You must specify this character in the destination field. In the example just given, the letter "I" is used to change the filename to its expanded form, README.WRI.

Description of Driver	Res[*]	Driver	A	B	C	D	E	F
8514/a	120x120	8514.drv	1	1	1	1		1
8514/a (Small fonts)	96x96	8514.drv	1	1	1	1		1
Compaq Advanced VGA	96x96	cpqavga.drv	2	2	1	2		1
Compaq Portable Plasma	96x96	plasma.drv	3	3	2	3		2
EGA	96x72	ega.drv	4	4	3	4	1	3
EGA Black-and-White (286 only)	96x72	egahibw.drv		4	2		1	2
EGA Monochrome (286 only)	96x72	egamono.drv		5	4		1	4
Hercules Monochrome	96x72	hercules.drv	5	6	5	5		5
IBM MCGA (286 only)	96x96	vgamono.drv		1	2			2
Olivetti/AT&T Monochrome	96x80	olibw.drv	3	7	2	3		2
Olivetti/AT&T PVC Display	96x80	olibw.drv	3	7	2	3		2
QuadVGA, ATI VIP VGA, 82C441 VGAs	96x96	vga.drv	6		1	6		1
TIGA (Small fonts)	96x96	tiga.drv	7	1	1	1		1
TIGA (Large fonts)	120x120	tiga.drv	7	1	1	1		1
VGA	96x96	vga.drv	8	1	1	7		1
VGA with Monochrome display	96x96	vgamono.drv	8	8	4	1		4
SuperVGA (800x600, 16 colors)	96x96	supervga.drv	8	1	1	7		1
Video Seven 640x480 (512K)	96x96	v7vga.drv	9	1	1	2		1
Video Seven 720x512 (512K)	96x96	v7vga.drv	9	1	1	2		1
Video Seven 800x600 (1MB)	96x96	v7vga.drv	9	1	1	2		1
Video Seven 1024x768 (1MB)	120x120	v7vga.drv	9	1	1	2		1
Video Seven 1024x768 (Small fonts)	96x96	v7vga.drv	9	1	1	2		1
XGA (640x480, 16 colors)	96x96	vga.drv	10	1	1	6		1
XGA (Small fonts)	96x96	xga.drv	11	1	1	2		1
XGA (Large fonts)	120x120	xga.drv	11	1	1	2		1
XGA (640x480, 256 colors)	96x96	xga.drv	11	1	1	2		1

[*] The resolution column lists the horizontal by vertical resolution per inch of the display.

Note: The numbers in columns A through F correspond to the drivers and files listed in the second part of this table, which follows.

Table 13-5. *Windows Video Drivers and Associated Files*

Column A** 386 Enhanced Mode Virtual Display Drivers	Column B 286 Grabbers	Column C Logo Files
1. VDD8514.386	1. vgacolor.2gr	1. VGALOGO.LGO
2. VDDAVGA.386	2. cpqavga.2gr	2. CGALOGO.LGO
3. VDDCGA.386	3. cga.2gr	3. EGALOGO.LGO
4. VDDEGA.386	4. egacolor.2gr	4. EGAMONO.LGO
5. VDDHERC.386	5. egamono.2gr	5. HERCLOGO.LGO
6. VDDCT441.386	6. hercules.2gr	
7. VDDTIGA.386	7. oligrab.2gr	
8. *VDDVGA.386	8. vgamono.2gr	
9. V7VDD.386		
10. VDDVGA30.386		
11. VDDXGA.386		

Column D 386 Grabbers	Column E EGA Driver	Column F Logo Data Files
1. VGADIB.3GR	1. EGA.SYS	1. VGALOGO.RLE
2. V7VGA.3GR		2. CGALOGO.RLE
3. PLASMA.3GR		3. EGALOGO.RLE
4. EGA.3GR		4. EGAMONO.RLE
5. HERC.3GR		5. HERCLOGO.RLE
6. VGA30.3GR		
7. VGA.3GR		

** This driver is listed on the display= line in the [386Enh] section of SYSTEM.INI.

Table 13-5.   *Windows Video Drivers and Associated Files (continued)*

Screen Display Versus Printed Output

The images you see on the Windows screen are not to scale with the actual output you see on the printer. If you open Windows Write, select Ruler, and then hold a real ruler up next to it, you notice a big discrepancy between your ruler and Write's. In fact, Write's ruler appears as 1.5 inches for every inch on the real ruler. All Windows programs use what's called a *logical-inch measure*, meaning that they approximate an inch on the screen (but produce accurate printouts). The size of a logical inch is measured in pixels. The pixels per inch for each of the standard video resolution monitor types is listed here:

	EGA	VGA	8514/a
Horizontal pixels/inch	96	96	120
Vertical pixels/inch	72	96	120

You can see from this table that both VGA and 8514/a monitors produce a square aspect ratio, whereas EGA is somewhat distorted on the vertical. How many users have held a printout up to their screen wondering why the resolution and size are not the same? The reason for the discrepancy has to do with the fact that the number of pixels on the screen cannot legibly display fonts below 10 or 12 points in size. So Windows expands the display size to make the characters readable. This is usually not a problem in text applications such as Write since the ruler is enlarged along with the text.

When working with graphics applications, you can apply the pixel width of the display when drawing or painting images to print at a specific resolution. For example, if you're using a VGA monitor and you want to print a one-inch square, just draw a box that is 96x96 pixels square. You can try this now by starting Paintbrush. Choose Cursor Position from the Display menu and select the Box drawing tool. Position the cursor at 100,100, then draw a box out to the 196,196 position. Print the box and measure. You'll see that it's one-inch square.

*If you are not sure what resolution you're using, you can determine the pixels per inch from the Image Attributes dialog box in Paintbrush. Choose Image Attributes from the Options menu, click Inch in the Units field, type **1** in the Width field, then click Pels (picture elements or pixels) in the Units field. The width value of "1" changes to the pels value of one inch, or the pixels-per-inch value.*

You may have noticed the Use Printer Resolution option on the Paintbrush Print dialog box. Click this option to print the pixel resolution of the display at the dot-resolution of the printer. For example, if your screen resolution is 96 pixels per inch, and you print the 1-inch square box at the resolution of a 300dpi laser printer, you'll get a box that's about 1/3 the size you intended. To print a 1-inch square box at the printer's resolution, you would need to create a box on the screen that is 300 screen pixels square.

Here's an interesting trick that takes advantage of a laser printer's resolution. Paint on the screen using a large canvas, and then print at the printer's resolution to create high-resolution images. For example, to print a high-resolution 1-inch square logo, create it onscreen in a box that is 300 pixels square, and then enable Use Printer Resolution on the Print dialog box when printing.

Other Display Files

Besides the video driver files, the grabbers, and the logo screens, screen fonts are used to display the text in Windows titles, menus, and some accessories. There are three sets of fonts each for EGA, VGA, and 8514 resolution.

Chapter 11 discusses how to customize the look of your screen by changing these fonts. They are mentioned next in case you need to upgrade your video driver. In addition, text fonts used to display characters in applications come in sets for each screen resolution. They are discussed here in case you're upgrading your video driver, but covered more fully in Chapter 16.

Screen Fonts

When a video driver is installed using Setup, a set of matching screen fonts for the display resolution of the driver are copied to the Windows SYSTEM directory. Don't confuse these system fonts with fonts that applications use to display the text of your documents. The screen fonts support the following resolutions:

    EGA resolution (650x350)
    VGA resolution (640x480)
    8514 resolution (1024x768)

While other resolutions are possible, such as 800x600, Windows only supplies the resolutions just listed. If you have an 800x600 resolution display, Windows installs the 8514 resolution fonts.

There are three fonts per screen resolution:

- *System Font* The System font is a proportionally spaced font used to display title bar names and menu options.

- *Fixed Fonts* Fixed fonts are fixed-pitch characters used in applications such as Notepad and SysEdit that do not support proportional fonts.

- *OEM Fonts* OEM fonts are fixed-pitch fonts related to the U.S. or foreign character set. OEM font sets contain special characters used by some applications.

Here are the font sets and the Windows disk where the files are located for each screen resolution:

Resolution	System font	Fixed font	OEM font
EGA (650x350)	EGASYS.FON	EGAFIX.FON	EGAOEM.FON
VGA (640x480)	VGASYS.FON	VGAFIX.FON	VGAOEM.FON
8514 (1024x768)	8514SYS.FON	8514FIX.FON	8514OEM.FON

These fonts are indicated to Windows with the following lines in the [boot] section of SYSTEM.INI:

fonts.fon=*system font filename*

fixedfon.fon=*fixed font filename*

oemfonts.fon=*OEM font filename*

Text Fonts

The text fonts used by applications come in sets that match the resolution of the screen. Each set is discussed in Chapter 16 and listed in Table 16-2.

These fonts are copied to the Windows SYSTEM directory during Windows setup, or when you install a new video driver using the Setup utility.

Windows Old Application Fonts (WOA)

The Windows Old Applications fonts (WOA) listed next define the text fonts used for non-Windows applications running in a resizable window in 386 enhanced mode. These fonts are largely replaced by the new ADP850.FON file which is accessed by choosing the Fonts option on the control menu of a DOS application running in a window. These fonts define the character set, with the 850 fonts defining multilingual characters.

CGA40WOA.FON	CGA40850.FON
CGA80WOA.FON	CGA80850.FON
EGA40WOA.FON	EGA40850.FON
EGA80WOA.FON	EGA80850.FON

Entries for these four fonts are found in the [386Enh] section of SYSTEM.INI as shown here:

EGA80WOA.FON=EGA80WOA.FON (or EGA80850.FON)

EGA40WOA.FON=EGA40WOA.FON (or EGA40850.FON)

CGA80WOA.FON=CGA80WOA.FON (or CGA80850.FON)

CGA40WOA.FON=CGA40WOA.FON (or CGA40850.FON)

Using Setup to Install Video Drivers

The Setup utility works fine when installing any of the video drivers provided on the Windows disks. Use caution when following instructions provided by manufacturers for setting up their video drivers. They sometimes require you to replace the SETUP.INF file in the Windows SYSTEM directory with a copy of SETUP.INF on the driver disk, and then run the Setup utility. When following this procedure, make sure to do the following:

1. Compare the dates of the screen and font files on the disk to those in our Windows SYSTEM directory. If they are older, you may prefer to manually install the drivers as discussed in the next section. Alternatively, you can run this setup procedure, then reinstall the new Windows screen and font files from the original Windows disks.

2. Rename the original SETUP.INF file so you can keep it for later. The new one from the video card manufacturer may not be appropriate for anything but installing the video card.

3. Run the Windows Setup utility from Windows. Choose Change System Settings from the Options menu, and then choose the name of the video card from the list.

4. You're then asked to specify the video driver disks and possibly some of the Windows disks.

5. When the installation is complete, you'll need to restart Windows.

Working with Video Drivers

Normally, you use the Setup utility to install new video drivers, or to change the driver of an existing card. The utility checks to see if the drivers are already in the Windows SYSTEM directory. If they are not, it asks you to insert the appropriate disks. In some cases, it may be preferable to install the video drivers yourself and make manual adjustments to the SYSTEM.INI file. For example, it's possible that Setup will copy older screen font files on the driver disk over more recent screen font files on your system. You should always compare the dates of the files on the driver disk with those in your system before using Setup. In some cases, Setup will ask you to verify before it copies an older file over a new one, but this feature is not always reliable.

To install a video card manually, follow the steps given next. This procedure assumes you're installing a new third-party video driver. Use Setup to install video drivers included on the Windows disks, as listed in Table 13-5.

1. Determine the names of the display driver and virtual display driver on the video driver disk.

2. Copy those files to the \WINDOWS\SYSTEM directory.

3. Update the system, fixed, and OEM screen fonts if necessary.

4. Update the Windows Old Applications files, if necessary.

5. Change SYSTEM.INI to specify the new driver files and fonts.

6. Reboot Windows.

The remainder of this section describes this process in detail. First, view the contents of the file OEMSETUP.INF on the video driver disk (if the file doesn't exist, check for SETUP.INF). A description of each available driver (some video cards allow different screen resolutions or color modes) is listed under a section called [display]. Note that the description of each video driver is on a line that's usually word-wrapped, so it looks confusing at first. The description of a driver starts with its name, followed by an equal sign, then the name of the driver file. This is followed by the description of the driver in quotation marks. Here's an example of the "Normal" video driver for the ATI Ultra video card.

```
ULTRA=u:ultra.drv,"ULTRA: Normal 1024x768","100,120,120",
u:vgacolor.2gr, u:vgalogo.lgo, u:vddultra.386, u:8514.3gr, ,
u:vgalogo.rle
```

The driver file is ULTRA.DRV. This is followed by the description of the driver, which you would see if you ran Setup. Following this is the aspect ratio and per-inch screen resolution of the driver, then the names of the logo files. Besides the driver file ULTRA.DRV, the other important file to look for is the .386 file. In the example just given, it's VDDULTRA.386. Copy these files from the disk to your \WINDOWS\ SYSTEM directory. Also note the names of the .2GR and .3GR grabber files and copy these from your Windows disks to the \WINDOWS\ SYSTEM directory. The .RLE and .LGO files can't be integrated into the startup using this method. Just use your existing startup logo files.

Next, copy the screen fonts from the Windows diskettes that match the resolution of the driver. The last two numbers in the resolution field indicate the screen font you should use, as shown here:

96,72	Use EGASYS.FON, EGAFIX.FON, and EGAOEM.FON
96,96	Use VGASYS.FON, VGAFIX.FON, and VGAOEM.FON
120,120	Use 8514SYS.FON, 8514FIX.FON, and 8514EOM.FON

Now list the WOA files on your system and compare the dates to those on the video driver disk. Only copy the files on the disk if they are newer.

The last step is to update the SYSTEM.INI file. Use Notepad or SysEdit to access the file, then make changes as described in these steps:

1. Locate driver.drv= under the [boot] section and type in the new driver name. In the previous example for the ATI Ultra, you would replace the line with:

```
driver.drv=ultra.drv.
```

2. Locate the grabber and screen font lines and update them with the new filenames. The following example shows entries made for the 8514 display resolution used by the ATI Ultra.

```
386grabber=8514.GR3
286grabber=VGACOLOR.GR2
oemfonts.fon=8514OEM.FON
fixedfon.fon=8514FIX.FON
fonts.fon=8514SYS.FON
```

3. Change the entry for the virtual display driver (VDD) in the [386Enh] section to the new .386 file. Notice how the entry was changed for the ATI Ultra:

```
display=VDDULTRA.386
```

4. Finally, if you need to change the Windows Old Application fonts, make the changes to the entries under the [386Enh] section. Usually, this is only necessary if you want to change to the multilingual fonts, as described earlier.

5. Save the changes, then restart Windows.

Troubleshooting Video Adapter Problems

Recall that video cards use memory locations in the first part of the adapter area (upper memory area) for their BIOS routines. The memory address range A000 to CBFF is dedicated to the video adapters (note that the range may go as high as CFFF). You can locate this range on the memory map shown earlier in Figure 8-3. Conflicts can occur if other devices or programs use memory in these areas used by your video card. In some cases, the conflicts don't become apparent until the memory is accessed, which is not always immediately after starting your system or Windows.

Remember to refer to README.WRI. It may contain important configuration information for your display adapter.

When the System Boots Incorrectly

If after installing a new video card, your system won't boot, a conflict exists between the video card and another driver in memory. Back up your CONFIG.SYS and AUTOEXEC.BAT files, and then edit them to remove all drivers and non-essential programs. Reboot your system and if the problem goes away, replace each driver one by one and reboot until the problem reemerges. Once you've found the problem, take steps to avoid the conflict by changing the memory area used by the driver or the card. This is done by editing the line that loads the driver or utility in CONFIG.SYS or AUTOEXEC.BAT and adding a parameter that changes its memory location, interrupt, or other conflicting option. If this still doesn't solve the problem, try removing hardware devices such as network cards, sound boards, CD-ROM adapters, and so on. If the problem goes away, you've got a hardware conflict. Change the settings of adapters to remove interrupt or I/O conflicts. Refer to the adapter's manual for instructions on changing these settings.

When Windows Won't Start or Your System Crashes

Windows makes a scan of the adapter area to look for available space when you start in 386 enhanced mode. If Windows doesn't properly detect an area used by the video card, it may set it aside for its own use. Later, when the video card accesses the area, a conflict occurs and the system halts. These problems usually occur when starting non-Windows applications. To resolve such problems, prevent Windows from using any of the video area by placing the following command in the [386Enh] section of SYSTEM.INI:

```
EMMExclude=A000-CFFF
```

When configuring EMM386 for your CONFIG.SYS file, make sure not to include any of the video memory areas unless you're sure they are not being used by your video card.

Some VGA display adapters, such as those manufactured by Video 7 and Paradise, or those that use the Tseng Labs, Chips and Technologies, Paradise, or Headland Technologies chip sets may use additional memory to enhance the performance of their cards. If the card is configured with the 8514 drivers, or if you have a card that uses additional memory besides those just listed, include the following line in the [386Enh] section of SYSTEM.INI. This procedure is documented in the README.WRI file.

```
EMMExclude=C400-C7FF
```

If the video conflict goes away, you can further experiment with the video adapter segment, whittling it down to just the area required by your video card. This opens addresses in the adapter segment for use by Windows, or as an area for loading device drivers high as discussed in Chapter 9. For example, the monochrome display area can often be used by placing the following command in the [386Enh] section of SYSTEM.INI:

```
EMMInclude B000-B7FF
```

Refer to Chapter 9 for an in-depth discussion of methods to free upper memory for use by Windows or device drivers.

Resolving Port Conflicts

Occasionally, a Windows video driver will conflict with an I/O port used by a hardware device. Everything seems to work until you start Windows and switch into a high-resolution mode. The system then halts. At first, you might view this as a memory conflict and go through the steps just described to resolve it. Instead, use Setup to install a different video mode that uses lower resolution, if one is listed for your card. Then restart Windows. If the problem goes away, the higher resolution video mode may conflict with system hardware or drivers.

For example, in one case, an ARCnet network card used I/O port E02h. The system ran fine until starting Windows, which used a high-resolution (1024x768) video driver. A blank white screen appeared and the system locked up. The Setup utility was used to pick a lower resolution video driver until the problem was determined to be the ARCnet card. In this case, the ARCnet card could not be switched to another I/O port and had to be replaced by a different network card so the monitor could be run in high-resolution mode.

To determine the cause of port problems, temporarily disable commands in CONFIG.SYS and AUTOEXEC.BAT as described earlier, or remove adapters such as network cards. If the problem goes away, reinstall your drivers and adapters using different interrupt or I/O settings, if possible, until the problem goes away.

Display Drivers

It is important that you always use the latest display drivers for your card. Updates resolve software problems and may enable features on your card that were previously inaccessible. Check with the card manufacturer for the latest drivers, or log onto bulletin board services like CompuServe and check the forum set up by the card's manufacturer.

You can resolve some video card problems by trying a different vendor's driver for your card. For example, you could run Setup and load the "QuadVGA, ATI VIP VGA, 82C441 VGA" driver instead of the normal VGA driver. This driver is required by some boards. See your video card manual for details. Another example is the Tseng drivers, which are usable on a wide variety of video cards that use the Tseng video chip set.

Where to Find Other Information

This chapter has dealt mainly with hardware issues related to video equipment. Chapters 9, 16, and 21 delve into related topics.

Chapter *14*

Multimedia

Multimedia integrates sound and graphics into an interactive medium for learning and entertainment on computers. This interaction is not only exciting but useful. Multimedia makes computer information easier to access and understand.

A computer that has a specific set of hardware devices and software drivers to support multimedia is called a Multimedia PC, or MPC for short. The specification for an MPC is defined by Microsoft and the Multimedia Marketing Council.

Minimum Requirements for Multimedia

You'll need each of the components listed on the left in Table 14-1 to *play* multimedia titles and record and play back sounds. The components of a full-blown system—everything you'll need to *author* multimedia titles—are listed on the right.

The playback system listed in Table 14-1 is the minimum system that you can use. A Musical Instrument Digital Interface (MIDI) synthesizer or sound module is useful if you need professional sound quality when playing MIDI files. You can even try authoring your own multimedia presentations using prerecorded sounds or sounds you capture with a microphone. If you don't have a sound board, you can still play sounds using the optional speaker driver that you can obtain from Microsoft.

You can build your multimedia PC in steps. After trying out the speaker driver, upgrade to one of the sound boards discussed later in this chapter. Then add a CD-ROM and you'll be ready to play multimedia productions.

Playback System	Authoring System
CPU	CPU
Color display	Color display
CD-ROM drive (optional)	CD-ROM drive
Sound board	Sound board
Speakers or headset	Speakers or headset
	Microphone
	Electronic synthesizer
	Video camera
	Capture board
	Video disc player
	Scanner

Table 14-1.   Multimedia Playback and Authoring Systems

The Multimedia Development Kit

In mid-1991, Microsoft announced the Multimedia Development Kit (MDK), which contains tools that software developers can use to make multimedia applications and productions available for Windows. Software and hardware developers as well as multimedia authors began designing and creating a whole new class of products, including multimedia titles. Windows 3.1 supports the Multimedia Extensions provided by the MDK through drivers, utilities, and programs.

The MDK and Windows 3.1 come with two accessories and two utilities that help you work with sound. (You'll learn about all of these in the "Multimedia Utilities in Windows 3.1" section later in this chapter.) Other multimedia extensions are provided by vendors when you purchase multimedia-compatible products. Generally, the MDK is used by programmers and developers for creating multimedia products; Windows 3.1 provides extensions that allow users to play multimedia titles but not to author them.

Types of Media

This section defines the types of media that multimedia encompasses. Windows with Multimedia Extensions supports a range of media types, some audio and some visual.

Audio Media

Sound support is included with Windows 3.1, as described in this section.

Waveform Audio

Waveform audio is a digital representation of sound waves. (You'll get a more technical explanation in the "Waveforms and Digital Recording" section later in this chapter.) You can record and play back sounds using a compatible sound board. System startup and message events can trigger the sounds, or you can include sound files in documents and electronic messages to other users.

MIDI Audio

Musical Instrument Digital Interface (MIDI) files contain commands, not a digital representation of sounds. Thus, they require less storage space and suffer no loss in performance through recording and storage. A MIDI command might instruct a synthesizer to play a note for a period of time. The synthesizer generates the sound.

Windows 3.1 does not provide tools for creating MIDI files, but allows you to play them on externally attached synthesizers or on a sound board. MIDI allows you to hook up electronic musical instruments to your system with a connection usually provided by a sound board, or a dedicated MIDI interface adapter. Most sound boards play MIDI files directly using their own sound sources, or let you attach MIDI devices to extend the range of sounds. (You'll learn more technical aspects of MIDI later in this chapter.)

CD Audio

Windows comes with a driver that lets you play CD audio discs if your system has a CD-ROM drive. Some multimedia presentation applications provide utilities for indexing and accessing music from CD audio discs during a presentation.

Visual Media

Support for animation and video is normally provided when you purchase animation software or multimedia video adapters.

Animation

Windows supports moving images within windows, but you'll need an appropriate application to create the images. The Multimedia Development Kit includes a utility called Movie Player that plays animation files created with MacroMind Director (a

Macintosh product). Other vendors are developing both authoring and playback tools to handle animation. Animation can be combined with waveform or MIDI sound.

Video

Video is supported under Windows, provided that you have the proper hardware. At its simplest, a video window lets you watch normal television broadcasts, but there are other uses. For example, you can watch instructional tapes at your computer. You could have a video camera installed in your children's room and keep an eye on them in a small window on your screen while you work. The video can also become part of a multimedia presentation. You could click a menu item to see a short video presentation played from video disc.

Multimedia Products

The following is a short list of multimedia titles and products. There are many other products on the market and even more in development—the purpose of this list is just to give you an idea of the types of products that are available. To play these products you need the minimum system for playback, given earlier. Most of these products are played using a program that comes on the disc, or you can use the Media Player (described later in this chapter).

- Compton's *Multimedia Encyclopedia for Windows*
- *Guinness Multimedia Disk of Records*
- The *Macmillan Dictionary for Children, Multimedia Edition*
- MIDI sounds tracks from Voyetra and Passport Designs
- *Multi Media Music Library* A collection of music, production elements, and sound effects from Killer Tracks
- Games: Almost all games take advantage of Ad Lib and Sound Blaster sound boards to provide more realism

The Microsoft Multimedia Extensions

The full Microsoft Multimedia Extensions as provided in the Microsoft Multimedia Development Kit (MDK) are listed next. Some of these components are also included in Windows 3.1. You obtain the others when you purchase Microsoft multimedia-compatible products. For example, when you buy a sound board, the full Multimedia Extensions are usually included. The extensions are a set of drivers and programs as listed here:

- Device drivers that can play disc-resident digital audio and MIDI files in the background while an application is running. These drivers are included with Windows 3.1.

- Recording of live audio and playback on compatible sound boards. Windows 3.1 provides this support; however, you'll need a sound board to record and play. A driver that plays sounds through your computer's built-in speaker is available from Microsoft. Call Microsoft at (800) 426-9400, and ask for the SPEAKER.DRV driver file. Sound is stored in files with the .WAV extension.

- Support for MIDI. Sound boards and MIDI keyboards or sound modules play files that have the .MID extension.

- The Media Control Interface (MCI). MCI is an interface for communicating with the device drivers that play and record audio, play compact discs and CD-ROMs, and control videodisc players. (MCI is discussed later in this chapter.)

- Enhanced timer services that are used when playing multimedia productions.

- Joystick support.

- Enhanced file input/output services. This includes support for the Resource Interchange File Format (RIFF), covered next.

The RIFF File Format

The RIFF file format is one of the most important contributions of the Microsoft Multimedia Extensions. The RIFF format is similar to the Electronic Arts IFF format and was codeveloped by Microsoft and IBM. RIFF represents information as separate sections or blocks of binary data, preceded by a header that identifies exactly what the data is. The sections in a file can include waveform audio, MIDI audio, bitmaps, and other multimedia information. The RIFF is essentially a universal file format. With RIFF, developers can include diverse types of multimedia information in one file, rather than using many files.

The RIFF file format and OLE (Object Linking and Embedding, covered fully in Chapter 4) add a whole new range of features that make it easy to incorporate many types of elements in your documents besides text and graphics. A compound document could include an icon to play sound or a video or animation clip. While many users will not have the capability to create sound, video, and animation, Windows 3.1 provides the tools to play the elements if they are embedded in documents, and it won't be long until many users also have the hardware necessary to create their own sound, video, and animation computer effects.

Enhanced Display Drivers

The following enhanced display drivers are included in the Multimedia Development Kit. You should get these drivers (or their equivalents) when you buy multimedia products:

- A 256-color driver with a resolution of 320x200, designed for quick display of bitmaps

- High-resolution driver for 8-bit VGA (256 color)

- VGA driver with custom 16-color palettes

- A monochrome driver that displays 256-color bitmaps in 16 shades of gray

Components of Multimedia Systems

This section discusses the components of a multimedia system. Some of these are optional.

The CD-ROM Drive

The CD-ROM drive is becoming a vital component in personal computer systems that provides a way to distribute large amounts of easily accessible information. You don't need to first copy it to your hard drive or shuffle through a large quantity of floppy disks. Software vendors are already taking advantage of this to add value to their products. Product differentiation through add-ons is becoming increasingly important since many competing applications now include similar features, especially if they run under Windows. Added value comes in the form of applications (CorelDRAW and Microsoft Word for Windows, for example) on CD-ROM that are easy to install and include enhanced utilities (for instance, audio dictionaries), sample files, templates, online documentation, and in some cases, multimedia tutorials.

The Microsoft Multimedia specification defines CD-ROM drive requirements. Generally, these ensure that CD-ROM drivers have adequate performance to transfer information to live animations and other multimedia presentations in real-time (the data is transferred directly to the application instead of being loaded in advance).

The Microsoft Multimedia requirements for CD-ROM drives are listed here:

- The drive must be able to access any data on the disc within one second and transfer data at a sustained rate of 150KB per second.

- The drive must handle data transfers on its own, leaving the system CPU relatively free to handle other tasks.

• The drive must have a front-mounted audio jack and volume control.

Many sound boards now come with a CD-ROM port that supports a drive sold by the board manufacturer, or various other CD-ROM drives on the market. A CD drive needs an adapter, cables, and a software driver. The adapters are often SCSI host interfaces, but they usually don't support the attachment of anything but another similar CD-ROM drive. (SCSI was discussed earlier in Chapter 12.) A driver called MSCDEX.EXE supports a CD-ROM under DOS and Microsoft Windows. It is loaded at boot time with a command in the AUTOEXEC.BAT file. In most cases the drive manufacturer will supply additional drivers.

Video Hardware

The minimum requirement for video hardware is a color VGA display, but this only allows 16 colors at a resolution of 640x480. Most pictures require 256 or more colors for a realistic appearance. Some multimedia products use a special driver that reduces the 256-color images to dithered 16-color images, but the quality of the image drops.

To get the most from multimedia, you need at least a Super VGA card that provides more colors and higher resolutions. Chapter 13 provides more information on video graphics displays.

Multimedia Cards and Sound Boards

This section uses the terms multimedia card and sound card interchangeably. Most so-called sound cards actually provide more functions than the recording and playback of sound. They also include CD-ROM connectors and other features related to multimedia. Future cards will include additional features such as the ability to compress and decompress files. Compression is an important feature for multimedia because it improves the flow of data to and from devices and reduces the requirements of data storage. Important features found on sound cards are covered in the following sections.

Sound Synthesis   Most sound boards synthesize sounds using technology called *FM (Frequency Modulation) synthesis*. Sound waves that mimic the waves produced by actual musical instruments are produced using digital oscillators. The best sounds are produced when six or more oscillators are used to produce a single sound. Sound cards such as the Pro Audio Spectrum and the Sound Blaster Pro only use two oscillators, so they are often inadequate for use in professional presentations but are fine for home or office use. Some sound cards and most external synthesizers and sound sources use actual digitized recordings of pianos and strings when playing MIDI files. The quality of these sounds is more appropriate for professional playback. They do not have the "toy music box" quality associated with some sound cards.

Sound Voices   The number of voices provided is one of the most important features to consider when you're shopping for sound cards or synthesizers. Each single note played in a MIDI file requires a separate voice. The best way to understand this is by looking at an electronic keyboard synthesizer. If it has eight voices, you can only press eight keys at once to form a chord. If you press ten keys, two of those keys will not be heard. The number of voices is not critical when playing waveform files, since a single wave includes all the frequencies and components to reproduce the sound. This is discussed in more detail under the "Waveforms and Digital Recording" section later in this chapter.

Sampling   *Sampling* is a recording method that turns analog sound waves into digital reproductions.

Most sound cards include a microphone input so you can sample and digitize sounds.

Sound boards must meet the following requirements for compatibility with the multimedia extensions:

- 8-bit digital-to-analog converter (DAC), linear PCM (Pulse Code Modulation) sampling, 11.025KHz and 22.05KHz sampling rate DMA/FIFO (Direct Memory Access/First In, First Out) with interrupts.

A PCM file contains uncompressed, sampled sound data.

- 8-bit analog-to-digital converter (ADC), linear PCM sampling, 11.025KHz sampling rate, microphone input.

- Music synthesizer chip capable of reproducing four or nine instrument sounds, depending on the quality of the sound.

- On-board analog audio mixing capabilities.

- MIDI-in and MIDI-out ports.

The mixing capabilities are used to combine and adjust the volume of waveform audio, CD, and synthesizer outputs to a speaker system. Most sound cards come with a mixer utility.

MIDI and Synthesizers

The MPC specification requires that a MIDI port be available on the MPC computer. MIDI provides the connection to electronic musical instruments such as MIDI keyboard synthesizers and MIDI sound modules. The MIDI specification, as discussed later in this chapter, clearly states how MIDI should be implemented, so all you need to know when looking at sound boards is that they have a MIDI-compatible connector. In some cases, you'll need to buy an external MIDI box that connects to the back of the sound card. This is because sound board manufacturers have little room left for the relatively large MIDI connectors (two or three are required).

A MIDI connector can consist of In, Out, and Thru ports; however, not all MIDI devices will have every port. For example, a device that only sends data and never receives it will have only an Out port. The Thru port simply passes MIDI information from one machine to the next and provides a way to daisy-chain MIDI devices together. This is discussed further under the "More on MIDI" section later in this chapter.

Selecting Multimedia Hardware

The following sections describe several popular multimedia sound boards. This is only a partial listing. Many other boards (or complete multimedia add-ons) are available. Be on the lookout for additional options and "goodies" such as CD-ROM connectors, or interesting attachments such as Ad Lib's "surround sound" option.

The Ad Lib Sound Cards   The original Ad Lib sound card has been upgraded significantly for Windows 3.1. Three new versions exist. The Ad Lib Gold PC-1000 for the XT bus uses a Yamaha YM262 sound chip with 20 stereo voices. Sampling is in stereo at 12 bits. The Ad Lib Gold AT-2000 is an AT-compatible board and the Ad Lib Gold MC-2000 is a Micro Channel bus architecture board. Both of these boards offer the same features as the PC-1000, with the addition of a standard SCSI interface port for connection to a CD-ROM drive.

Creative Lab's Sound Blaster   Creative Lab's original Sound Blaster has been up-graded to the Sound Blaster Pro, a product that better supports the new MPC standard. The Sound Blaster Pro exceeds the MPC standards and includes stereo microphone and speaker jacks. A CD-ROM controller exists on the card, but so far it supports only a Panasonic drive. The board's FM synthesizer provides 11 voices per channel. A MIDI adapter plugs into the board's joystick port.

Media Vision CDPC   The Media Vision CDPC is a fully integrated multimedia system, enclosed in a case that fits on top of your PC. The front panel consists of stereo speakers, a push-button control panel, microphone and headphone jacks, and a CD-ROM drive. The sound system consists of 100-watt speakers with low-noise audio and bass enhancement. The unit is Ad Lib, Sound Blaster, and Roland MPU-401 compatible and has four-operator FM synthesis with 20 voices.

Roland Products   Roland is a manufacturer of MIDI-compatible keyboard synthesizers and other musical equipment. In the computer world, they are most famous for designing the MPU-401, a MIDI interface board that set the standard for PCs. That board has been replaced by the Roland MPU-IPC and the SCC-1 sound card (with MIDI interface). It is common to refer to a MIDI interface as MPU-401 compatible.

It's important to distinguish the MPU-401 as a MIDI interface card, and not a sound card. It provides a MIDI connector for MIDI-compatible external synthesizers and handles the sending and receiving of MIDI commands between the two, but it does not meet the MPC specification for a sound card. However, if you're just interested in recording and playing MIDI files, the MPU-401 and its successors, the LAPC and SCC-1, are good bets. The latter two devices provide built-in sound synthesis for playing MIDI files, as well as a MIDI interface to external devices. However, they do not provide sampling and other MPC features.

Turtle Beach Systems   The sound cards made by Turtle Beach are aimed at the high-end professional who needs CD-quality sounds. Turtle Beach's MultiSound board provides 44.1KHz, 16-bit sampling. This rate will record sounds that are almost indistinguishable from the source. The board includes all the standard features and controls, and comes with software for recording, mixing, and playback of .WAV and .MID files.

Multimedia Utilities in Windows 3.1

Two multimedia accessories (the Sound Recorder and the Media Player) and two Control Panel utilities (MIDI Mapper and Sound) are included in Windows 3.1. The Sound Recorder is an accessory for recording, editing, and playing back sounds. The Media Player plays sound or multimedia productions, including .WAV and .MID (MIDI) files. Use the MIDI Mapper utility to configure an external MIDI device such as a keyboard synthesizer. The Sound utility lets you assign sounds to system events.

These are used to record or play sound, video, and animation files. Keep in mind that you play embedded files in compound documents by simply double-clicking the embedded icon or window. You use the utilities described here to open files and play them on their own (when you're not in a document). The utilities are covered shortly.

Why a Mixer Is Not Included

One thing not included with either the MDK or Windows 3.1 is a standard audio level (mixer) control utility that lets you control and equalize the volume of the individual units in a multimedia system. However, most multimedia boards and devices come with a mixer utility of their own. Microsoft did not include this utility because it anticipated future products from manufacturers that would include non-standard functions, such as television and radio control. Microsoft allowed each manufacturer to add their own components and create custom mixers to match. A typical mixing control panel is shown in Figure 14-1.

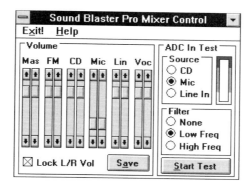

Figure 14-1.   *A mixer is used to control the sound level of all multimedia devices installed in a system*

The Sound Recorder

The Sound Recorder lets you record and play back wave files. Before learning how the Sound Recorder operates, let's first get a little background on digital recording and the wave file format.

Waveforms and Digital Recording

Sounds consist of vibrations that form a wave with a certain amplitude and period as shown in Figure 14-2. The *amplitude* is a measure of the height of the wave but is perceived as the loudness of the sound. The *period* is the distance between two waves in the sound. Finally, *frequency* is a measure of the number of periods per second, expressed as hertz (Hz). One hundred periods per second is 100Hz, for example. The range of human hearing is 20Hz to 20,000Hz and this is the range that high-fidelity sound equipment strives to reproduce.

To record a wave digitally, a *sample* must be made at various time intervals to determine its amplitude. The wave in Figure 14-3 is sampled 16 times. Assuming that this particular wave lasts one second (1 hertz), then the sampling rate is 16 hertz.

Sampling at such a low rate is impractical. Even sampling at 100Hz or 1000Hz produces sounds that have a very low quality when played back. That's because the digital representation of waves is not smooth. Filtering techniques can "smooth" the wave, but the real trick to quality digital recording is to increase the sampling rate. The Windows Multimedia specification requires three rates: 11.025KHz, 22.05KHz, and 44.1KHz. You use one of these rates depending on the type of sound you're recording.

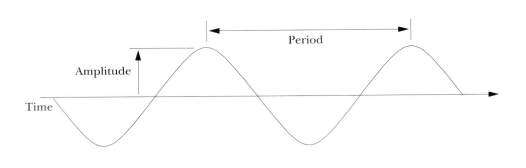

Figure 14-2.   *Ways of measuring a sound wave*

Sampling the wave pictured earlier 11,000 times produces a fairly accurate recording. However, the amount of disk space required to store sounds increases as the sampling rate and amount of recording time increases. A formula for calculating disk space is presented in a moment, but there's one other variable you need to know about before you can work with the formula, and that is the number of bits used to store the sampled information.

Each sample includes information about a small segment of the sound. The number of bits used to record each sample determines exactly how precise the sample is in terms of its vertical height. An 8-bit sample allows a vertical sampling of the wave that's divided into 256 equal units. A 16-bit sample allows a vertical sampling of the wave that's divided into 65,536 equal units. Obviously, 16-bit sampling is more accurate, but it also requires more disk space.

The previous discussion used a "pure" sound wave as an example. In reality, sound waves are never pure. They are a mix of many different and varying frequencies that represent the timbre of the sound. *Timbre* determines the unique sound of an

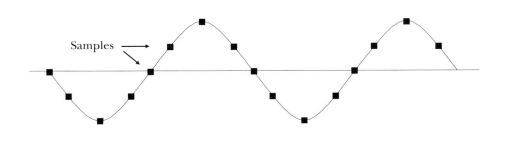

Figure 14-3.   *A digital sampling of a sound wave*

instrument. For example, the sound of a fine violin consists of the vibrating strings and the resonating sound box (some claim the unique sound of a Stradivarius is produced by ground jewels in the varnish). These sounds produce very complex waves as shown in Figure 14-4.

Now you see the importance of increasing the sampling rate and using high bit values to record sounds. Not only do you need to know the amplitude of each sample, you also need to know everything the wave is doing within the time frame of that sample. Capturing the very tiny frequencies within the larger frequencies is important to producing a quality digital sound, but of course, the trade-off is the amount of disk space used by the recorded sound.

Now that you're familiar with sampling rate and bits, here's the formula to figure out disk space:

(sampling rate * bits)/8 = bytes per sec

The following table shows the amount of disk space required for one minute of sound for each sampling rate when 8 bits are used. The last entry in the table is the rate and bit size used by Compact Disc Digital Audio.

Bits	Sampling	Rate	Bytes/Storage Required
8 bits	11.025KHz	0.66	MB/minute
8 bits	22.05KHz	1.32	MB/minute
8 bits	44.1KHz	2.646	MB/minute
16 bits	44.1KHz	5.292	MB/minute

If you record in stereo, double the disk requirements.

If you plan to do high-quality digital recording, these numbers show why it's important to purchase a sound board that has analog-to-digital and digital-to-analog

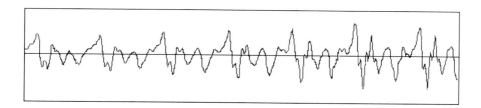

Figure 14-4. *Actual sound waves are complex and must be sampled thousands of times per second for accurate digital reproduction*

converters that handle high sampling rates. Generally, voice recording is suitable at 8 bit 22KHz, but 11KHz sampling is the absolute minimum for quality. Some boards offer filters that help smooth the digital representation of the sound wave. Activision, for example, claims better quality at 8KHz on a properly filtered DAC (digital-to-analog converter), than at 22KHz on a normal DAC.

Keep in mind that sampling at high rates is inappropriate if the recording and playback equipment is inferior. For example, a pocket microphone that's rated for voice would be a poor match when recording at 44KHz. Even if you do manage to record an accurate, high-quality sound, the playback system must be of equally high quality. The speaker in your computer is probably not this quality.

Using the Sound Recorder

The Sound Recorder is a handy but somewhat limited digital recorder that provides good introduction to digital recording. On a Sound Blaster, Sound Recorder records at 11.025KHz and 8 bits. However, editing the sound file is inconvenient. True sound editors let you use cut, copy, and paste techniques to actually move a block of recorded sound from one place to another in the file. Your sound board may come with such a utility.

The Sound Recorder is useful for creating small voice files to include in documents or send over electronic mail. You can use Object Linking and Embedding (OLE) techniques to include a sound in a document as discussed in Chapter 4. The Sound Recorder is also useful for recording the sounds used in system events. You assign those sounds using the Sound utility in the Control panel as discussed in Chapter 11.

Double-click the Sound Recorder icon in the Accessories group. The Sound Recorder dialog box appears as shown in Figure 14-5.

Playing an Existing Sound

Windows comes with four sounds you can play right away. Choose the Open command on the File menu, and then choose any of the .WAV files you see listed. The files are stored in the Windows directory.

Once the file is loaded, its name appears in the title bar. Click the Play button to play the sound all the way through. Use the other controls as follows.

- Click Pause to stop the sound temporarily.
- Click Rewind to go back to the beginning.
- Click Forward to go to the end of the sound.
- Move the slider button to any part of the sound.

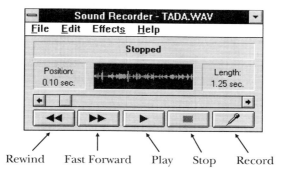

Figure 14-5. *The Sound Recorder dialog box*

- Click the left or right slider button to move through the sound .1 second per click. Click the scroll bar itself to move 1 second forward or backward through the sound.

Recording a New Sound

To record a sound, first attach a microphone to your sound board or run a patch cable from another sound source such as a CD audio player or your stereo. Sounds can be added to existing sounds, or you can record a new sound file. Choose New on the File menu to create a new sound. To add to an existing sound, first load the sound, and then do one of the following:

- Position the cursor where you want to start recording. The new sound copies over the existing sound from that point on.

- Position the scroll button at the end of the file and start recording. The new sound is appended to the existing sound.

Press the Record button when you've got everything set up. Recording starts immediately. The message bar indicates that the Sound Recorder is recording and displays the maximum amount of time you can record. Watch the Length panel if you're concerned about the recording time. Save the sound using the Save As option on the File menu.

Some sound files cannot be copied over or appended if they were recorded on equipment that has different specifications than your own.

Editing Sounds

Now that you've got some sounds, you can try editing them and inserting sounds from other files. It's possible to open more than one Sound Recorder panel, which can make recording and editing a little easier.

Inserting Another Sound   Use the Insert File option on the Edit menu to insert an existing sound file. First position the slider to where you want to insert new sounds, and then choose Insert File and type the name of the file you want to insert. The sound is inserted, preserving the existing sound. Note that you might want to prepare the sound to insert beforehand. You can open another copy of the Sound Recorder and create or edit the file, then save it, switch to your other window and insert it. This saves you the trouble of loading and unloading files several times to edit.

Mixing Another Sound   Use the Mix With File option on the Edit menu to mix in the sounds of another sound file. First, position the cursor where you want to mix in the new sound, and then choose the option and select the file to mix. Both sounds are mixed into the same time frame of the sound file.

Deleting Before or After the Current Position   Unwanted sounds or periods of silence can be removed. To delete sound at the beginning of the file, position the cursor at the end of the sound you want to delete and choose the Delete Before Current Position option from the Edit menu. To delete at the end of the sound, position the cursor and choose the Delete After Current Position option.

Changing the Volume   Choose the Increase Volume or Decrease Volume options from the Effects menu to change the volume of the entire sound. Repeat the option to further increase or decrease volume.

Changing the Speed   Choose the Increase Speed or Decrease Speed options on the Effect menu to change the speed of the entire sound. Repeat the option to further speed up or slow down the sound.

Adding an Echo   Choose the Add Echo option to add an echo effect to the sound. In most cases, you'll need to repeat this several times before you'll hear a reasonable echo.

Reversing the Sound   Choose the Reverse option to flip the sound around and play it backwards.

Sound Tricks

The four sounds that come with Windows (Chimes, Chord, Ding, and TaDa) can serve as a starting point for many other sounds. This section provides you with some tricks that will help you create a whole collection of new sounds. You can also obtain sounds from other sources, such as bulletin boards or other users.

Open one of the sounds (Chimes, for example), and then increase the speed and save the new sound. Increase the speed again and save it as yet another sound. You can also try decreasing the sound, but don't work with the sound you just sped up; speeding up a sound and then decreasing it adds too much distortion. Open Chimes again and decrease it, and then save that sound.

Slowing Chimes down produces a lot of interesting individual sounds that you can edit out to create single-strike gong sounds. Here's how to edit out an individual portion of Chimes:

1. Open Chimes and slow it down twice, and then play the sound and watch the amplitude of the wave in the oscilloscope window. You'll see the amplitude rise at each strike.

2. Now determine how many times you must click the mouse to position the cursor at the beginning of the sound you want. Rewind the sound, click until you see the beginning of the wave you want, and then click Play. If it sounds right, reposition the cursor by again clicking the appropriate number of times.

3. Choose Delete Before Current Position from the Edit menu.

4. Repeat the process to remove unwanted portions at the end of the sound, choosing Delete After Current Position from the Edit menu.

5. Save the new sound, and then try changing its speed or adding other effects such as echo or reverse.

Here are some more tricks for creating new sounds:

- You can create some eerie, low-frequency sounds by capturing a small portion (1 second or less) of a sound using the steps just given, and then slowing it down five or six times. Speeding up the sound creates interesting electronic beeps you might want to add to your system error messages.

- Create a repeating sound by positioning the cursor at the end of a sound, then inserting the same file from disk using the Insert File option on the Edit menu. Try changing the speed of this new sound, or adding echo.

- When you insert a sound, there is often an unpleasant gap between the existing sound and the new one. To smooth the gap, use the Mix File option instead of the Insert File option. Position the scroll bar at the end of the current sound, and then click the left scroll button once or twice. When you mix the new sound, it starts as the previous sound begins to fade out, making the transition more pleasant.

- You can mix in any sound from disk to your current sound. This is where it's helpful to have another Sound Recorder Window open. Use the second window to create or modify sounds and save them to disk, and then switch to the first window and insert or mix the sound.

- Before mixing in a new sound, change the volume of the current sound or the sound you want to mix in. Once they're mixed, you can only change both sounds together.

- If you need to mix two sounds together, but they differ in length, you can change the speed of one sound to change its length, but this also changes its pitch. An alternative is to mix in a sound more than once. Start by mixing in the sound, then mix it in again. To avoid gaps, overlap the end of the first mix with the new mix by clicking the left slider button once or twice.

There are an incredible number of sound possibilities, more than this book has space for. Keep experimenting. If you enjoy working with sounds, look for more advanced sound editors. Most sound boards also come with useful sound editing utilities. WaveEdit, included with the Microsoft Multimedia Development Kit, has sophisticated editing features such as cut, paste, and zoom.

Media Player

Media Player lets you play multimedia files like the sound files you create with the Sound Recorder, or MIDI files, which you can obtain from various sources such as bulletin boards. A selection of both types of files is often included with sound boards or as part of a multimedia production you can buy on disk, so you can take advantage of multimedia right away.

Keep in mind that Media Player is not the only device you use to play files. Most sound boards come with their own player programs that offer many more features than those available in Media Player. For example, MIDI files are really multitrack recordings that play several different sounds at once. Played on Media Player, all the sounds are heard at once. More advanced software lets you individually control the characteristics of each instrument. For example, you can single out the piano track, change its volume, add echo, or pan it from left to right if using stereo.

The following discussion assumes you have a sound board installed in your system, or at least the speaker driver (SPEAKER.DRV). A wave (.WAV) file is played in the examples. If you have other devices installed such as a CD-ROM drive or a videodisc player, the procedure for playing them is similar, except that you need to make sure to choose the correct device to play.

To play MIDI files, you must have a MIDI-compatible sound module or keyboard attached to a MIDI port on your system (that is, on the sound card). Alternatively, most sound cards let you map the sound channels in a MIDI file to the voices on the card itself. Mapping MIDI channels is discussed under "Using the MIDI Mapper" later in this chapter.

Normally, you don't need to use MIDI Mapper since most multimedia-compatible sound boards conform to a specification called General MIDI. (See the section by that name later in this chapter.) If you have an older synthesizer, you may need to use MIDI Mapper to match the sounds and keystrokes in your MIDI files with those produced by the synthesizer.

Using Media Player

Double-click Media Player in the Accessories group of the Program Manager. The following Media Player dialog box appears.

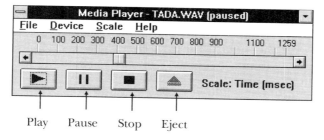

Media Player is easy to use. Like the Sound Recorder, Media Player has controls like a simple tape deck: Play, Pause, Stop, and Eject. A scale and slider bar indicate how far Media Player is into the playback. The scale can be adjusted manually to hear or see specific parts of the media.

Specifying a Device

Before you can play anything with Media Player, you must first specify the type of device to use (either simple or compound). Open the Device menu as shown here to see the types of devices available on your system:

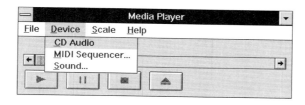

- A *compound device* opens and plays files. In the Device menu, an ellipsis follows the device name (so MIDI Sequencer and Sound in the illustration are both compound devices). When you select a compound device, Media Player displays the standard Open dialog box and lets you choose the file you want to play.

- A *simple device* is a "play-only" device, most typically a CD-ROM drive with an audio disc in it. If you place a CD music disc in the drive and choose CD Audio as shown in the illustration, Media Player scans the disc and displays information about its tracks in the slider bar. You can then click the Play button to play the disc.

 If the CD Audio option does not appear, use the Control Panel Drivers utility to install it. You must have a CD-ROM drive to do so.

Controlling Media Player

Once the compound device file is loaded, or the simple device is ready to play, click the Play button. Click the Pause button to temporarily halt playback or the Stop button to stop it. If the media is a CD-ROM, CD audio disc, or videodisc, click the Eject button to remove it from the drive.

The Scale

The scale is a slider bar with a time or track scale along the top. Media Player will display the most appropriate scale for the device you've selected, but you can change it by choosing a different scale (Time or Track) from the Scale menu. Track is used for CD audio, but you can change to Time to see how far you're into the CD timewise.

To move forward or backward through the time or track scale, click the scroll bar button and drag, or click the right arrow or left arrow buttons.

More on MIDI

As discussed previously, you can play prerecorded MIDI files that have the extension .MID with the Media Player, assuming you have a sound card that supports MIDI in your system. Most sound cards will play MIDI files using their internal sounds, or direct the MIDI sounds to an external MIDI synthesizer or sound module.

 MIDI is an important new feature of Windows. It can be used to add sound to presentations created with such applications as Microsoft Power Paint and ZumaGroup's Curtain Call.

MIDI is a specification developed in the early 1980s that defines how electronic musical instruments can interface and communicate with one another. The interface defines the physical connection (cables and connectors) among instruments, and the protocols for communications. MIDI also defines the type of information transmitted over the cables and how that information is stored in memory or on disk. MIDI information consists of messages, rather than the actual wave forms of sound. A message might instruct a synthesizer to play (turn on) middle C, then another message might turn it off. These on/off messages and other instructions provide a much more efficient way of storing musical information, when compared to saving digital waveforms, but it requires that you have a device that understands MIDI messages.

Because MIDI got its start as a way to connect keyboard synthesizers, let's look at how those connections are made. The need for MIDI arose because musicians often had several keyboards at their disposal, but only two hands with which to play them. By connecting keyboards with MIDI as shown in Figure 14-6, the musician can "play" the attached keyboard "remotely." Any key played on the main keyboard also plays on the remote unit. This doubling up of sounds helps to produce "fatter" notes. The notes played on the remote keyboard might be moved an octave up or down, or assigned a different sound altogether. You can combine a piano sound on the main with a string sound on the remote, for example.

As sequencing became popular, a need arose for more voices that could play sounds unassisted by the musician. One synthesizer could be set to automatically play a drum solo while the musician played the main keyboard. At the same time, another synthesizer could play a chorus whenever you press the middle C key (for example) on the main keyboard. Obviously, not all these units need to be keyboard synthesizers. That's where *sound modules* come in. Sound modules simply provide extra voices that are controlled from a main keyboard as shown in Figure 14-7, providing the musician with many sounds at little expense. The connection method used in the illustration is important. It shows how the three MIDI connectors (In, Out, Thru) are used. The Thru connection simply extends the MIDI connection to another device. The middle device does not alter the messages sent from the keyboard to the last device.

A computer can be added to this setup to provide enhanced control of the MIDI system. MIDI connections form a daisy-chain arrangement in which a large number of MIDI devices can be connected. Note that the keyboard can send its information to the computer. Thus, you can record the notes played at the keyboard using a

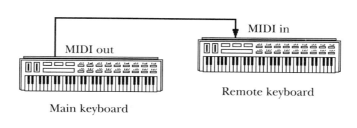

Figure 14-6.   *A main keyboard can control another keyboard*

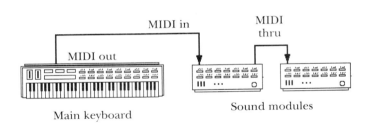

Figure 14-7.   *Keyboard and sound modules connected with MIDI*

computer program called a *sequencer*, which will be covered shortly. (A sequence is a series of notes and system event commands that is stored in memory when you record a score.) When you play the score back, you can direct the notes to any synthesizer or sound module by specifying which *channel* they will receive. You tune a synthesizer to a MIDI channel in the same way you tune a television or radio to a particular channel. One channel might contain the woodwind while another might have the string information. In this way, one cable transmits all the MIDI information, and each synthesizer plays only the notes of the channel it is tuned to.

System events are instructions used to change sounds and make other settings on a MIDI device. If a computer is used to record the sequence, it can be stored on disk as a MIDI file with the .MID extension. In fact, a computer creates an ideal MIDI sequence because the score is displayed graphically on the screen for editing. A sequencing package allows you to cut and paste notes from one location to another, and even print the musical score in some cases.

While MIDI is a standard that defines everything from the connector and cable to the transmission of messages to other systems, the best way to understand what MIDI is all about is to look at the process of creating a MIDI file. Windows 3.1 does not have an accessory to create MIDI files, but if you buy a sound card that conforms to the Multimedia specification, you'll probably get a sequencer application that does. Think of a sequencer as a multitrack tape recorder. You use it to record sounds onto tracks. If you have an externally attached MIDI keyboard, you can use it to play the notes for the recording. If you don't have a keyboard, you can create a score by adding notes manually with the mouse, almost as if you were creating sheet music. Typically, you record each track separately, and then play them back together.

A screen from the Voyetra sequencer included with the Sound Blaster Pro and Media Vision Pro Audio Spectrum is shown in Figure 14-8. Thirteen tracks out of a possible 64 are pictured under the "Trk" heading. Note that bass is recorded on track 1, melody on track 2, and so on. The Port heading indicates where the sounds will play. Assume a Pro Audio Spectrum is connected to Port 2. The MIDI port on a Pro Audio Spectrum is Port 1, so if you wanted to direct some of the tracks to play on an external synthesizer or MIDI sound module, you would change the Port number to 1 for that track.

```
┌─────────────────────────────────── Main ───────────────────────────────────┐
│ Song  CANNON_D                                                               │
│ Tk     1 Bass                    BPM 110              ▐STOP▌     Mem 144016   │
│                                                        1:0    THRU:OFF        │
│ Trk Name                   Port Chan Prg   Transpose  Quantize   Loop   Mute  │
│  ▐1▌ Bass                     2    2   2    ------      ---      ---    ▆▆▆▆  │
│   2  Melody                   2    3  75    ------      ---      ---    ----  │
│   3  Tenor                    2    4  58    ------      ---      ---    ----  │
│   4  Counter Melody           2    5  58    ------      ---      ---    ----  │
│   5  --------------------     1    1   0    ------      ---      ---    ----  │
│   6  --------------------     1    1   0    ------      ---      ---    ----  │
│   7  --------------------     1    1   0    ------      ---      ---    ----  │
│   8  --------------------     1    1   0    ------      ---      ---    ----  │
│   9  --------------------     1    1   0    ------      ---      ---    ----  │
│  10  --------------------     1    1   0    ------      ---      ---    ----  │
│  11  --------------------     1    1   0    ------      ---      ---    ----  │
│  12  --------------------     1    1   0    ------      ---      ---    ----  │
│  13  --------------------     1    1   0    ------      ---      ---    ----  │
├─────────────────────────────── Main Menu ───────────────────────────────────┤
│ Delete  Loop  Mute  Name  Quit  Record  Solo  Tempo  EDIT  FILES  OPTIONS    │
│ VIEW                                                                         │
└──────────────────────────────────────────────────────────────────────────────┘
```

Figure 14-8.   *An example of a sequencing program*

The sequencer has a zoom-in mode that lets you edit the notes of each track, as shown in Figure 14-9. This is a view of the notes for track 2 of the CANYON.MID file supplied with Windows 3.1. The notes are the black bars displayed from left to right and they play in that order. The note names are listed on the left and they have the same arrangement as a piano keyboard. Notice above the notes that this is the first bar and it's played in octave 4. You can copy, move, and delete individual notes or

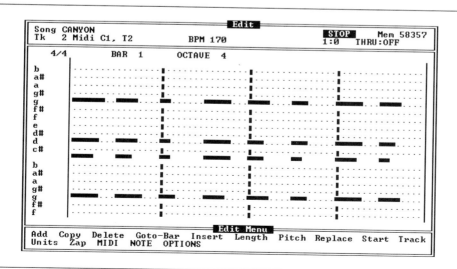

Figure 14-9.   *You zoom in on a track to edit its notes, which are displayed from left to right as they would play*

groups of notes. The mouse is used to scroll anywhere within the score, and to perform the note editing.

If you look again at Figure 14-8, you'll notice that each track also has a channel assignment. Recall that synthesizers receive messages and note information from specific channels. The MIDI specification provides for 16 channels of data. The MIDI Sound module in Figure 14-10 is tuned to channels 1, 2, and 3. The MIDI keyboard is tuned to channel 4 and plays whatever notes are recorded on track 4. Note that in this case, the synthesizer connected to channel 4 was also used to create the score and participates in the playback.

It's not necessary for tracks and channels to have a one-to-one relationship as shown in the illustration. If the MIDI keyboard is currently set to receive channel 4 and you want it to play track 1 instead (perhaps this synthesizer has a specific sound more suited to the instrument on track 1), you would change the channel mapping of track 1 to channel 4 in the sequencer software. Alternatively, you could set the keyboard to receive channel 1.

Keep in mind that a synthesizer or sound module can tune itself to several channels and play all the notes on the channels, up to the amount of internal sound-producing voices it has. A sound card such as the Sound Blaster that has 11 voices per stereo channel can play a single note from each of 11 channels, 11 notes from a single channel, or even five notes on one channel and six notes on another. The advantage of adding sound modules becomes obvious. The more voices you have, the better your scores sound because you can include more recorded tracks and play more instruments. A typical sound module may have from 16 to over 100 voices.

There's one more important setting on the screen shown in Figure 14-8. It's labeled Prg (Program), but is sometimes called "part" or "patch." This is the number of the sound on the playback device. A typical synthesizer has hundreds of sounds from pianos to horns to strings to drums. Each sound has a number and is listed in the synthesizer manual. You select the sound you want to play for that synthesizer by inserting its

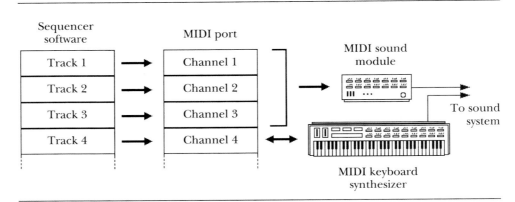

Figure 14-10.   *The flow of note information from a sequencer to a sound module and synthesizer*

number in the Prg field. When you play the score, a MIDI message is sent to the synthesizer instructing it to change its patch for that channel. Alternatively, you can select a different sound on the synthesizer for a particular channel while the song is playing.

About Base-Level and Extended Synthesizers

The Multimedia specification classifies synthesizers and sound boards into two levels: base-level synthesizers and extended synthesizers. This classification is based on the number of instruments and notes the synthesizer can play, not on the quality or the cost of the synthesizer. The following table shows the minimum capabilities of base-level and extended synthesizers:

Synthesizer	Melodic Instruments		Percussive Instruments	
	Number	*Polyphony*	*Number*	*Polyphony*
Base-Level	3 instruments	6 notes	3 instruments	3 notes
Extended	9 instruments	16 notes	8 instruments	16 notes

Polyphony is the number of notes the synthesizer can play simultaneously. The polyphony expressed above applies to each group of instruments, both melodic and percussive. For example, an extended-level synthesizer can play 16 notes distributed among nine melodic instrument sounds and 16 notes distributed among eight percussive sounds. MIDI channels are normally arranged as follows, depending on the level of the synthesizer:

- *Base-level synthesizers* MIDI channels 13 through 16 are used for melodic instruments, with channel 16 reserved for key-based percussion instruments.

- *Extended-level synthesizers* MIDI channels 1 through 10 are used for melodic instruments with channel 10 reserved for key-based percussion instruments.

Note the differentiation between melodic and percussive instruments. You can assign melodic instruments to different MIDI channels, and then assign a specific sound patch to that channel.

Percussive instruments are all on a single MIDI channel and *key-based*, which means that each key or note on the keyboard plays a different percussion instrument. For example, the middle C key is usually a high bongo, the D key in the same octave is a mute high conga, the E key is a low conga, and so on.

General MIDI

The MIDI Manufacturers Association (MMA) has a General MIDI specification that defines what percussive instrument each key on the keyboard plays, and what instrument is assigned to each patch number. The general MIDI specification is important because it helps standardize the way MIDI files will sound on any system. It defines the sounds for each patch number and the percussion sounds for keys on the keyboard. In this way, multimedia authors and MIDI musicians can create MIDI scores that can be played back on other systems with the assurance that those other systems will play the intended instruments. General MIDI ensures that a honky-tonk piano (general MIDI patch number 3) is played back as a honky-tonk piano on other systems. If a non-general MIDI keyboard is used that has a violin assigned to patch 3 instead, then the honky-tonk piano track (channel) will play with a violin sound. You use the MIDI Mapper utility in the Control Panel to correct these situations, as discussed next in this chapter. The MIDI Mapper rearranges the patch and percussion key mappings so MIDI files play correctly on keyboards that don't conform to the general MIDI specification.

Piano	Chromatic Percussion	Organ	Guitar
0 Acoustic Grand Piano	8 Celesta	16 Hammond Organ	24 Acoustic Guitar (nylon)
1 Bright Acoustic Piano	9 Glockenspiel	17 Percussive Organ	25 Acoustic Guitar (steel)
2 Electric Grand Piano	10 Music Box	18 Rock Organ	26 Electric Guitar (jazz)
3 Honky-tonk Piano	11 Vibraphone	19 Church Organ	27 Electric Guitar (clean)
4 Rhodes Piano	12 Marimba	20 Reed Organ	28 Electric Guitar (muted)
5 Chorused Piano	13 Xylophone	21 Accordion	29 Overdriven Guitar
6 Harpsichord	14 Tubular Bells	22 Harmonica	30 Distortion Guitar
7 Clavichord	15 Dulcimer	23 Tango Accordion	31 Guitar Harmonics

Bass	Strings	Ensemble	Brass
32 Acoustic Bass	40 Violin	48 String Ensemble 1	56 Trumpet
33 Electric Bass (finger)	41 Viola	49 String Ensemble 2	57 Trombone
34 Electric Bass (pick)	42 Cello	50 SynthStrings 1	58 Tuba
35 Fretless Bass	43 Contrabass	51 SynthStrings 2	59 Muted Trumpet
36 Slap Bass 1	44 Tremolo Strings	52 Choir Aahs	60 French Horn
37 Slap Bass 2	45 Pizzicato Strings	53 Voice Oohs	61 Brass Section
38 Synth Bass 1	46 Orchestral Harp	54 Synth Voice	62 Synth Brass 1
39 Synth Bass 2	47 Timpani	55 Orchestra Hit	63 Synth Brass 2

Table 14-2.   *The Standard MIDI Patch Assignments for MIDI Files Based on the General MIDI Mode Specification*

Reed	Pipes	Synth Lead	Synth Pad
64 Soprano Sax	72 Piccolo	80 Lead 1 (square)	88 Pad 1 (new age)
65 Alto Sax	73 Flute	81 Lead 2 (sawtooth)	89 Pad 2 (warm)
66 Tenor Sax	74 Recorder	82 Lead 3 (caliope lead)	90 Pad 3 (polysynth)
67 Baritone Sax	75 Pan Flute	83 Lead 4 (chiff lead)	91 Pad 4 (choir)
68 Oboe	76 Bottle Blow	84 Lead 5 (charang)	92 Pad 5 (bowed)
69 English Horn	77 Shakuhachi	85 Lead 6 (voice)	93 Pad 6 (metallic)
70 Bassoon	78 Whistle	86 Lead 7 (fifths)	94 Pad 7 (halo)
71 Clarinet	79 Ocarina	87 Lead 8 (brass + lead)	95 Pad 8 (sweep)

Synth Effects	Ethnic	Percussive	Sound Effects
96 FX 1 (rain)	104 Sitar	112 Tinkle Bell	120 Guitar Fret Noise
97 FX 2 (soundtrack)	105 Banjo	113 Agogo	121 Breath Noise
98 FX 3 (crystal)	106 Shamisen	114 Steel Drums	122 Seashore
99 FX 4 (atmosphere)	107 Koto	115 Woodblock	123 Bird Tweet
100 FX 5 (brightness)	108 Kalimba	116 Taiko Drum	124 Telephone Ring
101 FX 6 (goblins)	109 Bagpipe	117 Melodic Tom	125 Helicopter
102 FX 7 (echoes)	110 Fiddle	118 Synth Drum	126 Applause
103 FX 8 (sci-fi)	111 Shanai	119 Reverse Cymbal	127 Gunshot

Table 14-2.   *The Standard MIDI Patch Assignments for MIDI Files Based on the General MIDI Mode Specification (continued)*

The standard MIDI patch assignments for MIDI files, based on the General MIDI Mode specification, are listed in Table 14-2. The key-based percussion sounds are listed in Table 14-3.

The MIDI Mapper

The MIDI Mapper utility is located in the Control Panel. It is used to change the channel, patch, and key mappings if a synthesizer is attached that does not conform to the General MIDI specifications. Some older keyboards do not. Also note that if you're working with a sequencer and creating your own MIDI files, channel mappings and patch assignments are controlled within the sequencer software. The MIDI

Number	Sound	Number	Sound
35	Acoustic Bass Drum	59	Ride Cymbal 2
36	Bass Drum 1	60	High Bongo
37	Side Stick	61	Low Bongo
38	Acoustic Snare	62	Mute High Conga
39	Hand Clap	63	Open High Conga
40	Electric Snare	64	Low Conga
41	Low Floor Tom	65	High Timbale
42	Closed High-Hat	66	Low Timbale
43	High Floor Tom	67	High Agogo
44	Pedal High Hat	68	Low Agogo
45	Low Tom	69	Cabasa
46	Open High Hat	70	Maracas
47	Low-Mid Tom	71	Short Whistle
48	High-Mid Tom	72	Long Whistle
49	Crash Cymbal 1	73	Short Guiro
50	High Tom	74	Long Guiro
51	Ride Cymbal 1	75	Claves
52	Chinese Cymbal	76	High Wood Block
53	Ride Bell	77	Low Wood Block
54	Tambourine	78	Mute Cuica
55	Splash Cymbal	79	Open Cuica
56	Cowbell	80	Mute Triangle
57	Crash Cymbal 2	81	Open Triangle
58	Vibraslap		

Note: The keys are assigned numeric values; middle C is key number 60.

Table 14-3.   *MIDI Key Assignments for Percussion Instruments*

Mapper is mostly designed for users who play back MIDI files on non-standard equipment.

Using the MIDI Mapper

In the discussion of the MIDI Mapper, the term source (abbreviated "Src") refers to the input side of the Mapper. The term destination (abbreviated "Dest") refers to the output side of the Mapper. For example, if you're playing a MIDI file, it inputs MIDI information into the MIDI Mapper on the source channels and outputs it to your sound board or MIDI device on the destination channel. You use the MIDI Mapper to change the destination channel, but not the source channel because the source channel always stays the same. Also note the following:

- All references to MIDI channel numbers use the logical channel numbers 1 through 16. The actual MIDI specification refers to these as channels 0 through 15.

- All references to MIDI program/patch-change and key values use the physical values 0 through 127.

MIDI Mapper Startup and Overview

Double-click the MIDI Mapper icon in the Control Panel. The MIDI Mapper dialog box shown here appears.

In the Show field, you click either Setups to change channel mappings, Patch Maps to change the configuration of a patch, or Key Maps to change the assignment of percussion sounds on synthesizer keyboards. You can edit an existing channel, patch, or key map by choosing it in the Name field and clicking the Edit button. Click New to create a new map, after first selecting the type in the Show field.

The Channel Map

The channel map is accessed by clicking the Setups button in the Show field, and then choosing a setup in the Name field and clicking the Edit button. You'll see a MIDI Setup dialog box similar to the one shown in Figure 14-11. This dialog box is for a Sound Blaster card. To create a new MIDI setup, click the New button in the MIDI Mapper dialog box. You'll be asked for a name and description of the new MIDI map. When you respond you'll see a basic channel map with blank port and patch assignments.

MIDI Setup: 'Extended MIDI'

Src Chan	Dest Chan	Port Name	Patch Map Name	Active
1	1	Creative Labs Sound Blaster 1.5	[None]	☒
2	2	Creative Labs Sound Blaster 1.5	[None]	☒
3	3	Creative Labs Sound Blaster 1.5	[None]	☒
4	4	Creative Labs Sound Blaster 1.5	[None]	☒
5	5	Creative Labs Sound Blaster 1.5	[None]	☒
6	6	Creative Labs Sound Blaster 1.5	[None]	☒
7	7	Creative Labs Sound Blaster 1.5	[None]	☒
8	8	Creative Labs Sound Blaster 1.5	[None]	☒
9	9	Creative Labs Sound Blaster 1.5	[None]	☒
10	10	SB MIDI Out	MT32 Perc	☒
11	11	[None]	[None]	▓
12	12	[None]	[None]	▓
13	13	[None]	[None]	▓
14	14	[None]	[None]	▓
15	15	[None]	[None]	▓
16	16	[None]	[None]	▓

OK   Cancel   Help

Figure 14-11. *The MIDI Setup dialog box is used to change the channel mapping and patch assignments*

The MIDI Mapper uses a single channel map with an entry for each of the 16 MIDI channels. Each channel map entry specifies the information described in the following sections.

The Src Chan Column   Src Chan simply refers to the source channel.

The Dest Chan Column   Dest Chan is the destination channel for the MIDI message. You can change this channel if you have a synthesizer tuned to a specific channel and you want it to receive messages from another channel. The alternative is to change the channel setting of the synthesizer.

The Port Name Column   Port Name is perhaps the most important option in the MIDI Mapper if you have both a sound card and an external synthesizer attached. You use Port Name to define whether channels should be directed to the internal card or through the MIDI port to an external synthesizer. To direct a channel to a MIDI port, click the down arrow button and select a MIDI Out port. In Figure 14-11, note that channel 10 (the percussion channel) has been directed to the MIDI port of the sound blaster. A MIDI drum machine might be attached to this port.

The Patch Map Name Column   Table 14-2, seen earlier in this chapter lists the instruments and patch numbers defined by the general MIDI specification. If your synthesizer doesn't play the correct instruments when you play a MIDI file, or if you just want to change which instruments it plays, choose a different patch map in this field. You can use an existing patch map, but most likely, you'll need to create another, as discussed in the upcoming "Patch Maps" section.

The Active Column   You can disable the active field to turn off a channel. For example, if you don't want to hear a violin sound on channel 3, disable its Active option.

There are several ways you might use the channel mapping feature. Assume your system has a sound board and all the channels are assigned to a port name that matches the sound board. Now assume you have temporary use of a MIDI synthesizer. You could create a new channel map that directs all the channels to the MIDI port, while keeping your old settings in another channel map so you can revert back to the sound board only.

If your channel map has mixed port assignments in which some channels are directed to an internal sound board and others are directed to the MIDI port, you may need to change the patch maps for either the sound card or the MIDI port. Most sound cards conform to general MIDI specifications, so you can usually specify None in the Patch Map Name column settings.

Note that changing a patch map, even if a sound board or synthesizer doesn't need a change, can produce interesting results. Basically, the instruments in the MIDI score are changed to the instrument numbers in the new patch. Keep in mind that the results may not sound the way the composer intended.

Patch Maps

Each channel map entry can have an associated patch map. Patch maps affect the instrument sounds played by a sound card or synthesizer attached to the port. You can also adjust the volume of the channel using the patch map. Keep in mind that patch maps only need to be created if your synthesizer does not conform to the general MIDI instrument specifications listed in Table 14-2. You'll need to find out the numbers assigned to the instruments on your synthesizer, and then create a new patch map and reroute the MIDI Mapper source number to the correct destination number on your synthesizer. This will ensure that MIDI files play back with the instruments intended by the composer.

To access the Patch Map dialog box, click Patch Maps on the MIDI Mapper main dialog box, then click New to create a new patch map. To edit an existing patch map, choose it in the Name drop-down list box and click the Edit button. The patch map for Roland MT-32 is shown in Figure 14-12.

There are 128 patches (instrument types) defined in the patch map. Some synthesizers number these patches from 0 to 127 while others number the patches from 1 to 128. Click the button at the top of the dialog box to switch between 0-based or 1-based patches. The dialog box lists the source patch number and source patch

		MIDI Patch Map: 'MT32'			
		1 based patches			
Src Patch	Src Patch Name	Dest Patch	Volume %	Key Map Name	
0	Acoustic Grand Piano	0	100	[None]	
1	Bright Acoustic Piano	1	100	[None]	
2	Electric Grand Piano	3	100	[None]	
3	Honky-tonk Piano	7	100	[None]	
4	Rhodes Piano	5	100	[None]	
5	Chorused Piano	6	100	[None]	
6	Harpsichord	17	100	[None]	
7	Clavinet	21	100	[None]	
8	Celesta	22	100	[None]	
9	Glockenspiel	101	100	[None]	
10	Music Box	101	100	[None]	
11	Vibraphone	98	100	[None]	
12	Marimba	104	100	[None]	
13	Xylophone	103	100	[None]	
14	Tubular Bells	102	100	[None]	
15	Dulcimer	105	100	[None]	

OK	Cancel	Help

Figure 14-12. *The MIDI Patch Map dialog box is used to change the sounds played on MIDI channels*

name. You can't change these, but you can change the destination patch number to conform with the instrument on your synthesizer. For example, in Figure 14-12, note that patch 3, the honky-tonk piano, is reassigned to dest patch 7 on the external synthesizer, where that sound exists. As mentioned, you need to first determine the patch number for the instruments on your synthesizer, and then match them to the source patch numbers and names on the dialog box.

You can also change the volume of individual patches by adjusting the values in the volume fields. If a sound on one patch is louder than it should be, adjust the value by clicking the up arrow or down arrow button. You can use the Key Map field to select a different key mapping for the patch. For example, you can choose "+1 octave" in the list to adjust a sound one octave up the scale. Other values are "+2 octave," and "−1 octave." Additional key maps are used for percussive instruments. If you are creating a patch map for percussion instruments, specify a percussion key map name in the key map field for all instruments in the patch. Key maps are discussed next.

Once you have created a patch map, assign it to a channel using the channel mapping options discussed in the previous section.

Key Maps

There are two types of key maps. The first defines percussion sounds played by the keys on a synthesizer keyboard. The second adjusts the registration of melodic sounds up or down an octave. Windows 3.1 comes with three octave adjustment options (+1 octave, +2 octave, and –1 octave), which offer sufficient range so you won't need to create others. Choose one of these as a patch in the MIDI Patch Map dialog box discussed in the previous section.

The general MIDI specification assigns keys 35 through 81 to various percussion instruments. If your synthesizer assigns different numbers to the instruments, you need to determine what the numbers are and create a new key map. Choose Key Maps in the Show field of the main MIDI Mapper menu, and then click the New button. Some key maps already exist, such as the Roland MT-33. To view or edit those maps, select a name in the Name field and click the Edit button. The key map for Proteus/1 is shown in Figure 14-13. Note how some of the keys are remapped to match the percussion sounds on that synthesizer.

More About Multimedia and the MCI Interface

The multimedia interface in Windows 3.1 consists of a number of driver files, but its architecture is simple, consisting of just a few modules as shown in Figure 14-14. The

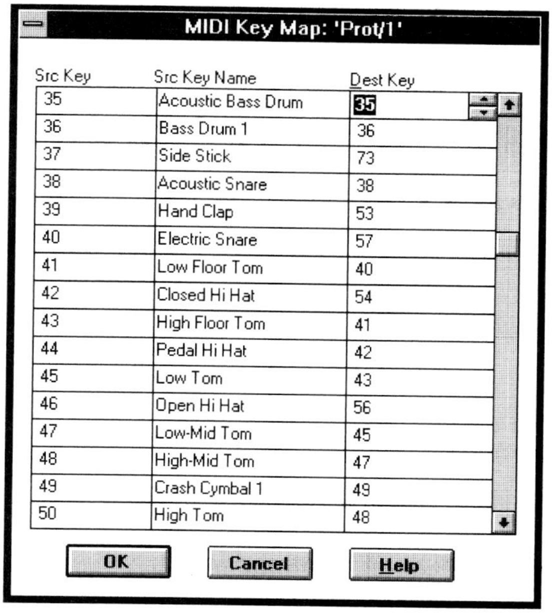

Src Key	Src Key Name	Dest Key
35	Acoustic Bass Drum	35
36	Bass Drum 1	36
37	Side Stick	73
38	Acoustic Snare	38
39	Hand Clap	53
40	Electric Snare	57
41	Low Floor Tom	40
42	Closed Hi Hat	54
43	High Floor Tom	41
44	Pedal Hi Hat	42
45	Low Tom	43
46	Open Hi Hat	56
47	Low-Mid Tom	45
48	High-Mid Tom	47
49	Crash Cymbal 1	49
50	High Tom	48

MIDI Key Map: 'Prot/1'

OK   Cancel   Help

Figure 14-13.   *Use the MIDI Key Map dialog box to change the key assignments for percussion sounds*

connection between modules illustrates the flow of control from an application to a physical device. The modules are described here:

- *MMSYSTEM.DLL* The MMSYSTEM.DLL module is a dynamic link library that provides Media Control Interface (MCI) services and low-level multimedia support functions.

- *Multimedia Device Drivers* The multimedia device drivers provide support for specific types of equipment such as sound boards. Some examples are MSADLIB.DRV (the Ad Lib sound board driver) and SNDBLST.DRV (the Sound Blaster driver).

- *Drivers for the Media Control Interface* Media Control Interface drivers provide high-level control of media devices. Examples are MCICDA.DRV (CD Audio driver) and MCISEQ.DRV (MIDI device driver).

The Media Control Interface (MCI)

MCI is a high-level command interface to multimedia devices and resource files. Programmers take advantage of MCI to access commands for controlling internal

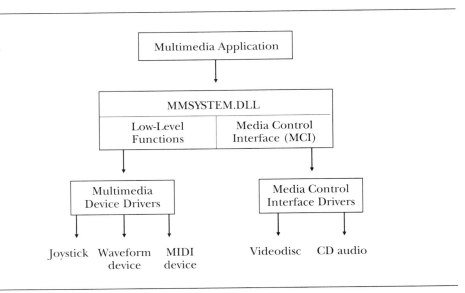

Figure 14-14.   *Windows multimedia architecture*

and external audio and visual peripherals. MCI coordinates activities and communicates with MCI device drivers. Some MCI device drivers, such as those for videodisc and movie players, control the target device directly. Others such as the MIDI and waveform services, indirectly control more intelligent devices such as sound boards and MIDI keyboards.

MCI device drivers can stream digital audio and MIDI data directly from a storage device to the appropriate device driver, allowing applications to play files too large to fit in available physical memory. This data streaming takes place in the background while an application is running. The application is responsible only for setting up MCI and telling it to start playing or recording.

MCI commands provide programmers with a generic interface to multimedia devices, making programming easier, and production faster. The advantage to the user is a wide selection of new multimedia products for Windows 3.1.

MCI Device Types

The following table lists the types of devices that are defined in the Microsoft Multimedia Development Kit and, on the left, the device type name associated with each device in the SYSTEM.INI file. The list represents the type of products supported by Windows 3.1.

Device Type Name	Device
cdaudio	CD audio (Red Book) player
dat	Digital audio tape player (DATs)
digitalvideo	Digital video in a window
mmmovie	Movie or animation player
other	Undefined MCI device
overlay	Video overlay device
scanner	Image scanner
sequencer	MIDI sequencer
vcr	Videotape recorder or player
videodisc	Videodisc player
waveaudio	Waveform audio device

MCI Components

The following list describes some of the device drivers that are fundamental to multimedia. The names on the left are the option names used in the [mci] section of the SYSTEM.INI file. The three devices listed here are included with Windows 3.1:

Option Name	Filename	Device
cdaudio	MCICDA.DRV	An MCI device driver for playing compact disc (Red Book) audio.
sequencer	MCISEQ.DRV	An MCI device driver for playing MIDI files.
waveaudio	MCIWAVE.DRV	An MCI device driver for playing and recording waveform audio.

The Windows MDK includes the following additional MCI drivers that you may get when purchasing multimedia products:

Option Name	Filename	Device
videodisc	MCIPIONR.DRV	An MCI device driver for controlling the Pioneer LD-V4200 videodisc player.
mmmovie	MCIMMP.DRV	An MCI device driver for playing multimedia movie files.

Multimedia drivers and MCI components are installed when Windows is installed or by using the Drivers utility in the Control Panel. The drivers may also be installed when you install multimedia devices and add the Multimedia Extensions.

If a device type is installed more than once, the device is appended with an integer to create unique names for each MCI device type entry. For example, if two audio devices are installed, the entries "cdaudio" and "cdaudio1" are made in the file. In this case, each name refers to a different CD audio player.

These lists do not represent all available drivers. Multimedia vendors create their own drivers and make entries into the SYSTEM.INI when you install their products.

SYSTEM.INI Entries for Multimedia

The SYSTEM.INI file contains the following sections related to multimedia:

Section	Function
[drivers]	Lists multimedia drivers
[mci]	Lists Media Control Interface drivers
[mmsystem]	Lists options used by MMSYSTEM.DLL
[Multimedia.Setup]	Lists audio and display drivers selected during setup of Windows with Multimedia Extensions

Media Vision Pro Audio Spectrum Example   Here's an example of the settings in SYSTEM.INI for the Media Vision Pro Audio Spectrum. Those drivers specific to Media Vision are labeled with a description between brackets. All other drivers are included with Windows or the Multimedia Extensions, which are supplied with the Pro Audio Spectrum.

```
[drivers]
midimapper=midimap.drv
joystick=ibmjoy.drv
timer=timer.drv
MIDI=mvfm.drv          Media Vision FM stereo driver*
MIDI1=mvmidi.drv       Media Vision MIDI interface driver
aux=mvaux.drv          Media Vision mixer volume control
mixer=mcimixer.drv     Media Vision mixer driver
wave=mvwave.drv        Media Vision waveform audio driver


[mci]
cdaudio=mcicda.drv
waveaudio=mciwave.drv
Sequencer=mciseq.drv
mixer=mcimixer.drv     Media Vision MCI mixer extension
```

*FM refers to Frequency Modulation, which is the method used by the Pro Audio Spectrum to create synthesized sounds.

There are several other settings made by the Pro Audio Spectrum setup routine. The DMA and IRQ settings for the board in your system are added to the [mvwave.drv] section. In the [386Enh] section, the line "device=vadmad.386" is added to provide virtual audio DMA support when running in 386 enhanced mode.

Sound Blaster Pro Setup Example   The following settings are included in the SYSTEM.INI file when you install the Sound Blaster Pro:

```
[drivers]
midimapper=midimap.drv
joystick=ibmjoy.drv
timer=timer.drv
MIDI=sbpfm.drv         Sound Blaster FM stereo driver*
MIDI1=sbpsnd.drv       Sound Blaster MIDI interface driver
aux=sbpaux.drv         Sound Blaster mixer volume control
wave=sbpsnd.drv        Sound Blaster waveform audio driver
```

The following settings in the [mci] section are made when Windows is installed:

```
[mci]
cdaudio=mcicda.drv
waveaudio=mciwave.drv
Sequencer=mciseq.drv
```

*FM refers to Frequency Modulation, which is the method used by the Sound Blaster to create synthesized sounds.

The Sound Blaster Pro also adds settings to a section called [sndblst.drv], in which you specify the I/O port, interrupt settings, and DMA channel used by the card in your system.

Chapter *15*

Printers

The information in this chapter will enable you to install new printers or change the default configuration of existing printers. You'll learn how to

- Install a new printer driver
- Configure an installed printer
- Select printers and control their features
- Print documents
- Work with the Print Manager

Configuring and using printers is easy in Windows. When multiple printers are installed, you simply choose the one to print on from a list in the Print Setup dialog box. The dialog box also has options for setting the printer's features.

The Print Setup dialog box shows up in two places: when you install and configure printers using the Printers icon in the Control Panel, and when you choose Print Setup on the File menu in a Windows application. While both boxes have similar features, their use is different:

- Use the Control Panel Printer utility and its Printer Setup dialog box to add new printers or reconfigure existing printers. Changes you make in this box become the default settings.

- Use the Printer Setup option in applications to select another printer or to change the default settings. Changes you make here only apply to the current session. The next time you open the application, printer settings revert to the defaults in the Control Panel.

If you plan to make permanent changes to printer settings that you want all applications to use, make them in the Control Panel Printer utility.

When a document is printed in Windows, it is first sent to the Print Manager, which queues the print job so you can continue working. This chapter discusses the pros and cons of using the Print Manager. You can disable the Print Manager to improve performance, but keeping it active lets you access your system immediately, if necessary. For example, you might need to open a file while your system is in the middle of a big print job. Without the Print Manager, you would need to stop the print job.

The type of printer installed determines which fonts are available to applications. TrueType fonts will always be available unless you've disabled them, but special printer fonts built into your printer are part of the printer driver. This is especially true of PostScript printers. Fonts are covered in Chapter 16.

 While you're setting up a printer, you can access detailed information about specific printers and their setup by looking in the PRINTER.WRI file and on the help menus.

Printer Setup

To add a new printer or change the settings of an existing printer, use the Printer utility on the Control Panel. This is the same utility you worked with during Windows installation if you installed a printer. Double-click the Printers icon to open the Printers dialog box shown in Figure 15-1.

This dialog box shows that four printers are currently installed. The Default Printer box lists the printer that applications will use, but you can change this setting when working in applications by opening the application's Printer Setup dialog box.

Note that three HP LaserJet printer drivers are connected to the LPT1 port in Figure 15-1. There are two reasons for this. One, a single printer with three possible setups requires three separate drivers. Two, a switchbox directs printing from one port to three printers. These topics are covered later in this chapter.

Adding a New Printer Driver

After adding a new printer to your system, follow the steps here to add the new printer driver. You'll need to know which port the printer is attached to. If it's connected to a serial port, you'll need to know the serial interface settings such as baud rate, bits, and parity. This will be covered shortly.

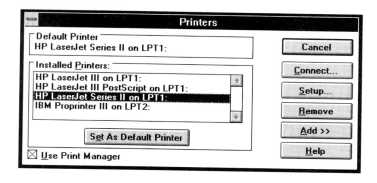

Figure 15-1. *The Printers dialog box*

Click the Add button to display the List of Printers box. Scan the list to find the name of your printer, and then highlight it and click the Install button.

Messages will appear asking you to insert one or more of the Windows disks. The driver files are copied and, in a moment, you see your new printer listed in the Installed Printers list box. The next step is to configure the printer, which you'll do shortly.

If You Can't Find a Printer Driver

If you don't see your printer listed, highlight Install Unlisted or Updated Printer, then insert a disk that contains the printer's driver in the floppy drive.

You can obtain this driver from the printer manufacturer or by calling Microsoft at (800) 426-9400 and asking for the Windows Driver Library (WDL) disk.

If you don't have the appropriate driver and you want to use your printer right away, try using a driver for a compatible printer. For example, many laser printers use the HP LaserJet driver, and many dot matrix printers are compatible with Epson drivers. The following sections can help you locate a compatible printer driver.

Laser Printer Drivers   The following are some possible driver substitutes for a variety of laser printers.

- For Hewlett-Packard-compatible laser printers, use the Hewlett-Packard LaserJet Plus driver.

- For color PostScript printers, use the QMS-ColorScript driver.

- For PostScript printers with 35-font Plus font set or superset, use the Apple LaserWriter Plus driver.

Dot Matrix Printer Drivers   The following are some possible driver substitutes for dot matrix printers.

- For IBM-compatible 9-pin dot matrix printers, use the IBM Proprinter driver.

- For Epson-compatible 9-pin dot matrix printers, use the Epson FX-80 driver for narrow-carriage printers or the FX-100 driver for wide-carriage printers.

- For IBM-compatible 24-pin printers, use the IBM Proprinter X24 driver.

- For Epson LQ-compatible 24-pin printers, use the Epson LQ-1500 driver.

Plotter Driver   If you have a Hewlett-Packard HPGL-compatible plotter, use the Hewlett-Packard 7475A plotter driver.

The Generic/Text Only Printer Driver   If you have a printer that is not listed in the previous sections or in the Printers dialog box, set up the Generic/Text Only printer driver until you can obtain a driver from the manufacturer. Using this driver does not necessarily mean you will be able to take advantage of all your printer's features. For step-by-step instructions on how to use the Generic/Text Only printer driver, refer to the section "Configuring Your Own Printer Driver" later in this chapter.

Configuring the Printer

Once the printer drivers are copied to your system and the printer name appears in the Installed Printers box, you're ready to configure the printer. Make sure the new printer is highlighted, then click the Connect button. The dialog box in Figure 15-2 appears.

Printer Port Settings

Use the Connect dialog box to choose the LPT or COM port that the printer is attached to. Here's the selection of ports you can choose from, with a description of each of the device names defined by DOS and Windows:

LPT1, 2, or 3	Parallel printer ports
COM1, 2, 3, or 4	Serial printer ports
EPT	Special IBM printer ports
FILE	Sends printed output to a file for printing at another time
LPT1.OS2	Parallel printer port 1 when using OS/2's DOS compatibility box

LPT2.OS2   Parallel printer port 2 when using OS/2's DOS
                      compatibility box

Most systems do not physically have all these ports. In most cases, the LPT1 parallel port and the COM1 serial port are present. New systems usually have both COM1 and COM2 attachments. LPT parallel ports have 25-pin female type connectors. COM ports have 9- or 25-pin male connectors.

If you pick a COM port, the Settings button becomes available. Click it to set the baud rate and other serial communications settings. If you're unfamiliar with the settings, refer to Chapter 23.

Timeout Options

The fields in the Timeout box have default settings that are appropriate in most cases. You may want to change them in these instances:

- The Device Not Selected field determines the amount of time that elapses before you see warning messages when a printer is off-line or not responding. Decrease this value for an earlier warning, or increase it to provide more time to fix a printer problem (like setting it online) before the warning message appears. The warning box does not impede your work, but it can be inconvenient if it appears too soon. For example, if a shared printer is often busy, you might want Windows to attempt access to it for a longer time before it displays its message.

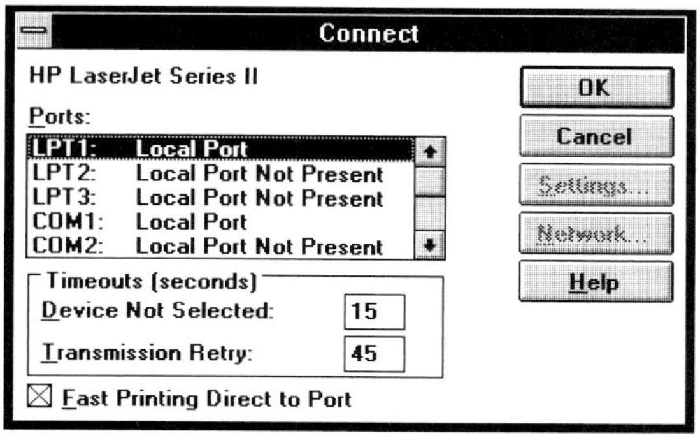

Figure 15-2.   The Connect dialog box

- The Transmission Retry option specifies the amount of time Windows will continue to retry access to a printer you are already using. It is often necessary to increase this option when printing large documents, graphics, or PostScript files that fill the printer's buffer and prevent Windows from sending more print information. Windows continues to retry sending to the printer, but if the buffer depletes slowly, Windows assumes the printer is stalled and displays an error message. You can continue printing in a few seconds by responding to the error message. Windows then continues transmitting, but the error messages are annoying, especially if you return from lunch and find that your print job is only 10 percent complete. Increasing the value makes Windows retry the printer for a longer period of time, thus allowing its printer buffer time to empty.

On serial printers, you can decrease the data transmission rate (baud rate) so Windows sends information to the printer at the same speed at which it prints.

At this point, you can save the configuration or continue setting the printer's features. To save the configuration, click the OK button on the Printers - Configure dialog box. This returns you to the Printers dialog box, where clicking the OK button returns you to the Control Panel.

Bypassing DOS

In most cases, the Fast Printing Direct to Port option on the Connect dialog box is enabled. When checked, Windows does not use DOS interrupts for printing. It prints directly to the printer to improve performance.

Using Multiple Drivers and Switchboxes

There are two situations in which you might have multiple printer drivers installed for the same port:

- You can install multiple drivers for a single printer on the same port to access different configurations for that printer. For example, Figure 15-1 shows two additional drivers installed for use with an HP LaserJet III. The PostScript printer driver provides support when the optional PostScript cartridge is installed. The HP LaserJet Series II driver has a useful intensity setting feature (discussed later in this chapter) that the LaserJet III driver does not have.

- If you have multiple printers attached to a switchbox coming off of one port, you install a driver for each printer, then set the same port for each. When printing, you first choose the printer driver to use, then switch to the appropriate printer on the switchbox.

Even if you don't have a PostScript printer, you should install its driver, then use that driver to create print files that you can print at copy shops or service bureaus. PostScript is common in the typesetting industry, so you shouldn't have any problem producing high-quality documents. Chapter 21 covers this in more detail.

Printing to a File

A *print file* contains all the information required to print a document at a later time, even if the application that created it is not running. A print file allows you to create a file with a Windows application, then send the file to a friend or associate to print on their printer even if they don't have the Windows application. You can create the file without actually having the printer, and they can print the file without starting the application that created it. You can print such a file using one of the following methods:

- Drag and drop the icon for the file from the File Manager to the running Print Manager.
- Use the Print command in the File Manager.
- Use the COPY or PRINT command at the DOS Prompt.

To create print files, first follow the instructions presented earlier for installing a printer driver. Then follow these steps:

1. Open the Printers utility (see Figure 15-1) in the Control Panel.
2. Click the Add button and choose a printer.
3. Click the Connect button, then choose File as the port for the printer.
4. Close the dialog box.

After you've installed the printer, you can select it in your application. To create the print file, choose Print from the File menu. You'll be asked to name the print file. All information required to print the document is then stored in the file, which you can print at another time or send to another user.

Creating Custom Ports

Instead of naming the file every time you use a printer connected to a File port, you can create a custom port that automatically saves your print file with a specific filename. The print file is overwritten every time you print to the port, so you only use this option to print after first backing up the previous file (or, you may not care if it's copied over).

In the following illustration, a port called H:PROJECTS.DOC is listed. This port is used to send a print document to a shared directory on a remote network hard drive where other users can access it. Users then print the file on their own printer.

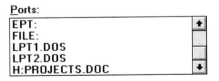

To create a custom port, insert a line similar to the following in the [ports] sections of WIN.INI. You can use your own drive and filename, but the equal sign must be included.

```
H:PROJECTS.DOC=
```

The Print Setup Dialog Box

Once a printer is installed, set its features by clicking the Setup button on the Printers dialog box. Since printers have different features, Print Setup dialog boxes don't always look the same, but they share many features. The Setup dialog box for an HP LaserJet printer is shown in Figure 15-3.

The Setup dialog box displayed by the Control Panel Printers option is the same one you see when choosing Print Setup from an application.

Some of the options you'll encounter on the Setup dialog box are described in the following sections. For additional help on any option, click the Help button.

Cartridges Select the cartridge fonts installed in the printer. You can select only from the cartridges your printer allows.

Fonts Click the Fonts button to install additional fonts. Fonts are covered in Chapter 16.

Resolution Choose a printing resolution in the Resolution box. Select a low resolution to print faster, draft-quality documents; then select a higher resolution to print the final pages.

Memory Specify the amount of memory installed in your printer.

Options The Options button may be available for some printers. Click it and change option settings according to instructions you can view by pressing the Help button.

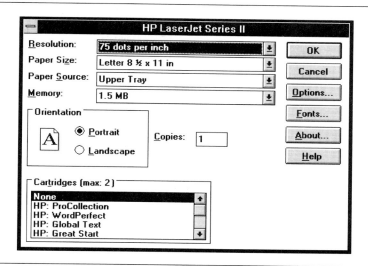

Figure 15-3.   *A typical Printer Setup dialog box*

Orientation   Select Landscape to print sideways and Portrait to print on the paper normally.

Paper Size (or Format)   Select the paper size used on the printer.

Paper Source (or Feed)   In the Source box, choose the paper tray where your printer will get paper, or the method it will use to advance paper as it prints. Different paper sizes or forms can be selected for a printer that has multiple trays. For example, one tray can hold company stationery while another can hold blank paper. When manual feed is selected, the printer waits for you to insert a sheet of paper or an envelope in the manual feed slot.

Printer   The Printer Setup dialog box often includes a Printer list box that displays a family of printers related to the printer you previously selected. Choose a printer from this list that exactly matches your printer. While most printers will have the same features, you should select the exact model of your printer if possible, since there may be subtle differences.

The Options Dialog Box

Click the Options button on the Print Setup dialog box to display the Options dialog box pictured in Figure 15-4. Use this dialog box to make resolution adjustments when printing graphic images. It sets the gray-scale on single-color printers.

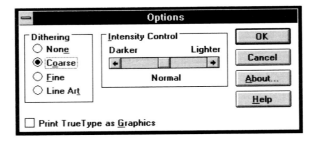

Figure 15-4.   *The Options dialog box is used to set printer resolution*

Dithering   The dithering options are used to specify the fineness of detail in graphic images when colors are printed on single-color printers. The options work in conjunction with the Intensity Control slider to control the conversion of colors to gray-scale. The maximum number of dots per inch is achieved when Fine or Line Art is selected in the Dithering box. When Coarse is selected, larger dots are used, and when None is selected, images are printed as either black or white (the lightest colors print white). Note that the Fine and Line Art options work best on high-resolution printers such as laser printers. The Line Art option converts some colors to patterns for special effects, so you'll need to experiment with the colors available in your applications when using this option.

Intensity Control   The Intensity Control slider is used to darken or lighten the dot pattern when Coarse, Fine, or Line Art is selected in the Dithering box. You'll need to experiment to get the intensity that's right for your art. For example, in Paintbrush, yellow is the lightest color, but sliding the Intensity Control slider to Darker causes it to print black. Sliding the control to lighter makes colors that normally print black appear in various shades of gray.

TrueType Fonts in Bitmapped Images   Click the Print TrueType Fonts as Graphics option when you want to overlap graphic images onto text. When checked, it prints TrueType fonts as if they are graphics. This is important in applications such as Excel where a TrueType font that is hidden behind a cell would print completely. If you use this option, only the part that shows will print.

Important Printer Setup Information

Because every printer is different, Microsoft supplies important information about installation and setup in the Printers dialog box help facility. After installing a printer, click the Help button on the main Printers dialog box, or in the Connect, Setup, or Options dialog box.

If you have a PostScript printer, you'll find an abundance of information on printer settings in the Help facility.

Printer Fonts

Many printers now allow you to install additional fonts along with the built-in fonts. These fonts may come in the form of cartridges or may be disk based. Disk-based fonts, or *soft fonts,* are copied from your computer to the memory of the printer; therefore a printer memory upgrade may be necessary to support soft fonts. Chapter 16 contains a complete discussion of printer fonts and system fonts.

Configuring Your Own Printer Driver

When you can't locate a driver to use for your particular printer, try using the driver of a compatible printer. If that fails, use the Generic/Text Only printer driver in the Printers dialog box until you obtain the correct printer driver. This section discusses how to configure the Generic/Text Only printer driver.

Start by selecting the Printers icon on the Control Panel. In the List of Printers box, choose the Generic/Text Only driver, then press the Install button. When the selection appears in the Installed Printers list box, select it and click the Setup button. In a moment, the Generic/Text Only dialog box shown in Figure 15-5 appears. You can enter some initial settings for your printer on the Generic/Text Only dialog box, such as Paper Size, Paper Feed method, and Carriage size.

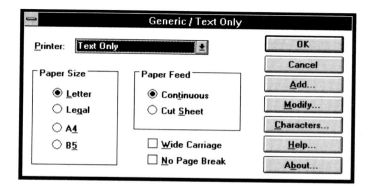

Figure 15-5.   *Use the Generic/Text Only dialog box to create your own printer driver*

Next, press the Add button to add the new printer description and supply other information. The dialog box in Figure 15-6 appears. Because you can set up as many generic printer descriptions as necessary, a name is important. Type it in the New Printer Name box.

Specify the control codes your printer uses to set fonts and other functions in the Printer Codes section. (You can find these codes in your printer manual.) Click an appropriate text box (under Printer Codes), then hold down the ALT key and type **0** and the three-digit code on the *numeric* keypad. Make sure the NUM LOCK key is on. Repeat this procedure for each item under Printer Codes, then click OK.

The Extended Character Set

Most printers have an extra set of characters from ASCII 128 to 255 called the *extended character set*. Because these characters may differ between printers, use the Characters dialog box to specify how the characters will print on your printer. Click the Characters button in the Generic/Text Only dialog box to display the Characters dialog box.

The On Screen list box shows an ANSI value and the character that displays on the screen. Scroll through the On Screen list to find the character you want to print, then enter your printer's code for the same value by holding the ALT key, while typing **0** and the three-digit number on the *numeric* keypad. Make sure the NUM LOCK key is on when you do this. Repeat these steps for each character you want to print. When finished, click OK until you return to the Control Panel to ensure that all changes are saved.

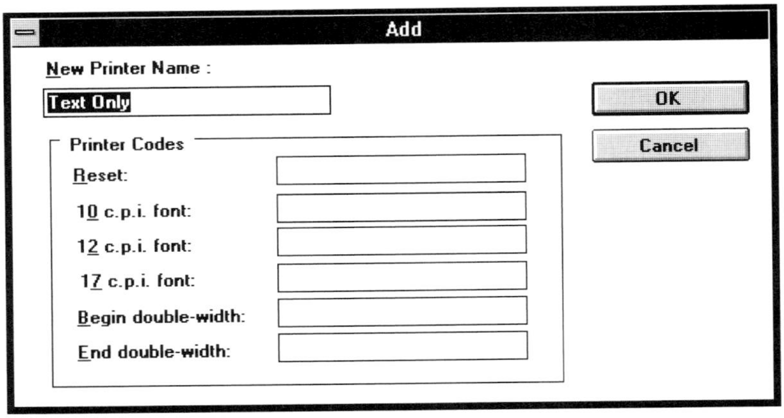

Figure 15-6.   *The Add dialog box*

Other Printer Options

The following options are set on the Printers dialog box.

Setting the Default Printer

You can set a default printer, which is the printer most applications automatically use when printing. Select the Printers icon on the Control Panel, then double-click the printer you want to be the default printer (or click the Set as Default Printer button). The printer will then appear in the Default Printer box.

The default printer is used by most applications the first time you start them. If you change the printer using the application's Printer Setup dialog box, the new printer will stay active for that application until changed or until you exit Windows.

The Print Manager

The Print Manager is a print job manager. It is useful when printing big jobs that tie up your computer for long stretches of time. The purpose of the Print Manager is to let you access your system while it prints. There's actually more to this than you might think. Without the Print Manager, you must stop a print job if you absolutely need to use your computer for other tasks. The Print Manager lets you share your system with your printer.

The Print Manager only works with Windows applications. Non-Windows applications automatically bypass the Print Manager. The Print Manager places files to print in queues, where they await printing. It holds the files in the queue if the printer is off or out of service and prints them at the next available time, unless you end your Windows session, which discards the queue. To view files in the queue, simply start the Print Manager. You can change the order of files in the queue when you want to print one file before another or you can remove any file from the queue.

The Print Manager operates automatically. You only open the Print Manager to manage files in the queue and change priorities. An example of the Print Manager window appears in Figure 15-7. These tasks are discussed in the following sections.

Handling Error Messages   When you print a file, the Print Manager icon appears on the desktop. If a printer is off-line, out of paper, or having other problems, Print Manager displays a message telling you that it's having problems printing your file. After fixing the printer problem, you click the message box's Retry button to resume printing. If you had to shut the printer off, and removed the Print Manager message, you'll need to open the Print Manager to either re-queue the file or delete it from the queue and reprint from your application. The Print Manager will display a "printer stalled" message in its message bar. Click the Resume button to resume printing on the stalled job.

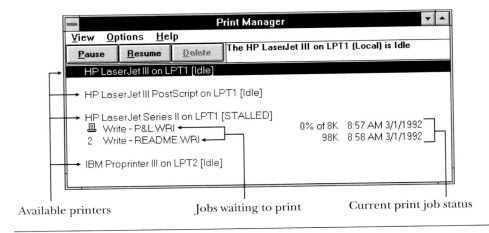

Figure 15-7.   *The Print Manager window*

Rearranging Print Jobs in a Queue   To rearrange print jobs in the queue, point to the print job to move, then click and drag it up or down through the queue list with the mouse. An icon that looks like an arrow appears. When you release the mouse button, the print job moves to its new location.

Deleting Print Jobs in a Queue   To delete a print job, simply click its name in the Print Manager queue and click the Delete button.

Print Manager Menu Options and Buttons

The Print Manager has two important menus. The first is the Options menu, which lets you change the priority and features of the Print Manager. The second is the View menu, which lets you set the display of file information on or off, or lets you work with network queues. These menus, their options, and the Print Manager buttons are discussed in this section.

The Options Menu

The following options are available from the Options menu. The priority settings are used to control how much time the Print Manager gives to each print file in the background as you work with other applications. In any multitasking environment, every running application is given a slice of the processor's time. The number of time slices you give the Print Manager is determined by assigning low, medium, or high priority to the print job.

Low Priority   In this mode, print jobs are given less of the processor's time while applications are given more of the processor's time. Use this option when you need to print, but you also want to work in a foreground application. This option ensures that your application is given the full attention of the processor when it's working on a task; print jobs continue printing when your application is not busy.

Medium Priority   In this mode, print jobs and applications are allocated processing time somewhat equally. Your application may slow down when more information is sent to the printer. You might want to start with this option, then switch to Low Priority if your application is running too slowly, or to High Priority if you need to quickly finish the print job.

High Priority   In this mode, print jobs are given a high priority while applications are given a low priority. Set this option when working in applications that don't require a lot of processor time, for instance when typing non-formatted text in an application such as Notepad.

Alert Always   When you select this option, the Print Manager's messages are displayed immediately.

Flash If Inactive   Select the Flash If Inactive option if you want the Print Manager title bar, or its icon on the desktop to flash when it needs to display a message. You then open the Print Manager or make it active to view the message.

Ignore If Inactive   If the Print Manager window is inactive or reduced to an icon, the Ignore If Inactive option prevents messages from being displayed.

Network   The Network option is available when connected to a network. Choose it to set the following options:

- *Update Network Display* Set this option to off to ignore the status of the network queue. Setting this option on will slow your system down, and increase network traffic. Turning Update Network Display on is not recommended unless you set it on to temporarily monitor a queue for availability.

- *Spool Net Jobs* Set this option to on to send print jobs directly to the network printer and bypass the Print Manager. You should set Spool Net Jobs to on if your network has its own spooling program, and most do.

   The printer priority setting depends a lot on the type of application you're using. A database application that is sorting a mailing list requires almost 100 percent of your processor's time so printing may pause until the sorting task is completed, depending on the priority mode and the application.

On the other hand, when working with a word processor, your system will idle every time you stop typing. This idle time can be put to use for printing. If Low Priority is set, the idle gaps of time are given to the Print Manager and you won't see much of a slowdown when you resume typing. If High Priority is set, you'll see interruptions as the Print Manager occasionally sends more text to the printer.

The View Menu

The following options are listed on the View menu, but some may not be available if you are not connected to a network.

Time/Date Sent   When the Time/Date Sent option is set, the time and date that the file was sent to the Print Manager is displayed.

Print File Size   When the Print File Size option is set, the file size is displayed in the Print Manager.

Refresh   When connected with a network printer, it may be necessary to refresh the list of files waiting in the queue since Windows does not monitor its status automatically. To automatically refresh the queue listing, use the Update Network Display on the Options menu as discussed earlier.

Selected Net Queue   Click the Selected Net Queue option to see a list of all files waiting in the queue of a network printer. This option is useful if you're looking for a printer on a network that's not too busy.

Other Net Queue   The Other Net Queue option displays a list of files on other network printer queues.

Exit   The Exit option closes the Print Manager window.

Print Manager Buttons

The buttons on the Print Manager window are described in the following sections.

Pause   Click a printer in the list, then click the Pause button to prevent it from printing jobs in the queue. Print jobs can still be sent to the printer, but they are not printed until you click the Resume button. Use this option if you need to change paper in a printer or service it.

Resume   Click the Resume button to resume printing on a paused printer, usually after changing paper or correcting printing problems.

Delete   Click the Delete button to delete print jobs in a queue. First select a print job, then click the Delete button.

Bypassing the Print Manager

The Print Manager can be bypassed when you want to print directly to a printer. This is sometimes necessary when printing complex jobs to avoid repeated error messages. Select the Printers icon from the Control Panel to display the Printers dialog box. Highlight the appropriate printer in the Installed Printers list box and click on the Use Print Manager check box.

The Print Manager can slow down the printing process, especially if you're printing small, one-page files. Files must be queued into the Print Manager, then saved into your temporary directory before they are printed. This process is bypassed if you disable the Print Manager. You'll learn a lot more about the Print Manager in the next section.

Troubleshooting

When your printer doesn't print or prints improperly, you can follow the procedure listed here to determine the problem. Most printer problems are hardware related and often easy to fix. Software problems are usually related to the use of an incorrect driver. Follow these steps to diagnose problems:

1. Start by checking the printer and its cables. Is the printer off-line? Did the cable fall off? Is the printer out of paper? Make sure the cable is connected to the correct port. Some systems have two LPT or COM ports. The port needs to match the setting you made when configuring the printer.

2. If the printer is a serial printer, you'll need a correctly configured serial cable. Make sure the serial communications settings in Windows match those of the printer.

3. Try printing from DOS using the command DIR > PRN. If a directory listing is printed, the problem is software related.

4. In Windows, make sure the correct printer driver is installed. If more than one driver is installed, make sure you're using the driver for the destination printer.

5. Try printing text from Notepad. If the text prints, the problem is in your application.

6. In the application, check all printer-related options. You may be printing to a file, rather than the printer, or the page setup options may be incorrect.

7. If the TEMP= variable in the AUTOEXEC.BAT file points to a RAM drive, the Print Manager may not have enough room in the RAM drive to place its temporary files. Try temporarily disabling the Print Manager. If your document prints, either create a larger RAM drive, set the TEMP= variable to point to a hard drive, or disable the Print Manager in the Control Panel Printers dialog box.

When you're able to print, but the output is not the way you intended, problems are usually related to an incorrect printer driver or incorrect settings in applications. If a printer driver was not available for your printer, and you selected another compatible printer, it may not be fully compatible. Try another printer driver. In some cases, the most compatible printer driver won't correctly print some of the formatting you've placed in your document. You may need to remove special or unusual formatting until you get the correct driver.

If text is not placed correctly on the page, make sure the page setup options are set correctly in your application. Some printers (HP LaserJet Series) will not print closer than a quarter of an inch to the edge of the paper. If the very edge of text is missing, change your margin settings.

If you're using TrueType fonts and they don't print on your printer, you're probably using a pre-Windows 3.1 driver for the printer. Obtain a more recent driver from the printer manufacturer, or call Microsoft at (800) 426-9400.

If your printer uses cartridge fonts or soft fonts and those fonts are not printing, make sure you've selected the fonts in the Control Panel's Printers dialog box. Make sure the font cartridge is completely inserted in the printer, but turn off the printer before fully connecting it. If you're using soft fonts, make sure they are properly installed and that they are compatible with Windows 3.1 printer drivers.

Soft fonts download from the computer to the printer when you print a document, or they may stay permanently resident in the printer to avoid the download process every time you print. If the printer was shut off, the fonts must be downloaded again, as discussed in Chapter 16. Soft fonts are downloaded to the memory of your printer, which must have adequate memory to hold the fonts. If you download too many fonts, you'll need to reset the printer and download only those fonts you use.

When printing graphics, shaded images may appear as rough dot patterns. You can adjust the intensity settings on Print Setup's Options dialog box as discussed previously under "The Options Dialog Box." If Paintbrush images are printing too small, try clicking the Use Printer Resolution check box in the Print dialog box. When printing large graphic images, the printer may lag behind while Windows continues to send it information. When the printer's buffer fills, an error message appears. Change the Transmission Retry settings to increase the amount of time between Windows' attempts to access the printer. This gives the printer time to catch up with Windows.

Chapter *16*

Fonts

The term *font* is widely misused. In traditional printing, font describes an entire set of characters for one size of typeface, for example, the alphabet and all symbols for 12-point Courier. Traditionally, *typeface* meant a specific design of type—Courier, for example—regardless of type size. Largely because of computers and the way they create letters on the screen or printer, the term has acquired new meaning. Most computer users call a typeface a font.

The most common typefaces are Roman, Helvetica, and Courier. Roman was originally designed by the Greeks who drew the characters with a slanted stylus. Later, the Romans added the *serif*, a decorative stroke at the ends of letters, as shown in the following illustration. The more common Times Roman was developed by the *Times* of London. Helvetica is a straight font without serifs (or *sans serif*, which is what typefaces without these flourishes are called today).

Derivatives of Helvetica are called Swiss or Univers. Similar-looking typefaces have different names to avoid copyright conflicts. Courier is a unique serif typeface that is fixed-pitch, which means that all characters are the same width; so the lowercase "i" and the capital "M" both are allotted the same space in a line. The text typed on a typewriter is fixed-pitch. In contrast, Roman and Helvetica are *proportional typefaces*, which means each character has a different horizontal spacing based on how much room each needs. The letters in this book are proportionally spaced.

A font can have various attributes added to it, such as bold and italic. The font definition dialog boxes in Windows applications let you add the following attributes to a selected set of characters:

- Normal
- Bold
- Italic
- Bold italic

 In this book, font *describes a complete set of characters in a specific typeface. Within a font are subsets of characters with variations in style (italic, bold, and so on) and size.*

Fonts in Windows

Windows contains an assortment of fonts for the screen and for printers that are designed to provide *WYSIWYG* (What You See Is What You Get) output. Ideally, the text you see on your screen should look as close as possible to the way it appears when printed. As mentioned in Chapter 13, there is a slight variation in size between the two. The screen tends to expand images to make them more readable; if it didn't, you wouldn't be able to read characters under 12 points in size. This slight expansion onscreen is something computer users must live with until display resolutions improve to match printed resolutions.

All displays and most printers produce images using a pattern of tiny dots. How the pattern of dots is formed depends upon the font technology in use. Windows 3.0 uses bitmapped fonts in which predefined characters are displayed on the screen. An exploded view of a bitmapped font is shown in this illustration, with the original size shown in the upper-left. Windows 3.1 includes TrueType outline fonts, which form characters on the screen using a font description language, which you'll read about shortly in the "Outline Fonts" section.

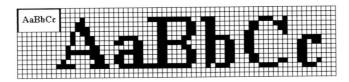

The next section includes a discussion of bitmapped fonts, but keep in mind that as TrueType and other outline fonts become more common, you will have less need to use the screen and printer fonts supplied with Windows. However, these fonts will probably remain with Windows for some time to support older Windows applications that cannot use TrueType.

Font Categories

Fonts used with personal computers fall into one of two technical categories, depending upon how they are created. The two categories, screen fonts and printer fonts, are described in the following sections.

Screen or Raster Fonts

Screen fonts—often called *raster fonts*—are bitmapped fonts. The font file contains a bitmapped image of each character in each size provided by the file. Bitmapped files display characters quickly on the screen because the characters are already formed; the disadvantage to this is that font files can be relatively large in size. Because including every font size possible would mean font files of impossible length, manufacturers make a limited number of font sizes available. The Windows screen fonts include the point sizes 8, 10, 12, 14, 18, and 24.

Choosing a size outside the normal range of a screen font can result in poor quality. The Windows screen fonts can only be sized in even multiples, and the larger the font size, the more jagged characters become. Only the original font sizes in the font file are designed with precision. Bold and italic are usually not designed into the screen font set. Instead, bits are simply added to the font to give it the appearance of bold or italic, as you can see in this illustration:

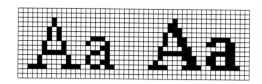

There are six sets of raster fonts, grouped as shown here:

- *Courier* A monospaced (fixed-width) font sized from 8 to 15 points for EGA resolution and from 10 to 15 points for other resolutions.

- *MS Serif* A proportionally spaced font with serifs similar to Times Roman.

- *MS Sans Serif* A proportionally spaced font without serifs, similar to Helvetica.

- *Symbol* A symbol font.

- *Small* A small font used to display page previews or other small text.

- *Special EGA Fonts* Two special raster fonts, Arial and Times, are included for EGA displays. The fonts are both 8 and 10 points in size.

Each typeface includes a set of files to match the resolution of most displays. A letter in the filename distinguishes each font and the display it is designed for, as shown in Table 16-1.

Table 16-2 lists the files on the Windows disks. The font names include the range of sizes available for that font. Using a size outside this range means that characters will be distorted. The Aspect/Res column lists the aspect ratio and resolution of the font. The aspect ratio, you'll remember from Chapter 13, is the ratio of width to height. The *resolution* is the number of dots per inch (horizontally and vertically) of the screen used to display the font. The more dots used, the clearer, darker, and sharper each character appears. As shown in Table 16-1, these numbers are used during Windows setup to determine which fonts to install on your system, based on the video driver you have selected.

Printing the Screen Fonts

The screen fonts can be printed if their resolution and aspect ratio are close to a printer's. Compare the printer's resolution and aspect ratio with Table 16-1. If you find a match you want to use, open the Fonts utility on the Control Panel and install the font (unless it's already installed) as discussed later in the section on "Installing Fonts."

For example, a 24-pin printer can print in 120x180 resolution (1:1.5 aspect ratio), 180x180 (1:1), and 360x180 (2:1). Some others provide 360x360 resolution. The E and F font sets will print on these printers using the 180x180 resolution. With the advent of TrueType, however, there's no longer much need to print the screen fonts.

One difference between screen fonts and printer fonts is the character set. Windows uses the ANSI character set that contains special characters coded higher than ASCII 128 (open the Character Map to see these characters). A printer will often use a different set of characters for values above 128. A character set used by a particular device is known as its *OEM font set*. The most common is the IBM OEM font set, originally built into the IBM Graphics Printer. It has line-draw characters,

Font Set	Display	H-Res	V-Res	Aspect Ratio H:V
B	EGA	96 dpi	72 dpi	1.33:1
E	VGA	96 dpi	96 dpi	1:1
F	8514/a	120 dpi	120 dpi	1:1

Table 16-1. *The Font Sets and Their Resolutions*

Font Name	Font File	Aspect/Res
B Font Files		
Arial 8,10 (EGA res)	ARIALB.FON	133,96,72
Courier 8,10,12,15 (EGA res)	COURB.FON	133,96,72
MS Sans Serif 8,10,12,14,18,24 (EGA res)	SSERIFB.FON	133,96,72
MS Serif 8,10,12,14,18,24 (EGA res)	SERIFB.FON	133,96,72
Small Fonts (EGA res)	SMALLB.FON	133,96,72
Symbol 8,10,12,14,18,24 (EGA res)	SYMBOLB.FON	133,96,72
Times New Roman 8,10 (EGA res)	TIMESB.FON	133,96,72
E Font Files		
Courier 10,12,15 (VGA res)	COURE.FON	100,96,96
MS Sans Serif 8,10,12,14,18,24 (VGA res)	SSERIFE.FON	100,96,96
MS Serif 8,10,12,14,18,24 (VGA res)	SERIFE.FON	100,96,96
Small Fonts (VGA res)	SMALLE.FON	100,96,96
Symbol 8,10,12,14,18,24 (VGA res)	SYMBOLE.FON	100,96,96
F Font Files		
Courier 10,12,15 (8514/a res)	COURF.FON	100,120,1
MS Sans Serif 8,10,12,14,18,24 (8514/a res)	SSERIFF.FON	100,120,1
MS Serif 8,10,12,14,18,24 (8514/a res)	SERIFF.FON	100,120,1
Small Fonts (8514/a res)	SMALLF.FON	100,120,1
Symbol 8,10,12,14,18,24 (8514/a res)	SYMBOLF.FON	100,120,1

Table 16-2. Screen Font Files

math symbols, and foreign characters, while the ANSI character set may contain other types of characters. Once again, when using TrueType, limitations of the character set are not a problem since TrueType instructs the printer to draw any character you request.

If you are printing the screen fonts, you may need to change the printer's switches to enable a font set that includes the characters you're using. For example, on HP LaserJet printers, enable the PC-8 setting on the printer control panel to print the IBM line-draw characters.

The Limitations of Screen Fonts

A disadvantage of screen fonts is that WYSIWYG is not always possible. Remember, WYSIWYG implies that the fonts on the screen resemble the printed output. With bitmapped fonts, this is only possible when a screen font exactly matches the font available at the printer. If you pick a printer font that does not have a corresponding screen font, Windows uses the next available screen font, but what you see is no longer what you get. Windows will stretch a screen font to imitate the printer font, thus giving accurate line breaks and spacing, at the same time introducing distortion into the characters.

It is possible to print screen fonts on graphic printers, if the horizontal and vertical dot size matches or closely approximates the matrix used by your printer. However, with TrueType fonts, there is little reason to print the raster fonts, as you'll see. Note that the raster fonts will not print on HP LaserJets, PostScript printers, or pen plotters.

Printer Fonts

A *printer font* is a bitmapped screen font that has been hard-coded into the printer or downloaded into the computer's memory. On laser printers, the bitmapped resolution is 300 dots per inch, providing high-resolution fonts. Most printers include a built-in set of bitmapped fonts. Windows displays the names of these fonts in the Font dialog box when the correct printer driver is installed. It then uses a closely matching screen font to depict the printer font on the screen. Some printers come with a set of screen fonts you copy to the Windows directory for use when working with the printer fonts. They more accurately depict the font than the screen fonts that Windows uses. These are installed using the Fonts utility.

When a printer driver that has printer fonts is installed, you see a listing of those fonts when you open the Fonts dialog box, as you can see in the following illustration. The printer symbol indicates that a font belongs to a printer. The name indicates its size. For example, 10cpi stands for 10 characters per inch. Note that these fonts are usually displayed on your screen using the raster fonts just discussed.

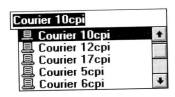

Not all printer fonts are hard-wired into the printer. Some are available on optional *cartridges* or by downloading a font definition file from your computer into the printer's memory. The latter method, using soft fonts, was explored in Chapter 15. When you specify a soft font for a print job, the font is automatically downloaded to the computer and stays in memory for the next print job. You can also preload soft fonts in memory when your system boots so they are available immediately to applications. Many font cartridges and soft fonts come with a set of matching screen fonts so what you see on the screen is very close to what is printed.

Types of Fonts

The types of fonts currently in use by the personal computer industry are described in the following sections.

Outline Fonts

Outline fonts are drawn by the computer, based on a mathematical description of each character. Such fonts our referred to as *scalable* fonts, because you can scale them to any size you want. Your computer's outlining of a character based on the font description is analogous to your tracing a character using a stencil. Outline font files take up much less room than bitmapped font files because they do not contain a representation of every character in every size. Instead, they contain character definitions that an *outline font language* (such as TrueType) uses to draw the character in any size you specify. The only drawback is that each character must be drawn on the spot, which can slow performance. TrueType is one brand of outline font language; others include PostScript fonts and those from third-party suppliers, such as Bitstream's FaceLift.

Many users will be happy with the TrueType fonts supplied with Windows, but if you do page layout or production work for other people, you may need to add more typefaces to your system. PostScript is an almost universal font description language used in many printers. You can take documents formatted with PostScript and print them on any PostScript printer, taking advantage of the resolution of that printer if it happens to be a high-resolution (2400dpi to 3600dpi) image setter. TrueType is somewhat comparable to PostScript as a font standard in this way.

TrueType Fonts

The TrueType fonts are installed in the \WINDOWS\SYSTEM directory when Windows is installed. Two files exist for each font as listed in Table 16-3. The .FOT file is a header file and the .TTF file contains the font description.

The WingDing font, shown in Figure 16-1, is a set of special symbols and characters that you can include in your documents. Use the Character Map utility to access these characters and paste them into your documents.

You can create a printout of WingDing characters to show which key each represents on your keyboard. First, type all the keys on the top row of your keyboard using a normal font. Then type all the keys on the top row after switching to the WingDing font. Repeat this for each row of keys (don't forget the SHIFT key), then print the list.

Fonts	Files
Arial (TrueType)	ARIAL.FOT and ARIAL.TTF
Arial Bold (TrueType)	ARIALBD.FOT and ARIALBD.TTF
Arial Bold Italic (TrueType)	ARIALBI.FOT and ARIALBI.TTF
Arial Italic (TrueType)	ARIALI.FOT and ARIALI.TTF
Courier New (TrueType)	COUR.FOT and COUR.TTF
Courier New Bold (TrueType)	COURBD.FOT and COURBD.TTF
Courier New Bold Italic (TrueType)	COURBI.FOT and COURBI.TTF
Courier New Italic (TrueType)	COURI.FOT and COURI.TTF
Times New Roman (TrueType)	TIMES.FOT and TIMES.TTF
Times New Roman Bold (TrueType)	TIMESBD.FOT and TIMESBD.TTF
Times New Roman Bold Italic (TrueType)	TIMESBI.FOT and TIMESBI.TTF
Times New Roman Italic (TrueType)	TIMESI.FOT and TIMESI.TTF
Symbol (TrueType)	SYMBOL.FOT and SYMBOL.TTF
WingDing (TrueType)	WINGDING.FOT and WINGDING.TIF

Table 16-3.   *TrueType Fonts and Their Associated Files*

Vector (Plotter) Fonts

Microsoft includes three scalable *vector fonts* designed for use with pen plotters. They are often referred to as *plotter fonts*. While similar to outline fonts in the way they are drawn, plotter fonts lack the precision of outline fonts, although they are suitable for their intended use. Plotter fonts are a remnant of previous versions of Windows. If you're choosing between a plotter font and a bitmapped font, the bitmapped font is always preferable if you're using one of the available sizes. The plotter fonts are useful when sizing outside the range of bitmapped fonts. The plotter fonts included with Windows are Modern, Roman, and Script.

The usefulness of plotter fonts is limited now that TrueType is available, but some Windows applications use them when sizing characters. For example, previous versions of Aldus PageMaker that don't recognize TrueType use bitmapped fonts until you request a font not in the bitmapped fonts range. PageMaker then switches to the plotter fonts.

The plotter fonts are automatically installed in the \WINDOWS\SYSTEM directory when Windows is set up. In the Font dialog boxes plotter fonts are referred to as "continuous scaling" fonts. The filenames are ROMAN.FON, SCRIPT.FON, and MODERN.FON.

Figure 16-1.   *The WingDing font*

Using the Control Panel Fonts Utility

The Fonts utility is used to view currently installed fonts, and to add or remove fonts. There are several things to keep in mind regarding fonts:

- Windows installs all TrueType fonts and plotter fonts during setup. It installs only the bitmapped fonts appropriate for your screen resolution. As new

TrueType fonts become available, you can use the Font utility to install them into your system.

- You can install other bitmapped fonts just to have them available for use, although with TrueType, there is little need to do so. If you have reason to believe that TrueType outlining is slowing the performance of your system, you can remove TrueType and use only bitmapped fonts.

- Font files need to be copied to the \WINDOWS\SYSTEM directory, but they don't become available to Windows until you use the Fonts utility. When Windows uses a font, it takes up memory, so there is good reason to remove those fonts you don't need. When removing a font, you can release Windows' use of that font and leave it on disk for later use, or you can remove it from disk as well.

- Fonts files are normally located in the \WINDOWS\SYSTEM directory, but if you've installed new third-party fonts in another directory, you can tell Windows to use that directory instead. Otherwise, the Fonts utility copies the fonts to the \WINDOWS\SYSTEM directory, using additional disk space.

Viewing Fonts

You can use the Fonts utility to browse through fonts. Open the Control Panel and double-click the Fonts icon. When the Fonts dialog box opens, it appears as shown in Figure 16-2.

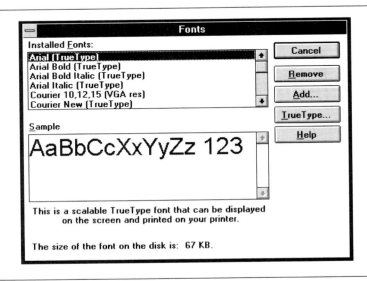

Figure 16-2. The Fonts dialog box

The Installed Fonts field displays a list of fonts currently in use by Windows. Click on any font to display it in the window. Also notice that the size of the font file on disk is displayed at the bottom of the dialog box.

Installing Fonts

To add fonts, click the Add button to open the Add Fonts dialog box, as shown in Figure 16-3. Initially, the dialog box may not list any files to add. You first select the floppy disk or hard drive directory where the font files are located. To install new fonts from floppy disk, select drive A or B in the Drives list box. To install fonts already on disk, choose a drive, and then choose a directory in the Directories list box. The Fonts utility scans the disk for available font files, and then displays them in the List of Fonts field.

Click one or more font files that you wish to install. Hold the CTRL key and click to select multiple font files, or click the Select All button to select all the fonts.

The Copy Fonts to Windows Directory is an important option. If the fonts are already on your hard drive in another directory, you should disable this option, otherwise a duplicate copy of the font is made in the \WINDOWS\SYSTEM directory. If you disable the option, Windows will find the fonts in their original directory. If the files are on a floppy disk, make sure this option is enabled. Click OK to install the fonts.

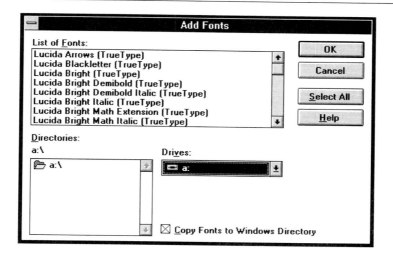

Figure 16-3.   *The Add Fonts dialog box*

TrueType Settings

Click the TrueType button to set the options detailed in the following sections. The dialog box shown in Figure 16-4 appears.

Enable TrueType Fonts   In most cases, make sure this box is enabled. Disabling it removes TrueType font names from the Fonts dialog boxes and drop-down list boxes in your applications. If you're using other high-resolution outline fonts or PostScript, you can disable the option to reduce the font list and free memory. If the TrueType outlining process seems to slow the performance of your system, you can disable TrueType and use bitmapped fonts. If you have a PostScript printer, you can use its built-in fonts for high-resolution printing.

Show Only TrueType Fonts in Applications   Enable this option if you only use TrueType fonts, and no other fonts. Usually this is a good idea since it reduces the list of fonts in dialog boxes and frees memory. Don't enable this option if you've installed special bitmapped character sets or are using PostScript fonts.

Font Settings in WIN.INI

The following settings are made during Windows installation and modified when you install new printers or use the Fonts utility.

Currently Installed Fonts

The [fonts] section describes font files that are loaded by Windows at startup. This section can contain one or more occurrences of the following setting:

   font-name=font-file

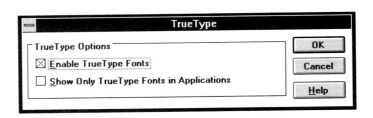

Figure 16-4.   *The TrueType dialog box*

For TrueType fonts, the font-file name must have the extension .FOT, which is the header file. For example, the following entry specifies that the Courier New TrueType font is active:

```
Courier New (TrueType)=COUR.FOT
```

Font Substitutions

The [FontSubstitutes] section describes fonts that Windows recognizes as the same typeface, which means Windows interchanges them. For example, Arial is substituted for Helvetica and MS Serif is substituted for Tms Rmn. Make settings under this header when you work on documents that include pre-Windows 3.1 screen fonts. The Helvetica, Times, Tms Rmn, and Helv settings are already made as shown in the following section, but you can make similar settings of your own.

The following entries are made in WIN.INI during setup to substitute the new Windows 3.1 fonts for the older fonts. Keep these settings as they are in most cases (unless you prefer to use the older fonts), but remember that the fonts must be installed on the hard drive.

```
[Font Substitutes]
Helvetica=Arial

Times=Times New Roman

Tms Rmn=MS Serif

Helv=MS Sans Serif
```

For example, for the setting Times=Times New Roman, Windows will consider the 3.0 Times and the 3.1 Times New Roman TrueType typefaces as identical. If you used the Times font in documents you created using Windows 3.0 applications, Windows 3.1 substitutes Times New Roman when displaying and printing the font.

TrueType Fonts Section

The [TrueType] section includes the settings you make on the Fonts dialog box when you click the TrueType button, as described in the "TrueType Settings" section earlier in the chapter. The following entry enables TrueType since it is set to 1. Setting this option to 0 disables TrueType.

TTEnable=1

The next entry enables only TrueType fonts since it is set to 1:

TTOnly=1

The last entry can only be changed by editing WIN.INI. Setting this value to 1 lists all non-TrueType fonts in all capital letters and setting it to 0 lists non-TrueType fonts with an initial capital and lowercase letters. The default is 0. Set this option for aesthetic reasons only.

nonTTCaps=0

More on TrueType Fonts

One of the reasons for the popularity of Windows is that it provides features that can be used throughout applications. Programmers need not worry about video and printer drivers, for example. They are created by the manufacturer to ensure that their product works with Windows. With Windows 3.1, fonts now become part of that scheme with the introduction of TrueType. TrueType provides every user with scalable WYSIWYG fonts. An important aspect of TrueType is *document compatibility*. Users can now interchange documents, knowing the fonts they use will work on another user's system and printer, and that the operating system will manage the entire interchange.

In TrueType, every straight line and curve is mathematically defined. TrueType then resizes the characters over a wide range with little loss of resolution. It then rasterizes the characters for display on the bitmapped display. *Rasterizing* is the process of converting the outline to a bitmapped image. Fonts are also rasterized when sent to a printer. The TrueType rasterizer adds additional instructions, called *hints*, which improve the screen or printed image by removing jagged edges and smoothing curves. It is this process that makes TrueType superior to other outline fonts. The result is true WYSIWYG because TrueType creates a perfect match between the fonts it creates onscreen and those it sends to the printer. If the printer is a laser printer or high resolution typesetter, the printout will be improved even further. The TrueType rasterizer is built directly into the Windows 3.1 interface, making the whole display and print process more efficient. Fonts are cached in memory.

The print driver provides TrueType with the specifications for rasterizing, based on the graphics resolution of the printer. Unlike PostScript printers, which rasterize using their own hard-wired circuitry, TrueType rasterizing takes place in your computer. A bitmapped image is then sent to the printer. Therefore, any bitmapped printer (and almost all printers are) can print TrueType images at a resolution determined by the highest resolution of the printer.

In some cases, TrueType uses the native format of a printer when printing fonts. On older LaserJet printers, a bitmapped font in the native PCL 4 (the Printer Control Language specific to the LaserJet) format is downloaded. On PostScript printers, to improve performance, type 1 outlines are sent when the point size is larger than 14; smaller sizes are sent as bitmapped fonts.

The following font or printer manufacturers support TrueType:

AGFA Compugraphics
Bitstream
Casady & Greene
Digital Typeface Corporation
Kingsly/ATF
Letraset
Linotype
MonoType
Varityper

LaserMaster, a manufacturer of high-speed, high-resolution printer controllers licensed TrueImage from Microsoft and developed a TrueImage "Turbores" printing engine that it resells to other manufacturers. You can expect wide support for TrueType in hardware over the next few years.

PostScript and TrueType

A big advantage of PostScript is that it's an industry standard. PostScript support surpasses that for TrueType as far as graphics drawing and shading commands are concerned. You can create "print files" on your system using a PostScript driver, and then send those files to a service bureau for printing on high-resolution printers. Simply install a PostScript driver using the Printer utility, and then designate its output port as FILE. When you're ready to send your PostScript file to the service bureau, simply print it. The FILE port causes Windows to ask for a filename. The information required to print the document is then copied to a disk file which you give to the service bureau. An added advantage is that you'll have access to the PostScript font set on your screen. Installing and working with PostScript in the context of graphics is covered further in Chapter 21.

Before creating the files, call the service bureau to determine exactly which PostScript printer they have, then choose that printer in the Control Panel Printers utility. While PostScript is a standard, the method used to implement it is different among manufacturers. The Printers utility includes drivers for several high-resolution PostScript printers including AGFA, Linotronic, and Varityper. Be sure to install the exact driver for the printer you intend to use.

AGFA, Linotronic, Varityper, and other "printing" devices are actually imagesetters that output film used as camera-ready copy for pasteup and other pre-press work.

If you send files to service bureaus, use TrueType fonts with caution. First determine whether the service bureau supports TrueType, and whether you can mix TrueType fonts and PostScript data. For best results, you should probably disable TrueType and use only PostScript when creating these files.

 Keep in mind that TrueType defines fonts only. PostScript defines both fonts and vector graphics, so it is superior if you are working with mixed documents. However, bitmapped graphics is commonly supported by most printers and imagesetters.

When TrueType is output to a PostScript device, it rasterizes the type into bitmapped type that matches the resolution of the printer. PostScript is sent to the printer as outline data (the mathematical description of the font) and the printer does the rasterizing. If a file contains both TrueType and PostScript data, you'll end up with a print file that has a mixture of bitmapped data created by TrueType and outline font and graphics commands for PostScript. Such a file may not print correctly if the driver used to create the print file (say 300 dpi) is different than the printer used to create the final printout (say 1200 dpi). The TrueType fonts may appear incorrectly sized because they've already been rasterized for 300 dpi. The PostScript data will size correctly because it is rasterized at the printer, based on that printer's resolution. As mentioned, check with your service bureau before creating such files, and make sure you use the Windows printer driver that matches the device you'll use to produce your documents.

More About PostScript

When you install a PostScript printer driver, you can set special options for it in the Printers utility of the Control Panel. Choose the printer, then click Setup. You see the setup dialog box that lets you specify the paper type and tray. Click the Options button to display a dialog box similar to the one in Figure 16-5. On this dialog box, you can click Encapsulated PostScript File and specify a filename to create print files to send to other printers. This option is covered in Chapter 21. Click the Advanced button to display the the Advanced Options dialog box pictured in Figure 16-6. There are several selections you can make on this dialog box related to TrueType fonts, as discussed next.

Send to Printer as   This option is used to specify how TrueType fonts are printed. Most TrueType fonts are converted to bitmaps in the computer, then sent to the printer. However, large fonts above 14 points are converted in the printer. You can specify that they be sent as bitmaps by choosing Bitmap (Type 3), or you can choose Adobe Type 1 to substitute Adobe Type 1 outline fonts for the TrueType fonts.

Use Printer Fonts for all TrueType Fonts   Click this option to always convert the TrueType fonts to the fonts that reside in the Printer. The PostScript driver makes the most appropriate match. If you want to specify which fonts are used, choose the Use Substitution Table option.

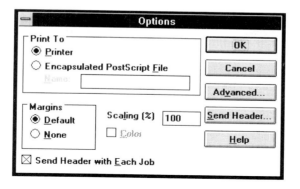

Figure 16-5.   *The Options dialog box for PostScript printers*

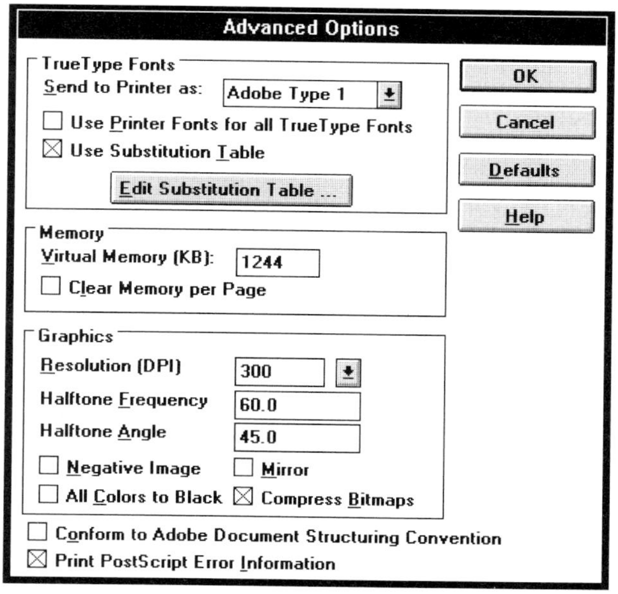

Figure 16-6.   *The Advanced Options dialog box for PostScript printers*

Use Substitution Table   Click this option to specify exactly which built-in printer fonts are substituted for your TrueType fonts. Click the Edit Substitution Table button to display the dialog box shown in Figure 16-7. Click a font on the left, then click a substitution font on the right.

Memory Box   Set the options in the Memory box to the amount of virtual memory your PostScript printer has. You determine this by printing the TESTPS.TXT file. This indicates the amount that you can place in the Virtual Memory (KB) field. Click the Clear Memory per Page option to clear memory and resend fonts to the printer after printing each page.

Other Fonts

One reason for all the hype over TrueType in this chapter is that it's included free with Windows. Why would you need any other font manager? Most of the companies who sold outline fonts for Windows 3.0 were forced to redesign their products for Windows 3.1 by making them compatible with TrueType. You can buy hundreds of different typefaces from companies such as Bitstream, Ares Software, Adobe, and others. But Adobe, one of the masters of font technology, has developed a new technology called Multiple Master that is worth looking at. It lets you "tune" fonts right on the screen to fit your needs. Multiple Master is one font, rather than sets of fonts. You create characters of any size, width, or weight by starting with a master typeface. You then expand or contract the font, or change its style. An additional feature lets you vary the serif of the font to fit your tastes.

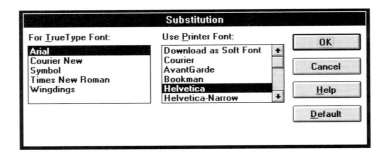

Figure 16-7.   *The Font Substitution dialog box for PostScript printers*

Installing Cartridge Fonts

If you've installed a cartridge font in your printer, you enable it in the Windows printer driver by first opening the Printers dialog box. Highlight the printer, then choose Setup. The Setup dialog box contains a list of supported cartridges. Pick the appropriate cartridge and click the OK button. There is a limit on the number of cartridges you can install, depending on the number of cartridge ports the printer has (usually it's two). Once the cartridge is installed, its fonts appear on the character formatting menus in most of your applications.

Some cartridges may be so new that their names do not appear in the Cartridges list. If that is the case, the font will come with a disk for installing font drivers. Follow the instructions in the next section to install new font drivers. After installation, you can select the new cartridge from the Cartridges list.

Installing Soft Fonts

A soft font is downloaded from your computer to a printer's memory. The process usually requires that the entire font be copied. Because of this, you might want to consider using TrueType instead, which keeps font descriptions in your system's memory and sends bitmap information to the printer. However, if you have special fonts, you'll need to download as discussed here.

To install soft fonts or screen fonts for printer cartridges, open the Printers dialog box, highlight the printer driver, and then click the Setup button. On the Setup dialog box, click the Fonts button to open the Font Installer dialog box. Use this dialog box to add new fonts from disk, or to copy installed soft fonts to the printer.

Permanent Fonts   When you designate a font as *permanent,* it is copied to the memory of your printer and remains available for use. When you print a document that needs the font, it does not have to be downloaded unless you turn off your printer, so it prints much faster. Keep in mind, however, that permanent fonts use printer memory, which may be needed to print graphics files or other complex printing jobs. In addition, if the printer is shared on a network, you may not want to load permanent fonts not required by other users because that might restrict others' use of the printer. Permanent fonts can be loaded every time your system and printer are turned on. You will be asked to designate this option when you exit the Fonts dialog box. Only one permanent font may be designated, so choose it wisely.

Temporary Fonts   *Temporary* fonts are copied to your printer's memory only when a document calls for the font. This is the preferred method if you don't use the font often, or if you are printing to a shared printer. When you are done with the font and need the printer's memory for other tasks such as printing complex documents, the font is removed, but may be reloaded again later for another print job. Temporary is the default setting.

Soft Font Installation Procedure

The procedure given here assumes the Printer Font Installer dialog box is visible on your screen. Keep in mind that the Help key provides important font information for your printer. You may wish to review this information as part of this procedure. Follow these steps to install a soft font:

1. Locate the disk with the soft fonts and place it in the floppy drive.

2. Click the Add button. The disk is scanned for available font files, which appear in the window on the right.

3. Highlight the font you want to copy. If it has the same name as one of your existing fonts, first rename it by clicking the Edit button.

4. To copy the font, press the Copy button.

5. Highlight the new font in the left box, and then click either the Permanent or Temporary button.

Repeat these steps for each font you wish to install, then click on the Exit button and exit the Printer Font Installer. If you installed a font related to a cartridge, be sure to select the new cartridge from the Cartridges list on the Printers dialog box.

Chapter *17*

Networks

A computer *network* connects computers and computer resources, allowing people to share information and equipment. Computer resources include disk storage devices, optical disks, printers, plotters, fax machines, modems, and any other shareable devices.

This chapter looks at using Windows with networks. The first part assumes Windows is already installed and gives you an overview of the utilities available in Windows when connected to a network. If you were attached to a network when you ran Setup, Windows would load the appropriate network support so you could immediately start using Windows to access the network. Later sections of this chapter are for network administrators, those who install or manage networks and who need to install and manage Windows on the network.

For important information about your specific network, refer to NETWORKS.WRI in the Windows directory (or the Setup disks), or start the Help system from any application and use the File Open option to open the .HLP file for your network.

Windows and Networks

Users with network connections can store files, access programs and large databases, or share peripherals such as printers. The network cabling system provides a link between users and the resources of the network server. Users can also communicate via electronic mail and messaging services.

Some networks provide a centralized and secure filing system, while others allow users to share their personal hard drives and peripherals with others. Novell NetWare is a *file server-based* system that provides high levels of security. The file sharing and much of the resource sharing is centralized at the server. On the other hand, IBM's LAN program and Microsoft's LAN Manager are *peer-to-peer* networks, which means a user shares his or her system (as if it were a server) with other users. Windows provides the following network services (regardless of which type of network you use):

- Displays network drives in the File Manager and provides facilities for mapping or changing drive mappings

- Provides access to network print queues

- Provides Control Panel functions for setting network options

- Provides messaging services to other users on the network

Accessing the Network

Centralized networks are managed by administrators who install software and ensure that users have access to it. The administrator manages security features and grants users access rights to directories and files. The administrator also backs up the server and makes sure shared resources such as printers are functioning.

On peer-to-peer networks, much of these activities are performed by the user, who makes his or her system available to other users. In either case, keep in mind that access to some directories and files may be restricted. A supervisor or users of a shared system may restrict access to directories or files.

To use network resources from Windows, first log into the server using the appropriate network commands. This must be done before starting Windows. For example, a batch file with the following commands initiates a Novell NetWare login procedure:

```
IPX
NETX
F:
LOGIN
```

The first command, IPX, loads the network interface driver and the second command, NETX, loads network command support. The third command, F:, switches to a network drive where the LOGIN command in the last line is executed. If the login is successful, a script runs that maps directories on the network server to drive letters visible in the user's Open and Save dialog boxes, or in the File Manager.

Mapping is the process of making directories on the network appear as drive letters. For example, a user named Cindy may have a personal network directory called \USERS\CINDY. If this directory is mapped to drive H, an icon for this drive letter appears in the File Manager. Usually, personal directories are only accessible to the person who owns them. An important thing to remember about mapped drives is that they are not always consistent from user to user. For example, Cindy's drive H may be mapped to \USERS\CINDY while Joe's drive H is mapped to \USERS\JOE. Shared directories, on the other hand, should be accessible with a common drive letter. For example, drive I might contain shared files accessed by all users, so this drive letter would be mapped to the same directory for all users.

Security is an important issue when working with networks. The login procedure prevents unauthorized users from accessing the shared files, and having personal directories restricts access to only the owner or users given special access to the directory. In some cases, you can see a directory in a file listing, but can't access the files in it because you don't have the proper file or directory access rights. The network administrator or the administrator of the drive you're accessing provides these rights.

File Sharing

When working with network files, be aware of file sharing. If an application is "network aware," it will prevent two users from accessing the same file at the same time (referred to as *file locking*). This is important to prevent one user's changes from overwriting another's. A database file, on the other hand, is almost always accessible by more than one user. In this case, individual records are locked to a user if they are already in use by another user.

Windows Network Options

The Windows network options are available once a system is connected to a network. Each option is discussed in this section, using Novell NetWare as an example. There are slight differences in how the dialog box looks from one operating system to another, but the functions are similar.

Some network operating systems install their own front-end utilities for accessing network resources. This eliminates the need to open the Control Panel or use other methods to set options. The NetWare Tools dialog box pictured in Figure 17-1 is an example. You simply double-click an icon for quick access to the utilities (covered in the following sections). NetWare Tools is installed when you install the Novell Windows Workstation software, available from Novell or Novell authorized dealers. You can also download the software from CompuServe.

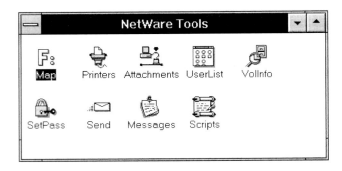

Figure 17-1. *Utilities available with the Novell Windows Kit*

Control Panel Options

The Control Panel Network icon displays a dialog box with options for controlling the network connection. The Network dialog box for Novell NetWare is shown in Figure 17-2.

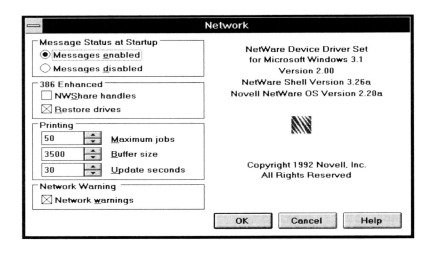

Figure 17-2. *The Control Panel Network utility for Novell NetWare*

The Message Status at Startup Field

You can enable or disable message popup from other users on the network with this field. Disabling this option is important if you're running applications that shouldn't be disturbed. You should also disable this option if you run Setup to change Windows' options.

The 386 Enhanced Field

The 386 Enhanced field lets you manage the mapping of network drives. Set the options as follows.

The NWShare Handles Option   When NWShare Handles is enabled, changes to drive mappings are saved for future sessions. When disabled, changes to drive mappings affect the current session only.

The Restore Drives Option   When the Restore Drives option is enabled, drive mappings are restored to their original state when you exit Windows. If disabled, drive mappings you make in Windows are also used at the DOS level.

The Printing Field

The Printing field has several options for setting printing parameters.

The Maximum Jobs Option   The Maximum Jobs option sets the number of print jobs that are listed in the Print Manager queue. Default: 50. Maximum: 250. Minimum: 1.

The Buffer Size Option   The Buffer Size option sets maximum buffer size (in bytes) of a print job. Default: 3500. Maximum: 30000. Minimum: 3500.

The Updates Option   The Updates option sets the time interval (in seconds) for the Print Manager to update the Print Manager queue. This change is reflected immediately. Default: 30. Maximum: 65. Minimum: 1.

The Network Warning Field

You decide whether to enable or disable warnings. If the network is not running or if the wrong network is running, messages can notify you of problems.

Working with the Network Filing System

The File Manager network options control drive mappings on network servers. Any drive mappings already established before starting Windows appear as icons on the File Manager window. These mappings are usually set by the networks login script or your personal login script. Use the drive mappings as you would any other drive.

 On NetWare networks, the MAP ROOT command must be used to map network drives prior to starting Windows; otherwise mapped drives will point to the root directory.

Adding New Connections

To change network connections in the File Manager, choose Network Connections from the Disk menu. A Network - Drive Connections dialog box similar to that shown in Figure 17-3 appears. The Data Drives field lists the current local or network drives. Available drive letters are listed at the bottom. To create a new drive mapping, use the Browse button to specify the directory to map, and then click the Map button.

The fields and operation of the Network - Drive Connections dialog box are listed in the next sections.

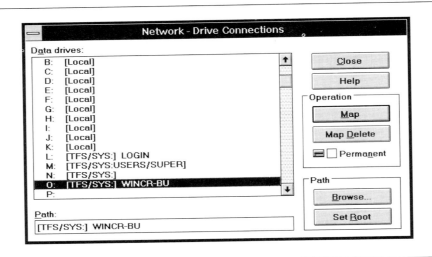

Figure 17-3.   *Use the Network - Drive Connections dialog box to make connections to directories on a network server*

The Data Drives Field

The Data Drives field lists the current drive mappings.

The Path Field

The Path field on the lower right of the Network - Drive Connections dialog box displays the path of a mapped drive. If you're creating a new map, click the Browse button to specify the path for that map. To delete or change a drive mapping, click a drive in the Data Drives field. That drive then appears in the Path field. Click the Map Delete button to remove it.

The Operation Field

You can either map a new drive or delete an existing drive with the Operation field.

The Map Button   Click the Map button when the correct path appears in the Path box to map a new drive.

The Map Delete Button   Click the Map Delete button to delete the drive mapping in the Path box.

The Path Box

The Path box on the lower right of the Network - Drive Connections dialog box lets you view network servers, volumes, and directories, and set root maps.

The Browse Button   Click the Browse button to view a list of network servers, volumes, and directories. The Browse Connections dialog box appears and displays servers you are attached to and the volumes and directories available on those servers. You can attach to or detach from servers by using the Attach or Detach buttons. When the path you want is listed at the top of the box, choose OK.

The Set Root Button   The Set Root Button allows you to map a drive as a *fake root* in NetWare. A fake root is a subdirectory that functions as a root directory. Even though there may be directories below it, the user sees it as the root. NetWare lets you map a search drive to a fake root (a directory where rights can be assigned to users). Enter the path in the path box, then place the cursor where you want to set the root. Then choose Set Root.

Printers

You establish connections to network printers by opening the Printers utility in the Control Panel. Select a printer (or install the driver for a network printer), then click the Connect button. On the Connect dialog box that appears, click Network to display a Network - Printer Connections dialog box similar to Figure 17-4.

The Available queues field lists network queues available on the current file server. To attach to other file servers, click the Attach button. To establish a printer connection, choose a queue in the Available queues list, choose a connection port in the Printer connections field, then click the Connect button. You can then click the Options button to change settings for the attached printer.

Note that the ports listed in the Printer connections field are not physical ports on your system. They are pseudo-ports that you can choose when printing a document from inside your application. The utility redirects printing from your physical port over the network (via these pseudo-ports) to the network printer. You choose these ports from inside your applications. Click Permanent to establish this printer connection every time you start Windows.

You can make the following settings on the Printer Options dialog box, shown in Figure 17-5, that appears when you press the Options button.

The Notify Option   If the Notify option is enabled, a message displays when printing is complete.

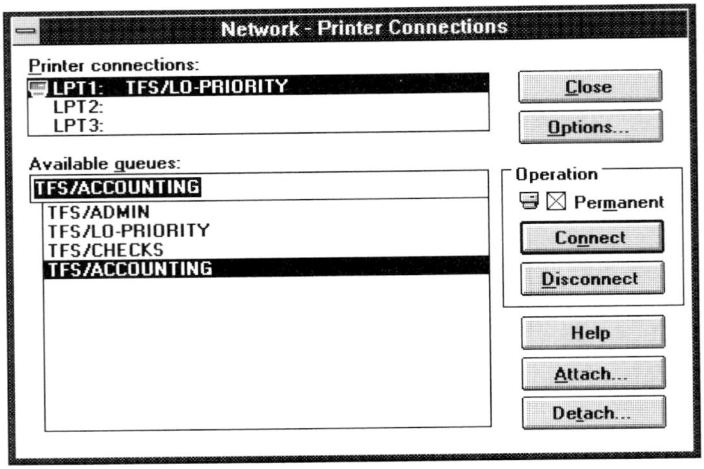

Figure 17-4.   *Use the Network - Printer Connections dialog box to establish connections with network printers*

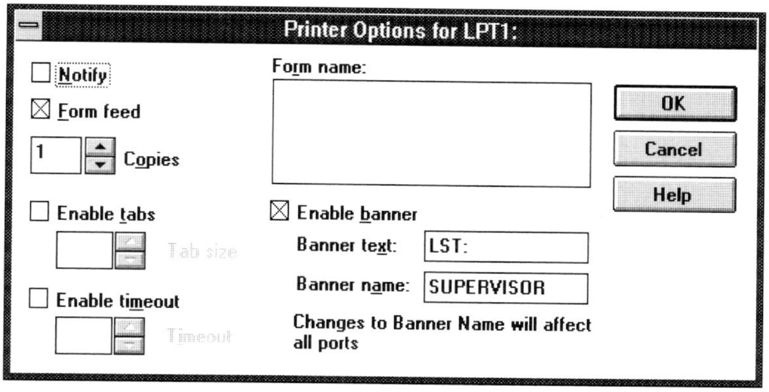

Figure 17-5. *The Printer Options dialog box*

The Form Feed Option   If you enable the Form feed option, all subsequent print jobs start at the top of a new sheet of paper.

The Copies Option   The Copies option lets you indicate the number of copies to print. Default: 1. Maximum: 255. Minimum: 1.

The Enable Tabs Option   You can specify the number of characters in one tab stop with the Enable tabs option. Enable this box if your application does not have print formatting capabilities (most applications do). Default: 8. Maximum: 18. Minimum: 0.

The Enable Timeout Option   The Enable timeout option increases the time a printer can handle a print file before an error is detected. Increase the timeout if only parts of files are being printed or if the files do not print at all. Default: 90. Maximum: 1000. Minimum: 0.

The Enable Banner Option   Specify the text of a banner page that separates print jobs with the Enable banner option. Enter the text to appear on the lower part of the banner page in the Banner text box. Your user name appears in the Banner name box; it will be printed on the top part of the banner page.

The Form Name Field   Use the Form name field to specify which form to print the job on.

The Connect Option   The Connect option simply connects a print queue to the selected port.

The Disconnect Option   The Disconnect option disconnects the print queue from the selected port.

The Other Servers Option   You can attach to or detach from other file servers using the Other Servers option.

Working with Printer Queues

You can use the Print Manager to track the print jobs you send to network printers. It will show a listing in its workspace for both local printers and network printers. However, the Print Server does not normally manage network print jobs—it simply displays their status.

To view the status of your network printer print jobs, simply open the Print Manager. You will see the status of the network printer and its print jobs, along with the status of your locally attached printers, if any. Note that it may be necessary to choose the Refresh option on the View menu to get the latest status information from the network printers.

Viewing the Network Queue Status

Use the following options to view network printer queues.

The Selected Net Queue Option   Select the Selected Net Queue option on the View menu to view the print jobs of all users in the queue.

The Other Net Queue Option   Select the Other Net Queue option on the View menu to view the status of network queues that you are not connected to. If you need a rush printing job, you might use this option to search for a printer with few print jobs in its queue.

Network Options   Select Network Options from the Options menu to set the following options:

- *Update Network Display* If you don't want the Print Manager to periodically check the net queue, clear this option to cut down on network traffic.

- *Print Net Jobs Direct* Normally, the Print Manager doesn't get involved in managing print jobs directed to network printers. If you want to use the Print Manager as a go-between, you can enable this option, but it will slow performance of your system.

Network Connections   This option displays the Network - Printer Connections dialog box discussed in the previous section. Use it to establish new network printer connections or remove existing ones.

Installing Windows on Networks

There are three ways to install Windows on a network and give users access to it. In all cases, you first expand all the Windows files to a network directory. In this way, users install from the files on the server, not from the original disks. This procedure is covered under "Expanding Windows Files to the Server."

Refer to NETWORKS.WRI for important setup information regarding your specific network.

The three possible installation scenarios are discussed next and illustrated in Figure 17-6.

- Windows installs completely on a user's workstation and does not require access to the server to run. However, users still access the server for other files.

- Only the files that are different for each user's installation are copied to the user's workstation. All other Windows files remain on the network in a directory where they are shared by other users. Windows accesses the network to load, but placing the configuration files on each users workstation prevents overlap.

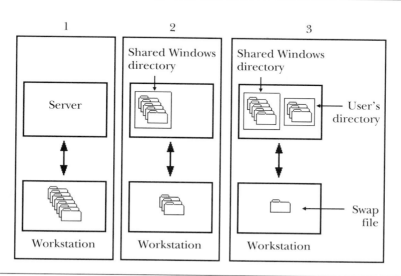

Figure 17-6. *Three different network installation methods*

- Users start Windows completely from the network. Their .INI files and other configuration files are kept in their personal directories on the network server. Shared Windows files are kept in a directory shared by all other Windows users.

The first method provides the best performance, but workstations must have enough hard disk space to hold the Windows files. A drawback to this method is that each individual user is responsible for updating the Windows files and applications on their own system. When Windows is installed on the server, network administrators can control and perform these tasks.

The second method saves disk space on local workstations since only a few Windows files are located there (such as the .INI files). However, network traffic increases since users now access the shared Windows files from the network. Network management is easy, however, since upgrades are performed at the server.

The third method is the easiest to manage from a network administrator's point of view, but it produces the most network traffic. The personal directory of each user contains the Windows .INI files and other Windows files, while the shared directory contains the remaining Windows files shared by all users. The last method must be used to run Windows on diskless workstations.

When the second and third methods are used, the following files are copied to the users' workstations or to their personal directories.

HIMEM.SYS	Extended memory manager
EMM386.SYS	Expanded memory manager
SMARTDRV.SYS	Disk cache manager
RAMDRIVE.SYS	RAM drive utility
WIN.COM	Windows startup file
*.INI	System and application initialization files
*.GRP	Program Manager group files

The other Windows files stay in the Windows shared directory where they are used by all Windows users. These files should be marked shareable and read-only, and Windows users should have rights in the directory.

Expanding Windows Files to the Server

To set up Windows for use on a network, you first copy the entire set of Windows disks to a shared directory. The files in this directory are not used to start Windows; instead, you use them to create executable copies of Windows on users' workstations or in their personal directories. Follow these steps to copy the files:

1. Insert the Windows 3.1 disk 1 in a floppy drive and switch to that drive.

2. Type **SETUP /A**.

(/A is the network install option.) The setup procedure prompts you for each disk, expands the files, and copies them to the drive and directory you specify. Remember that this directory contains all of the Windows files, so it takes a lot of disk space. You might want to remove those files you know users will never need. Refer to Appendix C for a detailed list of files.

Workstation Setup

The commands described in this section are executed at the user's workstation to install a working copy of Windows. Before proceeding, read through the remainder of this chapter. There are many setup options and variables. For example, you can specify exactly which hardware configuration gets installed at a workstation, or you can customize the Windows environment for individual workstations by including or excluding icons and groups in the Program Manager. Appendix G provides information on how to modify a user's Program Manager settings. You may want to refer to that appendix if you are setting up Windows for other users.

Users must have the correct access right in the shared Windows directory and in their personal directories to run Setup or Windows from the network.

Full Workstation Install From Server

The full installation method simply installs all the necessary files on the user's local workstation. It is no different from the normal setup from disks, except that no disk handling is required. All the files are copied from the expanded set of files on the server. Here are the steps:

1. Go to the workstation, or inform the user of this procedure.

2. Log into the network, and switch to the Windows directory on the server where you previously expanded the Windows files.

3. Type **SETUP**, then specify the user's local drive as the destination for the Windows files.

Shared Installation

The shared installation method copies only the necessary Windows files to the user's local hard drive or his or her personal directory on the server. The remaining Windows files are accessed in the shared windows directory. To set up a shared copy of Windows, follow these steps:

1. Go to the workstation, or inform the user of this procedure.

2. Log into the network, then switch to the shared Windows directory on the server.

3. Type **SETUP /N** to start the shared Windows setup program.

4. When prompted for the directory for personal files, indicate a directory on the local hard drive, or the user's personal directory on the server.

The Setup program copies only the relevant files to the user's directory, and then modifies the AUTOEXEC.BAT and CONFIG.SYS files on the workstation.

Automatic Installation

Decisions about video hardware and network connections are made during the Windows setup process. Network administrators must ensure that users make the correct decision, otherwise problems may occur. You can personally run the setup yourself, or guide the user through the setup over the phone. Another alternative is the automatic installation method described next.

During automatic setup, an information file is read that contains the exact specification for a particular setup. One file can specify a VGA display while another specifies an 8514/a display. When running Setup, the modified file is specified on the command line using the /h parameter. For example, the following command uses a setup file called 8514.AIF:

```
SETUP /h:8514.AIF
```

To install Windows using the shared directory method, include the /n parameter as shown here:

```
SETUP /h:8514.AIF /n
```

Once the .AIF file is created for various configurations, users can be given the appropriate command and parameters to run the setup themselves.

Note that this method of running Setup provides a relatively simple way of modifying a user's setup. Another method is to modify the SETUP.INF file, discussed in Appendix B, or to modify the Program Manager, discussed in Appendix G. You modify SETUP.INF to change the setup procedure for all users. The methods discussed here provide a way to specify a custom setup for a specific user or system.

Creating the .AIF File

To create the .AIF file, use an editor like Notepad and save the file under an appropriate name in the Windows shared directory. An example file listing can be found below. The .AIF file, like the .INI file should contain headers between square brackets. Each header is listed here:

```
[sysinfo]
[configuration]
[windir]
[userinfo]
[dontinstall]
[options]
[printers]
[endinstall]
```

You place specific commands under each header as described in the next few sections. A minimal .AIF file might look like this:

```
[sysinfo]
showsysinfo = yes

[configuration]
machine = ibm_compatible
display = vga
mouse = ps2mouse
network = lanman/01020000
keyboard = t4s0enha
language = enu
kblayout = nodll

[windir]
c:\windows

[userinfo]
"user's name"
"company name"

[dontinstall]
games

[options]

[printers]
"HP LaserJet III",LPT1:

[endinstall]
```

376 Windows 3.1: The Complete Reference

```
configfiles = modify
endopt = restart
```

[sysinfo]   The [sysinfo] section has only one entry. Specify showsysinfo=yes to display the System Configuration screen during setup. Specify showsysinfo=no to hide it. The default is No. It is not necessary to display this screen when automatically setting up a user's system.

[configuration]   Specify the hardware devices and configuration in this section. If an entry is not included, the detected or default value is used. During an update, the previous values for machine, display, mouse, and network are used, but you can force a new value by placing an exclamation point before the new value. Example: display=!8514/a.

You can specify a value for a third-party product if you know the device name. This can sometimes be found in the OEMSETUP.INF file on the disk that comes with the device.

Table 17-1 lists possible settings for each of the parameters. These values are found in the SETUP.INF file. If you don't find an appropriate value for your device, search the file. Updated versions may contain additional settings.

machine=

ibm_compatible	MS-DOS system
ast_386_486	AST 80386- and 80486-based machines
at_and_t	AT&T PC
everex_386_25	Everex Step 386/25 (or compatible)
hewlett_packard	Hewlett-Packard: all machines
ibm_ps2_70p	IBM PS/2 Model 70P
ibm_ps2_l40sx	IBM PS/2 Model L40sx
ncr_386sx	NCR 80386 and 80486-based machines
nec_pm_sx+	NEC PowerMate SX Plus
nec_prospeed	NEC ProSpeed 386
toshiba_1200xe	Toshiba 1200XE
toshiba_1600	Toshiba 1600
toshiba_5200	Toshiba 5200
zenith_386	Zenith 80386-based machines
att_nsx_20	AT&T NSX 20: Safari notebook
apm	MS-DOS system with APM
apm_sl	Intel 386SL-based system with APM

Table 17-1.   *Possible Settings for Configuration Parameters*

display=

8514	8514/a
8514s	8514/a (Small fonts)
cpqavga	COMPAQ Advanced VGA 640x480 256 colors
plasma	Compaq Portable Plasma
egahires	EGA
egahibw	EGA black-and-white (286 only)
egamono	EGA Monochrome (286 only)
hercules	Hercules Monochrome
mcga	IBM MCGA (286 only)
olibw	Olivetti/AT&T Monochrome or PVC display
ct441	QuadVGA, ATI VIP VGA, 82C441 VGAs
tiga1	TIGA (Small fonts)
tiga2	TIGA (Large fonts)
vga	VGA
vgamono	VGA with Monochrome display
svga	Super VGA (800x600, 16 colors)
v7vga	Video Seven 640x480, 256 colors (512K)
v7c	Video Seven 720x512, 256 colors (512K)
v7d	Video Seven 800x600, 256 colors (1Mb)
v7e	Video Seven 1024x768, 256 colors (1Mb)
v7f	Video Seven 1024x768 (Small fonts)
xga16	XGA (640x480, 16 colors)
xgasm	XGA (Small fonts)
xgalg	XGA (Large fonts)
xgalo	XGA (640x480, 256 colors)

mouse=

hpmouse	HP Mouse (P-HIL)
lmouse	Logitech
ps2mouse	Microsoft, or IBM PS/2
genius1	Genius serial mouse on COM1
genius2	Genius serial mouse on COM2
msmouse1	Mouse Systems serial mouse on COM2
msmouse2	Mouse Systems serial or bus mouse
nomouse	No mouse or other pointing device
kbdmouse	Olivetti/AT&T Keyboard Mouse

Table 17-1.   *Possible Settings for Configuration Parameters (continued)*

network=

nonet	No network installed
3open/xx010000	3Com 3+Open versions 1.xx3open1
3open/00020000	3Com 3+Open version 2.0 Basic
3open/01020000	3Com 3+Open version 2.0 Enhanced
3share	3Com 3+Share
lantastic/xx000000	Artisoft LANtastic versions below 3.00
lantastic/xx030000	Artisoft LANtastic version 3.xx
lantastic/xx040000	Artisoft LANtastic version 4.xx
banyan/xx000000	Banyan Vines versions below 4.00
banyan/xx040000	Banyan Vines version 4.0x
banyan/xx041000	Banyan Vines version 4.1
dlr/xx000000	IBM OS/2 LAN Server versions below 1.2
dlr/xx012000	IBM OS/2 LAN Server version 1.2
dlr/xx012001	IBM OS/2 LAN Server version 1.2 with CSD
dlr/xx013000	IBM OS/2 LAN Server version 1.3
pclp/xx000000	IBM PC LAN Program version below 1.32
pclp/xx013200	IBM PC LAN Program version 1.32
lanman/xx000000	Microsoft LAN Manager version 1.xx
lanman/00020000	Microsoft LAN Manager version 2.00 Basic
lanman/01020000	Microsoft LAN Manager version 2.00 Enhanced
lanman/00021000	Microsoft LAN Manager version 2.10 Basic
lanman/01021000	Microsoft LAN Manager version 2.10 Enhanced
msnet	Microsoft Network (or 100% compatible)
novell/00000000	Novell Netware versions below 3.01
novell/00030100	Novell Netware versions below 3.21
novell/00032100	Novell Netware version 3.21 and above
pathworks/xx000000	DEC Pathworks versions below 4.0
pathworks/xx040000	DEC Pathworks version 4.0
pathworks/xx040100	DEC Pathworks versions 4.1 and above
10net/xx000000	TCS 10Net versions below 4.1
10net/00041000	TCS 10Net version 4.1x
10net/01041000	TCS 10Net version 4.1x with DCA 1M card
10net/xx042000	TCS 10Net version 4.2 and above
10net/xx050000	TCS 10Net version 5.0

Table 17-1.   *Possible Settings for Configuration Parameters (continued)*

keyboard=

t3s0alat	All AT type keyboards (84 to 86 keys)
t1s2at&t	AT&T "301" keyboard
t1s4at&t	AT&T "302" keyboard
t4s0enha	Enhanced 101 or 102 keys (U.S. and Non U.S.)
t3s0hp1	Hewlett-Packard Vectra keyboard (DIN)
t4s40oliv	Olivetti 101/102 A keyboard
t1s0oliv	Olivetti 83-key keyboard
t3s10oliv	Olivetti 86-key keyboard
t2s1oliv	Olivetti M24 102-key keyboard
t1s42oliv	PC-XT 83-key keyboard
t1s0pcxt	PC/XT - Type keyboard (84 keys)

language=

dan	Danish
nld	Dutch
enu	English (American)
eng	English (International)
fin	Finnish
fra	French
frc	French Canadian
deu	German
isl	Icelandic
ita	Italian
nor	Norwegian
ptg	Portuguese
esp	Spanish (Classic)
esn	Spanish (Modern)
sve	Swedish

kblayout=

beldll	Belgian
bridll	British
cafdll	Canadian Multilingual
dandll	Danish
dutdll	Dutch
findll	Finnish

Table 17-1.   *Possible Settings for Configuration Parameters (continued)*

kblayout= *(continued)*

fredll	French
candll	French Canadian
gerdll	German
icedll	Icelandic
itadll	Italian
latdll	Latin American
nordll	Norwegian
pordll	Portuguese
spadll	Spanish
swedll	Swedish
swfdll	Swiss French
swgdll	Swiss German
nodll	U.S.
usadll	U.S.
usddll	U.S.-Dvorak
usxdll	U.S.-International

Table 17-1.   *Possible Settings for Configuration Parameters (continued)*

[windir]   Insert a line that specifies where to install the Windows files under the [windir] heading. For example, inserting **c:\windows** places them in the WINDOWS directory on the user's local hard drive.

[userinfo]   Specify the user and company name under the [userinfo] heading. The first line is the user name and is required unless a shared copy of Windows is set up using the /n parameter. The second line is the company name and is optional. Place the names between quotes. See the earlier example.

[dontinstall]   Specify any components that should not be set up under this heading. Here is a list of components you can specify.

readmes	The readme informational text files
accessories	The accessories (Write, Notepad, and so on)
games	The games (Solitaire and Minesweeper)
screensavers	The screen saver files
bitmaps	The wallpaper bitmaps

[options]   Three options can be specified in this section, as follows.

setupapps	Use setupapps to set up applications; user chooses from dialog box.
autosetupapps	Use autosetupapps to set up all applications on the user's system.
tutorial	Use tutorial to start the Windows tutorial at the end of setup.

[printers]   Use [printers] to specify the names of printers to install during setup. These names are listed in CONTROL.INF, found in the Windows shared directory. If the printer name contains blank spaces, enclose it in quotation marks. Specify a port name after the printer name, but separate the two with a comma. An example is shown here:

```
"HP LaserJet",LPT1:
```

Here are the possible port names. If special printer ports have been created in WIN.INI, they can also be specified.

    LPT1:
    LPT2:
    LPT3:
    COM1:
    COM2:
    COM3:
    COM4:
    EPT:
    FILE:
    LPT1.OS2
    LPT2.OS2

[endinstall]   Insert one of the following to specify what should happen at the end of the install routine:

- *configfiles=modify*   Use configfiles=modify to make all changes to CONFIG.SYS and AUTOEXEC.BAT. The previous files are renamed with the .OLD extension, or if that extension is in use, .000 is used (or a consecutive number following that).

- *configfiles=save*   Use to save changes to CONFIG.SYS and AUTOEXEC.BAT in CONFIG.WIN and AUTOEXEC.WIN. The user can then rename or edit these files later.

If you do not specify one of these configfiles entries, the CONFIG.SYS and AUTOEXEC.BAT files will be modified by Setup. The endopt entries below specify what happens at the end of Setup. You can specify one of the following:

endopt=exit	Return to DOS
endopt=restart	Restart Windows
endopt=reboot	Restart the system unless a shared copy is being set up

Other Setup Options

The SETUP.INF file tells the Setup utility how Windows is set up. The options are related to the Program Manager group windows, icons, available applications, and other features. A complete discussion of this file is covered in Appendix B. Typically, the changes you make to the file are used for all network installations, but you create several different copies, and then rename the files before a user does an installation, or create a setup batch file that users can run to rename the files based on the version of SETUP.INF they need for their installation. Here's a list of options you can specify in SETUP.INF:

- Add groups to the Program Manager.

- Add applications to any Program Manager group.

- Include additional files in the setup process, such as special drivers, TSRs, .PIF files, or special .INI files for applications.

- Set up third-party device drivers.

- Set Program Manager features. You can disable the Run, Exit Windows, Save Settings on Exit, and set restrictions on what users can modify in the Program Manager. You can disable the File menu, if necessary.

The Program Manager can also be changed by setting the options in PROGMAN.INI as discussed in Appendix G.

General Network Considerations

Every large network will surely have users who want or need Windows. The strategy may be to use Windows throughout. The network administrator must decide whether users run Windows from their local workstations or over the network. The main issue is *network traffic versus network management*. If Windows files are stored on the server, and users access those files every time they start Windows, you can easily make changes to setups and operating features. If Windows runs completely from the user's workstation, network traffic decreases, but servicing Windows is harder. This discussion tackles the issues involved when Windows runs in a shared directory on the server, and each user's files are either stored at their workstation or in a personal network directory.

Running Windows (and other programs) entirely from the server is cost-effective when diskless workstations or floppy drive-only systems are used. This frees up funds for more important things, such as memory upgrades. The magic number for Windows is 4MB. If the network is large, improve its performance by upgrading to fast network cards (16-bit), or change to a network cabling system with fast through-put (such as Ethernet).

Performance can be improved dramatically by using several network cards in the server. This lets you divide the network into multiple trunks. For example, use a fast Ethernet trunk for users who access large graphic files, and then place the "slow" users who only access an occasional file on slower-performing (and less-expensive) trunks.

Here are some important points to consider when setting up Windows for network users:

- Create a shared directory name such as \APPS\WINDOWS, and then flag the directory and files *shareable* and *read-only*. You don't want users accidentally changing these files since all Windows users need them.

- Create a special Windows users group, and then assign that group access to the shared directory.

- Use commands in the system login script that execute if a user is a member of the Windows user group. The "IF MEMBER OF" login script command is well documented in the NetWare manuals.

- When creating the search path mappings for users in the login script, insert the map command for the user's personal Windows directory before the map command for the shared Windows directory. This order is important because both directories contain files with the same name. Those files in the user's personal directory are customized for the user's configuration. That directory must be searched first to ensure execution of the correct files. Place the map commands in the "If member of Windows group" section of the system login script.

- Minimize the number of drive mappings for users. Each map appears as an icon in the File Manager; these soon clutter the screen. Consider branching application directories from a single directory, such as APPS, and then map a drive to APPS. Give users rights to APPS and its subdirectories. In the File Manager, they'll see all the branching subdirectories of APPS as folders. Let them access files by moving through the directory structure in the File Manager, rather than assigning a lot of drive maps. Be aware of how the Windows utilities change, save, and restore drive mappings during a Windows session. Use the Control Panel to set these options. They get stored in the network's .INI file (NETWARE.INI and WIN.INI), so you can set these values, and then copy the .INI files to user's directories during setup.

- MAP ROOT is important when running NetWare. If you don't use it, all drive icons in the File Manager point to the root directory. If you MAP ROOT a user's personal directory, he or she can't see parent directories, only sub-directories. This keeps them from "exploring" other directories and from inadvertently changing his or her mappings. MAP ROOT also speeds searching. The File Manager starts its searches at the root; MAP ROOT shortens that search by specifying only one branch of the directory tree. An example of the correct form for the MAP command is shown here. The Ins (Insert) option preserves the DOS path settings, adding the new path settings after them.

```
MAP INS ROOT F:=SYS:USERS\ASHLEY
```

- On NetWare networks, create a SHELL.CFG file that includes the following SHOW DOTS line. It makes the parent directory [..] visible when listing subdirectories. If not used, the parent directory icon is not visible and users will have trouble getting back to the directory in the File Manager.

```
SHOW DOTS = ON
```

Also include the following option to increase file handles from the default of 40 to approximately 60, making sure the value matches the value of FILES= in the CONFIG.SYS file.

```
FILE HANDLES = 60
```

- The location of the swap files used by the Virtual Memory system in 386 enhanced mode is an important consideration. It should be located on a local hard drive. Swapping to the server drive puts too much traffic on the network. If the workstation doesn't have a local drive, increase its memory to minimize its need to ever use a swap file.

- Be sure to use the latest drivers for network interface cards and for Windows. When installing NetWare, use the Windows Workstation Utilities. These are self-installing utilities that automatically make changes to the WIN.INI and SYSTEM.INI files. These utilities are available from Novell or you can download them from CompuServe's NetWire forum.

- Make sure users always have the same drive mappings to the directories they use. If a mapping is changed, program icons in the Program Manager that access network drives may not work.

Hardware Considerations

The NETWORKS.WRI file contains the latest information on the various networks supported by Windows. Refer to this document for information regarding startup settings and other problems. Note the following:

- If a network interface card uses IRQ 2 or 9, make sure you have the file VPICDA.386 when running Novell NetWare. Replace device=*vpicda in the [386Enh] section of SYSTEM.INI with device=vpicda.386 to avoid interrupt conflicts. Note that the commands are automatically placed in SYSTEM.INI when you install the Windows Workstation software.

- Memory base address C0000h and I/O port base address 02Eh have been known to cause problems with Windows. Avoid these addresses when configuring network interface cards.

- Use the EMMExclude= line in the [386Enh] section of SYSTEM.INI to avoid memory conflicts with the memory address used by network cards. Alternatively, use the EMM386 (CONFIG.SYS) /x option to exclude the memory as discussed in Chapter 9.

- Some NetWare utilities may not run in 386 enhanced mode unless you create a PIF file. Use the parameters shown here as a starting point. On the main PIF screen, set the following:

    KB Required: 256
    KB Desired: 640
    Display Usage: Full Screen
    Execution: Exclusive

  Click the Advanced button and set the following parameters:

    Background Priority: 1
    Foreground Priority: 1000
    EMS Memory KB Limit: 1024 and Locked
    XMS Memory KB Limit: 1024 and Locked
    Video Memory: High Graphics
    Monitor Ports: Mark all options in this field

Switching applications in Windows may cause network problems. Choose the Prevent Program Switch option when you create a PIF for the program.

SYSTEM.INI Settings

Listed next are network-related settings in SYSTEM.INI. Changes to these settings are optional, but if problems occur, review this list.

NetAsynchFallback=   If NetAsynchFallback= is enabled, Windows attempts to save a failing NetBIOS request. When an application issues an asynchronous NetBIOS request, Windows will attempt to allocate space in its global network buffer to receive the data. If there is insufficient space in the global buffer, Windows will normally fail the NetBIOS request. If this setting is enabled, Windows will attempt to save such a request by allocating a buffer in local memory and preventing any other virtual machines from running until the data is received and the timeout period (specified by the NetAsynchTimeout setting) expires. To change: Use Notepad to edit the SYSTEM.INI file.

NetHeapSize= A Windows application may not run properly if it requires a larger buffer for transferring data over the network than Windows normally provides. You can increase the NetHeapSize setting in the SYSTEM.INI file [standard] or [386Enh] sections from the default value of 8K (standard mode) and 12K (386 enhanced mode).

NetDMASize= The NetDMASize= setting specifies how much memory Windows should reserve for direct memory access. The default value is 0 for ISA machines and 32 for Micro Channel machines.

AllVMsExclusive= If enabled, AllVMsExclusive= forces all applications to run in exclusive full-screen mode, which helps avoid network-related problems when running non-Windows applications. Settings in an applications program information file (PIF) are ignored when this option is on. Enabling this setting might prolong the Windows session when you are running network or memory-resident software that is incompatible with Windows.

CachedFileHandles= Windows keeps 14 handles open by default. If users are having problems running a shared copy of Windows from a server, decrease this number, but doing so may slow Windows down.

FileSysChange= The FileSysChange= setting indicates whether the File Manager automatically receives messages any time a non-Windows application creates, re-names, or deletes a file. If disabled, a virtual machine can run exclusively, even if it modifies files. Enabling this setting can slow down system performance significantly. You can try setting this option off to prevent Windows from being alerted every time a file is manipulated. The default setting is on in 386 enhanced mode and off in standard mode.

InDOSPolling= If enabled, InDOSPolling= prevents Windows from running other applications when memory-resident software has the InDOS flag set. Enabling this setting is necessary if the memory-resident software needs to be in a critical section to do operations off an INT21 hook, but will slow down system performance slightly. The default is No.

INT28Critical= INT28Critical= specifies whether a critical section is needed to handle INT28h interrupts used by memory-resident software. Some network virtual devices do internal task switching on INT28h interrupts. These interrupts might hang some network software, indicating the need for an INT28h critical section. If you are not using such software, you might improve Windows' task switching by disabling this setting.

MaxPagingFileSize=   You can't completely disable swapping since the Windows memory management scheme requires it, but you can reduce swapping to disk by increasing the memory available to each workstation's memory. Try including the statement MaxPagingFileSize=512 in the SYSTEM.INI file.

ReflectDosInt2A=   The ReflectDosInt2A= setting indicates whether Windows should consume or reflect DOS INT 2A signals. The default means Windows will consume these signals and therefore run more efficiently. Add this option and enable it if you are running memory-resident software that relies on detecting INT2A messages.

TimerCriticalSection=   The TimerCriticalSection= setting instructs Windows to go into a critical section around all timer interrupt code, and specifies a timeout period (in milliseconds). Specifying a positive value causes only one virtual machine at a time to receive timer interrupts. Some networks and other global memory-resident software may fail unless this setting is used. However, it slows down performance and can make the system seem to stop for short periods of time. The default is 0.

TokenRingSearch=   If TokenRingSearch= is enabled, Windows searches for a token ring network adapter on machines with IBM PC/AT architecture. Disable this setting if you are not using a token ring card and the search interferes with another device.

Part *III*

Working with Applications

Chapter *18*

Installing and Organizing Applications

This chapter discusses how to install and organize your applications. You'll learn various ways to organize with the Program Manager, the File Manager, and directories, and you'll see how your programs modify the .INI files.

Installing Applications

Installation of Windows applications is straightforward. First, you should always follow the instructions in the owner's manual. This normally involves executing the application's setup or install program from the Run dialog box in Windows, as shown in Figure 18-1. Typically, you type **A:INSTALL** or **A:SETUP** in the dialog box and click OK. The installation procedure handles the rest, asking you for the name of the directory where it should place files.

Most installation procedures for Windows applications create a separate group window in the Program Manager and place startup icons in it. This is fine if the application contains several associated applications and you want to keep their startup icons together in the same group. As an alternative, you can copy the icons into a larger group, and then remove the group window. For example, instead of keeping separate groups for a drawing program, a paint program, and a scanning program, you could copy all the icons to a single group called Graphics.

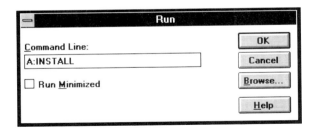

Figure 18-1.   *Use the Run dialog box to start an application's install utility*

If you already have applications on your system, and you don't see startup icons for those applications in the Program Manager, run the Setup program. Choose Setup Applications from the Setup Options menu and follow the procedure discussed in Chapter 6. The Setup program finds the executable files on your system and displays them in a window so you can select the files you want to set up as icons in the Program Manager. Alternatively, you can use the Setup utility to set up a single program with its own icon if you know the program's directory and filename. See Chapter 6 for details.

Organizing Application Directories

Most of the applications that are bundled with Windows are stored in the Windows directory. By default, any files you create with those applications are also stored in the Windows directory. The section "Organizing Documents" later in this chapter shows you how to specify another directory for data files so you don't clutter the Windows directory.

When installing new applications, never install them in the Windows directory. Instead, specify a directory that branches from the root. For example, when installing Word for Windows, the directory \WINWORD is specified. However, you can create a directory structure that's easy to back up by appending all application directories to a single directory called \APPS or \PROGRAMS. Then when you back up, simply specify the \APPS or \PROGRAMS directory and their subdirectories. For example, you could create a directory called \PROGRAMS\WINWORD for Word for Windows and another called \PROGRAMS\PUBPB for ZSoft's Publishers Paintbrush as shown here:

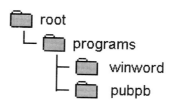

When you specify application directories during the setup of a Windows application, Program Manager icons are created to call the program from the directory you specified. You can specify where the program should store its documents by altering the properties of the icon as discussed in a moment.

If you reorganize your applications by moving their directories to other locations, be sure to update any files that refer to those applications in the old directory. Change the properties of the startup icon for the application in the Program Manager, and also check the WIN.INI file for entries related to the application. The application itself may have internal settings that refer to the old directory, or it may create its own .INI file that may require updating.

Installing Non-Windows Applications

Non-Windows applications should be installed from the DOS prompt using the procedure documented in the application's manual. After you've installed the application, you can start Windows and create a startup icon for it in the Program Manager, or use the Setup utility.

The Setup utility has descriptions for a large number of third-party applications, which you can see if you list the APPS.INF file in the Windows \ SYSTEM directory. (This procedure also creates a PIF for the program). If Windows doesn't recognize the program, it recommends that you use the New option on the Program Manager File menu to create a startup icon for the file. You should then create a PIF file for the application, following the procedures described in Chapter 19.

Using Program Information Files (PIFs)

Non-Windows applications run more efficiently if the proper startup and operating parameters are specified for the application in a Program Information File. If you don't create a PIF file for an application, Windows uses the settings in its default PIF (_DEFAULT.PIF) when you run the application. This may pose a problem for some applications if the default settings are not the optimum ones. You can change the settings of the default PIF, but it's best just to create a PIF for each application using the PIF Editor. Before doing so, check to see if the application came with a PIF of its own. Manufacturer-supplied PIFs contain settings that optimize the application for Windows. Check the disks or program directory of the application.

Adding Protection

Once you've installed either a Windows or non-Windows application, you can protect its files from accidental deletion or modification by applying the Read Only attribute. Files that have this attribute cannot be altered or deleted. However, be careful not to apply the attribute to files that the application needs to change while it runs. The .INI files used by Windows are a good example. These files are updated on a regular basis, so never give them the Read Only attribute (unless you want to prevent unauthorized tampering with your Windows settings).

To apply the Read Only attribute, follow these steps:

1. Start the File Manager, and then open a directory window on the directory that holds the program files.

2. Select the files you want to protect. To select all, click the first file, and then hold SHIFT and click the last file. To select specific files, hold CTRL and click the files you wish to select.

3. Choose Properties from the File menu, and then enable the Read Only box and click OK.

Later, if you need to remove the Read Only property, follow the same steps, but disable the Read Only box in step 3.

 Don't forget where you've applied the Read Only attribute. Later, when updating a program, you may see messages saying that the installation can't proceed. Your first step would be to unprotect the files in the directory.

Organizing Documents

There are many ways to organize the documents created by your applications. You could create one directory called \ DOCS and store all documents created by all applications in it. However, you won't be able to use the same filenames, and similar filenames can be confusing. A better way to organize is to create directories that reflect the way you work or the projects that you're working on.

For backup reasons, it's a good idea to create directories that branch from a single directory, such as \ DATA. Typical directory structures are shown in the following illustration:

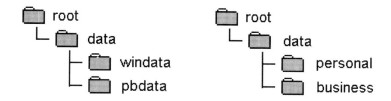

The directory structure on the left is organized according to the documents created by each application. The structure on the right is organized by the types of files you create and their use. You could also create directories such as \ PROJECT1, \ GRAPHICS, or \ NEWSLET (newsletter). For example, the newsletter directory would contain all the files you use (graphics and text) to create a newsletter.

Once you've created the directory structure, you need to change the properties of your program icons to ensure that document files are stored in the correct document directory. Click the program icon, choose Properties, and then specify the directory in the Working Directory field. You should do this for all your applications, including the Windows accessories. For example, to ensure Write documents are stored in a directory called \ BUSINESS, change the Program Item Properties dialog box as shown in Figure 18-2.

But what if you want to store personal files in another directory called, for example, \ PERSONAL? Just create another Write icon, then change its properties to point to the \ PERSONAL directory. To create a copy of an icon, hold the CTRL key, and then click and drag. You will be dragging off a copy of the icon. You then

Program Item Properties		
Description:	Write	OK
Command Line:	WRITE.EXE	Cancel
Working Directory:	\DATA\BUSINESS	**B**rowse...
Shortcut Key:	None	Change **I**con...
	☐ **R**un Minimized	**H**elp

Figure 18-2.   *The Program Item Properties dialog box*

choose Properties from the File menu and change both its Description and Working Directory fields as shown in Figure 18-3.

Change the name of the previous Write icon (the one that saves files in the \ BUSINESS directory) to Business. As you can see, multiple icons are created to help you direct exactly where files are stored. In addition, when you start the application and choose the Open option, you'll get a listing of the files in the specified directory.

Document Icons

Recall that documents can have their own startup icons. If the document is associated with a Windows application, all you need to do is specify the document's name; Windows will find the right application to start. The following illustration shows a Program Manager group that contains both program and document icons.

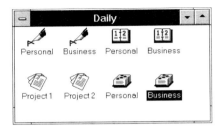

This group follows our theme of personal and business files. Note that the icons still reflect the type of application to run, but the icon names are changed to indicate the document file that will open when the icon is executed.

Figure 18-3. *Changing the Description and Working Directory fields shown in the Program Item Properties dialog box*

The easiest way to create document icons is to drag File Manager file icons to a Program Manager group, as outlined in Chapter 6. The names of each document then appear as document icons. You can also create document icons using the New option on the Program Manager File menu. On the Properties dialog box, specify the program and document name on the Command Line field. Use this method to create startup icons for DOS applications, or for unassociated documents. For example, to create a startup icon for a Word for DOS document called REPORT.DOC in the \ BUSINESS directory, you would type the following line on the Command Line field:

```
C:\WORD55\WORD   C:\DATA\BUSINESS\REPORT.DOC
```

Don't forget to change the icon if necessary to reflect the type of document or application that runs when the icon is double-clicked. Remember that third-party icons like those used for DOS applications are found in the MOREICONS.DLL file. Setup uses this file when it creates application icons.

Chapter 19

Running DOS and DOS Applications

This chapter is about running non-Windows (DOS) applications under Windows. There are advantages to doing so. In standard mode, Windows lets you quickly switch among DOS and Windows applications and even cut and paste text between them. In 386 enhanced mode, DOS and Windows applications can run simultaneously, and you can run a DOS application in a resizable window, instead of full screen. This lets you work with applications side by side to compare information or perform cut-and-paste operations more easily.

DOS applications running under Windows require special treatment, however, because they don't share system resources (such as a processor, memory, ports, and so on) in a cooperative way like Windows-specific applications do. DOS applications expect to have the whole system to themselves. For example, a DOS application takes a certain amount of memory and doesn't release it until you close the application. Windows applications, on the other hand, share memory with other applications, taking only what they need. Windows tames DOS applications by making them share system resources.

You can make adjustments to the way a DOS application uses system resources by creating a Program Information File (PIF). PIF settings can specify how much memory a DOS application gets, or how much of the processor's time it gets when running with other applications. PIF settings can also specify whether DOS applications run full screen, or in a window in 386 enhanced mode. When you execute a DOS application, Windows searches for a matching PIF file and executes the application using the settings in the PIF. If a PIF doesn't exist, Windows uses its default PIF, which is called _DEFAULT.PIF. The default PIF has generic settings designed to help a wide variety of applications run under Windows. You'll probably need to create special PIFs for your applications to make them run efficiently.

 Use Setup to automatically create PIFs and icons for non-Windows applications. The utility knows the settings for most popular third-party applications.

Considerations for DOS Applications

As mentioned, DOS applications need special treatment under Windows. One way to ensure they run properly and at their highest performance is to run them exclusively and full screen. When an application runs *exclusively*, it gets all your system's processing power. Running full screen instead of in a window (386 enhanced mode only) improves performance since Windows doesn't need to handle the extra processing required by having a window on the desktop. When a DOS application runs exclusively, Windows steps aside and removes almost all of itself from memory.

DOS applications are handled differently in the two operating modes of Windows:

- *Standard Mode*   In standard mode, DOS applications can only run exclusively and full screen. You can't place them in a resizable window and all other applications stop processing. However, you can quickly switch back to Windows applications if necessary, and perform crude cut-and-paste operations. Press CTRL-ESC or CTRL-TAB to switch between Windows and the DOS application.

- *386 Enhanced Mode*   In 386 enhanced mode, DOS applications can multitask and run in resizable windows. Several DOS applications and Windows applications can run at once; the only limitation is the amount of memory your system has. You can control how much processing time each application gets. Press CTRL-ESC or CTRL-TAB to switch between Windows and the DOS application, or press ALT-ENTER to place the application in a resizable window.

Memory Issues

One of the biggest issues when running DOS applications is memory. Drivers and applications loaded before Windows starts use memory in the conventional memory area where DOS applications run. When you start Windows and then run a DOS application, the existing DOS environment is re-created for the application. Any memory used by drivers and utilities is still in use, but at the same time, the drivers and utilities are available for use by the application. Chapter 9 covers the topic of optimizing conventional memory in detail. Using DOS 5, you can move drivers into high memory, thus freeing conventional memory for applications.

If your DOS applications (or even Windows applications) require that you run specific utilities, run them from DOS before starting Windows so they are available to the applications you run from Windows. Keep in mind that the utility reduces the amount of memory available to each DOS application. If a utility is needed by only one application, run the utility from Windows before starting the DOS application. You can create a batch file that starts the utility and the program at the same time, and then run the batch file from Windows. The advantage of this method is that the memory used by the utility and the application is freed up when you exit the application.

Expanded Memory Considerations

Applications that require expanded memory require special memory configurations, depending on the mode you run:

- *Standard Mode*   If you intend to run a DOS application that requires expanded memory in standard mode, you'll need to configure part of system memory as expanded memory. This is done by adding a special expanded memory board and loading the EMS memory manager. You only need to configure as much expanded memory as the application needs. Configure all other memory as extended memory.

- *386 Enhanced Mode*   Windows provides the best support for expanded memory applications when you run 386 enhanced mode. 386 enhanced mode simulates expanded memory for the application so you don't need to configure any memory as expanded memory. This topic is covered fully in Chapter 9.

Using Batch Files

Use DOS batch files to start DOS applications and utilities at the same time from Windows. The batch file can contain one or more commands you need to load when starting the application. As mentioned previously, this helps save memory because the utility and application are removed from memory when you exit the application. For example, to start a utility, then an application, create a batch file that contains the following:

```
UTIL.EXE
PROGRAM.EXE
```

The first line is the utility and the second is the program. You then create a PIF for the batch file by following the steps discussed under "Using the PIF Editor" later in this chapter. For example, if the batch file is called STARTUP.BAT, you would open the PIF Editor, type **STARTUP.BAT** in the Program Filename field, set other PIF options as necessary for the DOS session, and then save the PIF using the filename STARTUP.PIF. You can then create a startup icon for the PIF or the batch file. If you start the batch file, Windows automatically finds and uses the PIF. If you start the PIF, Windows runs the batch file specified in the PIF.

To preserve memory, Windows closes DOS sessions when you exit a DOS application, or after the completion of commands in a batch file. If text from a command listing is displayed on the screen, you may not have a chance to see it if Windows immediately restores itself. For example, choose Run from the Program Manager or File Manager File menu and type **MEM /P** (to list memory statistics). Windows executes the command, then immediately restores itself before you get a chance to see the listing. To keep a DOS session open when running a batch file, insert COMMAND as the last line in the batch file as shown here:

```
echo off
prompt Windows DOS Session - $p$g
mem /P | more
command
```

COMMAND.COM loads a secondary command processor and prevents an immediate return to Windows until you type **EXIT**.

The second line sets a DOS prompt that reminds you you're in a DOS session—many users forget they've switched out to DOS, then type WIN in an attempt to start Windows. There are some commands that should not be executed while working at the DOS level. These are listed under "Incompatible DOS Commands," later in this chapter.

Using the MS-DOS Prompt

Start the MS-DOS Prompt when you prefer to work at the DOS prompt with familiar DOS commands. You might use this mode to execute useful commands such as MEM as mentioned previously, or DOS file manipulation commands instead of the File Manager commands. The MS-DOS Prompt executes the PIF file called DOSPRMPT.PIF. You can edit this file to change various settings. For example, you can specify that MS-DOS run in a resizable window (386 enhanced mode), or that any applications in it run exclusively.

When you start the MS-DOS Prompt a message box appears, with instructions on how to exit and switch away from the MS-DOS Prompt. If you want to disable this message, include or change the DOSPromptExitInstruc= line in the [386 Enhanced] section of SYSTEM.INI. It should appear as shown here if you want to disable the message:

```
DOSPromptExitInstruc=0
```

Incompatible DOS Commands

The following DOS commands are not compatible with Windows 3.1, or should be used with caution or not used at all. Refer to SETUP.TXT on the Windows disk 1 for information about other commands and third-party utilities that may not run correctly with Windows.

APPEND   The APPEND command interferes with the ability of Windows and Windows applications to build valid filenames for the files they need to access. Do not use APPEND when running Windows 3.1.

CHKDSK   Do not run the CHKDSK command with the /F option when working in a Windows DOS session. CHKDSK would attempt to modify part of the operating system that cannot be changed while Windows is running.

FASTOPEN   In low-memory situations, Windows 3.1 may not run properly if FASTOPEN is in use. Also disable this command when running disk defragmenting utilities.

GRAPHICS   If you run multiple DOS sessions from Windows (that is, more than one virtual machine) and use the GRAPHICS command to print from each session, you may experience printing problems since each session can send documents to the printer simultaneously.

JOIN   If JOIN is in use, do not change the state of the joined drives while Windows is running.

MIRROR   If you run MIRROR while in a Windows DOS session, you must type **MIRROR** /U before exiting the DOS session to remove MIRROR from memory.

SUBST   As with the JOIN command, do not change the state of the substituted drives while Windows is running.

In general, never run commands that delete files in the Windows directory, or delete temporary files that might be in use by Windows or a Windows application. Do not run disk defragmenting programs while Windows is running. In addition, as a continuing reminder, disable SmartDrive and FASTOPEN *before* running disk defragmenting programs.

Creating Startup Icons and PIFs

Use the Setup utility to create startup icons and PIFs for DOS applications. The APPS.INI file contains PIF settings for hundreds of third-party applications, and defines the icons used for those applications. The icons are in the MORICONS.DLL file.

Choose the Setup Applications option from the Setup Options menu to set up a new application. This procedure is covered in Chapter 6, but reiterated briefly here. The first dialog box you see after choosing the command contains the options discussed next.

The Search for Application Option   If you choose Search for Application, Setup searches the path and/or specified drives in your system. It locates all DOS applications it knows how to install and presents you with a list. You then pick the ones for which you wish to create icons and PIFs. The icons are placed in a Program Manager group called Applications.

The Ask You to Specify an Application Option   If you choose Ask You to Specify an Application, Setup asks for the path and name of the application. You can also click the Browse button to pick a drive, directory, and filename using standard Open dialog box options. Once you've specified the application name, you choose in which Program Manager group to have Setup place the icon.

Setup will not create icons and PIFs for applications not listed in the APPS.INF file. If you specify an application not in the file, Setup tells you to create the icon and PIF yourself. Use the PIF Editor discussed later in this chapter to create a PIF for the application, and then create a startup icon in the Program Manager for the PIF.

Running DOS Applications in Standard Mode

DOS applications started in standard mode run exclusively and in full-screen mode. That means Windows removes all but a small part of itself from memory and gives your system's full processing power to the application. You can easily switch back to Windows by pressing ALT-TAB, ALT-ESC, or CTRL-ESC. CTRL-ESC displays the Task List. When you switch back to Windows, you'll see the application's icon on the desktop. You then double-click the icon to return to the application.

You can start additional DOS applications, but they do not multitask as they would in 386 enhanced mode. Standard mode provides *program switching* rather than multitasking. You double-click the icon of the DOS application you want to use, and then switch back to Windows to use another DOS application or Windows application. When you switch back to Windows, your current DOS application is temporarily suspended.

When a non-Windows application runs in standard mode, it is displayed in a full screen. There are no window borders or menu options. A Control menu exists, but only when you switch back to Windows and click the application icon. Use the options on the menu to perform three actions: restoring, pasting, and moving.

Restore   Use Restore to restore the application to full-screen display.

Paste   Use Paste to attach information from the Clipboard into the non-Windows application.

Move   Use Move to manipulate the icon on the Windows desktop.

Copy and Paste Operations in Standard Mode

You can copy text-only information (not graphics) from a DOS application in standard mode by pressing the PRINT SCREEN key. The information is placed on the Clipboard. You then return to Windows and paste it into another application. If you have an older keyboard, you may need to press ALT-PRINT SCREEN to copy text.

To paste text information on the Clipboard into a DOS application, first open the DOS application and position the insertion point. Switch back to Windows and click the icon of the application to open its Control menu, then choose Paste.

Running DOS Applications in 386 Enhanced Mode

386 enhanced mode provides many useful options for running DOS applications. Press ALT-ENTER to switch from a full-screen to a windowed mode. When the application runs in a window, you can change its font and window size, move it around on the desktop, more easily work with other applications, and cut and paste with more control.

Starting a DOS application in 386 enhanced mode is the same as starting any other application. You double-click its icon, or the icon of its PIF if one is available. PIF settings are more important and diverse for DOS applications running in 386 enhanced mode. You can control multitasking features that determine how much processing time the application gets, and whether it starts in a window or full screen.

Using Resizable Windows

You can start a DOS application in full-screen mode, and then press ALT-ENTER to switch it to a resizable window. Keep in mind that using a window makes your system run slower. In addition, the application itself runs faster in full-screen mode. You should use full-screen mode whenever possible, then switch to a window to cut and paste, or work with other application windows. When you're done with the window, press ALT-ENTER again to return to full-screen mode.

To run an application in a window every time it starts, you can modify its PIF file. For example, to change the PIF setting so the MS-DOS Prompt runs in a window, start the PIF Editor in 386 enhanced mode (the PIF menu is different in standard mode), and then choose Open from its File menu. Open the DOSPRMPT.PIF file, and then click the Windowed option in the Display Usage field. Save the changes, and then double-click the MS-DOS Prompt icon to open it in a window.

The fonts and size of a DOS application window are changed by choosing the Fonts option on the window's Control menu, as discussed in the next section.

The Control Menu

The Control menu of the MS-DOS Prompt running in 386 enhanced mode is shown in Figure 19-1. If your DOS application is in full-screen mode, press ALT-ENTER to switch to a window so you can access the Control menu.

The first few options are used to resize and move the window. You can choose the Switch To option to return to Windows and the Task List. Choose Edit to open the edit options menu so you can cut and paste. Settings is used to control the multitasking options for the application, or to change it from full screen to a Windows application.

Settings Options

When you choose the Settings option, the dialog box in Figure 19-2 appears. You change settings on this dialog box to override those specified by the application's PIF file. Keep in mind that this menu is used to control the settings of an application

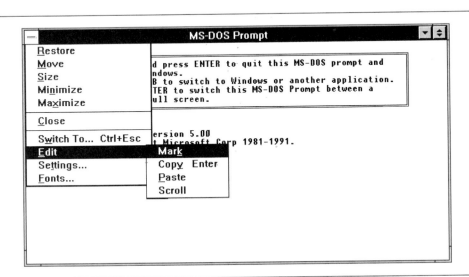

Figure 19-1.   *The Control menu of a DOS application running in a window in 386 enhanced mode*

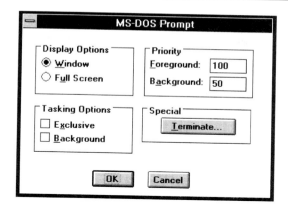

Figure 19-2.   *386 enhanced mode settings dialog box for DOS applications*

during its current session only. Make changes within a PIF to create permanent settings.

The Display Options Box   Click either Windowed or Full Screen to change the display mode. Note that you can press ALT-ENTER to switch between full screen and windowed mode from the keyboard.

The Tasking Options Box   Click Exclusive or Background or both. Select Background to run the application in the background when working on other tasks in the foreground. If you don't enable this option, the application is suspended when you work on other tasks. If you select Exclusive, all other applications are suspended when the application is active. If both Exclusive and Background are selected, the application runs exclusively when active in the foreground, and continues processing when it's in the background and you're working on other tasks. If you run the application exclusively, click Full Screen in the Display Options box as well to maximize the application's performance.

The Priority Box   The priority options determine the amount of processor time the application gets in relation to other active tasks. You'll learn more about this in the "Multitasking Options" section later in this chapter.

The Special Box   Click the Terminate button to quit a DOS application that is not responding. *Only use this option as a last resort.* Switch to another application and save your work, and then terminate the application, reboot, and restart Windows since it may become unstable.

It's important to remember that the Control menu options are used to change the settings of a running application. Use PIF files to specify the initial startup settings. For example, if you're running a DOS application and its performance seems slow, you can click Exclusive on the Control menu or change its Foreground priority. If a DOS application is processing in the background and is slowing down other applications, you can open the Control menu and disable the Background option or reduce the Background priority setting. These features are covered in a moment.

Fonts and Window Size

Choose the Fonts option on the Control menu to change the Fonts and Window size. If you don't see the Fonts option on the menu, open SYSTEM.INI for editing and add the following line under the [NonWindowsApp] section, and then restart Windows:

```
FontChangeEnable=1
```

The Font Selection dialog box shown in Figure 19-3 lets you change the font and size of windows. In the Font box, choose a different font size. Both the Selected Font and the Window Preview fields change to show the new size. Enable Save Settings on Exit if you want the new setting to be used the next time you start the application.

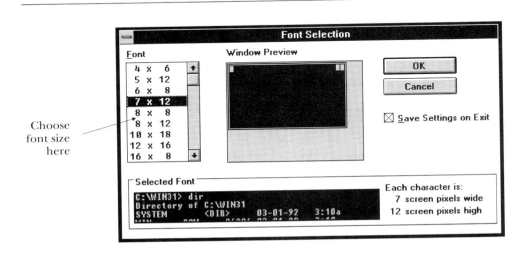

Figure 19-3. *Use the Font Selection box to change the font size and window size for DOS applications running in a window in 386 enhanced mode*

By default, the Save Settings on Exit check box is enabled. That means any changes you make to fonts take effect the next time you open the DOS application. Disable this setting if you don't want font changes saved. If you want the Save Settings on Exit box disabled for all new applications you open, add the following line to the [NonWindowsApp] section of the SYSTEM.INI file:

```
DisablePositionSave=1
```

Note that the default for this option is 0 because Windows does not place the line in your SYSTEM.INI file. To reenable font changes, remove the line or set its value to 0. Changes to the fonts of DOS application windows are logged in the file DOSAPP.INI. You can view this file to see the history or status of DOS applications you've opened, but there's not much need to change its settings since the Fonts utility does an adequate job of that.

You can change the foreground and background colors in DOS application windows using ANSI.SYS commands as documented in your DOS manual.

Using a Mouse in a DOS Window

Windows 3.1 now supports the use of a mouse in a windowed DOS application. If you're running a DOS application in a DOS window and you can't use the mouse, first make sure MOUSE.COM is loaded at the DOS level. There should be a MOUSE command in your AUTOEXEC.BAT file, or a DEVICE=MOUSE.SYS command in your CONFIG.SYS file. Either option loads the mouse driver at the DOS level before Windows is started. If you still can't use the mouse in a window, include the following line in the [NonWindowsApp] section of the SYSTEM.INI file and restart Windows:

```
MouseInDosBox=1
```

Cut-and-Paste Operations

The procedure for cutting and pasting for 386 enhanced mode DOS applications is the same as for standard mode if the application is running full screen. Press PRINT SCREEN to capture the entire screen when the DOS application is active. To paste to a DOS application, first open the DOS application and position the insertion point. Switch back to Windows and click the icon of the application to open its Control menu, and then choose Paste from the Control menu.

If the application is running in a resizable window, you can copy specific portions of the application's screen to the Clipboard using commands on the Control menu. If the window is running full screen, press ALT-ENTER to display it in a window. Then open its Control menu and choose Edit to access the Mark, Copy, and Paste options.

Choose the Mark option to highlight a specific area to copy to the Clipboard. A rectangular cursor appears in the upper-left corner of the window. Move the cursor to the beginning of the area you want to copy, then, while holding down the SHIFT key, press the arrow keys to select an area. When done, choose Edit from the Control menu again, and then choose the Copy option to place the selected text or object on the Clipboard. Press ALT-TAB or use the mouse to switch to another application and paste in the normal way.

To paste information on the Clipboard into a DOS application, first place the application in a window by pressing ALT-ENTER, then position the insertion point and choose Paste from the Edit section of the DOS application's Control menu.

If text pasted into a DOS application is missing characters, the Clipboard is probably sending characters faster than the application can receive them. If so, disable the Allow Fast Paste option in the application's PIF. If a PIF doesn't exist, create one and disable this option.

Multitasking Options

Multitasking within DOS applications is possible when running Windows in 386 enhanced mode. Windows applications automatically multitask, but non-Windows applications require special parameters and settings that help them cooperate and share your system resources when running in a multitasking mode.

You set multitasking options in several places. Open the Control Panel's 386 Enhanced utility, as shown in Figure 19-4 to set the amount of processing time allocated to Windows applications, but only if a DOS application is running—that is, if two or more virtual machines have been created. (These settings have no effect if DOS applications are not running). To specify the amount of processing time DOS applications get, create a PIF file for the applications and make changes on the PIF. When a DOS application is running, you can change its multitasking options by opening the Control menu and choosing the Settings option.

The rest of the text in this section discusses the 386 Enhanced dialog box shown in Figure 19-4 and provides a general overview of multitasking terminology. (Some of these terms will be familiar to you from the discussion in Chapter 8.)

The Device Contention Box

Because DOS applications don't share resources cooperatively, one application may try to access printer or serial ports in use by another. You may need to specify how these contentions between devices are handled if you're running applications that access the same ports.

DOS applications access system devices such as the COM (serial communications) and LPT (parallel printer) ports as if they have exclusive use of those devices. If another DOS application tries to access a device that's in use, a conflict occurs.

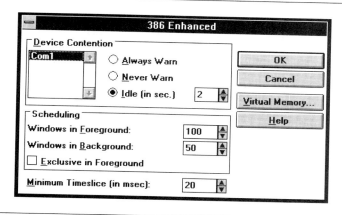

Figure 19-4.   *The Control Panel 386 Enhanced utility*

Windows monitors ports and can warn you when device contentions occur. Use the Device Contention options to specify how you want to be warned. You first click the device that may experience device contention, and then set one of the following options:

- *Always Warn*   Enable the Always Warn option if you want Windows to warn you when a device contention occurs. You can then arbitrate the conflict by choosing which device gets access.

- *Never Warn*   Enable the Never Warn option only when you're sure no device conflicts will occur, such as when only one DOS application is running.

- *Idle (in sec.)*   Enable the Idle option and set the time interval (in seconds) that you want to elapse before you're notified that an application is waiting to access a port that is already in use. Windows won't display a warning message until after the allotted time goes by and the device still can't safely access the port. Use this option if you often switch between applications and printing. You might forget that the printer port is in use, in which case, Windows will make the latest print job wait until the first is complete, or else will display a message once the idle time has passed.

The Scheduling Box

Before covering the options in this field, let's define some of the terms you'll use. You'll also see these terms on the settings dialog box for DOS applications, as shown earlier in Figure 19-2.

Exclusive Processing An application running exclusively has all the processor's resources. All other applications temporarily suspend processing. You can set this feature by enabling the Exclusive option.

Foreground Processing When an application is running in the foreground, it is the active application and may have exclusive use of the processor, or may share processing with other DOS or Windows applications running in the background, depending upon the settings.

Background Processing Applications running in the background continue processing while you work on other tasks.

The Minimum Timeslice Field

A time slice is the percentage of processing time given to each multitasking application. Each application is processed in turn. Think of a card game in which each person at the table gets to play their hand in turn during the "time slice" allocated to them. Play continues around the table until the game ends. If one person goes out, play still continues with other players, but the speed of the round increases because there are fewer players.

Setting Multitasking Priorities

We can continue our analogy of a card game to describe how priority settings are made for multitasked applications. You enter a value that represents the percentage of processor time an application gets on the Control Panel for Windows applications, or in a PIF for DOS application. In addition, you can change a DOS application's settings on its Control menu while the application runs. Each application gets two values: one for when it runs in the foreground and one for when it runs in the background.

Recall that each DOS application runs in its own virtual machine, so when you allocate processing time, you allocate how much time the processor spends in each of the virtual machines. Also recall that Windows runs in its own virtual machine so the processing time you allocate it is used by all Windows applications.

Now let's look again at that card game. You can compare a time slice assigned to each virtual machine to the amount of time each player gets to play their hand during each round. In the computer, a time slice is the amount of time the processor spends in each application. You can increase or decrease this value. Increasing the value improves performance because the processor spends less time switching between each application and more time processing. Decreasing the value gives an appearance of smoother operation, but decreases performance. The default value is 20. Decrease it if your screen seems to constantly pause; however, note that decreasing the time-slice value will decrease overall performance. The time-slice value is changed by opening the 386 Enhanced Mode icon in the Control Panel.

Figuring Foreground and Background Allocations

Now look at the foreground and background values (or index). These values refer to the percentage of total processor time each virtual machine gets, not the number of time slices. You use these values to calculate the percentage of processor time an application gets when running with other DOS or Windows applications. First, get the foreground or background values of each running application. Let's assume three applications are running and the active foreground application has a fore-ground value of 100. The two background applications have background values of 50 each. You add these together to determine the total processing time, then divide each value by the sum to come up with the percentage allocated to each application, as you can see here:

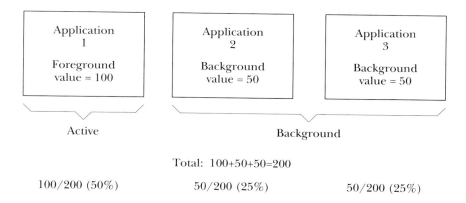

When you divide the foreground application's value of 100 by the sum of 200, you get 1/2, or 50 percent of the allocation. When you divide each background application's value of 50 by 200 you get 1/4, or 25 percent of the total allocation.

Of course, these values change if you make another task active, or add a new task. As another example, assume that Application 2 is made active and has a foreground value of 300 while Application 1 has a background value of 200. When combined with Application 3's value of 50, this gives a total processing value of 550 (200+300+50=550). When you divide Application 1's background value of 200 by 550 you get 36 percent. So 36 percent of the allocation will go to Application 1. When you divide Application 2's value of 300 by the 550 you get 54 percent. When you divide 50 by 550 (for Application 3) you get 10 percent of the total allocation going to Application 3.

Adding another application into the equation changes the percentage values again. Assume you have the three applications from the previous example, with the same values. Add another background application with a background value of 100.

This gives a total processing value of 650 (200+300+50+100=650) and the following results:

$$200/650 = 31 \text{ percent allocation for Application 1 (background)}$$
$$300/650 = 46 \text{ percent allocation for Application 2 (foreground)}$$
$$50/650 = 7 \text{ percent allocation for Application 3 (background)}$$
$$100/650 = 16 \text{ percent allocation for Application 4 (background)}$$

As you can see, assigning priority values ahead of time (in a PIF file) only makes sense when you know which other applications will be running with the application. You may be better off assigning values once an application is running and you know and can calculate the values of the other running applications. Simplifying this even further, only concern yourself with these values when a multitasked application seems to run too slowly or switching seems erratic. If applications run slowly, open the Control menu of the application and increase its foreground (or background) value by one-quarter to one-half, then see if it runs faster. If not, increase the values further.

To give an application exclusive use of the processor, choose Settings on its Control menu and enable the Exclusive option.

Rebooting a Non-Windows Application

Windows 3.1 vastly improves the way non-Windows applications are handled in 386 enhanced mode. Performance is improved, and a new reboot feature lets you recover from locked or hung applications without rebooting your entire system. You can terminate the application and still return to Windows to save your other work.

A *hung application* is one that no longer responds to keyboard or mouse commands and won't allow you to quit. Before Windows 3.1, pressing CTRL-ALT-DEL was the method used to quit the application, but this caused the entire system to reboot. Any unsaved work in other virtual machines was lost. With Windows 3.1, you can now quit a hung application by pressing CTRL-ALT-DEL without causing the entire system to reboot. CTRL-ALT-DEL has the same effect in Windows 3.1 as choosing the Terminate command on the Settings dialog box.

You should only use CTRL-ALT-DEL *and the Terminate command as last resorts.*

You can take any one of the following three actions after pressing CTRL-ALT-DEL. You'll see a message on the screen reminding you of these actions.

- Press ESC to return to the application, which may be usable.

- Press ENTER to close the application.

- Press CTRL-ALT-DEL again to reboot the system.

If you press ESC or ENTER, it is recommended that you save all your work and restart Windows since it may be unstable.

Settings in SYSTEM.INI

The following settings in the SYSTEM.INI file control how non-Windows applications run in Windows. You may need to alter these settings if your applications don't run correctly or you need to change the way they run. You should refer to the SYSINI.WRI file for complete details on each setting.

Only the settings you can change manually in SYSTEM.INI are listed here. Other settings are changed from the Control Panel. If an option is listed as Boolean, set it to 1 to enable it and 0 to disable it.

The [standard] Section

Two settings in the [standard] section are used when running non-Windows applications in standard mode.

Int28Filter=*number*   Int28Filter= specifies the percentage of INT 28h interrupts, generated when the system is idle, that are made visible to software loaded before Windows. Increasing this value improves performance but may interfere with some memory-resident software. The default is 10.

Stacks=*number*   This line specifies the number of interrupt reflector stacks used by standard mode to map MS-DOS or BIOS API from real mode to protected mode. Change this setting if you receive a "Standard Mode: Stack Overflow" message. The default is 12, but you can set it to anything from 8 to 64.

The [NonWindowsApp] Section

[NonWindowsApp] lets you control the general settings of non-Windows applications used in standard and 386 enhanced modes.

CommandEnvSize=*bytes*   CommandEnvSize= specifies the size in bytes of the COMMAND.COM environment. (This setting also applies to batch files.) It must be set to 0 or between 160 and 32,768. A value of 0 disables this setting, and any PIF setting overrides it. The value is normally set to the value of the /E: parameter of the SHELL statement in CONFIG.SYS.

DisablePositionSave=*Boolean*   DisablePositionSave= determines whether the font and window size are saved (for the next session) for DOS applications running in a window. These are the settings you make when choosing the Fonts option on the Control menu of the window. This setting simply sets the default for the Control menu option.

FontChangeEnable=*Boolean*   FontChangeEnable= allows font changes for DOS applications running in a window. You may need to add this option for some video cards if the Fonts option doesn't appear on the Control menu.

MouseInDosBox=*Boolean*   MouseInDosBox= allows the mouse to be used in DOS applications running in a window. The default is 1.

NetAsynchSwitching=*Boolean*   NetAsynchSwitching= lets you set whether you can switch away from an application that has made an asynchronous network BIOS call. The default is 0, which protects against system failures that might occur when switching from some applications. Set it to 1 only if you are sure an application won't receive the BIOS calls.

ScreenLines=*number*   With ScreenLines= you specify the number of lines displayed on the screen when a non-Windows application runs. The default is 25, which is normally adequate.

SwapDisk=*path*   SwapDisk= specifies the name of the disk (or RAM disk) used for swapping. The default is the directory set with the TEMP environmental variable in your AUTOEXEC.BAT file.

The [386Enh] Section

The settings in the [386Enh] section determine how non-Windows applications run in 386 enhanced mode. These settings control memory and other features and may override the settings in the PIF files.

AllEMSLocked=*Boolean*   AllEMSLocked= prevents expanded memory used by DOS and Windows applications from swapping to disk. The setting here overrides PIF settings. Set to 1 (on) if using a disk cache that uses expanded memory.

AutoRestoreScreen=*Boolean*   AutoRestoreScreen= determines whether the display of a non-Windows application is restored by the application or by Windows. This setting applies only to VGA displays and applications that notify Windows that they can update the display themselves. The default is 1 (on).

BkGndNotifyAtPFault=*Boolean*   Refer to BkGndNotifyAtPFault= if your screen is corrupted when running or switching between non-Windows applications. The default is 1 for VGA displays and 0 for 8514 displays.

FileSysChange=*Boolean*   FileSysChange= sets whether the File Manager is automatically updated (which slows performance) whenever a non-Windows application makes a file change. The alternative is to manually refresh a directory window by pressing F5. The default is 1 for 386 enhanced mode and 0 for standard mode.

MouseSoftInit=*Boolean*   Refer to MouseSoftInit= if you are having problems with the mouse cursor. The default is 1 (on). Set this option to 0 if the cursor and screen information appear distorted when you are using the mouse with an application.

ReservePageFrame=*Boolean*   If you run low on conventional memory when running non-Windows applications, and you're using expanded memory, refer to ReservePageFrame=. The default is 1. Set this to 0 if you are not running Windows applications that use expanded memory.

VideoBackgroundMsg=*Boolean*   VideoBackgroundMsg= sets how messages are displayed if a background application is not running properly. The default setting of 1 (on) causes Windows to display messages when a background application is suspended.

WindowUpdateTime=*milliseconds*   Use WindowUpdateTime= to specify the time Windows takes between updates of the display for a windowed DOS application.

WOAFont=*font filename*   Use WOAFont= to specify which font files are used for DOS applications.

Using the PIF Editor

Use the PIF Editor to create program information files that specify the startup parameters of a DOS application. To start the PIF Editor, double-click its icon in the Program Manager. The dialog box that appears depends upon your current Windows mode. Figure 19-5 shows the PIF Editor dialog box for standard mode. Figure 19-6 shows the PIF Editor dialog box for 386 enhanced mode. The Advanced Options dialog box for 386 mode is shown in Figure 19-7.

To create a PIF, use the information provided in the remainder of this chapter to fill out the PIF Editor dialog box. The next sections lead you through the first four fields. Then, for assistance in completing the rest of the fields, flip to either "The Standard Mode PIF Settings," or "The 386 Enhanced Mode PIF Settings." (The default settings are appropriate in most cases.) After the appropriate options are set,

```
┌──────────────────────────────────────────────────────────┐
│ ─ │              PIF Editor - [Untitled]           │ ▼ │ ▲ │
├──────────────────────────────────────────────────────────┤
│ File   Mode   Help                                         │
├──────────────────────────────────────────────────────────┤
│ Program Filename:    ┌─────────────────────────────────┐   │
│                      └─────────────────────────────────┘   │
│ Window Title:        ┌─────────────────────────────────┐   │
│                      └─────────────────────────────────┘   │
│ Optional Parameters: ┌─────────────────────────────────┐   │
│                      └─────────────────────────────────┘   │
│ Start-up Directory:  ┌─────────────────────────────────┐   │
│                      └─────────────────────────────────┘   │
│ Video Mode:          ⦿ Text      ○ Graphics/Multiple Text  │
│ Memory Requirements:  KB Required  ┌─────┐                 │
│                                    │ 128 │                 │
│                                    └─────┘                 │
│ XMS Memory:      KB Required ┌───┐   KB Limit ┌───┐        │
│                              │ 0 │             │ 0 │        │
│                              └───┘             └───┘        │
│ Directly Modifies:  ☐ COM1   ☐ COM3   ☐ Keyboard          │
│                     ☐ COM2   ☐ COM4                        │
│  ☐ No Screen Exchange      ☐ Prevent Program Switch        │
│  ☒ Close Window on Exit    ☐ No Save Screen                │
│  Reserve Shortcut Keys:  ☐ Alt+Tab   ☐ Alt+Esc   ☐ Ctrl+Esc│
│                          ☐ PrtSc     ☐ Alt+PrtSc           │
├──────────────────────────────────────────────────────────┤
│ Press F1 for Help on Program Filename                      │
└──────────────────────────────────────────────────────────┘
```

Figure 19-5.   *The PIF Editor dialog box for standard mode*

save the PIF file using the Save option on the File menu. You can save the PIF in the directory of the application, or in the Windows directory.

 Windows uses the PIF called _DEFAULT.PIF if it can't locate a PIF for an application. You can edit this PIF to change the default setting Windows uses for applications.

The First Four Settings

Fill out the first four fields of the PIF Editor dialog box (your responses to these should be the same whether you're in standard mode or 386 mode). Then enable or disable the remaining settings as described in subsequent sections.

Program Filename

In the Program Filename field type the drive, path, and filename of the application you wish to execute. Files can be executable files with the extensions .EXE and .COM, or they can be batch files with the extension .BAT. If you're running a batch file, type the following command, which loads a secondary command processor and expands the environment to 512 bytes:

COMMAND.COM /E:512 /C *batch filename*

Window Title

The Window Title text box is optional. You can type a descriptive name for the PIF in this box. The name you type will appear under the application's icon on the desktop. You'll probably want to keep the icon name short so it doesn't overlap other icon names.

Optional Parameters

In the Optional Parameters field, type parameters you normally use when running the command from the DOS prompt. Include "?" if you want to be prompted for parameters when the PIF runs. For example, some versions of Microsoft Word for DOS can be started in graphics mode by typing **WORD** /**G**. To start Word in this way from a PIF, type /**G** in the Optional Parameters box. If you are creating a PIF to start a program, then load an existing file in its workspace. You can include the filename in the Optional Parameters box. Be sure to include the drive and path, if necessary.

Start-up Directory

In the Start-up Directory field, type the path of the directory the application must access in order to run. This will also be the current directory when the application runs. You can create several PIFs for a single application, each pointing to different data directories. In this way, you can start an application with one PIF to access business files, and another PIF to access personal files. If you create an icon in the Program Manager for a PIF, then specify a directory in the Working Directory field of the Program Item Properties dialog box for the icon in the Program Manager. Note that the Program Manager settings override the PIF settings.

The Standard Mode PIF Settings

While the first four fields in the PIF Editor dialog box for enhanced mode and the PIF Editor dialog box in standard mode are the same, the remaining settings differ slightly.

The parameters that appear on the PIF Editor window in standard mode are illustrated in Figure 19-5. If you're working in 386 enhanced mode, refer to "The 386 Enhanced Mode PIF Settings" later in this chapter.

Video Mode

Use the Video Mode option to specify the memory requirements for screen switching between the application and Windows. Use text if the application is text based, but if you can't switch back to Windows, use the Graphics/Multiple Text option. (*Multiple text* refers to applications that use more than one video page to display text.)

The Video mode ensures that enough memory will be available when switching between applications. Windows saves the full contents of the DOS application's screen in a buffer when you switch. This buffer uses part of the memory available to the DOS application, reducing the amount of memory available to the application.

Recommended setting: If you're not sure which to use and you have plenty of available memory, use the Graphics/Multiple Text option. If you are low on memory, choose text.

Memory Requirements

The Memory Requirements settings specify how much memory must be free before the application can be started. The setting of 128 is usually appropriate for most applications. This value does not limit the amount of memory available to an application, it simply specifies how much must be available before Windows will start it. Do not use the memory requirements listed in the application's documentation.

Recommended setting: Leave at 128K.

XMS Memory

When running a non-Windows application that uses extended memory, specify the minimum amount of extended memory the program will require to get started in the KB Required box. You must also specify the maximum amount of extended memory the application can use in the KB Limit box, or enter –1 if you don't want to specify a limit. If a non-Windows application that uses extended memory is making your other Windows applications run slowly, try entering a reduced value in the KB Limit box.

Recommended setting: Leave at default settings or set to 0 to prevent the use of extended memory.

Directly Modifies

The Directly Modifies option is used to prevent hardware conflicts, such as when two or more applications attempt to gain access to a communications port or keyboard shortcut keys. While most non-Windows applications behave well when it comes to sharing these ports, some may need to be tamed by enabling one of the Directly Modifies options. If you get garbled information from a communications port, you can give an application exclusive use of the port while it is running by checking one of the port options in the application's PIF. Select the Keyboard option if the application takes direct control of the keyboard and prevents you from switching between Windows.

Recommended setting: Click a COM port the application can use that doesn't contend with another application. Don't enable the Keyboard option unless you're low on memory.

No Screen Exchange

To conserve memory, you can enable the No Screen Exchange option to prevent information from being copied onto the Clipboard using ALT-PRINT SCREEN or PRINT SCREEN. This is the same as reserving PRINT SCREEN and ALT-PRINT SCREEN.
   Recommended setting: Leave disabled unless you're low on memory.

Prevent Program Switch

To conserve memory, you can select the Prevent Program Switch option. If it is selected, you will not be able to switch from one application to another in Windows. You will need to exit your applications to return to the Program Manager. Use this option only if you are running low on memory. It is the same as reserving all shortcut keys or selecting any Directly Modifies option.
   Recommended setting: Leave disabled. Set only as a security measure if the application crashes when switching to Windows.

Close Window on Exit

Enable the Close Window on Exit option to return directly to Windows when exiting an application. This prevents the information from being left on the screen. Turn this option off if you want to view any messages left by the application, such as those that might indicate an error.
   Recommended setting: Disable if you want to keep a screen visible after exiting an application so you can read any exit messages it may have displayed.

No Screen Save

This option prevents Windows from updating the screen when you switch back to the application, thus saving memory.
   Recommended setting: Leave disabled unless the application can save its own screen information.

Reserve Shortcut Keys

You can normally only use Windows' shortcut keys such as ALT-ESC (which lets you switch between windows) and ALT-PRINT SCREEN (which copies the screen to the Clipboard) with Windows when you are working in an application. In some cases, you may need to use the same key combination within your application. If so, click on the key you want the application to respond to and until you disable that key, Windows will not respond to it.
   Recommended setting: Depends on the application's use of shortcut keys.

Alt+Tab   If this box is empty, Windows toggles between applications when ALT-TAB is pressed. If this option is enabled, your application will respond to the keystroke.

Alt+Esc   If this box is left empty, Windows will switch to the next application window. If this option is enabled, your application will respond to the keystroke.

Ctrl+Esc   If this box is left empty, Windows displays the Task List when you press the keys. If this option is enabled, your application will respond to the keystroke.

PrtSc   If this box is left empty, Windows copies a full screen to the Clipboard when you press PRINT SCREEN. If this option is enabled, your application will respond to the keystroke.

Alt+PrtSc   If this box is left empty, Windows copies the active window to the Clipboard. If this option is enabled, your application will respond to the keystroke.

The 386 Enhanced Mode PIF Settings

This section covers the options in the PIF Editor dialog box for 386 enhanced mode as shown in Figure 19-6.

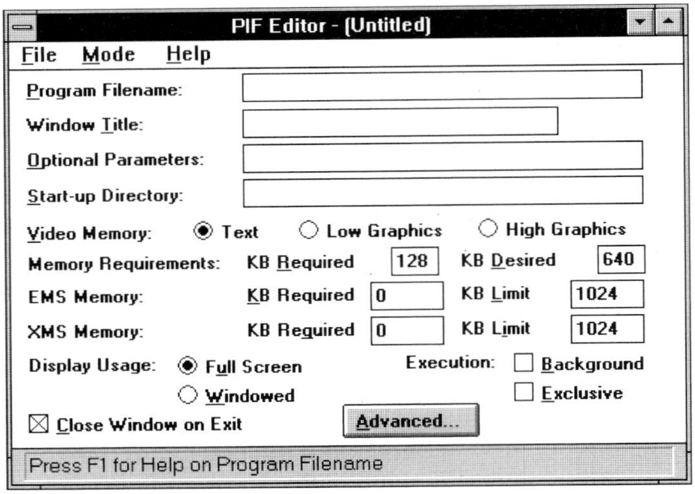

Figure 19-6.   *The PIF Editor dialog box for 386 enhanced mode*

Video Memory

Use the Video Memory settings to specify how much memory must be available to the application for video. The text settings provide the least memory for video but keep memory free and available to the application. The amount of memory used by each setting is listed here:

Text	16K
Low Graphics (CGA)	G932K
High Graphics (EGA)	128K

Recommended setting: Use Text if possible. If you have trouble switching back to Windows, use one of the graphics settings. To reserve the most memory for an application, choose High Graphics and enable Retain Video Memory.

Text   Enable this option to set aside enough memory for text mode if you have a text-only monitor or if you will be running text-only non-Windows applications. This option uses the least memory; it sets aside 16K for video memory.

Low Graphics   Enable this option if you have a CGA video adapter and will be running applications in graphics mode. This option sets aside 32K for video memory.

High Graphics   Enable this option if you have an EGA or VGA video adapter and will be running applications in graphics mode. This option sets aside 128K for video memory.

   If you have plenty of memory and you're not sure which option to use, enable High Graphics. If you're sure the application is text based, or can be switched to text mode, Windows will free memory that it doesn't need if you choose Low Graphics or High Graphics, and then run a Text application.

Memory Requirements

The Memory Requirements settings are used to specify how much conventional memory (640K maximum) must be free before the application can be started, and the maximum amount of memory Windows will give to the application. There are two options in this field: KB Required and KB Desired.

The KB Required option does not limit the amount of memory used by an application. It simply specifies how much memory must be available to start the application.

KB Required   In the KB Required field, type the amount of conventional memory Windows must have available before the application will start. This prevents error messages that might occur if you start an application when there isn't enough memory available. Keep in mind that the number entered in this field is not a memory limit.

KB Desired   In the KB Desired field, type the amount of conventional memory you want Windows to allocate to the application. You can limit the use of memory to keep it available for other applications. If you enter −1, Windows will give the application as much conventional memory as possible, up to the maximum of 640K.

Recommended setting: Leave at 640K or reduce if possible to free memory for other applications.

EMS Memory

Use this option to specify how much memory must be available to expanded memory applications. In the KB Required field, specify how much expanded memory must be available to start the application. In the KB Limit field, specify the maximum amount of expanded memory that can be allocated to the application. Use this option to limit expanded memory to applications that may take as much as Windows will give it, thus reducing available memory for other applications.

Recommended setting: Use the default settings if you plan to use expanded memory. Set both fields to 0 to prevent the use of expanded memory.

XMS Memory

When using a non-Windows application that can use extended memory, specify the minimum amount of extended memory the program will require to get started in the KB Required box. You must also specify the maximum amount of extended memory the application can use in the KB Limit box, or enter −1 if you don't want to specify a limit. If a non-Windows application that uses extended memory is making your other Windows applications run slowly, try entering a reduced value in the KB Limit box.

Recommended setting: Leave at default settings or set to 0 to prevent the use of extended memory.

Display Usage

Select either Full Screen or Windowed for the display usage. The default is Full Screen, but if you want the application to always load into a separate resizable window, select Windowed. Remember that a windowed application will require more memory (about 2K). If you only need a window occasionally, keep this option at Full Screen, then switch the application to a window while it is running by selecting Windowed from its Control menu.

Recommended setting: You choose whether you want the application to run in full-screen mode or in a window, but remember that full-screen mode is always more efficient.

Execution

The Execution option is used to control how an application cooperates with other loaded or running applications. Enable the Background option to allow the application to run when in the background. If disabled, the application is suspended when it is not the active window.

Enable the Exclusive option to give an application exclusive use of the system resources and to suspend all other applications. If you intend to run an application in Exclusive mode, you should also select Full Screen in the Display Usage field. This provides some improvement in performance.

Recommended setting: Choose whether the application should run in the background or exclusively.

Remember, you can set these options on the window's Control menu while using the application only when you need it.

Close Window on Exit

If the Close Window on Exit option is checked, Windows will close its window automatically when you quit the application. In some cases, you want to clear the option to mark and copy information from an application that runs only in full-screen display. If you select the Full Screen display option discussed earlier, and clear the Close Window on Exit option, Windows will try to display the application in a window when you quit so you can mark and copy information onto the Clipboard before closing the window.

Recommended setting: Enable this setting whenever you need to save screen information.

Advanced PIF Options for 386 Enhanced Mode

Click the Advanced button to display the Advanced dialog box shown in Figure 19-7. This dialog box is divided into four areas as discussed in the following sections.

The Multitasking Options Box

Use the Multitasking options to specify how an application shares processing time with other applications. The values you can specify in the Background and Foreground Priority fields range from 0 to 10,000. The foreground and background values of all applications are totaled and a percentage of the processor's time is given to an application based on its share of the total when running in foreground or background mode. (See the previous discussion on "Setting Multitasking Priorities" for information about setting these options.)

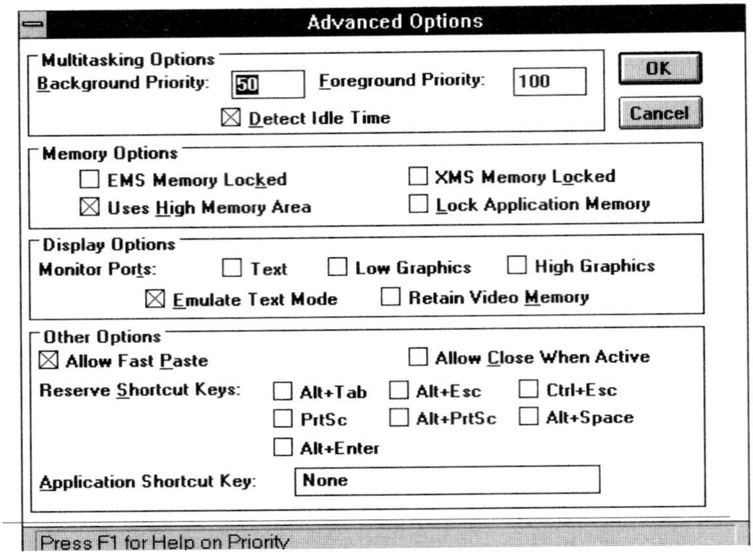

Figure 19-7.   *Advanced PIF options*

Background Priority   In the Background Priority field, specify the amount of processor time an application receives when it is operating in the background. The value is only valid if the Background option is set on the main PIF dialog box. Note that this option becomes meaningless if another active foreground application is processing in exclusive mode.

Foreground Priority   In the Foreground Priority field, specify the amount of the processor's time an application gets when processing in the active foreground window. The actual percentage of time the application receives depends on how many applications are running in the background, if any.

Detect Idle Time   Enable Detect Idle Time if you want to allocate time from an active application to other applications. Leave the option enabled to enhance performance. In cases when an application runs abnormally slowly, Windows may incorrectly perceive the application as idle. You may need to clear this option to speed up the application.

Recommended setting: Enable this option in most cases. Do not enable this option for 3270 and 5231 emulation applications.

The Memory Options Box

Use the Memory Options settings to control how an application uses your computer's memory when running in 386 enhanced mode.

EMS Memory Locked   Enable the EMS Memory Locked option to prevent Windows from swapping the application's expanded memory to hard disk, thus increasing performance of the application at the cost of slowing down the rest of the system.

Recommended setting: Enable this option if you have plenty of memory and/or you don't switch to other applications.

XMS Memory Locked   Enable the XMS Memory Locked option to prevent Windows from swapping the application's extended memory to hard disk, thus increasing performance of the application at the cost of slowing down the rest of the system.

Recommended setting: Enable this option if you have plenty of memory and/or you don't switch to other applications.

Uses High Memory Area   Enable the Uses High Memory Area option to allow the application to use the high memory area (HMA), which is the first 64K of extended memory.

Recommended setting: Enable this option if you have plenty of memory and/or you don't switch to other applications. If you're using DOS 5 and loading it high, disable this option. If the high memory area is available, enable this option.

Lock Application Memory   Enable the Lock Application Memory option to speed up some applications. It keeps the application in memory and prevents it from being swapped to disk; however, a slowdown in the rest of the system may occur.

Recommended setting: Enable this option if you have plenty of memory and/or you don't switch to other applications.

The Display Options Box

The Display Options box contains options to set how an application appears on the screen and how Windows allocates memory to display the application. Note that the video memory setting you choose is the initial memory setting made when an application first starts. Windows may adjust the setting as necessary.

Text   Enable the Text option only for text mode applications that interact directly with your system's hardware input and output ports to control display adapters. Few applications require this option.

Low Graphics   Enable the Low Graphics option only for low-resolution graphics mode applications that interact directly with your system's hardware input and output ports to control display adapters. Few applications require this option.

High Graphics   Enable the High Graphics option only for high-resolution graphics mode applications that interact directly with your system's hardware input and output ports to control display adapters. Few applications require this option.

Emulate Text Mode   Enable the Emulate Text Mode option to increase the rate at which applications display text. If text is garbled, or the cursor appears in the wrong place, try clearing the option.

Retain Video Memory   Enable the Retain Video Memory option to instruct Windows not to release the application's extra video memory to other applications. Windows may release extra video memory to applications that allow you to change to a different video mode that requires less memory. Enabling the option ensures that the video memory will still be available when you switch back to the other mode but doesn't free up memory.

The Other Options Box

The Other Options box contains several unrelated options used to make your applications run properly in the 386 enhanced mode.

Allow Fast Paste   Enable Allow Fast Paste to allow an application to paste from the Clipboard using the fastest method. However, if you are having problems pasting, you may want to try disabling the option. Enabling the option lets Windows decide which Paste method is the best.

Allow Close When Active   Enable Allow Close When Active to allow Windows to exit without requiring you to also exit from the application. This option is convenient because it lets you quit Windows without closing each application separately. If the application does not use MS-DOS file handles in the standard way, clear the option.

Reserve Shortcut Keys   You normally only use the Windows shortcut keys such as Alt+Esc (which switches between windows) and Alt+PrtSc (which copies a screen to Clipboard) with Windows when you are working in an application. In some cases, you may need to use the same key combination for your application. If so, click the key you want the application to respond to, and Windows will not respond to that key until you clear this option.

If any of the following options are checked, your application will respond to the keystrokes, not Windows.

- *Alt+Tab* Windows recognizes this as a switch-windows command. If disabled, your application may use the keystroke for its own use.

- *Alt+Esc* Windows recognizes this as a switch-windows command. If disabled, your application may use the keystroke for its own use.

- *Ctrl+Esc* If disabled, Windows displays the Task List.

- *PrtSc* (Print Screen) If disabled, Windows copies a full screen to the Clipboard.

- *Alt+PrtSc* If disabled, Windows copies the active window to the Clipboard.

- *Alt+Space* If disabled, Windows displays the Control menu for the application.

- *Alt+Enter* If disabled, Windows toggles the application in or out of a window.

Application Shortcut Key   The key sequence you specify in this field can be used to quickly make an application the current active window. For example, you could specify CTRL-F10 or ALT-F1 as a shortcut key. The keys you select should not be in use by any other application. To make an entry in the field, press the key combination you want. Windows will interpret your keystrokes and display them in the field.

Other Recommendations

- Be sure the High Graphics check box in the Monitor Ports section of the Display Options box is disabled. This will improve performance of DOS text applications.

- Do not check any of the Port settings under Display Options (Advanced Options in 386 enhanced mode) unless the application is causing problems. Then only check the options as a test to see if the application reacts favorably.

- Most DOS applications run in text mode, so check the Text option. Also, check Emulate Text Mode to improve performance for text applications.

- Under Multitasking Options in the Advanced Options dialog box for 386 mode, change Foreground Priority to 10,000 to give the active application the highest priority possible.

- Always disable Uses High Memory Area if you've loaded DOS 5 into the HMA.

- Set EMS Memory KB Required and XMS Memory KB Required to 0 unless the application needs expanded or extended memory.

Chapter **20**

Writing and Editing

Both Notepad and Write are text editing programs included with Windows. Notepad is an ASCII text editor, which means it loads and saves files without special formatting codes or control characters. Write, on the other hand, has extensive character and paragraph formatting capabilities. In addition, Write lets you control page layout by adjusting the margins, indents, and page numbers, as well as the headers and footers of a document. Write does not have editing tools such as spelling and grammar checkers, or a thesaurus like more advanced word processors do, but it is an extremely useful word processor, and it's included with Windows.

This chapter discusses Notepad and Write, with more emphasis on Write because it has more features. What you learn about Notepad can also be applied to the SysEdit system editor, which is used to edit the startup files and Windows .INI files.

Notepad Features

The Notepad window shown in Figure 20-1 consists of a title bar and workspace. The following menu options are available.

The File Menu

The Notepad File menu has all the standard Open, Save, and Print options discussed in Chapter 3.

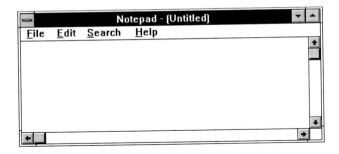

Figure 20-1.   *The Notepad window*

The Edit Menu

The Edit menu has the standard Clipboard options of Cut, Copy, and Paste discussed in Chapter 3. You can also click the Undo option to restore any editing changes you made. The following options are also on the Edit menu.

The Select All Option   Choose Select All to select all the text in the Notepad workspace so you can copy it to the Clipboard.

The Time/Date Option   Choose Time/Date to insert the current time and date at the location of the insertion point.

The Word Wrap Option   Choose Word Wrap to wrap the text at the current window border. You can resize the window to change the current word wrap. The text fits into the new window size and prints using that width.

The Search Menu

The following options are available on the Search menu:

The Find and Find Next Options   After specifying the text you want to find in the Find dialog box, you choose Find Next, or press F3 to find the next occurrence. When using Find, the dialog box stays open so you can continue to search for the next occurrence, or specify new search text. Enable the Match Case option to locate text that has the exact upper- and lowercase specifications you type. Click the Up or Down option to change the direction of the search.

Notepad has a time logging feature that will insert the current time and date whenever you open a file. Refer to Chapter 5 for more on the time logging feature.

Remember, if you need help with editing keys or keyboard methods that move you through the document, refer to the Help menu.

Windows Write

Windows Write is a complete word processing program that you can use to create formatted letters and documents. In addition, Write is an excellent program to use for document exchange with other Windows users. Since it is part of every Windows package, you can format text with TrueType fonts and know that your document will look the same when opened on another user's system. In addition, since TrueType prints on all graphics printers, the printed document will resemble what you created when printed on another user's system. The Write window is pictured in Figure 20-2.

You've already learned about most of the features of the File and Edit menus in Chapter 3. This section covers a few more options on those menus. For more about object linking and embedding options, see Chapter 25. This chapter concentrates on the remaining options used to search for and replace text, format characters, change paragraph formatting, and design your page layout. Load the README.WRI file now so you can easily follow along with the examples given here.

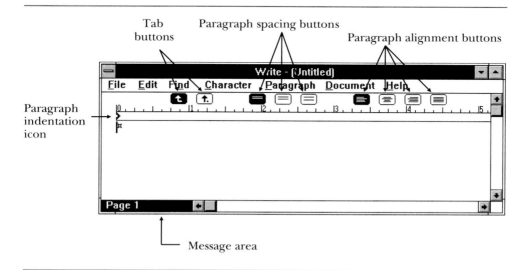

Figure 20-2. *The Write window*

The Write Window and Workspace

The Write workspace is where you enter the text of your documents or insert pictures from Paintbrush or other graphics programs. It consists of an insertion point (the I-beam) and an end-of-document marker, which moves down as you type.

The Ruler

One of the first things to do is turn the Ruler on. Choose Ruler On from the Document menu if it is not already visible. The Ruler helps you align text and includes icons that help you quickly format paragraphs. Click the icons when you want to set tabs, change the spacing of paragraphs, or change the alignment of paragraphs against the left and right margins.

Tabs and margins are set for the entire document. Set Margins by choosing Page Layout from the Document menu.

Paragraphs

The paragraph is an important concept in Write. The traditional definition of a paragraph is simply one or more sentences joined together to discuss an idea. In Write, a paragraph is technically defined by a paragraph end marker. Paragraphs end and new paragraphs begin when you press the ENTER key. Paragraph text is automatically word-wrapped, so you never press ENTER at the end of a line to start a new line unless you want the new line to begin a new paragraph.

The importance of paragraphs in Write is that paragraph styles are applied to each paragraph individually. You can center one paragraph, left align another, and double-space still another paragraph. As a unit, paragraphs are also easier to select. For example, to center a paragraph, click anywhere in it, then click the Center icon on the Ruler. Paragraphs are also easy to select when applying character formats, as discussed in the next section.

To start a new line, but keep it as part of the existing paragraph, press SHIFT-ENTER. *This is useful when creating tables or name and address information.*

Selecting Text

Before you can apply a character style to a particular section of text, copy the text to the Clipboard, or delete it, you must first select it. Selecting text is the same as highlighting text.

The selection bar is the space between the left edge of text and the left window border. When you point in the selection bar, the mouse pointer changes to an arrow that points to the upper-right.

Use the following methods to select text in a document for editing or deletion. These methods assume you have a mouse. Refer to the Help menu for keyboard selection techniques.

- Click and drag through any text to select.

- Double-click a word to select it, and then hold the mouse button and drag through other words to select them.

- To highlight and select an entire paragraph, double-click in the selection bar to the immediate left of the paragraph.

- To select a line, point to the line in the selection bar and click once.

Page Breaks and Repagination

You insert page breaks when you want a section of your document to begin printing on a new sheet of paper. Page breaks are essential when you want to start a new section or chapter. To insert manual page breaks into a document, choose the Repaginate option on the File menu. You can insert your own page breaks at any one place in the document by pressing CTRL-SHIFT-ENTER. A dotted line appears in the text to indicate a page break.

Use the Repaginate option on the File menu to automatically repaginate your document. If you don't use this option, Write inserts page breaks automatically when you print a document. Repaginate lets you determine where a page should break. This is important to prevent section headers or other titles from printing at the bottom of a page. In addition, you may want to prevent a table from being split over two pages.

If you haven't done so already, load the README.WRI file into Write's workspace. Choose the Repaginate option from the File menu to try this example. The Repaginate Document dialog box appears, as shown here:

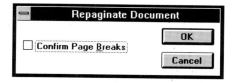

To have Write show you the location of page breaks, and to be able to move those page breaks, click the Confirm Page Breaks check box, then click the OK button. You'll see the following dialog box when Write locates the first page break.

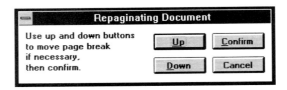

You can click Up or Down to move the page break; however, in most cases, you won't be able to move it further down than it already is. Click Down if you've moved the page break up, then decide to move it down. Click Confirm to accept the page break and move to the next, or Cancel to stop repagination.

You must repaginate a document before you can use the Go To Page option on the Find menu to jump to a specific page number.

Jumping to Pages

To quickly position the insertion point on a specific page, choose Go To Page from the Find menu. Type the number of the page you want to jump to and click the OK button.

This technique is only accurate immediately after repaginating a document. If you've inserted text since the last repagination, the page numbering will have changed for all pages following the text insertion.

Using Optional Hyphens

You use hyphens to specify where a multisyllabic word should break at the end of a line. Using hyphens can give your text a more balanced look on the printed page and give you more control over where pages break. Paragraphs that are justified at both the left and right margins often have extra spaces between words to make the text reach the right margin evenly. This space will be excessive if long words wrap to the next line. Inserting a hyphen breaks the word and helps fill the line properly with characters, rather than blank spaces.

Press CTRL-SHIFT-HYPHEN to place an optional hyphen in a word. The hyphen is only used if the word falls at the end of the line. In some cases, you might not know whether a word will fall at the end of the line until you've repaginated and justified the text. Insert optional hyphens only when you're sure a word will fall at the end of a line and you don't want it to completely word-wrap to the next line. If you add a hyphen to a word and it causes an additional line to be inserted, you'll need to repaginate.

Find and Replace Techniques

Use the Find option on the Find menu to quickly locate text within a document. Use the Replace option to replace text that has been found. There are many useful ways to use these commands; listed here are just a few possibilities:

- Find all occurrences of a word, phrase, or sequence of characters
- Find and replace words, phrases, or characters
- Find and replace special characters such as tabs and paragraph markers

Using Find

Choose Find from the Find menu to display the Find dialog box shown here:

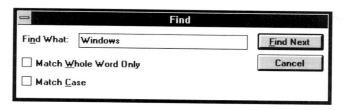

To search for the word "Windows", type **Windows** in the Find What field, and then click the Find Next button. The first instance of Windows is highlighted. You can leave the Find dialog box open and click its Find Next button to find the next occurrence, or you can type some other text that you wish to find. Note the following:

- You can close the Find dialog box, and then press F3 to find the next occurrence of the text you typed in the Find What field. Find retains this text until you change it.

- Find starts its search from the current position of the insertion point. To begin a search at the top of your document, scroll to the top and click at the beginning of the text, and then choose the Find command.

Find provides an easy way to jump back to a particular place in your document. For example, you can search for the title of a section. Before jumping to another section, mark your current place in the document with a set of unusual characters such as "***". Later you can quickly jump back to where you left off by searching for "***".

Use the two check boxes on the Find dialog box to more exactly specify the text you want to find. Each check box is covered next.

The Match Whole Word Only Option   Click Match Whole Word Only to find just the text you've specified when it's a complete, entire word, not part of another word. For example, if you're searching for "kit," Find will highlight occurrences of "kitten" and "skit" unless you click this option.

The Match Case Option   Click Match Case to find text that exactly matches the uppercase/lowercase you gave for the text in the Find field.

Using Replace

The Replace option is useful for updating documents, changing mistakes, or replacing text codes with full text strings. A text code might be an acronym that you expand after the document is complete (you'll read more about text code shortly under "Using Replace with Text Code"). Choose Replace from the Find menu to display the dialog box in Figure 20-3. Use the Replace dialog box in the same way you use the Find dialog box, but also specify replacement text. Specify the text you want to find in the Find What field, and the text you want to replace it with in the Replace With field, and then take one of the following steps:

- Click Find Next to find the first occurrence.

- Click Replace to replace the highlighted text that was found.

- Click Find Next again to keep the highlighted text and find the next occurrence. Doing so does not replace the selection.

- Click Replace All if you're sure you want to replace all remaining occurrences of the text. It's a good idea to first test your search and replace by clicking Find Next and Replace a few times before clicking Replace All.

- Click Close to stop the replace procedure.

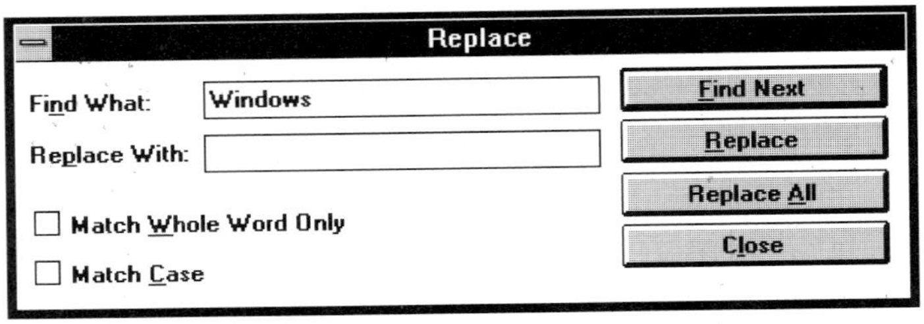

Figure 20-3.   *Use the Replace dialog box to quickly change text in a document*

For example, to change the name of a character in a script from "Jim" to "John," just specify "Jim" in the Find field of the Find What dialog box and "John" in the Replace With field.

Using Replace with Text Code   The code replacement procedure mentioned earlier is a good way to save yourself a lot of typing. Instead of typing long strings of text, type a code instead. When the document is done, use the Replace command to replace all occurrences of the code with its equivalent text string. For example, type **NASA** when writing a document, then later replace all occurrences of NASA with "National Aeronautics and Space Administration." You can selectively replace using the Find Next and Replace buttons, so in the example using NASA, you might replace only those instances that appear at the beginning of a new section, and let the NASA acronym remain in use in the document, once you're sure your readers know what it stands for.

Special Character Searches

To search for text that includes tabs, paragraph markers, manual page breaks, or spaces, use the following characters in the Find What box:

Type	To Search For
^d	A page break inserted with CTRL-ENTER
^p	A paragraph mark
^t	A tab character
^w	A space character
?	Any character or string of characters in a file

You can use these codes in a number of ways. For example, if the search text is hea?, Write finds every occurrence of hea followed by at least one character, such as theater, figurehead, or heat.

Documents that you obtain from bulletin boards or other sources often contain paragraph markers at the end of every line. A good example of this is the README.WRI file. Open it, and then search for ^p. Click Find Next several times and notice that every line ends with a paragraph mark. To save paper when printing, these paragraphs could be wider, so it makes sense to remove all the paragraph markers in a paragraph except for the last one. You can do this by selecting, finding, and replacing paragraph markers with space characters. However, notice that some lines (such as those in the bulleted lists) are indented using five space characters. Removing the paragraph markers would join the lines but leave wide gaps that precede these indents, so you need to search for each occurence of a paragraph marker (^p) plus five spaces and replace it with one space (or search for ^p and four spaces and don't specify any replacement text).

Tables are always good candidates for search and replace operations. For example, say you used five spaces to align columns on the screen; when you print the table, you find the columns don't align, usually because you're printing with a proportionally spaced font rather than a monospaced font. The trick when preparing any table is to use tabs, so in this case you could search for five spaces in the table and replace them with the tab character (^t).

To limit your search to a specific area, place the cursor just above it, then click the Close button after the area has been searched. With some Windows applications (not Write), you can highlight an area and limit the search to that area.

Designing the Page Layout

Now that you've learned a few basic techniques, you can start a new document by choosing New from the File menu. This section describes the options and settings you use to define how and where the document is printed on the page, the location of headers, and how to set tabs.

Printer Settings

One of the first things to do when designing your page layout is to specify the size and orientation of the paper you want to use. Choose Page Setup from the File menu, and then choose Portrait or Landscape in the Orientation field and a paper size and source in the Paper field.

You also use this box to change printers or specify the intensity of printing if your document contains graphic images. See Chapter 3 for more about working with these features.

Setting Margins and the First Page Number

To set document margins, choose Page Layout from the Document menu. The Page Layout dialog box shown in Figure 20-4 appears on the screen.

Use this dialog box to adjust the boundaries for printed text on the page and the starting page numbers. Follow these guidelines:

- Most documents will have a starting page number of 1, but if you're creating continuous text that consists of several document files, adjust this number. For example, if Chapter 1 of a document ends on page 10, set this field to 11 for Chapter 2.

- Click the cm box in the Measurements field if you prefer to work in centimeters. The Ruler converts when you do so, and values in the Margins fields convert to centimeters.

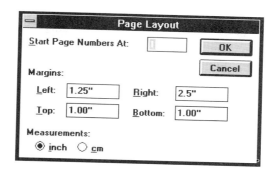

Figure 20-4.   *The Page Layout dialog box*

- Enter the values for the margins in the Margins fields. You don't need to insert the " character, just type the value for the margins. Write inserts it when you press OK. Keep in mind that .25" is the minimum for most laser printers since they will not print closer to the edge of the paper.

Note that the left and right margin settings determine the default width of all paragraphs in the text. To further reduce the width of individual paragraphs, use the indenting options discussed under the section on "Formatting Paragraphs" later in this chapter.

Setting Tabs

The default tab stops on the Ruler determine the movement of the insertion point when you press the TAB key. Default tab stops are placed every half-inch. If these settings work for your needs, you'll never need to set custom tabs. To set custom tabs, use the tab buttons on the Ruler, or choose Tabs from the Document menu. Keep the following in mind regarding tabs:

- Tab changes apply to the entire document, not just the current paragraph. If you adjust tabs, you'll need to scan through your document to see how other tabs have been affected.

- When you set a custom tab, all the default tabs to its left are removed, but default tabs to the right remain.

- Use a decimal tab to align columns of numbers on their decimal points as shown here:

9.9

99.99

999.999

9999.9999

To set a tab stop, click either the normal or decimal tab button in the Ruler, and then click just below the measure bar in the Ruler to set the tab. An arrow representing the tab appears. You can click and drag this tab marker left or right to adjust the tab. To remove it, click and drag it all the way to the right and off the Ruler. Alternatively, you can click the Clear All button on the Tabs dialog box as discussed next to remove all custom tabs.

The Tabs Dialog Box   Choose Tabs from the Document menu to open the Tabs dialog box shown in Figure 20-5. You use this dialog box to enter the exact numeric position of a tab stop on the Ruler. Click the Decimal check box under each tab stop that you want to have formatted as a decimal tab. To clear all the custom tabs and restore the default tabs, click the Clear All button.

Headers and Footers

Headers and footers include text that prints at the top or bottom, respectively, of every page. Typically, you include a chapter or section title in a header or footer, along with the date and a page number. You specify the header or footer by choosing the Header or Footer option on the Document menu. When you choose one of the

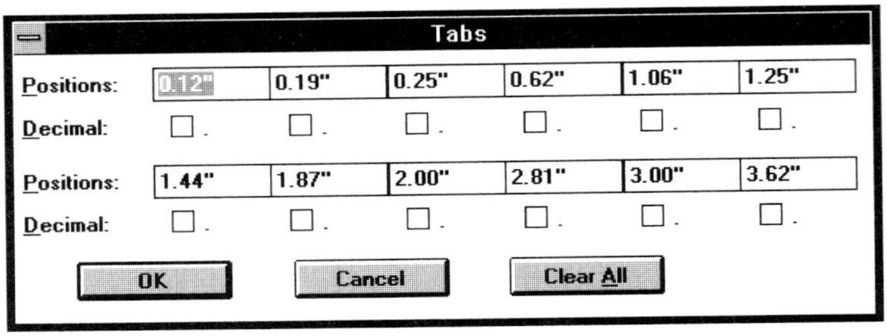

Tabs
Positions:	0.12"	0.19"	0.25"	0.62"	1.06"	1.25"
Decimal:	□ .	□ .	□ .	□ .	□ .	□ .
Positions:	1.44"	1.87"	2.00"	2.81"	3.00"	3.62"
Decimal:	□ .	□ .	□ .	□ .	□ .	□ .
OK	Cancel	Clear All

Figure 20-5.   *Use the Tabs dialog box to enter the exact position of tabs*

options, the Write window title bar converts to HEADER or FOOTER and a Page Header or Page Footer dialog box overlaps it. Figure 20-6 illustrates the Header window and its overlapping Page Header dialog box.

The following discussion concentrates on headers, but you set up footers in exactly the same way. Follow these steps:

1. Type the text for the header in the HEADER window. You can format the text using character or paragraph formatting as discussed later in this chapter.

2. In the Page Header dialog box, enter the distance you want the header to be from the top of the page (this would be from the bottom of the page for a page footer).

3. In the Distance from Top (or Bottom) field, type the amount of space between the header (or footer) and the page edge. Keep in mind that laser printers have a nonprinting zone about a quarter-inch from the paper's edge. Also, if you specify a value that is too large, the header may overlap the body text.

4. Click the Print on First Page option to print the header or footer on the first page of your document. If the first page is a title page, you'll probably want to disable this option.

5. Click the Insert Page # button to insert a page number at the insertion point. This page number will automatically update as the document prints. For example, you could type **Page-**, then click the Insert Page # button to precede the page number with text.

6. To clear the current header information, click the Clear button.

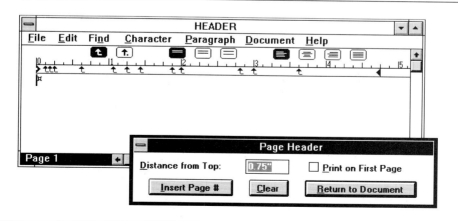

Figure 20-6. *The Page Header dialog box overlaps the Header window*

7. When the header information is complete, click the Return to Document button.

Follow the same procedure to create a footer.

Formatting Characters

Character formatting is applied to selected text only. You can click and drag through text with the mouse, or click in the selection bar to select lines or paragraphs of text as discussed earlier in the "Selecting Text" section. There are also keyboard techniques for selecting one or more words, sentences, or paragraphs. You may want to review these key functions in the Help menu.

Once text is selected, choose one of the formatting options on the Character menu as shown in Figure 20-7, or choose Fonts to open its Fonts menu. Refer back to Chapter 3 for more information on the Fonts menu.

Note that the most common options also have quick keys, so for example, you can press CTRL-B to boldface, CTRL-I to apply italics, and so on. To return to normal text, press F5. The typical procedure when typing text is to enter a quick key sequence to select a format, type the text, then press F5 to return to normal mode.

Use the Reduce Font and Enlarge Font options to decrease or increase the size of a font. However, to gain better control over font sizing, it is best to open the Fonts dialog box and specify the exact font size you want.

Creating a Font Test Sheet

It's a good idea to print out all of the fonts available on your system. When you're creating documents, you can then refer to the font test sheet to determine the best font style and size to use. Follow the steps given next to create the test sheet. This

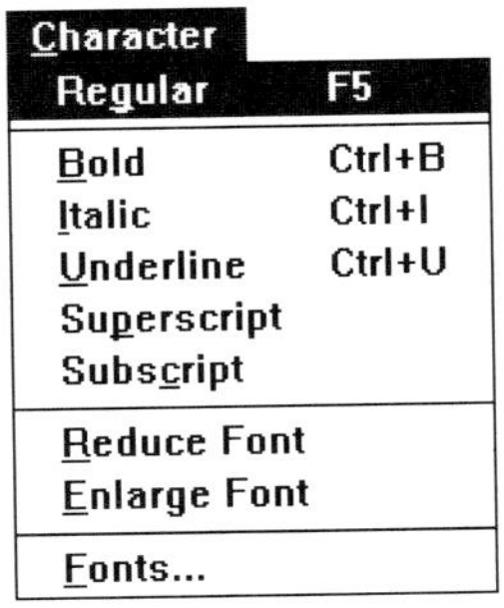

Figure 20-7.   *The Character formatting menu options*

example assumes you have the TrueType fonts enabled. If not, substitute any fonts you prefer that are available on your system.

1. Choose New on the File menu to start a new document.

2. Choose Fonts from the Character menu to open the Fonts dialog box.

3. Click Arial in the Font list box, click 12 in the Size box, and finally click OK.

4. Now type the following line, which indicates the font and style you've selected.

```
Arial 12 point normal
```

Repeat steps 1 through 4 for Courier New, Times New Roman, and any other fonts you want to print on the test sheet. Keep the font size at 12; next, you'll copy the 12-point text and resize it. The Write Window should look similar to Figure 20-8.

Once you've typed samples of all the 12-point fonts, highlight all of them by dragging through with the mouse. Choose Copy from the Edit menu, and then click at the end of your document, insert an extra line, and paste the text. Now highlight all the pasted text and choose Enlarge Font from the Character menu. The sample text is enlarged to 14 points, so change the text in the selected box to read 14 point, not 12 point.

You can continue this process of pasting and enlarging (or reducing) the font to create a sample of the various font sizes available. After creating a complete set of fonts in different sizes, select the entire block, copy it to the Clipboard, and then paste a copy at the end of your document, highlight the pasted text, and choose Italic from the Character menu.

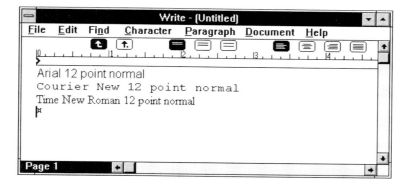

Figure 20-8.   *Creating a font test sheet*

As you can see, this process of copying and pasting makes it easy to quickly create many different examples of font styles and sizes. Once you've got the test sheet complete, print it and keep it handy when working with Write or any other application that uses the fonts you've printed.

Formatting Paragraphs

As was mentioned earlier, a paragraph is a string of text that may wrap at the end of a line and that ends when you press the ENTER key. Each paragraph is a separate entity that can have its own spacing and alignment setting. You apply these settings by clicking anywhere in the paragraph to select it, and then clicking one of the paragraph spacing or alignment buttons in the Ruler. You can also adjust the indent markers on the measure bar, or choose options from the Paragraph menu. Note that the Paragraph menu duplicates many of the features already on the Ruler, so this discussion focuses on the Ruler.

To experiment with the paragraph formatting options, type a paragraph that is several lines long, and then click each of the alignment buttons and the spacing buttons.

Applying Indents

The measure bar has three symbols, as shown in the following illustration. The *left indent marker* is a triangle that points right. You move it to adjust the left edge of text away from or closer to the left margin.

The *first-line indent marker* (referred to as the *tick*) is a small square that you click and drag to adjust the indent of the first line of text.

The *right indent marker* is the triangle that points left and is used to adjust the right edge of text away from or closer to the right margin.

 The tick initially overlaps the left indent marker. You need to click and drag it off before you can adjust the left indent, and then you can readjust the tick.

The following section explains how to create several types of paragraphs using the measure bar on the Ruler. Note that after adjusting indents with these markers, you can choose indents on the Paragraph menu to see their numeric settings and fine-tune alignment if necessary.

First-Line Indented Paragraphs   To create a paragraph with an indented first line, simply click the tick marker and drag it to the right in the measure bar. An example is shown here:

```
0. . . . | . . . . |1. . . | . . . |2. . . | . . . |3. . . | . . . |4. . . |
▶
```
```
        Slide the tick to the right on the
measure bar to adjust the first line indent.
It is at the half-inch mark here.|
```

Hanging Indents   A *hanging indent* might more appropriately be called a hanging outdent because the first line hangs out to the left of the normal paragraph indent. You use hanging indents to create numbered or bulleted lists. Remember to use the Character Map utility to add bullets to your documents. The following example shows how the tick is dragged to the left of the left indent marker:

```
0. . . | . . . . |1. . . | . . . |2. . . | . . . |3. . . | . . . |4. . . |
  ▶
```
```
1.   Slide the tick to the left and the left
     indent marker to the right to create
     hanging indents used for numbered and
     bulleted lists.
```

Left and Right Indents   You can adjust both the left and right indents to create paragraphs used for quotations or that stand out from the rest of the text. Screen-writers create paragraphs of this sort to describe scenes or insert dialog. An example is shown here:

```
0. . . . | . . |1. . . | . . . |2. . . | . . . |3. . . | . . . |4. . . |
         ▶                                    ◀
```
```
         Slide both indent markers to
         create left and right indented
         paragraphs. Also adjust the
         tick if necessary|.
```

Inserting Pictures

You can insert into your document pictures that were created in Paintbrush or other drawing or painting programs. Recall from Chapter 4 that pasted pictures may be static, embedded, or actively linked to the application that created them. To change a static picture, you must delete it and repaste a new copy of the picture. To change an embedded picture, double-click it to open the application that created it, then make your changes and exit. Linked pictures change automatically if you change the original picture or drawing.

This section focuses on positioning pictures in your document. After a picture is pasted, you can move it left or right on the line, or size it. Try the following examples by first starting Paintbrush, and then opening the file LEAVES.BMP. The file is located in the Windows directory. Use the Paintbrush Pick tool (the scissors in the upper right of the toolbox) to outline part of the leaves image. Choose Copy from the Edit menu, and then return to your Write document. Position the insertion point where you want to paste the image and choose Paste on Write's Edit menu.

Sizing a Picture   To size the pasted picture, first click it with the mouse, and then choose Size Picture from the Edit menu. A shadow frame appears around the picture and the mouse pointer converts to a box. Before moving the mouse, decide which corner or side you want to change, and then position the mouse cursor over it. Any further movements of the mouse adjust the shadow frame. Click the mouse to accept the new size. If it's not what you want, choose Undo from the Edit menu and try again.

Note that image sizing information appears in the lower-left corner of the Write window (in the status bar). Use this information to size the image proportionally. The image starts out with the coordinates 1x and 1y. To reduce the size of the image by 50 percent, move the mouse until these coordinates are .5x and .5y. To enlarge an object by 50 percent, move the mouse until the coordinates are 2x and 2y.

Moving a Picture   Now that you've got a picture in the Write document, click it, and then choose the Move Picture option on the Edit menu. A shadow frame appears around the image and the mouse pointer turns into a small box. Simply drag the mouse left or right to position the shadow frame where you want to place the picture, or press the LEFT ARROW or RIGHT ARROW key for more accurate positioning. Click the mouse when the picture is where you want it.

Using Prewritten Text

The Copy and Paste commands of the Clipboard provide a useful way of reusing text you've already written. For example, you can create a document that contains blocks of standard text like that used in legal documents or form letters. These blocks of text are often called boilerplates, as you may recall from Chapter 5. To create a new document, you open the document that contains the boilerplates, copy and paste them throughout as necessary, and then save the document under a new name. It's important to save with a different name to protect the original boilerplate text.

In fact, you can create whole sets of prewritten documents that you use on a regular basis, and then just change the appropriate part or parts of each document and print it. To protect these documents from accidental erasure or changes, apply the Read Only attribute to them using the File Manager. Start the File Manager, click the files you want to protect, and then choose Properties from the File menu. When the Properties dialog box opens, click the Read Only attribute and the OK button. Now when you attempt to save the file after making changes, a message appears that the file is protected. Use the Save As option on Write's File menu to save the file with a different name.

Chapter *21*

Graphics

Graphics is an important topic for Windows users because of the graphical nature of the Windows environment. Users find that incorporating graphics into their documents is simple and easy. Most Windows applications automatically provide this support. Windows Paintbrush is an excellent application for creating simple pictures or logos to add to Write or other Windows' application documents. Microsoft Excel is good for creating graphs and charts from spreadsheet data. But if you're working with page layout programs such as Aldus PageMaker or Ventura Publisher, you'll probably need to incorporate photographs and art that requires scanning. This chapter covers the steps required to get graphics, edit and convert them, and finally, print them using your local printer, or a high-resolution typesetter at a service bureau or print shop.

Of course, some users may have more sophisticated graphics needs than others. Working with black-and-white or color photographs that have continuous tones and potentially millions of gray shades or colors requires special video hardware. Such images must retain their natural colors throughout the process, from input (using a scanning device) through editing, to the final printout or production. You'll need 16-bit or 24-bit video cards that support 32,000 or 16.7 million colors, respectively. You'll also need lots of memory and disk space to hold and store the images.

This chapter focuses on low-end graphics production and is aimed especially at users who print images on laser printers at 300 dots per inch. The process of converting color images for printout on a black-and-white printer presents some interesting challenges in itself, as you'll see later in this chapter. Working with high-resolution color images is also discussed, but it is assumed that most users will send this type of work out to service bureaus for final production work due to the fact that most laser printers can't handle such images properly.

The Graphics Production Process

The world of graphic design and production is becoming more and more digital and involved less with pasteup and manual techniques. Advertisements, brochures, newspapers, and magazines are now created as a whole using page-layout programs in which pictures and text are manipulated on a computer screen. The resulting files can be sent directly to a printer as drafts or finals, or to phototypesetting machines that produce prepress output such as camera-ready copy or film.

Ultimately, what you plan to do with a graphic image dictates the type of hardware you should use to capture the image, display it, and edit it. The following list describes several uses for graphics and helps introduce methods for obtaining the images.

- You want to display a simple black-and-white image of your company's logo on your screen and print it as part of your letterhead.

- You need to include blueprints or part of a diagram in a document.

- You want a color picture of your family as a desktop background image.

- You're creating an onscreen presentation or a multimedia production that requires high-resolution, full-color graphic images.

- You're creating a newsletter that requires some black-and-white photos.

- You're creating a brochure that requires full-color images. You plan to manipulate the images in your system, and then send them to a service bureau that can separate the colors for professional printing.

These are only a few examples, but you can see the transition from simple black-and-white line drawings to full-color images. The line drawing (called *line art*) consists of a single-color graphic that is easy to create with most paint or drawing programs, or is easily input using a scanning device. You can print line art on most laser printers with little or no loss of resolution. Photographic-quality images are the next step up. Are they black-and-white or color? Do you need to display them on the screen only for presentations or multimedia programs, or do you need to print them? If you only plan to display the images, then you need a scanner that captures the continuous tones in color or gray-scale photographs. If your system won't handle the colors, then it's not worth scanning at a high resolution. Typical requirements for video display systems to handle color are listed in Table 21-1.

If you have this type of video equipment, then you can work with high-color images and prepare them for printing on high-resolution color output devices. As you move up to full-color graphics, the input and output equipment and methods become more complex. You'll need a high-resolution color scanner or access to one (or you can buy images on disk), and you'll need a color printer or the ability to produce color separations, which many Windows-based graphics packages now do. Many users simply rely on service bureaus to do all this *pre-press* work (pre-press refers to the

4-bit systems	16 colors or gray-scales
8-bit systems	256 colors or gray-scales
16-bit systems	32,000 colors or gray-scales
24-bit systems	16.7 million colors or gray-scales

Table 21-1.   *Color Requirements for Video Display Systems*

production of high-resolution film, negatives, or other media that are used by print shops in the final production).

If the final destination for your images is a black-and-white printer like a local laser printer, you'll need to reduce the image in both its resolution and color content. If this is the case, you should probably start by scanning at a lower resolution and with lower color values since high-resolution images require a lot of memory for manipulation, and this resolution is lost in the final process anyway. The reduction process converts color or gray-scale images to *dithered patterns* or *halftones*. These are patterns of dots that approximate the colors or grays, as you'll see.

The graphic production process is illustrated in Figure 21-1 and discussed in the following sections.

The Input Stage

You can obtain graphic images from many sources. Several methods are listed here:

- *Create them yourself* You can create your own graphics by using paint and draw programs.

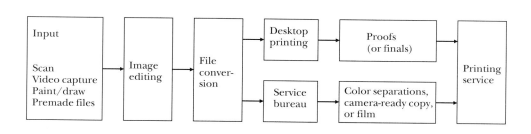

Figure 21-1.   *The graphics production process*

- *Scan them in*   A scanner is a device that converts black-and-white or color images on paper to digital information that you can display on your screen as bitmapped images.

- *Capture with a video camera*   A video-capture system combines a video camera with a "frame grabber" board that digitizes the video image and displays it on your screen.

- *Obtain from a graphic service*   Images are available from a variety of sources. You can purchase single images or an entire library of images on CD-ROM.

Editing and Conversion

You have full control over the creation and editing process if you create your own graphic images. Images captured from scanners and video systems almost always need adjustments and touch-ups. There are several categories of applications that let you do this:

- *Paint applications*   These provide tools for painting dot-by-dot (bitmapped) pictures and editing scanned images.

- *Draw applications*   These are another class of tools that you can use to create graphics using object-oriented commands. For example, a command of this type might be interpreted as "draw a circle of this size." The underlying commands are created by the drawing tools and stored with the file. What you see are the images.

- *Image enhancement applications*   These are designed primarily for touching up scanned photos and artwork. They use many of the same tools and techniques a photographer would use to bring out the details or change the appearance of a photograph.

- *Conversion utilities*   These are often required because there are many different graphic file formats. The conversion utility converts one type of file format so it can be used in an application that supports another file format.

Output

Images can be printed on a local printer, or sent to a service bureau for output on high-resolution imagesetters. If the images are color, separations (images of each color) can be produced either on your local printer or at a service bureau, depending on the resolution of the images and the capabilities of your hardware and software. A portion of this chapter discusses output to imagesetters like the high-resolution Linotronic series. These devices output paper film that is used in paste-up or as final proofs. Imagesetters typically accept PostScript files that you can create with many Windows applications. Windows provides several PostScript printer drivers that work with a number of these high-resolution systems. You simply install these printer drivers and then "print" your images to files, which can then be sent to the service bureau for output.

Types of Graphics

The art you see in books and magazines falls into two categories. The first is line art (mentioned earlier), which is a single-color image or image with multiple solid colors. The next, *halftone images*, are dot patterns that simulate shadings of gray or colors. Black-and-white or color photographs are *continuous tone images*, with potentially millions of color gradations, produced by the minute particles of the photographic film's emulsion. Printed paper material consists of line art or halftone images. The reason for this is that printers use one color at a time and have no way to adjust that color except to print more or less of it using minute dots. You can see these dot patterns if you look at a printed page with a magnifying glass.

Once these images are in your computer, they are classified as either *bitmap* or *vector* (*object-oriented*) graphics. The methods used to create and manipulate these images are different, as is the way your system displays and prints them.

Bitmapped Graphics

You can picture a bitmapped image in a grid pattern as shown next. Each block in the grid represents a screen pixel and is either off (white) or on (black or a specific color). On a monochrome display that displays only black or white, a single bit in memory can hold the information for each pixel. If the bit is 0, the pixel is off and if the bit is 1, the pixel is on.

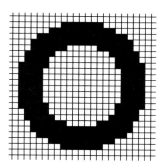

If the image contains colors, more than one bit is required to represent each "pixel." The number of pixels used to store a color defines the range of possible colors the pixel will display. If 4 bits are used to define each pixel, up to 16 colors are possible. This is because 4 bits can hold up to 16 different combinations of 0's and 1's to represent a digital value for a color. Increasing the *bit-plane* (number of pixels used) lets you define more colors as listed previously. But doing so also increases the amount of memory you'll need to display and store the image. Images with more than 256 colors are unwieldy to work with and cause a decrease in performance. If performance is more important than color range, choose a 4-bit or 8-bit video card or use a card with a graphics accelerator. Keep in mind that 16 colors (or gray shades) is really only suitable for creating line art or cartoon-like images. There is not enough color range to represent an image that looks natural. Even 256 colors or gray shades may be inadequate.

Here are important features of bitmapped files:

- Bitmapped images are created and edited using "paint" programs, as opposed to "draw" programs, which are used to create and edit vector graphics.

- Scanners and digitizers produce bitmapped images. They convert the light and dark areas of a scanned image into 0s and 1s, or, if the image is full color, into binary representations of those colors.

- Bitmapped image files can be quite large because every bit within the boundary of the image is saved, even if it appears blank. For example, saving the entire screen area of a VGA display (640x480) produces a file with 371,200 pixels. If the image is black-and-white line art, that's about 38K in size. A 4-bit color image requires 153K.

- Bitmapped images do not enlarge well. In the previous illustration, notice the "stair stepping" on the curves in the "O." Making the image larger only emphasizes the stair stepping unless you manipulate the image to smooth out the curves.

- Distortions are introduced when altering bitmapped images. In the following illustration, the square box is tilted as shown on the right. Notice the unevenness of the angled lines.

While bit-mapped images have some drawbacks, you have superior control over the individual elements of a picture. You can easily erase or change the color of individual or groups of pixels using brush tools or zoom in editing modes. Chapter 22 covers the Windows Paintbrush bitmap editor program.

Object-Oriented Graphics

Object-oriented graphics are often called vector graphics, (a *vector* is simply a line or curve from one point to another). The vectors are defined by mathematical expressions. Typically, a single action with a drawing tool creates an object like a box or circle that is defined internally by vector commands. Unlike a bitmapped image in which lines consist of many side-by-side dots (screen pixels or printer dots), a vector graphic file consists of point-to-point drawing instructions. The instructions in the file are "replayed" whenever the file is opened, drawing the image on the screen following the same order used to create it. The commands to draw a triangle might consist of the following simple statements:

Draw line A to B
Draw line B to C
Draw line C to A

Compare how those commands are stored in a file with a bitmap file, which consists of a continuous series of binary numbers that represent the color value of each pixel on the screen. Obviously, the bitmap file is going to be much larger, but complex vector graphic files that define multiple layers of objects in different colors and textures can also become quite large because of the number of commands required to define the image. The triangle created with the previous commands becomes an object that you can click on to select, then drag to another location, resize, or delete. Thus vector graphic drawing commands create object-oriented graphics. Drawing programs such as CorelDRAW, Adobe Illustrator, and Micrografx Designer are vector graphics programs.

Many of the tools used in vector graphic applications are similar to those used in bitmapped graphics applications. For example, drawing a box in a bitmapped application creates a box composed of individual bits that you can edit one by one. You could use an eraser tool to remove the upper-right corner of the box in a bitmap graphics file as shown here:

Creating the same box in a vector graphics application creates a single object. You can't edit individual bits in the object, but you can select it entirely by clicking anywhere on the object. Once selected, you can use various tools and commands to flip it, stretch it, change its color, or change its shape. In addition, you can press the DEL key to remove the object entirely. Objects can overlap one another. In the object-oriented graphic shown next, the three objects can be moved separately from one another. For example, the rectangle with rounded corners is selected. The dotted lines indicate that it is an underlying object. It can be dragged elsewhere, or brought to the top of the other objects. If the same drawing were a bitmap graphic, you could not move the rounded-corner rectangle away from the other two objects; instead, you would have to erase each line separately and redraw it.

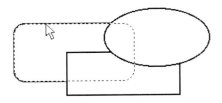

Objects have *handles* that you click and drag to resize the objects. In the following example, the oval on the left is clicked, displaying its handles. You then click a handle and drag to resize the object as shown on the right.

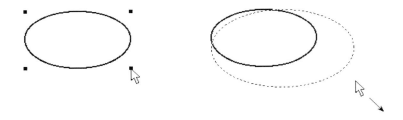

PostScript and Object-Oriented Graphics

CorelDRAW, Adobe Illustrator, and many other packages provide tools that create PostScript commands in the background. PostScript is a widely accepted font and graphic-producing language that provides device independence for files. As you'll recall from Chapter 15, device independence in PostScript files refers to their "portability," meaning that you can take them to any PostScript-compatible display or printer device and view or print the graphic exactly as it was created. Most high-resolution imagesetters such as those in service bureaus support PostScript.

Colors and Gray-Scales

Black-and-white and color photographs have a large amount of color or gray information that is difficult to reproduce accurately on computer displays and printers. Transitions between boundaries may consist of hundreds of variations in color or gray. To display these colors as smooth transitions, a display needs to have a resolution of 300 to 500 pixels per inch, or more—well above the 72 to 120 pixel-per-inch range of current VGA and Super VGA monitors. With low-resolution monitors, these color transitions are abrupt and appear as bands of closely matched colors.

For example, consider the number of color variations in the blue of an evening sky. Displaying this type of scene on a computer monitor is extremely difficult, especially if the video system only supports 16 colors. Even 256-color capability is not enough to prevent the discerning eye from seeing the banding of color transitions in the sky when it is displayed. Printing is even more difficult because the printer itself is limited to one color (assuming a black-and-white printer for this discussion) and a constant dot size. You'll need a printer with a resolution of 2400 to 3600 dots per inch to print such an image at near-photograph quality. This section looks at methods used to display and print gray-scales and colors.

Displaying Colors

If your picture has 256 colors but your monitor only provides 16 colors, some of those colors are converted to the next available color, or they are dithered. Dithering is a technique of representing an image using fewer colors than it originally had. The transition from one color to another is shown by mixing dots of the two colors in various patterns. You can see this by opening the Color utility in the Control Panel. Click the Color Palette button, then the Define Custom Colors button to display the Custom Color Selector dialog box shown in Figure 21-2.

You can see the dithering in the progression of solid basic colors at the top to the darker colors at the bottom. Unfortunately, this color scheme is the default for Windows, even if you have a 256-color display. It represents a compromise by Microsoft to provide compatibility for applications designed to use 16-color displays

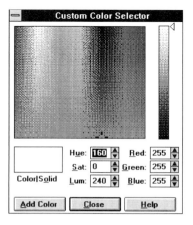

Figure 21-2.   *Dithered colors are created on the Custom Color Selector dialog box*

and those designed to use 256-color displays. Windows actually provides 20 solid colors as its default palette, but a VGA monitor can only display 16 of those colors at a time. The only time you can use a full-color palette (no dithered colors) is if you have a 256-color video card and monitor and are using an application that is specifically written to use the full color palette, such as Aldus PageMaker or Microsoft PowerPoint. Alternatively, video cards with the Sierra RAM DACs (discussed in Chapter 13) can provide 256 colors to some applications.

Printing Colors and Gray-Scales

A color display device, even if it supports only 16 colors, does a pretty good job of approximating transitions between colors, if you can stand the dithering. However, printing the images is another matter. Black-and-white printers use only one primary color, usually black. You can see how Windows displays solid and dithered colors by printing the Paintbrush color palette. Doing so gives you an idea of how your printer handles colors. The object of the following steps is to get a cutout of the color palette that you can zoom in to look at or print. These instructions assume you've got some knowledge of Paintbrush; if you don't, refer to Chapter 22.

1. Start by opening Paintbrush, and then make sure the palette is visible by enabling the Palette option on the View menu.

2. Press ALT-PRINT SCREEN to capture the Paintbrush window on the Clipboard.

3. Now choose Zoom Out on the View menu, choose Paste on the Copy menu, and click on another tool to lock the pasted image down. You see the Paintbrush window within the Paintbrush window!

4. Now choose Zoom In on the View menu to return to normal mode, and then use the Pick tool to outline the color palette.

5. Choose Copy To from the Edit menu, and then save the cutout with the name COLORBAR.BMP.

This last step saves the color palette; since you outlined just the palette itself, none of the other bits on the screen are saved in the file, thus saving disk space. Now you have a color bar you can print to use as a guide for testing color output. It also serves as a test strip for adjusting the Intensity control on the Printer Setup Options box. Adjusting this control lets you specify how light or dark each color prints.

There are two things you should do at this point. First, choose Zoom In from the Edit menu. The mouse pointer turns into a rectangle. Place this over the colors on the right side of the color bar and click the mouse button. These are the dithered colors and you can see in zoom-in mode how Windows creates them by intermixing different colors of pixels. Scan to the left to see other mixes. As you approach the left side of the color bar, the colors become solid. Now choose Zoom Out from the Edit menu and print the color bar on your printer. You'll end up with an image that has dithered patterns on the right, and relatively smooth, grid-like patterns for the solid colors on the left, as shown here:

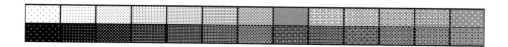

When painting pictures you intend to print, choose colors that will print well on your printer, based on how these patterns appear in the test strip you just made.

If you have an HP LaserJet or similar printer, you can try adjusting the Intensity slider on the Print Setup dialog box (click the Options button to see it) to lighten or darken how the colors print. The Intensity Control slider is shown in Figure 21-3. For best results, set the Dithering option to Fine, and then set the Intensity Control slider to the middle position. Try several printouts, adjusting this slider left or right slightly.

Using the Printer's Resolution

In bitmap editors such as Paintbrush, the image you draw on the screen is closely approximated in size on the printer (assuming that the Use Printer Resolution check box is not enabled). If you have a high-resolution laser printer, more dots are used to print the image than correspond to pixels on the screen. In fact, if you compare the screen image, it's just a little larger than the printed image. If you hold a real ruler up to the Ruler in Windows Write, you'll notice that an inch on the Write Ruler is really about 1.5 inches, although text prints correctly. Windows does this to make small fonts visible on the screen. Otherwise, font sizes below 10 points would be illegible.

You can work with bitmaps using the resolution of the printer if you want exact control over the final output. In Paintbrush, you click the Use Printer Resolution

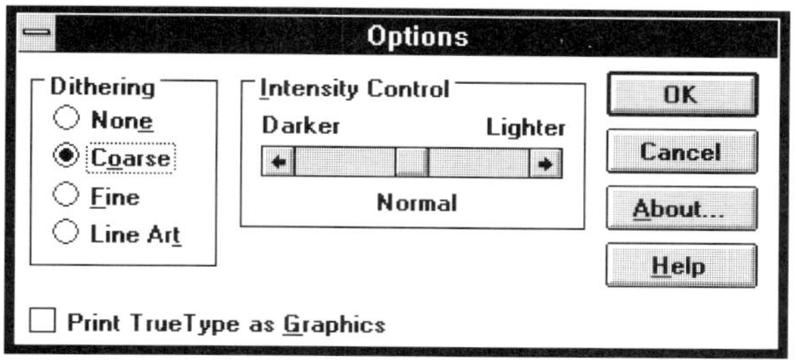

Figure 21-3. *Adjusting how colors print with the Options dialog box*

check box on the Print dialog box. Screen pixels are then matched one-on-one to printer dots. This usually tends to shrink the image, depending on the screen and printer resolution. For example, if you're using a 300 dots-per-inch laser printer and you draw an image that's 100 pixels wide, it will be 1/3 of an inch wide when printed at the printer's resolution. These techniques are useful when creating small printed images such as logos.

Halftoning Gray-Scale and Color Images

Displaying and printing black-and-white or gray photographs poses some interesting challenges. You'll need video equipment that can display all the subtle transitions in grays or colors, and a printer output device with enough resolution to simulate those transitions using a single color. If your final output device is a 300 dots-per-inch laser printer, you'll need to convert the color image for suitable black-and-white output using a process called dithering or *halftoning*. Most paint applications have commands for doing both. Basically, the colors are converted into pseudo-random dot patterns (dithering) or dot screens (halftoning) that simulate variations in gray.

The following image is from a black-and-white photograph that has been dithered. The subtle shades of gray are converted to dot patterns that simulate the transitions between light and dark, but the image is basically line art.

The next image shows a close-up of an image that has been halftoned. You can see the difference between this and the dithered image. However, halftoning requires high printer resolutions to look acceptable.

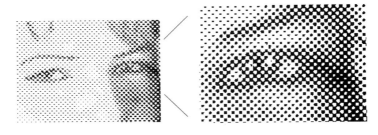

If you're working with high-resolution images with thousands of colors, and you want to maintain those colors, or gray-scale versions of them to the final printout, you'll need more elaborate equipment and techniques. Assume that you can capture and display such images accurately. If you only need to print a few copies, you can send the output to a color laser printer or some of the new color copy machines. But to mass-produce the images in magazines or advertising brochures, you'll need to first separate each primary color. Remember that a printing press only prints one color at a time. It can't mix colors on the fly like a video display. The printer uses the separation to print each color separately with a resulting mix that looks like your original photograph. To maintain tonality, a fine pattern of dots must be used. In this way, colors are mixed at the printer, not by overlapping them, but by placing tiny dots of varying colors and size next to each other.

Halftoning and color separation are vital to accurate color reproduction. While many graphics packages now have the ability to separate colors, most laser printers are limited in their ability to maintain image resolution and gray shades at the same time. The reason for this has to do with how halftones are printed, as discussed next. Many graphic artists send their work as disk files to service bureaus that can produce accurate color separations at high resolution on camera-ready film.

Let's look at how a halftone dot is produced on a printer. The printer may be your desktop laser printer or a phototypesetter that produces pre-press output. Assume for simplicity that your image has only five color/gray levels, from white to black with three levels of color or gray between. If you use a 2x2 dot matrix on the printer to represent one pixel on screen, you can simulate these grays as shown in Figure 21-4.

This block of pixels is often called a *super-dot, halftone cell,* or *meta pixel.* Let's refer to it as simply a cell from here on. By varying the fill of the cell, various shades of gray are simulated. This is best seen when a large number of cells are grouped together, as you can see on the right side of the previous illustration. You can use a completely unrelated utility in Windows to see how this works. Open the Desktop dialog box in the Control Panel and click the Edit button. Reproduce the patterns of the color palette in the Edit box while watching the sample window on the left. An example of a 50 percent pattern is shown in Figure 21-5. Try the 25 percent or 75 percent pattern as well.

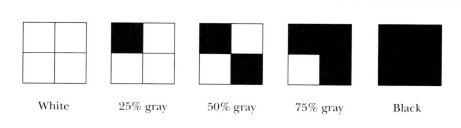

| White | 25% gray | 50% gray | 75% gray | Black |

Figure 21-4. *A 2x2 dot matrix prints three shades of gray as well as white and black*

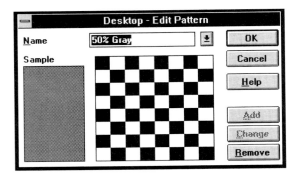

Figure 21-5.   *Seeing how halftoning works using the Edit Pattern dialog box*

But what if your picture has more than five colors or grays? You simply increase the size of the cell to provide more dots in the fill. An example of a 4x4 cell that provides 15 gray shades, plus all white and all black is shown here:

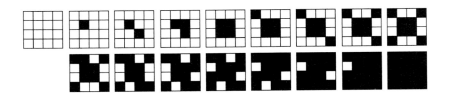

Try creating 4x4 cells in the Edit Pattern dialog box as discussed in the previous section, but notice that the larger cell size produces larger dots in the sample box on the left.

The larger the matrix, the more levels of gray you can obtain. An 8x8 matrix will provide 64 shades of gray, plus all white and all black. When the cells of varying intensity are placed side by side and at a high enough resolution, they produce acceptable looking gray-scales.

Compare the halftoning method to the dithering method, as shown in Figure 21-6. While halftoning simulates grays using halftone cells, dithering simply interprets a color as either black or white at the pixel level, producing a high-contrast image. Figure 21-6 shows an exploded view of the pixels with the actual image size in the upper-left corner.

While increasing matrix sizes provides more gray shades, it can decrease the quality of the image. Because a halftone cell has a height of two or more printer dots, there can no longer be a one-to-one relationship between screen pixels and printer dots. Using an 8x8 cell that allows 64 gray shades translates to a screen pixel that

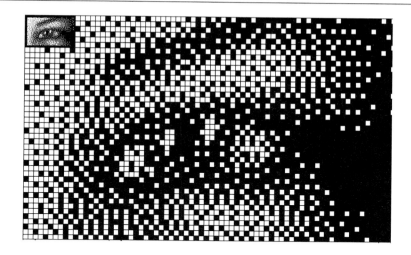

Figure 21-6.   *Dithering (to black and white) doesn't use halftone cells; it converts each color pixel to either black or white, producing a line art image.*

prints with a height of 8 dots. Thus a row of pixels forms a line that is 8 dots high. Printers and typographers use this line height to gauge the lines-per-inch (lpi) resolution of images (not the dots-per-inch resolution). Listed here are the lines-per-inch resolutions you can achieve with a 300dpi laser printer:

Halftone Cell	Lines Per Inch
2x2	150 lpi
4x4	75 lpi
8x8	37.5 lpi

Obviously, the more gray shades you require, the lower the printed image's resolution quality. The size of the image plays a part as well. Assume you've created an image that has a height of 300 pixels. Without halftoning, this image would be 1 inch high when printed on a 300dpi laser printer at the printer's resolution. If a 2x2 cell is used to represent each pixel, that image grows to 2 inches in height without a loss in resolution—it just increases its size. However, if you must constrain the image to a height of 1 inch, the printing resolution must drop to 150 lines per inch to accomodate the new cell size. For best results, you'll need a printer with 1200dpi resolution or greater when working with halftones.

There are several other factors to consider. If you are scanning color or gray-scale images that you plan to print on a 300dpi laser printer, be careful not to "overscan" the images because the extra resolution will be lost during the printing stage. Set your scanner resolution to approximately 75dpi and set its color or gray-scale setting to 16 or 64. In this way, your images won't be large in size and take up a lot of disk space. If you have access to a Linotronic Imagesetter or equivalent with resolutions of 1270dpi or higher, you can set scanning levels higher (150dpi with color/gray-scale settings at 64 to 256). If the image is reduced in size when printed, use a lower scanning resolution, but if it's enlarged, use a higher scanning resolution. Don't assume that higher scanning resolutions are always best. Your files will take up more room on disk and the extra resolution is often lost in the halftoning process. However, high-resolution scanning is useful if the image is black-and-white line art.

Obtaining Graphics

You can obtain graphic images (clip-art) from service bureaus, bulletin boards, or off-the-shelf image libraries. Many paint and draw programs come with their own set of pictures that you can use for in-house use. The alternative is to scan photographs and art using scanners or video capture techniques.

Scanners

Scanners provide a way of converting images on paper or film into graphics on your screen. There is a wide range of scanner types, from inexpensive hand scanners to high-resolution film scanners that produce color separations. These high-end scanners are typically found in prepress shops and production houses and are not discussed in this book. A typical flatbed scanner can detect up to 256 levels of gray. Color scanners that offer higher resolution are becoming more prevalent as prices drop. Once you've scanned an image, you use image editing software to "touch up" images, and then save it to disk. All scanners convert scanned images to bitmaps.

A hand scanner will have screen controls similar to those shown in the following illustration, or have similar controls in software. The switch on the left is used to set the level of gray-scales the scanner will capture. The middle switch is used to set the dots-per-inch resolution. Lower settings translate to smaller file sizes, but less detail. The dial on the right is used to control contrast. Adjustment of this control depends on the image you are scanning. Note that scanning software usually has options for adjusting the lightness or darkness of an image after it has been scanned.

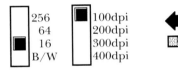

Color scanners are increasing in popularity because their prices are coming down, but keep in mind that color information may be lost if the image is printed on a low-resolution device. However, if you're preparing images for onscreen display or multimedia presentations, capturing colors is important to make the image look as life-like as possible.

There are several types of scanners; each is described in the following sections.

Flatbed Scanners   A flatbed scanner contains a plate of glass on which you place the image. Photosensors under the glass then scan the image. Flatbed scanners are usually the most accurate.

Sheetfed Scanners   A sheetfed scanner moves the photograph or image past the photosensors (many FAX machines use this process). While you can stack a number of sheets for scanning, you are limited to two-dimensional sheets. Books and large images cannot be scanned with these unless you first photocopy them or rip out the pages.

Hand-Held Scanners   Hand-held scanners are inexpensive, and quite accurate. Rollers under the scanner help keep it positioned on the paper as you drag it over an image. While this type of scanner has a limited width (usually 4 inches), most scanner software provides a "stitching" feature that accurately pastes together the images you've obtained from several scans over the picture.

FAX Machines   Some FAX machines provide a serial port that provides a way to transfer the image scanned by the built-in FAX scanner into your computer.

Video Capture and Digital Cameras

A *video capture system* consists of a video camera and an interface card. The video camera captures the image and the interface card digitizes it and displays it as a still image on the screen. Some systems display live video and let you capture any portion of the video by clicking a button.

An alternative to the video capture system is the *digital camera*, a portable device like a film camera, that has a built-in floppy disk to store images, or enough memory to hold images that you then download to a computer. The images are captured digitally.

The results of both systems are the same once you get the image into your computer; however, the color capabilities of either is something to watch for. You can use various image-editing software packages to touch up or edit the images as discussed next.

Image-Editing Software

Once you've captured an image, you'll probably need to touch it up. For example, you can remove a scratch that might have been in the original photo or you can reduce excessive highlights. Touch-ups can apply to an entire image or to individual elements. You could darken or lighten the entire image, change its contrast, or apply special effects that soften or sharpen the image.

Most scanners come with software for editing bitmapped scanned images. In some cases, an image-editing application is really a full-blown paint package, as discussed in the next section. For example, Zsoft's Publisher's Paintbrush provides professional bitmap editing features and scanner support. This section lists some of the features you can expect to find in image-editing software such as Image-In (CPI), PhotoShop (Adobe), and Ansel (Logitech). These features are specifically designed for editing scanned images such as photographs and often simulate the techniques used by professional photographers.

The Zoom-in Feature   The Zoom-in feature lets you zoom into any portion of the image and do spot touch-ups. Using brush tools of various shapes, you can convert a range of pixels to another color.

The Darken/Lighten Feature   The Darken/lighten feature lets you brush an area to darken or lighten it in small increments. The longer you brush the area, the darker or lighter it gets, an effect similar to burning-in an area of a photograph.

The Brighten Feature   The Brighten feature lets you increase the brightness of the entire image.

The Contrast Feature   The Contrast features lets you increase or decrease the contrast of an image by replacing gray areas with black or white.

The Sharpen Feature   With the Sharpen feature, you can bring out details of an image by mathematically distinguishing edges.

The Smooth Feature   The Smooth feature lets you reduce the sharpness of an image and blend its grays more smoothly.

Halftoning Options   Use the halftoning options to convert colors or gray-scales to dot patterns. An image editor should have a wide range of halftoning options so you can convert color photographs for printing on black-and-white printers.

The Histogram Equalization and Gamma Correction Feature   The Histogram Equalization and Gamma Correction feature lets you view and change the distribution of gray shades in an image. This "equalization" helps bring out details in areas that appear too light or too dark. Scanners often have a limited "dynamic range" which means they have trouble perceiving white highlights or dark blacks. Colors or grays may be bunched together, giving the image the appearance of high contrast. Correcting this brings out the details hidden in the dark areas without dropping out the rest of the image.

The De-Interlacing Feature   Some editors provide this feature to remove distortions in video captures caused by the interlacing of the video circuitry. Interlacing is defined in Chapter 13.

These are just a few of the available features; there are, of course, many additional features available in image-editing applications. Some may offer more features than others; many even have begun to take on the features of paint applications, as discussed next.

Paint and Draw Programs

Graphics software comes in three categories: bitmapped (paint), object-oriented (draw), and software that supports both. (Windows Paintbrush is a bitmapped graphics application covered separately in Chapter 22.) Some of the most common tools and features of these applications are discussed here. Both types of applications provide the following:

- A canvas or drawing area.

- A set of drawing tools used to create boxes, circles, curves, and lines that are drawn by hand.

- Color tools used to fill areas or convert colors.

- Text tools for adding labels and editing text.

- Line width and style selectors.

- Zoom-in modes that let you work with individual pixels in paint packages, or create and edit small objects in draw packages.

- Special effects such as rotate, resize, reverse, tilt, and many others.

- Gradient fills, which fill enclosed areas with a smooth transition of color from light to dark or dark to light.

- Some packages offer multiple drawing layers so you can create a picture by painting or drawing on several different layers, and then combine those layers in the final picture.

In many respects, it's difficult to tell the difference between a paint and draw application. Many of the tools are the same. For example, the process of drawing boxes, rectangles, ellipses, lines, and curves is similar and the tools often look the same. However, draw applications create objects that you can select by clicking with the mouse. Paint applications simply paint pixels.

Conversions and File Formats

Once you've scanned, painted, or drawn your graphics image, you can paste it into a page layout program or other document. But this step may require a file format conversion before the target applications will accept the image. Many applications provide their own file conversion routines. In some cases, you may need to convert a bitmapped image into an object-oriented image. Programs that use vectorization features often let you do this conversion, as discussed later in this chapter in the "Vectorizing (Autotracing)" section.

Windows 3.1 Clipboard Conversion

The Windows Clipboard provides a form of file conversion that is handled in the background by applications that copy information to the Clipboard and receive information from it. You don't need to be too concerned with this process since applications handle the conversion automatically, but it may shed some light on how graphics are translated between applications.

When you cut or copy a graphic image to the Clipboard, the application that created the image often copies several different file formats with it. You can start the Clipboard and open the Display menu to see these formats when an image is on the Clipboard. When you switch to another application and choose Paste, that application first reviews the available formats and chooses the one it can best handle.

Image Capture and File Conversion

Paintbrush is an application that you can use to create and edit graphics, even though it has some limitations. (Chapter 22 is devoted entirely to Paintbrush, so this section is just to introduce it.) Paintbrush supports two common file formats, but not the more common TIFF file format used by scanners and professional paint and draw programs. If you need to create PostScript graphics for output to high-resolution imagesetters, you need more sophisticated draw applications such as Adobe Illustrator and CorelDRAW.

The need for file conversion usually arises when you upgrade to a new paint or draw program, or need to transfer images to another user. Some service bureaus may require that you convert your files to a more standard format. That's where image capture and conversion utilities come in. Two common image capture and conversion utilities, Paint Shop and DoDot, are described next.

Paint Shop   This utility by JASC, Inc. of Eden Prairie, Minnesota provides picture viewing and conversion. It will open files in many different formats, and then let you save the files in a different format. Paint Shop provides options for flipping, rotating, stretching, and trimming an image. In addition, you can convert a color image to gray-scale, dither a 256-color image to 16 colors, or convert it to black-and-white.

There are also options for changing the contrast and brightness, or adjusting the red, green, or blue components of an image. Paint Shop is also an image-capture utility. You can capture the entire screen, or drag a box around any part of the desktop to capture it. Paint Shop is available on most bulletin boards as a shareware product. You pay for it if you use it.

DoDot   DoDot is a popular package made by Halcyon Software of Cupertino, California and sold in retail stores. It provides conversion of bitmapped files to the most common formats and provides many image enhancement options like Paint Shop. DoDot can "vectorize" bitmapped images into object-oriented graphics and supports output to PostScript printers. (See the section on "Vectorizing (Autotracing)" later in this chapter.)

File Formats

The following sections give the most common file formats used by personal computers. Refer to Table 21-1 earlier in this chapter for the necessary information regarding bits per pixel.

The BMP Format   The BMP (for bitmap) format is the standard Windows Paintbrush format. Paintbrush saves files as 1 or 4 bits only but will display 8-bit files. There are Windows and OS/2 versions of this file format.

The DIB Format   The DIB (for device independent bitmap) format is really another form of the BMP file, but you'll see more of it as multimedia grows in popularity. The data in the file can be displayed regardless of the characteristics of the current display or the display used to create the file.

The GIF Format   The graphic interchange format is a CompuServe format that supports 1, 4, and 8 bits per pixel. The GIF file format was designed for uploading and downloading to and from bulletin boards. An *interlacing* method transfers and displays the file in four passes. This has the advantage of letting you see the image at 1/4 resolution on the first pass and decide whether you want to continue the download. On the first pass, only every fourth line is displayed.

The EPS Format   An EPS (for encapsulated PostScript) file is a text file that stores commands used to re-create a graphic image. The EPS format is device independent, meaning you can print the files on any PostScript printer and take advantage of whatever resolution that printer has. (You'll learn more about the EPS format later in the "Printing" section of this chapter.)

The PCX Format   The PCX format is a popular graphic format originally created by Zsoft but now used by many applications. It supports 1, 4, and 8 bits per pixel.

The RLE Format   The RLE (for run length limited encoding) file is a bitmapped file that has been compressed using the RLE technique. A compressed file may reduce in size by 50 percent or more. The Windows logo screen is an RLE file.

The TIFF Format   TIFF (for tagged image file format) is a recognized standard for image files. A form of this file format is an international standard used in FAX transmissions. Several types of compression are supported. Most scanners create TIFF files. TIFF files support 1, 4, 8, and 24 bits per pixel resolution. The TIFF format differentiates between black-and-white, gray-scale, and color pictures.

Vectorizing (Autotracing)

Vectorizing or *autotracing* is the process of outlining a bitmapped image and converting it to an object with control points as shown in the lower part of the following illustration. The actual bits are traced with a line. You can then edit and scale the object using object-oriented drawing techniques. In addition, some of the problems associated with printing bitmapped images are removed since the image obtains vectors that print as smooth curves.

File Compression

Graphic images, whether bitmapped or object-oriented, can take up quite a bit of disk space. At some point, you'll need to consider a file compression utility to reduce the size of your graphics files. Compression frees up space on your hard disk and also makes the files more manageable if you need to send them to another user on diskette or over a modem. Some files are automatically compressed, or are easily compressed using the file conversion utilities discussed earlier. The most notable is the TIFF format, which supports RLE (run length limited encoding) compression.

A popular compression utility is PKZIP from PKWARE, Inc, which is a shareware product that you pay for if you use. PKZIP is available on most bulletin boards and is the software standard for packing and unpacking (PKUNZIP) files on CompuServe and many other online services. You can contact PKWARE in Glendale, Wisconsin.

Printing

After you've created or scanned your graphic images, you're ready to print. There are two areas of concern. First, if you are printing to a local black-and-white printer, you'll need to dither or halftone the image to produce acceptable results. Second, if you're sending your output to high-resolution printers like Linotronic Imagesetters, you'll need to know a little bit about PostScript.

Preparing an Image for Printing

We've already discussed ways you can prepare a color or gray-scale image for printing. If you're printing on a local printer with relatively low resolution, you can either dither it to a pattern of dots, or use a halftoning method that provides a greater range of gray-scales. If the image is being sent to a service bureau for printing on a high-resolution printer, you should not dither or halftone the image. Let the service do that, but check ahead to make sure.

In some cases, the image you see on the screen will already be dithered. For example, if you open a 256-color image on a display that can only support 16 colors, the application will dither the image or convert non-displayable colors to the next solid color. The standard Windows color palette supports only 20 solid colors and dithers the rest, so in this respect, all 256-color images will have some dithering or color conversion in Paintbrush, which does not support more than the standard colors. Keep in mind that the full-color information in a file is retained unless you save the file after opening it in an application that doesn't support full colors, so be careful.

If you need to work with natural colors, be sure to use an application and video equipment that support 256 or more colors under Windows.

To prepare your images for printing on your local printer, you'll need a suitable image editor, or an application that provides dithering or halftone options. Figure 21-7 shows several dithering options available in Paint Shop Pro for reducing a color or gray-scale image to two colors. All images are *error diffused*, which means they are converted using an algorithm in which the difference between the original color and black or white is diffused to the neighboring pixels. There are three popular error diffusion algorithms: Floyd-Steinberg, Burkes, and Stucki, which are shown from top to bottom, respectively. The images on the left are dithered using a *weighted palette*, which produces less dithering and gives the appearance of fewer grays and a sharper image. The images on the right are *non-weighted*, which results in normal dithering with less sharpness and the appearance of more gray levels.

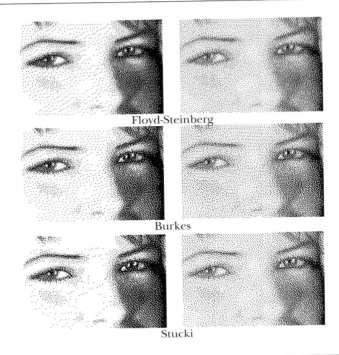

Floyd-Steinberg

Burkes

Stucki

Figure 21-7. *Different dithering methods affect the conversion of colors to black and white. The images on the left are weighted and those on the right are non-weighted.*

The error-diffusion method tends to follow the contours of the image, and looks best when there are many different colors or gray shades. There are many other types of conversions available; check your graphic application or file conversion utility for more information.

PostScript

PostScript is a command language created by Adobe Systems that provides a way to describe how graphics and text are printed on a PostScript-compatible printer (or displayed on a PostScript-compatible display device). When using PostScript illustration packages such as Adobe Illustrator, CorelDRAW, or Micrografx Designer, you draw images on the screen in the normal way. While those images are displayed using the pixels of your screen, in the background the application creates a PostScript text file that contains a series of commands that let you print the file at any time, on any PostScript-compatible printer, and at the highest resolution of that printer. This last point, *resolution independence*, is an important feature of PostScript.

You can create PostScript files even if you don't have a PostScript printer. Simply install any of the PostScript drivers provided by Windows, and then create your graphic image while the driver is active. You then print the image to a file and take that file to your nearest service bureau or other location where a high-resolution Linotronic Imagesetter or other PostScript-compatible printer is available. The service can create color separations and camera-ready copy. Because PostScript is a widely accepted industry standard, you'll get the kind of output you expect.

PostScript defines fonts on a page and any graphics that go with those fonts, such as boxes that surround text, underlines, or bold blocks in headers and footers. This type of PostScript file can be called *normal* because it does not contain special Encapsulated PostScript (discussed in a moment) graphics that might be imported from another application. Printing a PostScript file on a PostScript printer is not much different from printing any other file. You don't need to be concerned with the PostScript commands since the printer handles everything in the background.

A PostScript print file can be listed like any text file when you want to view the commands within. The file starts off with a *header* that provides information about what is in the file and the application used to create it. The header also contains the file's creation date, the fonts used, and any fonts needed, as well as the paper size and number of pages. Header information sets up the printer for the print job and is necessary if you're sending files to a shared network printer that may be in another print mode from a previous job. Following the header is the actual imaging information. PostScript experts may want to change this information to make fine adjustments in a PostScript file, but in most cases, if you need to make changes it's best to go back to the original application to edit and reproduce the file.

Encapsulated PostScript Files

An encapsulated PostScript (EPS) file is a special version of a PostScript file that supports graphics. It was developed by Altsys, a company that developed an illustration program called Freehand for Aldus. The EPS file format is unique in that it contains the PostScript commands to print the graphic, and a displayable bitmap of the graphic. When the EPS file is pasted into a document, the bitmap displays the image, but the PostScript information is used to print it. On PCs, the bitmapped image is usually in the TIFF format and is embedded in the EPS file.

The EPS format is supported by most illustration packages such as CorelDRAW, Micrografx Designer, and others. An EPS file is created by *exporting* it to a separate file and giving it the .EPS extension. For example, the Export command in Micrografx Designer is a file conversion utility that lets you save images in a number of formats. Besides PCX, TIFF, and several others, there are two EPS formats, one with the TIFF preview image and one without. Page layout programs such as Aldus PageMaker and Ventura Publisher have *importing* options used to paste EPS files into documents. Note that export and import provide the same functionality as copy and paste, but are quite different since a separate file is created during an export.

The TIFF preview bitmap is optional, but recommended if you are pasting a number of graphics into a document. As you scroll through the document, you'll be able to see what the image looks like and visually scale and crop it if necessary. In addition, the TIFF format displays the graphic image quickly. The alternative is that the image simply displays as a gray mask that approximates the size of the image.

As always, if you plan to send your files to an outside service, check with them to determine the compatibility of your PostScript files. It's best to create some test files in advance and send them to the service bureau before starting full production on your documents and graphics.

Installing a PostScript Driver

As mentioned, you don't need to have a PostScript printer to use a PostScript driver. You can install a PostScript driver and use it to create print files for PostScript printers at other locations. Windows supports a wide range of PostScript printers. You can view the list by opening the Printers utility in the Control Panel and clicking the Install button.

Before installing a PostScript printer driver, first call the service bureau you plan to use and find out what brand and model of PostScript system they have. The Linotronic Imagesetter series is discussed in the following sections since it is commonly used. There are four drivers, each with different resolutions. Click the Install button and scroll to the Linotronic options in the listing, and then pick the appropriate printer. Except for the resolution, the options described next are the same for all the printers.

When the printer appears in the Installed Printers list, click it, and then click the Setup button. The dialog box for setting paper and orientation appears. Click the Options button to display the dialog box shown in Figure 21-8.

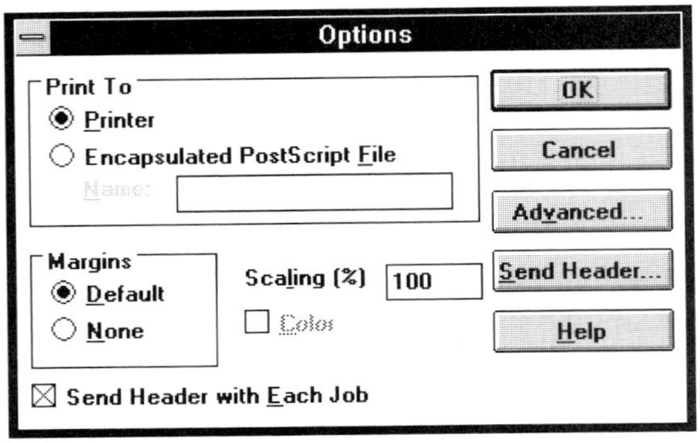

Figure 21-8.   *The PostScript Options dialog box*

Each option in the Options dialog box is described next, but keep in mind that a full description of the options on this dialog box are available by clicking the Help button. Space does not allow full coverage here.

Print To   Choose Printer if your system is directly connected to the printer, or Encapsulated PostScript File to print to a file that you can take to a service bureau.

Margins   Select Default to use the area in which the printer can print (1/4 inch from the edge of the paper) or None to use the paper size.

Scaling   Type in the percentage you want to scale the document.

Color   If the printer supports color, the Color option will be available. Enable it to print the image in color.

Send Header with Each Job   Typically, leave this option enabled. It is required if you're sending the files to network printers that might be in use by other users since it resets the printer for your specific jobs. You can speed performance if your printer is local and dedicated by disabling it after sending at least one print job with a header to the printer, assuming your print jobs are similar.

Pressing the Advanced button opens the Advanced Options dialog box shown in Figure 21-9. This options is used to set how TrueType fonts are handled, the graphics resolution, and the halftone settings.

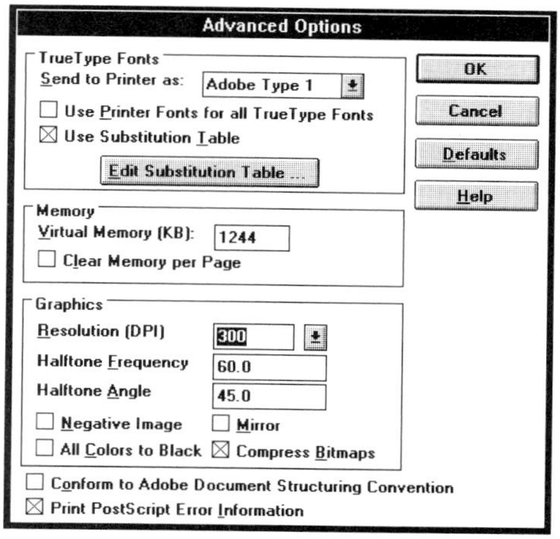

Figure 21-9.   *The PostScript Advanced Options dialog box*

TrueType Fonts   If your document has TrueType fonts, you set options in this field to specify how they should be handled by the PostScript printer. You can specify PostScript or Adobe Type 3 font replacements for TrueType fonts. Click the Help button for specific information.

Memory   You may need to adjust the Virtual Memory option if printer errors occur. Test the printer by sending the file TESTPS.TXT to the printer. This file is located in the Windows directory. Complete instructions are available on the help menus.

Graphics   The Graphics field has options for setting the printer resolution, halftone frequency (number of lines per inch), and the halftone angle. You must experiment with the halftone options; settings will depend on the type of image you are printing. The halftone angle is important. When halftones are set at a 45-degree angle, they tend to be less visible and give the image a more natural appearance.

Conform to Adobe Document Structuring Convention   Enable this check box to create a document print file that you can use with a program that supports the Adobe Document Structuring Conventions (DSC). This option is also useful if you want to share the document file with others, or if you want to use a printing service to print the file. When enabled, the Halftone Frequency, Halftone Angle, and Clear Memory Per Page options are dimmed, indicating that you cannot use them. Clearing this check box may speed up printing. You do not need to select this option if you are creating Encapsulated PostScript (EPS) files.

Print PostScript Error Information   Enable this check box to debug printer problems. Errors are then printed as part of the document.

Resources

There are of course many other topics related to graphics that are much too involved to discuss here. One of those topics is the color-separation and printing process. Producing full-color graphics for magazine layouts, advertising, and other printed material is beyond the scope of this book. However, there are many excellent resources to which you can refer. The following provides a list of reference books for more information on graphics in general.

> *An Introduction to Computer Graphics Concepts.* Sun Microsystems, June 1991. While this book was published by a non-Windows vendor, it provides an excellent overview of graphic concepts and techniques. It's well illustrated with clear explanations of technical concepts.

Beale, Stephen, and James Cavuoto. *Linotronic Imaging Handbook.* Micro Publishing Press, 1990. This book is a must if you're using Linotronic Imagesetters.

Busch, David D. *The Complete Scanner Handbook for Desktop Publishing, PC Edition.* Dow Jones & Company, 1990. David Busch provides an excellent description of the scanning, editing, and printing process.

Glober, Gary. *Running PostScript from MS-DOS.* Windcrest Books, 1989. This is a useful primer for those interested in editing PostScript files.

McClelland, Deke. *Drawing on the PC, A Non-Artist's Guide to CorelDRAW, Micrografx Designer, and Many Others.* Business One Irwin, 1991. The book is written by a graphic artist for aspiring graphic artists, so it contains many tricks and techniques for using the paint and draw tools you'll find in graphics applications. It contains hundreds of graphics examples, and is well illustrated and indicates the author's knowledge of graphics.

Sosinsky, Barry. *Beyond the Desktop, Tools and Technology for Computer Publishing.* Bantam Books, 1991. Barry Sosinsky provides a broad overview of the graphics process.

Chapter 22

The Bitmap Editor: Paintbrush

Windows Paintbrush is a bitmap painting program that offers a full set of painting tools and a wide range of colors for creating business graphics, company logos, illustrations, maps, and many other types of artwork. Enjoy yourself as you work through the chapter by experimenting with Paintbrush.

Startup and Overview

Start Paintbrush now by double-clicking its icon in the Accessories group window of the Program Manager. The Paintbrush window opens as shown in Figure 22-1.

The Paintbrush window consists of a work space or canvas where pictures are created. To the left of the canvas is the Toolbox, which contains a set of painting tools. At the bottom of the canvas is the color palette, where you select the color you want to paint with. To the left of that is the Linesize box, where you select the width to use for the Brush, Line, and other tools. To paint, select a tool, color, and line width, and then point to the canvas and click and drag the mouse.

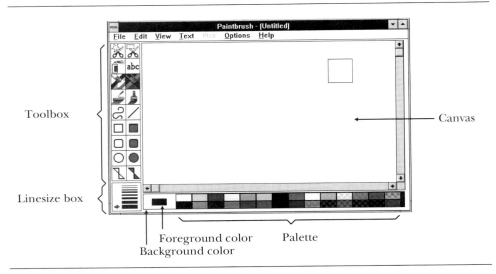

Toolbox

Canvas

Linesize box

Foreground color
Background color   Palette

Figure 22-1.   *The Paintbrush window*

Working with the Color Palette

The color palette is the strip of color boxes at the bottom of the Paintbrush window. When a color is selected, it appears on the left in the color selection box. If you click a color with the left mouse button, that color appears in the foreground box. If you click a color with the right mouse button, the color appears in the background box.

The background color and the canvas color have an important relationship. When you erase a color with the Eraser tool, the color of the canvas shows through unless a different background color is selected. To change the canvas color, click a color with the right mouse button and choose New from the File menu.

If you erase with the Eraser tool, the canvas color always shows through.

Most tools paint with the foreground color; however, when painting filled boxes, circles, and polygons, the background color becomes the border and the foreground color becomes the fill. If you can't remember which mouse button is used for the border and fill when creating filled objects, think of the foreground/background color box as a filled object itself. Notice how the box mimics the color arrangement of the box you just painted.

Foreground and background colors are especially important when using the Color Eraser, which replaces the foreground color with the background color.

The Toolbox

The Toolbox contains a full set of tools for painting in the workspace. Simply click a tool, and then point to the canvas and start painting by clicking and dragging the mouse. Keep in mind that most tools paint with the current colors in the color palette and the width selected in the Linesize box. Here is a list of the tools and what each does:

- *Scissors*   You use the Scissors to select irregularly shaped cutouts.

- *Pick*   Use the Pick to select rectangular cutouts.

These first two tools are used to define cutouts, *which are selected parts of the drawing that you can move, copy, or delete.*

- *Airbrush*   The Airbrush sprays a dot pattern of the currently selected foreground color.

- *Text*   Type text for captions and titles using the Text tool.

- *Color Eraser*   The Color Eraser erases the foreground color and changes it to the background color.

- *Eraser*   The Eraser erases/converts all colors to the canvas or background color.

- *Paint Roller*   The Paint Roller tool fills enclosed areas with the foreground color.

- *Brush*   The Brush is a tool that you "paint" with using a freehand style.

- *Curve*   The Curve is a freehand painting tool for creating curved shapes.

- *Line*   You create straight lines with the Line tool.

The remaining Paintbrush tools come in pairs. The tool on the left side of the Toolbox is used to create a hollow object that is outlined with the current foreground color. The corresponding tool on the right side of the Toolbox is used to create an object filled with the current foreground color and outlined with the current background color. Select the line width for the object from the Linesize box before painting. To paint symmetrical shapes, hold down the SHIFT key while dragging the mouse.

To create a filled object without a border, select the same foreground and background color.

- *Box*   The Box tools create square or rectangular shapes.

- *Rounded Box*   The Rounded Box tools create squares or rectangles with rounded corners.

- *Circle*   The Circle tools create circles or ellipses.

- *Polygon*   The Polygon tools create irregularly shaped triangles, boxes, and other multi-sided objects.

Painting Techniques

The following sections offer a few techniques to help you improve the quality of your pictures and the efficiency of painting methods.

Making Corrections

To erase part of what you've just painted, press the BACKSPACE key. A box with an X appears. Drag over the object you just created to erase it. The same technique that you use to work the Eraser tool works with most of the drawing tools. Also note that the current canvas color always shows through when erasing, even if another background color is selected in the color palette.

Another way to make corrections is to choose the Undo command on the Edit menu. Select this command after pasting an object you don't want or after making radical changes to an object such as tilting or inverting it.

When Undo is selected, all changes you've made with the current tool are undone. For example, if you draw three boxes with a Box tool and choose Undo, all three boxes are removed, not just the last box.

The Cursor

The mouse pointer shape is an arrow when selecting menus, tools, and colors. When on the canvas, it changes to a cross hair when working with the Cutout tools, Line tools, and hollow or filled tools. When working with the Text tool, the cursor is an I-beam. When one of the Eraser tools is selected, the cursor is a box that matches the size of the current line width. To select a "tip" for the Brush tool, double-click the Brush in the Toolbox. The Brush Shapes dialog box shown in Figure 22-2 appears. Double-click the brush shape you want to use, and then choose an appropriate line width in the Linesize box.

Viewing Cursor Positions

Choose the Cursor Position option on the View menu to display the cursor position box shown here:

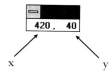

It displays the x and y coordinates of the cursor on the canvas. The coordinates displayed in the Cursor Position box are useful in the following cases:

- To create objects of an exact size

- To create multiple objects that match in size

- To align objects such as boxes or circles

- To move objects with precision

Arrow Key Techniques

To work with precision when using any tools, use the arrow keys on the keyboard. Each press of the key adjusts the pointer or moves a selected object one pixel at a time. For example, to carefully erase the very edge of an object, position the Eraser close to it, and then press the arrow keys to move the Eraser tool into position and click the mouse button to erase.

You can also use the arrow keys to position an object. Drag the object into place, then, while still holding the mouse button, press the arrow keys to move it one pixel width at a time.

Painting with Constraint

While this may sound like a frustrating way to paint, the technique described here is essential to creating orderly pictures. To paint circles rather than ellipses, and paint

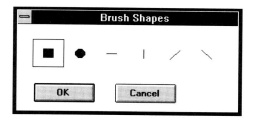

Figure 22-2.   *The Brush Shapes dialog box; access this box by double-clicking the Brush tool*

squares rather than rectangles, hold the SHIFT key while dragging with the mouse. A box or circle shape is retained as you drag the mouse. When the Line or Polygon tool is selected, holding SHIFT restricts mouse movements to 45-degree increments.

Zooming In for Detail

While the arrow keys and SHIFT key help you paint more precisely, the Zoom In command lets you magnify a part of the picture so you can change its individual picture elements (pels). When you zoom in, the color of individual elements can be changed by clicking them with the mouse. To see how the zoom mode works, and to see how Paintbrush colors are formulated, follow these steps:

1. Select the thickest line in the Linesize box.

2. Select the reddish-brown color on the top-right end of the palette.

3. Select the Brush tool.

4. Paint a wide horizontal line on the upper-left corner of the canvas. If you're a perfectionist, hold the SHIFT key to constrain the line.

Now select dark brown and repeat step 4. Continue selecting colors and painting strips in this way until you get to the lavender shades in the palette. The lavenders and all colors to the left of them are solid and are not of interest in this discussion, since we want to see how dithered colors are mixed. Now zoom in to take a look at the components of the colors by following these steps:

1. Choose Zoom In from the View menu. A rectangular cursor appears. Position it over the top colors as shown here:

2. Click the mouse to zoom in on the area inside the rectangle. The area selected for zoom is displayed on the canvas, similar to that shown here. Notice that the box in the upper-left corner shows the normal view.

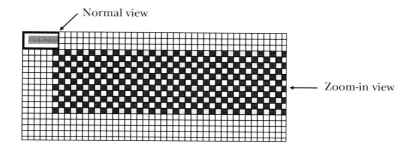

3. Click the vertical slider and drag down, watching the colors scroll in the box. When another set of colors is visible, release the mouse button.

Repeat step 3 until you've scanned all the colors. Note that these colors are mixtures of the solid colors on the left of the color palette. Now you can try changing the individual elements of the colors by following these steps:

1. Scroll back to the top colors, then click black in the color palette with the left mouse button and white with the right mouse button.

2. Now click the red picture elements, or try dragging a horizontal line across the canvas. As you do, watch the box in the upper-left corner.

3. Click with the right mouse button to erase pixels.

4. Choose Zoom Out from the View menu to return to normal view mode.

Those are the basic steps for using the zoom mode. Typically, you paint in normal mode, and then zoom in to add detail or erase colors you don't want.

The Paintbrush Canvas

The canvas is your painting area. You can change its color, change its size, and zoom out to see the entire canvas.

The View Picture Mode

Choose the View Picture option from the View menu to see the picture on the canvas in full-screen mode, without the borders, Toolbox, and color palette. You can't do any editing in this mode—just stand back and admire your masterpiece. To return to normal mode, click anywhere in the picture, or press CTRL-C.

Canvas Settings

To set the size of the canvas, the unit of measure, and the type of palette you want to use, choose Image Attributes from the Options menu. The Image Attributes dialog box like the one shown in Figure 22-3 appears.

The Image Attributes dialog box contains the following fields:

- *Units* Click the unit of measure you want to work in, either inches, centimeters, or pels. Pels are the picture elements or bits you see when you choose Zoom In from the View menu.

- *Width and Height* Enter the width and height for the canvas in these fields. The value should correspond to the measure you picked in the Units field.

- *Colors* Normally, you'll work in color, but Black and White mode can be used to paint with dot patterns that may look better when printed on your printer.

Keep these things in mind when changing the settings on the Image Attributes dialog box:

- Initially, Paintbrush establishes a default canvas size that matches the pixel width and height of your screen, but if you're low on memory, the canvas may be smaller. To gain more workspace, close other applications if possible, and then click Default on the Image Attributes dialog box and open a new canvas by choosing New on the File menu.

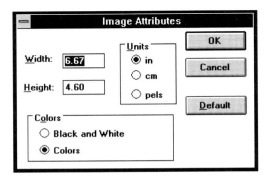

Figure 22-3.   *Use the Image Attributes dialog box to create a new canvas size, change the unit of measure, or switch from Colors to Black and White mode*

- The smaller the settings in the Width and Height boxes, the less disk space required by the file when saved. Even excess white space is saved to disk. However, don't feel you need to work on a small canvas all the time. In fact, it's sometimes easier to work on a large canvas so you can move cutouts around, or place them at the bottom of the canvas for later use. When you're ready to save the picture, use the Cutout tool to surround just the part you want, and then choose Copy To from the Edit menu to save only the cutout.

About Image Resolution

If you need to use exact measurements when creating pictures, you'll first need to find out how many pels (picture elements or pixels) there are per inch or centimeters on your screen. To specify measurements, choose Image Attributes from the Options menu. Click the Units box for inches or centimeters and type 1 in the Width field. Now click pels in the Units field and note the value in the Width field. Click Cancel to close the Image Attributes box.

Use the value you found in the previous steps to paint objects that conform to the inch or centimeter scale. For example, if your screen has 96 pels per inch, create a line or box 96 pels in width and print it. This assumes that the Use Printer Resolution check box on the Print dialog box is not enabled. If it is, the pixels on the screen are matched one-to-one with the dots of your printer. In that case, you would need to draw a line or create a box to match your printer. For example, if you have a 300dpi laser printer, draw a box on the screen that is 300 pixels wide, then print it at the printer's resolution to create a 1-inch box.

Clearing the Canvas

You can clear the canvas at any time to start a new painting or remove unwanted art by using one of the following methods:

- Double-click the Eraser. You'll be asked if you want to save the current image if it has been edited since last saved.

- Choose the New option on the File menu.

- Select one of the Cutout tools and surround the image you want to clear, and then choose Cut from the Edit menu.

When New is selected from the File menu, the canvas becomes the color of the currently selected background color. Be sure to select a white background, or the color you want as a canvas, before opening a new document.

When You Need More Room

Canvases that are larger than your screen size will not be completely visible in the Paintbrush window; however, you can use the scroll bars to bring other parts of the picture into view, or you can try one of the following techniques:

- Temporarily remove the Toolbox and Linesize box by choosing Tools and Linesize from the View menu.

- Temporarily remove the color palette by choosing Palette from the View menu.

 Select the tool and color you'll need before removing the Toolbox and color palette.

- Choose Zoom Out from the View menu. In this mode, the entire canvas is visible, but at a reduced size. Use this mode to paste large objects or move objects that are too large to be selected in the normal view. Zoom-out mode techniques are covered later under Pasting Large Objects.

Once you're done moving and pasting objects, you can restore the Paintbrush window to its normal size and put the Toolbox and color palette back in place.

Securing Objects on the Canvas

Objects you paint or objects you paste are not secured or pasted down on the canvas until you click another Paintbrush tool or click elsewhere on the canvas. Until then, you can move them elsewhere or remove them by pressing the BACKSPACE key. In some cases, changes to a painting may be accidentally removed when you scroll or select a zoom mode. Always click another tool or click elsewhere on the canvas after pasting or moving an object.

Copying, Moving, and Saving Cutouts

Use the Scissors and the Pick tool to create *cutouts*. A cutout is a selected object that you can move, copy, and save to disk. Use the Scissors tool to drag around an irregularly shaped object (as shown on the left in the following illustration) and the Pick tool to drag a box around a large area or an item that can be selected without selecting other parts of the canvas (as shown on the right side).

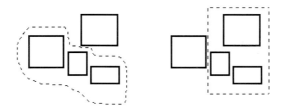

Copying Transparently

You've already seen how to move and copy a cutout. Simply click and drag to move the cutout, or hold the SHIFT key and click and drag to copy the cutout. Notice that cutouts copied in this way are transparent and allow underlying art to show through. You don't need to do anything special to copy cutouts transparently since the default mode is to copy them transparently when dragging cutouts elsewhere on the canvas.

Copying Opaquely

You copy opaquely by clicking with the right mouse button and dragging. The cutout overlaps existing art and does not allow it to show through. The entire area within the cutout border, including the canvas color, is copied. Since the entire area in the cutout is copied, it's best to use the Scissors in most cases to define cutouts, so you can outline the edges of the object.

Saving Cutouts

Save cutouts that you'll need in the future by choosing the Copy To option from the Edit menu. Cutout files saved in this way have the .BMP extension unless you specify otherwise. Use the Paste From command on the Edit menu to paste a previously saved cutout. A pasted cutout can be moved anywhere on the canvas before you paste it down by clicking elsewhere on the canvas.

Use the Copy To option instead of the Save or Save As option to save your paintings. In this way, you can define only the most essential part of the drawing and reduce the amount of disk space it requires.

Using the Painting Tools

The painting tools are used on the canvas to paint boxes and circles or fill them. You can also paint freehand shapes with a brush or an airbrush, and erase any art with the eraser tools.

The Eraser Tool

The Eraser replaces everything in its path with the background color currently selected in the color palette. In most cases, you will set the background color to the canvas color before erasing. To erase small areas, choose the smallest line width in the Linesize box; to erase large areas, choose a large line width. The following illustration shows how the eraser removes all colors. Compare this to the Color Eraser, described next.

To erase small details, choose Zoom In from the View menu and remove colors bit by bit.

The Color Eraser Tool

The Color Eraser replaces the foreground color with the background color. You can drag the Color Eraser on the canvas, or double-click the tool in the Toolbox to replace all instances of the color in the visible window. The following illustration shows how the Color Eraser removes only a specific color.

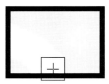

Only the visible part of the canvas is converted when using the double-click method. You must scroll other parts of the painting into view, and then double-click the Color Eraser again.

Airbrush Techniques

The Airbrush sprays a dot pattern of the current foreground color onto your painting. Simply point, click, and drag to paint with the Airbrush. Hold down the

SHIFT key to spray straight along a line and select a line width in the Linesize box to change the width of the spray pattern, as shown here:

Brush Techniques

Use the Brush to paint in a freehand style with different brush shapes and sizes. Double-click on the Brush to open the Brush Shape dialog box, or choose Brush Shapes on the Options menu. Click any one of the brush shapes, and paint in the drawing area for different effects as shown here:

Be sure to select a color in the Palette before you begin painting with the brush and trying different line widths. You can erase with the brush by selecting white as the foreground color. Hold down the SHIFT key to constrain brush strokes.

Roller Techniques

The Roller is used to fill closed areas with the foreground color. Closed areas are completely surrounded by a border, such as a box or circle, or a solid color surrounded by another color. Point the Roller tip into an enclosed area and click. Choose the Undo command if the color spills out of the closed area. You may need to zoom in and add pixels to areas that aren't completely closed up. The following illustration shows the tip of the roller in an enclosed area.

The Text Tool

The Text tool is used to add captions and other text to your paintings. You click the tool, then select a font and font style from the Font menu. As long as the Text tool is still selected, you can make font and style changes to the text you've typed. If a different font is selected, all the text in the current selection changes to that font. You can also change colors while the Text tool is still in use.

Once you click another tool, the text is pasted down and cannot be edited without erasing and starting over. Pasting the text causes it to convert to a graphic image on the canvas. The Text tool uses the currently selected foreground color. Text can only be painted in solid colors, not the mixed colors on the right of the Palette. Paintbrush will select the closest solid color if you choose a mixed color.

The Line Tool

The Line tool is used to paint a straight line at any angle with the currently selected foreground color. To constrain a line, hold down the SHIFT key. The Line tool (like the Curve tool, described next) is used to paint lines using the current color in the palette and the line width selected in the Linesize box.

The Curve Tool

The Curve tool is one of the most interesting tools in Paintbrush. It paints curves using a simple "anchor and pull" technique. You'll need to experiment with the Curve tool to become familiar with its use. Think of the Curve tool as a rubber band stretched between two posts. You first designate the location of the posts, then stretch the line like a rubber band between the posts. Try painting a curved line now by following these steps:

1. Select the Curve tool, a foreground color and a line width.

2. Move the pointer to the canvas, and then click where the first post should be.

3. Hold the mouse button and drag to create a line. Release the mouse to create the second post.

4. Click and hold above or below the line. The line bows out toward the pointer position as shown here:

5. Drag the mouse around on the canvas, and then release the button to set the curve.

6. You can add one more curve. Click below the line as shown here:

7. Drag the mouse around, and then release the button when the curve looks the way you want it to.

You can create an enclosed curve that has a teardrop or airfoil shape by following these steps:

1. For this technique, you don't hold the mouse button and drag a line to the second post. Just click in the canvas to create the first post.

2. Click elsewhere on the canvas to create the second post.

3. Click at a third location on the canvas, then hold and drag the mouse to reshape the curve, as shown here:

4. Release the mouse when the object looks the way you want it to.

Using the Box, Circle, and Polygon Tools

The Box, Circle, and Polygon tools can be either hollow or filled, and can take on the colors in the palette and the width in the Linesize box, as discussed previously. You've already had experience creating boxes and circles. Try the following to create a polygon shape:

1. Click the Hollow Polygon tool in the Toolbox.

2. Click in the canvas, and then drag to another point to draw the first line.

3. Click at another point on the canvas to create a line that connects with the previous line.

4. Continue clicking at random points to expand the polygon, and then click the original starting point.

Clicking at the starting point closes the polygon to form an enclosed space or spaces that can be filled. You must click exactly on the original starting point for the polygon to "close up." Choose the Filled Polygon tool and follow the steps again, creating several sides for the polygon. End by clicking at the starting point. All enclosed spaces created by the polygon are filled. The following illustrates how the tips of a five-pointed star are filled when using the Filled Polygon tool:

Special Techniques

The following techniques can be used to enhance the use of the tools or manipulate objects you've painted on the canvas.

Pasting Large Objects

If you attempt to paste a large object and it doesn't fit, the edges that don't fit are cropped. Zoom-out mode is the only way to paste such objects on your canvas. When you choose Zoom Out from the View menu, the entire canvas is displayed in a reduced size. You can then use the Paste command to place large objects on the canvas and the Pick tool to position them. To move an existing large object, select it with the Pick tool in Zoom-out mode, and then move it.

Sweeping a Cutout

You can "sweep" a cutout across the screen and leave a trail of the cutout in the mouse path. Try it with these steps:

1. Create an object with a Paintbrush tool.

2. Cut out the object with the Scissors or Pick tool.

3. Click the selected object, and hold down the SHIFT key while dragging.

Quickly dragging the mouse pastes the cutouts further apart, as shown on the top row of the following illustration. Slowly dragging the mouse pastes the cutouts closer together, as shown on the bottom in the following illustration:

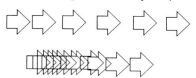

Moving the mouse quickly

Moving the mouse slowly

Cutouts can be swept transparently by holding the left mouse or opaquely by holding the right mouse button.

Shrinking and Enlarging a Cutout

When a cutout is selected, the options on the Pick menu become available. Use the Shrink and Grow option to resize the cutout, and if you want to replace the original cutout with the resized cutout, choose the Clear option. Select the object to size with the Scissors or Pick tool. Choose Shrink + Grow from the Pick menu. Point to a blank area of the canvas, then drag out a small frame with the Pick tool and release the mouse. The selected object is resized within the frame and the original cutout remains intact. Note that Shrink + Grow remains active until you select another tool or click the option on the Pick menu again. Choose the Clear option from the Pick menu to replace the original cutout when you resize it. In this way, you can try several sizes without cluttering the canvas with all your experiments.

You can maintain the proportions of the cutout by holding the SHIFT key when selecting and resizing the cutout.

Tilting Objects

The Tilt option on the Pick menu is used to tilt an object horizontally. Like Shrink + Grow, it stays active until you click another tool or choose Tilt again on the Pick menu to turn it off. Choose the Clear option on the Pick menu to clear the most recent attempt at tilting the cutout. Clear keeps the canvas from becoming cluttered so you can tilt the cutout several times until it looks the way you want it to.

Flipping Cutouts

A cutout can be flipped several ways using the Flip Horizontal and Flip Vertical options on the Pick menu. First select an object with the Scissors or Pick tools, and then select one of the options. Note that you can flip an object four ways by combining the horizontal and vertical flip options.

The best way to learn about the Flip commands is to experiment. Type some text with the Text tool, then select it and choose each flip option.

Inverting Cutouts

The Inverse option on the Pick menu is used to invert the colors of a cutout. One practical use of this feature is to reverse text—that is, change black text against a white background into white text with a black background. Inverting also gives you a way to make copies of cutouts look different by changing their colors.

When inverted, black changes to white and white changes to black. Dark gray changes to light gray and light gray changes to dark gray. Other color changes are as follows.

- Reds and light blues invert respectively
- Yellows and dark blues invert respectively
- Greens and lavenders invert respectively

Parts of the canvas included inside the cutout area are also inverted, so you may need to use the Eraser (or Zoom-in mode) to remove unwanted colors around an object after inverting it.

Creating Custom Colors

You can create (mix) your own colors for use in Paintbrush. When special colors are created, they replace the colors in the color palette. However, color palettes can be saved to disk for future use so you can define several palettes for use in different painting situations.

Editing Colors

To open the Edit Colors dialog box, double-click on the color in the color palette you want to change, or choose Edit Colors from the Options menu. The Edit Colors dialog box in Figure 22-4 is displayed.

The color and numeric value of the current color are displayed in this dialog box. Click and drag the Red, Green, and Blue slider bars to adjust colors until the color you want is displayed in the sample box on the right. You can also type color values

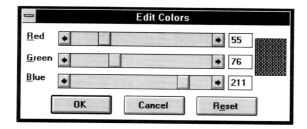

Figure 22-4. *Use the Edit Colors dialog box to create your own custom palette colors*

between 0 and 255 in the number boxes when you know the values of a color you want to create. When the color looks the way you want it to, click OK or press ENTER. The new color then replaces the original color in the palette.

Saving and Retrieving Colors

Save the color palette after you've made changes to it by choosing the Save Colors option on the Options menu. When the Save dialog box appears, type the name for the color palette file. Paintbrush recommends the .PAL extension for the file. To load a customized palette at any time, choose Get Colors from the Options menu.

Saving Your Work

The Save and Save As commands on the File menu are used to save your Paintbrush canvas to a disk file. To save cutouts, choose the Copy To option on the Edit menu.

When saving a file, Paintbrush automatically saves files in the BMP (bitmap) format. You can check one of these other options in the Save File as Type drop-down list box:

- *PCX Paintbrush File* Choose this option when you need to transfer your art to an application that supports the PCX format, but not the Paintbrush .BMP format.

- *Monochrome Bitmap with BMP Extension* Pick this option if your art does not include colors. Files saved in this format use less disk space.

- *16-Color Bitmap with BMP Extension* This is the default Paintbrush file format that supports 16 colors.

The other options on the Save File as Type drop-down list box are not relevant when saving Paintbrush files. They are used when importing art from other applications. After you've picked a file format, type a name for the file in the Filename field, and then click the OK button or press ENTER to save it to disk.

Printing Pictures

The Print option on the File menu is used to print your paintings. The Print dialog box is shown in Figure 22-5.

The following sections explain the features of the Print dialog box:

- To print a selected portion, click the Partial button in the Window box, and then click the OK button. The entire image becomes visible. Drag over the portion of the painting you want to print. When you release the mouse button, the selected portion is printed.

- To print with a different quality, select Draft or Proof in the Quality box. Draft mode is a low-quality, high-speed print mode available with some printers.

- To print multiple copies, type a value other than 1 in the Number of Copies field.

- Graphics can be scaled up or down by entering a new value in the Scaling box. For example, to print art at half its normal size, type **50** in the Scaling box. To double the size of a picture, type **200** in the Scaling box. Art can be scaled to a size that is larger than the paper size. The image will be printed on several sheets that you can tape or paste together.

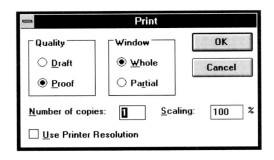

Figure 22-5.   *The Print dialog box for Paintbrush*

- Select the Use Printer Resolution box if you want your painting to print at the resolution of your printer rather than at screen resolution. This sets up a one-to-one relationship between the pixel on the screen and the dot resolution of your printer. On low-resolution printers, the image may print larger than that on the screen, and on high-resolution printers, the image will print smaller.

Since colors are converted to dithered patterns on black-and-white printers, you may want to adjust the intensity controls on the Printer Setup dialog box as discussed under the "Controlling Color Output" section later in this chapter.

Headers and Footers

You can include headers and footers on the printout of your painting by choosing the Page Setup option on the File menu. Type the header or footer in the appropriate box. You can use the following listed codes to include various system parameters or text alignment options:

&d	Inserts the current date
&p	Inserts a page number
&f	Inserts the current filename
&l	Aligns the text to the left margin
&r	Aligns the text to the right margin
&c	Centers the text (default)
&t	Inserts the current time

The Page Setup dialog box also has options for setting the margins on the printed page. The numbers entered in the boxes indicate the amount of space in the margins from the edge of the paper to the text.

Tips and Tricks

Now that you've learned about the features of Paintbrush, you may find the following of interest.

Controlling Color Output

When pictures are printed on black-and-white printers, colors are converted to dot patterns that simulate various shades of gray. The dot patterns may be course or fine, depending on your printer and the setting of the Printer Setup dialog box. You can control the way colors are converted to grays by adjusting the Intensity slider in the Printer Setup dialog box. Chapter 21 described the steps necessary to capture the Paintbrush color palette and print it, and then adjust the printer Intensity Control slider for your printer. If you read through Chapter 21, you may have saved the file with the name COLORBAR.BMP. Refer to Chapter 21 for more information on this subject.

Creating Desktop Tiles

Recall that you can repeat various graphic images on the desktop in a tiled formation. Use Paintbrush to create the graphics, then use the Desktop utility in the Control Panel to tile them on the desktop. Put on your artist's cap and follow these steps:

1. Open a new canvas by choosing New from the File menu.

2. Draw a picture on an area of the canvas that is approximately two inches square. Don't worry about being exact. Remember that images are placed directly next to each other when tiled, so consider how objects or colors will look when organized this way.

3. When you're done painting, choose the Pick tool and select the image. Only select the part you want tiled. You should create objects that will connect properly when tiled. In the following illustration, notice how pillars are carefully selected with the Pick tool so that when placed side-by-side in a tile arrangement, they will connect. This image produces a "Greek condominium" effect when tiled.

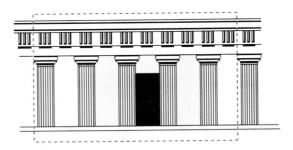

4. Choose Copy To from the Edit menu, and then save the cutout in the Windows directory with the filename extension .BMP.

5. Open the Control Panel and choose the Desktop utility.

6. In the Wallpaper field, pick the file you just created, then click the Tile option and the OK button. Your images will be tiled on the desktop.

Creating Desktop Images

Desktop images can be created in the same way as tiled images, except that you create one image that fills the entire screen, and choose the Center option in the Wallpaper field of the Desktop utility. Follow these steps:

1. Choose Image Attributes from the Options menu.

2. Click the Default button and then click OK. This creates a new canvas that is the size of your screen.

If the canvas is smaller than the screen size, you don't have enough available memory and should not install wallpaper.

3. Paint the image to appear on the desktop. You can also use a scanner or import pictures from other sources.

If you have a scanner, you can create personalized cards or screens by scanning pictures of your kids (or dogs, cats, birds, and so on), and then adding captions under the pictures, such as birthday wishes or important achievements.

4. Save the image using the Save As option on the File menu. Be sure to save the file in the Windows directory with the extension .BMP.

5. Open the Control Panel and choose the Desktop utility.

6. In the Wallpaper field, pick the file you just created, and then click the Center option and the OK button. Your image becomes the desktop wallpaper.

Another idea is to create a file in Write that has important phone numbers and days you can update easily. Capture the Write window by pressing ALT-PRINT SCREEN, *then paste it into Paintbrush and erase the window borders. Save the file, then display it on the desktop. Whenever the information changes, just reopen the Write file you created earlier, make editing changes, and repeat the steps to capture and display the image on the desktop.*

Chapter *23*

Connections and Communications

There are a number of ways you can connect your system to external computers or devices. A few of those ways are listed here:

- A parallel connection to a printer or plotter
- A serial connection to a printer or plotter
- A serial connection to another local computer
- A serial connection to a remote computer over the phone lines using modems
- A network connection to a network file server using special network cabling
- A connection to a mainframe system using various cabling and communications schemes
- A MIDI (Musical Instrument Digital Interface) connection to a piece of musical equipment

The list goes on, but in this chapter we're mainly interested in serial and parallel connections to other systems, to output devices such as printers, and to modems. This chapter begins with the basics of serial and parallel connections, then discusses modems and communications, and finally covers important settings in Windows.

Types of Connections

Chapter 8 explained bits and bytes. Remember that a byte consists of 8 bits (bits are like switches that represent on or off states) and a byte can generally be considered the amount of memory required to store a single character. Sending a character from one place to another requires transfer lines, whether you're transferring that character inside the computer or externally. These transfer lines form the *data bus* of the computer or the external cables that connect peripheral devices. The method used to transfer information depends to some extent on the number of transfer lines or wires. We'll concentrate on the external connections from here on.

If a data transfer is done over a single wire, it is referred to as a *serial* transfer because each bit of a byte is sent over the cable in single file. This is a very elementary description of the process since various encoding and compression schemes are normally used to send data serially over a telephone line, thus increasing throughput. However, for this discussion, it's easier to envision the bits "marching" across the line in single file. Serial communications requires that bytes be "unassembled" by the serial interface card, sent across the line, and reassembled by the receiving system's serial interface card. This takes time, and the transfer rate is slow compared to the parallel method discussed next. However, as you'll see, various methods of encoding and compressing data dramatically improve transmission speed.

 This does not imply that a serial cable has only one wire. In fact, up to 25 wires are used to send various signals besides the data itself. For example, some wires are used to signal a pause or resumption of data transfer by the receiving device.

If you picture a serial transfer as taking place on a single-lane highway, you can picture a *parallel* transfer as taking place on a multilane freeway. A parallel cable consists of multiple data transfer wires. The de facto standard for parallel data exchange between computers and peripherals such as printers is the Centronic parallel interface used on the first IBM Personal Computer. It provides eight parallel data lines plus additional lines for control and status information. The important point is that 8 bits are sent across the cable at the same time.

The transfer lines between the chips on the motherboard of your computer are typically parallel lines 16 or 32 bits wide. There is an obvious speed advantage to parallel transfer lines and they are used almost exclusively for local communications between devices. Serial communications methods are used more commonly when connecting with the outside world over the phone lines. In this case, a *modem* is required to convert the computer's digital signal into the analog signals that can be carried between computers via phone lines. You'll learn more about modems later in this chapter under the "Telecommunications and Modems" section.

Connection Ports

Your computer has both parallel and serial ports with which to connect to external devices. Almost all personal computer systems have at least one parallel and one serial port. These are named LPT1 (line printer 1) and COM1 (communications port 1). Some systems have a second serial port called COM2. DOS reserves the port names LPT2, LPT3, COM3, and COM4 for any additional ports you might add to your system.

As the name implies, the LPT ports were designed as connectors for printers. Sometimes they are used for other devices such as network connectors or even the Disney Sound Source (an external sound device). You'll find parallel port connections to be trouble free because they have become so standardized.

The connection of serial devices is a different matter. The interface is defined by a standard (Electronic Industries Association RS-232-C), but manufacturers of serial equipment often implement it differently. The RS-232-C standard defines the specific lines and signal characteristics used to transfer data between devices. Additional standards (RS-422/423/449) define transmissions over 50 feet.

When making serial connections, always purchase a cable that is specifically designed for the equipment you are connecting. The pins and lines required for a successful connection may be defined differently by various equipment manufacturers. You also need to check the connectors required for the equipment. Some are 9-pin and some are 25-pin. Generally, the cable connector that plugs onto the back of your PC is either a 9-pin or 25-pin female connector. The modem side of the connector uses a 9-pin or 25-pin male connector.

Connecting Two Computers Together

File transfers are possible between systems connected with the right cables and using the right software. The first step is to connect the serial ports of both systems together. You can then start a communications package on each system and use file transfer options and commands to send or receive files between the two. This method is useful when you need to transfer a large number of files. Of course, if the systems are connected to a network, you can transfer files over the network, eliminating the need for serial connections.

Windows Terminal provides options for doing this type of file transfer using serial cables. (The last section of this chapter is devoted to Windows Terminal, so you'll learn what it is and how to use it shortly.) Even better are utilities such as hDC Disk Share, which has an easy-to-use menu specifically designed for transferring files between systems. If you plan to share files in this way, you'll need a cable that lets the two computer ports connect together. The hDC utility lets you transfer files via the serial or parallel port, provided you have the correct cable. The cables are available from hDC.

To connect the serial ports between two systems, purchase a *null-modem* cable with the appropriate connectors from your local electronics store. This type of cable connects the transfer line of one system to the receive line of another. Order either a 9-pin or 25-pin female connector for each end.

Telecommunications and Modems

As mentioned in the beginning of the chapter, a modem is the device that lets you connect with other systems via telephone. The primary job of the modem is to convert the digital data of your computer into analog signals like those used on phone lines. The digital information is *modulated* into waveforms by a modem at one end and *demodulated* by another modem at the other end. ("Modem" is short for modulator/demodulator.)

The world of telecommunications is filled with concepts and terminology that easily confuse. You may have heard stories from other users who had problems connecting to other systems using modems, but don't worry. If you follow two simple rules, you'll avoid many problems:

- Always make sure the cable that connects the modem to your computer has the correct configuration.

- Make sure the communications protocols and settings (baud rate, number of bits, and so on) for your system match the settings of the remote system. If you're not sure, call the administrator of the remote system before starting your session.

Communication Settings

When discussing communications on personal computers, computer users generally refer to *asynchronous transmissions.* This is a form of data transmission that sends information one character at a time. Each character is separated by bits that indicate the start of a new character to the receiving system. This eliminates the need to synchronize a clock signal between the two systems (using a clock signal, or determining the separation of characters based on a time factor is called *synchronous communications*). In asynchronous transmissions, each transmitted character consists of a start bit, data bits, and a stop bit as shown in Figure 23-1. (There's also a parity bit, which you'll learn about soon.)

The settings of a communication session determine exactly how the serial data is sent and received, and how it is checked for errors. Both systems must be in agreement on these settings, otherwise communications will fail. The settings are

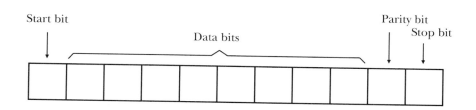

Figure 23-1. *Asynchronous transmission coding scheme*

made when you start your communications software and set up for a communication session. Each setting is described next, and is followed by a few recommendations.

Baud and Bits-per-Second

The term *baud* comes from telegraphy and was originally used when measuring the dots and dashes used to transmit messages. In serial communications, baud is a measure of the number of times the line changes states to represent either a binary 0 or binary 1. This change in state is actually a change in frequency on the line. Picture the serial cable as a neon light, flashing rapidly between two levels of brightness with each flash representing either a 0 or 1. You can think of a baud as measuring the speed at which the light switches between dim and bright. So keeping in mind that baud measures only the rate of change between two states, you'll see why a more accurate method of measuring data by the number of bits per second (bps) is used.

Transfer rates above 300 baud are typically measured using bits per second rather than baud. Bits per second must be used when measuring the *throughput* (transfer rate) of high-speed modems because the modems encode each baud (change of state) to represent 2 or more bits. Not only does this give a higher transfer rate, but it's also necessary because public telephone lines restrict the modulation of the line to about 1200 baud. Encoding helps achieve higher transfer rates. Modem manufacturers use a technique called *phase shift keying* that varies the phase of a signal, rather than its frequency. This method can represent 2 or more bits with each change in the state of the line. It is handled automatically by the modem. For example, a typical 1200 bits-per-second modem really operates at 600 baud using the phase shift keying method. Each change in the line can represent 2 bits, so the modem is rated as 1200 bps.

The important point is that a baud can represent more than one digital bit when encoding is used. This encoding technique has expanded to provide even higher data rates. In fact, a single baud can contain up to 16 bits and thus represent up to

16 values using the *quadrature amplitude modulation* (QAM) technique defined by the CCITT (Comité Consultatif Internationale de Télégraphie et Téléphonie). The CCITT is a Geneva-based standard organization established as part of the United Nations International Telecommunications Union. Its recommendations have become the standard for worldwide communications, as you'll see later in this chapter.

Each of the 16 values or states of the line in a QAM transmission can represent one of 16 binary values (0000, 0001, 0010, and so on). The techniques can provide transfer rates on normal analog telephone lines up to 9600 bps. Other methods for compressing data and improving data transmission exist, but full coverage of telecommunications is a book in its own right.

Note that the term baud is still commonly used to specify the initial transmission settings when establishing a communications session. Set the values to the highest rate your system can handle and forget about it. Once the two modems start talking to each other, they determine exactly what transmission rate and method are appropriate and set themselves accordingly.

Other Values

There are a few other values you'll need to set when establishing a communications session, but in most cases, these values are only important when you're first calling the remote system. Modems that use encoding and compression methods ignore some of these settings once the connection is established. Refer to Figure 23-1.

The Start Bit   A single bit is used in a transmission to signal the start of another character. Set start bits at 1 if you're not sure.

Data Bits   Data bits are a group of bits, usually 7 or 8, that represents the character or the encoding of the data being transmitted.

The Parity Bit   The parity bit is used as an error-checking mechanism. The sending system sets a bit to specify whether the total number of data bits, plus the parity bit, is even or odd. The receiving system then determines whether the number of data bits it receives is even or odd. Depending on the method used, a lack of parity indicates a transmission error and signals the sending system to retransmit the data. The most commonly used parity methods are described next, but keep in mind that most modems today use their own error-checking routines, so "no parity" is a typical setting.

- *Even parity*   The parity bit is set to 1 to make the total number of 1s in the data bits group, plus the parity bit, even.

- *Odd parity*   The parity bit is set to 1 to make the total number of 1s in the data bits group, plus the parity bit, odd.

- *No parity* Parity checking is not used.

You'll often see two additional parity options, Space and Mark. Space always sets the parity bit to 0 and Mark always sets it to 1. Set these options only if the remote system is set the same way.

Stop Bits Stop bits are one or more bits that signal the end of a character. Stop bits usually immediately follow the data bits of a character. There may be 1, 1.5, or 2 stop bits, depending on the convention used. Set stop bits at 1 if you're not sure.

Recommended Settings

The use of 7 data bits and even or odd parity checking is a somewhat dated standard for data communications that is still sometimes used. You may need to set these values to initially establish communications with a remote system. Use 8 data bits and no parity checking if possible. Always use the highest baud rate that both systems will support unless the telephone lines in your area are "noisy" and produce a lot of communications errors. Parity checking is not required when using 8 data bits, and in most cases, error checking is handled by software or the modem at higher levels in the transmission, not at the bit level. Here are the two most likely settings:

Start bits=1, data bits=7, parity=even, stop bits=1

Start bits=1, data bits=8, parity=none, stop bits=1

Most communications software automatically sets the start and stop bits to 1 as a default. All you need to do is specify the baud rate, data bits, and parity method to initially establish the session.

Communications Protocol or Handshaking

The communications settings discussed previously determine how data is assembled for transmission. A communications protocol, or *handshaking method*, sets the rules for the exchange of data between the two computers. A protocol called XON/XOFF is a basic handshaking method used to start or stop transmissions of data. In the case of a printer connected to your system with a serial cable, the printer sends an XOFF signal using a specific wire (pin) on the cable when its buffer is full. This signals the computer to stop sending data until the printer can catch up. When the printer is ready for more data, it sends an XON signal.

A software handshaking method is used when modems talk to other modems. The XON/XOFF signals are part of the data transmitted over the lines, not a hardware signal on a separate wire. Remember that telephone transmissions are accomplished using only one wire, so all the information, including the data and the protocol signals or messages, are part of the data stream.

When the computer needs to send commands to the modem, a standard set of commands is normally used. These commands were originally defined by Hayes and are called the *Hayes Standard AT Command Set*. They are used to get the attention of the modem and control it. You can send the commands yourself from the DOS command line. For example, you could send a command to make the modem dial a number, or to make it stand by and wait to answer an incoming call.

Typically, these commands are handled by the communications software, however. While not all modems support the AT command set, it's a feature you should look for to maintain compatibility with software packages.

When a session is first established, the modems negotiate to determine the transfer rate, error-correction method, compression, and protocols required to maintain and manage the session. The transfer rate is usually the highest rate common to both modems. Once the settings are made, the communications software package takes over and makes itself available to the user. The user can then communicate with the remote system or user and exchange files.

Encoding and Compression Techniques

As mentioned previously, the CCITT has been responsible for establishing worldwide modem standards for communications. The CCITT is largely responsible for the standardization of the encoding schemes used over telephone wires. Without such a standard, high-speed transfers would be limited to modems made by the same manufacturer unless you established, in advance, the exact encoding and compression you wanted to use with the owner or manager of the remote system. Communications standards like those defined by the CCITT turn this task over to the modems.

The most important standards defined by CCITT are listed next. You don't absolutely need a modem that supports these standards to communicate with another system. However, to get the highest transfer rates that include data compression and worldwide support, make sure the modem you purchase supports these standards. Note that this is only a partial list. Other standards support special-purpose leased lines and synchronous communications (based on time intervals), rather than asynchronous (based on number of characters at a time).

A duplex transmission *is one that takes place simultaneously between sender and receiver. In contrast, a* simplex transmission *transmits in just one direction at a time.*

Standard Protocols

The following protocols are widely used and do not include enhanced error checking or compression techniques as discussed in the next sections.

- *V.22* A 1200 bps, full-duplex protocol.

- *V.22bis* A revision of the V.22 protocol that provides 1200 and 2400 bps transmission.

- *V.32* A full-duplex 9600 bps protocol.

- *V.32bis* A revision of the V.32 standard that provides full-duplex modulation standard with rapid renegotiation and speeds of 7200, 12,000, and 14,400 bps.

Error-Checking Protocols

The following error-checking routines provide enhanced performance in error checking.

- *MNP 2, 3, and 4* Proprietary, licensed error-checking protocols developed by Microcom that are widely implemented.

- *V.42* A CCITT-developed, MNP-compatible error-checking protocol.

Compression Protocols

The data compression protocols are important because they offer a method of increasing throughput that goes beyond encoding. Compression removes excess space and replaces commonly repeated data with tokens or place holders. When data compression is used with a 9600bps modem, throughput can increase to 38,400 bps.

- *MNP 5* A Microcom-developed, proprietary, licensed protocol for data-compression.

- *V.42bis* An international standard for data compression. Throughput with V.42bis can be almost four times greater than with normal V.42.

Other Compression Methods

If you don't have a modem that compresses data, you can use software that compresses files before you send them. Compression software has the added benefit of combining a group of files into a single file, making the transfer session easier to handle. Data compression can reduce the transmit time by 50 percent in most cases. You can also use compression utilities to archive old files by packing them, then copying them to floppy disks.

A popular compression utility is PKZIP from PKWARE, Inc. It is a shareware product that you pay for if you use it. PKZIP is available on most bulletin boards and is the software of choice for packing and unpacking (PKUNZIP) files you upload or download from bulletin boards. You can contact PKWARE in Glendale, Wisconsin.

File Transfer Protocols

Communications programs implement one or more of the file transfer protocols listed next. These protocols manage the transfer of the file and perform error checking to ensure that the file is not altered in any way during the transmission. The protocols listed are industry standards and are in the public domain, meaning they are available for all to use without a license. The protocols must match between the systems. Of course, you can transfer a simple ASCII text file without using a protocol, but there will be no error detection and correction. You should always use a protocol when transferring compressed files, program files, or any file with control characters.

CSERVEB+   The CSERVEB+ protocol was designed for use on the CompuServe information system. The remote system controls the entire file transfer process.

KERMIT   The KERMIT protocol is used widely as a means of transferring information between microcomputers and mainframes. Information is transmitted in variable-length units (packets) up to 96 bytes long. Each packet is checked for errors. Control characters in text files are transmitted as normal ASCII characters, which prevents them from being misinterpreted.

XMODEM   XMODEM is the first widely accepted file transfer protocol and is supported by most systems. Use XMODEM if you're unsure which protocol to use. XMODEM transfers 128-byte blocks of information and assigns each frame a sequential block number that is used to report errors or duplications in transmission. Each block contains a 1-byte checksum (a sum of the data-bits) used to detect errors.

XMODEM CRC   XMODEM CRC is an enhanced XMODEM protocol that uses a 2-byte cyclical redundancy check (CRC) to detect transmission errors. CRC error checking calculates a number based on the data to transmit and the receiving system compares this number to its own calculation on the data bits to check for transmission errors.

XMODEM 1K   XMODEM 1K is another version of XMODEM that is specifically designed for large, long-distance file transfers. Transmissions are made in 1024-byte (1K) blocks and completely error checked.

YMODEM   YMODEM is a variation of XMODEM 1K. It transfers files in 1024-byte blocks and provides CRC (cyclical redundancy checking) just like XMODEM CRC does. In addition, it can send multiple files (batch-file transmission) and has the ability to abort transfer by transmitting two cancel characters in a row.

ZMODEM ZMODEM is another enhancement to the XMODEM protocol. It includes a feature called checkpoint restart that resumes transmission where an interrupt occurs, rather than at the beginning of the file, if the communications link is lost and then restored.

Terminal Emulations

Windows uses *terminal emulation* to imitate a terminal, which is a standard screen and keyboard device that conforms to various industry standards. Terminal emulation is used primarily to make a microcomputer look like a specific type of terminal to the remote system, thus simplifying communications. The primary terminal emulations are VT-52, VT-100, VT-200, and VT-320. The VT terminals were originally manufactured by Digital Equipment Corporation. Use one of them when connecting a personal computer with a mainframe system. If you're not sure which to use, try VT-100.

Most communications software packages also offer an ANSI terminal emulation that you use when connecting to bulletin boards. The ANSI mode is defined by the American National Standards Institute, an organization that develops standards in areas ranging from hard drive interfaces to programming languages. ANSI terminal emulation has the ability to display colors and reverse or flashing text.

A bare-bones emulation called TTY (teletypewriter) treats your system as if it is a basic teletypewriter. No special characters or color modes are possible, but it's your best bet if the other emulation modes won't work.

The UART

Most users of the original IBM PC didn't pay much attention to the lowly serial port in their system. If they connected a modem (usually 300 or 1200 bps), the board did its job of transferring data between the modem and the system. The serial card that the port is attached to is the active element in the data transmission process. It converts blocks of data into serial streams for transmission, and then sends that data out to the modem, which modulates it for transfer over phone lines. The work of converting the data to serial I/O is handled by a device called a *Universal Asynchronous Receiver/Transmitter*, or UART for short.

The UART relieves the processor in your system of the need to handle bit transfers for serial communications. Characters sent to the UART can essentially be forgotten. The UART handles the byte conversion in the background. It contains both a transmitter and receiving section to handle the two-way transfer of data between systems. The UART is almost universally used for serial communications and it is safe to say that where there's an RS-232 (or higher) interface, there's a UART.

To determine what type of UART your system has, run the MSD (Microsoft Diagnostic) utility, as discussed in Appendix F.

Upgrading the UART

The UART most commonly found on the serial cards of PC and XT systems is the National Semiconductor 8250, and the UART on the serial card of 80286 and above systems is typically the National Semiconductor 16450. The latest chip in this series is the 16550, and it offers vastly improved performance for serial communications. What's more, it is pin-compatible with the older chips, so in most cases you can replace the slower chips on your existing serial interface cards with the 16550. Note that IBM PS/2 systems with Micro Channel Architecture already use the 16550. If the chip is soldered on the board, you can't replace it, and on older PCs, it probably is not worth upgrading because the slow 8088 and 8086 processors can't handle the faster throughput provided by a 16550 chip.

You'll also need a modem that operates at 9600 bps or above to make the upgrade worthwhile. If your transmission speed is slower than 9600 bps, say 2400 bps, you'll do just as well by keeping the existing UART in your system.

As mentioned, the UART converts parallel data to serial data, and vice-versa. In addition, the UART generates interrupts (requests to the CPU for servicing) that tell the CPU that it either needs more data that it can send or has data from a receive operation. UARTs produced prior to the 16550s generate one of these interrupts for every byte of data they receive or need to send. The constant interruption of the CPU can slow performance. The 16550 adds a pair of 16-byte buffers (one for send, one for receive) so it's capable of sending or receiving 16 bytes at a time. Since the data is processed on a first in/first out (FIFO) basis, the buffers are referred to as FIFO buffers. With the FIFO buffer, the CPU has to service the UART less so performance increases. To paraphrase Intel's Thom Culbertson, it's like making one trip to the store to get five items instead of making five trips and getting one item each trip.

Multitasking under Windows benefits from the added 16550 FIFO buffer, but only under Windows version 3.1. Previous versions of Windows used the chip as if it were an 8250. The FIFO buffers must be accessed by software; therefore, a Windows communications package must specifically provide 16550 support to take advantage of its features. Windows Terminal does not provide 16550 support. (More about Windows Terminal shortly.) However, most of the popular communications packages for Windows have been or are being upgraded to support the chip.

Replacing the UART

If you decide to upgrade the UART, first make sure the UART is unsoldered. Pull the chip off, then pick up a new 16550 at your local electronics store and slip it into the vacant socket. Here are the numbers for the UARTs and some compatible models:

- National Semiconductor 16550AFN

- Silicon System 73M550

- Texas Instruments 16c550

If the UART is soldered, you can try another approach. Replace your existing serial card with an inexpensive model that has a socketed chip, and then replace the chip. If your system has a multifunction card that includes a disk drive controller, parallel port, and serial port, disable one of the serial ports and add a separate serial card.

Hayes Microcomputer Products makes a board called the ESP that includes two serial ports for simultaneously sending and receiving data. It has an Intel 8031 coprocessor and 1K of buffer memory, and includes special drivers that send incoming data directly to the memory of your system.

The FIFO buffers are automatically recognized by Windows. However, if for some reason you need to set the FIFO buffer off for a specific serial port, set the COMxFIFO lines in the [386Enh] section of SYSTEM.INI to false (0). Replace x with a number (1, 2, 3, or 4) to refer to COM1, COM2, COM3, and COM4 respectively. For example, to set the FIFO buffer off for COM1, change the COM1FIFO= line to the following:

```
COM1FIFO=0
```

Recall that Windows applications automatically use the 16550 UART. However, Windows does not enable the 16550 for MS-DOS applications. When running in 386 enhanced mode, 16550-aware DOS communication applications may not detect the chip and use it properly, because Windows is buffering the port for the application. To enable the 16550 for the DOS application, disable the buffering by changing the COMxBuffer= line in the [386Enh] section of SYSTEM.INI. The x refers to the port number (1, 2, 3, or 4). For example, to set buffering off for COM1, change the COM1Buffer= line to the following:

```
COM1Buffer=0
```

Some communications applications will replace the Windows COMM.DRV file with their own file, which may not provide proper UART support. Always use the

Windows COMM.DRV file unless the application's driver has features required by your application or is specifically described as being superior to the Windows driver. If you have to use a Windows 3.0 driver to make your application run, add the following line to the [386Enh] section of SYSTEM.INI:

```
COMdrv30=1
```

COM Ports and Interrupts

The COM ports are configured in Windows with the Ports utility on the Control Panel as shown here:

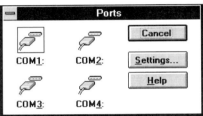

The four potential serial ports your system can have are shown in the dialog box. To change a port's settings, double-click its icon, or highlight it and click the Settings button. A dialog box similar to the one shown here appears.

In general, you only need to change these settings when configuring a serial printer. Use the options in a communications package to change serial port settings if you are connecting with a local computer or remote system. Each setting was described in the section called "Other Values." Click the down arrow button on each field to see a list of options. In the Flow Control field, select Xon/Xoff in most cases, unless the printer or other device specifically controls the flow of data.

The Advanced Settings

The advanced settings are important if you have more than two serial ports in your system. The original IBM PC supported COM1 and COM2 and provided standard I/O port addresses and interrupts for them. COM3 and COM4 were added later, but they were assigned interrupts that can conflict with COM1 and COM2 as shown in Table 23-1.

Notice that COM1 uses the same interrupt as COM3, and COM2 uses the same interrupt as COM4. This is only a problem when you install the extra ports and then attempt to run multiple applications in Windows 386 enhanced mode, or when you have a mouse connected to one of the ports. For example, a device on COM1 such as a modem would conflict with a mouse on COM3. This interrupt conflict was allowed because the early PCs had a shortage of interrupts, and usually only ran one application at a time anyway, so conflicts were rare except in the case of the mouse.

IBM PS/2 Micro Channel systems and EISA bus systems allow interrupt sharing and do not have a problem with interrupt conflicts in Windows 386 enhanced mode.

To avoid the conflicts when running applications in 386 enhanced mode on ISA (not MCA or EISA systems), change the hardware settings of the COM3 and COM4 ports and use the Ports utility to specify their new settings to Windows. You need to have a card that allows you to change the settings by moving jumpers or setting switches. After changing the interrupt or I/O address, use the Advanced options on the Port utility to specify the new interrupts and addresses to Windows.

Port	Address	IRQ
COM1	03F8h	4
COM2	02F8h	3
COM3	03E8h	4
COM4	02E8h	3

Table 23-1.   *Common I/O Port Addresses and Interrupts*

Click the Advanced button on the Settings dialog box to display the Advanced Settings for COM1: dialog box shown here:

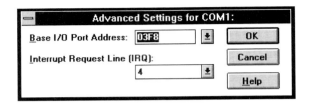

Click the down arrow buttons on the field to change the settings of the I/O port address and interrupt. These settings should not conflict with any other devices you have in your system. If you're not sure which settings to use, you can run the MSD utility discussed in Appendix F. If you make a setting that conflicts with another, your system may fail to boot. Look in the owner's manual of each adapter card, or look at the jumper settings on the card itself.

Microsoft recommends that you always use the lower numbered ports before using the higher numbered ports. Place the devices that need the best performance on the port that has the lowest interrupt number (COM2 or COM4 if using the defaults) to gain better service from the CPU.

Settings in SYSTEM.INI

The following settings can be made in the SYSTEM.INI file. Some are automatically set using the Ports utility, or the 386 Enhanced Mode icon in the Control Panel. Some are set during Windows setup. Note that the x in some settings is used to indicate the serial port number, as in COM1, COM2, COM3, and COM4. If a Boolean operator is required, use 1 to enable the option and 0 to disable it.

COMBoostTime=*milliseconds*   This option specifies the amount of time (in milliseconds) to allow a virtual machine to process a COM interrupt. If a communications application is losing keyboard characters on the display, increase this setting using Notepad. The default is 2.

COMdrv30=*Boolean*   Enable this setting only if you are using a Windows 3.0 serial communications driver. Leave the option disabled (its default) if you are using the standard Windows 3.1 serial communications driver (COMM.DRV). When this option is enabled, the Virtual COM Driver (VCD) will use its own copy of the serial communications driver's interrupt handler and improve the performance of your COM ports.

COMIrqSharing=*Boolean*   This option is enabled for Micro Channel and EISA machines, which share interrupts cooperatively. It should be disabled, however, for ISA machines.

comm.drv=*filename*   This option specifies the filename of the serial communications driver you are using.

COM*x*Buffer=*Boolean*   As discussed previously, set this option to 0 to disable Windows' buffering of a serial port when a DOS communication application can't access a 16550 UART.

COM*x*Base=*address*   This option determines how contentions for devices by non-Windows applications are handled. Set this option using the 386 Enhanced utility in the Control Panel. Pick the port, then specify its contention value as discussed in Chapter 19.

COM*x*FIFO=*Boolean*   Use this option to specify whether the FIFO buffer of a COM port's 16550 Universal Asynchronous Receiver Transmitter (UART) should be enabled or disabled. The FIFO buffers are enabled by default. If a serial port does not have a 16550 UART, this setting is ignored.

These values are used by Windows for both standard and enhanced modes.

COM*x*Irq=*n*   Set *n* to one of the default interrupt values of the I/O ports listed in Table 23-1. Use the Ports utility to change these settings.

COM*x*Protocol=XOFF   Set this option for a port to XOFF if a communications application using that port is losing characters while doing text transfers at high baud rates. Leave this setting disabled if the application is doing binary data transfers. Enabling this switch might suspend binary transmissions. If the application continues to lose characters after this setting is properly set, try increasing the COM*x*Buffer value.

Int28Filter=*n*   Set *n* to the percentage of INT28h interrupts, generated when the system is idle, that are made visible to software that is loaded before Windows. The default is 10. Windows will reflect every *n*th interrupt, where *n* is the value of this setting. Increasing this value might improve Windows' performance, but may interfere with some memory-resident software such as a network. Set this value to 0 to prevent INT28h interrupts. Note that setting this value too low might interfere with communications applications. Use Notepad to edit the SYSTEM.INI file.

MaxCOMPort=*n*   This option specifies the maximum number of COM ports supported in enhanced mode. The default is 4. Change this value if you have more than four COM ports installed in your computer.

Windows Terminal

Windows Terminal is a communications program you can use to connect with local or remote systems to exchange files or use the resources of the remote system. To use Terminal, you'll need a null-modem cable to connect to another system in your office, or a modem to connect over phone lines.

To start Terminal, double-click its icon in the Program Manager. The first time you start it, the Default Serial Port dialog box shown here appears, asking what serial port it should use:

Click a port name and the OK button.

Next, you see the Terminal window. It contains a set of menu options and a workspace. The workspace holds the dialog between your system and the system you're attached to. As you type text during a session, you'll see the text appear in the workspace. Any messages received from the remote system also appear in the workspace.

A communications session with another user usually begins by calling that user and agreeing on the initial settings for baud rate, parity, and stop bits. After you've agreed on these settings, choose Communications from the Settings menu to open the Communications dialog box shown in Figure 23-2.

Set these options according to the previous discussion in the "Baud and Bits-per-Second" section. Remember that for most high-speed modems, these settings are

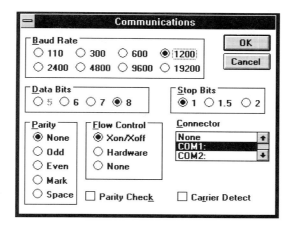

Figure 23-2.   *Use the Communications dialog box to change modem settings*

only used to get the communications session going. After making a connection, the modems usually synchronize themselves to the best communication settings.

When the proper settings are made and you're ready to dial the remote system, choose the Dial command on the Phone menu. The Phone Number dialog box shown here appears:

Type the phone number, along with any codes you may need if dialing an outside number. Separate these codes with a comma. For example, to dial an outside number, you might type **9,,19998887777**. Note that the 1 is included for long-distance access. The commas provide a four-second delay (two seconds per comma). The Timeout If Not Connected In field specifies how long Terminal should ring the remote system. The default is 30 seconds. Enable Redial After Timing Out if you want it to keep dialing if the system is currently busy. Enable Signal When Connected if you want to hear a beep when connected.

If your system initiates a call, then the remote system must stand by in auto-answer mode, which means it must be ready to answer your call when it comes in. Bulletin boards such as CompuServe are already waiting for your call. If a remote user calls your system, and thus incurs the phone charges of the session, type the following command in Terminal's workspace and press ENTER to place Terminal in auto-answer mode.

```
ATQIEOSO=1
```

This sends a Hayes command language auto-answer command to the modem. If your modem is not Hayes compatible, refer to your owner's manual for the correct command.

Once you're connected with a remote system, you can proceed with your online activities. If you are transferring files, refer to the section on "Online Activities" later in this chapter. To end a session, choose Hang-Up from the Phone menu, but if you're connected to an online service such as CompuServe, first make sure it knows you are hanging up. Otherwise, it may continue to charge you for connect time until it realizes you are no longer connected. In most cases, type **BYE** or **EXIT** to end your session, and then choose the Hang-Up command.

Customizing Terminal

There are a number of ways to customize Terminal. You can change the features of the window itself, or set options for a communications session. You can save settings to reuse them at a later time. Each option is discussed next.

The Session Timer

Before you begin a session, set the Session Timer on to time the session. To see the Timer, you'll also need to turn the function key display on by choosing Show Function Keys from the Settings menu. A set of ten boxes will appear at the bottom of the screen. The lower-right box contains the system timer. Initially, it shows the normal time. To begin timing a session, choose Timer Mode on the Settings menu. To turn the timer off, select Timer Mode again.

 The timer itself will toggle from clock to timer if you click it. Doing so does not reset the timer.

The Modem Commands Option

Use the Modem Commands option on the Settings menu to select a modem. If you have a Hayes-compatible modem and a touch-tone phone, you don't need to change settings on this menu. Only change the settings in the following cases:

- If you have a dial phone and a Hayes-compatible modem, change the ATDT dialing command to ATDP in the Dial Prefix box, which will initiate pulse dialing.

- If you have a MultiTech, TrailBlazer, or other non-Hayes modem, select one of the options under Modem Defaults. The correct settings are made when you choose MultiTech or TrailBlazer. If you choose None, you'll need to fill in the Commands options with the codes listed in your modem's instruction manual.

Terminal Emulation

Because of the diversity of computer systems, online services and remote systems usually treat your system as if it were a DEC VT-100 ANSI terminal. This lets the remote system interact with your system without having to define any special features. To switch to a different emulation, select Terminal Emulation from the Settings menu. Leave the Terminal Emulation setting at DEC VT-100 unless the remote system specifically requests DEC VT-52 or TTY (TTY is an abbreviation for teletypewriter). Choose TTY to emulate a no-frills "dumb" terminal that displays text only. Special commands that change the screen color or other features are not supported in TTY mode. Use TTY only when connecting to systems that do not support the other modes.

Terminal Preferences Option

Terminal Preferences are set to specify how you want your system to perform during a communications session. The settings are used to control sound, line wrap, and other features. Choose Terminal Preferences from the Settings menu to display the Terminal Preferences dialog box shown in Figure 23-3.

In most cases, you won't need to change these options. However, you can make Terminal display text in a different font by changing the selected font in the Terminal Font box. Refer to the last section of this chapter if you need more details about these settings. Note the following:

- If the remote system is sending lines longer than your system will display, set Line Wrap on.

- If you don't see the characters you type in the Terminal window, set Local Echo on. If you see duplicates of everything you type, set Local Echo off. Duplicate characters may be displayed if the remote system is echoing characters you send back to you for verification.

- If text types over itself after each carriage return instead of starting on a new line, the line-feed portion of a carriage return is missing. If this occurs on your system, click the Inbound box in the CR-> CR/LF box to add a line-feed. If the remote user complains of this problem, check the Outbound box.

- If you are communicating with systems in other countries, you may need to choose a country in the Translation box.

Online Activities

Once you've connected with a remote system, you can begin transferring files, chat with another user, or engage in other online activities. The following sections discuss the various types of file transfers you can perform with Terminal.

Receiving a file from another system is called downloading *a file. Sending a file to a remote system is called* uploading *a file.*

Terminal supports two types of file transfers. The first is the standard text file transfer and the second is the binary file transfer.

Text Files   A *text file* contains standard ASCII characters. ASCII is an industry-wide standard that codes numbers and letters of the alphabet with numeric values. Almost

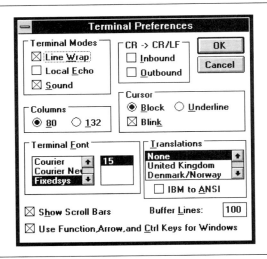

Figure 23-3.   *Use the Terminal Preferences dialog box to change the communication settings for your system*

every computer system recognizes ASCII characters, so you can use Terminal to send text files just about anywhere. Notepad and many other programs create text files.

Binary Files   A *binary file* is typically a program file, or a document file with special formatting and control codes. Binary program files (typically files with the extensions .COM and .EXE) contain executable code that does not conform to ASCII coding schemes. You must send these files using binary protocols.

In most cases, you should transmit all your files, including text files, using binary transfer methods. These provide several advantages over text transfer methods. For example, errors are more thoroughly tested and corrected in binary transfers. In addition, document files that contain formatting codes like those created with Windows Write can be sent to other users with the formatting codes intact.

Sending and Receiving Binary Files

You can choose the XMODEM-CRC protocol or the KERMIT protocol to transfer binary files. Choose Binary Transfers from the Settings menu to make one of these selections.

Remember to use a file compression utility when sending files. A compressed file transmits faster, and you can combine a group of files into a single compressed file. If you receive a compressed file, use a utility to uncompress it. As mentioned earlier under the "Other Compression Methods" section, PKZIP (compress) and PKUNZIP (uncompress) are the most common utilities. Files you download from bulletin boards with the .ZIP extension must be "unzipped" using PKUNZIP.

Uploading Files   To send (upload) a binary file, make sure the remote system is ready to receive the file by issuing an upload command for the service, and then choose Send Binary File from the Transfers menu. The Send Binary File dialog box appears, which looks just like the standard Open dialog box. Select the file to send and click OK.

Downloading Files   To receive a binary file, first select the file you want to receive on the remote system using its commands. The service will notify you that it is ready to download the file. Choose Receive Binary File from the Transfers menu, and then type the name you want to use for the file on your system.

Transmitting Text Files

You may need to transfer a text file using the text transfer method, rather than the binary file method, if the remote system is incapable of transmitting binary files.

Follow the procedure in this section to transmit the files. Choose the Text Transfers option on the Communications menu to display the Text Transfers dialog box shown in Figure 23-4.

Enable the appropriate Flow Control option as discussed in the following sections.

The Standard Flow Control Option

Click the Standard Flow Control option to use the flow control currently selected on the Communications dialog box.

The Character at a Time Option

Click the Character at a Time option to send text files as slowly as possible when there are line problems or the remote system can't keep up with the transfer. When this option is enabled, the additional options below become available.

- *Delay Between Characters* Enable the Delay Between Characters option to transmit at a slow, even rate without verification. If you still have problems with the transmission, increase the delay rate.

- *Wait for Character Echo* Enable the Wait for Character Echo option if you want to verify the transfer of each character. Terminal sends the character to the remote site, then receives it back to verify accuracy.

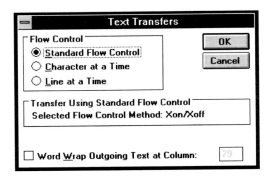

Figure 23-4. *Use the Text Transfers dialog box to change settings when transferring standard text files*

The Line at a Time Option   Enable the Line at a Time option to send text files one line at a time. It is faster than using the Character at a Time option, but if the file is not sent properly, you may need to revert to Character at a Time. When the Line at a Time option is selected, these additional options appear.

- *Delay Between Lines*   Enable the Delay Between Lines option to transmit at a slow, even rate without verification. If you still have problems with the transmission, increase the delay rate.

- *Wait for Prompt String*   Enable the Wait for Prompt String option to wait for a response from the remote system before sending each additional line.

Make sure the settings on the Text Transfer dialog box are set the way you want, and then choose Send Text File from the Transfers menu. Type the name of the file to send in the File Name field. In the Following CR field, enable Append LF Select to add a line-feed to the end of each line of text, or enable Strip LF to remove extra line-feeds from text. Click OK to begin sending the file. As the file is sent, it will appear in the Terminal window.

The control buttons that appear at the bottom of the screen can be used to pause, resume, or stop the transmission of data during a file transfer session.

The Receive Text File Option

To receive a file, make sure the settings on the Text Transfers dialog box are correct, then choose Receive Text File from the Transfers menu. In the File Name field, type the name you want to assign to the file you'll receive. Set the options given next, if necessary, depending on how text should be handled in the file.

The Append File Option   Check the Append File option if you want to append the incoming text to an existing file. You must specify the existing file's name in the Filename box.

The Save Controls Option   If formatting codes are being transmitted with the file, such as those used to change fonts or styles, select the Save Controls option to save the codes. Not all codes can be transmitted.

The Table Format Option   Check the Table Format option if you want Terminal to replace two or more consecutive spaces with a tab.

Click OK to begin receiving text. The file will scroll on the Terminal window as it is received.

You can print incoming data by choosing Printer Echo from the Settings menu.

Viewing a Text File

The View Text File option on the Transfer menu can be used to look at a text file before sending it or after one has been received. Choose View Text File from the Transfer menu, then type the name of the file you want to view. You can specify whether line-feeds should be added or removed by checking the Append LF or Strip LF boxes, respectively. Click OK to view the file.

Working in the Terminal Window

You can type messages or paste information from the Clipboard into the Terminal window to send to the remote location. To send the contents of the Clipboard, choose Paste from the Edit menu. The pasted information is then sent to the remote site. You can also type text in the window, highlight it, then choose Send from the Edit menu to send it to the remote site.

Terminal's Buffer

The Terminal screen is really a large buffer that can be scrolled to see the text and messages of a communication session. You can scroll back through the text and use Cut and Copy commands to copy text to the Clipboard, and then paste it into other documents.

The Printer Echo Option

You can instruct the printer to print all information received during a communications session by choosing Printer Echo on the Settings menu. You'll need to select the option to stop printer echo after the session has ended.

Defining Function Keys

You can define special commands for up to 32 function keys in Terminal. These keys can hold frequently typed text, or commands you execute often when logged onto a system. For example, you can assign the login key sequence for an online service, such as CompuServe, to one of the keys.

To display Terminal's function key labels, select Settings and choose Show Function Keys. Then you can click the buttons or press the function keys on the keyboard to execute their assigned operations. The labels on the screen correspond to function keys F1 through F8. The upper-left label is F1, the lower-left label is F2, and so on. There are four levels of key labels that you can access by clicking the Level label. In Figure 23-5, note the key assignments. Login is the F1 key, Download is F2, and so on. Up to four sets of these buttons can be made visible by clicking on the Level button for a total of 32 function key assignments.

To assign functions or commands to the buttons (and the function keys), choose Function Keys from the Settings menu. You'll see the Function Keys dialog box shown in Figure 23-6. If function keys have already been assigned, their names and commands will appear in this dialog box. To assign a function to a key, type the name you want to appear on the key in the Key Name field, and then type the command or text string in the Command field. The Command field can contain codes as described in "Codes for Defining Function Key Assignments," next.

The Function Keys dialog box shows eight key assignments at a time. To work with the next set of eight key assignments, click the 2 button in the Key Level box. If you want the key labels to appear at the bottom of the screen, enable the Keys Visible check box.

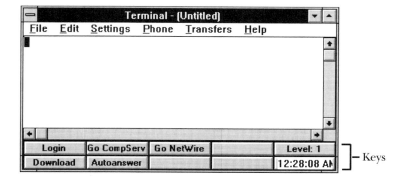

Figure 23-5.   *Key label examples*

Codes for Defining Function Key Assignments

Use the following codes in the Command field of the Function Keys dialog box. You can enter any text after the codes where appropriate.

Code	Result
^M	A carriage return
^A to ^Z	Sends a control code, A to Z, to the remote computer
^$D*nn*	Causes Terminal to delay the specified number of seconds before continuing
^$B	Causes Terminal to transmit a break code of 117 milliseconds in duration
^$C	Chooses Dial from the Phone menu
^$H	Chooses Hang-up from the Phone menu
^$L1 to ^$L4	Changes to another level of key groups in which keys are defined

As an example, look at the command shown here:

^M^$D03^M^$D03*ttt*^M^$D03*nnnnn,nnnn*^M

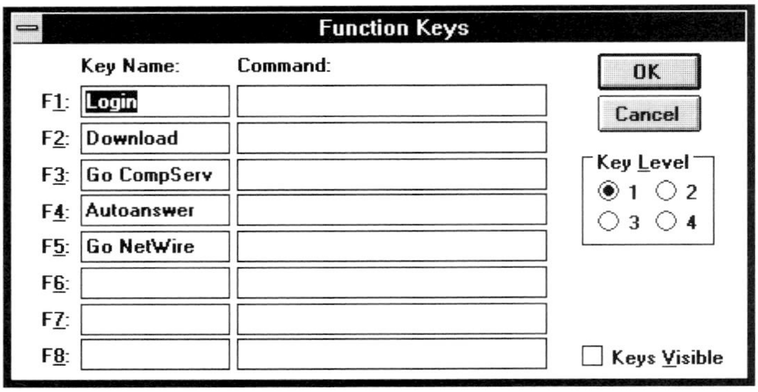

Figure 23-6. The Function Keys dialog box

This is an example of a command assigned to a function key that logs into the CompuServe information service after a connection has been established.

The first command, ^M, is used to type a carriage return, which is usually necessary to get attention from the system. The $D03 command then causes a three-second wait while CompuServe requests the host's name. The variable *ttt* in the command would be the host's name. The next ^M then types a carriage return to accept the host's name, followed by another three-second wait. The *nnnnn,nnnn* variable is the login identification, and the last ^M types another carriage return. CompuServe then asks for a password; however, it is not advisable to keep your password anywhere but in your own head. Don't include it in login scripts.

Chapter 24

Windows Desktop Accessories

Windows comes with the Calculator, Calendar, and Cardfile accessory programs, which provide features and functions very similar to the accessories you might have on your real desktop. You can start each accessory and keep it handy as an icon on the desktop for use at any time during the day.

The Calculator

The Windows Calculator has two operating modes, a Standard Calculator and a Scientific Calculator. Use the Standard Calculator for simple arithmetic. It has a memory feature for storing and accumulating numbers. Use the Scientific Calculator to perform number base conversions, statistical analysis, and trigonometric functions.

Startup and Overview

Load the Calculator by double-clicking its icon in the Program Manager Accessories window. When the Calculator appears, choose either Scientific or Standard from its View menu, depending on which you prefer to work with. The Standard Calculator is shown in Figure 24-1 and the Scientific Calculator is shown in Figure 24-2.

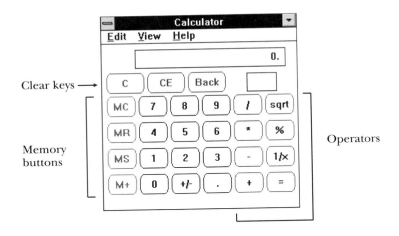

Clear keys

Memory
buttons

Operators

Figure 24-1.   *Choose Standard from the Calculator's View menu to display the Standard
Calculator*

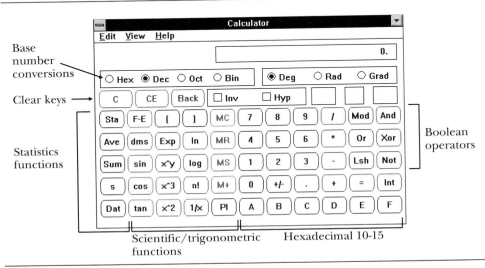

Base
number
conversions

Clear keys

Statistics
functions

Boolean
operators

Scientific/trigonometric
functions

Hexadecimal 10-15

Figure 24-2.   *Choose Scientific from the Calculator's View menu to display the Scientific
Calculator*

The Calculator's Edit menu provides copy and paste functions so you can paste numbers to the Calculator's display from another application, or copy results from the display to other applications.

Using the Keyboard

While you can click any Calculator button with the mouse, you can also perform most functions using keyboard methods, which may be preferable for quick data entry. You can also access most of the function keys from the keyboard. For example, the basic operators (+, −, *, /, =) are available on the keypad.

To use the numeric keypad, make sure NUM LOCK is on.

Function Used by Both Calculators

The standard functions used by both Calculators are shown in Table 24-1.

Button	Key	Function
+	+	Adds
−	−	Subtracts
*	*	Multiplies
/	/	Divides
M+	CTRL-P	Adds the display value to any value already in memory
MC	CTRL-C	Clears any value in memory
MR	CTRL-R	Recalls the value stored in memory (and retains the value in memory)
MS	CTRL-M	Stores the displayed value in memory
+/-	F9	Changes the sign of the displayed number
.	.	Inserts a decimal point in the displayed number
%	%	Calculates percentages
=	=	Executes an operation (or press ENTER)
1/x	R	Calculates the reciprocal of the displayed number
Back	BACKSPACE	Deletes the rightmost digit
C	ESC	Clears the current calculation
CE	DEL	Clears the displayed number
sqrt	@	Calculates the square root of the displayed value

Table 24-1. *Standard Functions Used by Both the Standard and Scientific Calculators*

The square root button is missing in the Scientific Calculator. You can calculate the square root by raising a number to the power of 1/2 using the x-to-power-of-y (x^y) key. Type in the value of x, click the x^y key, and then type in .5 and press ENTER.

Calculation Techniques

Calculations are performed in the normal way by clicking numbers on the calculator keyboard with the mouse, or by using the numeric keypad. The mouse method is assumed for this discussion. For example, to add two numbers, follow these steps:

1. Click the first number.
2. Click the operator (+).
3. Click the second number.
4. Click the Equals button to view the results in the display.

Clearing the Calculator

To clear the Calculator's display and memory so you can start new calculations, do one of these steps:

*   To clear the Calculator's current entries, click on the C (Clear) button, or press ESC.
*   To clear the number currently being entered without clearing previously entered numbers, click CE (Clear Entry), or press DEL.
*   To remove the most recently typed digit, click the Back button on the Calculator, or press BACKSPACE on the keyboard.

Using the Memory Keys

Use the Calculator's memory keys to store numbers for later use or to accumulate totals. There is only one memory. New values placed in memory either replace it, add to it, or subtract from it. The buttons are as follows.

*   *Memory Store (MS)*   The MS button puts the current value in the Calculator's display into memory, replacing any existing value in memory.
*   *M+*   The M+ button adds the current value in the Calculator's display to the value in memory and stores the sum in memory.
*   *Memory Recall (MR)*   The MR button displays the contents of memory.
*   *Memory Clear (MC)*   The MC button clears memory.

Scientific Calculator Functions

The Tables 24-2 through 24-5 explain the use of the advanced functions on the Scientific Calculator. You can click on the Calculator button with the mouse, or use the keystroke listed in the key column.

Scripts for the Calculator

The Calculator Edit menu has options for copying and pasting from the Clipboard. The Copy option is used to copy a calculated result from the Calculator's display that you can then paste to another application. The Paste option can be used to paste a number from another application.

The paste characters listed here are interpreted as key sequences, or function keys, if pasted from the Clipboard. You can take advantage of this feature by creating scripts in Notepad. A *script* is a line of text that the Calculator will interpret as a command.

Paste Characters	Function
:	If placed before a number from 1 to 12, a function key is simulated; for example, 1 becomes F1.
:C	Equivalent to the MC (Memory Clear) button.
:E	If you're in decimal mode, :E allows entry of numbers in scientific notation. Can be followed by + or – to indicate the sign of the exponent.
:M	Equivalent to the MS (Memory Store) button.
:P	Equivalent to the M+ button. Adds the currently displayed value to memory.
:Q	Clears the display. Equivalent to the C button.
:R	Equivalent to the MR (Memory Recall) button.
\	Same as Data button on the Scientific Calculator.

In Figure 24-3, the Notepad accessory is placed on the desktop, next to the Calculator, to create scripts.

The scripts are copied to the Clipboard from Notepad and pasted to the Calculator. In this example, the script multiplies the contents of memory by 10, and displays the result each time they are pasted. The script shown in Notepad uses :R to recall memory which is multiplied by 10; :M is then used to store the new value back in memory, and the result remains in the Calculator's display. Note that 100 was initially stored in memory and that the display shows the results after several iterations.

Button	Key	Function
(	(	Starts a new level of parentheses. The current level appears below the display. The maximum number of levels is 25.
)	)	Closes the current level of parentheses.
And	&	Calculates bitwise AND.
Int	;	Displays the integer portion of a decimal value. Inv+Int displays the fractional portion of a decimal value.
Lsh	<	Shifts left. Inv+Lsh shifts right.
Mod	%	Displays the *modulus*, or remainder, of x/y.
Not	~	Calculates bitwise inversely.
Or	|	Calculates bitwise OR.
Xor	^	Calculates bitwise exclusive OR.

Table 24-2. *Operators on the Scientific Calculator*

Of course you can create more complicated scripts and even create a whole Notepad file full of scripts that you use on a regular basis. Type each script on a separate line so you can easily select and copy it to the Clipboard. For clarity, precede each script with a descriptive name. When using scripts keep in mind that variables are stored in the Calculator's memory.

Button	Key	Function
Bin	F8	Converts to the binary numbering system.
Byte	F4	Displays the lower 8 bits of the current number.
Dec	F6	Converts to the decimal numbering system.
Dword	F2	Displays the full 32-bit representation of the current number.
Hex	F5	Converts to the hexadecimal numbering system.
Oct	F7	Converts to the octal numbering system.
Word	F3	Displays the lower 16 bits of the current number.

Table 24-3. *Number Base Functions on the Scientific Calculator*

Button	Keys	Function
Ave	CTRL-A	Calculates the mean of the values displayed in the Statistics box. Inv+Ave calculates the mean of the squares.
Dat	INS	Enters the displayed number in the Statistics box.
s	CTRL-D	Calculates the standard deviation with the population parameter as n–1. Inv+s calculates the standard deviation with the population parameter as n.
Sta	CTRL-S	Activates the Statistics box and the Ave, Sum, s, and Dat buttons.
Sum	CTRL-T	Calculates the sum of values in the Statistics box. Inv+Sum calculates the sum of the squares.

Table 24-4. *Statistical Functions on the Scientific Calculator*

Number Base Conversions (Scientific Calculator Only)

The Scientific Calculator can be switched from its default base 10 number system to binary, octal, or hexadecimal by clicking one of these buttons:

- Hex (hexadecimal)

- Dec (decimal)

- Oct (octal)

- Bin (binary)

Button	Key	Function
cos	O	Calculates the cosine of the displayed number. Inv+cos calculates the arc cosine. Hyp+cos calculates the hyperbolic cosine. Inv+hyp+cos calculates the hyperbolic arc cosine.
Deg	F2	Sets trigonometric input for degrees. This function is available in degrees only.
dms	M	Converts the displayed number to degree-minute-second format. Calculator assumes the displayed number is in decimal format. Inv+Dms converts the displayed number to decimal format. Calculator assumes the displayed number is in degree-minute-second format.

Table 24-5. *Other Functions on the Scientific Calculator*

Button	Key	Function
Exp	X	Allows entry of scientific notation numbers. The exponent has an upper limit of +307. You can continue to enter numbers as long as you do not use keys other than 0-9. Exp can only be used with the decimal numbering system.
F-E	V	Toggles scientific notation on and off. Numbers bigger than 10^{15} are always displayed exponentially. F-E can only be used with the decimal numbering system.
Grad	F4	Sets trigonometric input for gradients when the Calculator is in decimal mode.
Hyp	H	Sets the hyperbolic function for sin, cos, and tan. The different functions automatically turn off the hyperbolic function after a calculation is completed.
Inv	I	Sets the inverse function for sin, cos, tan, PI, x^y, x^2, x^3, In, log, Ave, Sum, and s. The different functions automatically turn off the inverse function after a calculation is completed.
In	N	Calculates natural (base e) logarithm. Inv+In calculates e raised to the xth power, where x is the current number.
log	L	Calculates common (base 10) logarithm. Inv+log calculates 10 raised to the xth power.
n!	!	Calculates the factorial of the displayed number.
PI	P	Displays the value of PI (3.1415...). Inv+PI displays 2 * PI (6.28...).
Rad	F3	Sets trigonometric input for radians, when in decimal mode. Input can be from 0-2*PI.
sin	S	Calculates the sine of the displayed number. Inv+sin calculates the arcsine. Hyp+sin calculates the hyperbolic cosine. Inv+hyp+sin calculates the hyperbolic arcsine.
tan	T	Calculates the tangent of the displayed number. Inv+tan calculates the arctangent. Hyp+tan calculates the hyperbolic tangent. Inv+hyp+tan calculates the hyperbolic arctangent.
x^y	Y	Computes x raised to the yth power. Inv+x^y calculates the yth root of x.
x^2	@	Squares the displayed number. Inv+x^2 calculates the square root.
x^3	#	Cubes the displayed number. Inv+x^3 calculates the cube root.

Table 24-5.   *Other Functions on the Scientific Calculator (continued)*

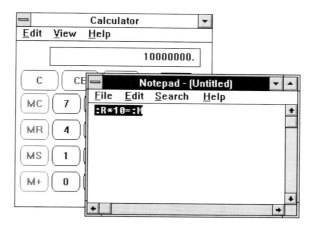

Figure 24-3. *The Notepad accessory placed next to the Calculator on the desktop*

To convert a number from one number base to another, click the button of the starting number base (decimal for example). Type the value to be converted, and then click the button of the target number base. The number is converted. Select a unit of measurement for displaying the results. When converting to hexadecimal, octal, or binary numbers, click Dword to display the full 32-bit representation of the number, click Word to display the 16-bit representation of the number, or click Byte to display the 8-bit representation of the number.

The buttons A through F on the Scientific Calculator are used to enter hexadecimal numbers 10 through 15.

Statistical Functions (Scientific Calculator Only)

The Scientific Calculator can perform averaging and standard deviations. Values are entered in a special Statistics box that appears when the Sta button is pressed. The Statistics box can be moved onto the desktop, where you can then enter a list of numbers or data points. To see how this works, follow these steps:

1. Switch to the Scientific Calculator if it is not already in use by choosing Scientific from the View menu.

2. Click the Sta button to display the Statistics box as shown here:

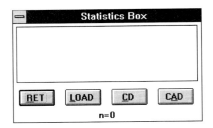

3. Move the Statistics window to the side, and then click on the Calculator and start typing numbers such as 100, 200, 300, and so on, clicking the Dat button or pressing the INS key after each number, to insert it into the Statistics box.

4. Now click the Ave (average), Sum, or s (standard deviation) button to display statistical results for the numbers in the Statistics box.

The buttons on the Statistics box are used as follows.

- *RET* Use RET to jump to the main calculator so you can type numbers.

- *LOAD* Use LOAD to copy the highlighted number in the Statistics box to the calculator's display.

- *CD* Use CD to delete the currently selected number in the Statistics box.

- *CAD* Use CAD to delete all numbers in the Statistics box.

The Calendar

The Windows Calendar provides a month-at-a-glance or daily view of appointments and schedules. In daily view, you can add messages and set alarms on the hour, half-hour, quarter-hour, or any special time you wish. In monthly view, you can click on a specific day to view its schedule.

Startup and Overview

To start the Calendar, double-click the Calendar icon in the Program Manager Accessories window. The Calendar window appears, as shown in Figure 24-4.

The appointment area contains a list of times. These are initially set in one-hour increments but you can change the increments to 30 minutes or 15 minutes. You can also insert special times when necessary. The status bar shows the current time and

Scroll days

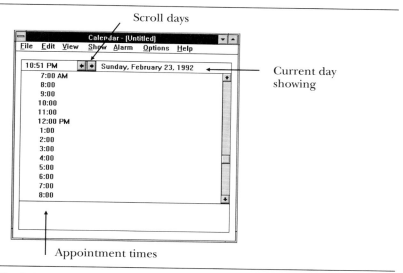

Current day
showing

Appointment times

Figure 24-4.   *The Calendar window*

the day being viewed. To view the previous or upcoming day, click the right arrow or left arrow buttons.

The Calendar date range is from January 1, 1980 to December 31, 2099. The dates are formatted using one of the following schemes:

mm/dd/yy
mm/dd/yyyy
mm-dd-yy

Leading zeros are not required when typing a date.

Using the Calendar

When Calendar first starts, the current day is displayed in its work area. You can advance to another day to view upcoming appointments or enter new appointments. Once the correct day is highlighted, you can view appointments, add new appointments, or remove appointments. The following section leads you through the use of the Calendar.

Calendar Setup

Before you start using Calendar for the first time, you can set some of its features to suit your own needs. For example, you can change the appointment interval (to 15, 30, or 60 minutes) the time format (to standard or military), and the starting time on the Day Settings dialog box as follows. Choose Day Settings on the Options menu to display the Day Settings dialog box:

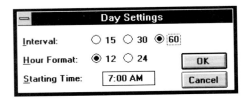

Click the time interval you want to use between appointments. Keep in mind that special times that don't conform to the interval can be inserted whenever necessary. Click either 12 or 24 in the hour format and enter a time in the Starting Time field. This should be the time you normally start your day. It will always appear at the top of the appointment list, although you can still scroll up to earlier times if necessary.

Jumping to a Day or Month

To enter an appointment, you need to select the correct day view. To do this, use any of the following techniques:

- Click on the left arrow or right arrow button in the status bar to jump forward or backward among the days.

- Choose Previous, Next, or Today from the Show menu to return to the appointments for yesterday, tomorrow, or the current day.

- Choose Date from the Show menu, and then type the date you want to see in the Show Date field and press ENTER.

- Choose Month from the View menu to display the month view as shown in Figure 24-5, and then double-click a day to return to the correct day view.

To jump to another month, you can either choose the Date option from the Show menu and type the date you want to view, or choose Month from the View menu, then click the left or right arrow button to move between months.

Typing Appointments

After selecting a day, you can view, add, or remove appointments. To enter appointments, first click the time for the appointment, or press the UP ARROW or DOWN ARROW key on the keyboard to move the insertion point to the appropriate time. The scroll bars can also be used to scroll through the time list.

Once you've positioned the insertion point, type a message of up to 80 characters. The message text scrolls to the left when the right Calendar border is reached. The following keys can be used to move around in the Calendar window:

- Press END to jump to the end of a line and HOME to jump to the beginning of a line. Use the arrow keys to scroll through the text of a message.

- Press PGUP and PGDN to move up or down one screen in the appointment list.

- Press CTRL-HOME to move to your daily starting time.

- Press CTRL-END to move 12 hours past the starting time.

Typing Notes and Reminders

Each daily appointment window has a note area at the bottom of the screen where you can type a message of up to three lines. Click the mouse button in the note area, then type the text of the note. Alternatively, you can press the TAB key to jump to the note area, then TAB again to jump back to the appointment area.

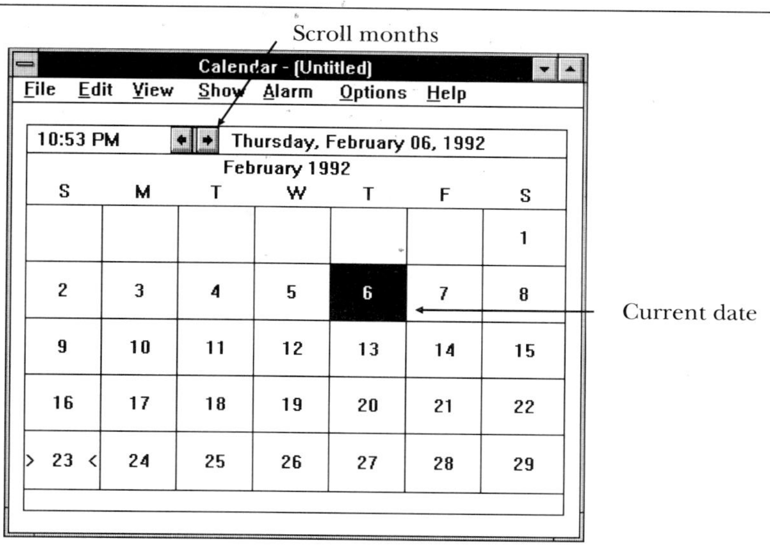

Figure 24-5.   *The month view lets you quickly jump to any day or month by double-clicking it*

Removing Appointments

You can remove the appointments for a day or a range of days by choosing the Remove option from the Edit menu. When the Remove dialog box appears, type the beginning date in the From box and the ending date in the To box, then choose OK to remove the days.

Adding Special Times

You can insert special times in the appointment listing for any day by first jumping to the day's appointment date. Make sure the day view is active by choosing Day from the View menu, then choose Special Time from the Options menu to open the Special Time dialog box:

Type in the special time and click the AM or PM button, then click Insert to insert the new time. To remove a special time, follow the same steps, but click the Delete button when the Special Time dialog box is opened.

Saving and Printing Appointments

To save an appointment calendar, choose Save or Save As from the File menu. Calendar files are saved with the .CAL extension unless you specify another extension. You can create any number of Calendar files and then create a special startup icon for each in the Program Manager. For example, you can create a general appointment calendar with one-hour increments, and then create a detailed schedule with 15-minute increments.

Setting Page Layout and Printing

The Page Setup command is used for setting margins, headers, and footers when printing appointments. Choose Page Setup from the File menu, and then highlight the fields to change and type the new settings. The following codes can be used in the Header or Footer field.

Code	Function
&d	Inserts the date
&p	Inserts the page number
&f	Inserts the current filename
&l	Left-justifies the text that follows
&r	Right-justifies the text that follows
&c	Centers the text that follows
&t	Inserts the time

For example, to print a header showing a centered title, you could type **&cAppointments for the Week of September 2, 1991**.

To print a footer with a centered page number, you could type **&cPage &p** (note that Page is printed before the page number itself).

To print appointments, select the Print option from the File menu. The following Print dialog box appears.

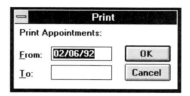

Type the beginning date in the From box and the ending date in the To box, and then choose OK to print the appointments.

Calendar Messages and Alarms

You can set an alarm for any time in the daily appointment window. When the alarm goes off, Calendar displays a message or alerts you in one of the following ways:

- If the Calendar window is active, a dialog box appears to display the alarm message.

- If the alarm sound is set on, a beep sounds for a few seconds.

- If the Calendar window is inactive, the alarm will sound and the title bar will flash. The message is displayed when you select the window.

- If the Calendar is reduced to an icon, the icon flashes. When you select the icon, the message is displayed but the Calendar window is not opened.

To set an alarm, move the insertion point to the appropriate time. Choose the Set option on the Alarm menu. A bell appears in front of the time to indicate that an alarm has been set.

To change the amount of advance warning time and sound for alarms, follow these steps:

1. Choose the Controls option from the Alarm menu to display the following Alarm Controls dialog box

2. In the Early Ring text box, type the amount of time (from 0 to 10 minutes) for the early warning.

3. Click the Sound box to turn the alarm sound on or off.

4. Click OK to save the changes.

Marking Dates

The Calendar provides a set of five different marks you can use to call attention to certain dates. When a day is marked, it appears in the month view with the special characters used for marking. To mark a day, choose Month from the View menu, and then click on the day you wish to mark. To mark days in other months, click the left arrow or right arrow button in the status bar. Select Mark from the Options menu to display the Day Markings dialog box shown here:

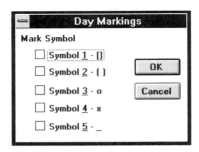

Click the mark you want to add and press OK. To remove a mark, you use the same procedure except you click on the mark you want to remove when the Day Markings dialog box appears.

There are five different marks. You may find it helpful to write down what these marks will designate on your calendars. For example, the box symbol (symbol 1) could represent birthdays, and the x symbol could represent deadlines.

The Cardfile Accessory

The Cardfile is an electronic index card filing system used to store text and pictures. Figure 24-6 shows the initial Cardfile screen. Each card has a title that is used for sorting and searching, while additional text and graphics is typed or pasted in the body of the cards. You can display cards by searching for text in the Index header or text in the body of the card.

Several different sets of index card files can be stored on your system. For example, you can keep a name and address list, a list of your music collection, or a household inventory list. The Cardfile is also an excellent tool for cataloging graphic images created in drawing programs. For example, objects used often in your drawings can be placed on index cards for quick retrieval.

Startup and Overview

To start the Cardfile, double-click its icon in the Program Manager's Accessories window. Take a moment to look over the Cardfile's features and menus. The status bar indicates how many cards are in the stack. It also shows the view method—you view either the cards or the index headers. The status bar also includes the left arrow and right arrow buttons, with which you move back and forth through the card stack.

Using the Cardfile

When the Cardfile is first started, a single, blank index card appears in its work area. You add new cards by choosing the Add command on the Card menu. Any new card added to the stack is alphabetically sorted into the stack based upon the information in the index header.

Because the index header information is used to sort the cards in the stack, use care when typing it. You might want to create a coding scheme to categorize the information. For example, names in a business card file can be coded based on the profession of each person. In this scheme, Attorneys are coded "A" and doctors are coded "D." This leaves room in the index header for more important information.

The following sections explain how to use each of Cardfile's features.

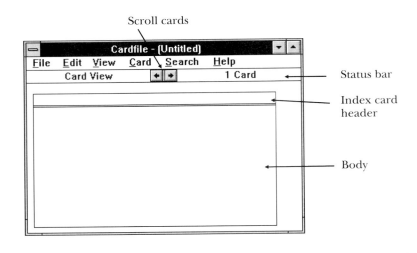

Figure 24-6.   *The Cardfile is designed to look and work like an index card filing system*

Adding New Index Cards

To add new index cards, use the Add command on the Card menu. Choose the command, and then enter the index header information for the new card in the Add field. Click OK to add the card to the stack. Once the card appears, you can type information in its text area.

To change the index header information for an existing card, choose the Index option on the Edit menu.

Typing Index Card Text

Once a new card has been added to the stack, you can put text or graphics on the card. To add text, make sure the card you want to edit is at the top of the stack by clicking the card, or by pressing the scroll buttons in the status bar until it appears on top. The text insertion point will be in the body of the card, so you can begin typing immediately.

Cardfile wraps the text to a new line when you reach the right edge of the card. You can't type more text than will fit on the card. Keep in mind that the Search command can be used to locate words in the body text, so be sure to include important keywords when appropriate.

Scrolling Through Cards

To edit or make other changes to a card, first bring it to the top of the card stack. If the card is visible in the Cardfile window, simply click it with the mouse. Another method is to scroll through the cards using the left arrow and right arrow buttons on the status bar. Since cards are arranged in a circular order, clicking the buttons repeatedly wraps the card stack around to where you started. The following keys can also be used to move through the card file:

PGDN	Scrolls forward one card in card view and one page in list view
PGUP	Scrolls backward one card in card view and one page in list view
CTRL-HOME	Restores the first card to the top of the stack
CTRL-END	Brings the last card to the top of the stack

Jumping Between Cards

To quickly jump to a card, hold down the CTRL key and type the first letter in the index header of the card. The card will appear at the top of the stack, or if there is more than one card with the letter, you'll see the first card with that letter. If the card you want is not on the top of the stack, scroll to it using the Advance button in the status bar.

The Go To option on the Search menu can also be used to locate a card by its index header information. When you choose the option, you can type the text that appears in the index header of the card you want to see. Note that you only need to type as much text as will be needed to locate the card.

Listing Cards

Another way to view and jump to specific cards is to choose the List option from the View menu. Each index header in the card stack is listed in alphabetical order on its own line. To view the information on any card in the stack, click its header in the list view, and then choose the Card option on the View menu. The card view is restored, and the card you selected will be on top.

Duplicating Cards

Another way to add a card is to duplicate one that already exists. This saves time and keystrokes when one card already has information you need for a new card. For example, you can type the city, state, and zip code on one card, then duplicate it for use with other cards that need the same information. To duplicate a card, first click to select it, and then choose the Duplicate option on the Card menu. Next, choose the Index option on the Edit menu and change the header information for the card as necessary.

Remember that the Clipboard can be used to copy text from one card to another as well.

Restoring a Card

Cards can be restored to their original condition after an edit if you change your mind or make a mistake. To do this, choose the Restore option on the Edit menu.

You cannot restore a card once you click another card.

Deleting Cards

To delete a card, bring it to the top of the stack, and then choose Delete from the Card menu. You will be asked to confirm the deletion of the card. If the card has some useful information, use the Clipboard commands to move the information to another card before deleting the card.

Searching for Text

You can search for text in the body area of index cards using the Find option on the Search menu.

You must be in Card view instead of List view to perform a search.

To search for text, choose Find from the Search menu. When the Find dialog box appears, type in the text you want to find. Notice that the other options are not available because Cardfile doesn't distinguish between uppercase and lowercase or whole words. Click the Find Next key. The first card with matching text is placed at the top of the stack. To find the next occurrence, click the Find Next button again, or if the dialog box is closed, choose Find Next from the Search menu.

Printing and Saving Card Files

You can print cards using one of the three methods described here:

- To print just the top card in the stack, choose Print from the File menu. The cards must be in Card view, not List view.

- Choose Print All to print all cards. They must be in Card view, not List view.

- To print just the index headers, choose List from the Edit menu, and then select the Print All command.

Choose the Save or Save As command to save a card file. Card files are saved with the .CRD extension unless you specify another extension.

Other Cardfile Techniques

You can include graphic images on your cards using Clipboard copy and paste techniques. In addition, you can combine two card files and have your system dial a telephone number listed on a card. These techniques are covered in the following sections.

Cutting and Pasting Graphics

In some cases, you may want to paste graphics on a card. You can easily do this using Clipboard commands. To add a picture to a card, open Paintbrush or another painting or drawing program and capture the image you want using the Copy or Cut command on the Edit menu. Return to the Cardfile window, and then bring the appropriate card to the top of the stack. Choose the Picture option from the Edit menu, and then choose the Paste option from the Edit menu to paste the picture on the card.

When the picture appears, you can drag it to any position on the card. You can also add text to the card by choosing the Text option from the Edit menu. If you type text on a card that a graphic image has been pasted to, the text will be typed underneath the image. You can click Picture at any time, and then point and click on the graphic image to move it elsewhere on the card.

Be sure to choose Text from the Edit menu after pasting or moving graphics, otherwise you won't be able to type text in a card.

Merging Card Files

You can merge the cards in one file with the cards in another using the Merge option on the File menu. The File Merge dialog box is similar to the Open dialog box in that it displays a list of card files in the current directory. You can specify other directories and drives where card files might be located.

To merge cards, open one card file, then merge the other into it. When two card files are merged, they are sorted alphabetically on the index header. You may want to save the merged file under a new name using the Save As option on the File menu.

Automatic Dialing

If your system is connected to a Hayes-compatible modem, you can have your system dial telephone numbers on index cards. When the Autodial option is selected from the Card menu, the Cardfile reads the first number it finds on the index card at the top of the card stack, and displays the Autodial dialog box with the number in its number field, as shown here:

Click the OK button to dial the number. Click the Setup button to select Tone or Pulse dialing and the communications port of the modem.

The telephone number must always be the first number to appear on a card. Other numbers can then be typed after it.

Cardfile Scrapbooks

You can create a scrapbook of graphic images by pasting pictures and images you use often onto individual cards in a card file. When you need an image while working in another application, you can switch to the Cardfile graphics catalog, locate the card containing the image, copy it to the Clipboard, and then return to your application and paste it.

Chapter 25

Compound Documents
and OLE

Chapter 4 showed you how to use object linking and embedding (OLE) along with the Clipboard to copy pictures from Paintbrush into Write and Cardfile. When applications support OLE in programs such as Paintbrush, Write, and Cardfile, the pasted image or other information (called an object) maintains an association with the application used to create it. If the object is linked, changes you make to the original file are also made to the pasted links in other documents. If the object is pasted as a simple embedded object, you can double-click it in the document to quickly edit it. The document appears in the workspace of the application that created it. You'll recall from Chapter 4 that images pasted into applications that don't support OLE are pasted as static objects, which you can only change by replacing them with updated objects.

Compound documents change the approach users take when creating documents. A *compound document* is a document that contains elements from other applications. In the old application-centered view, a user needed to be concerned with the features available in an application. When creating a document, individual components, such as graphs, spreadsheets, and text, were produced and possibly even printed separately. The user jumped from one application to the next. OLE provides a document-centered view in which the document itself holds all the components of the project. The features of an application are no longer important, because the application that holds the document can simply "borrow" features from other applications as needed.

For example, when you paste a graphic image into Write as an embedded object, and then double-click the object, it appears in the Paintbrush window for editing, making Write appear as if it has graphic editing capabilities. Write, Paintbrush, and

Cardfile will serve to get you started with OLE and help you learn about its features. More advanced applications such as Microsoft Word, Excel, and PowerPoint really put OLE to use.

OLE and Business Information

To understand the potential of OLE and compound documents, let's look at how you might use it in your office. As an example, this section examines the creation of compound documents by several users over a network. Let's assume you are a department or group manager and you need to create a business report that includes charts, tables of numbers, and text.

Start by compiling a rough draft that includes a table of numbers from Excel and some quickly sketched diagrams in Paintbrush. You will link these document elements into the main document, making it a compound document. Since you're working on a network, each element exists on the shared network disk as a separate file. If you were working in a firm with separate departments, you would call the graphics department and tell them to improve the appearance of your diagrams, and call the financial department and have them check the validity of the numbers in your spreadsheet. The users in these departments simply open the file(s) that contain the graphic or spreadsheet, not the entire compound document. Any changes they make are reflected in your compound document the next time you open it because it is linked with OLE.

This example illustrates a truly powerful use for OLE, but you can do the same thing on a local level, making all the changes yourself on your own machine. Or, for a mid-level use of OLE, you could copy any of the linked files to a floppy disk and give them to another user to update. Once updated, you copy them back to your system where the changes get integrated into your compound document. The document-centered view of managing and tracking the information in a project becomes apparent.

Keep in mind that the full OLE specification was not completed when Windows 3.1 was announced, so using it on a network as described earlier is not fully supported, and future versions of OLE will have more features. In addition, more packages will support OLE. The problem with using OLE on a network is that linked files can be hard to track if the drive mappings change. Eventually, controlling how and when linked files are changed, and by whom can be a problem.

OLE Components

To create compound documents, you use various components of Windows that provide OLE support. These components are included as options on the Edit menu of most applications, or may be integrated into the functions of a program. For example, the File Manager's OLE features are integrated. When you click a file icon and drag it to a document in an OLE-compatible application, the icon becomes embedded as an OLE object. When you double-click the object, it opens or plays the document.

An *object* (in this instance) is a package of information that originates in a *source* document and is pasted to a *destination* document. The source and destination documents are created in server and client applications respectively, as discussed next.

Servers and Clients

A compound document is as easy to create as any other document. You use the same Clipboard cut and paste options that you use when copying information such as pictures and graphs into a document. If the originating application supports OLE, the information is pasted as an object that can be manipulated by the user. That application is a *server* of OLE data, and the application receiving the pasted data is a *client*. Double-clicking on an embedded object opens the server application. Note that applications are not restricted to being either servers or clients. Some applications are both. Here are some examples.

Paintbrush   Paintbrush is a server application that only provides OLE graphic objects to client applications. The object appears as an image in the client document.

Write   Write is solely a client application.

The Cardfile Accessory   The Cardfile is solely a client application.

Sound Recorder   Sound Recorder is a server application. Use Sound Recorder to create sounds and embed them in your documents. Embedded sounds are displayed as Sound Recorder icons.

Microsoft Excel   Microsoft Excel is both a server and a client. You can paste Excel spreadsheet data into most client applications. You can also paste sound files, graphics, and other information into an Excel spreadsheet.

Microsoft Word   Word is primarily a client application; however, you can paste Word document icons in other applications.

Microsoft PowerPoint   PowerPoint is another application that can be either a server or client, but is primarily a client. PowerPoint is used to create graphic presentations.

Some objects can only be pasted as icons or packages. For example, when pasting a Sound Recorder sound into a document, a Sound Recorder icon is displayed because you can't conveniently display a sound.

Verbs

A *verb* is the action an object takes when double-clicked; the type of action that results depends on the type of object it is. The most typical is the *play* verb. An object such as a sound file or an animation routine in a multimedia document plays. An icon for a program more correctly "runs," but "play" also applies. The other important verb is *edit*. An edit object, when double-clicked, opens for editing in the workspace of the application that created it.

The type of document dictates whether objects are played or edited. In the previous example, graphics and spreadsheets were placed in a report document that was going through revisions. These objects are edited objects. On the other hand, you can create documents in which objects are played by the end user or recipient. For example, you can add voice annotation to an electronic mail message and send it to another user on your network, who then plays it. You could also create an educational "picture and sound" document for students. They see a picture of a cow or a horse, then double-click a sound icon to hear the animal. Later, when working with objects, you'll see the significance of verbs.

Linking and Embedding

By now, you're probably already familiar with linking and embedding, but this section defines the two explicitly because how an object is pasted into a document depends first on whether the source and the destination support OLE.

Normal Objects   If neither the source nor the destination support OLE, then the paste results are non-OLE. You must repaste an updated version of the information.

Packaged Objects   If the destination supports OLE, but the source does not, the Clipboard contents are pasted as normal information into the document. However, you can use Packager (discussed later in this chapter) to create OLE-compatible packages for these non-OLE objects. They then appear as icons that, when double-clicked, play, run, or edit a specific file.

Embedded Objects   If both the source and the destination are OLE-compliant, a pasted object is embedded into the destination document. If you double-click the object, it plays, runs, or opens for editing, depending on the object type. The object maintains an "association" with the application that created it, much like the association filename extensions have in the File Manager. It is important to understand that embedded objects are not associated with any file once they're embedded. They become part of the document and maintain an association to the source application only. This link is used by OLE to determine which application to open when you double-click the object.

Linked Objects   A linked object maintains a two-way dynamic link between a file and the pasted object. You choose the Paste Link command from the Edit menu of an OLE-compatible application to paste an object as a linked object. When the file is updated, the pasted link also changes, so it's important that the file not be moved to another location or removed from disk, otherwise the link is broken and must be repaired with the Links command on the Edit menu.

Clipboard Methods of Linking and Embedding

The most common method for linking and embedding objects is with the Clipboard. In the source application, you highlight or select the information to copy, and choose the Copy command from the Edit menu. You then switch to the destination application and choose one of the following Paste commands from the Edit menu. Note that Paste Link will not be available if the source document is not saved as a file.

The Paste Command   Choose Paste to embed the object as it is on the Clipboard. If the information is from an OLE source application, it is embedded.

The Paste Special Command   Paste Special is similar to Paste, except that a dialog box similar to the following opens. You choose which format you want to use to paste the object. In this example, a Paintbrush image is on the Clipboard. Only the top item pastes an embedded object. The other options paste the image on the Clipboard as a normal image. The Paste Link button is available if the source image is saved as a file.

When a server places information on the Clipboard, it does so in one of the following formats. The order of these formats determines how the object is displayed and the type of object it becomes.

- *Native Data*   The Native Data format defines the format used to embed an object.

- *OwnerLink Data* If the first item is OwnerLink, the object can be paste-linked or embedded.

- *Presentation Data* The Presentation Data format allows the client only to display the object in a document. Presentation formats might be CF-MetaFilePict, CF_DIB, or CF_Bitmap.

- *ObjectLink Data* The ObjectLink Data format identifies the class, document, and item that is the source for the linked object. This is used if you choose Paste Link.

The importance of these options has to do with whether the client can display or handle the object in the same way as the server. The first option in the list is always the preferred option, but if it can't be used, the others are used in the order listed.

The Paste Link Option

If the object on the Clipboard is from an existing file, the Paste Link option is available. Choose it to paste the object and maintain a link to the disk file so that any changes to the file are reflected in the compound document.

When working with OLE-compatible applications, several other options appear on the Edit menu as discussed in the following sections.

The Links Option

The Links option is used to change the links of an object, such as when a link has been lost (because the file was moved). This is discussed later under "Editing Links."

The <Class> Object Option

<Class> is replaced with the type of object selected (Paintbrush graphic, Word document, Sound Recorder package, and so on), so the wording of this option changes. For example, if it is a Paintbrush object, you'll see "Edit Paintbrush Object." If the object is a package, you'll see "Object Package." If you click on Object Package, you can choose to run or edit it from a submenu.

The Insert Object Option

Use the Insert Object option to create a new object or link. It displays the Insert Object dialog box shown next, which gives a list of the current OLE-compatible applications in your system and serves as an alternate method of starting the application.

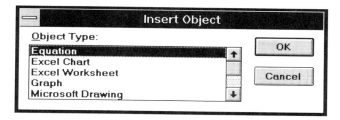

Changing Embedded and Linked Objects

When you double-click an object in a client document, the object appears in its source application for editing. After making changes, you choose one of the following options from the File menu.

The Update Option   Choose Update to bring up to date the object in the destination with your changes and then remain in the source application for further editing.

The Exit and Return To Option   Choose the Exit and Return To option to return to the destination application. If you've made changes, you'll be asked if you want to update the destination with those changes.

Packaged Objects

A *packaged object* is an embedded or linked icon that, when double-clicked, does one of the following.

- Opens a file for editing

- Plays a sound or animation file

- Starts a program file

There are two ways to create packages. The first is to drag the icon of the source file from the File Manager to the destination document. The second method is to use the Object Packager utility, which gives you more control over the startup command, the icon used, and the label for the icon. If using the File Manager, you access Clipboard commands to copy a file and its information, rather than dragging the icon. This is useful if your windows are not in a convenient arrangement for dragging and dropping. Basically, you click a file icon, and then choose Copy from the File Manager File menu. You then click the Copy to Clipboard option. Finally, you switch to the destination application and paste.

A packaged object is often called an *encapsulated* icon. It is not much different from the icons you use in the Program Manager to start applications, except that the icon is in your documents. For example, you could create a packaged object that opens another document related to the document you're working on. This is a convenient way to give the readers of the file quick access to other related documents. You could also create a set of instructions for new employees who double-click icons that contain further instructions for tasks they are not familiar with.

Sound Recorder files can be embedded using the File Manager, or using the Object Packager. As mentioned earlier, you could create a document for young students that contains animal pictures next to icons that they double-click to hear the sounds of the animals. A document could contain sound icons that pronounce foreign language translations of words.

The Object Packager also provides a method of creating embedded objects for files created with applications that do not directly support OLE, such as Windows 3.0 applications. The process is similar to creating a startup icon for a program in the Program Manager. You specify the path and filename of the object, and the Object Packager manages the task of opening it when the icon is double-clicked in the compound document. You'll see more about the Object Packager later in this chapter.

Using OLE

The following examples will guide you through the use of OLE commands and help you build compound documents using Windows Paintbrush, Sound Recorder, Write, and Cardfile. These instructions assume you have the Speaker driver installed or are using a sound board that can play Sound Recorder wave files. You've already seen how to do some of the tasks presented here, but this section will show you some of the menu options and OLE controls you use when creating compound documents.

Creating Embedded Objects

Start Paintbrush and Write, and then open one of the Paintbrush .BMP files, or create your own image. You might want to create a company logo or add some artistic touches to your address to create stationery. Use the Pick tool to highlight the object you painted, and then choose Copy from the Edit menu.

Now switch to Write and open the Edit menu, which looks similar to Figure 25-1. Note that Paste and Paste Special are available since an object is on the Clipboard. Choose Paste Special to see the Clipboard formats for the object. You'll see Paint-brush Picture Object as the first item in the list. Choose this item to paste the Clipboard contents as an embedded object.

Paste Link is not available until you save the image in the source application's workspace as a file.

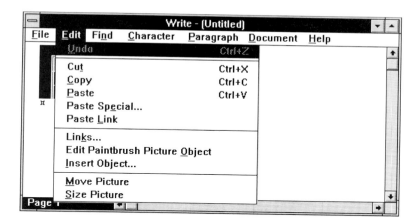

Figure 25-1.   *The Edit menu in OLE-compatible applications includes special linking and embedding commands*

The object is pasted in the normal way. However, since it came from an OLE server, it is still associated with it. Double-click the object you just pasted to open Paintbrush and edit the image. If Paintbrush is already open, another version is started. Note the title bar of the Paintbrush window. If you had saved the Write document where the picture was pasted, the name of that document appears in the title bar; otherwise it reads "Paintbrush Picture in (Untitled)."

Now make some minor changes to the image. You can try changing its colors or enlarging it. When you're done, position the Paintbrush window so you can see the Write window beneath, and then choose Update from the File menu. Notice the change takes effect immediately in the other document. Choose "Exit and Return" from the Paintbrush File menu to return to Write. Your original copy of Paintbrush should still be open for the next example.

Creating a Link

In the previous example, you had to double-click the object in the Write document to make changes to it. In this example, you'll paste a linked object, and then make changes to the object and watch them be dynamically updated in the compound document.

First, return to Paintbrush and save the graphic image to disk. Now use the Pick tool to select part of the image and choose Copy from the Edit menu. Return to the Write document, position the cursor, then choose Paste Link from the Edit menu.

Now position the Write and Paintbrush windows so you can see both, and then start making changes to the object in the Paintbrush window. As you make changes, the object in the Write window is updated automatically!

You could save the Write document and close its window, continue to make changes to the Paintbrush image, and then reopen Write to see those changes. This illustrates how you can update objects by editing the source, or by opening the compound document and double-clicking its embedded image.

Editing Links

You can view and edit the link information for linked objects by choosing the Link command on the Edit menu. You'll see a dialog box similar to the one shown in Figure 25-2. Every link in the document is listed.

The Links field shows the type, name, size, and update method for the linked object. You can make the following changes from the dialog box:

- In the Update field, enable the Automatic option to have the object automatically update when changes are made to the source file.

- If you choose Manual, you'll need to click the Update Now button on the Links dialog box whenever you want to update the image. Some OLE applications have a quick-key sequence you can use to update an object.

- Click the Cancel Link button to remove the link. The object remains in the document as an embedded object.

- Click the Change Link button if the linked file has been moved and you need to specify its new location. A dialog box similar to the Open dialog box opens. You then specify the new drive and directory where the source file is located.

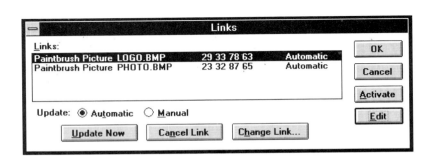

Figure 25-2.   *The Links dialog box displays a list of linked items in a document*

- Click Activate to play or run the file linked to the object. This is the same as double-clicking an object. If the object can only be edited, click the Edit button.

- Click Edit to edit the object.

Using Microsoft Excel and Word Together

Microsoft Excel and Word for Windows were written specifically to take advantage of OLE. You can copy a range of cells from Excel to quickly create a table in Word. If you've created a chart in Excel using spreadsheet data, you can copy the chart to your Word document. The most important aspect is the link. Changes made to the Excel spreadsheet are automatically made to the copy in the Word document.

To copy data from Excel into a Word table, select the range of cells containing the data to copy, and then choose the Copy command from the Edit menu. Switch to the Word document and choose Paste to embed the object, or Paste Link to link the object. A table is inserted into the Word document.

To copy a chart from Excel into a Word document, first create the chart in Excel and size it appropriately. Select the chart and choose Copy from the Edit menu. Switch to the Word document, position the insertion point, and choose the Paste or Paste Link option from the Edit menu.

Remember that you can specify automatic or manual updates for linked objects by clicking the object and choosing Links from the Edit menu. If you choose Manual update, you can press the F9 key in Word to update the tables or charts whenever necessary.

Creating Packaged Objects

Now you're ready to try creating some packaged objects. First, open the File Manager, and then locate the .WAV files in the Windows directory. You can sort the list based upon the file type by choosing Sort by Type from the View menu; next scroll to the bottom to locate the .WAV files. Hold CTRL and click on each file, and then click and drag the selection to the Write window. In a moment, icons for the files appear in the document as shown in Figure 25-3. Double-click each icon to hear its sound.

You can add any file in this way. Open Cardfile and try the same thing, though you can only paste one object per card (you must choose the Picture option on its Edit menu before dragging the icon from the File Manager or pasting an image onto its cards).

Another way to copy file icons from the File Manager to your application is to first click the files you want to copy, and then choose Copy from the File menu. Enable the option Copy to Clipboard, and then switch to the destination application and choose the Paste command.

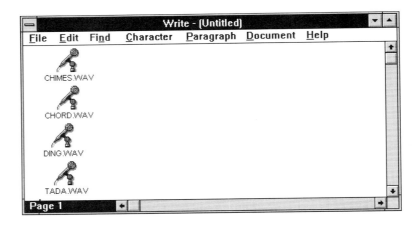

Figure 25-3.   *An OLE client application with OLE sound packages from Sound Recorder*

Think about how you might use these features. In Cardfile, you could create an index to the files on your system. Each card would describe the contents of a file and below that description would be an icon you double-click to open the file. In a Write document, you could add voice annotations and pictures to create a multimedia presentation.

The Object Packager

Use the Object Packager to create packages to embed as icons into your documents. The Object Packager is an alternative to the click-and-drag method you can use if the File Manager is not open. You can also create icons for Windows applications that don't support OLE. Still another technique is to create packages for DOS commands that you can embed in a document.

You can open Object Packager by double-clicking its icon in the Accessories group, but the best method is to choose Insert Object on the Edit menu of the document you're working in. Do this now in the Write document. When the Insert Object dialog box appears, choose Package from its Object Type list. The Object Packager dialog box shown in Figure 25-4 appears.

The Object Packager contains all the tools you need to create your own embedded or linked icon in a document. Since you opened the Object Packager in Write, the icon you package will be placed at the location of the insertion point. Create a package for the README.WRI file in the Windows directory by following these steps:

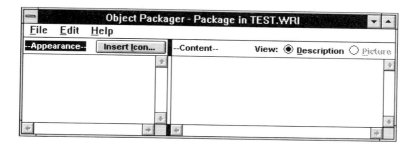

Figure 25-4.   *Use the Object Packager dialog box to create packaged icons instead of using the File Manager drag-and-drop method*

1. Choose the Command option from the Edit menu and then type **C:\WINDOWS\README.WRI** in its field. The path and filename appear in the Content window.

2. Click the Insert Icon button to add an icon to the file.

3. Choose an icon from the list. The icon appears in the Appearance window.

4. Choose Label to add a label under the icon.

5. Type **READ ME** in the Label field. The packaged object is now complete.

6. Choose Update from the File menu to add it to the Write document.

An even easier method is to choose Import from the File menu, and then choose the README.WRI file from the Open dialog box. The necessary information is automatically placed into the fields of the Object Packager. You can then change the command, icon, or label using the previously discussed options.

When you open Object Packager from within an OLE application, it assumes you want to place the package into the client document. If you want to copy the package to another application, choose Copy Package from the Edit menu, then click on the application and choose paste. The object package is inserted at the insertion point.

If the object is a graphic, click the Picture button to see the graphic instead of the description.

The Registration Editor

The Registration database contains the information that Windows needs to recognize an OLE application and provides drag-and-drop services for opening and printing documents. To start the Registration Editor, choose Run from the Program Manager or File Manager File menu, then type **REGEDIT** in the Run field and press ENTER. The Registration Info Editor dialog box shown in Figure 25-5 appears. A companion registration database called REG.DAT is associated with the editor.

Every time you work with an OLE object, Windows checks the Registration database to determine what to do with the object. For example, the list of object types displayed in the Insert Object dialog box comes directly from the Registration database. If you double-click on one of the listed items in the Registration Info Editor windows, such as Paintbrush Picture (scroll down to select it), a Modify File Type dialog box similar to Figure 25-6 opens, listing the information for Paintbrush.

The fields of the Modify File Type dialog box are listed next. These are the same fields you'll see when adding or modifying an entry in the Registration Info Editor window.

The Identifier Field   The Identifier field lists a unique keyword that identifies the file type in the registration database.

The File Type Field   The File Type field lists a text description of the file type. It appears in the Registration Editor's listing and also in the Associate dialog box in the File Manager.

The Action Field   The Action field specifies the action that occurs for this option. Open specifies that options in the Command field and the DDE section are used to play, run, or edit the file. Print specifies that the commands in the Command and DDE fields are used to print a file.

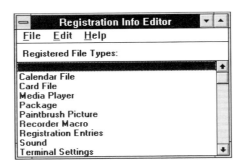

Figure 25-5.   *The Registration Info Editor dialog box*

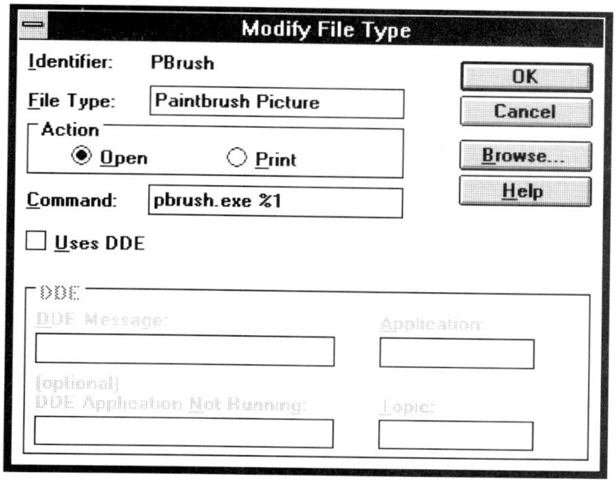

Figure 25-6. *The Modify File Type dialog box lists registration information for a particular OLE application*

The Command Field   The Command field holds the commands to execute when an object is selected. The field contains the command of the source application. The %1 option is a replaceable parameter. The name of the current linked object file is inserted in its place.

The DDE Field   If the application supports DDE messages and application strings, the Uses DDE box is enabled. These options are fully documented in the Help system.

Installing and Adding New Types

Most Windows applications that support DDE will automatically add an entry to the Registration database. If this doesn't happen, choose Merge Registration File from the File menu, and then choose the .REG file in the File Open dialog box. You may need to insert a disk in the floppy drive and switch to that drive in the File Open dialog box.

To add a new file type, you can choose Add File Type from the Edit menu. Make the appropriate entries based on the previous descriptions of the Modify File Type dialog box, which is the same as the Add dialog box. You can choose Copy File Type to make a duplicate of an existing file type, or Delete to remove a File Type.

Restoring the Registration Database

If the registration database ever becomes corrupted because you've made incorrect entries or it is accidentally deleted, you can restore it by following these steps:

1. Quit Windows and delete the file REG.DAT in the Windows directory (unless it has already been deleted).

2. Restart Windows and run the Registration Info Editor. Its list will be empty.

3. Choose Merge Registration File from the File menu and select SETUP.REG from the File Name list in the dialog box. This updates the registration database with the default values.

4. If you need to add other types, choose Add File Type from the Edit menu.

Chapter 26

Windows Command and Option Reference

1 1/2 Space (Write Paragraph menu)   Changes line spacing to 1 1/2 lines. Affects only the currently selected paragraph.

386 Enhanced (Control Panel utility)   Use to set options for running applications in 386 enhanced mode. The options on this dialog box are global settings for Windows applications if one or more non-Windows applications are running. Use a PIF to set non-Windows application settings.

Activate button (Links dialog box (common))   Click this button to play or run an OLE object. It is the same as double-clicking the object in the document.

Add (Add dialog box, Cardfile)   Type in this field the text of the index card header.

Add (Cardfile Card menu)   Adds a new card to a Cardfile stack. You are asked to enter the index header information.

Add Echo option (Sound Recorder Effects menu)   Adds an echo to the current sound file. You can repeat this option to enhance the echo effect.

Add/Remove Windows Components (Windows Setup Options menu)   Use this utility to add or remove some of the Windows accessories, help, and information files to save disk space. Alternatively, if a component was not installed during setup, you can use this option to install it.

Alert Always (Print Manager Options menu)   Displays messages if there is a printer problem or the printer needs servicing (that is, needs paper). The message appears even if the Print Manager is not the active application.

All File Details (File Manager View menu)   Displays all information about the files and directories in the currently active directory window.

Always Warn (386 Enhanced utility)   Displays a warning when two non-Windows applications attempt to access the same port. Windows applications do not have this problem.

Analog (Clock Settings menu)   Displays the time in analog form (that is, as a clock with hands as opposed to digital time).

Archive (Properties for Windows dialog box, File Manager)   Set the Archive attribute for a file and prevent it from being included in a backup.

Arrange Icons (Program Manager Window menu)   If a group icon is currently highlighted, choosing this option arranges the group icons. If a program icon is selected in an open group window, choosing this option arranges the icons in the group.

Associate (File Manager File menu)   Use this dialog box to create file associations so you can open a document for editing by double-clicking it. You associate a particular file extension with a program.

Associate with (Associate dialog box, File Manager)   Type or select the program name to associate the specified filename extension.

Auto (Clipboard Viewer Display menu)   Displays the original format of the Clipboard contents. Choose other options on the Display menu to see how the information looks in other formats. The viewer can only be used to view the contents of the Clipboard.

Auto Arrange (Program Manager Options menu)   Set to automatically arrange group icons whenever you resize a group window. Disable to manually arrange icons.

Autodial (Cardfile Card menu)   Dials a phone number on the selected card. The first number on the card is dialed; any other numbers are ignored.

Backup (Save As dialog box, Write)   Enable this option to create a backup file when saving files. A backup file is the most recent version of the file, saved with the .BAK extension.

Base I/O Ports Address (Ports utility)   Select the base I/O address for a serial card based on its jumper or switch settings. The I/O address is the hexadecimal memory address the card uses for input and output with the processor.

Baud Rate (Communications dialog box, Terminal)   The baud rate is the number of signal changes in one second of a communications transfer. One or more bits of information may be included in a single baud, depending on the encoding method used. Set the baud rate to match the remote system, although most modems will find their own matching transfer rates once a connection is established.

Baud Rate (Settings dialog box, Port utility)   *See* Baud Rate (Communications dialog box, Terminal).

Binary Transfers (Terminal Settings menu)   Set the protocol for transferring non-ASCII, binary files. Binary files are usually in a form readable only by a program and may be compressed.

Bold (Paintbrush Text menu)   Converts selected characters to bold type style or switches to bold typing mode.

Bold (Write Character menu)   *See* Bold (Paintbrush Text menu).

Border Width (Desktop utility)   Increase or decrease the width for window borders. You can change the width to make windows more discernible on the desktop or easier to click on with the mouse.

Brush Shapes (Paintbrush Options menu)   Changes the shape of the Brush tool. You can double-click on the brush tool to display this dialog box. Choose a width for the brush in the Linesize box.

Buffer Lines (Terminal Preferences dialog box, Terminal)   The number of lines of received or transmitted information that the computer retains in memory. The higher this value, the more information you'll be able to scroll through and review. Has the opposite effect of reducing system memory.

By File Type (File Manager View menu)   Displays the By File Type dialog box. Set the options on this box to display specific files in the current directory window. Use wildcard characters in the Name field, or click one of the file options in the File Type box.

Cancel Link button (Links dialog box (common))   Click this button to remove an OLE link. The object becomes embedded and you can still double-click it for editing purposes. You remove a link if you no longer want an object to automatically update every time you change its source file. This improves performance.

Capacity (Format Disk dialog box, File Manager)   Specify the type of disk you want to format. The options in the list box depend on the drive type (whether 5.25-inch drive or 3.5-inch drive).

Card (Cardfile View menu)   Displays the index cards as a series of cards. The list option displays the card index headers only in descending order.

Carrier Detect (Communications dialog box, Terminal)   When enabled, Terminal uses the carrier-detect signal to determine whether the modem is online. When disabled, Terminal looks at the modem response string to determine whether the modem is connected.

Cascade (Program Manager and File Manager window menus)   Arranges open windows so they overlap, displaying only the title bar of underlying windows.

Center (Desktop utility)   Centers the wallpaper image on the desktop. Use this option for large, non-repeating pictures. Use Tile if you want the image to repeat over the desktop.

Centered (Write Paragraph menu)   Centers paragraphs or pictures between the left and right margins, or within the current indent settings.

Change Link button (Links dialog box (common))   Click this button to change or repair the link an OLE object has to its source file, if that file has been moved. A file dialog box opens so you can specify the new drive and directory of the source file.

Change System Settings (Windows Setup Options menu)   Choose this option to change the settings of your display, keyboard, mouse, and network. You must restart Windows after changing the settings in order for them to take effect.

Clear (Paintbrush Pick menu)   Removes the current cutout when you are using the Shrink+Grow or Tilt command. Typically, you resize or tilt a cutout several times before you find the correct form. The Clear command removes any attempts you don't like.

Clear Buffer (Terminal Edit menu)   Clears the contents of the scroll buffer, freeing up memory. The scroll buffer contains the text of a communications session that you can review by scrolling.

Clear button (Page Header or Footer dialog box, Write)   Click this button to delete the header or footer text.

Collapse Branch (File Manager Tree menu)   Collapses subdirectories below current directory in tree. Use this option to reduce the size and clutter of the directory tree. You can collapse any individual branch by clicking the folder icon for the branch and choosing the command.

Collate Copies (Print dialog box, Write)   When printing multiple copies of a document, organizes pages so they are all in proper numeric order.

Color (Control Panel utility)   Use to change the colors of the desktop and the windows on the desktop. Drop-down menu colors and button colors can also be changed.

Color Palette button (Color utility)   Click to create custom colors that you can use when creating new desktop and window color settings.

Color Schemes (Color utility)   Choose a color scheme from the drop-down list box. The Color utility comes with a set of predefined color schemes. Press the DOWN ARROW key on the keyboard to scroll through the schemes. They appear in the Sample window as you scroll.

Colors (Image Attributes dialog box, Paintbrush)   Use this to enable either color or black-and-white palettes. *See also* palette in the Glossary.

Columns (Terminal Preferences dialog box, Terminal)   Specify either 80 or 132 columns (characters per line) of text on the screen. If you have a high-resolution monitor, and/or have selected a small font, you can enable the 132 Column option to see more text.

Command (Command Line dialog box, Object Packager)   Specifies the command that is executed when an OLE package is activated. The command can be a program name, document name, batch filename, or other DOS command.

Command Line (Object Packager Edit menu)   Use this to specify the DOS command that executes when the package is selected. The command can be a program, associated document name, PIF file, or batch file. An associated document opens in the workspace of the application that created it if you double-click its file icon in the File Manager.

Command Line (Program Item Properties dialog box, Program Manager)   Type the DOS command you want to execute when an icon is selected. This field can include the name of a program file, associated document, PIF file, or batch file.

Command Line (Run dialog box, Program Manager and File Manager)   Type the DOS command to execute. You can specify filenames and parameters on the command line in much the same way that you type commands at the DOS prompt.

Commands (Modem Commands dialog box, Terminal)   Specify the commands that control your modem, typically Hayes-compatible commands. Refer to your modem manual for the commands to enter in these fields. The commands are executed when you dial, hang up, or issue other commands from Terminal.

Communications (Terminal Settings menu)   Use this dialog box to set the communications parameters (baud rate, parity, stop bits, data bits) for establishing a communications session.

Confirm Page Breaks (Repaginate Document dialog box, Write)   Enable this option if you want to view and change where pages break during a repagination.

Confirmation (File Manager Options menu)   Set the type of file delete, copy, and move confirmation messages you want displayed. You may want to disable some options temporarily when rearranging the directory structure of your hard drive or removing a large number of files.

Connect Network Drive (File Manager Disk menu)   Use this option to connect your computer to a network drive. *See also* network drive in the Glossary.

Connector (Communications dialog box, Terminal)   Specify the physical port the modem is attached to. This is usually COM1 or COM2, but may also be COM3 or COM4.

Continuous Loop (Record Macro (and Properties) dialog box, Recorder)   Enable this option to loop a macro continuously until CTRL-BREAK is pressed. This option is often used to play running demonstrations or tutorials.

Control+Break Checking (Recorder Options menu)   Enable this option to prevent a macro from being stopped with the CTRL-BREAK key combination. You must turn the computer off to stop the macro, so make sure all work has been saved before enabling this option.

Controls (Calendar Alarm menu)   Opens a dialog box to set the features of the Calendar alarm.

Copies (Print dialog box, Write)   Enter in this field the number of copies you want to print.

Copy (Edit menu (common))   Places a copy of the highlighted text or graphics on the Clipboard so you can paste it into another application with the Paste command on the Edit menu.

Copy (File Manager File menu)   Use to specify the source and destination of files or directories to copy instead of dragging with the mouse.

Copy (Object Packager Edit menu)   Copies the contents of the selected window (Appearance or Content), not the complete package, and places it onto the Clipboard. An icon must exist in the Appearance window.

Copy (Program Manager File menu)   Copies a program item icon to another group. You can type the source icon, or click it before choosing the command. You then pick the destination group from a list of those available.

Copy Disk (File Manager Disk menu)   Makes a backup copy of a floppy disk by copying the source disk to a destination disk.

Copy Package (Object Packager Edit menu)   Copies the contents of the Appearance and Content windows onto the Clipboard so you can paste it in an OLE-compatible document.

Copy System Files to Disk (Make System Disk dialog box, File Manager)   Copies the hidden files IO.SYS and MSDOS.SYS as well as COMMAND.COM to a formatted floppy disk, making it bootable, which means you can use the disk to start a system from the floppy drive. The system files are not necessary on data disks and simply take up room.

Copy To (Paintbrush Edit menu)   Use this option to save a cutout defined by the Scissors or Pick tool. The method saves disk space since it saves only the part of the picture you select. The normal Save option on the File menu saves the entire workspace, including blank areas that take up room.

Copy to Clipboard (Copy dialog box, File Manager)   Copy the selected file as an OLE object to the Clipboard. You can paste the file as an icon (similar to a Program Manager icon) into an OLE-compatible application, and then double-click the icon to start the application or open the file. If the file is a sound file, animation, or video clip, it is activated and immediately runs.

Country (International utility)   Select which country code you want to use. Selecting this option is usually sufficient to set all other options on the International dialog box.

Create Directory (File Manager File menu)   Creates a subdirectory that branches from the currently selected directory. You can also specify the exact path for the new directory if you want it to branch from another location.

Currency Format (International utility)   Choose the currency format for the selected country by clicking the Change button.

Cursor (Terminal Preferences dialog box, Terminal)   Choose a cursor type and whether or not it should blink.

Cursor Blink Rate (Desktop utility)   Move the slider button left or right to change the blink rate of the cursor. Watch the sample box on the right.

Cursor Position (Paintbrush View menu)   Displays the x-y position of the cursor. Use this option when drawing exact objects or placing the cursor.

Cut (Edit menus (common))   Removes highlighted text or graphics and places it on the Clipboard where it can be pasted elsewhere using the Paste command on the Edit menu.

Cut (Object Packager Edit menu)   Deletes the contents of the selected window (Appearance or Content), not the complete package, and places it onto the Clipboard. An icon must exist in the Appearance window.

Data Bits (Communications dialog box, Terminal, or Settings, Ports utility)   The number of bits used in a data transfer, usually 7 or 8.

Date (Calendar Show menu)   Use this dialog box to enter a date that you want to show in the Day or Month view.

Date (Clock Settings menu)   Enables or disables the display of the date when the clock is set to digital display.

Date (Date & Time utility)   Click the up arrow or down arrow button to change the date, or type a time in one of the fields.

Date Format (International utility)   Select the date format for the selected country by clicking the Change button.

Date/Time (Control Panel utility)   Use this to set the date and time for the system. This date and time is stamped on files when they are created or changed.

Day (Calendar View menu)   Switches from the Month view to the Day view.

Day Settings (Calendar Options menu)   Use this dialog box to change the intervals between appointments, the type of clock (12- or 24-hour), and the starting time that appears at the upper-left of the window.

DEC VT-52 (Terminal Emulation dialog box, Terminal)   Enables your system to emulate a DEC VT-52 terminal. Emulation makes your computer appear to be a terminal that the remote system recognizes.

DEC VT-100 (ANSI) (Terminal Emulation dialog box, Terminal)   Choose this option to emulate a DEC VT-100 terminal. This is the most common setting. Emulation makes your computer appear to be a terminal that the remote system recognizes.

Decimal (Tabs dialog box, Write)   Click this box to specify a decimal tab. *See also* decimal tab in the Glossary.

Decrease Speed command (Sound Recorder Effects menu)   Increases the length of a sound and changes its pitch.

Decrease Volume command (Sound Recorder Effects menu)   Decreases the amplitude of the sound.

Define Custom Colors button (Color utility)   Click this button to define custom colors. Any colors you mix appear in the Custom Colors palette.

Delay (Screen Saver field, Desktop utility)   Choose the amount of time from the last mouse or keyboard action before the screen save becomes active.

Delay Before First Repeat (Keyboard Speed field, Keyboard utility)   Adjust the slider to change the delay, and then test in the Test box.

Delete (Cardfile Card menu)   Deletes a card from the Cardfile stack.

Delete (Clipboard Viewer Edit menu)   Clears the Clipboard. You can choose this option to free up system memory. Alternatively, you can copy a single character to the Clipboard to copy over its current contents.

Delete (Delete dialog box, File Manager)   Type the drive, path, and filename of file(s) to delete, or select files before opening the dialog box.

Delete (File Manager File menu)   The drive, path, and filename of file(s) to delete, or if a file is highlighted before selecting the command, its name appears in the dialog box.

Delete (Notepad Edit menu)   Deletes selected text from a document, but does not place the text onto the Clipboard.

Delete (Object Packager Edit menu)   Deletes the contents of the selected window.

Delete (Program Manager File menu)   Choose this option to remove the selected group or startup icon.

Delete (Recorder Macro menu)   Deletes a selected macro.

Delete After Current Position (Sound Recorder Edit menu)   Use this option to remove all unwanted sound after a specific point in the sound. First position the slider button in the slider bar, and then choose the command.

Delete Before Current Position (Sound Recorder Edit menu)   Use this option to remove all unwanted sound before a specific point in the sound. First position the slider button in the slider bar, and then choose the command.

Description (Program Item Properties dialog box, Program Manager)   Type in this field the name you want to appear under the program item icon.

Description (Record Macro dialog box, Recorder)   Type in this field a description of the macro for future reference.

Desktop (Control Panel utility)   Use this to change the desktop options such as wallpaper, screen savers, icons spacing, sizing grid, and others.

Destination In (Copy Disk dialog box, File Manager)   Type the destination drive where files should be copied. It can be the same as the source. If so, Windows will ask you to switch disks during the copy.

Device Not Selected (Connect dialog box, Printers utility)   Enter the time to wait before Windows displays a warning that the printer is off-line.

Dial (Phone Number dialog box, Terminal)   Type in this field the phone number of the remote system. Enter any dial-out codes (such as 9) followed by a comma, and then the phone number. If you need more time between the dial-out code and the phone number, add more commas.

Dial (Terminal Phone menu)   Choose this command to dial the phone number and connect to a remote system.

Digital (Clock Settings menu)   Displays the time as numbers (as opposed to analog, which shows time using traditional hour and minute hands).

Direction (Find dialog box (common))   Choose the direction to search through the document (either up or down) when finding or replacing text.

Directories (By File Type dialog box, File Manager)   Enable this option to show subdirectories of the current directory in the contents list of a directory window. You can then double-click the icons to list the files in the subdirectories.

Directories (Open dialog box (common))   Type the name of a directory, or choose a directory in the tree. If a directory has subdirectories you need to access, double-click the directory icon to expand its branch and show the subdirectories. If the directories are on another drive, be sure to choose the correct drive in the Drives field.

Directories (Save As dialog box (common))   *See* Directories (Open dialog box (common)).

Directory Delete (Confirmation dialog box, File Manager)   Enable this option to have Windows warn you before deleting directories and subdirectories.

Directory Only (File Manager View menu)   Choose this option to display only the directory tree in a directory window. This command affects only the current directory window.

Disconnect Network Drive (File Manager Disk menu)   Disconnects your computer from a remote hard drive on a network file server.

Disk Commands (Confirmation dialog box, File Manager)   Enable this option to have Windows warn you before it executes disk commands that might erase existing files on a disk.

Disk In (Format Disk dialog box, File Manager)   Specify the drive letter where the disk to format is located.

Display (Change System Settings dialog box, Windows Setup utility)   Select a new display driver to install. You can choose one of the drivers in the list, or scroll to the bottom and choose "Unlisted driver" if your driver does not appear. Setup then asks you to place the driver disk in the floppy drive.

Distance from Bottom (Page Footer dialog box, Write)   Type the distance of the footer from the bottom edge of the paper. Too large a value may cause it to overlap the body text.

Distance from Top (Page Header dialog box, Write)   Type the distance of the header from the top edge of the paper. Too large a value may overlap the header on the body text.

Dithering (Options dialog box (common))   Choose how graphics are printed, either as coarse or fine dots, or as simple line art. Choose None to prevent dithering. Dithering adjusts the lightness or darkness of the pattern by using pseudo-random dot patterns. Use the Intensity slider to adjust the lightness or darkness of the dithered pattern.

Documents (By File Type dialog box, File Manager)   Enable this option to list associated documents in the file listings of the Program Manager directory windows.

Double Click Speed (Mouse utility)   Slide the button left or right to adjust the double-click speed. Test by double-clicking in the Test box.

Double Space (Write Paragraph menu)   Changes line spacing to double-spaced.

Drive (Virtual Memory dialog box)   Specify the drive where the virtual memory file should be located.

Drivers (Control Panel utility)   Use this option to install and configure device drivers for Windows.

Drives (Open and Save As dialog boxes (common))   Click the icon of the drive where you want to open or save files.

Drives (Select Drive dialog box, File Manager)   Select the drive you want to switch to for the active directory window. Use this command if you don't have a mouse. Alternatively, double-click the drive icon of the drive you want to switch to.

Duplicate (Cardfile Card menu)   Duplicates the selected card. Use Index on the Edit menu to change the duplicated card's index header. Use this option to duplicate cards that have common features such as city or zip code, and then edit each card individually.

Early Ring (Alarm Controls dialog box, Calendar)   Type the number of minutes for an early ring of the alarm.

Edit button (Links dialog box (common))   Click this button to edit an OLE object. Alternatively, you can double-click the object to display it in the workspace of the application that created it. Use this option to edit objects that normally play (like sounds or animation) when double-clicked.

Edit Colors (Paintbrush Options menu)   Opens a dialog box for creating custom colors. The colors are added to the palette. You can then save the palette with custom colors for later use.

Edit Pattern button (Desktop utility)   Click to edit your own desktop patterns. The pattern repeats over the desktop. Note that the pattern colors are affected by the color settings you set in the Control Panel Colors utility. The Windows Text setting determines the color of the pattern. The Desktop setting determines the color that shows through the pattern.

Enable Shortcut keys (Playback Field, Record Macro (and Properties) dialog box, Recorder)   Enable to use the macro shortcut keys. Disable if the shortcut keys interfere with shortcut keys used by other Windows applications.

Enable System Sounds (Sound utility)   Enable this option to use sound for system events. When disabled, the normal system beep is used when you make an operational error.

Enable TrueType Fonts (TrueType dialog box)   Enable this option to show True-Type fonts in character formatting menus and Font dialog boxes. Disable if you use other fonts such as PostScript-compatible outline fonts and don't need TrueType.

Enlarge Font (Write Character menu)   Enlarges the font size of the selected text in the document, or causes all subsequent characters you type to be in a larger font size. Choose the option multiple times to increase the font size in increments if necessary. The font size typically increases 2 points (in even values) every time you choose the option.

Events (Sound utility)   Click the system event to assign a sound to, and then click the name of a sound file in the Files field to play when that event occurs. Click the Test button to test the sound.

Exclusive in Foreground (386 Enhanced utility)   Enable this option to specify that Windows applications get exclusive use of the processor when operating in the foreground. A similar option appears on the Control menu of non-Windows applications. This option affects only Windows applications, and all at the same time.

Exit command (Media Player File menu)   Exits Media Player, but some devices such as audio CDs may continue to play.

Exit option (common)   Closes the current application. If files are still open and unsaved, you'll be asked if you want to save them.

Exit Windows (Program Manager File menu)   Choose to exit from Windows. Be sure to check the status of the Save Settings on Exit option on the Options menu. If it is enabled, your current Program Manager arrangement is saved for the next session.

Expand All (File Manager Tree menu)   Expands all the branches in the directory tree of the current drive. Choose Expand Branch if you only want to expand the currently selected directory, or double-click its icon.

Expand Branch (File Manager Tree menu)   Expands all the subdirectories of a directory in the tree. You can also double-click the icon to expand its branching subdirectories.

Expand One Level (File Manager Tree menu)   Expands a collapsed directory tree one level.

Fast "ALT-TAB" Switching (Desktop utility)   When enabled, the name of each open application appears when switching with ALT-TAB. When disabled, the title bar of the window appears. Enabling this option allows faster switching between windows on the desktop.

Fast Printing Direct to Port (Connect dialog box, Printers utility)   When enabled, Windows does not use MS-DOS interrupts for printing. Instead, it bypasses MS-DOS and prints directly to your printer, which speeds printing. Some applications may require that this option be disabled.

File (Wallpaper Field, Desktop utility)   Choose the name of a file to display as wallpaper on the desktop.

File Attributes (Partial Details dialog box, File Manager)   Enable this option to display the attributes of files in the File Manager directory windows.

File Delete (Confirmation dialog box, File Manager)   Enable this option to have Windows warn you before it deletes files.

File Name (Open dialog boxes (common))   Type the name of the file you want to open or choose a file from the list below the field. To show other files in the list, type wildcard (using * and ? characters) file specifications, and then choose from the lists. Choose a different drive and directory on the dialog box to list files in other locations, if necessary.

File Name (Save As dialog box (common))   Type the name of the file you want to save. Use the other options on the menu to specify a different drive and directory where the file should be saved.

File Replace (Confirmation dialog box, File Manager)   Enable this option to have Windows warn you before replacing a file.

Files (Sound utility)   Select a sound file to play when the event listed in the Events field occurs. Click the Test button to test the sound.

Files with Extension (Associate dialog box, File Manager)   Type the filename extension of the file you want to associate to a program. You can then double-click the file type in a File Manager directory window to automatically open the document in the application's workspace. Note that if you select a file before choosing the command, its filename extension appears in the field.

Find (common)   Use Find to search for text in a document. Type the text you want to find in the Find What field.

Find Next (common)   Repeats the last search without opening the Find dialog box. You can also press F3 in most cases to repeat a find.

Find What field (Find and Replace dialog boxes)   Type the text you want to find in this field. You can include special search characters in the text as follows: ^d, page break; ^p, paragraph marker; ^t, a tab character; ^w, a space character; ?, any character or string.

First Line (Indents dialog box, Write)   Type how far the first line indent should be from the left margin. Use a negative number to hang the indent out to the left of the paragraph's indent when creating bulleted or numbered lists. You can also slide the tick on the measure bar to adjust the first line indent. These options only affect the currently selected paragraph(s).

Flash If Inactive (Print Manager Options menu)   Enable this to make the Print Manager icon or title bar flash when the Print Manager needs to display a message.

Flip Horizontal (Paintbrush Pick menu)   Flips a cutout from side to side. You choose a cutout with the Pick or Scissors tool.

Flip Vertical (Paintbrush Pick menu)   Flips a cutout from top to bottom. You choose a cutout with the Pick or Scissors tool.

Flow Control (Text Transfers dialog box in Terminal or Settings dialog box in the Ports utility)   Choose a flow control type based on that used by the remote system. Flow control is a signaling method that acknowledges the transfer of information in a communications session. Standard flow control uses Xon/Xoff which sends until the receiving computer signals a stop because its buffers are full. Character at a time sends one character, then waits for an echo from the receiving system. Line at a Time transmits a line at a time and waits for a response.

Following CR (View Text File dialog box, Terminal)   Enable this option to append a line-feed to each line if incoming text overwrites previous lines.

Font (File Manager Options menu)   Displays the Font dialog box, in which you can change the font used to list files in directory windows.

Font (Font dialog box (common))   Choose a font in the font list, or type its name.

Font Style (Font dialog box (common))   Choose a style from the list.

Fonts (common)   Opens the Fonts dialog box used to change fonts, font styles, and font size.

Fonts (Control Panel utility)   Use this to manage fonts and TrueType options. The utility lets you install new fonts, or remove fonts from memory, or remove them completely from disk.

Footer (Write Document menu)   Opens the Footer window and dialog box where you type the footer text and specify its position on the printed page.

Format Disk (File Manager Disk menu)   Formats a floppy disk. You must specify the drive and disk size. You can also specify a label for the disk and, if it was previously formatted, you can specify a quick format, which simply erases the disk.

From (Copy dialog box, File Manager)   In this field, type the name of the file you want to *copy* to another disk or directory. If you click a file before executing the command, it appears in the From field. You can specify more than one file by using wildcard characters (* and ?) or by selecting multiple files before choosing the command.

From (Move dialog box, File Manager)   In this field, type the name of the file you want to *move* to another disk or directory. If you click a file before executing the command, it appears in the From field. You can specify more than one file by using wildcard characters (* and ?) or by selecting multiple files before choosing the command.

From (Remove dialog box, Calendar)   In this field, type the beginning date of appointments that you want to delete.

From (Rename dialog box, File Manager)   *See* From (Remove dialog box, Calendar).

Function Keys (Terminal Settings menu)   Opens a dialog box for defining commands and text strings to assign to the function keys.

Get Colors, Paintbrush Options menu)   Retrieves previously saved color palettes that you have customized with special colors created using the Edit Colors option.

Go To (Cardfile Search menu)   Quickly jump to a specific card by typing all or part of its index header text. This option only searches the index header, not the body text. Use the Find option to search for text in the body of the card.

Go To Page (Write Find menu)   Type the number of a page to jump to in a document. The document must be paginated correctly by choosing the Repaginate option on the File menu.

Granularity (Sizing Grid field, Desktop utility)   Use this to set the spacing between icon and other desktop objects. The granularity is initially 0, but you can set it from 1 to 49, with each increment representing 8 pixels. To get an idea of pixel size, note that the default border width is 3 pixels.

Hangup (Terminal Phone menu)   Disconnects from the phone line. Be sure to log off the remote system before choosing this command, otherwise you may be charged for time until it detects you have stopped the connection.

Header (Write Document menu)   Opens the Header window and dialog box where you type the text of a header and specify its position on the printed page.

Height (Image Attributes dialog box, Paintbrush)   Enter the new height in inches, centimeters, or pixels for the canvas. Choose a measure to use in the Units field before entering a height value.

Hidden (Properties for Windows dialog box, File Manager)   Enable this to hide a file or disable it to show hidden files. DOS hides some of its system files to protect them from accidental deletion. Windows hides swap files for similar reasons. You can see these files by enabling the option.

High Priority (Print Manager Options menu)   Assigns a high priority (more processing time) to printing and a low priority to any running applications.

Hour Format (Day Settings dialog box, Calendar)   Specify 12-hour or 24-hour time format.

Idle (386 Enhanced utility)   Specify the amount of time after an application uses a port (LPT or COM) before another application can access the port. This option is designed to prevent non-Windows applications, which do not share devices cooperatively, from contending for the same port.

Ignore If Inactive (Print Manager Options menu)   Enable to ignore messages if the Print Manager window is inactive or is running as an icon.

Image Attributes (Paintbrush Options menu)   Use to set the size, measurement, and color settings of a new painting. Choose New after setting these options to open a new canvas with the attributes you set.

Import (Object Packager File menu)   Places the path and filename of a selected file in the Content window of Object Packager.

Inbound CR-> CR/LF (Terminal Preferences dialog box, Terminal)   Enable this option to add a line-feed to incoming text. This option is necessary if incoming text is writing over itself.

Increase Speed command (Sound Recorder Effects menu)   Shortens the wavelength of the sound by 50 percent.

Increase Volume command (Sound Recorder Effects menu)   Increases the amplitude of the soundwave by 25 percent.

Indents (Write Paragraph menu)   Opens a dialog box where you can set alignment options for the current paragraph. If you choose Ruler on the Document menu, you can set indents using the ruler bar.

Index (Cardfile Edit menu)   Choose this option to edit the index header for the currently selected card.

Index Line (Index dialog box, Cardfile)   Type the text of the index card header.

Indicate Expandable Branches (File Manager Tree menu)   Marks expandable directories with a plus sign (+) and expanded directories with a minus (−). Setting this option on may cause File Manager to run slower, but gives you an indication of directories that hold subdirectories without first opening them.

Insert File command (Sound Recorder Edit menu)   Use to insert another sound into the current sound. All sound after the insertion point moves to the right and the length of the entire sound file is extended. If you want to mix a sound file, choose the Mix with File option.

Insert Object (Write Edit menu)   Displays a list of server applications on your computer that can supply OLE (object linking and embedding) objects. You can then choose an application from the list to retrieve an object you want to embed or link in the current document. This produces the same results as starting a server application and using the Clipboard to copy and paste the object into the current document.

Insert Page # button (Page Header or Footer dialog box, Write)   Click this option to insert a marker that prints the page number in the header text.

Installed Fonts (Fonts utility)   Click an installed font to see it displayed in the Sample window. If you want to remove a font, first select it in this field.

Installed Printers (Printers utility)   Choose a printer in this list, then click the Connect or Setup button to change its settings.

Intensity Control (Options dialog box (common))   Slide the button to adjust how colors in graphic images print on black-and-white printers. A middle setting is usually appropriate. Slight adjustments remove perceptible dither patterns from some colors to produce solid grays on some printers. For best results, choose Fine in the Dither field and use a high-resolution printer, such as a laser printer.

International (Control Panel utility)   Use this to change the keyboard layout, measurement system, and date/time, currency, and number formats.

Interrupt Request Line (Ports utility)   Select the interrupt setting for a serial card based on its switch or jumper settings.

Interval (Day Settings dialog box, Calendar)   Specify the time interval to use when displaying the daily schedule.

Inverse (Paintbrush Pick menu)   Reverses the colors in a cutout as follows: blacks convert to white and vice versa; dark gray and light gray reverse; light blue and reds switch; dark blues and yellows switch; lavenders and greens switch.

Italic (Paintbrush Text menu)   Converts selected characters to italic or switches to italic typing mode.

Italic (Write Character menu)   *See* Italic (Paintbrush Text menu).

Justified (Write Paragraph menu)   Aligns paragraphs with both the left and right margins.

Kermit (Binary Transfers dialog box, Terminal)   A communications protocol used to transfer data files. Popular for mainframe transfers.

Key Maps (MIDI Mapper)   Click this option to create or edit a key map. A key map defines which percussive sounds are assigned to the keyboard of an electronic keyboard synthesizer. A key map can also adjust the sounds in a patch map up or down one or more octaves.

Keyboard (Change System Settings dialog box, Windows Setup utility)   Select a new keyboard type to install.

Keyboard (Control Panel utility)   Use to set the keyboard repeat rate and delay. The delay is how long you hold the key before it starts repeating and the repeat rate adjusts how fast a key types characters when held down.

Keyboard Layout (International utility)   Choose a keyboard layout appropriate for the country you have selected in the Country field of the International dialog box. Usually, the most appropriate keyboard is already selected.

Label (Label Disk dialog box, File Manager)   Type an electronic label (name) you want placed on the disk being formatted. This name appears in directory listings of the disk and is often used to verify that the proper disk has been inserted in the drive.

Label (Object Packager Edit menu)   Changes the label (title) of the icon in the Appearance window. Use this option to assign a new title to an icon that you are pasting as a package.

Label Disk (File Manager Disk menu)   Assigns or changes the volume label (name) for a floppy or hard disk. This name appears in directory listings of the disk and is often used to verify that the proper disk has been inserted in the drive.

Language (International utility)   Choose a specific language to use within the selected country. This field is usually set according to the country selected in the Country field, but you can change it if necessary.

Last Modification Date (Partial Details dialog box, File Manager)   Enable this option to list the date stamp of files in directory listings.

Last Modification Time (Partial Details dialog box, File Manager)   Enable this option to list the time stamp of files in a directory listing.

Left (Write Paragraph menu)   Aligns paragraphs or pictures with the left margin.

Left Indent (Indents dialog box, Write)   Specify the distance of the left indent from the left margin. You can also slide the left indent marker on the measure bar to set this.

Line Wrap (Terminal Preferences dialog box, Terminal)   Enable this option to wrap incoming text.

Links (common)   Opens a dialog box that lets you change the settings of a linked OLE object. You can change the drive, path, and filename of the object.

Links (Object Packager Edit menu)   Changes the settings of linked objects.

List (Cardfile View menu)   Displays the index headers of cards in alphabetical order.

List Files of Type (Open dialog boxes)   Choose one of the options in the drop-down list box to change the file list in the File Name field. Alternatively, you can type a wildcard (* and ?) specification in the File field.

List of Drivers (Drivers utility)   Select a driver to install from this list and click the OK button. If you don't see the appropriate driver listed, choose Unlisted or Updated Driver and click the OK button. You are then asked to insert the disk containing the new drivers. Note that if you are updating a driver, you may need to first remove the existing driver.

List Separator (International utility)   Specify the character you want to use as a separator between elements in listings. This separator is set according to the country settings, but you can change it if necessary.

Local Echo (Terminal Preferences dialog box, Terminal)   Enable to display keystrokes in the Terminal workspace if nothing appears when you type.

Low Priority (Print Manager Options menu)   Assigns a low priority (less processor time) to printing and a higher priority to running applications.

Lowercase (Font dialog box, File Manager)   Choose this option to display all filenames in directory windows in lowercase type.

Macro Name (Macro Properties dialog box, Recorder)   Type the name of the macro you want to record.

Make System Disk (File Manager Disk menu)   Adds the operating-system startup files (IO.SYS, MSDOS.SYS, and COMMAND.COM) to a previously formatted disk. This option makes the disk bootable, but leaves less disk space for other files.

Margins (Page Layout dialog box, Write)   Type the value for the left, right, top, and bottom margins.

Mark (Calendar Options menu)   Use this dialog box to choose a reminder mark for the current day. Reminder marks appear in the Month view to remind you of special events such as birthdays.

Match Case (Find and Replace dialog box, Write)   Enable to find only text that exactly matches the uppercase and lowercase specifications that you typed in the Find What box.

Match Whole Words Only (Find and Replace dialog box, Write)   Enable to find only occurrences of the text when it's not part of another word (such as "Wind," not "win").

Measurement (International utility)   Choose a measurement system to use when displaying rulers and other settings. This field is set according to the country selected in the Country field, but you can change it if necessary.

Measurements (Page Layout dialog box, Write)   Specify the measurement system to use, either inches or centimeters. The measure bar changes to match the setting you select, as well as the margin settings in the Page Layout dialog box.

Memory (Setup, Printers utility)   Specify the amount of memory installed in the printer.

Merge (Cardfile File menu)   Use this option to merge another Cardfile stack with the current stack. The cards from both files are merged and sorted according to their index headers.

Merge (Recorder File menu)   Merges another Recorder file into the existing file. The macro list expands to show macros from both files.

Medium Priority (Print Manager Options menu)   Assigns a medium priority to printing and to running applications. Both are given an equal amount of the processor's time.

MIDI Mapper (Control Panel utility)   Use to control the MIDI (Musical Instrument Digital Interface) output channels, instrument patches, and key assignments for devices attached to a MIDI port.

Minimize On Use (common)   When enabled, causes the window of the host application to reduce to an icon when a program or macro starts.

Minimum Timeslice (386 Enhanced utility)   Specify the time slice value used when multitasking all applications. Reducing this value enhances the perceived performance but increases the switching between devices and may slow processing.

Mix with File command (Sound Recorder Edit menu)   Mixes (blends) another sound file with the current sound file. The mix is inserted at the current location of the slider button in the existing sound file, so you should adjust it before choosing the command if necessary.

Modem commands (Terminal Settings menu)   Use these to specify the type of modem and its settings. Most modems comply with the Hayes command set, but if not, refer to the modem manuals for the specific commands used by the modem to activate dial, hangup, and other commands.

Modem Defaults (Modem Commands dialog box, Terminal)   Specify the command strings your modem uses. Refer to your manual. The default is the Hayes AT command set.

Month (Calendar View menu)   Switches from the Day view to the Month view.

Mouse (Change System Settings dialog box)   Select a new mouse to install.

Mouse (Control Panel utility)   Use to change the speed, click rate, and other settings of the mouse.

Mouse Action (Confirmation dialog box, File Manager)   Enable this option to have Windows ask you to confirm mouse copy and move commands.

Mouse Tracking Speed (Mouse utility)   Slide the button left or right to adjust the mouse tracking speed. Test immediately by moving the mouse.

Mouse Trails (Mouse utility)   Enable this option on LCD screens to more easily locate the mouse. It leaves a short trail of mouse pointers when you move the mouse.

Move (File Manager File menu)   Use this dialog box to move files from one disk or directory to another. Moving files removes them from their original location (as opposed to copying, which keeps files in their original spot). Specify the drive, path, and filenames of the source files or select the files before choosing the command, then specify the destination drive and directory. You can specify wildcard characters (* and ?) for the source files.

Move (Program Manager File menu)   Moves a program item icon to another group. You can click an icon before choosing the command, and then specify the target group for the icon in the dialog box.

Move Picture (Write Edit menu)   This option lets you adjust a pasted picture horizontally on the line. Drag the mouse or press the LEFT ARROW or RIGHT ARROW key to adjust the picture.

Name (By File Type dialog box, File Manager)   Type the wildcard specification of the files you want to list in the directory window.

Name (Create Directory dialog box, File Manager)   Type the name of the new directory. Specify its full path if it should branch from a directory other than the one listed in the Current Directory field.

Name (File Manager View menu)   Display filenames only in the active directory window.

Name (Pattern field, Desktop utility)   Select a pattern in the list box or type a name for an existing pattern. To see and test the patterns, choose the Edit Patterns button.

Name (Screen Saver field, Desktop utility)   Choose a screen saver in the drop-down list. After selecting a screen saver, click the Setup button to adjust its settings.

Network (Change System Settings dialog box, Windows Setup utility)   Select a network type to install from the drop-down list.

Network (Control Panel utility)   Use this utility to add or remove connections to remote drives on network servers, or change other network settings.

Network Connections (Print Manager Options menu)   Enables or disables connection to a network printer.

Network Settings (Print Manager Options menu)   Use these to set the Print Manager's interaction with network printers.

Never Warn (Device Contention field, 386 Enhanced utility)   Enable this if you don't ever want to see a warning when two devices access the same port. Only enable if you're sure this contention won't occur.

New (PIF Editor File menu)   Opens a new Program Information File with default settings.

New (Program Manager File menu)   Use New to create a new group or add an icon to a group. The first dialog box you see lets you choose to create a group or program item icon. You then see a dialog box for specifying the parameters for a group or icon.

New Size (Virtual Memory dialog box)   A recommended size is in this box, but you can change it to increase or decrease the size of the virtual memory file. Virtual memory (a feature of 386 enhanced mode) lets Windows run as if there is more memory than actually present by using hard disk space as if it were memory.

New Window (File Manager Window menu)   Opens another directory window like the currently active window. Alternatively, you can double-click a drive icon to open a directory window on that drive.

Next (Calendar Show menu)   Move to the next day in the Day view or the next month in the Month view. Alternatively, you can click the right arrow button on the status bar to move ahead a day or month, depending on the current view.

No Title (Clock Settings menu)   Removes the title bar from the clock so you can reduce its size more effectively.

Normal (Write Character menu)   Reverts selected characters back to normal style, which is a style that is not boldfaced or italic.

Normal (Write Paragraph menu)   Reverts a formatted paragraph back to normal alignment and spacing. The paragraph aligns with the current margin settings.

Number (Autodial dialog box, Cardfile)   Type the telephone number to dial in this field. If a prefix or dial-out code is required, type it followed by a comma. The comma introduces a two-second delay. Add more commas if necessary.

Number Format (International utility)   Select the number format for the selected country by clicking the Change button. This field is preset according to the country setting in the Country field, but you can change it if necessary.

Object (Write Edit menu)   Plays, runs, or opens an OLE object for editing.

Object Type (Insert Object dialog box, Write)   When inserting a new object, click the type of object to insert in this field. It contains a list of OLE-compatible servers that can supply OLE objects for embedding or linking into your current document.

Omit Picture Format (Paintbrush Options menu)   Limits the formats that Paintbrush copies to the Clipboard. Some applications cannot read all the formats Paintbrush supplies and you may need to limit the formats before copying a picture between Paintbrush and the applications.

Open (Clipboard Viewer File menu)   Opens a previously saved Clipboard file so you can paste it in a document.

Open (File Manager File menu)   Opens a directory window if a directory is selected and starts a program or application if a file is selected.

Open (Media Player File menu)   Opens a file to play with the specified device. This command is only available when a compound device has already been specified by choosing an option under the Device menu.

Open (PIF Editor File menu)   Open an existing PIF for editing.

Open (Program Manager File menu)   Opens a selected group or starts a selected program icon.

Options, Make System Disk (Format Disk dialog box, File Manager)   Click this option if you want to format a disk and add the system files (IO.SYS, MSDOS.SYS, and COMMAND.COM) to the disk, thus making it bootable. System disks have less room available for other files.

Options, Quick Format (Format Disk dialog box, File Manager)   Enable this option to erase a previously formatted disk.

Orientation (Print Setup dialog box, Write)   Choose Portrait to print the page vertically or Landscape to print the page horizontally.

Other Files (By File Type dialog box, File Manager)   Enable this option to list all other non-associated document files in file listings.

Other Net Queue (Print Manager View menu)   Choose to display a list of files in network queues besides the one you're connected to. You usually choose this option to check the status of other queues when you're looking for a printer to print on.

Outbound CR-> CR/LF (Terminal Preferences dialog box, Terminal)   Enable this option to add a line-feed to outgoing text. Enable this option if lines are overlapping on the receiving system.

Outline (Paintbrush Text menu)   Produces an outline of the characters you type.

Page Layout (Write Document menu)   Opens a dialog box in which you set the margins, page number, and measurement system for the document.

Page Number (Go to Page dialog box, Write)   Type the number of the page you want to jump to. Choose Repaginate on the File menu to establish or reestablish page numbers.

Page Setup (Paintbrush File menu)   Opens a dialog box used to set the margins and headers or footers for a Paintbrush file.

Palette (Paintbrush View menu)   Removes or restores the Palette on the Paintbrush window. You remove the palette to gain more workspace. Be sure to pick the foreground and background colors you anticipate using before removing the palette.

Paper (Print Setup dialog box, Write)   Choose the paper size and its source in this dialog box.

Paper Size (Setup, Printers utility)   Use this to select a paper size.

Paper Source (Setup, Printers utility)   Use this to select the tray or other paper input method.

Parity (Communications dialog box, Terminal)   Specify the type of parity checking you want to use during a communications session. Use the same setting that the remote system uses.

Parity (Settings dialog box, Ports utility)   Select an error-checking method in the list box to match the parity-checking method used by the device attached to the port (that is, a printer).

Parity Check (Communications dialog box, Terminal)   Specify whether parity checking should be used during a communications session.

Partial Details (File Manager View menu)   Opens a dialog box so you can specify which file details to list in a directory window.

Paste (Object Packager Edit menu)   Embeds the object on the Clipboard into Object Packager.

Paste (Write Edit menu)   Places the information on the Clipboard into a document. Use the Copy or Cut command to place information on the Clipboard.

Paste From (Paintbrush Edit menu)   Retrieves a previously saved cutout and pastes it into your current document. The cutout remains selected so you can position it before pasting it down. Click elsewhere to paste it down. Click Info to see the cutout measurements.

Paste Link (Object Packager Edit menu)   Links the object on the Clipboard into Object Packager. This creates a linked package that you can paste in other documents.

Paste Link (Write Edit menu)   Pastes the information on the Clipboard into the current document. The information maintains a link with a file created by an OLE server application and will change when that file changes.

Paste Special (common)   When pasting OLE objects, choose this option to specify how you want the object pasted (that is, as an OLE object, a normal object, or another listed object).

Patch Maps (MIDI Mapper dialog box)   Click this option to create or edit patch maps. Patch maps define the sounds produced by each MIDI channel. After you click this button, click the Edit or New button. If you're editing an existing patch map, choose its name in the Name field before clicking the Edit button.

Pause (Terminal Transfers menu)   Pauses a text-file transfer.

Phone Number (Terminal Settings menu)   Set the options for dialing a remote computer on this dialog box.

Picture (Cardfile Edit menu)   Enable this option to paste, move, or delete pictures on a card. If it is not selected, you can only type or edit text on the card.

Portrait (Orientation field, Setup, Printers utility)   Enable this option to print a page vertically.

Ports (Control Panel utility)   Use this dialog box to change the settings of the COM serial ports. You typically change these settings when configuring serial printers, plotters, or other devices on the ports. Modems are normally configured in the software application you use to communicate.

Ports, Connect button (Printers utility)   Select the port the printer is attached to from the list.

Positions (Tabs dialog box, Write)   Type the numeric position of tabs.

Preferences (Recorder Options menu)   Opens a dialog box where you can change the default settings for recording a macro. The default settings will appear in the Record Macro dialog box whenever you record a new macro.

Prefix (Autodial dialog box, Cardfile)   Type a dial-out prefix, if any (that is, dial a 9 or 1 if necessary to get an outgoing line).

Previous (Calendar Show menu)   Move to the preceding day in the Day view or the preceding month in the Month view. Alternatively, you can click the left arrow button on the status bar to move to a previous day or month.

Print (File Manager File menu)   Prints a file on the default printer. Type the name of the file to print, unless the file was selected before choosing the command, in which case it appears in the dialog box.

Print (Write File menu)   Prints the current document and lets you specify the number of copies, which pages to print, and the quality of printing.

Print All (Cardfile File menu)   Prints all the cards in the Cardfile stack.

Print File Size (Print Manager View menu)   Enables the display of the file size for files sent to the print queue.

Print on First Page (Page Header or Footer dialog box, Write)   Enable this option to print a header or footer on the first page.

Print Quality (Print dialog box, Write)   Choose a print quality from the drop-down list box. This varies from printer to printer.

Print Range (Print dialog box, Write)   Choose All to print all of the document, Selection to print a highlighted portion, or Pages to specify the page range to print.

Print To File (Print dialog box, Write)   Check this box to print to a file. You'll be asked to specify a filename after you click OK. When you print documents to files, they contain all the formatting codes required to print a document on a specific printer. You can then take the print file to a location where that printer exists and print it without requiring the application that created it.

Print TrueType as Graphics (Options dialog box)   Choose this option to print TrueType text exactly as it appears in a graphic image or spreadsheet, even if the text is overlapped by graphics or objects that appear to mask or clip the type.

Printer (Print Setup dialog box)   Enable the default printer, or click Specific Printer and choose another printer from the drop-down list box.

Printer Echo (Terminal Settings menu)   Choose this option to print incoming text and your keystrokes.

Printer Setup (Print Manager Options menu)   Use this to specify a printer and its setup options. This option is primarily used to specify the printer you want to use when you drag file icons from the File Manager and drop them onto the Print Manager for printing (drag-and-drop).

Printers (Control Panel utility)   Use to add and configure printers.

Programs (By File Type dialog box, File Manager)   Enable this option to display program files in file listings.

Properties (File Manager File menu)   Opens a dialog box for changing the file attributes of a selected or specified file.

Properties (Program Manager File menu)   Opens a dialog box so you can change the properties of a group or program item icon. Use this option to edit existing icons, or if you've made a copy of an icon that you plan to use for another purpose.

Properties (Recorder Macro menu)   Opens the Macro Properties dialog box so you can edit the settings of the currently selected macro.

Read Only (Properties for Windows dialog box, File Manager)   Enable this option to protect the selected or specified file from being changed or deleted. If you need to edit or delete the file in the future, use this option to turn the attribute off. You can specify multiple files using wildcard (* and ?) characters.

Receive Binary File (Terminal Transfers menu)   Choose this option to receive a binary (non-ASCII) file from the remote computer. *See also* Binary Transfers.

Receive Text File (Terminal Transfers menu)   Choose this option to receive an ASCII text file from the remote computer. *See also* Text Transfers.

Record (Recorder Macro menu)   Opens the Record Macro dialog box so you can start recording a macro.

Record Macro Name (Record Macro dialog box, Recorder)   Type the name of the macro you want to record.

Record Mouse (Default Preferences dialog box, Recorder)   Specify the default settings as to how mouse movements should be recorded.

Record Mouse (Record Macro dialog box, Recorder)   Specify how mouse movements should be recorded.

Redial After Timing Out (Phone Number dialog box, Terminal)   Specify how long Terminal should wait to redial if the line was busy.

Reduce Font (Write Character menu)   Reduces the font size of the selected text 2 points, or switches to a reduced size so all subsequent letters you type are reduced in size. You can choose the option several times in a row to reduce the font as necessary.

Refresh (File Manager Window menu)   Updates the active directory window. Use this option if the files in a directory have changed but the directory window is not aware of those changes. This normally occurs when a non-Windows application makes changes to files, or if you switch a disk in the floppy drive.

Refresh (Print Manager View menu)   Choose to manually refresh the list of files waiting to print at the network queues. You should choose this option before printing to a network queue to see how many files will be ahead of your print job in the queue. If the queue is busy, you may want to try another queue.

Regular (Paintbrush Text menu)   Restores text to "normal" style. Normal font does not have bold or italic styles.

Relative to (Default Preferences dialog box, Recorder)   *See* Relative to (Record Macro dialog box, Recorder).

Relative to (Record Macro dialog box, Recorder)   Specify whether the macro plays back in the same window or over the entire desktop. Use this option to prevent a macro from playing outside the current window if the window size changes.

Remove (Calendar Edit menu)   Removes all appointments between a range of appointment days.

Remove button (Drivers utility)   Select a driver and click this button to remove the driver. You may need to remove a driver before installing an updated version of the driver.

Remove Scheme button (Color utility)   Choose a color scheme in the Color Schemes list box, then click this button to remove the scheme.

Rename (File Manager File menu)   Choose this command to rename the selected file, or you can specify a file to rename when the Rename dialog box opens.

Repaginate (Write File menu)   Automatically inserts page breaks and page numbers. You need to use this option before you can use the GoTo Page command on the Find menu.

Repeat Last Find (Write Find menu)   Choose this option to repeat the last find without reopening the Find dialog box. You can also press F3 to repeat the Find command.

Repeat Rate (Keyboard utility)   Adjust the slider to change the repeat rate, and then check it in the Test box. The repeat rate is how quickly the key retypes letters when held down.

Replace (Write Find menu)   Use to search for and replace text in a document.

Replace With (Replace dialog box, Write)   Type the text that will replace the found text.

Resolution (Printer utility)   Choose a printing resolution for the printer. Lower resolutions print faster but may not give high-quality output.

Restore (Cardfile Edit menu)   Undoes all changes you have made on a card if the card is still at the top of the stack and the file has not been saved.

Resume (Terminal Transfers menu)   Resumes a text-file transfer after you paused it with the Pause command on the Transfers menu.

Reverse command (Sound Recorder Effects menu)   Plays the current sound backwards.

Revert command (Sound Recorder File menu)   Reverts the sound file to its last saved state, removing any changes you made. Choose this option if you don't like the changes you've made to a sound and you want to start over.

Right (Write Paragraph menu)   Right-aligns paragraphs or pictures.

Right Indent (Indents dialog box, Write)   Type how far the right indent should be from the Right margin. You can also click and drag the right indent marker on the measure bar. Only the current paragraph is affected, but you can select multiple paragraphs to apply indent changes to them all.

Ruler On (Write Document menu)   Displays the Ruler and the measure bar at the top of the Write window. You should always enable this option since it's easier to change indents, line spacing, and tabs on the Ruler and measure bar than it is to do so with menu options.

Run (Program Manager and File Manager File menus)   Type a command to execute in the Command field. If you select an icon before opening the dialog box, its command appears in the field.

Run (Recorder Macro menu)   Replays a macro.

Run Minimized (Program Item Properties dialog box, Program Manager)   Enable this option if you want the program to minimize to an icon whenever it starts.

Run Minimized (Run dialog box)   Click this option to reduce the program to an icon on the desktop when it starts.

Save (PIF Editor File menu)   Saves an edited PIF file.

Save As (File menu)   Saves a new or existing document. If the file has already been saved, choosing this option lets you save it under a new name to preserve the original document. You can use this feature when working with template files.

Save Colors (Paintbrush Options menu)   Saves the color palette and any changes you have made to it.

Save Contents (Object Packager File menu)   Saves the displayed object to a new file if you opened Object Packager from within an application.

Save File as Type (Save As dialog box (common))   Choose one of the options in the drop-down list box to change the file list in the File Name field. This lets you see the names of existing files to avoid duplicates.

Save Scheme button (Color utility)   Click this button to save a custom color scheme. A dialog box appears asking for the name you want to save the scheme as.

Save Settings on Exit (File Manager Options menu)   Enable this option if you want to save the current arrangement of the File Manager windows and icons for the next session. The arrangement is saved when you exit. Alternatively, you can hold the SHIFT key and choose Exit from the File menu to save the scheme without exiting the File Manager and Windows.

Save Settings on Exit (Program Manager Options menu)   Enable this option if you want to save the current arrangement of the Program Manager windows and icons for the next session. The arrangement is saved when you exit. Alternatively, you can hold the SHIFT key and choose Exit from the File menu to save the scheme without exiting the Program Manager and Windows.

Scientific (Calculator View menu)   Switches to Scientific Calculator mode.

Screen Element (Color utility)   Choose the screen element to change when redefining the colors of a color scheme, or click an element in the Sample screen located on the left of the Colors dialog box.

Search (File Manager File menu)   Use this command to search for files on the current drive. You can specify wildcard characters (* and ?) and the starting directory. The files appear in a separate window and you can select any files in the resulting list and execute commands on them such as Copy, Delete, Rename, and others.

Search for (Search dialog box, File Manager)   Using wildcard specifiers if necessary, type the names of all the files you want to search for.

Seconds (Clock Settings menu)   Enables or disables the display of seconds when the clock is set to digital display.

Select All (Notepad Edit menu)   Selects all the text in a document for copying to the Clipboard.

Select All (Terminal Edit menu)   Selects all text in the Terminal window and scroll buffer. You can then copy the text to the Clipboard and paste it into a Write document to format and save it for later use. Alternatively, you could select the text in the buffer and transfer it to the remote system by choosing Send from the Edit menu.

Select Drive (File Manager Disk menu)   Choose a disk drive to switch to from a list. Alternatively, you can double-click a disk drive icon.

Select Files (File Manager File menu)   Use wildcard characters to select or deselect files in the current directory. You use this option as an alternative to or in conjunction with mouse selection techniques.

Selected Net Queue (Print Manager View menu)   Choose this option to display a list of all the files in the queue of the network printer to which you are connected.

Send (Terminal Edit menu)   After highlighting text in the workspace, choose this command to send it to a remote computer. You can use the Select All command to highlight all the text in the buffer space.

Send Binary File (Terminal Transfers menu)   Choose this option to send a binary (non-ASCII) file to the remote computer. *See also* Binary Transfers.

Send Text File (Terminal Transfers menu)   Choose this option to send a text file. *See also* Text Transfers.

Set (Calendar Alarm menu)   Use this option to set alarms in Calendar. First place the blinking cursor in the appropriate time field, and then choose the command.

Set Font (Clock Settings menu)   Changes the font of the clock.

Set Up Applications (Windows Setup Options menu)   Choose this option to create the Program Manager startup icons for applications already on your hard disk. If the application is a non-Windows application, Setup will create a PIF file for it if the application is listed in the APPS.INF file (most are). If the application is not known to Windows, you'll see a message that you should create the .PIF and icon manually. Refer to Chapter 19 for details.

Settings button (Ports utility)   Click this button to change the settings of the selected port. Typically, printers attached to serial ports are configured using this option. Modems are configured within the software application you use to communicate with remote systems.

Setups (MIDI Mapper utility)   Click this option to edit or create new channel mappings for MIDI devices. A channel mapping directs the musical score on a specific MIDI channel to a MIDI port, which may be a sound card or an external MIDI device. You also choose the patch map for the channel, which determines the sound played on the channel. If you're creating a new channel map, click the New button. To edit an existing channel map, choose its name in the Name field, then click the Edit button.

Shadow (Paintbrush Text menu)   Creates a shadow around text, using the selected background color.

Shortcut Key (Program Item Properties dialog box, Program Manager)   Lets you specify a shortcut key that will start the program specified by the program item icon. CTRL-ALT is automatically inserted with the key you press to prevent conflicts with system key assignments.

Shortcut Key (Record Macro (and Properties) dialog box, Recorder)   Type the shortcut key you want to use and specify whether it uses CTRL, SHIFT, or ALT.

Shortcut Keys (Recorder Options menu)   Use this option to enable or disable shortcut keys. You disable shortcut keys if they conflict with the shortcut keys currently in use by another application.

Show Date (Show Date dialog box, Calendar)   Type the date of the day you want to view.

Show Hidden/System Files (By File Type dialog box, File Manager)   Enable this option to show hidden and system files in directory listings. Hidden and System files don't normally appear in DOS file listings (this is to prevent users from accidentally deleting them). The DOS system files IO.SYS and MSDOS.SYS are hidden in the root directory and should never be deleted since they are used to boot the hard drive. Windows swap files are hidden and should never be deleted while Windows is running. You can set this option on if you are trying to determine the disk space used by swap files.

Show Only TrueType Fonts in Applications (TrueType dialog box)   Enable this option to show only TrueType fonts in character menus and in the Fonts dialog box.

Show Scroll Bars (Terminal Preferences dialog box, Terminal)   Enable or disable the scroll bars using this option.

Show/Hide Function Keys (Terminal Settings menu)   Displays or hides the function keypad, and the session timer or system time along the lower edge of the Terminal window.

Shrink+Grow (Paintbrush Pick menu)   Changes the size of a cutout. You first select an object with the Scissors or Pick tool, and then choose Shrink+Grow. Draw a new selection box with the mouse pointer and the selected object resizes itself to fit within the box. Choose Clear from the Pick menu if you want the previous cutout to be removed when you resize a new one.

Signal When Connected (Phone Number dialog box, Terminal)   Sounds a beep when a connection is made to a remote system. Use this option if the line has been busy and you set Terminal to redial until a connection is made.

Single Space (Write Paragraph menu)   Changes the line spacing of the current paragraph to single-spacing.

Size (Font dialog box)   Choose a font size in the list, or type the font size in the box.

Size (Partial Details dialog box, File Manager)   Enable this option to display the size of files listed in directory windows.

Size Picture (Write Edit menu)   Changes a pasted picture's size.

Sort by Date (File Manager View menu)   Sorts files in the active directory window by last modification date, with the most recently modified file listed first.

Sort by Name (File Manager View menu)   Sorts files in the active directory window alphabetically by filename.

Sort by Size (File Manager View menu)   Sorts files in the active directory window by size, from largest to smallest.

Sort by Type (File Manager View menu)   Sorts the active file list alphabetically by filename extensions. Choosing this option makes file selection easier since it groups files by type.

Sound (Alarm Controls dialog box, Calendar)   Enable this option if you want to hear sound when an alarm goes off; otherwise a Calendar icon blinks or its title bar flashes.

Sound (Control Panel utility)   Use this to assign sounds to system and application events, assuming you have the Speaker driver installed or a sound board installed.

Sound (Terminal Preferences dialog box, Terminal)   Enable this option to turn on the system bell for the remote computer.

Source In (Copy Disk dialog box, File Manager)   Type the drive letter where the source disk is located. Its contents are copied to the drive specified in the Destination In field.

Spacing (Desktop utility)   Choose the number of pixels used to space icons on the desktop.

Special Time (Calendar Options menu)   Choose this option to set or remove special times between the current time intervals. Use this option if you have an appointment that does not fall into the normal time categories or if you want to set an alarm at a non-standard time.

Special Time (Special Time dialog box, Calendar)   Type in a special time to insert between the normal time intervals.

Speed (Playback Field, Default Preferences dialog box, Recorder)   Specify whether the macro plays back at fast speed or at recorded speed. When you set this option, you are setting the default option used when new macros are recorded. However, you can change the setting before recording the macro or afterward.

Speed (Playback Field, Record Macro (and Properties) dialog box, Recorder)
Specify whether the macro plays back at fast speed, or at recorded speed for demonstrations. If you enable recorded speed, the viewer is able to follow the mouse movements on the screen and see how an action is performed.

Split (File Manager View menu)   Use the arrow keys to move the split bar left or right. The split bar separates the directory tree from the contents list. Typically, you move it left to see more files in the contents list and remove white space from the directory tree.

Standard (Calculator View menu)   Switches to the Standard Calculator.

Standard (PIF Editor Mode menu)   Choose this option to edit the PIF settings used by an application when it runs in Windows standard mode.

Start From (Search dialog box, File Manager)   Specify the drive and directory where the search for files should start. You can specify the root directory (\) to search the whole drive.

Start Page Numbers At (Page Layout dialog box, Write)   Type the beginning page number for the document. The default is 1, but you can specify another page number if the document is a section or chapter of a larger document that is split into several files.

Starting Time (Day Settings dialog box, Calendar)   The starting time is the time that is displayed by default whenever the Calendar is opened. The default is 7:00.

Status Bar (File Manager Options menu)   Choose this option to set the status bar on or off. The status bar displays file sizes and other information about the File Manager.

Stop (Terminal Transfers menu)   Stops a text- or binary-file transfer.

Stop Bits (Communications and Settings dialog box)   Specifies the number of stop bits, usually 1. Stop bits specify the number of timing units between characters in a data transmission.

Strikeout (Effects, Font dialog box, Paintbrush)   Enable this option to add strike-out to text.

Strip LF (View Text File dialog box, Terminal)   Enable this option to remove the line-feed at the end of each line from ASCII files. You do so if the transmission includes extra lines.

Subscript (Write Character menu)   Positions selected text below other text, or switches to subscript typing mode.

Superscript (Write Character menu)   Positions selected text above other text, or switches to superscript typing mode.

Swap Left/Right Buttons (Mouse utility)   Enable this option if you are left-handed to swap the functions of the mouse buttons.

System (Attributes field, Properties for Windows dialog box, File Manager)   Enable this option to mark the selected file as a system file, or display the option to unmark system files.

Tabs (Write Document menu)   Opens a dialog box from which you can specify where tab settings should be by entering their numeric value.

Terminal Emulation (Terminal Settings menu)   Opens a dialog box for setting the preferred terminal emulation type.

Terminal Font (Terminal Preferences dialog box, Terminal)   Choose a typeface and size from the list to display text in the Terminal workspace.

Terminal Preferences (Terminal Settings menu)   Opens a dialog box for specifying the terminal settings used during a communication session.

Text Transfers (Terminal Settings menu)   Sets the options for transferring simple text files.

Text (Cardfile Edit menu)   Enable this option to work with text on cards.

Tile (File Manager Window menu)   Places directory windows side by side.

Tile (Program Manager Window menu)   This option arranges open group windows side by side.

Tile (Wallpaper field, Desktop utility)   Choose this option to repeat a graphic image over the desktop.

Tilt (Paintbrush Pick menu)   Tilts a cutout. You first choose a cutout using the Scissors or Pick tool, and then choose the option. Click the cutout then drag left or right to tilt it. Enable the Clear option on the Pick menu if you want your previous attempts at tilting cleared.

Time (Date & Time utility)   Click the up or down arrow button to change the time, or type a change in one of the fields.

Time command (Media Player Scale menu)   Changes the scroll bar scale to show time intervals. If a CD audio disk is playing, you see the time listed for each track.

Time Format (International utility)   Select the time format for the selected country by clicking the Change button. This option is usually set properly based on the country selected in the Country field, but you can change it if necessary.

Time/Date (Notepad Edit menu)   Inserts the time and date into a document.

Time/Date Sent (Print Manager View menu)   Enables the time and date on print queues.

Timer Mode (Terminal Settings menu)   Enables the session time, which records how long you are logged on to a remote system.

To (Copy dialog box, File Manager)   Specify the destination of a file to copy. Include the drive and path in the field. Copy makes duplicates of the current files in the location specified by To.

To (Move dialog box, File Manager)   Specify the destination of a file to move. Include the drive and path in the field. Move removes the files from their current location and places them in the location specified by To.

To (Playback field, Default Preferences dialog box, Recorder)   Specify the default settings as to whether the macro plays back in any application or only the one in which it was recorded. This setting is used for all new macros, but you can change it at the time you record the macro, or later by editing the macro's properties.

To (Playback field, Record Macro (and Properties) dialog box, Recorder)   S p e c i f y whether the macro plays back in any application or only the one in which it was recorded. Use this option to prevent play of a macro in an application it was not meant for, which could cause unexpected results.

To (Remove dialog box, Calendar)   Type the ending date of appointments you wish to remove.

To (Rename dialog box, File Manager)   Type the new name for a file you want to rename in this field.

To Group (Copy/Move Program Item, Program Manager)   Specify the group to which you want to move the selected icon.

Today (Calendar Show menu)   Highlights the current day in the Day or Month view.

Tools and Linesize (Paintbrush View menu)   Remove or redisplay the Toolbox and Linesize box. You remove the options to make more workspace available.

Tracks (Media Player Scale menu)   Changes the scroll bar scale to show track numbers. This option is used when a CD audio disk is in the CD-ROM drive.

Translations (Terminal Preferences dialog box, Terminal)   Choose the country setting for the file transfer.

Transmission Retry (Connect dialog box, Printers utility)   Enter the amount of time Windows should continue to retry the printer when sending data and the printer is not responding. Increasing the time is useful when printing large jobs like graphics or PostScript. It prevents an error message from displaying if the printer's buffer fills. The increased time may give the printer a chance to catch up with the computer.

Tree and Directory (File Manager View menu)   Displays both the directory tree and the directory contents in the active directory window.

Tree Only (File Manager View menu)   Displays the directory tree only in the active directory window.

TTY (Terminal Emulation dialog box, Terminal)   Choose this option to emulate a basic dumb-terminal (text only).

Type (Virtual Memory dialog box)   Specify the type of virtual memory drive (permanent or temporary) that you want to use. A permanent drive retains its place on the disk even when Windows is not running. A temporary virtual drive uses whatever disk space is available and releases it when you exit Windows. A permanent drive is much more efficient, but permanently uses disk space until you remove it.

Underline (Effects, Font dialog box, Paintbrush)   Choose this option to underline the selected text, or switch to underline typing mode.

Underline (Paintbrush Text menu)   Choose this option to underline the text to type.

Undo (Object Packager Edit menu)   Undoes the last change made in the selected window.

Undo (Write Edit menu)   Undoes your last typing, editing, or formatting action.

Units (Image Attributes dialog box, Paintbrush)   Click a unit of measure to use in the width and height fields.

Update (Links dialog box (common))   Choose Automatic to update the document whenever a change is made to the source file in the server application, or choose Manual to update the object only when you click the Update Now button.

Update (Object Packager File menu)   Updates an OLE package with the changes you made in the document from which Object Packager was opened.

Update Now button (Links dialog box (common))   Click to manually update a linked object.

Use 32-Bit Disk Access (Virtual Memory dialog box)   This is the FastDisk option described in Chapter 12. Enable this option to have Windows access the drive directly, bypassing BIOS, when running in 386 enhanced mode. Disable this option if your drive does not allow 32-bit access, as per the manufacturer's recommendation.

Use Prefix (Autodial dialog box, Cardfile)   Enable to use the specified prefix when dialing out.

Use Print Manager (Printers utility)   Enable to use the Print Manager as a print queue; disable to print directly to a printer, bypassing the Print Manager and possibly increasing printing speed.

View Picture (Paintbrush View menu)   Displays the current canvas on the entire screen without window borders or the Paintbrush toolbox and palette. You use this option to get a quick view of your entire picture, and then click the picture to return to regular view mode.

View Text File (Terminal Transfers menu)   Displays a text file in the Terminal window before you send it. To send the file, choose Select All from the Edit menu, and then Send.

Width (Image Attributes dialog box, Paintbrush)   Enter the new width in inches, centimeters, or pixels for the canvas. Choose New from the File menu to set up a new, blank canvas with the dimensions you selected.

Windows in Background (386 Enhanced utility)   Specify a value to represent the percentage of processing time all Windows applications get when operating in the background.

Windows in Foreground (386 Enhanced utility)   Specify a value to represent the percentage of processing time all Windows applications get when operating in the foreground.

Word Wrap (Notepad Edit menu)   Wraps text in a document at the current window border.

Word Wrap Outgoing Text at Column (Text Transfers dialog box, Terminal)   Enter a value to specify how wide the document should be and where lines should wrap.

Working Directory (Program Item Properties dialog box, Program Manager)
Type the drive and path of the directory where the application should read and save files. Use this option to separate program files from data files. Specify the directory where the data files are stored in this field.

Wrap Title (Desktop utility)   Enable this option to wrap icon titles. This lets you place icons closer together without their icon titles overlapping.

XModem/CRC (Binary Transfers dialog box, Terminal)   A standard file transfer protocol.

Zoom In (Paintbrush View menu)   Displays a close-up view of the pixels of a painting. You can do detailed work on a picture in zoom-in mode.

Zoom Out (Paintbrush View menu)   When in zoom-in mode, returns to normal view. From normal view, fits the picture on the screen and lets you paste large objects.

Chapter *27*

Glossary

386 enhanced mode   A Windows operating mode that takes advantage of features on Intel 80386 and greater processors. These features include virtual memory, multitasking, and the ability to run non-Windows applications in a window.

accelerator   A video card that boosts video performance using proprietary chips or industry standard coprocessors.

active window   The current window. Its title bar is highlighted. All keyboard activity takes place in this window. To make another window the active window, just click it.

adapter segment   The area of conventional memory that starts at address A000 (640K) and extends to EFFF (1024K).

ADC   *See* analog-to-digital converter.

aliasing   The jagged-edge effect produced when a computer's display resolution is not high enough to display smooth edges.

amplitude   The size of the peaks and troughs in a waveform, usually associated with a sound's volume.

analog   A term that applies to continuously variable physical properties, such as a natural waveform. *See also* digital.

analog-to-digital converter (ADC)   A device that translates analog signals to digital signals. A sound board with sampling capabilities is an example.

ANSI character set   The American National Standards Institute 8-bit character set. It contains 256 characters. To display an ANSI character, hold down the ALT key and type a four-digit number starting with 0. It's best to use the Character Map to access the characters. *See also* ASCII character set.

anti-aliasing   A process that removes jagged edges on curved and angled lines caused by coarse display resolution. Anti-aliasing is also used on some printers to produce higher-quality printouts without increasing resolution.

API   *See* Application Programming Interface, next.

Application Programming Interface (API)   A set of routines that an application program uses to request and carry out services provided by the computer's operating system. The Windows API manages windows, menus, icons, and other graphical user interface elements.

application swap file   A temporary file created by Windows that runs in standard mode and that stores a non-Windows application when you switch away from it. The file can be on disk or in a RAM drive.

archive attribute   A flag assigned to a file that indicates whether it has been backed up or not.

ASCII character set   The American Standard Code for Information Interchange 7-bit character set. This character set consists of 128 (0-127) characters represented by a three-digit number. ASCII characters are recognized worldwide for the exchange of text files. *See also* ANSI character set.

aspect ratio   Usually associated with a computer display, aspect ratio is the relationship of the horizontal pixels to vertical pixels.

associate (or association)   The process of associating a document's filename extension with an application so that when you double-click the document, it automatically loads in the application's workspace.

asynchronous transmission   A form of data transmission, usually over a modem, in which information is sent one character at a time, with a time interval between characters. *See also* synchronous transmission.

attributes   Flags assigned to a file that indicate whether it is archived, read-only, hidden, or a system file.

automatic link   An OLE object with an automatic link is updated whenever changes are made to the original file in the server application.

background   In a multitasking environment in which multiple applications get a share of the processor's time, a background application is one that runs while a user actively uses another application in the foreground.

bank switching   A method of providing more memory to an application by switching between banks of RAM on an expanded memory card. Frames of memory 64K in size are brought in from the external card as needed.

baud rate   The speed at which information can be transferred through a COM or serial port. Not to be confused with bits-per-second, a single baud, or signal change, can be encoded to hold many bits, thus improving transmission rates.

binary   The numbering systems used by computers, it consists only of 0 and 1, which correspond to the on and off states of digital electronic devices.

binary file   A machine-readable file, typically a program or compressed file.

BIOS   The Basic Input/Output System, usually coded onto a chip in a computer. Provides support for hardware and peripherals in a computer system and an interface to the operating system.

bit   A binary digit, or single memory location. A bit is the smallest unit of information handled by a computer.

BITBLT   (Bit Block) transfer. A GUI function that moves or resizes a block of bits on the screen. It is basic to moving and sizing Windows.

bit-depth   The number of bits used to hold the color value of a pixel on a video display. The more bits used, the wider the range of colors.

bitmap   A computer graphic stored as a series of bits. The bits represents the on/off or color state of the pixels on a video display.

buffer   A memory area that temporarily holds information that is in transit to another location, or that may be required later for another use.

burn-in   Damage inflicted on the screen when the same image is displayed for too long. A screen saver that takes over after about a minute will protect the screen from burn-in.

cache   A memory area that holds frequently used data accessed from a hard drive. When information is needed, the cache is checked first before going to the disk, thus improving access. SMARTDrive is the Windows disk caching program.

cascade   An overlapping window arrangement in which the title bars of underlying windows are visible. *See also* tile.

CCITT   The Comité Consultatif Internationale de Télégraphie et Téléphonie, a Geneva-based organization that recommends communications standards.

CD-ROM   Acronym for compact disk read-only memory, a form of storage with high-capacity and write-only capability. A laser is used to read the disk.

channel map   In the MIDI Mapper utility, the channel map specifies destination channels, output devices, and patch maps for MIDI channel messages.

Character Map   Character Map is a Windows accessory that lets you choose non-standard characters (e.g., foreign symbols) and paste them into text.

check box   Check boxes appear on dialog boxes and contain a check mark if enabled. You click the box to enable or disable it, depending on its current state.

checksum   A calculated value used to test integrity in a data transmission.

client application   In Windows, a client application is one that accepts OLE (object linking and embedding) objects.

Clipboard   A temporary memory area used when transferring information with Cut, Copy, and Paste commands.

collapse   To conceal the subdirectories that branch from directories in the File Manager directory tree.

color separation   The process of printing an image as several documents, each representing different basic colors in the image. These separations are then taken to a print shop and recombined in the final process to give full-color results. Each color separation must be halftoned.

COM port   A serial communications port with the device names COM1, COM2, COM3, and COM4. *See also* parallel port and serial port.

command line   The DOS prompt, or a field in a Windows dialog box where you type executable commands.

communications protocol   A set of rules that defines how a data transmission takes place between two devices.

compound device   A Multimedia device that uses disk files, as opposed to a simple device, which plays a medium such as a CD audio disk. The Media Player is used to access and play compound devices. *See also* simple device.

compound document   A document that contains information from multiple OLE server applications.

confirmation message   A message that appears when you attempt an action that is not allowed or an action that affects files or directories.

contention   A conflict when two applications attempt to access the same device (usually a serial or parallel port) at the same time.

Control menu   The menu that appears when you click the upper-left button of a window. It contains commands for moving and sizing the window if you don't have a mouse, or for closing the window.

conventional memory   The first 640K of memory that MS-DOS uses for running applications.

CPU   The central processing unit of a computer system.

CRC   *See* cyclical redundancy check.

cursor   The insertion point, not to be confused with the mouse pointer. Characters typed at the insertion point are inserted into the text. The mouse pointer is used to move the cursor elsewhere.

Cut   A command that removes highlighted text or graphics and places it on the Clipboard where it can be pasted elsewhere or discarded.

cutout   In Paintbrush, an area defined by the Scissors or Pick tool. You can move, copy, cut, resize, tilt, and invert a cutout. You can also save a cutout using the Copy To command or retrieve a cutout using the Paste From command.

cyclical redundancy check (CRC)   An error-checking routine that attempts to ensure the accuracy of transmitted data.

data file   A document file created while working in an application.

DDE   *See* dynamic data exchange or Object Linking and Embedding.

decimal tab   A decimal tab is used to align a column of numbers on their decimal points.

default printer   The printer that applications use unless you specify another. Specify the default printer with the Printer utility on the Control Panel.

Desktop   The Windows screen on which windows, icons, and dialog boxes appear.

destination   The common term used to refer to the location where files, objects, or other information will be after a command is executed.

device   Any hardware component in a computer system, such as a display, printer, disk drive, mouse, or keyboard.

device contention   *See* contention.

device driver   The software that the system uses to communicate with a device such as a display, printer, plotter, or communications adapter.

DGIS   The Direct Graphics Interface Specification, an interface developed by Graphics Software Systems that allows a program to display graphics on a video display through an extension of the IBM BIOS Interrupt 10H interface.

dialog box   A window used to specify further information and options before executing a command.

digital   Related to digits and the way they are represented. In computing, digital is synonymous with binary numbering because computers process information in 0s and 1s, which refer to the on and off states of electronic devices. *See also* analog.

digital-to-analog converter (DAC)   A device that converts digital data to an analog signal. A compact disk player uses DACs to convert the digital information on the disk to analog signals that are sent to an amplifier. *See also* analog-to-digital converter.

digitize   The process of scanning an image such as a photograph and converting it to digital information. A video may also be digitized.

Direct Memory Access (DMA)   A method of accessing memory that does not involve the processor and improves performance. An interface card that performs DMA must have the ability to access memory on its own.

directory   Part of a file management structure used to hold and organize files. A directory has a name, similar to a filename, and may have branching subdirectories.

directory icon   In the File Manager, an icon that represents a directory on a hard disk.

directory path   *See* path.

directory tree   In the File Manager, a graphic display of the directory structure of a disk. Directory tree also refers to the branching structure of directories and subdirectories.

directory window   A window in the File Manager that displays a list of files for a specific directory.

disk cache   *See* cache.

display resolution   The number of pixels per inch and the size of a display screen.

dithering   A graphics technique that creates the illusion of varying gray shades or colors when a full range of those colors is unavailable. Also, a varying mixture of black or colored dots that the eye sees as a smooth transition from one shade to the next.

DLL   *See* dynamic-link library.

DMA   *See* Direct Memory Access.

document   A file created by an application. Document files created by Windows applications are associated and thus open automatically when double-clicked.

document-file icon   An icon in the Program Manager or File Manager that opens an application when it is double-clicked, assuming that the file is associated with an application.

DOS   An acronym for disk operating system. MS-DOS is the operating system used on most systems that run Windows 3.1.

dot matrix   A grid of dots that form an image, depending on which dots are on and which are off. Display devices and printers use dot matrices.

double-buffering   The use of two buffers (instead of one) to temporarily hold data that is being transferred from one device to another. One buffer fills while the other empties. Double-buffering slows performance but prevents a loss of data on SDSI disk devices.

downloadable fonts   Fonts stored as files on hard drives and copied to the memory of a printer when requested by an application.

DPMI   An acronym for DOS Protected Mode Interface. This is an industry standard that allows MS-DOS applications to execute code in the protected operating mode of the 80286 or 80386 processor.

draw program   As opposed to a paint program, a draw program creates objects by describing them mathematically, and then redraws the object using the description the next time the file is opened.

drive icon   In the File Manager, a graphic representation of a disk drive that you can click once to list the files on that drive, or double-click to open a new directory window that lists the files on the drive.

driver   A program that controls a device. A driver file must be loaded when a system boots to support the device.

dynamic data exchange (DDE)   Supports the exchange of commands and data between two applications running simultaneously. In Windows 3.1, DDE is further enhanced with object linking and embedding (OLE).

dynamic-link library (DLL)   A module that contains code that one or more applications can access if necessary. DLLs keep the size of programs small since shared code can be kept in one file.

EISA   Acronym for Extended Industry Standard Architecture, a bus standard introduced in 1988 by a consortium made up of AST Research, Compaq, Epson, Hewlett-Packard, NEC, Olivetti, Tandy, Wyse, and Zenith.

embedded object   In object linking and embedding (OLE), an OLE object that has been pasted into a document and that maintains an association with the application that created it. You can then simply double-click the object to open the application with the object in its workspace ready to be edited.

EMM386.EXE   The Microsoft 386 expanded memory manager.

EMS memory   *See* expanded memory.

Encapsulated PostScript (EPS) file   A PostScript graphic file that contains a TIFF file used to present the image in an application.

EPT port   An IBM Personal Pageprinter port.

exclusive mode   An application running in Windows' exclusive mode has access to all the system resources. Other applications are temporarily suspended.

expanded memory   An older memory standard that some DOS applications use. It pages blocks of information in and out of conventional memory from an expanded memory board. Also called EMS memory.

extended memory   Memory greater than one megabyte in 80286-, 80386-, and 80486-based computers. Windows uses extended memory to provide additional memory to applications. Also called XMS memory.

flow control   A signaling method that acknowledges the transfer of information in a communications session.

font   A set of characters of the same typeface, style, and size.

foreground   In Windows, the active application is in foreground windows. Other windows are in the background.

frequency   A measure of how often a periodic event occurs. Sound waves are measured in hertz, which is the number of times per second a signal repeats.

full-screen application   Applications running full screen take up the entire screen. Non-Windows applications running in standard mode run full screen only. In 386 enhanced mode, applications can run full screen or in a window.

General MIDI specification   Defines a standard setup for MIDI files, including channel settings, instrument patch settings, and key assignments.

grabber   A Windows driver that supports exchange of data in video memory between non-Windows applications and Windows.

granularity   On the Windows desktop, this refers to an invisible grid that Windows and other objects "snap to" when moved or resized. You can control the size of the granularity with the Desktop utility in the Control Panel.

graphic primitives   A drawing element such as a line or arc that can be combined with other elements to form an image.

Graphical User Interface (GUI)   A user interface such as Windows that presents a pictorial representation (icons) of commands, programs, and other features. Usually associated with a mouse pointing device.

graphics coprocessor   A special chip on a video card that handles graphic instructions and relieves the CPU so it can handle other tasks.

graphics resolution   A measure of the number of display pixels and printer dots available to display or print images. Higher resolution produces better quality images.

gray-scale   A progressive series of shades ranging from black to white. The range of shades handled by a monitor depends on the available memory and the ability of the monitor and video card to display them.

Group window   A window in the Program Manager that holds program item icons.

GUI   *See* Graphical User Interface. Windows is a GUI operating system.

halftone   A pattern of dots that simulate shades of gray or color on a printout.

handshake   A signaling method used between a computer and a printer or modem to indicate readiness to send and receive data.

hertz   The measure of frequencies per second, usually abbreviated Hz.

High Memory Area (HMA)   The first 64K of extended memory, which is addressable by DOS applications running under DOS 5. Typically, DOS files are loaded into the HMA to make more conventional memory available for applications.

I/O addresses   Memory locations used by devices to communicate with the CPU and software.

icon   A small graphic image that is used to represent a program or file.

imagesetter   A typesetting device, usually with high resolution output, that is used to produce camera-ready copy.

inactive window   The window you are working in is the active foreground window. All others are inactive and in the background. However, an application running in a multitasking environment may continue to process in the background.

insertion point   The location of a blinking cursor where text will be inserted when you type.

interlacing   A video display technique that continually refreshes first odd-numbered scan lines and then even-numbered scan lines. Some users may find such screens unpleasant to look at over long periods.

interrupt   When a device needs the attention of the CPU, it sends an interrupt signal. Each device uses a specific interrupt signal line, of which there is usually a limited number available. Conflicts can occur if two devices use the same interrupt signal.

IRQ   An interrupt request. *See also* interrupt.

ISA   Abbreviation for Industry Standard Architecture, an unofficial designation for the bus design of the IBM PC/XT.

kernel   The core dynamic-link libraries that make up Windows.

key map   A MIDI patch map entry that translates key values for certain MIDI messages—for example, the keys used to play the appropriate percussion instrument or a melodic instrument in the appropriate octave.

LAN   *See* local area network.

LIM (Lotus/Intel/Microsoft)   *See* expanded memory.

link   In Object Linking and Embedding, a communication between an object pasted in a client document and a source file created by a server application. Changes to the source file are automatically updated in the client.

local area network (LAN)   A communications system between many different computer workstations, usually characterized by a file server (shared hard disk). Workstations communicate with one another and share files, or access files stored on the file server. Devices on networks such as printers and modems are usually shared by all workstations.

local bus video   A technique of placing video circuitry directly on the motherboard to improve performance.

LPT port   A parallel printer port.

macro   A series of keystrokes, recorded and stored in a file for later use. Windows Recorder is used to record macros.

manual link   In Windows object linking and embedding, a manual link is one that you must update by opening the Links dialog box and clicking the Update Now button. In contrast, automatic links update a linked object when you open the file that contains it.

mapped drive   On Novell Netware networks, a directory on the file server that has been "mapped" to a drive letter and appears to the user as if it is a disk drive.

Media Control Interface (MCI)   A multimedia control interface that lets applications control a variety of multimedia devices and files. Multimedia devices may be sound boards, CD-ROM drives, videodisc players, or MIDI devices.

memory-resident utility   A program that loads into memory and remains available for use during a computing session. Also called a terminate-and-stay-resident (TSR) program.

MFM   *See* modified frequency modulation encoding.

Micro Channel Architecture (MCA)   The bus standard for IBM PS/2 computer systems. It is characterized by a 32-bit design.

MIDI   The Musical Instrument Digital Interface standard that defines communications and hardware connections between electronic musical instruments.

MIDI channels   MIDI sends messages out over 16 channels. MIDI devices can "tune" themselves to any of these channels and play the song parts on the channel.

MIDI file   A file containing MIDI messages that plays a song on a MIDI device.

MIDI sequencer   A program similar to a multitrack tape recorder that records songs and plays them back over MIDI channels.

modem   A communications device that enables a computer to transmit information over a telephone line.

modified frequency modulation encoding (MFM)   A technique used to store information on hard drives. A similar method that encodes data and allows more storage is RLL encoding.

mouse pointer   An arrow or other icon that appears on the screen for a mouse pointing device. It moves when the mouse is moved.

multimedia   The combination of graphics, sound, animation, and video on a single computer system.

MultiSync monitor   A video display that can respond to a wide range of horizontal and vertical synchronization rates, and thus can be used with a wide variety of video adapters. Such monitors synchronize themselves with the video card signal.

multitasking   A process that allows a CPU to run several applications by giving each a certain amount of computer time, called a time-slice.

NetBIOS   An API that provides developers with a standard set of commands to request network services.

network   *See* local area network.

network drive   A network drive is a shared disk drive on a network server or a hard drive on a remote file server to which you are connected.

non-Windows application   An application that was not designed specifically to run in the Windows environment and cannot take full advantage of Windows features such as memory management, user interface, or data exchange.

object   A pasted graphic image, text, chart, sound file, animation, or other information in an OLE-compatible client application that maintains an association or link to the OLE server application where it originated.

Object Linking and Embedding (OLE)   An enhancement to the DDE protocol that allows embedding and linking of data created from server applications to client applications.

package   An icon that contains an embedded or linked object. You can double-click the icon to play, open, or edit the object, depending on the type of object it is.

page   *See* paging.

page-description language (PDL)   A programming language such as PostScript that describes output to a printer or a display device. The instructions are in a file that can be edited. The file can be created manually, but more often is automatically created by an application such as a drawing program. PDL files are device-independent, meaning that any device that understands the PDL language can display or print them.

page frame   A physical address in the upper memory block where a page of expanded memory can be mapped. The page frame itself can be a maximum of four 16K pages.

paging   A virtual memory technique in which the virtual address space is divided into fixed-sized blocks called pages, each of which can be mapped onto any physical addresses available on the system.

paint program   A paint program creates graphic images using pixels. The resulting image is known as a bitmap. Scanners and digitizers create bitmaps that are manipulated by Paint programs. Each pixel can be manipulated. *See also* draw program.

palette   The computer version of a painter's palette—this is where you choose which color you want to paint or draw with.

parallel port   Computer ports with the device names LPT1, LPT2, and LPT3. A printer is normally attached to a parallel port. *See also* serial port.

parity   An error-checking procedure in which the number of 1s must always be the same (even or odd) for each group of bits transmitted without error.

Paste   A command on the Edit menu of most applications that places the contents of the Clipboard into a document at the current cursor position.

patch map   A map that defines which instrument sounds are played on a channel. Use the MIDI Mapper utility in the Control Panel to change patch maps.

path   The location of a file within the directory structure of either a hard disk or a floppy disk.

pels   Picture elements. *See* pixel.

period   The length of time required for an oscillation to complete one full cycle.

phototypesetter   A high-resolution output device that applies light directly to photographic film or photosensitive paper to produce copy for final pasteup and production.

PIF   *See* program information file.

pixel   The smallest graphic unit that can be displayed on the screen, usually a single-colored dot. Sometimes referred to as pels (picture elements).

port   A connection on a computer used to attach printers and serial devices such as modems.

PostScript   A page-description language developed by Aldus and used in many laser printers and high-resolution imagesetters. *See* page-description language.

printer font   A font that is hard-wired in a printer. You can use the font if a driver that matches the printer is installed in Windows.

print file   A file that contains all the information necessary to print a document without first opening the application that created it.

print queue   Files waiting to be printed are placed in a holding area called a queue.

program information file (PIF)   A file that provides Windows with information about how to load and run a non-Windows application in Windows. Each non-Windows application can have its own PIF file. The PIF Editor is used to edit PIF files for either standard mode or 386 enhanced mode.

program-item icons   In the Program Manager, a startup icon for a program is referred to as a program-item icon. Double-click the icon to start the application.

protected mode   A computer's (Intel 80286 or higher) operating mode that is capable of addressing extended memory directly and providing memory protection to applications when multitasking.

protocol   A set of rules that define how devices communicate with one another.

queue   In terms of Windows printing, a queue is a holding area where documents await printing. A queue normally operates on a first-in/first-out basis.

RAM DAC   An acronym for random access memory digital-to-analog converter. Converts digital information into analog video signals for display on a computer monitor.

RAM drive   A simulated disk drive in computer memory not to be confused with a cache. Data in a RAM drive must be saved to a physical disk, whereas a cache is automatically managed by the operating system and any changes in the data are written to disk at the most convenient time. *See also* cache.

raster fonts   Bitmap fonts that are stored in a file with specific sizes and styles.

raster image processor (RIP)   A device that converts (rasterizes) vector graphics and text into a raster image (bitmapped). Usually part of a high-resolution imagesetter. Most RIPs accept PostScript files.

read-only file   A file with the read-only attribute. You cannot change or delete the file without first removing the attribute.

real mode   The operating mode of Intel 80286, 80386, and 80486 processors that support MS-DOS. It is a single-tasking mode (one-program-at-a-time) that limits applications to one megabyte of memory. Under previous versions of Windows, this referred to an operating mode of Windows that used the real mode of the processor. *See also* protected mode.

refresh rate   A measure of how often the entire screen is repainted per second. The refresh rate depends on the horizontal scanning rate, but is measured as the vertical refresh rate. Rates above 70Hz (hertz) are required in most cases to reduce noticeable flicker.

register   A memory location on a microprocessor that stores binary numbers. Similar to a memory on a desktop calculator, a register is used to manipulate numbers or perform mathematical operations.

reminder marks   Reminder marks appear in the Month view to remind you of special events such as birthdays.

repeat rate   How quickly a key retypes letters when held down.

resolution   *See* display resolution.

RIP   *See* raster image processor.

RLL   *See* Run Length Limited.

root directory   The top-level directory of a disk. All other directories branch from the root directory.

Run Length Limited (RLL)   A technique used to store information on hard drives in which an encoding scheme is used to gain 50 percent more storage space than MFM methods.

sampling   The process of gathering data from a source. In multimedia Windows, audio waves are sampled and stored as digital information by an analog-to-digital processor on an optional sound card.

scalable typeface   A set of letters, numbers, punctuation marks, and symbols that are a given design but can be scaled to any size.

screen font   A font that is displayed on the screen to approximate the look of a printer font.

screen saver   A moving image that appears on the screen following a period of non-activity to protect the screen from damage that might be caused by displaying the same image for too long (this damage is called burn-in).

scroll bar   A bar at the bottom and/or right edge of a window that contains buttons for scrolling through the contents of the windows.

sequencer   The software equivalent of a multitrack tape recorder, a sequencer records musical notes produced by a MIDI keyboard synthesizer or by manual editing, and then plays them back through a MIDI device.

serial port   A connection port for transmitting data over a single line. A modem is usually attached to a serial port, but some printers also connect in this way. Serial ports have the device names COM1, COM2, COM3, and COM4. *See also* parallel port, port.

server   A network computer that shares its disk space and provides resources used by workstations attached to the network. The server often holds the network control programs that manage the flow of data over a network and access to network resources. *See also* local area network.

shadowing   A process of mapping ROM BIOS on a video adapter card into faster 32-bit RAM memory on the system board.

simple device   In MIDI, a simple device is one that does not use disk files. It plays directly. An example is a CD-ROM drive that plays a CD audio disk. *See also* compound device.

soft font   A soft font is stored on disk and sent to the memory of a printer when needed.

sound file   A digital audio file that can play on a sound board. The sound board then converts digital information to analog waveforms, which can be heard through a speaker.

source   The location of a file to be copied to a new destination and/or the name of the file.

standard mode   A Windows operating mode that provides access to extended memory and that allows program-switching between Windows and non-Windows applications. A non-Windows application can only run full screen and all other application suspend while it runs.

stop bits   Specify the number of timing units to occur between characters in a data transmission.

subdirectory   A directory that branches from another directory. All directories are subdirectories of a disk's root directory.

swap file   In 386 enhanced mode, an area on the hard drive that is used to hold information in memory so that memory can be freed up for other uses. Swap files can be temporary (removed when you exit Windows) or occupy a permanent place on the disk (which provides better performance). *See also* application swap file.

synchronous transmission   Data transfer in which information is transmitted in blocks of bits that are separated by equal time intervals. *Compare to* asynchronous transmission.

synthesizer   An electronic keyboard (like a piano) or device that generates sounds. Such devices typically have a MIDI interface and are used to record or play back MIDI files using sequencer software. MIDI files can also be played back using the Media Player accessory.

Task List   A switching utility that you can access by double-clicking the desktop or by pressing CTRL-ESC. Task List displays a list of running applications that you can switch to.

terminal emulation   Enables your computer to act like a terminal that is compatible with a remote computer.

terminate-and-stay-resident (TSR) program   *See* memory-resident utility.

text file   A file containing ASCII characters that can be displayed on a wide variety of computer systems.

tile   A window arrangement that places all open windows side by side (like tiles on a floor) so you can see part of the contents of each. *See also* cascade.

timeout   This is the amount of time a device has to respond to another device (such as your computer) before it is assumed to be busy or out of service.

transfer rate   The rate at which a communication channel can send information, usually quoted as bits per second.

transmission   The transfer of information from one device to another, usually over the phone lines using modems.

TrueType fonts   Scalable fonts that can be sized to any height and that print exactly as they appear on the screen. *See also* screen font, printer font.

TSR (terminate-and-stay-resident software)   *See* memory-resident utility.

UART   *See* universal asynchronous receiver-transmitter, next.

universal asynchronous receiver-transmitter (UART)   An integrated circuit that receives and transmits serial transmissions. It is usually located on the serial interface card.

upper memory area (or adapter segment)   The block of memory that starts at 640K and ends at 1024K (hexadecimal addresses A000 through FFFF). The system hardware components use this area; however, drivers or memory-resident utilities can be loaded into addresses not used if the operating system permits (DOS 5 does so).

vector fonts and graphics   Fonts or graphic images that are created using lines or curves between points rather than bitmaps. Such images are often created by object-oriented drawing packages.

VESA (Video Electronics Standard Association)   An organization that is standardizing Super VGA and other types of video display resolutions, including local bus on-board video.

video RAM (VRAM)   A special type of dynamic RAM memory that speeds video applications. The chips are dual-ported, and they accept data from a video controller while sending data to a RAM DAC.

virtual device   A device that exists in software, but does not physically exist. A RAM drive is a good example; it appears to be a physical disk drive, but exists only in memory.

virtual machine (VM)   The emulation of a computer within another computer. For example, Windows 386 enhanced mode creates 8086 machines with 640K of memory to allow non-Windows applications to run in a window.

virtual memory   A technique of simulating additional memory for an application by mapping memory to a physical disk. The application sees more memory than is physically available. Virtual memory is available in Windows 386 enhanced mode and provides a way to run multiple applications at once without running out of memory.

VRAM   *See* video RAM.

wallpaper   A graphic image placed on the desktop for aesthetic reasons. You can also place images that contain useful information, such as birthdates.

waveform   A term that refers to the way a natural wave (that is, a sound wave) changes its amplitude in time.

workspace   The area of a window that is used to display and edit documents. Some applications have multiple document windows, and thus multiple workspaces.

XMS   *See* extended memory.

Part IV

Appendixes

Appendix A

Setup

This chapter gives you an overview of the Windows setup procedure. Rather than providing step-by-step instructions, you'll get a behind-the-scenes look at the setup process so you can better manage setup on your system or other systems. This appendix is written for anyone interested in how Setup works, such as system administrators who need to modify setup for installation on many machines. It also introduces you to the SETUP.INF file covered more fully in Appendix B.

View the SETUP.TXT file for additional Windows setup information before proceeding with the setup procedure. It is located on Windows disk 1 and is a text file.

    The Setup utility installs Windows on your hard drive, and is also used to change the configuration of your setup any time after the installation. To change the configuration, you can run Setup from the Windows directory in DOS, or from inside Windows. This appendix focuses on installing Windows. Chapter 11 tells you how to change the configuration.

    Setup follows a setup "script" in the file SETUP.INF. This file specifies exactly how Windows should be set up on specific types of hardware. For example, if Setup detects a VGA color display, it copies only the files designed for that display. Normally, you don't need to be concerned with this file, but it can be modified to give you added control over the setup process. The individual sections of SETUP.INF are covered in Appendix B. Although the techniques are similar, don't get the procedure for modifying SETUP.INF mixed up with the procedure for modifying Setup for installation on a network, as discussed in Chapter 17.

Starting Setup from DOS

To start the Setup program, first place Windows disk 1 in a floppy drive, then switch to that drive and type **SETUP**. You can type the options (described individually next) on the Setup line; note that some of these options are designed for system administrators who are installing Windows on a Network. If you type an option on the command line, Windows enters custom setup. If you type **SETUP** without one of these parameters, you get a choice between custom setup or the faster express setup. The difference between custom and express setup is discussed following the startup parameters given here.

The /a Option   The /a option is used for the administrative (network) setup. Having this option in the command line expands and copies all the Windows files to a directory on a network server, where they are shared by network users who wish to set up and use Windows. Refer to Chapter 17 for information on this topic.

The /b Option   The /b parameter sets up Windows for a monochrome display adapter.

The /i Option   Use /i when you want to turn off (or ignore) automatic hardware detection. Setup normally tries to determine the type of hardware your system has. If Setup fails during its first phase, use the /i option to prevent it from trying to detect hardware. When /i is used, you'll need to manually specify the hardware settings on the System Information screen once Setup starts.

The /n Option   The /n parameter sets up a shared copy of Windows on a network. See Chapter 17 for more information.

The /t Option   The /t parameter causes Setup to search the setup drive for incompatible software that should not run at the same time Setup (or Windows) is running. Use this option if Setup fails the first time you run it. Also see the /i option, explained earlier in this appendix.

The /h:*filename* Option   Use /h:*filename* to specify a filename that contains setup parameters and options used to set Windows up in a specific, predefined way. While this method is normally used by network administrators to install shared copies of Windows for users on a network, you can also use the method to control your own Windows setup. The procedure for doing so is covered in Chapter 17.

The /o:*filepath* Option   If you've created an alternative SETUP.INF file as discussed in Appendix B, use /o:*filepath* to direct the Setup utility to use the alternate file. For example, if the alternative file is called ALTSETUP.INF and it is located in the Windows directory, you would type the following to start Setup:

SETUP /o:C:\WINDOWS\ALTSETUP.INF

The /s:*filepath* **Option**   Use /s:*filepath* to specify an alternate location for the Windows setup files. For example, they may be on the disk in drive B, a network drive, or even on a CD-ROM drive. Type the full path to the Windows files.

Upgrading

If you have a copy of Windows 3.0, Microsoft recommends that you upgrade it, rather than install Windows 3.1 in a new directory. Setup preserves existing Windows 3.0 settings during the upgrade. If you prefer to install Windows 3.1 in a separate directory and preserve your Windows 3.0 installation, simply specify another directory for Windows 3.1 during the Setup procedure. You'll need to choose Custom installation as discussed in the upcoming "Express and Custom Setup" section.

Setup maintains certain settings and options when you upgrade, as listed here.

Program Manager Groups   Windows maintains the groups and arrangements in the Program Manager.

The .INI Files   The existing SYSTEM.INI, WIN.INI, and other .INI files are preserved. Any settings in those files are retained, or upgraded with new and appropriate settings.

Device Drivers   Setup keeps existing drivers but updates those drivers if they are old or not compatible with Windows 3.1. Unknown drivers or those supplied by another manufacturer are left unchanged. You may need to run Setup from Windows after the installation to upgrade some drivers, such as video drivers.

Memory Settings   Windows does not change any settings you have that configure upper-memory. Usually these are DOS 5 loadhigh= and devicehigh= commands, as discussed in Chapter 9. Third-party memory manager commands are also left as is unless they are incompatible with Windows. Setup displays a warning message during Setup if it detects incompatible drivers.

Express and Custom Setup

As previously mentioned, typing **SETUP** without any startup parameters displays a screen that lets you choose between custom and express setup. Express setup automatically determines the type of machine in use (to the best of its knowledge), and then asks what type of printer to install and the port it is attached to. No other information is requested. If Setup determines the installed equipment incorrectly, Setup can be run from the Windows directory to modify the installation.

Custom setup gives you more control over the setup process than express setup does. You can change the following during your setup when you use the custom setup method:

- *The directory to hold the Windows files*

- *The system hardware* Custom Setup lets you specify third-party displays, mouse, keyboard, and other drivers.

- *Language* You can specify a language other than U.S. English.

- *Network setup*

- *The printers and the ports the printers are attached to*

- *Installation of supporting files* Whether you want to install all or some of the supporting accessory, help, and text files that come with Windows.

- *Icons* Whether you want to create startup icons for applications already installed on your system. If the applications are non-Windows applications, Setup creates PIFs for them using an extensive parameter list in the file APPS.INF file.

In some cases, custom setup is necessary to ensure that the correct equipment is detected. For example, Setup may select MS-DOS System when one of the following is more appropriate and necessary for proper operation on your system. You can choose any of these models using custom setup:

AST Premium 386/25 and 386/33 (CUPID)
AT&T NSX 20: Safari notebook
AT&T PC
Everex Step 386/25 (or compatible)
Hewlett-Packard: all machines
IBM PS/2 Model L40sx
IBM PS/2 Model P70
Intel 386SL-based system with APM
MS-DOS System with APM
NCR: all 80386- and 80486-based machines
NEC PowerMate SX Plus
NEC ProSpeed 386Toshiba 1200XE
Toshiba 1600
Toshiba 5200
Zenith: all 80386-based machines

The Setup Process

Setup starts out in DOS mode. You'll see several text screens before Setup displays the Windows interface. Once the Windows portion of Setup is available, you can use the mouse to make selections from dialog boxes. The following sections cover the custom installation procedure; however, they may also be helpful if Setup fails during an express setup.

The DOS Setup Phase

During the DOS mode setup phase, Setup asks what type of setup you want, either express or custom. If you choose express, Setup proceeds on its own, asking for floppy disks and eventually for the type of printer you want to set up.

If you choose custom setup, the system confirms the directory where you want to install Windows, and then displays the System Configuration screen for your system and gives you a chance to change settings if necessary. At this point you can specify third-party drivers. If you install by typing **SETUP /i**, Windows does not identify your system and you must manually choose a machine type, display, mouse driver, and network on the System Configuration screen.

Behind the scenes, Setup checks to make sure the SETUP.INF file is available and not corrupted. It also checks to make sure the MS-DOS version is equal to or greater than version 3.1 and that at least 386K of memory is available. If one of these is not true, Setup fails and displays an appropriate message. If Setup gets past this stage, it then checks for previous versions of Windows, first on the path, then over the entire drive. This is an efficient search method since Windows is likely to be on the search path. If Windows Setup finds another copy of Windows, it asks if you want to upgrade it or leave it as is.

After you've confirmed the configuration and setup directory, Setup copies the files necessary to display the Windows interface. It also checks to ensure that the files it copies are newer than those on your system if you're installing into an existing Windows directory. If newer versions of any file exist on your system, Setup does not copy the older files on the floppy disk. During an upgrade, Windows installs new files and deletes unnecessary files, maintaining your existing setup and Program Manager groups. It also keeps your existing WIN.INI and SYSTEM.INI Files, but makes changes where appropriate. For example, Setup adds new options for TrueType, multimedia, OLE, and others.

The [boot] section of SYSTEM.INI is updated to reflect the hardware changes you specified on the System Configuration screen. The following lines are updated to include the settings for your system.

```
system.drv=
display.drv=
keyboard.drv=
mouse.drv=
fonts.fon=
eomfonts.fon=
sound.drv=
comm.drv=
fixedfon.fon=
language.dll=
network.drv=
```

In addition, the [keyboard] section is updated, but only the type= setting is needed if the U.S. setting is used. The 286grabber= section is updated to include the name of the video grabber used to run non-Windows applications. If the system is an 80386 or above, the 386grabber= entry is updated, and various driver entries are added to the [386Enh] section of the file.

At this point, Setup is ready to build WIN.COM in the specified directory. This file is a combination of WIN.CNF and the logo code file and logo data file associated with the selected display type. WIN.COM is executed by Setup. You see the logo screen, and the remainder of Setup runs in the Windows environment.

Troubleshooting

If Windows fails at this point, there are several likely problems. The first is that a terminate-and-stay-resident (TSR) utility is interfering with Setup. Disable the TSR in your startup files and run Setup again.

Another possible problem is that Setup has detected the wrong configuration. If your system is listed in the "Express and Custom Setup" section, be sure to select it in the Computer field of the System Configuration screen. You can also try running setup with the auto-detection feature off by typing **SETUP /i**.

The Windows Setup Phase

If the DOS phase was successful, Setup displays the Windows logo and eventually the Windows setup screen. At this point, Windows is running in standard mode. It reduces the size of the SETUP.INF file by locating the [blowaway] section and trimming it there. This reduces the file in size so that it uses less memory.

Setup asks if you want to run the tutorial for the mouse and the Windows interface. Next, Setup asks for a user name and company name, which is appended to the serial number and registration information.

The next thing you see is the Windows Setup dialog box, which is used to specify exactly which Windows components to install during setup, as shown in Figure A-1. If you don't need certain components, use this dialog box to disable their installation.

There are two ways to disable the installation of files. First, the dialog box splits files into groups, such as README files, Accessories, and Games. You can disable the entire group by clicking (disabling) the check box of that group.

Alternatively, you can disable the installation of individual files within a group by clicking the File button for that group. You then pick files that you want to install (or that you don't want to install) on the dialog box that appears, which should be similar to the Accessories dialog box shown in Figure A-2.

The dialog box in Figure A-2 shows the files for Accessories. All the Accessories files are listed in the right field for installation because the check box under the Component column on the Windows Setup dialog box in Figure A-1 was enabled when the Files button was pressed. In this case, you click the items you don't want to install in the right list, and then click the Remove button. Alternatively, you can disable the check box for a group on the Windows Setup dialog box before you click the Files button, and then add individual components. The end results are the same, but the number of individual files you want to install determines the method you use.

After you've selected files, click the OK button on the Windows Setup dialog box to continue installation. Setup copies the files necessary to run Windows, along with any component files selected. The WIN.INI and SYSTEM.INI files are further updated as necessary to support the files you selected. The TrueType font files are also copied, as well as screen fonts. You're then asked to install printers. Follow the procedures in Chapter 15 to select a printer and configure its settings.

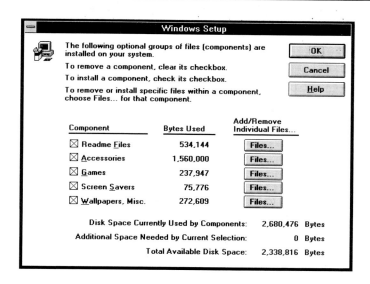

Figure A-1.   *The Windows Setup dialog box specifies which components to install*

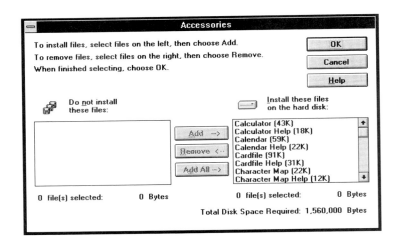

Figure A-2.   *Choosing the files that you want to install (or not install) in the Accessories dialog box*

Finally, Setup starts the Program Manager and builds its groups if this is a new installation. If you are updating a previous version of Windows, Setup maintains your existing groups. It also adds the Startup group. You can set up Windows with a group configuration similar to that on another system by simply copying the *.GRP files and the PROGMAN.INI file from the other system to the new system. If this is a new installation, create an appropriate Windows directory on the target drive, and then copy those files into the directory before running Setup. During setup, specify the directory to which the files were copied as the new Windows directory. Setup then maintains the groups when it installs Windows.

As Setup continues, it adds the HIMEM.SYS command to the CONFIG.SYS file and the SMARTDRV.EXE command to the AUTOEXEC.BAT file. Setup also makes sure the FILE= setting in CONFIG.SYS is at least 30. If your hard drive requires double-buffering, a SMARTDRV.EXE command is added to the CONFIG.SYS file as discussed in Chapter 12.

Setup checks the list of incompatible drivers in the SETUP.INF file; if it locates similar drivers on your system, Setup displays a message indicating that the drivers cannot be used. Included in this check are the MS-DOS commands APPEND, SUBST, and JOIN.

Finally, you are asked how you want to make the changes to the CONFIG.SYS or AUTOEXEC.BAT file. You can have Setup make the changes automatically, or you can review and edit the file later. The last window asks if you want to reboot Windows or return to MS-DOS. In most cases you should reboot the system to enable the new settings in the startup files.

Troubleshooting

A failure in any part of the Windows Setup phase usually indicates an improper System Configuration setting. For example, the display driver may be incorrectly selected, or the driver itself may not be compatible with Windows 3.1. Some adapters cause Setup to incorrectly detect the type of adapter. Try selecting either the EGA or VGA display adapters, since they usually work under any condition. If Setup then works through the entire setup procedure using this driver, you'll need to obtain an updated driver and install it later using the Setup routine from inside Windows.

A Post-Setup Checklist

This section lists the things you should check after a setup. Each topic here lists the chapter in the book to which you can refer for specific information.

FastDisk If you have an 80386 or higher system and a hard drive that can support FastDisk, be sure to enable 32-bit access on the Virtual Memory dialog box. Access this box by opening the 386 Enhanced utility in the Control Panel, then click the Virtual Memory button, and then the Change button. See Chapter 12 for more information. This option should not be enabled on some battery-powered portables that automatically shut down the hard drive to conserve power.

SMARTDrive If your hard drive requires double-buffering, make sure a SMARTDRV.EXE command with the double-buffering option is located in the CONFIG.SYS file. See Chapter 12 for details.

Drivers If you have additional drivers to install such as those supplied with a sound board, CD-ROM drive, or other peripheral, use the Drivers utility in the Control Panel or follow the procedure recommended in the owner's manual to install them. Refer to Chapter 11 for details.

Ports If you have a serial printer attached to a serial port, open the port's utility and configure its settings. Refer to Chapter 23 for details.

Printers Choose the Printer icon in the Control Panel and add additional printers if necessary, or make sure the configuration is correct for those installed. Refer to Chapter 15 for details.

Fonts Open the Fonts utility and add or remove fonts, or set the options for TrueType fonts. You might want to add TrueType fonts you've obtained from other sources. Refer to Chapter 11 for details.

The Mouse and Keyboard   Open the Mouse and Keyboard utilities in the Control Panel to adjust the settings of these devices to fit your needs. See Chapter 11 for details.

Desktop   Open the Desktop utility in the Control Panel and set customization options for your system as discussed in Chapter 11.

The Setup Information Files

This appendix describes the three information files used by Setup or Windows to install Windows, printers, or applications. These files run the equivalent of "scripts" that provide detailed instructions on how setup is handled. This appendix is written for system administrators who configure Windows on many different systems. It describes how to change the files and provides a road map to each of the sections they contain. General Windows users who set up Windows for their own use won't normally need the information presented here.

- *SETUP.INF* The information file used to set up Windows or upgrade a previous version of Windows.

- *APPS.INF* The information file used by Setup to create icons and PIFs for non-Windows applications. It contains PIF settings and icon specifications for a large number of non-Windows applications.

- *CONTROL.INF* This information file holds instructions on how to set up printers and change international settings.

The .INF files are located in the \WINDOWS\SYSTEM directory.

File Structure

The .INF files are text files. You can edit them with any text editor but you must be sure to save them without any formatting or other codes. If you use Write, you'll be asked if you want to convert the files to Write format when opening the document. Do not convert the file; it must remain in text-only format. Always keep a backup copy of the original handy.

The files contain multiple sections that start with a header in square brackets as shown here. You'll see comments below the headers in most cases, and then a set of commands or options. Comments always start with a semicolon (;) and are optional. Commands and options always start with a keyname, as shown here:

```
[section header]
;comments and descriptive notes (optional)
keyname=value ;comment
```

SETUP.INF

Let's first look at the sections of SETUP.INF. You should open the file in Write or another word processor and scan through the setting as you read this section. Alternatively, you can print the file and make notes as necessary for future use.

[setup]

The name and location of the help file that a user can access during the Setup procedure is specified in the [setup] section. To disable help, place a semicolon in front of the entry.

[run]

If you want to run a program when Setup completes, enter its name in the [run] section. For example, to run a tutorial program called TUTOR at the end of setup, place the following command in the section:

```
[run]
tutor
```

[dialog]

The [dialog] section specifies the text strings used to display messages to the user during setup. There are several examples in the SETUP.INF file to which you can refer.

[data]

The [data] section is comprised of two parts. The first part specifies the amount of hard disk space and memory required to perform the setup. The first number is the hard disk space and the second number is the memory requirement. If you add the names of additional files to install during setup (as discussed later in this appendix), you should increase these values to ensure there is enough space on the hard disk for the installation. The second section specifies default settings used during setup. Those you might want to change are described next.

deflang=   deflang= is the default language code. You can find this code in the [language] section at the very end of the SETUP.INF file.

defxlat=   defxlat= is the default translation mode (xlat means translate). Refer to the [codepages] section for alternate codes.

defkeydll=   defkeydll= is the default keyboard layout. Refer to the [keyboard.tables] section for alternate codes.

NetSetup=   Set NetSetup= to 1 (true or on) to force Setup to do a network install if Setup is being run by a user at a network workstation. Chapter 17 provides additional information about installing Windows on a network.

[winexec]

The [winexec] section defines the location and names of the Windows kernel files and is not normally changed. The kernel files are described in Chapter 8.

[disks]

The [disks] section names each of the disks Setup will ask for. Each disk is assigned a number or letter that is referred to later in Setup. You can add other disk names to this section. For example, you could name the disk that contains a special driver called for later in Setup. To request a disk later in Setup, ask for the disk number or letter followed by a colon. If you're viewing the SETUP.INF file, you'll see lines that have the following parameters in this section.

n	Disk number 1 through 9 or A through Z (do not use 0)
path	The path of disk *n*, usually ".", to specify the root directory
diskname	The label of disk *n*, enclosed in quotes
disktag	The volume name for disk *n* that determines if the correct disk is installed

[oemdisks]

Specify any additional disks required to install third-party drivers or applications in the [oemdisks] section. Use the same format as described in the [disks] section above. If you have additional programs and you want to prompt the user for those disks during setup, include the disk names in this section.

[user]

[user] defines the installation disk that contains the user and company identification.

[windows]

The files copied to the Windows directory during the MS-DOS phase of the setup are specified in the [windows] section. Note that the .SRC files are the templates for the WIN.INI and SYSTEM.INI files as described in Appendixes C and D. The Net entry specifies that these files are only copied during network installation when **SETUP /A** is typed at the DOS prompt.

[windows.system]

The files copied to the \WINDOWS\SYSTEM directory during the MS-DOS phase of the setup are specified in the [windows.system] section.

[windows.system.386]

The files that appear in the [windows.system.386] section are copied to the \WINDOWS\SYSTEM directory if the system is an 80386 or above.

[386max]

The files listed in the [386max] section are copied if the system is running the 386max memory manager by Qualitas.

[bluemax]

The files listed in the [bluemax] section are copied if the system is running the BlueMax memory manager (IBM PS/2 version) by Qualitas.

[shell]

The [shell] section specifies which application to install as the Windows shell. The shell is the program that starts when Windows starts (as described in Chapter 11). Normally this is the Program Manager, but you can specify WINFILE.EXE if you want the File Manager to load as the shell instead.

[display]

The [display] section defines the display drivers and the associated grabbers, virtual display driver (VDD), and logo files to load with it. You can make your own entries in this section to install other display drivers. If so, the files for the drivers must be copied to the \WINDOWS\SYSTEM directory. To do so, specify the disk where the files are located in the [disks] section, and then add an entry that conforms to the following format. (If you're not familiar with the terminology in this section, refer to Chapter 13.)

keyname=driver,description,resolution,286grabber,logocode,VDD,386grabber,ega.sys,logo data,optional section

keyname The *keyname* is the profile name of the driver used throughout the remainder of the SETUP.INF file.

driver *driver* stands for the driver name, preceded by its disk number.

description *description* gives the drivers' description in quotes. This name appears in the System Settings menu. Do not change this description for existing drivers.

resolution *resolution* stands for the pixel resolution (horizontal and vertical) displayed on the screen. These numbers are used to define the type of screen fonts to install, as defined in the [sysfont], [oemfont], and [fixedfont] sections.

286grabber   *286grabber* signifies the disk location and name of the 286 display grabber.

logocode   *logocode* tells you the disk location and name of the logo code.

VDD   *VDD* stands for the disk location and name of the virtual display driver.

386grabber   *386grabber* gives the disk location and name of the 386 grabber.

ega.sys   If EGA support is required, list the EGA filename here; otherwise replace it with two commas.

logo data   *logo data* gives the disk location and name of the Microsoft logo bitmap.

optional section   This entry may list the name of an additional section following [display] that provides other display driver information. Typical section headers are [v7vga], [vgamono], [8514], and so on. An entry in an optional section has the following format:

> *file,destination,ini file,section,OldLine,NewLine*

- *file*   This indicates an optional file to copy. Type a comma if the file is already installed.

- *destination*   This gives the directory where the file should be copied. Type a comma if the file is already installed. Type **0:** to copy it to the Windows directory and **0:system** to copy it to the \WINDOWS\SYSTEM directory.

- *ini file*   This is the name of the .INI file to modify.

- *section*   This indicates the section name to modify in the .INI file.

- *OldLine*   This marks an entry that you want to remove. Place the entry in quotes.

- *NewLine*   This marks an entry that you want to add. Place the entry in quotes.

One custom change that you can make in this section is to remove any line for devices that you do not want to display during the setup process.

[*.3gr]

The [*.3gr] section defines which WOA (Windows Old Application) fonts to copy, depending on the 386 grabber entry for the selected display. These are defined by the entries in the [display] section. Note that each line lists two files. The first is copied if code page 437 (U.S. character support) is used and the second is copied if foreign support is specified.

[keyboard.drivers]

The [keyboard.drivers] section maps a keyname to the keyboard drivers.

[keyboard.types]

The [keyboard.types] section defines a short name for each of the keyboard types. The name of the required DLL (Dynamic Link Library) file is specified at the end of the line. A nodll (no dynamic link library) entry specifies a U.S. keyboard since that library is built into Windows. Alternate entries are found in the [keyboard.tables] section, discussed next. One custom change that you can make in this section is to remove any line for devices that you do not want to display during the setup process.

[keyboard.tables]

The [keyboard.tables] section defines the short names for the DLL (Dynamic Link Library) files. The short names are included in the [keyboard.types] entries and in the defkeydll= entry in the [data] section.

[codepages]

The [codepages] section defines the files required for codepages other than the standard code page 437 (U.S.). An alternate codepage is specified with the defxlat= line (xlat means translate) in the [data] section. The entries in this section have the following format:

codepage=xlat table, OEM font, WOA font, description

codepage is the number, *xlat table* is the filename for the translation table, *OEM font* is the OEM screen font, *WOA font* is the Windows Old Application font file, and *description* is a string in quotations that describes the country.

[pointing.device]

The [pointing.device] section provides the following information on the pointing device in the format shown here:

keyname=mouse driver, description, VMD, optional section

keyname is the profile name, *mouse driver* is the name of the mouse file, *description* is a driver description that must be enclosed in quotation marks, *VMD* specifies the mouse driver for non-Windows applications in 386 enhanced mode, and *optional section* contains additional information about the mouse driver. One custom change that you can make in this section is to remove any line for devices that you do not want to display during the setup process.

[lmouse]

The [1mouse] section defines support for the Logitech MS-DOS mouse driver.

[dos.mouse.drivers]

The [dos.mouse.drivers] section assigns the Windows mouse driver to an MS-DOS mouse driver.

[network]

The [network] section assigns the following entries for a network profile name, using the format shown shortly. One custom change that you can make in this section is to remove any line for devices that you do not want to display during the setup process.

keyname=driver,description,help file,optional file,win section,sys section,VDD

keyname   *keyname* is the profile name.

driver   *driver* is the driver filename.

description   *description* indicates a description between quotations.

help file   *help file* gives the name of an associated help file.

optional file   The *optional file* section indicates additional files to install.

win section   *win section* gives the section name in WIN.INI that should be modified.

sys section   *sys section* gives the section name in SYSTEM.INI that should be modified.

VDD   *VDD* signifies the virtual display driver filenames for non-Windows applications in 386 enhanced mode.

Network-Version Sections

The sections that follow the [network] section provide information about specific networks. The section names take the form [3open.versions], [lantastic,versions], and so on. The information is in the following format:

version #=description,optional files,optional sections

The parameters specify the network driver version number, its description, any required optional files, and one of the optional sections that have the name of the network as defined under the [network] section.

Network-Specific Sections

There are a number of sections for specific network versions. The sections take the names [10net41], [ban4], and so on. These sections provide additional information required for the specified network in the following format.

ini-keyname=section,entry-keyname,value

ini-keyname   *ini-keyname* gives either the WIN.INI or SYSTEM.INI file where the entries are made.

section   *section* gives the section in the .INI file.

entry-keyname   *entry-keyname* is the keyname value to place as the entry.

value   *value* is the value for the keyname entry.

[sysfonts]

The [sysfonts] section specifies the location of the system fonts and defines their description and aspect ratios (resolution).

[fixedfonts]

The [fixedfonts] section specifies the location of the fixed fonts and defines their description and aspect ratios (resolution).

[oemfonts]

The [oemfonts] section specifies the location of the OEM fonts and defines their description and aspect ratio.

[win.copy], [win.copy.net], [win.copy.win386]

The format of this section is *from,to*. *From* indicates the location and name of a file, and *to* indicates its destination. Destination 0: is the Windows directory and destination 0:system is the \WINDOWS\SYSTEM directory. If the *from* entry contains a pound sign (#), it specifies a list of files in the indicated sections that follow. For example, if you input **#win** it indicates that all files under the [win] heading should be copied.

[net], [net.386], [win.other], [win.shell], [win386]

These are the sections that contain lists of files to copy as specified in the [win.copy], [win.copy.net], and [win.copy.win386] sections.

If you are setting up special third-party applications, you can create a custom section called [custom.apps] for example, and then specify this section in the [net], [win.copy], and [win.copy.386] sections. Insert lines in the [net] section to copy files during a network setup. Insert lines in the [win.copy] section to copy files for single-user setup on a 286 machine. Insert the lines in the [win.copy.386] section if the setup is on a 386 machine. If the files are on floppy disk, be sure to assign a disk number and name in the [disks] section, and then specify the disk number in the appropriate sections.

If those files go in a special directory, you would include a command similar to the following, which specifies a directory called APPS that branches from the Windows (0:) directory:

```
#custom.apps,0:appdir
```

Your [custom.apps] section would then contain entries that specify the disk number (defined in the [disks] section), and the program name. Here's an example:

```
[custom.apps]
7:CUSTAPP.EXE,"A custom application",365,000,custapp
```

If you specify additional files, be sure to increase the disk requirements in the [data] section up to the amount required by the new files. If a custom application requires a special DLL file, add a line similar to the following to the [win.dependents] section. Note that the profile name matches the name specified at the end of the previous example.

```
custapp=7:custapp.dll
```

[DelFiles]

The files listed in the [DelFiles] section are deleted when Windows 3.0 is upgraded to Windows 3.1. You can add or remove items in this list.

[RenFiles]

The files listed in the [RenFiles] section are renamed when Windows 3.0 is upgraded to Windows 3.1. If you want to keep some configuration files on your system instead of having them copied over, make entries in this section using the format *current name, new name*. Note that upgrade saves the existing MIDIMAP.CFG file by renaming it MIDIMAP.OLD.

[win.apps], [win.dependents], [win.games], [win.scrs], [win.bmps], [win.readme]

These sections describe the disk location and filenames of the Windows accessories, games, screen savers, bitmaps, and other files to copy to the Windows directory. The entries include the disk number, a description, the file size, and a profile string. The profile string is used later to specify in which Program Manager group to create an icon for the file, and also specifies which dependent files are required, if any, in the [win.dependents] section.

You can add or remove entries in this section to customize the setup process on your system, or for other users.

[new.groups]

The [new.groups] section specifies the new groups to create in the Program Manager during an upgrade. The lines take the following format:

section name=group name, min/max

section name is the name of one of the [group*x*] sections listed later, *group name* is the name assigned to the group window, and *min/max* indicates whether the group is minimized (0), or maximized (1). To create custom groups, add an entry in this section that specifies a groups section like those defined under [group*x*] shortly.

[progman.groups]

The [progman.groups] section defines the groups built for new installations. The lines in the section use the same format as the [new.groups] section described previously. To create custom groups, add an entry in this section that specifies a groups section like those defined under [group*x*] next.

[group*x*]

There are several groups within [group*x*], each specifying the profile name and program name of the programs to add to the specified group. The group name is defined in the [new.group] section. To create a special group with custom icons, specify a new group header and add the names and parameters of the programs that go in the group.

[fonts]

The [fonts] section defines the disk location, filename, description, and resolution of screen fonts. The resolution is matched to the display device resolution.

[ttfonts]

The [ttfonts] section defines the TrueType font installation. The lines have the following format:

font header file,description,font file,fontfamily/flags

font header file is the .FOT file associated with the .TTF file, *description* is a description of the font enclosed in quotations, *font file* is the filename for the TrueType font, and *fontfamily/flags* indicates the family and weight of the font. The *fontfamily/flags* option indicates normal-weight fonts if 0000, bold fonts if 0100, and italic fonts if 1000. This option must be in quotation marks.

[compatibility]

The [compatibility] section checks for incompatible commands in the CONFIG.SYS file. If a match is found with one of the commands under the header, the command is removed from CONFIG.SYS. You can add the command later if the incompatibility issue is resolved. You can also edit this section to remove names of commands that are no longer compatible, or add those that are.

[incompTSR1]

The [incompTSR1] section lists TSRs and drivers that prevent Setup from running and should be removed from memory before starting Setup. You can edit them out of your CONFIG.SYS and AUTOEXEC.BAT files until Setup is finished.

[incompTSR2]

The [incompTSR2] section lists TSRs and drivers that prevent both Setup and Windows from running. You should edit such items out of the CONFIG.SYS or AUTOEXEC.BAT file until you obtain an updated version that is compatible with Windows.

[block-devices]

The [block-devices] section specifies block devices that are not compatible with Windows 3.1.

[Installable.Drivers]

The [Installable.Drivers] section lists which drivers to install for multimedia windows. The format of the lines in the section takes the following form:

keyname=filename,types,description,VxDs,default parameters

The *keyname* provides the profile name used elsewhere in the Setup. The *filename* describes the file's location and filename. The *types* and *description* options specify the type and description of a device between quotation marks. The *VxDs* field defines any virtual device files required to support the device in 386 enhanced mode. Finally, the *default parameters* option specifies the parameters that you use initially, if any.

[translate]

The [translate] section specifies translated OEM filenames, with their disk locations and filenames.

[update.files]

The [update.files] section describes drivers that must be updated if earlier versions exist on the hard drive. The format of the line specifies the location of the files and their filenames. A 0 indicates the Windows directory and a 0:system indicates the \WINDOWS\SYSTEM directory.

[update.dependents]

[update.dependents] specifies dependent files for any entries in the [update.files] section that require updating.

[ini.upd.patches]

This section temporarily renames profile strings for .INI entries if a similar string already exists in the file. This renaming is only temporary. The lines in the section take the following form:

ini file,section,temporary profile,original profile

ini file names either WIN.INI or SYSTEM.INI, *section* specifies the section in the file to change, *temporary profile* specifies the profile to replace, and *original profile* specifies the value to add to the .INI file.

[blowaway]

The [blowaway] section marks the end of the installation information and the beginning of the configuration section. Setup deletes the previous sections in memory in order to save space since it doesn't need them to complete the setup.

[ini.upd.31]

The [ini.upd.31] section specifies which lines in WIN.INI and SYSTEM.INI get replaced with new values during an upgrade from Windows 3.0 to Windows 3.1. The lines in this section have the following format:

ini file,section,OldLine,NewLine

ini file indicates the file, *section* indicates the section within the file, *OldLine* specifies the existing line to replace, and *NewLine* specifies the line to replace it with.

[system]

The [system] section assigns profile names to several drivers that do not have special selections in the Setup menus. The names are used in the [machine] section. One custom change that you can make in this section is to remove any line for devices that you do not want to display during the setup process.

[machine]

The [machine] section defines which files are installed for specific machines. The machines listed in the section are those that appear when a computer type is selected on the Setup Configuration menu. Do not change the order of the entries in this section. The lines in the section have the following form:

> *keyname=description,system drv,kbd drv,kbd type,mouse drv,disp drv,sound drv,comm drv,himem switch,ebios,Cookz*

Each option is described next.

keyname   *keyname* is the profile string for the system.

description   *description* is the description of the system enclosed in quotations.

system drv   *system drv* is the name of the system driver defined in the [system] section.

kbd drv   *kbd drv* is the name of the keyboard driver in the [keyboard.drivers] section.

kbd type   *kbd type* is the name of the keyboard type in the [keyboard.types] section.

mouse drv   *mouse drv* is the name of the mouse driver in the [pointing.device] section.

disp drv   *disp drv* is the name of the display driver defined in the [display] section.

sound drv   *sound drv* is the name of the sound driver defined in the [system] section.

comm drv   *comm drv* is the name of the communications driver defined in the [system] section.

himem switch   *himem switch* is a number that identifies the A20 line so HIMEM.SYS can access extended memory.

ebios   *ebios* is the EBIOS (Extended Basic Input/Output System) support defined in the [ebios] section.

Cookz   *Cookz* defines how .INI entries are modified.

One custom change that you can make in this section is to remove any line for devices that you do not want to display during the setup process.

Cookie Entries

The Cookz entries follow the [machine] section and include the profile name of the machine they define. For example, [apm_cookz], [ast_cookz], and [t5200_cookz] are a few of the sections. They have the following format:

> *ini file, section, cookie, needed file*

ini file is either the WIN.INI or SYSTEM.INI file, *section* is the section in the file to modify, *cookie* is a specific entry to add in the section (in quotation marks), and *needed file* is any file that might be needed. Refer to WININI.WRI or SYSINI.WRI for possible entries.

[special_adapter]

The [special_adapter] section is read during the MS-DOS setup phase to provide additional support for special adapters.

[ebios]

The [ebios] section is used by the [machine] section to indicate which files to copy when a system needs extended BIOS (Extended Basic Input/Ouput System) support.

[language]

The [language] section defines the language libraries that come with Windows. The entry deflang= in the [data] section uses one of these values. The lines have the following format:

> *keyname=language DLL, description, language ID*

keyname is the profile string, *language DLL* is the filename and location of the DLL file, *description* describes the country name, and *language ID* is the numeric code that identifies the DLL.

APPS.INF

The APPS.INF file is used by Windows Setup to create Program Information Files for applications, and to create startup icons for the applications in the Program Manager. Keep in mind that you can run Setup from inside Windows after the main installation. This file directs setup when you choose Setup Applications from the Setup Options menu. The individual sections of this file are explained here.

[dialog]

[dialog] contains the title text displayed when Setup displays the Setup Applications dialog box.

[base_PIFs]

[base_PIFs] defines a batch file used to create the _DEFAULT.PIF file. This is the default Program Information File. This section also defines the settings for the MS-DOS Prompt icon and its associated PIF.

[enha_dosprompt]

The [enha_dosprompt] section defines memory requirements for the MS-DOS Prompt icon when it runs in 386 enhanced mode.

[dontfind]

The [dontfind] section specifies which applications Setup should ignore when searching the hard drive because they already have icons in the Program Manager.

[pif]

The [pif] section defines the parameters used to create a PIF when you run the Setup utility. A PIF is always created for non-Windows applications when you run Setup, and an icon is placed in a Program Manager group. Setup specifies icons in the PROGMAN.EXE or MORICONS.DLL files. Do not change the order of lines in the file. They have the following format:

> *exe file=pif name,window title,startup directory,close-window flag,icon filename,icon n,*
> *standard pif, 386 pif,ambiguous exe,optimized pifs*

Each of the settings is defined in the following sections.

exe file   *exe file* is the executable file for the application.

pif name   *pif name* is the name for the PIF file.

window title   *window title* gives the name to appear on the title bar.

startup directory   *startup directory* is the directory the application should use.

close-window flag   The *close-window flag* value should be cwe (close window on exit) if the application window should close on exit, and left blank if the window should not be closed.

icon filename   *icon filename* is the name of the file where the icon should be obtained. Normally the filename is PROGMAN.EXE, but MORICONS.DLL is an alternate.

icon n   *icon n* is the number from the icon extraction table with the default at 0.

standard pif   *standard pif* is the section in the APPS.INF file where standard mode PIF settings are obtained, usually [std_dflt].

386 pif   *386 pif* is the section in the APPS.INF file where 386 enhanced mode PIF settings are obtained, usually [enha_dflt].

ambiguous exe   *ambiguous exe* is the APPS.INF section that lists applications with the same executable filename specified in the exe file section.

optimized pifs   *optimized pifs* give other APPS.INF sections that contain optimized PIF settings.

The settings in the [std_dflt] and [enha_dflt] sections are the same settings you make when creating a PIF file as described in Chapter 19.

CONTROL.INF

The CONTROL.INF file contains information used by the Control Panel when installing or configuring printers and setting international support. The individual settings in the CONTROL.INF file are described next.

[io.device]

The [io.device] section lists the printers supported by Windows 3.1. When you start the Printers utility in the Control Panel and click Add to add new printers, the printers listed in this section appear. The lines have the following format:

filename, description, scaling string, scaling string

filename defines the disk number and name of the file, *description* defines the filename, and *scaling string* defines one or two scalings for the device.

One custom change that you can make in this section is to remove any line for devices that you do not want to display during the setup process.

[io.dependent]

The [io.dependent] section specifies any other files to copy that support the printer. These files include help files and dynamic link libraries (DLLs).

[country]

The [country] section defines international formats. Microsoft recommends only making international modifications by choosing an appropriate country in the International utility.

Appendix *C*

The Windows Files

This appendix provides a listing and description of the Windows files. The files are grouped according to the component or feature they support in the Windows system. The types of extensions are described in the next section. The section "Producing a Disk List" describes a way to produce an alphabetical listing that indicates the disk on which each file is located.

Extensions

The filename extension provides the best description of what a file is for. The extensions described in this section are the most common Windows extensions, however, this is not a complete list.

.WRI   The .WRI extension indicates Write files. These files contain descriptive information about Windows.

.SYS   .SYS files are files supplied with Windows, DOS, or other applications that get loaded at the DOS level with commands in CONFIG.SYS.

.EXE   .EXE files are used at the DOS level or to start programs or accessories within Windows.

667

.COM   .COM files are supplied with Windows and used at the DOS level.

.INF   .INF files are information files that contain scripts and instructions for running setup routines.

.INI   .INI files are initialization files that hold startup and operating parameters for Windows and Windows applications.

.386   Files with the .386 extension are virtual device drivers that support various modes or devices in virtual machines running in 386 enhanced mode.

.DRV   .DRV files are driver files used to supply information to Windows about using devices.

.LGO   The .LGO extension indicates logo files used during Windows startup. Each screen resolution has its own .LGO file.

.RLE   The .RLE extension indicates compressed logo files used during Windows startup. RLE stands for run length limited encoding, a compression technique.

.DLL   DLL stands for dynamic link libraries. These files contain code and commands shared by one or more applications.

.2GR   The .2GR extension indicates grabber files for standard mode. Used in conjunction with WINOA286.MOD, these files support data exchange between non-Windows applications and Windows.

.3GR   The .3GR extension indicates grabber files for 386 enhanced mode. Used in conjunction with WINOA386.MOD, these files support data exchange, displaying data in windows, copying graphics to the Clipboard, and PrintScreen.

.HLP   The .HLP extension indicates a help file.

.FON   The .FON extension indicates screen, printer, and plotter font files.

.FOT   The .FOT extension indicates a TrueType resource file. There is a .FOT file for each .TTF file.

.TTF   The .TTF extension indicates a TrueType font description file. Note that each .TTF file has a corresponding .FOT file.

.WPD   The .WPD extension indicates PostScript description files for printers.

Producing a Disk List

When you buy Windows, the package can contain one of four types of floppy disks: 3.5-inch or 5.25-inch disks at either high or low density. Therefore, the disk location of each Windows file is different, depending on the disk set you have. To produce your own disk list, follow the steps given next. There are two methods. The first produces a simple list by directing the listing of a DIR command to the printer. The second requires an advanced word processor that allows sorting and, although not essential, multicolumn layout to reduce the amount of paper required to print the disk list.

To print the simple list, turn your printer on, and then type the following command at the DOS prompt for each floppy disk. It sorts the disk directory and sends it to the printer.

```
DIR | SORT > PRN
```

(On laser printers, you'll need to eject the last sheet before printing the contents of the next disk.) This command produces a separate list for each disk. Using the next method, you can produce a list that sorts all the files on all the disks together, and tags each file with its source disk number. To do this, you need a word processor that allows sorting.

1. Place Windows disk 1 in the floppy drive and type the following command. You can use any filename besides DISKLIST.DOC, but first make sure a file with that name does not exist on your system. Note that the double arrows append the directory listing to the file.

   ```
   DIR A: >> DISKLIST.DOC
   ```

2. Next, remove Windows disk 1, insert Windows disk 2, and press the F3 key to repeat the previous command. Repeat this step for each Windows floppy disk.

3. Once the disk list is complete, start your word processor and open the file. You'll see the Windows disk 1 listing followed by listings for other disks. The header information for each listing separates the files.

4. Before removing the header information and sorting the entire list, add a disk number to the end of each line. Highlight all the files for Windows disk 1, and then use your word processor's Replace command to replace the carriage return at the end of each line with a space, type the number 1, and press the carriage return.

By highlighting a specific group of files, you can restrict the replacement to only those files. If this feature is not supported by your word processor, start replacing at the beginning of the section and make sure not to replace past the last file in the section.

5. Repeat step 4 for each block of files, changing the number to represent the disk number where the files are located.

6. Once you've tagged each file with its disk location, you can sort the entire list. But first, scan through and remove the directory listing header text that separates each section. To sort the list, highlight the entire file and choose your word processor's Sort command.

7. If your word processor supports multiple columns, place the list in two columns before printing. You'll need to reduce the font size as well as the left and right margins to get the list to fit in two columns.

8. Print the list.

Expanding Files

Most of the files on the Windows floppy disks are compressed. Those that are have an extension ending in an underline (_) character. To copy individual files and decompress them, use the EXPAND.EXE utility. It is located in the Windows directory or on Windows disk 2. To expand a file, type the source file's name and its new destination name. This requires that you know what the full extension should be (you should be able to find it in one of the tables given later in this chapter). In the following example, the README.WR_ file is expanded to the Windows directory and given the name README.WRI.

    EXPAND A:\README.WR_ C:\WINDOWS\README.WRI

Readme Files

The following Readme files contain important information that you should review. In most cases, you just refer to specific sections in each file that pertain to your setup. Setup places the files in the Windows directory.

NETWORKS	.WRI	Network information file
PRINTERS	.WRI	Printer information file
README	.WRI	General information file
SETUP	.TXT	Setup information file
SYSINI	.WRI	Description of SYSTEM.INI
WININI	.WRI	Description of WIN.INI

DOS-Level Files

The following files are included with Windows for use at the DOS level. The .COM and .EXE files are executable from the DOS prompt, or you can include them in the AUTOEXEC.BAT file. Commands with the .SYS extension go in the CONFIG.SYS file.

EGA	.SYS	Driver required in CONFIG.SYS for EGA systems
EMM386	.EXE	Expanded memory manager for 80386 or above systems
EXPAND	.EXE	Decompress utility for Windows floppy disk files
HIMEM	.SYS	Extended memory manager
IPXODI	.COM	Novell NetWare workstation communications driver (ODI model)
LMOUSE	.COM	Logitech mouse driver
LSL	.COM	Novell NetWare workstation link support layer (ODI)
MOUSE	.COM	Microsoft Mouse driver
MOUSE	.SYS	Microsoft Mouse driver (for CONFIG.SYS)
MOUSEHP	.COM	HP HIL mouse driver
MOUSEHP	.SYS	HP HIL mouse driver (for CONFIG.SYS)
NETX	.COM	Novell Netware workstation shell
RAMDRIVE	.SYS	RAMDrive utility (include in CONFIG.SYS)
SMARTDRV	.EXE	SmartDrive disk caching utility
TBMI2	.COM	Novell NetWare task switcher support

Setup Files

The following files are used during the Windows setup process, or after Windows is installed. The .INF files hold script information that Setup or Windows uses when installing components.

APPS	.INF	Used to create non-Windows application PIFs
CONTROL	.SRC	Template for CONTROL.INI file
CONTROL	.INF	Control Panel and printer information file
PRTUPD	.INF	Printer Update information file
SETUP	.EXE	Setup command
SETUP	.HLP	Setup help file
SETUP	.TXT	File containing important pre-setup information
SETUP	.INF	Setup information file

SETUP	.REG	Registration Database template
SETUP	.INI	Initialization file for Setup
SETUP	.SHH	Template for automated setup
SYSTEM	.SRC	Template for SYSTEM.INI
WIN	.SRC	Template for WIN.INI
XMSMMGR	.EXE	Extended memory manager used during setup

Windows Core Components and Operating Files

WIN.COM is created using WIN.CFG and an appropriate logo file. It is the Windows loader. When executed, it checks the available memory size and device drivers to determine the appropriate startup mode. It then executes DOSX.EXE to start standard mode or WIN386.EXE to start 386 enhanced mode. As described in Chapter 8, the kernel files (KRNL286.EXE or KRNL386.EXE) are executed to provide memory and resource management. USER.EXE maintains the user interface, and GDI.EXE controls the graphics device interface.

386MAX	.VXD	Qualitas 386MAX virtual device standard systems
BLUEMAX	.VXD	Qualitas BlueMAX virtual device for IBM PS/2 systems
COMM	.DRV	Communications driver
CONTROL	.EXE	Control Panel executable file
CPWIN386	.CPL	386 enhanced Control Panel extension
DOSX	.EXE	Windows standard mode executable
DRIVERS	.CPL	Provides support for the Control Panel driver's utility
DSWAP	.EXE	Task swapper for standard mode non-Windows sessions
GDI	.EXE	Windows graphics device interface core component
HPEBIOS	.386	EBIOS virtual device for HP machines in 386 enhanced mode
HPSYSTEM	.DRV	HP Vectra system driver for standard mode
KRNL286	.EXE	Kernel for standard mode
KRNL386	.EXE	Kernel for 386 enhanced mode
MAIN	.CPL	Provides support for the Control Panel
POWER	.DRV	Device driver that manages battery power
SND	.CPL	Provides support for the Control Panel Sound utility

SYSTEM	.DRV	Main system driver
TASKMAN	.EXE	Task Manager switching utility
TIGAWIN	.RLM	Code for Texas Instruments Graphics Interface firmware
USER	.EXE	Provides Windows interface support
VPOWERD	.386	Virtual device that manages battery power
WIN	.CNF	Startup code file used to create WIN.COM
WIN386	.EXE	Windows 386 enhanced mode core components
WIN386	.PS2	PS/2 BIOS data for 386 enhanced mode
WINDOWS	.LOD	Qualitas 386MAX/BlueMax loadable module
WINOA386	.MOD	Non-Windows application component for 386 enhanced mode
WINOLDAP	.MOD	Non-Windows application component for standard mode
WSWAP	.EXE	Task swapper for standard mode

Keyboard Files

The keyboard drivers are listed next. These drivers provide standard keyboard support for all systems. International support is provided by specific .DLL files listed in the Dynamic Link Library section. All keyboard DLLs start with the letters KBD. Note that the keyboard DLL type is selected during Setup by specifying a different country.

KBDHP	.DRV	Hewlett-Packard keyboard driver
KBDMOUSE	.DRV	Olivetti/AT&T keyboard and mouse driver
KEYBOARD	.DRV	Windows keyboard driver

Keyboard Language Support

The following files provide additional support for the keyboard drivers. They provide specific keyboard key configuration information.

XLAT850	.BIN	International (850) code page support
XLAT860	.BIN	Portuguese (860) code page support
XLAT861	.BIN	Icelandic (861) code page support
XLAT863	.BIN	French-Canadian (863) code page support
XLAT865	.BIN	Norwegian and Danish (865) code page support

Mouse Files

The mouse drivers shipped with Windows are listed next. If you have a mouse other than those listed here, use Setup to install its driver.

HPMOUSE	.DRV	HP HIL mouse driver
LMOUSE	.DRV	Logitech mouse driver
LVMD	.386	Logitech virtual mouse device
MOUSE	.DRV	Microsoft Mouse driver
MSC3BC2	.DRV	Mouse Systems 3 button mouse for COM2
MSCMOUSE	.DRV	Mouse Systems Serial/Bus mouse driver
MSCVMD	.386	Mouse Systems virtual mouse device
NOMOUSE	.DRV	No mouse driver

Diagnostic Utilities

The following files provide diagnostic information for Windows or your system. DRWatson is used to log information when you're having problems running Windows or Windows applications. Microsoft's technical support hotline may have you run this utility if you call them for service. The MSD utility provides extensive information about your system, such as interrupts, BIOS versions and dates and port settings.

DRWATSON	.EXE	Windows Fault detection utility (must be running)
MSD	.EXE	Microsoft Diagnostics utility
MSD	.INI	Microsoft Diagnostics utility initialization file

Startup Logo Files

The startup logo files are displayed when Windows starts. The file used depends on your screen resolution.

CGALOGO	.LGO	Logo code for CGA display
CGALOGO	.RLE	Compressed logo file for CGA display
EGALOGO	.LGO	Logo code for EGA display
EGALOGO	.RLE	Compressed logo file for EGA display
EGAMONO	.LGO	Logo code for EGA monochrome display
EGAMONO	.RLE	Compressed logo file for EGA monochrome display
HERCLOGO	.LGO	Logo code for Hercules monochrome display
HERCLOGO	.RLE	Compressed logo file for Hercules display
VGALOGO	.LGO	Logo code for VGA display
VGALOGO	.RLE	Compressed logo file for VGA display

DLL Files

The dynamic link library (DLL) files provide applications with a library of functions they can "borrow" while running. DLLs are usually shared by several programs. They help reduce the size of programs by storing often-used functions and routines.

COMMDLG	.DLL	Windows common dialogs library file
DDEML	.DLL	DDE management library file
KBDBE	.DLL	Belgian keyboard library file
KBDCA	.DLL	French-Canadian keyboard library file
KBDDA	.DLL	Danish keyboard library file
KBDDV	.DLL	US-Dvorak keyboard library file
KBDFC	.DLL	Canadian multilingual keyboard library file
KBDFI	.DLL	Finnish keyboard library file
KBDFR	.DLL	French keyboard library file
KBDGR	.DLL	German keyboard library file
KBDIC	.DLL	Icelandic keyboard library file
KBDIT	.DLL	Italian keyboard library file
KBDLA	.DLL	Latin-American keyboard library file
KBDNE	.DLL	Dutch keyboard library file
KBDNO	.DLL	Norwegian keyboard library file
KBDPO	.DLL	Portuguese keyboard library file
KBDSF	.DLL	Swiss-French keyboard library file
KBDSG	.DLL	Swiss German keyboard library file
KBDSP	.DLL	Spanish keyboard library file
KBDSW	.DLL	Swedish keyboard library file
KBDUK	.DLL	British keyboard library file
KBDUS	.DLL	U.S. keyboard library file
KBDUSX	.DLL	U.S.-International keyboard library file
LANGDUT	.DLL	Dutch language library file
LANGENG	.DLL	General International language library file
LANGFRN	.DLL	French language library file
LANGGER	.DLL	German language library file
LANGSCA	.DLL	Finnish-Icelandic-Norwegian-Swedish language library file
LANGSPA	.DLL	Spanish language library file
LZEXPAND	.DLL	Windows file expansion library file
MMSYSTEM	.DLL	Multimedia System library file
MORICONS	.DLL	Icons for non-Windows applications
NETAPI20	.DLL	Microsoft LAN Manager API library file
OLECLI	.DLL	Object Linking and Embedding client library file

OLESVR	.DLL	Object Linking and Embedding server library file
PBRUSH	.DLL	Paintbrush library file
PMSPL20	.DLL	Microsoft LAN Manager Printer library file
RECORDER	.DLL	Recorder library file
SHELL	.DLL	Shell library file
SL	.DLL	Battery management library file
TOOLHELP	.DLL	Windows tool help library file
VER	.DLL	Version library file
WIN87EM	.DLL	80x87 math coprocessor emulation library file

Video and Screen Files

The following files support various types of display devices. The .DRV files are the standard drivers. The .386 files are virtual display drivers for 386 enhanced mode. The .2GR and .3GR files are grabber files. The grabber files work in conjuction with WINOA286.MOD (standard mode) and WINOA386.MOD (386 enhanced mode) to provide data exchange between non-Windows applications and Windows. The 386 grabbers also provide graphic cut-and-paste support.

8514	.DRV	IBM-compatible 8514/a display driver
CGA	.2GR	CGA standard mode display grabber
EGA	.3GR	EGA 386 enhanced mode display grabber
EGA	.DRV	EGA display driver
EGACOLOR	.2GR	EGA standard mode display grabber
EGAHIBW	.DRV	EGA black-and-white display driver
EGAMONO	.2GR	EGA monochrome standard mode display grabber
EGAMONO	.DRV	EGA monochrome display driver
HERC	.3GR	Hercules monochrome 386 enhanced mode display grabber
HERCULES	.2GR	Hercules monochrome standard mode display grabber
HERCULES	.DRV	Hercules display driver
OLIBW	.DRV	Olivetti/AT&T PVC display driver
OLIGRAB	.2GR	Olivetti/AT&T PVC standard mode display grabber
PCSA	.DRV	DEC Pathworks network driver
PLASMA	.3GR	Compaq Portable plasma 386 enhanced mode display grabber
PLASMA	.DRV	Compaq Portable plasma display driver
SUPERVGA	.DRV	Super VGA display driver (800x600, 16 colors)

TIGA	.DRV	TIGA display driver
V7VDD	.386	Video Seven virtual display driver (VDD)
V7VGA	.3GR	Video Seven 386 enhanced mode display grabber
V7VGA	.DRV	Video Seven display driver (256 colors)
VDD8514	.386	8514/a virtual display driver (VDD)
VDDCGA	.386	CGA virtual display driver (VDD)
VDDCT441	.386	VGA virtual display driver (VDD)
VDDEGA	.386	EGA virtual display driver (VDD)
VDDHERC	.386	Hercules monochrome virtual display driver (VDD)
VDDTIGA	.386	TIGA virtual display driver (VDD)
VDDVGA30	.386	VGA virtual display driver (VDD) (version 3.0)
VDDXGA	.386	XGA virtual display driver (VDD)
VGA	.3GR	VGA 386 enhanced mode display grabber
VGA	.DRV	VGA display driver
VGA30	.3GR	VGA 386 enhanced mode display grabber (v3.0)
VGACOLOR	.2GR	VGA standard mode display grabber
VGADIB	.3GR	DIB 386 enhanced mode display grabber (8514/a monochrome)
VGAMONO	.2GR	VGA monochrome standard mode display grabber
VGAMONO	.DRV	VGA monochrome display driver
XGA	.DRV	XGA display driver

Network Files

The network driver files provide support for network utilities in the File Manager, the Control Panel, and the Print Manager. These utilities let you work with files and view or manage print queues on a remote file server.

BANINST	.386	Banyan VINES 4.0 virtual network support
DECNB	.386	DEC Pathworks virtual NetBIOS support
DECNET	.386	DEC Pathworks virtual network support
IPX	.OBJ	Novell NetWare workstation communications driver
LANMAN	.DRV	Microsoft LAN Manager 2.0 network driver
LANMAN10	.386	Microsoft LAN Manager 1.x virtual support
MSNET	.DRV	Generic network driver
NETWARE	.DRV	Novell NetWare network driver
VIPX	.386	Novell NetWare IPX virtual support
VNETWARE	.386	Novell NetWare interface virtual support

Multimedia Files

The Multimedia files support various third-party sound boards, Musical Instrument Digital Interface (MIDI) adapters, CD-ROM drives, and other multimedia related devices. MCI (Media Control Interface) devices provide a high-level, device-independent software interface for controlling media such as audio and animation resources, audio/visual peripherals, and external devices such as videodisc players.

MCICDA	.DRV	CD Audio driver for CD-ROM drive
MCISEQ	.DRV	MCI driver for MIDI devices
MCIWAVE	.DRV	MCI driver for waveform audio
MIDIMAP	.CFG	Information file for Control Panel MIDI Mapper
MIDIMAP	.DRV	Extensions for Control Panel MIDI Mapper
MMSOUND	.DRV	Multimedia Sound driver
MMTASK	.TSK	Multimedia background task application file
MPU401	.DRV	MIDI driver for MPU401 compatibles
MSADLIB	.DRV	MIDI driver for Adlib compatibles
SNDBLST	.DRV	SoundBlaster 1.5 driver
SNDBLST2	.DRV	SoundBlaster 2.0 driver
TIMER	.DRV	Multimedia timer driver
VADLIBD	.386	Virtual direct memory access (DMA) device for Adlib
VSBD	.386	SoundBlaster virtual device
VTDAPI	.386	Multimedia virtual timer device

Applications and Accessories

The Windows applications and accessories files are executed when you double-click icons in the Program Manager, or by typing one of the executable filenames given next in the Run command field. Most files have an associated help file, and some create their own .INI initialization files.

CALC	.EXE	Calculator
CALENDAR	.EXE	Calendar
CARDFILE	.EXE	Cardfile
CHARMAP	.EXE	Character Map
CLIPBRD	.EXE	Clipboard Viewer
CLOCK	.EXE	Clock
MPLAYER	.EXE	Media Player
NOTEPAD	.EXE	Notepad

NWPOPUP	.EXE	Novell NetWare standard mode message popup utility
PACKAGER	.EXE	Packager
PBRUSH	.EXE	Paintbrush
PIFEDIT	.EXE	Program Information File Editor
PRINTMAN	.EXE	Print Manager
PROGMAN	.EXE	Program Manager
RECORDER	.EXE	Recorder
REGEDIT	.EXE	Registration Editor
SOL	.EXE	Solitare game
SOUNDREC	.EXE	Sound Recorder
SYSEDIT	.EXE	Windows System Editor
TERMINAL	.EXE	Terminal
WINFILE	.EXE	File Manager
WINHELP	.EXE	Windows help utility
WINMINE	.EXE	MineSweeper game
WINPOPUP	.EXE	LAN Manager standard mode network popup utility
WINTUTOR	.DAT	Windows tutorial data file
WINTUTOR	.EXE	Windows tutorial file
WINVER	.EXE	Windows-version utility
WRITE	.EXE	Write

Help Files

The following help files are copied to the Windows directory for the Windows programs and accessories. Some of the printer help files provide installation instructions and information on setting options. Note that a help file is only installed if its accompanying program is installed.

APPS	.HLP	Applications Setup help
CALC	.HLP	Calculator help
CALENDAR	.HLP	Calendar help
CARDFILE	.HLP	Cardfile help
CHARMAP	.HLP	Character Map help
CLIPBRD	.HLP	Clipboard Viewer help
CONTROL	.HLP	Control Panel help
GLOSSARY	.HLP	Windows Help glossary
HPPCL5A	.HLP	HP LaserJet III Series printer driver help
HPPCL5OP	.HLP	HP LaserJet III Series printer driver help
LANMAN	.HLP	Microsoft LAN Manager 2.0 network driver help

MPLAYER	.HLP	Media Player help
NETWARE	.HLP	Novell NetWare network driver help
NOTEPAD	.HLP	Notepad help
PACKAGER	.HLP	Packager help
PBRUSH	.HLP	Paintbrush help
PIFEDIT	.HLP	Program Information File Editor help
POWER	.HLP	Battery manager device driver help
PRINTMAN	.HLP	Print Manager help
PROGMAN	.HLP	Info for printer driver updates
PSCRIPT	.HLP	PostScript printer driver help
RECORDER	.HLP	Recorder help
REGEDIT	.HLP	Registration Editor help
REGEDITV	.HLP	Registration Editor help
SL	.HLP	Battery manager for SL help
SOL	.HLP	Solitare game help
SOUNDREC	.HLP	Sound Recorder help
TERMINAL	.HLP	Terminal help
TTY	.HLP	Generic/text-only printer driver help
WINFILE	.HLP	File Manager help
WINHELP	.HLP	Windows help file
WINMINE	.HLP	MineSweeper game help
WINPOPUP	.HLP	Windows Popup utility help file
WRITE	.HLP	Write help

Display Font Files

The following files display system, fixed, OEM, and DOS application fonts. These fonts display text in the Windows interface and come in EGA, VGA, and 8514 (1024x768) resolution. The following list is alphabetical. You'll find a complete description of these fonts and their categories in Chapter 16.

8514FIX	.FON	Monospaced system font for 1024x768 resolution
8514OEM	.FON	Terminal font for 1024x768 resolution
8514SYS	.FON	System font for 1024x768 resolution
APP850	.FON	Non-Windows application font for 386 enhanced mode (code page 850)
ARIALB	.FON	Arial font 8-10 (EGA resolution)
CGA40850	.FON	Non-Windows application font for 386 enhanced mode (code page 850)

CGA40WOA	.FON	Non-Windows application font for 386 enhanced mode (code page 437)
CGA80850	.FON	Non-Windows application font for 386 enhanced mode (code page 850)
CGA80WOA	.FON	Non-Windows application font for 386 enhanced mode (code page 437)
COURB	.FON	Courier font 10-12-15 (EGA resolution)
COURE	.FON	Courier font 10-12-15 (VGA resolution)
COURF	.FON	Courier font 10-12-15 (8514/a resolution)
DOSAPP	.FON	Non-Windows application font for 386 enhanced mode (code page 437)
EGA40850	.FON	Non-Windows application font for 386 enhanced mode (code page 850)
EGA40WOA	.FON	Non-Windows application font for 386 enhanced mode (code page 437)
EGA80850	.FON	Non-Windows application font for 386 enhanced mode (code page 850)
EGA80WOA	.FON	Non-Windows application font for 386 enhanced mode (code page 437)
EGAFIX	.FON	EGA or AT&T system font
EGAOEM	.FON	EGA (640x350) or AT&T (640x400) terminal font
EGASYS	.FON	EGA (640x350) or AT&T (640x400) system font
HERC850	.FON	Non-Windows application font for 386 enhanced mode (code page 850)
HERCWOA	.FON	Non-Windows application font for 386 enhanced mode (code page 437)
MODERN	.FON	Modern font (all resolutions)
ROMAN	.FON	Roman font (all resolutions)
SCRIPT	.FON	Script font (all resolutions)
SERIFE	.FON	MS Serif font 8-10-12-14-18-24 (VGA resolution)
SERIFF	.FON	MS Serif font 8-10-12-14-18-24 (8514/a resolution)
SMALLB	.FON	Small fonts (EGA resolution)
SMALLE	.FON	Small fonts (VGA resolution)
SMALLF	.FON	Small fonts (8514/a resolution)
SSERIFB	.FON	MS Sans Serif font 8-10-12-14-18-24 (EGA)
SSERIFE	.FON	MS Sans Serif font 8-10-12-14-18-24 (VGA)
SSERIFF	.FON	MS San Serif font 8-10-12-14-18-24 (8514/a)
SYMBOLB	.FON	Symbol font 8-10-12-14-18-24 (EGA resolution)
SYMBOLE	.FON	Symbol font 8-10-12-14-18-24 (VGA resolution)
SYMBOLF	.FON	Symbol font 8-10-12-14-18-24 (8514/a resolution)
TIMESB	.FON	Times New Roman font 8-10 (EGA resolution)

VGA850	.FON	VGA (640x480) terminal font (code page 850)
VGA860	.FON	VGA (640x480) terminal font (code page 860)
VGA861	.FON	VGA (640x480) terminal font (code page 861)
VGA863	.FON	VGA (640x480) terminal font (code page 863)
VGA865	.FON	VGA (640x480) terminal font (code page 865)
VGAFIX	.FON	VGA (640x480) resolution monospaced system font
VGAOEM	.FON	VGA (640x480) resolution terminal font
VGASYS	.FON	VGA (640x480) resolution system font

TrueType Fonts

Windows 3.1 supports TrueType scalable fonts. The fonts come in pairs. The .FOT font is the resource file that Windows uses to access TrueType, and the .TTF file is the font description file.

ARIAL	.FOT	Font resource for ARIAL.TTF
ARIAL	.TTF	Arial font
ARIALBD	.FOT	Font resource for ARIALBD.TTF
ARIALBD	.TTF	Arial Bold font
ARIALBI	.FOT	Font resource for ARIALBI.TTF
ARIALBI	.TTF	Arial Bold Italic font
ARIALI	.FOT	Font resource for ARIALI.TTF
ARIALI	.TTF	Arial Italic font
COUR	.FOT	Font resource for COUR.TTF
COUR	.TTF	Courier New font
COURBD	.FOT	Font resource for COURBD.TTF
COURBD	.TTF	Courier New Bold font
COURBI	.FOT	Font resource for COURBI.TTF
COURBI	.TTF	Courier New Bold Italic font
COURI	.FOT	Font resource for COURI.TTF
COURI	.TTF	Courier New Italic font
SYMBOL	.FOT	Font resource for SYMBOL.TTF
SYMBOL	.TTF	Symbol font
TIMES	.FOT	Font resource for TIMES.TTF
TIMES	.TTF	Times New Roman font
TIMESBD	.FOT	Font resource for TIMESBD.TTF
TIMESBD	.TTF	Times New Roman Bold font

TIMESBI	.FOT	Font resource for TIMESBI.TTF
TIMESBI	.TTF	Times New Roman Bold Italic font
TIMESI	.FOT	Font resource for TIMESI.TTF
TIMESI	.TTF	Times New Roman Italic font
WINDING	.FOT	Font resource for WINDING.TTF
WINDING	.TTF	Dingbat fonts for TrueType

Sample Files

Windows provides a set of sample files you can use to customize your system or try out various new features of Windows 3.1. These files include graphics images, sounds, and screen savers.

Paintbrush Bitmap Files

The following bitmap images are provided with Windows for use as wallpaper. To install wallpaper, open the Desktop utility in the Control Panel.

ARCADE	.BMP	Arcade wallpaper
ARCHES	.BMP	Arches wallpaper
ARGYLE	.BMP	Argyle wallpaper
CARS	.BMP	Cars wallpaper
CASTLE	.BMP	Castle wallpaper
CHITZ	.BMP	Chitz wallpaper
EGYPT	.BMP	Egypt wallpaper
FLOCK	.BMP	Flock wallpaper
HONEY	.BMP	Honeycomb wallpaper
LEAVES	.BMP	Leaves wallpaper
MARBLE	.BMP	Marble wallpaper
REDBRICK	.BMP	Red brick wallpaper
RIVETS	.BMP	Rivets wallpaper
SQUARES	.BMP	Squares wallpaper
TARTAN	.BMP	Tartan wallpaper
THATCH	.BMP	Thatch wallpaper
WINLOGO	.BMP	Logo wallpaper
ZIGZAG	.BMP	Zigzag wallpaper

Wave (Sound) Files

The following sound files are digital representations of sound waves. You can play them using the Media Player or Sound Recorder if the optional Speaker driver is installed, or a sound board is installed.

CHIMES	.WAV	Exit sound
CHORD	.WAV	Question sound
DING	.WAV	Default beep
TADA	.WAV	Start sound

MIDI Files

The Media Player will play Musical Instrument Digital Interface files that have the extension .MID. A single file, CANYON, is provided with Windows as an example. Additional files are available from manufacturers of sound boards and musical instruments.

CANYON	.MID	Canyon	MIDI sound

Screen Saver Files

The following screen savers are provided with Windows. You use the Desktop utility in the Control Panel to install screen savers.

SCRNSAVE	.SCR	Generic screen saver
SSFLYWIN	.SCR	Flying font screen saver
SSMARQUE	.SCR	Marquee screen saver
SSMYST	.SCR	Mystify screen saver
SSSTARS	.SCR	Stars screen saver

Printer Files

Printers are supported by a set of dynamic link library files, specific drivers, and, if the printer is a PostScript printer, description files with the extension .WPD. Note that some printer drivers and description files include an associated help file listed in the Help Files section.

Soft Font Installers

The following soft font installers are used when installing new fonts on the printers listed:

CAN_ADF	.EXE	Soft Font installer for LBPIII.DRV and LBPII.DRV
FINSTALL	.HLP	Soft Font installer for HPPCL5/a driver help
SF4019	.EXE	Soft Font installer for IBM Laser Printer 4019
SFINST	.EXE	Soft Font installer for PG 306 Printer

Dynamic Link Libraries

The following dynamic link library files provide additional printer support for some printer drivers:

DMCOLOR	.DLL	Universal printer driver color printing support library
FINSTALL	.DLL	Soft Font installer for HPPCL5/a driver library
GENDRV	.DLL	Generic printer driver library
UNIDRV	.DLL	Microsoft Universal printer driver library

Drivers

One or more of the printer drivers listed next, along with an associated .DLL file, font installer, and help file, if any exist, are copied to your system when you install a printer.

CANON10E	.DRV	Canon Bubble-Jet BJ-10e printer driver
CANON130	.DRV	Canon Bubble-Jet BJ-130e printer driver
CANON330	.DRV	Canon Bubble-Jet BJ-300/330 printer driver
CIT9US	.DRV	Citizen 9-pin printer driver
CIT24US	.DRV	Citizen 24-pin printer driver
CITOH	.DRV	C-Itoh 8510 or AT&T 470/475 printer driver
DICONIX	.DRV	Kodak Diconix printer driver
DM309	.DRV	Olivetti DM 309 printer driver
EPSON9	.DRV	Epson 9-pin printer driver
EPSON24	.DRV	Epson 24-pin printer driver
ESCP2	.DRV	Epson ESCP2 dot matrix printer driver
EXECJET	.DRV	IBM ExecJet printer driver
FUJI9	.DRV	Fujitsu 9-pin printer driver
FUJI24	.DRV	Fujitsu 24-pin printer driver

HPDSKJET	.DRV	HP DeskJet Series printer driver
HPPCL	.DRV	HP LaserJet II Series printer driver
HPPCL5A	.DRV	HP LaserJet III Series printer driver
HPPLOT	.DRV	HP Plotter printer driver
IBM4019	.DRV	IBM Laser Printer 4019 printer driver
IBM5204	.DRV	IBM Quickwriter 5204 printer driver
LBPII	.DRV	Canon LBP-8 II printer driver
LBPIII	.DRV	Canon LBPIII printer driver
NEC24PIN	.DRV	NEC 24-pin printer driver
OKI9	.DRV	Okidata 9-pin printer driver
OKI24	.DRV	Okidata 24-pin printer driver
OKI9IBM	.DRV	Okidata 9-Pin IBM Model printer driver
PAINTJET	.DRV	HP PaintJet printer driver
PANSON9	.DRV	Panasonic 9-pin printer driver
PANSON24	.DRV	Panasonic 24-pin printer driver
PG306	.DRV	PG 306 printer driver
PROPRINT	.DRV	IBM Proprinter series printer driver
PROPRN24	.DRV	IBM Proprinter 24-pin series printer driver
PS1	.DRV	IBM PS/1 printer driver
PSCRIPT	.DRV	PostScript printer driver
QWIII	.DRV	IBM QuietWriter III printer driver
THINKJET	.DRV	HP ThinkJet (2225 C-D) printer driver
TI850	.DRV	TI 850/855 printer driver
TOSHIBA	.DRV	Toshiba p351/1351 printer driver
TTY	.DRV	Generic/text-only printer driver

PostScript Description Files

The following files provide PostScript description information for printers that support PostScript.

TESTPS	.TXT	PostScript Test Text File
40291730	.WPD	IBM LaserPrinter 4029 (17 fonts)
40293930	.WPD	PostScript, IBM LaserPrinter 4029 (39 fonts)
DEC1150	.WPD	Digital DEClaser 1150
DEC2150	.WPD	Digital DEClaser 2150
DEC2250	.WPD	Digital DEClaser 2250
DECCOLOR	.WPD	Digital ColorMate PS
DECLPS20	.WPD	Digital LPS Print Server
EPL75523	.WPD	Epson EPL-7500

HERMES_1	.WPD	Hermes H 606 PS (13 Fonts)
HERMES_2	.WPD	Hermes H 606 PS (35 Fonts)
HP_3D522	.WPD	HP LaserJet IIID PostScript
HP_3P522	.WPD	HP LaserJet IIIP PostScript
HPELI523	.WPD	HP LaserJet IIISi PostScript
HPIID522	.WPD	HP LaserJet IID PostScript
HPIII522	.WPD	HP LaserJet III PostScript
HPIIP522	.WPD	HP LaserJet IIP PostScript
IBM17521	.WPD	IBM 4019 (17 fonts)
IBM39521	.WPD	IBM 4019 (39 fonts)
L200230&	.WPD	Linotronic 200/230
L330_52&	.WPD	Linotronic 330
L530_52&	.WPD	Linotronic 530
L630_52&	.WPD	Linotronic 630
N2090522	.WPD	NEC Silentwriter2 90
N2290520	.WPD	NEC Silentwriter2 290
N2990523	.WPD	NEC Silentwriter2 990
N890_470	.WPD	NEC Silentwriter LC890
N890X505	.WPD	NEC Silentwriter LC890XL
NCM40519	.WPD	NEC Colormate PS/40
NCM80519	.WPD	NEC Colormate PS/80
O5241503	.WPD	OceColor G5241 PS
O5242503	.WPD	OceColor G5242 PS
OL840518	.WPD	Oki OL840/PS
OLIVETI1	.WPD	Olivetti PG 306 PS (13 Fonts)
OLIVETI2	.WPD	Olivetti PG 306 PS (35 Fonts)
P4455514	.WPD	Panasonic KX-P4455
PHIIPX	.WPD	Phaser II PX
Q2200510	.WPD	QMS-PS 2200
Q820_517	.WPD	QMS-PS 820
SEIKO_04	.WPD	Seiko ColorPoint PS Model 04
SEIKO_14	.WPD	Seiko ColorPoint PS Model 14
TIM17521	.WPD	TI microLaser PS17
TIM35521	.WPD	TI microLaser PS35
TKPHZR21	.WPD	Phaser II PX I
TKPHZR31	.WPD	Phaser III PX I
TRIUMPH1	.WPD	PostScript, Triumph Adler SDR 7706 PS (13 Fonts)
TRIUMPH2	.WPD	Triumph Adler SDR 7706 PS
U9415470	.WPD	Unisys AP9415

Appendix **D**

The WIN.INI File

The WIN.INI file contains entries used to customize the Windows interface and environment. Changes you make using the Control Panel accessories are recorded in this file. In addition, many applications write their own settings in WIN.INI. Microsoft now encourages third-party application developers to use their own .INI files instead of making updates to WIN.INI. This reduces the size of the file, which is especially important since it's held in memory at all times.

This appendix does not explain each option that may be in your WIN.INI file. These settings are normally altered automatically when you run the Control Panel utilities, so there is little reason to edit them in the WIN.INI file. However, some options can only be added or changed by editing WIN.INI. They have already been covered in Chapter 11 and are listed here again for your convenience. For a complete description of all settings in the WIN.INI file, refer to WININI.WRI in the Windows directory of your system. This file also describes the new entries for Windows 3.1 if you are familiar with the Windows 3.0 WIN.INI file.

The Structure of WIN.INI

This portion of the chapter lists the basic sections in the WIN.INI file. Each section name is in square brackets and should not be changed.

[Windows]

[Windows] contains settings that control the general Windows environment, such as border width, printing features, keyboard settings, and mouse settings. Use the Control Panel utilities to make changes to these settings.

[desktop]

[desktop] contains settings that control the appearance of the desktop, usually set with the Desktop utility in the Control Panel.

[extensions]

[extensions] contains a list of applications and document file associations. You use the Associate command in the File Manager to make changes to this section.

[intl]

[intl] contains the current keyboard, language, number, and date format settings. These options are set with the International utility in the Control Panel.

[ports]

[ports] contains settings for the serial ports. These settings are made with the Ports utility in the Control Panel.

[fonts]

[fonts] contains font settings made with the Fonts utility in the Control Panel.

[fontSubstitutes]

[fontSubstitutes] lists interchangeable fonts and describes how to substitute old Windows 3.0 fonts with new Windows 3.1 fonts.

[TrueType]

[TrueType] contains settings for TrueType fonts. These settings are made by the Printer and Font utilities.

[mci extensions]

[mci extensions] contains settings for Multimedia Command Interface (MCI) devices. These settings are normally made when you install drivers using the Drivers utility.

[networks]

[networks] contains settings for networks. These settings are made when you install network support or use the Networks utility in the Control Panel.

[embedding]

[embedding] contains settings for Object Linking and Embedding (OLE). These settings are made at boot time, or by applications that support OLE.

[Windows Help]

[Windows Help] contains settings for the Help system.

[sounds]

[sounds] lists the sounds assigned to system events. Use the Sounds utility in the Control Panel to change these settings.

[printerPorts]

[printerPorts] describes how printer ports are handled. Use the Printers utility in the Control Panel to change these settings.

[devices]

[devices] describes the compatibility of output devices with earlier versions of Windows applications. These settings are made during installation.

[colors]

[colors] contains color settings for windows. You change these settings using the Color utility in the Control Panel.

The Rules of Editing

The rules and methods for changing the WIN.INI file are simple, as described here:

- *Always make a backup before changing the file*   The WIN.INI file is unique to your system. It contains settings that describe its specific setup. You can't simply update from the orginal diskette if you accidentally corrupt the file or erase it. Make a backup before each editing session.

- *Some settings require Boolean values*   These values enable or disable an option. You can enable an option by typing **True**, **Yes**, **On**, or **1**; in this book **1** is used in all cases. To disable an option you can type either **False**, **No**, **Off**, or **0**; this book uses **0** in all cases.

- *Comments are preceded with a semicolon (;)*   Never remove the semicolon from a comment. You can temporarily disable an option by placing a semicolon in front of it. This is an easy way to test settings that you might want to reset later without removing them completely from the file. Keep them in the file as a reminder that you've disabled them. However, don't keep too many of these nonfunctional settings since they increase the size of the file and the amount of memory it consumes.

- *Use the Control Panel to change settings whenever possible*   It won't make mistakes (at least in theory).

User-Definable WIN.INI Settings

The following settings can only be made by editing WIN.INI. Other settings are made with the Control Panel or Setup utility, and are described in previous chapters. In particular, Chapter 11 covers the Control Panel utilities used to change the Windows environment.

Documents=*extension*

In this setting you replace *extension* with the filename extension of any files you want to be considered "documents." Such files will appear in the File Manager listings when you enable the Documents option on the By File Type dialog box. Use this entry to define only document file extensions not listed in the [extensions] section of WIN.INI. Those extensions are automatically considered documents. You specify multiple extensions on the same line by separating them with a space. Do not include the period in the extension. This topic was covered in Chapter 7.

DoubleClickHeight=*pixels*, DoubleClickWidth=*pixels*

These entries specify the height and width (in pixels) that the mouse pointer can move between clicks in a double-click. This feature was discussed in Chapter 11 under the "Mouse" section.

DragFullWindow=*Boolean*

Enable this option (set to 1) to drag the complete image of a window instead of a gray outline.

Load=*filename(s)*

Specify the names of applications to load and place on the desktop as icons when Windows starts. This is a setting left over from Windows 3.0. In Windows 3.1, place icons in the Startup group and enable the Run Minimized option in the icons properties box to achieve the same results. You should be aware of this option since some applications make changes to it when installed. This topic was covered in Chapter 7.

MenuDropAlignment=*Boolean*

This option specifies the right or left alignment of menu titles. When disabled (set to 0), menus open in a left-aligned format. When enabled (set to 1), menus open in a right-aligned format.

NullPort=*string*

Use this entry to specify the name of a null port. The null port is not a real port. It is sometimes used for testing since any information sent to it goes nowhere. The default is None, which is appropriate in most cases.

Programs=*extension*

Replace *extension* with the filename extension of any files you want to be considered "programs." Such files will appear in the File Manager file listings when you enable the Programs option on the By File Type dialog box. You specify multiple extensions on the same line by separating them with a space. Do not include the period in the extension. The default is

    programs=com exe bat pif

Run=*filename(s)*

Specify the names of applications you want to run. These applications appear as open windows when Windows starts. This is a setting left over from Windows 3.0. In Windows 3.1, place icons in the Startup group to achieve the same results. You should be aware of this option since some applications make changes to it when installed.

IconTitleFaceName=*fontname*

Use this setting to change the font used to display icon titles. Refer to Chapter 11 under the section "Icons" for more information.

IconTitleSize=*number*

Use this setting to change the font size used to display icon titles. The default size is 8-point type. Refer to Chapter 11 under the section "Icons" for more information.

IconVerticalSpacing=*pixels*

Use this setting to change the number of pixels that will appear vertically between icons. The default setting depends on the display type and the font used. Refer to Chapter 11 under the section "Icons" for more information.

MenuHideDelay=*milliseconds*

This entry specifies how long to wait before hiding a cascading menu once it is displayed. The default is 0.

MenuShowDelay=*milliseconds*

This entry specifies how long to wait before displaying a cascading menu. The default is 0 for 80386 computers; 400 for 80286 computers.

WallpaperOrigin=*number*

These entries adjust the initial offset of a tiled wallpaper. The x-origin is the left side of the screen and the y-origin is the top of the screen. The default is 0 for both. Refer to Chapter 11 under the "Wallpaper" heading for more details.

There are a number of settings for adjusting the appearance and colors of the Help system. These settings are covered completely in Chapter 11. You can also add a print filename in the [ports] section of WIN.INI to create a printer output device that prints your documents to a file. Refer to Chapter 15 for details on how to do this.

Application Entries in WIN.INI

Applications store initialization information in the WIN.INI file, or in their own .INI files. The current Microsoft policy is for applications to create their own .INI files, so you'll probably have an .INI file for every application on your system. These are usually stored in the Windows directory; however, some applications store them in their own directory. In the past, all applications created entries in WIN.INI, causing the file to become large and cumbersome. What's more, WIN.INI is held in memory during normal operations, which reduces the amount of memory available to applications.

To explore initialization information for applications, you can look in WIN.INI or in the .INI file created by the application. Some applications, including Word for Windows, still make numerous entries in WIN.INI. For example, the entries for Word for Windows are found under the [Microsoft Word 2.0] entry if you have version 2.0. It includes the location of the program's directory, as well as the location of spelling- and grammar-checking programs. Word also creates entries related to file conversions, graphic import methods, and text conversions. In addition, a WINWORD.INI file is created in the program directory to hold settings from the last session, such as which files were open so you can quickly open those files again.

Applications make entries in WIN.INI or their own .INI files the first time you use the application. You can scan through the file to find these entries, but use care when making changes and always work with a backup copy. Most entries are made by the application so you won't need or want to change them. However, if you remove an application from your system, edit the WIN.INI file to remove any references to that application. Each application reference is under a heading in square brackets.

Some pre-Windows 3.1 applications use .INI file entries to specify the location of data files. Specifying a directory in the Working Directory field of the Properties dialog box for the application's icon has no effect because the application does not read those settings. Look for an entry like FileSpec= in the WIN.INI file or the application's own .INI file, and then enter the directory where you want applications to be stored.

Take a few minutes to open the .INI files on your system. Many entries are immediately apparent and you can often make interesting changes to the operating parameters of a program.

Keep several different copies of a program's .INI file, each with different settings. You can then run the program in different modes by activating a particular .INI file before starting the program. Save one file with the extension .IN1 and another with the extension .IN2, then copy the one you want to use to .INI.

Appendix E

The SYSTEM.INI File

The SYSTEM.INI file contains a record of your system's hardware and the settings necessary for Windows to run on that hardware. It also contains settings used to run virtual sessions and DOS applications in those sessions. Most SYSTEM.INI files do not contain every possible setting, only those required for the system. A complete description of every setting is found in the SYSINI.WRI file. This appendix provides an index to that file.

The Rules of Editing

If you need to make changes to SYSTEM.INI, be sure to follow the rules and methods described here:

- *Always make a backup before changing the file* The SYSTEM.INI file is unique for your system. It contains settings that describe its specific setup. You can't simply update from the original diskette if you accidentally corrupt the file or erase it. Make a backup before each editing session.

- *Settings that require Boolean values* These values enable or disable the option. To enable an option you can type **True**, **Yes**, **On**, or **1** (in this book we've used 1 in all cases). To disable an option, type **False**, **No**, **Off**, or **0**. (We use 0 in all cases.)

- *Comments are preceded with a semicolon (;)* Never remove the semicolon from a comment. You can temporarily disable an option by placing a semicolon in front of it. This is an easy way to test settings that you might want to reset later without removing them completely from the file. Keep them in the file as a reminder that you've disabled them. However, don't keep too many of these nonfunctional settings since they increase the size of the file and the amount of memory it consumes.

- *Use the Control Panel to change settings whenever possible* It doesn't make mistakes (at least in theory).

SYSTEM.INI Settings

Use the following index to quickly locate entries in the SYSTEM.INI file.

Description	Section and Option
16550 FIFO buffer enable	[386Enh] COMxFIFO=*Boolean*
32-bit access page setting	[386Enh] PageBuffers=*number*
32-bit disk access	[386Enh] 32BitDiskAccess=*Boolean*
386 enhanced mode permanent swap file path	[386Enh] PermSwapDOSDrive=*drive-letter*
386 enhanced mode permanent swap file size	[386Enh] PermSwapSizeK=*kilobytes*
386 enhanced mode temporary swap file path	[386Enh] PagingFile=*path-and-filename*
386 enhanced mode mouse enable, DOS applications	[NonWindowsApp] MouseInDosBox=*Boolean*
8042 keyboard controller password setting	[386Enh] KybdPasswd=*Boolean*
80283 C2 stepping	[standard] PadCodeSegments=0 | 1
A20 enable count	[386Enh] A20EnableCount=*number*
ALT key delay problem fix	[386Enh] AltKeyDelay=*seconds*
ALT key paste delay setting	[386Enh] AltPasteDelay=*seconds*
Application swap file location identifier	[NonWindowsApp] SwapDisk=*drive*:*directory*
Asynchronous NetBIOS setting	[386Enh] NoWaitNetIO=On | Off
Background application suspended message enable/disable	[386Enh] VideoBackgroundMsg=*Boolean*

Description (*continued*)	Section and Option (*continued*)
Background applications, suspend if display corrected	[386Enh] VideoSuspendDisable=*Boolean*
Batch file environment size	[NonWindowsApp] CommandEnvSize=*bytes*
BIOS setting for 386 enhanced mode	[386Enh] EBIOS=*filename-or-*devicename* (*see* Device=)
Break point instruction search	[386Enh] SystemROMBreakPoint=*Boolean*
Break points, virtual device driver	[386Enh] MaxBPs=*number*
Buffer, 16550 FIFO buffer enable	[386Enh] COMxFIFO=*Boolean*
Buffer, specify DMA buffer memory placement	[386Enh] DMABufferIn1MB=*Boolean*
Buffer, DMA hard disk	[386Enh] HardDiskDMABuffer=*kilobytes*
Buffer, keyboard	[386Enh] KeyBufferDelay=*seconds*
Buffer, keyboard (lost characters during pasting)	[386Enh] KeyPasteCRSkipCount=*number*
Buffer, memory size for DOS call mapping	[386Enh] XlatBufferSize=*kilobytes*
Buffer, standard mode	[NonWindowsApp] GlobalHeapSize=*kilobytes*
Buffer (transfer) allocation	[386Enh] ReservePageFrame=*Boolean*
Buffer allocation for networks in standard mode	[standard] NetHeapSize=*kilobytes*
Buffer size, COM port	[386Enh] COMxBuffer=*number*
Buffer size, DMA	[386Enh] DMABufferSize=*kilobytes*
Buffer size setting, network DMA	[386Enh] NetHeapSize=*kilobytes*
Buffer size setting, network NetBIOS DMA	[386Enh] NetDMASize=*kilobytes*
C2 stepping, 80286 chip	[standard] PadCodeSegments=0	1
Cache, expanded memory setting for disk cache	[386Enh] AllEMSLocked=*Boolean*
Cached file handle setting	[boot] CachedFileHandles=*number*
CGA no snow setting	[386Enh] CGANoSnow=*Boolean*

Description (*continued*)	Section and Option (*continued*)
Character set identifier, OEM	[keyboard] oemansi.bin=*filename*
Clipboard paste delay, DOS applications	[386Enh] KeyPasteDelay=*seconds*
Clipboard paste settings, DOS applications	[386Enh] KeyPasteTimeout=*seconds*
Code-page translation table identifier	[keyboard] oemansi.bin=*filename*
Color Graphics Adapter no snow setting	[386Enh] CGANoSnow=*Boolean*
Color setting for error message box	[386Enh] MessageBackColor=*vga-color-attribute*
Color setting for error message text	[386Enh] MessageTextColor=*vga-color-attribute*
COM driver, enable virtual interrupt handler	[386Enh] COMdrv30=*Boolean*
COM interrupt line share enable (MCI and EISA only)	[386Enh] COMIrqSharing=*Boolean*
COM port address values	[386Enh] COMxBase=*address*
COM port buffer size	[386Enh] COMxBuffer=*number*
COM port contention settings	[386Enh] COMxAutoAssign=*number-or-seconds*
COM port enable (when greater than 4)	[386Enh] MaxCOMPort=*number*
COM port interrupt processing time	[386Enh] COMBoostTime=*milliseconds*
COM port interrupt setting	[386Enh] COMxIrq=*number*
COM port protocol setting	[386Enh] COMxProtocol=XOFF	*blank*
COMMAND.COM environment size	[NonWindowsApp] CommandEnvSize=*bytes*
Communications driver	[boot] comm.drv=*filename*
CONFIG.SYS, define drivers as global	[386Enh] Global=*device-name*
Conventional memory limit for Windows	[386Enh] WindowMemSize=*number*	*kilobytes*
Conventional memory required	[386Enh] WindowKBRequired=*kilobytes*
CTRL-ALT-DEL reboot setting	[386Enh] KybdReboot=*Boolean*

Description (*continued*)	Section and Option (*continued*)
Device, BIOS type setting	[386Enh] EBIOS=*filename-or-*devicename* (*see* Device=)
Device, virtual device assignment	[386Enh] Device=*filename-or-*devicename*
Device assignment, display	[386Enh] Display=*filename-or-*devicename* (*see* Device=)
Device contention settings, COM port	[386Enh] COMxAutoAssign=*number-or-seconds*
Device driver memory allocation	[386Enh] MapPhysAddress=*range*
Device driver setting, mouse	[386Enh] Mouse=*filename-or-*devicename* (*see* Device=)
Disk, 32-bit access page setting	[386Enh] PageBuffers=*number*
Disk, enable multiple requests	[386Enh] OverlappedIO=*Boolean*
Disk, terminate interrupts enable/disable	[386Enh] VirtualHDIrq=*Boolean*
Disk access, FastDisk option	[386Enh] 32BitDiskAccess=*Boolean*
Disk cache expanded memory setting	[386Enh] AllEMSLocked=*Boolean*
Disk space requirements setting, temporary swap file	[386Enh] MinUserDiskSpace=*kilobytes*
Disk swap file, virtual memory	[386Enh] Paging=*Boolean*
Display, CGA no snow setting	[386Enh] CGANoSnow=*Boolean*
Display, dual support	[386Enh] DualDisplay=*Boolean*
Display, force exclusive full-screen mode	[386Enh] AllVMSExclusive=*Boolean*
Display, notify settings when switching apps.	[386Enh] BkGndNotifyAtPFault=*Boolean*
Display, route printer interrupts to system virtual machine	[386Enh] SGrabLPT=*port-number*
Display, suspend background application if corrupted	[386Enh] VideoSuspendDisable=*Boolean*
Display device assignment	[386Enh] Display=*filename-or-*devicename* (*see* Device=)
Display driver	[boot] display.drv=*filename*
Display font identifier, DOS apps.	[386Enh] CGA40WOA.FON=*filename*

Description (*continued*)	Section and Option (*continued*)
Display font identifier, DOS apps.	[386Enh] CGA80WOA.FON=*filename*
Display font identifier, DOS apps.	[386Enh] EGA40WOA.FON=*filename*
Display font identifier, DOS apps.	[386Enh] EGA80WOA.FON=*filename*
Display font identifier (proportional)	[boot] fonts.fon=*filename*
Display fonts for DOS applications	[386Enh] WOAFont=*font filename*
Display fonts identifier, OEM	[boot] oemfonts.fon=*filename*
Display grabber for enhanced mode	[boot] 386grabber=*filename*
Display grabber for standard mode	[boot] 286grabber=*filename*
Display lines, number of	[NonWindowsApp] ScreenLines=*number*
Display memory location setting	[386Enh] ReserveVideoROM=*Boolean*
Display ROM font usage setting	[386Enh] UseROMFont=*Boolean*
Display switching of DOS applications	[386Enh] AutoRestoreScreen=*Boolean*
Display update, scroll lines	[386Enh] ScrollFrequency=*number*
Display update time, DOS apps.	[386Enh] WindowUpdateTime=*milliseconds*
DMA buffer, hard disk	[386Enh] HardDiskDMABuffer=*kilobytes*
DMA buffer memory placement setting	[386Enh] DMABufferIn1MB=*Boolean*
DMA buffer size	[386Enh] DMABufferSize=*kilobytes*
DMA buffer size setting, NetBIOS	[386Enh] NetDMASize=*kilobytes*
DMA buffer size setting for networks	[386Enh] NetHeapSize=*kilobytes*
DMA maximum page address	[386Enh] MaxDMAPGAddress=*address*
DMA operating mode on EISA systems	[386Enh] EISADMA=*Boolean* or *channel,size*
DMA setting for MCA systems	[386Enh] MCADMA=*Boolean*
DOS 5 UMB support setting	[386Enh] LocalLoadHigh=*Boolean*
DOS application, allow switch after NetBIOS call	[NonWindowsApp] NetAsynchSwitching=0	1
DOS application, display switch notify setting	[386Enh] BkGndNotifyAtPFault=*Boolean*

Description (*continued*)	Section and Option (*continued*)
DOS application, Fonts dialog box option	[NonWindowsApp] DisablePositionSave=*Boolean*
DOS application, force exclusive mode	[386Enh] AllVMSExclusive=*Boolean*
DOS application, suspend if corrupted display	[386Enh] VideoSuspendDisable=*Boolean*
DOS application, TSRs	[NonWindowsApp] LocalTSRs=*list-of-TSR-applications*
DOS application buffer size setting (standard mode)	[NonWindowsApp] GlobalHeapSize=*kilobytes*
DOS application display font identifier	[386Enh] EGA40WOA.FON=*filename*
DOS application display font identifier	[386Enh] EGA80WOA.FON=*filename*
DOS application display grabber (enhanced mode)	[boot] 386grabber=*filename*
DOS application display grabber (standard mode)	[boot] 286grabber=*filename*
DOS application DOS call mapping buffer size	[386Enh] XlatBufferSize=*kilobytes*
DOS application file handle setting	[386Enh] PerVMFILES=*number*
DOS application font identifier	[386Enh] CGA40WOA.FON=*filename*
DOS application font identifier	[386Enh] CGA80WOA.FON=*filename*
DOS application font setting	[386Enh] WOAFont=*font filename*
DOS application font size change	[NonWindowsApp] FontChangeEnable=*Boolean*
DOS application interrupt 28 allocation	[standard] Int28Filter=*number*
DOS application interrupt timeout settings	[386Enh] TimerCriticalSection=*milliseconds*
DOS application keystroke priority setting	[386Enh] KeyBoostTime=*seconds*
DOS application minimum time-slice setting	[386Enh] MinTimeSlice=*milliseconds*
DOS application mouse enable	[NonWindowsApp] MouseInDosBox=*Boolean*

Description (*continued*)	Section and Option (*continued*)
DOS application mouse interrupt setting	[386Enh] MouseSoftInit=*Boolean*
DOS application paste delay setting	[386Enh] AltPasteDelay=*seconds*
DOS application paste timeout setting	[386Enh] KeyPasteTimeout=*seconds*
DOS application screen line setting	[NonWindowsApp] ScreenLines=*number*
DOS application screen switching	[386Enh] AutoRestoreScreen=*Boolean*
DOS application swap file location identifier	[NonWindowsApp] SwapDisk=*drive*: *directory*
DOS application time-slice settings	[386Enh] WinTimeSlice=*number,number*
DOS application update time	[386Enh] WindowUpdateTime=*milliseconds*
DOS call mapping buffer size	[386Enh] XlatBufferSize=*kilobytes*
DOS device memory allocation	[386Enh] MapPhysAddress=*range*
DOS driver XMS memory allocation	[386Enh] SysVMXMSLimit=*number-or-kilobytes*
DOS Prompt exit message enable/disable	[386Enh] DOSPromptExitInstruc=*Boolean*
DOSAPP.INI enable/disable	[NonWindowsApp] DisablePositionSave=*Boolean*
DOSAPP.INI, save settings enable/disable	[NonWindowsApp] FontChangeEnable=*Boolean*
Driver, enable Virtual COM driver interrupt handler	[386Enh] COMdrv30=*Boolean*
Driver, grabber for enhanced mode	[boot] 386grabber=*filename*
Driver, grabber for standard mode	[boot] 286grabber=*filename*
Driver identifier, display	[boot] display.drv=*filename*
Driver identifier, keyboard	[boot] keyboard.drv=*filename*
Driver identifier, keyboard	[386Enh] Keyboard=*devicename*
Driver identifier, mouse	[boot] mouse.drv=*filename*
Driver identifier, network	[boot] network.drv=*filename*
Driver identifier, serial	[boot] comm.drv=*filename*
Driver identifier, sound	[boot] sound.drv=*filename*

Description (*continued*)	Section and Option (*continued*)
Driver identifier, system	[boot] system.drv=*filename*
Driver setting, Network	[386Enh] Network=*filename-or-* *devicename* (*see* Device=)
Drivers, define global drivers	[386Enh] Global=*devicename*
Drivers, Installable	[boot] drivers=*filename-or-aliasname*
Drivers (DOS), extended memory allocation	[386Enh] SysVMXMSLimit=*number-or-kilobytes*
Drivers, local to virtual machines	[386Enh] Local=*devicename*
Dynamic link library, keyboard	[keyboard] keyboard.dll=*filename*
Dynamic link library, language	[boot] language.dll=*library-name*
Dynamic link library file handles	[boot] CachedFileHandles=*number*
Dynamic link library installer	[boot] drivers=*filename-or-aliasname* (*see* [Drivers] section for alias)
EISA DMA operating mode settings	[386Enh] EISADMA=*Boolean* or *channel,* *size*
Enhanced Mode grabber	[boot] 386grabber=*filename*
Environment size	[NonWindowsApp] CommandEnvSize=*bytes*
Error message color setting, background	[386Enh] MessageBackColor=*vga-color-attribute*
Error message text color setting	[386Enh] MessageTextColor=*vga-color-attribute*
Exclusive full-screen mode enable	[386Enh] AllVMSExclusive=*Boolean*
Exclusive setting for Windows apps.	[386Enh] WinExclusive=*Boolean*
Executable file handles	[boot] CachedFileHandles=*number*
Exit message enable/disable, MS-DOS Prompt	[386Enh] DOSPromptExitInstruc=*Boolean*
Expanded memory, excluded from Windows use	[386Enh] EMMExclude=*paragraph-range*
Expanded memory, included for Windows use	[386Enh] EMMInclude=*paragraph-range*
Expanded memory allocation method	[386Enh] ReservePageFrame=*Boolean*
Expanded memory allocation size	[386Enh] EMMSize=*kilobytes*

Description (*continued*)	Section and Option (*continued*)
Expanded memory availability requirement	[386Enh] SystemVMEMSRequired=*kilobytes*
Expanded memory lock setting	[386Enh] SysVMEMSLocked=*Boolean*
Expanded memory lock when using disk cache	[386Enh] AllEMSLocked=*Boolean*
Expanded memory manager, ignore unknown manager	[386Enh] IgnoreInstalledEMM=*Boolean*
Expanded memory off setting	[386Enh] NoEMMDriver=*Boolean*
Expanded memory page frame placement	[386Enh] EMMPageFrame=*paragraph*
Expanded memory use setting	[386Enh] SysVMEMSLimit=*number-or-kilobytes*
Extended memory A20 enable count	[386Enh] A20EnableCount=*number*
Extended memory allocation to DOS drivers	[386Enh] SysVMXMSLimit=*number-or-kilobytes*
Extended memory lock	[386Enh] AllXMSLocked=*Boolean*
Extended memory management routines for UMB enable/disable	[386Enh] XMSUMBInitCalls=*Boolean*
Extended memory required to start Windows	[386Enh] SysVMXMSRequired=*kilobytes*
FastDisk access	[386Enh] 32BitDiskAccess=*Boolean*
FastDisk page setting	[386Enh] PageBuffers=*number*
FIFO buffer enable, 16550	[386Enh] COMxFIFO=*Boolean*
File, enable/disable updates to File Manager	[386Enh] FileSysChange=*Boolean*
File handle setting for virtual machines	[386Enh] PerVMFILES=*number*
File handles	[boot] CachedFileHandles=*number*
File Manager file update enable/disable	[386Enh] FileSysChange=*Boolean*
File size of permanent swap file	[386Enh] PermSwapSizeK=*kilobytes*
Fixed system font identifier (ver 2.X apps.)	[boot] fixedfon.fon=*filename*

Description (*continued*)	Section and Option (*continued*)
Floppy disk, IRQ9 handling	[386Enh] IRQ9Global=*Boolean*
Font (proportional) used by Windows	[boot] fonts.fon=*filename*
Font identifier, fixed system (ver 2.X apps.)	[boot] fixedfon.fon=*filename*
Font identifier, DOS apps.	[386Enh] CGA40WOA.FON=*filename*
Font identifier, DOS apps.	[386Enh] CGA80WOA.FON=*filename*
Font identifier, DOS apps. display fonts	[386Enh] EGA40WOA.FON=*filename*
Font identifier, DOS apps. display fonts	[386Enh] EGA80WOA.FON=*filename*
Font identifier, OEM display	[boot] oemfonts.fon=*filename*
Fonts, changing of in DOS apps.	[NonWindowsApp] FontChangeEnable=*Boolean*
Fonts dialog box, DOS apps.	[NonWindowsApp] DisablePositionSave=*Boolean*
Fonts for DOS applications	[386Enh] WOAFont=*font filename*
General Protection errors, allow local reboot	[386Enh] LocalReboot=On | Off
Global drivers, defining	[386Enh] Global=*devicename*
Grabber (enhanced mode)	[boot] 386grabber=*filename*
Grabber (standard mode)	[boot] 286grabber=*filename*
Handles, cached file	[boot] CachedFileHandles=*number*
Handles, file handle setting	[386Enh] PerVMFILES=*number*
Hard disk DMA buffering	[386Enh] HardDiskDMABuffer=*kilobytes*
Hard disk interrupt enable/disable	[386Enh] VirtualHDIrq=*Boolean*
Hard drives, maximum DMA page address	[386Enh] MaxDMAPGAddress=*address*
Hardware driver identifier	[boot] system.drv=*filename*
HIMEM.SYS A20 enable count	[386Enh] A20EnableCount=*number*
I/O address, COM ports	[386Enh] COMxBase=*address*
I/O overlap allowed setting	[386Enh] OverlappedIO=*Boolean*
IBM PS/2 password setting	[386Enh] KybdPasswd=*Boolean*

Description (*continued*)	Section and Option (*continued*)
IBM PS/2 standard mode mouse settings	[standard] MouseSyncTime=*milliseconds*
Idle delay, keyboard	[386Enh] KeyIdleDelay=*seconds*
InDOS flag setting	[386Enh] InDOSPolling=*Boolean*
Installable drivers	[boot] drivers=*filename-or-aliasname* (*see* [Drivers]section for alias)
INT2A consume or reflect	[386Enh] ReflectDosInt2A=*Boolean*
INT16 setting (lost characters during pasting)	[386Enh] KeyPasteCRSkipCount=*number*
INT21 handling	[386Enh] InDOSPolling=*Boolean*
INT28 handling	[386Enh] INT28Critical=*Boolean*
INT33 mouse setting	[386Enh] MouseSoftInit=*Boolean*
Interrupt 28 allocation	[standard] Int28Filter=*number*
Interrupt handling, IRQ9	[386Enh] IRQ9Global=*Boolean*
Interrupt line (COM) share enable (MCI and EISA only)	[386Enh] COMIrqSharing=*Boolean*
Interrupt of virtual machine	[386Enh] IdleVMWakeUpTime=*seconds*
Interrupt processing time, COM port	[386Enh] COMBoostTime=*milliseconds*
Interrupt reflector stack size allocation	[standard] StackSize=*kilobytes*
Interrupt reflector stacks, map allocation in standard mode	[standard] Stacks=*number*
Interrupt settings, COM port	[386Enh] COMxIrq=*number*
Interrupt timeout period	[386Enh] TimerCriticalSection=*milliseconds*
Interrupts (keyboard), delay time	[386Enh] AltKeyDelay=*seconds*
Interrupts (printer), route to system virtual machine	[386Enh] SGrabLPT=*port-number*
Interrupts from hard drive, enable/disable	[386Enh] VirtualHDIrq=*Boolean*
IRQ9 handling	[386Enh] IRQ9Global=*Boolean*
Keyboard, ALT key problem fix	[386Enh] AltKeyDelay=*seconds*

Description (*continued*)	Section and Option (*continued*)
Keyboard buffer	[386Enh] KeyBufferDelay=*seconds*
Keyboard buffer setting (for lost characters)	[386Enh] KeyPasteCRSkipCount=*number*
Keyboard definition file	[keyboard] keyboard.dll=*filename*
Keyboard driver identifier	[boot] keyboard.drv=*filename*
Keyboard driver identifier setting	[386Enh] Keyboard=*devicename*
Keyboard identifier	[keyboard] type=*number*
Keyboard layout identifier	[keyboard] subtype=*number*
Keyboard paste delay	[386Enh] KeyBufferDelay=*seconds*
Keyboard problem, Zenith Z-248	[standard] FasterModeSwitch=*Boolean*
Keyboard scan code translation	[386Enh] TranslateScans=*Boolean*
Keyboard speed setting	[386Enh] KeyIdleDelay=*seconds*
Keystroke priority during multitasking	[386Enh] KeyBoostTime=*seconds*
Language library identifier	[boot] language.dll=*library-name*
Local drivers in virtual machines	[386Enh] Local=*devicename*
Local reboot enable setting	[386Enh] LocalReboot=On I Off
Lock expanded memory when using disk cache	[386Enh] AllEMSLocked=*Boolean*
MCA systems DMA setting	[386Enh] MCADMA=*Boolean*
MDA memory address ignore setting	[386Enh] VGAMonoText=*Boolean*
MDA memory area enable/disable	[386Enh] DualDisplay=*Boolean*
Memory, amount of expanded memory required as available	[386Enh] SystemVMEMSRequired=*kilobytes*
Memory, DMA buffer size	[386Enh] DMABufferSize=*kilobytes*
Memory, DMA maximum page address	[386Enh] MaxDMAPGAddress=*address*
Memory, DMA setting for MCA systems	[386Enh] MCADMA=*Boolean*
Memory, enable/disable MDA area	[386Enh] DualDisplay=*Boolean*
Memory, excluding from Windows use	[386Enh] EMMExclude=*paragraph-range*

Description (*continued*)	Section and Option (*continued*)
Memory, expanded memory allocation size	[386Enh] EMMSize=*kilobytes*
Memory, expanded memory page frame placement	[386Enh] EMMPageFrame=*paragraph*
Memory, extended memory lock	[386Enh] AllXMSLocked=*Boolean*
Memory, including for Windows use	[386Enh] EMMInclude=*paragraph-range*
Memory, linear address space setting	[386Enh] PageOverCommit=*megabytes*
Memory, lock expanded memory setting	[386Enh] SysVMEMSLocked=*Boolean*
Memory, lock expanded memory when using disk cache	[386Enh] AllEMSLocked=*Boolean*
Memory, UMB setting for DOS 5	[386Enh] LocalLoadHigh=*Boolean*
Memory, virtual machine unique memory address (PSP) setting	[386Enh] UniqueDOSPSP=*Boolean*
Memory, virtual memory enable/disable setting	[386Enh] Paging=*Boolean*
Memory, virtual memory paging drive	[386Enh] PagingDrive=*drive-letter*
Memory (conventional) limit for Windows	[386Enh] WindowMemSize=*number-or-kilobytes*
Memory (conventional) required to start Windows	[386Enh] WindowKBRequired=*kilobytes*
Memory (expanded) off setting	[386Enh] NoEMMDriver=*Boolean*
Memory (expanded) use setting	[386Enh] SysVMEMSLimit=*number-or-kilobytes*
Memory (extended) required to start Windows	[386Enh] SysVMXMSRequired=*kilobytes*
Memory (video) location setting	[386Enh] ReserveVideoROM=*Boolean*
Memory address (MDA) ignore setting	[386Enh] VGAMonoText=*Boolean*
Memory allocation, expanded and transfer buffers	[386Enh] ReservePageFrame=*Boolean*
Memory allocation (XMS) to DOS drivers	[386Enh] SysVMXMSLimit=*number-or-kilobytes*
Memory allocation for device driver	[386Enh] MapPhysAddress=*range*

Description (*continued*)	Section and Option (*continued*)
Memory amount to reserve in virtual machines	[386Enh] PSPIncrement=*number*
Memory in UMB to avoid setting	[386Enh] ReservedHighArea=*paragraph-range*
Memory management, maximum physical page number	[386Enh] MaxPhysPage=*hexadecimal-page-number*
Memory management (UMB) routines enable/disable	[386Enh] XMSUMBInitCalls=*Boolean*
Memory manager (expanded), Ignore unknown manager	[386Enh] IgnoreInstalledEMM=*Boolean*
Memory-resident software	[NonWindowsApp] LocalTSRs=*list-of-TSR-applications*
Memory-resident software, INT2A setting	[386Enh] ReflectDosInt2A=*Boolean*
Memory-resident software, INT21 handling	[386Enh] InDOSPolling=*Boolean*
Memory-resident software, INT28 handling	[386Enh] INT28Critical=*Boolean*
Memory-resident software interrupt allocation	[standard] Int28Filter=*number*
Memory scan range setting	[386Enh] UseableHighArea=*paragraph-range*
Memory setting, minimum available for virtual machine	[386Enh] MinUnlockMem=*kilobytes*
Message background color	[386Enh] MessageBackColor=*vga-color-attribute*
Message (exit) enable/disable, DOS prompt	[386Enh] DOSPromptExitInstruc=*Boolean*
Message enable/disable for suspended background apps.	[386Enh] VideoBackgroundMsg=*Boolean*
Message text color	[386Enh] MessageTextColor=*vga-color-attribute*
Monochrome Display Adapter memory area enable/disable	[386Enh] DualDisplay=*Boolean*

Description (*continued*)	Section and Option (*continued*)
Monochrome memory address ignore setting	[386Enh] VGAMonoText=*Boolean*
Mouse device driver setting	[386Enh] Mouse=*filename-or-*devicename* (*see* Device=)
Mouse driver identifier	[boot] mouse.drv=*filename*
Mouse enable in DOS apps. window	[NonWindowsApp] MouseInDosBox=*Boolean*
Mouse interrupt setting	[386Enh] MouseSoftInit=*Boolean*
Mouse problem, Olivetti M-250	[standard] FasterModeSwitch=*Boolean*
Mouse settings (PS/2), standard mode	[standard] MouseSyncTime=*milliseconds*
MS-DOS Prompt exit message enable/disable	[386Enh] DOSPromptExitInstruc=*Boolean*
Multitasking, force exclusive mode	[386Enh] AllVMSExclusive=*Boolean*
Multitasking, minimum available memory setting	[386Enh] MinUnlockMem=*kilobytes*
Multitasking, minimum time slice	[386Enh] MinTimeSlice=*milliseconds*
Multitasking, suspended application message enable/disable	[386Enh] VideoBackgroundMsg=*Boolean*
Multitasking, suspend background application on corrupted display	[386Enh] VideoSuspendDisable=*Boolean*
Multitasking, Windows exclusive setting	[386Enh] WinExclusive=*Boolean*
Multitasking priority during keystrokes	[386Enh] KeyBoostTime=*seconds*
Multitasking time-slice settings	[386Enh] WinTimeSlice=*number,number*
NetBIOS call, allow switching on	[NonWindowsApp] NetAsynchSwitching=0	1
NetBIOS DMA buffer size setting	[386Enh] NetDMASize=*kilobytes*
NetBIOS request failed setting	[386Enh] NetAsynchFallback=*Boolean*
NetBIOS service setting	[386Enh] NetAsynchTimeout=*seconds*
NetBIOS synch to asynch setting	[386Enh] NoWaitNetIO=On	Off
Network, allow switch on NetBIOS call	[NonWindowsApp] NetAsynchSwitching=0	1
Network, INT28 handling	[386Enh] INT28Critical=*Boolean*

Description (*continued*) | **Section and Option** (*continued*)

Network, DOS application interrupt timeout setting

[386Enh] TimerCriticalSection=*milliseconds*

Network, reserved memory setting

[386Enh] PSPIncrement=*number*

Network, Token Ring setting

[386Enh] TokenRingSearch=*Boolean*

Network, virtual machine unique memory address (PSP) setting

[386Enh] UniqueDOSPSP=*Boolean*

Network buffer allocation

[standard] NetHeapSize=*kilobytes*

Network DMA transfer buffer size setting

[386Enh] NetHeapSize=*kilobytes*

Network driver identifier

[boot] network.drv=*filename*

Network driver setting

[386Enh] Network=*filename-or-*
*devicename (*see* Device=)

Network file handle limits

[boot] CachedFileHandles=*number*

Network NetBIOS conversion setting

[386Enh] NoWaitNetIO=On | Off

Network NetBIOS DMA buffer size setting

[386Enh] NetDMASize=*kilobytes*

Network NetBIOS request failed

[386Enh] NetAsynchFallback=*Boolean*

Network NetBIOS service setting

[386Enh] NetAsynchTimeout=*seconds*

Nonmaskable reboot setting

[386Enh] NMIReboot=*Boolean*

OEM character set identifier

[keyboard] oemansi.bin=*filename*

OEM display fonts identifier

[boot] oemfonts.fon=*filename*

Olivetti M-250-E mouse problem

[standard] FasterModeSwitch=*Boolean*

Page address, maximum for DMA

[386Enh] MaxDMAPGAddress=*address*

Page frame placement of expanded memory

[386Enh] EMMPageFrame=*paragraph*

Page number, maximum in memory for virtual memory

[386Enh] MaxPhysPage=*hexadecimal-page-number*

Page setting for 32-bit access

[386Enh] PageBuffers=*number*

Paging drive, enable/disable

[386Enh] Paging=*Boolean*

Paging drive, virtual memory

[386Enh] PagingDrive=*drive-letter*

Password settings, IBM PS/2 systems

[386Enh] KybdPasswd=*Boolean*

Paste delay, DOS applications

[386Enh] KeyPasteDelay=*seconds*

Description (*continued*)	Section and Option (*continued*)
Paste delay, keyboard	[386Enh] KeyBufferDelay=*seconds*
Paste delay when using ALT	[386Enh] AltPasteDelay=*seconds*
Paste setting, keyboard buffer (lost characters during pasting)	[386Enh] KeyPasteCRSkipCount=*number*
Paste settings, DOS application	[386Enh] KeyPasteTimeout=*seconds*
Path of permanent swap file	[386Enh] PermSwapDOSDrive=*drive-letter*
Path of temporary swap file	[386Enh] PagingFile=*path-and-filename*
Performance, screen switching	[386Enh] AutoRestoreScreen=*Boolean*
Permanent swap file path	[386Enh] PermSwapDOSDrive=*drive-letter*
Permanent swap file size	[386Enh] PermSwapSizeK=*kilobytes*
Port, COM port buffer size	[386Enh] COMxBuffer=*number*
Port, COM port interrupt share enable(MCI and EISA only)	[386Enh] COMIrqSharing=*Boolean*
Port, COM port protocol settings	[386Enh] COMxProtocol=XOFF I *blank*
Port, interrupt setting of COM port	[386Enh] COMxIrq=*number*
Port address values	[386Enh] COMxBase=*address*
Ports, COM port interrupt time	[386Enh] COMBoostTime=*milliseconds*
Ports, contention settings on COM port	[386Enh]sec: COMxAutoAssign=*number-or-seconds*
Ports, enable virtual COM driver interrupt handler	[386Enh] COMdrv30=*Boolean*
Ports greater than four	[386Enh] MaxCOMPort=*number*
Printer interrupt to system virtual machine	[386Enh] SGrabLPT=*port-number*
Program Manager (or other) shell identifier	[boot] shell=*filename*
Proportional font used by Windows	[boot] fonts.fon=*filename*
Protocol settings, COM port	[386Enh] COMxProtocol=XOFF I *blank*
PS/2 password setting	[386Enh] KybdPasswd=*Boolean*
PS/2 standard mode mouse settings	[standard] MouseSyncTime=*milliseconds*
RAM drive memory allocation	[386Enh] MapPhysAddress=*range*

Description (*continued*)	Section and Option (*continued*)
Reboot, allow local	[386Enh] LocalReboot=On | Off
Reboot message background color	[386Enh] MessageBackColor=*vga-color-attribute*
Reboot message text color	[386Enh] MessageTextColor=*vga-color-attribute*
Reboot setting	[386Enh] KybdReboot=*Boolean*
Reboot setting, nonmaskable	[386Enh] NMIReboot=*Boolean*
Reflector stacks, interrupt mapping	[standard] Stacks=*number*
ROM, bypass hard drive ROM interrupts enable/disable	[386Enh] VirtualHDIrq=*Boolean*
ROM font (video) usage setting	[386Enh] UseROMFont=*Boolean*
ROM search for break point	[386Enh] SystemROMBreakPoint=*Boolean*
Scan codes (keyboard) translation	[386Enh] TranslateScans=*Boolean*
Screen, route printer interrupts to system virtual machine	[386Enh] SGrabLPT=*port-number*
Screen lines, specify number of	[NonWindowsApp] ScreenLines=*number*
Screen switching of DOS applications	[386Enh] AutoRestoreScreen=*Boolean*
Screen update time, DOS apps	[386Enh] WindowUpdateTime=*milliseconds*
Scroll lines, number of	[386Enh] ScrollFrequency=*number*
Segment limit, 80286 chips	[standard] PadCodeSegments=0 | 1
Serial driver	[boot] comm.drv=*filename*
Serial port, enable another driver	[386Enh] COMdrv30=*Boolean*
Serial port address values	[386Enh] COMxBase=*address*
Serial port buffer size	[386Enh] COMxBuffer=*number*
Serial port contention settings	[386Enh] COMxAutoAssign=*number-or-seconds*
Serial port interrupt processing time	[386Enh] COMBoostTime=*milliseconds*
Serial port interrupt setting	[386Enh] COMxIrq=*number*
Serial port interrupt share enable(MCI and EISA only)	[386Enh] COMIrqSharing=*Boolean*

Description (*continued*)	Section and Option (*continued*)
Serial port protocol setting	[386Enh] COMxProtocol=XOFF	*blank*
Serial ports greater than four	[386Enh] MaxCOMPort=*number*
Shell environment size	[NonWindowsApp] CommandEnvSize=*bytes*
Shell program	[boot] shell=*filename*
Sound driver identifier	[boot] sound.drv=*filename*
Stack Overflow message fix	[standard] Stacks=*number*
Stacks size in standard mode	[standard] StackSize=*kilobytes*

Standard mode, allow switch after
    NetBIOS call
	[NonWindowsApp]
	    NetAsynchSwitching=0
		1

Standard mode buffer	[NonWindowsApp] GlobalHeapSize=*kilobytes*
Standard mode grabber	[boot] 286grabber=*filename*
Standard mode interrupt 28 allocation	[standard] Int28Filter=*number*
Standard mode mouse settings (PS/2)	[standard] MouseSyncTime=*milliseconds*
Standard mode network buffer allocation	[standard] NetHeapSize=*kilobytes*
Startup program identifier (shell)	[boot] shell=*filename*
Swap file, maximum size setting	[386Enh] MaxPagingFileSize=*kilobytes*
Swap file, virtual memory	[386Enh] Paging=*Boolean*
Swap file, virtual memory	[386Enh] PagingDrive=*drive-letter*
Swap file 32-bit access page setting	[386Enh] PageBuffers=*number*
Swap file disk space requirements setting	[386Enh] MinUserDiskSpace=*kilobytes*

Swap file location identifier, DOS
    apps.
	[NonWindowsApp] SwapDisk=*drive* :
	    directory

Swap file (permanent) path	[386Enh] PermSwapDOSDrive=*drive-letter*
Swap file (temporary) path setting	[386Enh] PagingFile=*path-and-filename*
Swap file (permanent) size	[386Enh] PermSwapSizeK=*kilobytes*
Switcher identifier	[boot] TaskMan.Exe=*filename*
Synchronous NetBIOS setting	[386Enh] NoWaitNetIO=On	Off

Description (*continued*)	Section and Option (*continued*)
System driver	[boot] system.drv=*filename*
System fixed font identifier (ver 2.X apps.)	[boot] fixedfon.fon=*filename*
TASKMAN.EXE	[boot] TaskMan.Exe=*filename*
Temporary swap file disk space requirements setting	[386Enh] MinUserDiskSpace=*kilobytes*
Temporary swap file maximum size setting	[386Enh] MaxPagingFileSize=*kilobytes*
Temporary swap file path setting	[386Enh] PagingFile=*path-and-filename*
Terminate-and-stay-resident software	[NonWindowsApp] LocalTSRs=*list-of-TSR-applications*
Time, synchronize with system clock enable/disable	[386Enh] SyncTime=*Boolean*
Time setting	[386Enh] TrapTimerPorts=*Boolean*
Time-slice minimum setting	[386Enh] MinTimeSlice=*milliseconds*
Time-slice settings	[386Enh] WinTimeSlice=*number,number*
Timer interrupt for virtual machines	[386Enh] IdleVMWakeUpTime=*seconds*
Token Ring setting	[386Enh] TokenRingSearch=*Boolean*
Transfer buffer allocation	[386Enh] ReservePageFrame=*Boolean*
UMB management routine enable/disable	[386Enh] XMSUMBInitCalls=*Boolean*
UMB memory avoid setting	[386Enh] ReservedHighArea=*paragraph-range*
UMB scan range setting	[386Enh] UseableHighArea=*paragraph-range*
UMB setting for DOS 5	[386Enh] LocalLoadHigh=*Boolean*
Unrecoverable error, allow local reboot	[386Enh] LocalReboot=On I Off
VGA switching of DOS applications	[386Enh] AutoRestoreScreen=*Boolean*
Video Display, *see* Display	
Video driver	[boot] display.drv=*filename*
Video memory address (MDA) ignore setting	[386Enh] VGAMonoText=*Boolean*

Description (*continued*)	Section and Option (*continued*)
Video memory location setting	[386Enh] ReserveVideoROM=*Boolean*
Video ROM font usage setting	[386Enh] UseROMFont=*Boolean*
Virtual device assignments	[386Enh] Device=*filename-or-*devicename*
Virtual device driver break points	[386Enh] MaxBPs=*number*
Virtual machine, enable/disable Windows exclusive mode	[386Enh] WinExclusive=*Boolean*
Virtual machine available memory setting	[386Enh] MinUnlockMem=*kilobytes*
Virtual machine break points	[386Enh] MaxBPs=*number*
Virtual machine drivers	[386Enh] Local=*devicename*
Virtual machine file handle setting	[386Enh] PerVMFILES=*number*
Virtual machine minimum time-slice setting	[386Enh] MinTimeSlice=*milliseconds*
Virtual machine overlapped I/O enable setting	[386Enh] OverlappedIO=*Boolean*
Virtual machine reserved memory setting	[386Enh] PSPIncrement=*number*
Virtual machine TSRs	[NonWindowsApp] LocalTSRs=*list-of-TSR-applications*
Virtual machine UMB setting for DOS 5	[386Enh] LocalLoadHigh=*Boolean*
Virtual machine unique memory address (PSP) setting	[386Enh] UniqueDOSPSP=*Boolean*
Virtual machine "wake up"	[386Enh] IdleVMWakeUpTime=*seconds*
Virtual memory enable/disable setting	[386Enh] Paging=*Boolean*
Virtual memory FastDisk option	[386Enh] 32BitDiskAccess=*Boolean*
Virtual memory paging drive	[386Enh] PagingDrive=*drive-letter*
Virtual memory swap file maximum size setting	[386Enh] MaxPagingFileSize=*kilobytes*
Windowed DOS apps. mouse enable	[NonWindowsApp] MouseInDosBox=*Boolean*
XOFF serial port protocol setting	[386Enh] COMxProtocol=XOFF | *blank*
Zenith Z-248 keyboard problem	[standard] FasterModeSwitch=*Boolean*

Appendix F

Windows Diagnostics Utilities

Windows comes with two programs that help you obtain vital information about your system, and about application errors if they occur.

Microsoft Diagnostic Utility (MSD)

The MSD (Microsoft Diagnostic) utility displays information about your computer's ROM, memory, video, and other hardware. It also displays information about the operating system and any drivers and TSRs that might be loaded. To start MSD, exit Windows and type **MSD** at the DOS prompt. A screen appears, similar to the one in Figure F-1.

Use MSD to obtain vital information about your system when adding new hardware, configuring upper memory, or installing new drivers. Each button on the screen provides useful information that helps you avoid adapter, memory, and application conflicts. The MSD also helps you diagnose problems. Microsoft technical support may have you run MSD if you call them with a problem.

The MSD Screen

Each item available on the MSD screen is described next.

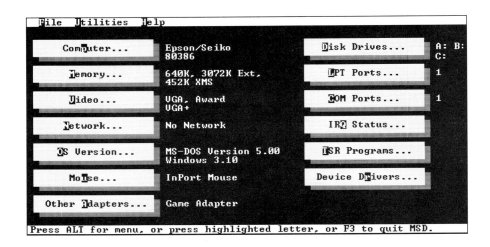

Figure F-1.   *The Microsoft Diagnostics utility main screen*

Computer   Use Computer to display the name of your system, its BIOS type, the processor type, keyboard type, and other information.

Memory   Memory displays a memory map of the upper memory area. You can use this map to determine the areas that are in use, and those that are available for loading TSRs and drivers high, as discussed in Chapter 9.

Video   Display the type of video your system has and its BIOS information with the Video option.

Network   Network displays information about your network connection.

OS Version   Use OS Version to display information about the operating system such as its serial number, version number, and location in memory. The current environment strings are also displayed.

Mouse   Use Mouse to access information about the mouse hardware, the interrupt port it uses, and the software drivers that support it.

Other Adapters   The Other Adapters option displays information about any other adapters in your system.

Disk Drives   Disk Drives displays a listing for each drive on your system, including RAM drives and CD-ROM drives, and provides vital information about each drive's cylinders, heads, tracks, and sectors, as well as its free space and total size.

LPT Ports   Use LPT Ports to display the port address and other information for each available LPT port.

COM Ports   Use COM Ports to display the port address and communication settings for each available COM port. The type of UART chip used on the COM port is also listed.

IRQ Status   The IRQ Status option provides vital information about the status of Interrupts in use by your system and any optional adapters. Use this information when installing new adapters that use interrupts.

TSR Programs   Activating TSR Programs displays a list of resident programs currently in memory. If the programs are loaded high, their upper memory block locations are listed. You can use this information when loading other programs high in place of using the MEM command as described in Chapter 9.

Device Drivers   The last option on the MSD main screen, Device Drivers, displays a list of resident programs currently in memory. This listing is similar to and can be used in the same way as the TSR Programs option (described just prior to this one).

Additional MSD Functions

The MSD menus provide some additional functions. The File menu has options for locating files and printing the MSD report. In addition, it lists the DOS startup and Windows .INI files. You can edit one of the files by choosing it from the list. The Utilities menu has options that programmers and others with technical abilitiy can use to display and browse memory. In addition, you can automatically insert some of the most common commands and options in the DOS startup and Windows .INI files. Choose Insert Command and select the command that you want to insert from the list. It is automatically placed in the file.

You can generate a report of the MSD information and print it or save it to a file. Choose Print Report, and then select the items you want to include in the report. In the Print To field, choose an appropriate port to print to, or choose File and type the name of the file that will hold the MSD information. Microsoft Technical Support may request you follow this procedure if you call them with problems.

Dr Watson

Dr Watson is a diagnostics tool designed to provide information as to the cause of a General Protection (GP) fault. A GP fault occurs when a Windows application writes to a memory space outside of its range, corrupting any code that exists in that space. Windows 3.1 has a new internal feature called Parameter Validation that checks for invalid parameters. If a GP fault occurs, you'll see a message that provides information about what happened. You should write down the message, save your work, and exit Windows. If an application is hung and does not respond, press CTRL-ALT-DEL. You'll then see instructions on how to close the application.

Dr Watson provides detailed information about the state of Windows when a system error occurs. The data generated by Dr Watson is technical in nature. Information about the current state of your system and memory are saved in a file called DRWATSON.LOG. Programmers or those with a technical background may want to browse the file. Microsoft or the vendor of the application producing problems may request a copy of the log.

To load Dr Watson, first expand it from the Windows disk set using the following command:

```
EXPAND A:DRWATSON.EX_ C:\WINDOWS\DRWATSON.EXE
```

Start Windows and load Dr Watson before starting the application that is producing problems. Choose the Run option from the Program Manager File menu and type **DRWATSON** in the Command box. Alternatively, you can create an icon for Dr Watson using the New command on the File menu, and then place the icon in the Startup group to start it whenever Windows starts.

If an application error occurs, Dr Watson automatically creates the DRWATSON.LOG file in the Windows directory. It then prompts you for a brief description of what you were doing when the fault occurred. You should then immediately exit Windows and back up the DRWATSON.LOG file. If additional errors occur, they are appended to the DRWATSON.LOG file.

Appendix **G**

Adding Restrictions to the Program Manager

If you are a system administrator who needs to control users' access to Windows features, you can do so by changing some of the settings of the PROGMAN.INI file. PROGMAN.INI contains the settings for the Program Manager and a list of groups it opens when started. The file has three sections: [settings], [groups], and [restrictions]. The [restrictions] section is of primary interest here, but you should also familiarize yourself with the entries in the [settings] section in case you ever need to create a custom PROGMAN.INI file to copy to users' systems. In particular, the Startup= option is of interest since it lets you specify a different group (other than Startup) as the startup group. Each section is described in this appendix and listed in the following sample file:

```
[Settings]
Window=44 75 539 375 1
SaveSettings=1
MinOnRun=1
AutoArrange=1
Startup=

[Groups]
Group1=C:\WINDOWS\MAIN.GRP
Group2=C:\WINDOWS\ACCESSOR.GRP
Group1=C:\WINDOWS\GAMES.GRP
Group1=C:\WINDOWS\STARTUP.GRP
```

```
[Restrictions]
NoRun=
NoClose=
NoSaveSettings=
NoFileMenu=
EditLevel=
```

 It's easier to let Windows make some of the settings described here by updating the file based on the current Windows settings. You can save the current Program Manager setup without exiting by holding the SHIFT key and choosing Exit from the File menu.

The [settings] Section

The [settings] section contains these entries, which you can change manually or set from within the Program Manager.

Window=*n* The first four numbers indicate the position and size of the Program Manager window, followed by a 1 if it starts maximized, or 0 if minimized. The position numbers depend on the resolution of your screen and the size and position of the window when it was last saved. There is little reason to change the settings unless you are creating a master file for many users. It's easier to let Windows save the settings when you exit (or you can press SHIFT and choose Exit to save changes without exiting).

SaveSettings=*Boolean* Set SaveSettings= to 1 if the Save Settings on Exit option on the Options menu should be enabled, or 0 if it should be disabled.

MinOnRun=*Boolean* Set MinOnRun= to 1 if the Maximize on Use option on the Options menu should be enabled, or 0 if it should be disabled.

AutoArrange=*Boolean* Set AutoArrange= to 1 if the Auto Arrange command on the Options menu should be enabled, or 0 if it should be disabled.

Startup=*name* The Startup= option specifies the name of the group windows containing icons that automatically start when Windows starts. The default is Startup. You can specify another group, or leave Startup= blank to prevent any applications from starting.

The [groups] Section

The [groups] section simply specifies the name, path, and load order of the [groups] windows in the Program Manager.

The [restrictions] Section

You can add or modify the following settings in the PROGMAN.INI file to restrict the access users have to the program. To enable the commands, set their value to 1. To disable, set the value to 0 or remove the line from the file.

NoRun=*Boolean*   When NoRun= is set to 1, the Run command is disabled on the File menu. It appears dimmed and users can't access it.

NoClose=*Boolean*   When NoClose= is set to 1, it disables the use of the Exit Windows command on the File menu and all other methods used to exit Windows. The system must be restarted to return to DOS.

NoSaveSettings=*Boolean*   When set to 1, NoSaveSettings= disables the Save Settings on Exit command on the Options menu. It appears dimmed. Any changes the user makes to the Program Manager are not saved. This setting overrides the SaveSettings= entry in the [Settings] section.

NoFileMenu=*Boolean*   When NoFileMenu= is set to 1, the File menu is unavailable. All its options appear dimmed. Note that users can still exit Windows by pressing ALT-F4 unless the NoClose= option is also set. The system must be restarted to return to DOS.

EditLevel=*n*   EditLevel=*n* sets the restriction level that users can modify Program Manager as follows:

- 0 is the default setting. It allows users to make changes.

- 1 prevents the user from creating, deleting, or renaming groups. The New, Move, Copy, and Delete options on the File menu are dimmed when a group is selected.

- 2 makes the New, Move, Copy, and Delete options unavailable if either a group or program item icon is selected.

- 3 has all the restrictions of 2, plus it prevents users from changing text in the Command Line field of the Properties dialog box. Using this option lets users change the working directory, icon title, icon type, and quick keys.

- 4 has all the restrictions of 3, plus it prevents users from changing any program item information on the Properties dialog box.

Index

Network dialog box, for Novell NetWare, 364
Network drives, 626
  assigning drive letters for, 190
  managing the mapping of, 365
Network files, 677
Network filing system, 366-367
Network management, versus network traffic, 382
Network options, Windows, 363-365
Network printer, displaying list of files in the
  queue, 338
Network printer print jobs, viewing the status of,
  370
Network traffic, versus network management, 382
Network utility, 212, 595
Networks, 361-387
NETWORKS.WRI file, 361, 371, 384, 670
New option, on the File menu, 47, 596
New Program Object dialog box, 95
No parity, 511
No Screen Exchange option, in the PIF Editor
  dialog box, 421
No Screen Save option, in the PIF Editor dialog
  box, 421
/noems parameter, 171
Non-palette device, 262-263
Non-weighted images, 473
Non-Windows applications. *See* DOS applications
Noncontiguous files, 121
Normal objects, 560
Normal PostScript files, 475
Notepad, 77-78, 431-433
Notes, typing in Calendar, 547-548
Novell Netware, Control Panel Network utility for,
  364
Novell Windows Workstations software, 363
Null-modem cable, 508
NUM LOCK key, 537
Number base conversions, 541-544

O

Object Linking and Embedding (OLE). *See* OLE
Object Packager utility, 563-564, 568-569, 577,
  579, 592
Object-oriented graphics, 455-456, 457-458
ObjectLink Data format, 562
Objects, 66, 559, 597, 627
  embedded, 560-561
  embedding, 68-69
  linked, 561
  linking between applications, 66-71
  normal, 560
  packaged, 560
  pasting in Paintbrush, 496
  securing on the canvas in Paintbrush, 490
  tilting, 497
Oct (octal), converting to, 541

Odd parity method, 510
OEM (Original Equipment Manufacturer), 205
OEM font set, 344
OEM fonts, 277
OEMSETUP.INF file, 207-208, 376
OLE (Object Linking and Embedding), 557,
  558-564, 627
  and business information, 558
  components of, 558-564
  linking applications with, 63-71
One-time only macro, 85
Open command, 125
Open dialog box, 39, 47-50, 582, 586
Operating modes, 3
Option buttons, enabling or disabling, 16
Optional Parameters field, in the PIF Editor
  dialog box, 419
Options
  on menus, 12
  unavailable, 13
Options dialog box
  for PostScript, 476
  for printing, 59, 331-332
Orientation
  selecting, 331
  of wallpaper, 224-225
Original Equipment Manufacturer (OEM), 205
Oscillators, 291
Out connection, 305, 306
"Out of memory" messages, 181
  preventing, 249
Outline font language, 347
Outline fonts, 347
Output, graphics, 454-455
Overtype mode, 52
.OVL (overlay) extension, 42
OwnerLink data format, 562

P

Package, 627
Packaged objects, 560, 563-564
  creating, 567-569
Packets, 514
Page break, inserted with CTRL-ENTER (^d), in
  Write, 439
Page breaks, in Write, 435-437, 578
Page frame, 179, 627
Page Header dialog box, in Write, 443, 576, 583
Page icon, 30
Page layout
  designing in Write, 440-444, 598
  setting in Calendar, 548-549
Page numbers
  inserting in Paintbrush, 501
  inserting in Write, 443, 598
  starting in Write, 440

Windows Update Notes

The update notes provide the latest information on Windows and Windows products. They are continually updated. The first update note will be available approximately 2 months after the release of Windows 3.1.

Send a $10 check or money order to the following address.
California residents add 72 cents sales tax.
Make checks payable to Tom Sheldon.

Tom Sheldon
P.O. Box 947
Cambria, CA 93428

Send the Windows Update Notes to:

Name: _____

Company/Phone: _____

Address: _____

City/State/Zip: _____

If you received previous update notes, write their date here: _____
There may be a slight delay as we prepare the next set.

NEW:
FOR MICROSOFT WINDOWS DEVELOPERS

WINDOWS DEVELOPER LETTER

THE TECHNICAL NEWSLETTER FOR ADVANCED WINDOWS PROGRAMMING

Windows Developer Letter is a unique newsletter for advanced Microsoft Windows developers. It is neither a marketing letter nor an introduction to basic Windows programming. Rather, it is packed with in-depth technical know-how, tips, techniques, secrets and undocumented knowledge that will turn you into a Windows guru. The sort of knowledge only a few individuals possess, and even fewer are willing to share. The know-how that will give you and your programs a unique advantage in the market. *Windows Developer Letter* is a hands-on newsletter that explains new and complex issues in full detail, with full source-code examples. No hand waving, no fluff, just the facts – and lots of them.

Each issue of *Windows Developer Letter* takes a detailed look at some of Windows' newest and most advanced features, with special emphasis on Windows 3.1 and a look toward the 32-bit future. Topics include DDE, DDELM, OLE, TrueType, Drag & Drop, using DPMI, the compression DLL, common dialogs, using Toolhelp to access Windows internals, and similar cutting-edge topics. Articles include a discussion and full working source code that show exactly how to use each advanced feature. In addition, each issue includes a diskette with the royalties-free source code for all the examples, so that you can put your new knowledge to work at once, building on the examples to create your own powerful programs.

Windows Developer Letter includes in-depth discussions of Windows architecture, internal structure, and the delicate interaction between the various elements of the system. It covers such topics as IOPL and protection rings, writing TSRs that work with Windows, the interaction between GDI and display device drives, optimizing graphics performance, how to write and take advantage of the power of virtual device drives (VxDs), intercepting DLL calls, and much more.

NOTE: This newsletter is not for beginners! It is for seasoned Windows developers who want to gain a comprehensive understanding of the newest, most advanced and most powerful Windows features and techniques.

No-risk double guarantee:
We are so sure you will find *Windows Developer Letter* to be an indispensable source of advanced technical information that we guarantee your complete satisfaction in two ways:
1. We will not charge your credit card or cash your check until 21 days after we mail your first issue. If it falls short of your expectations, you can simply drop us a note and we will cancel your subscription, without charging your credit card or cashing your check. The first issue, including the diskette, is yours to keep – **free!**
2. If you decide to cancel your subscription at any time after 21 days, you will receive a refund for all unmailed issues.

SUBSCRIPTION ORDER FORM

Please start my subscription to *Windows Developer Letter* **at $300.00 for one year (12 issues). Outside the U.S. and Canada add $50.00 for airmail shipping and handling. In California add sales tax.**

I will have 21 days to evaluate my first issue before my credit card is charged or my check cashed. If I cancel my subscription within 21 days, I will owe nothing. I may also cancel my subscription at any time after 21 days and receive a refund for any unmailed issues.

Please print

Diskette size: ❏ 3½"   or   ❏ 5¼"

❏ Check enclosed (U.S. funds drawn on a U.S. bank)
   made **payable to**: Wisdom Software, Inc.
Charge my: ❏Visa ❏MasterCard ❏AmEx

Card number: _____ Exp date: _____

Signature: _____

Name: _____

Company: _____ Title: _____

Address: _____

City: _____ State: _____ ZIP: _____

Country: _____

Phone: _____ FAX: _____

Mail to:

Wisdom Software, Inc.

322 Eureka Street

San Francisco, CA 94114

Tel: (415) 824-8482